BATGIRL

VOLUME **1**

Silent Knight

BATG

VOLUME 1

Silent Knight

Scott Peterson
Kelley Puckett
Chuck Dixon
Writers

Damion Scott
Coy Turnbull
Dale Eaglesham
Mike Deodato
Pablo Raimondi
Pencillers

Robert Campanella
Dan Davis
Andrew Hennessy
John Stanisci
Walden Wong
Inkers

Jason Wright
Rick Taylor
Gloria Vasquez
Colorists

John Costanza
Albert T. Guzman
Letterers

Jamison
Separations

Damion Scott &
Robert Campanella
Collection cover artists

Batman created by Bob Kane with Bill Finger

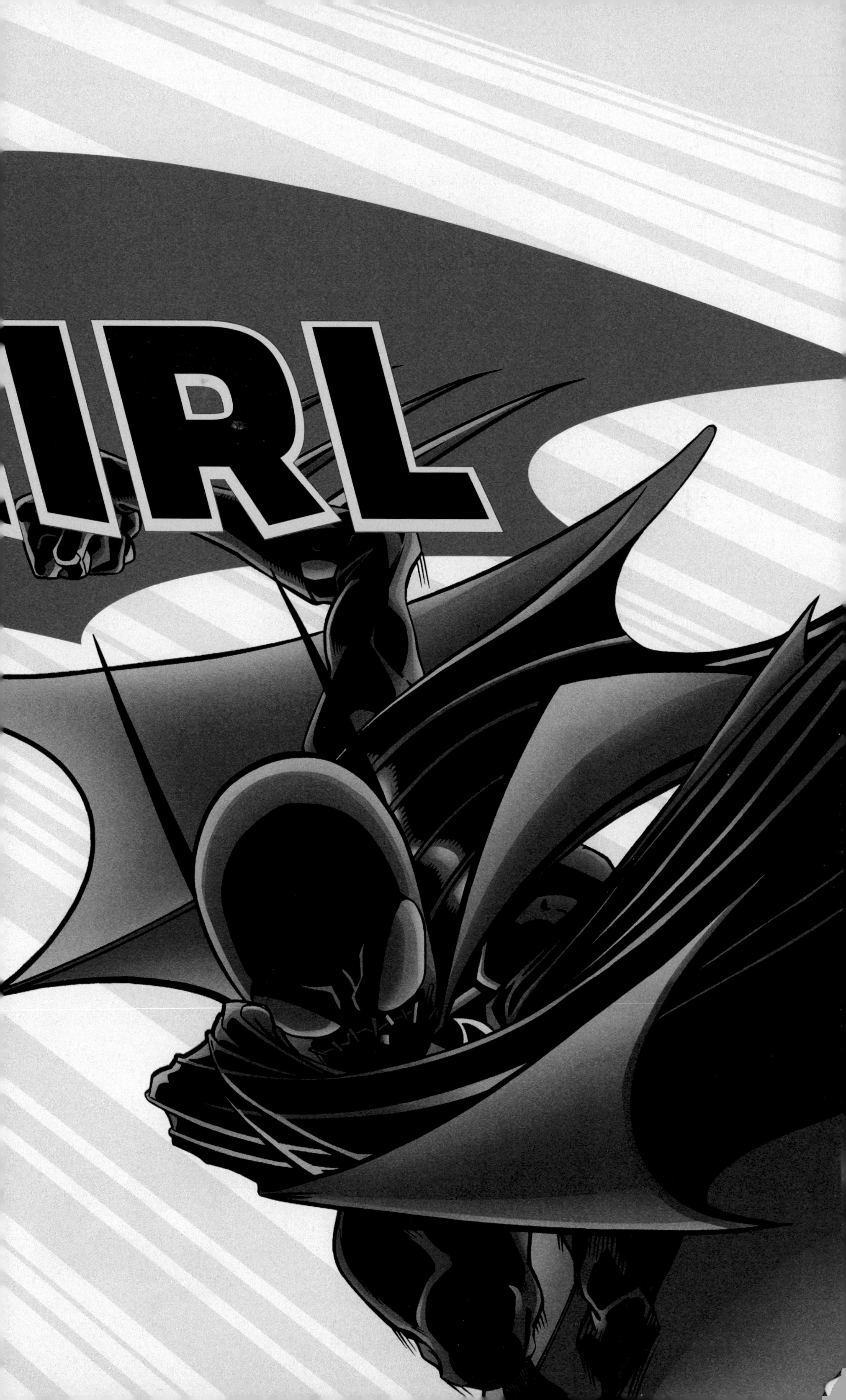
IRL

Batgirl Volume 1: Silent Knight

Published by DC Comics. Compilation Copyright © 2015 DC Comics.
All Rights Reserved. Originally published in single magazine form in
BATGIRL 1-12; BATGIRL ANNUAL 1 © 2000, 2001 DC Comics. All Rights
Reserved. All characters, their distinctive likenesses and related elements
featured in this publication are trademarks of DC Comics. The stories,
characters and incidents featured in this publication are entirely fictional.
DC Comics does not read or accept unsolicited submissions of ideas,
stories or artwork.

DC Comics, 2900 West Alameda Avenue, Burbank, CA 91505
Printed by RR Donnelley, Owensville, MO, USA. 12/11/15.
First Printing. ISBN: 978-1-4012-6627-1

PEFC Certified

Printed on paper from
sustainably managed
forests and controlled
sources

PEFC/29-31-75   www.pefc.org

Puckett, Kelley.
    Batgirl. Volume 1, Silent Knight / Kelley Puckett.
        pages cm
    ISBN 978-1-4012-6627-1 (paperback)
    1. Graphic novels. I. Title. II. Title: Silent Knight.
    PN6728.B358P75 2016
    741.5'973--dc23
                                            2015034652

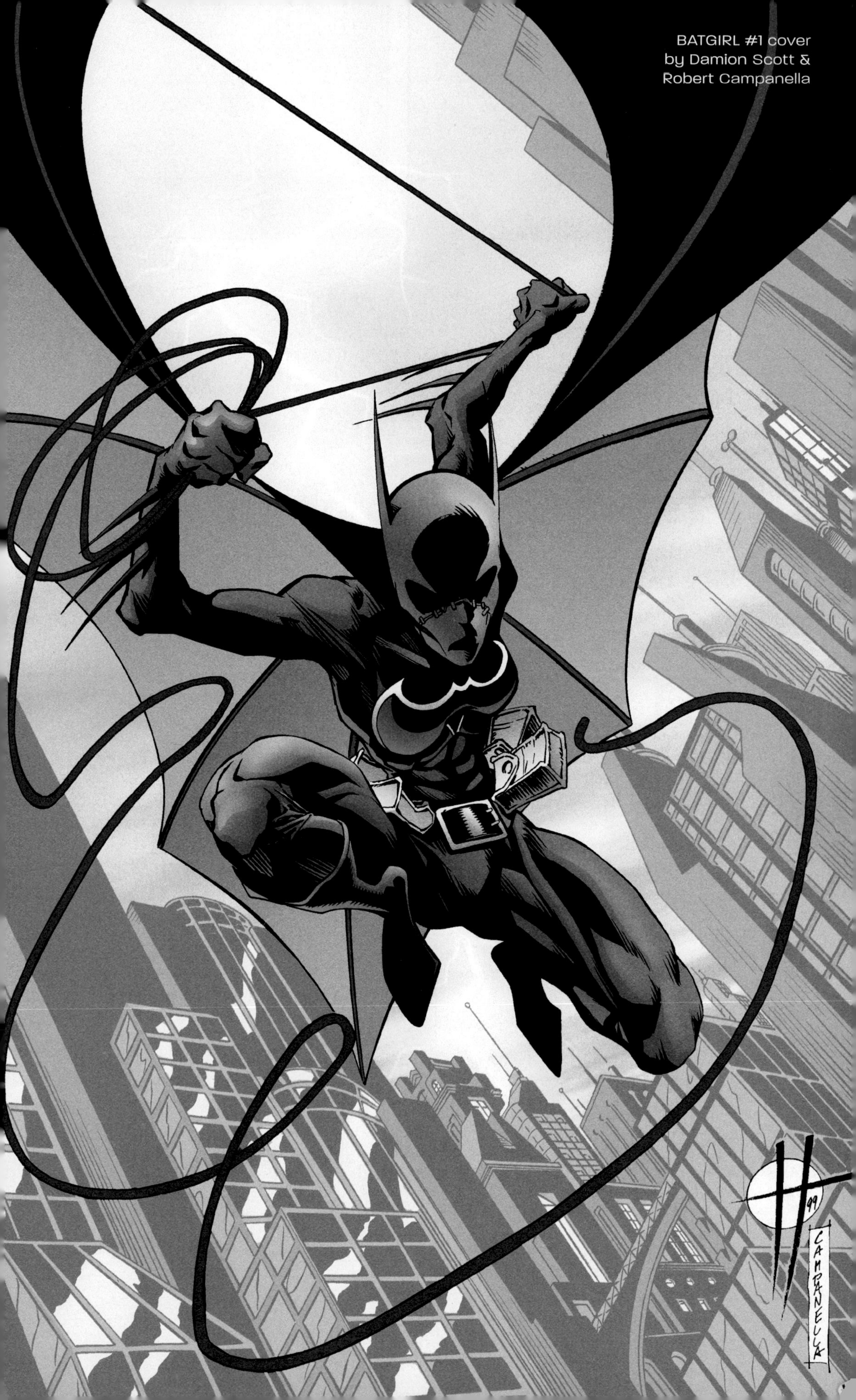

BATGIRL #1 cover
by Damion Scott &
Robert Campanella

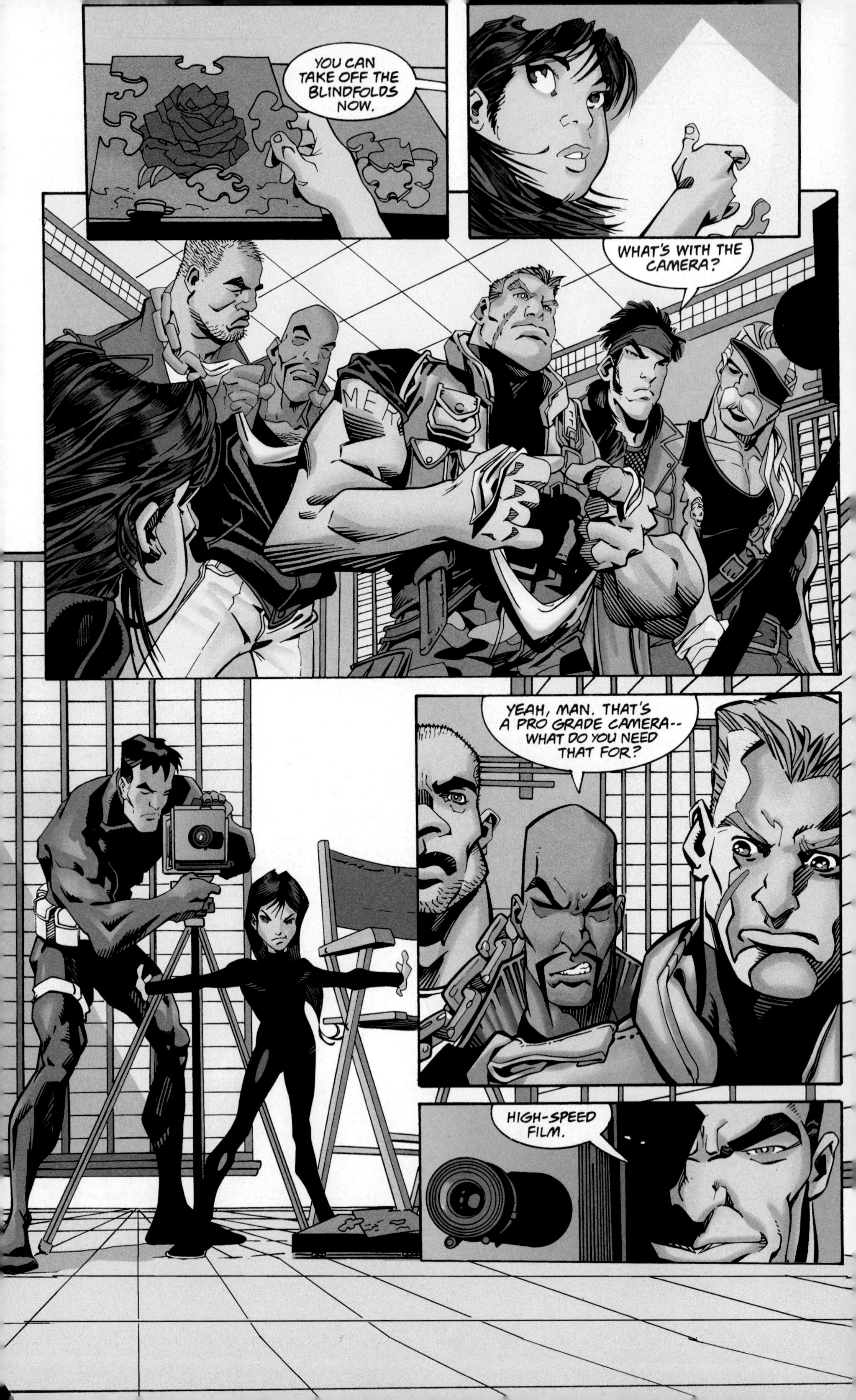
YOU CAN TAKE OFF THE BLINDFOLDS NOW.
WHAT'S WITH THE CAMERA?
YEAH, MAN. THAT'S A PRO GRADE CAMERA-- WHAT DO YOU NEED THAT FOR?
HIGH-SPEED FILM.

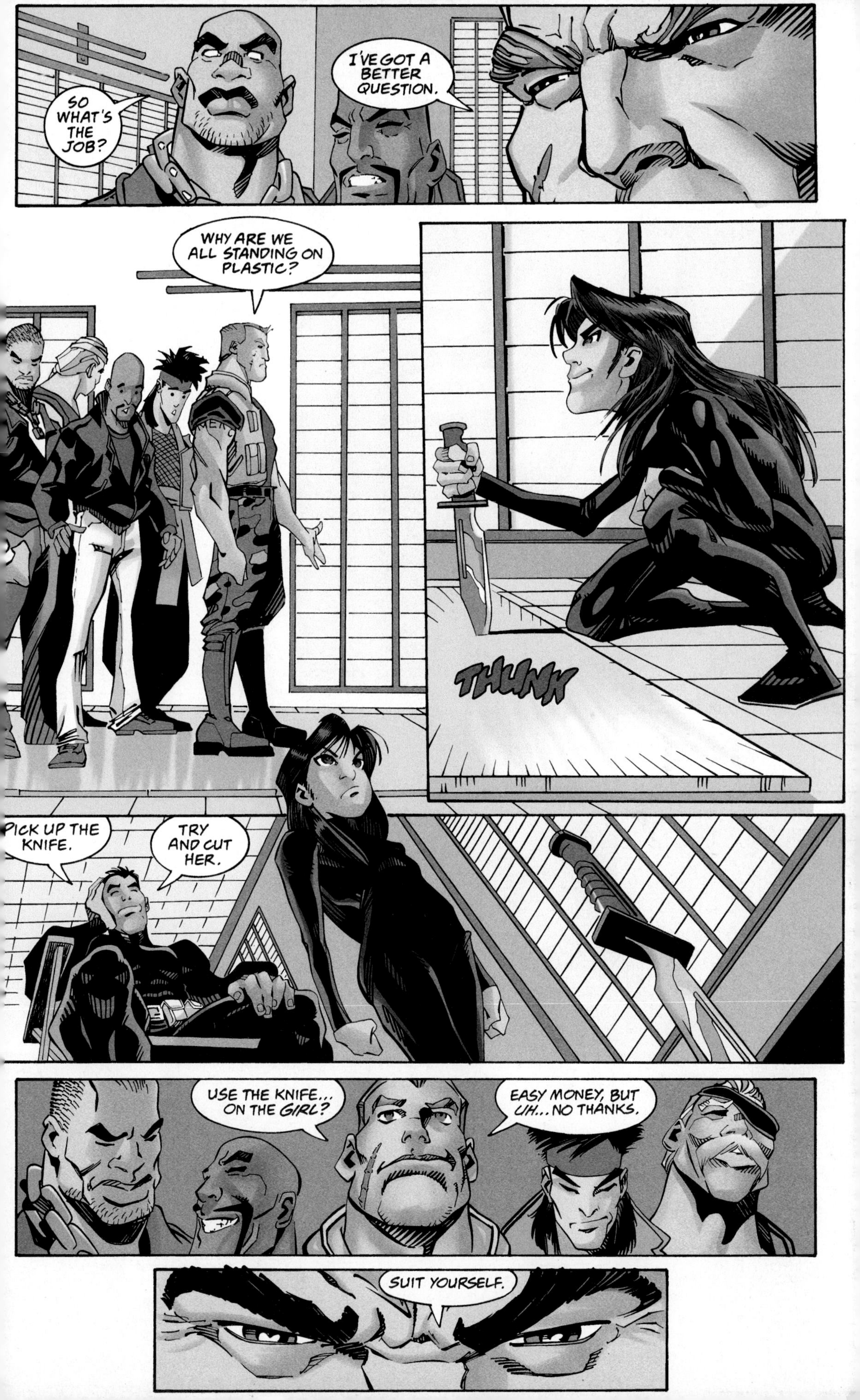
SO WHAT'S THE JOB?
I'VE GOT A BETTER QUESTION.
WHY ARE WE ALL STANDING ON PLASTIC?
THUNK
PICK UP THE KNIFE.
TRY AND CUT HER.
USE THE KNIFE... ON THE GIRL?
EASY MONEY, BUT UH... NO THANKS.
SUIT YOURSELF.

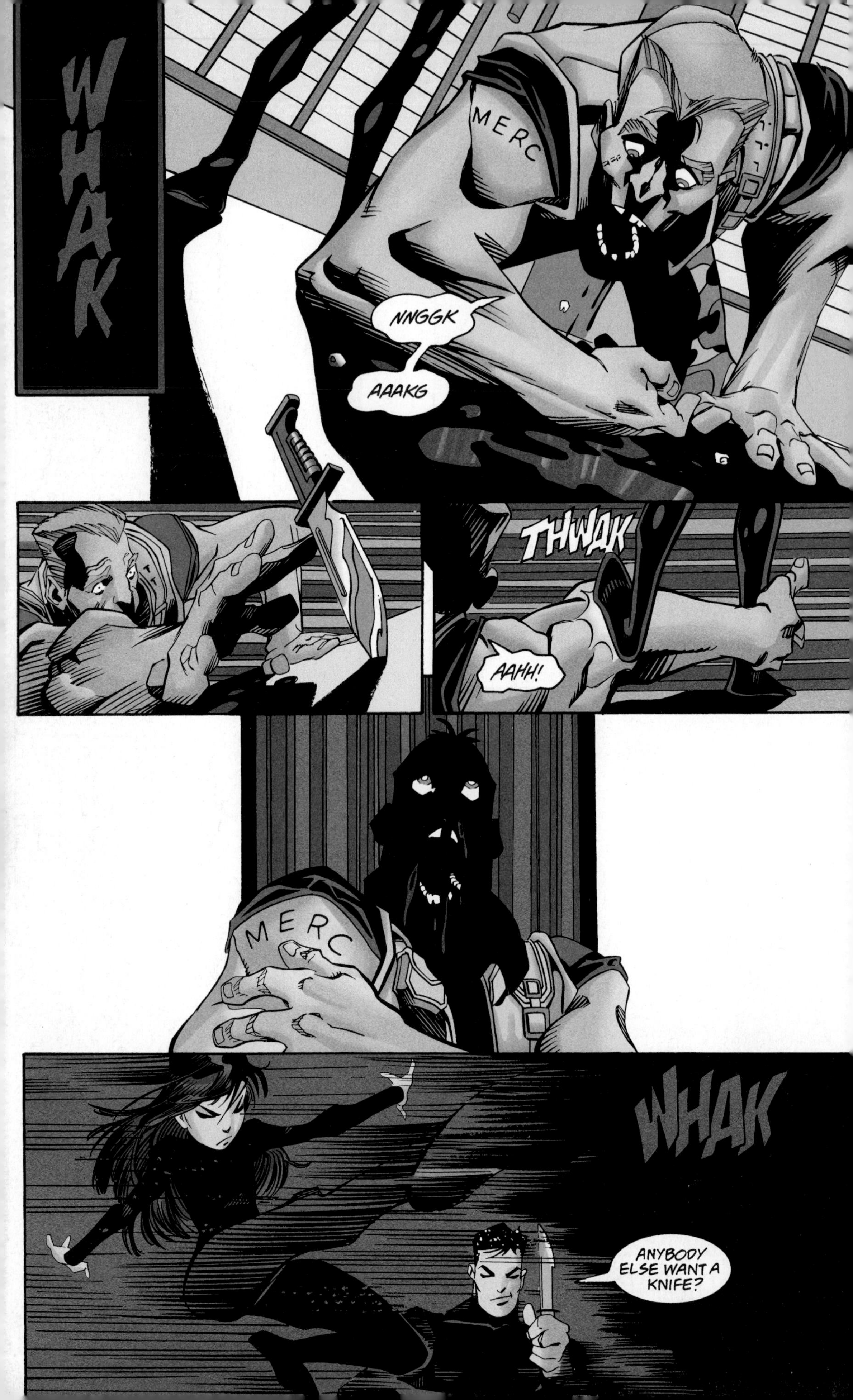
WHAK
MERC
NNGGK
AAAKG
THWAK
AAHH!
MERC
WHAK
ANYBODY ELSE WANT A KNIFE?

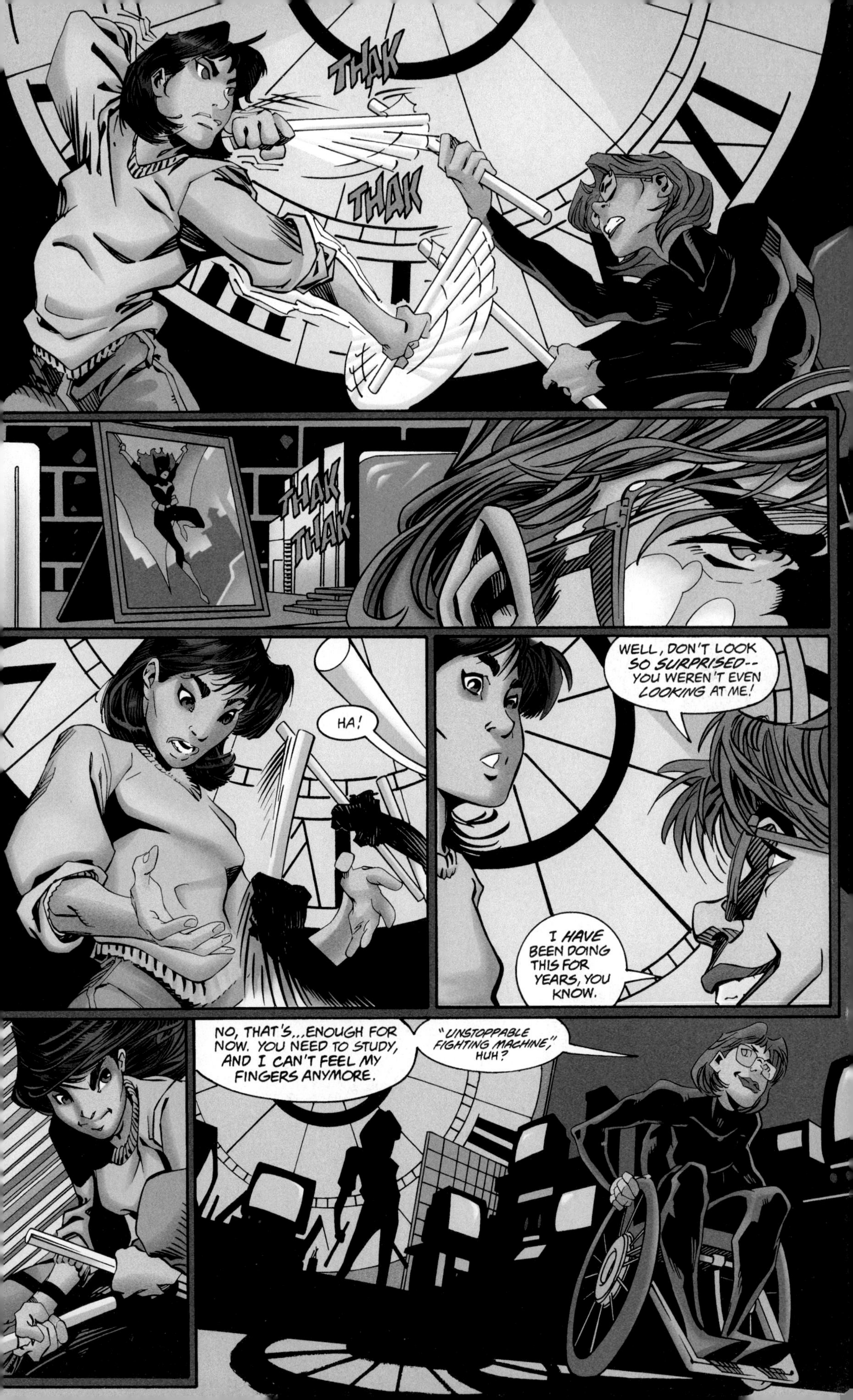
THAK
THAK
THAK
THAK
HA!
WELL, DON'T LOOK SO SURPRISED-- YOU WEREN'T EVEN LOOKING AT ME!
I HAVE BEEN DOING THIS FOR YEARS, YOU KNOW.
NO, THAT'S...ENOUGH FOR NOW. YOU NEED TO STUDY, AND I CAN'T FEEL MY FINGERS ANYMORE.
"UNSTOPPABLE FIGHTING MACHINE," HUH?

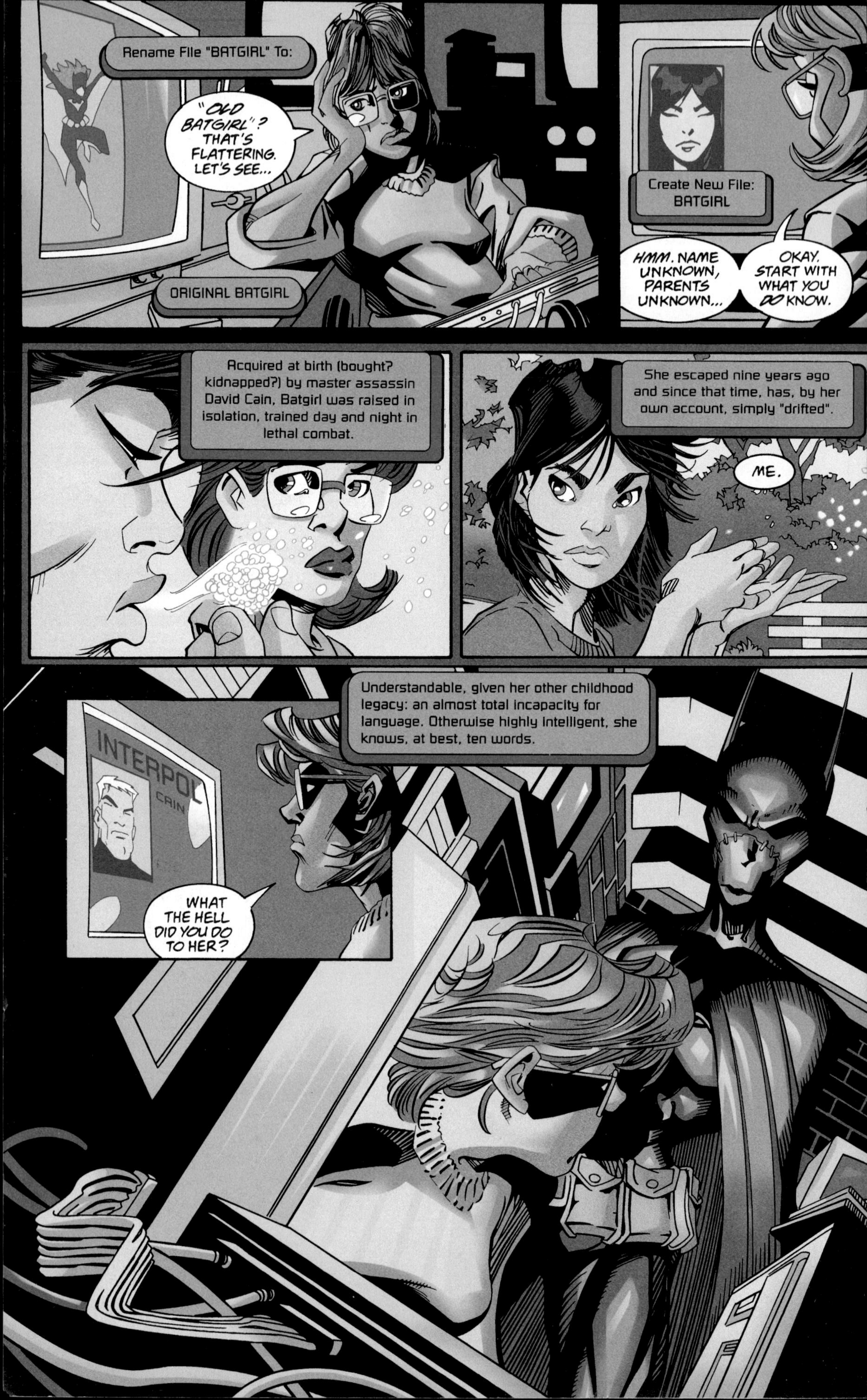

Rename File "BATGIRL" To:
"OLD BATGIRL"? THAT'S FLATTERING. LET'S SEE...
ORIGINAL BATGIRL
Create New File: BATGIRL
HMM. NAME UNKNOWN, PARENTS UNKNOWN...
OKAY. START WITH WHAT YOU DO KNOW.
Acquired at birth (bought? kidnapped?) by master assassin David Cain, Batgirl was raised in isolation, trained day and night in lethal combat.
She escaped nine years ago and since that time, has, by her own account, simply "drifted".
ME.
Understandable, given her other childhood legacy: an almost total incapacity for language. Otherwise highly intelligent, she knows, at best, ten words.
INTERPOL
CAIN
WHAT THE HELL DID YOU DO TO HER?

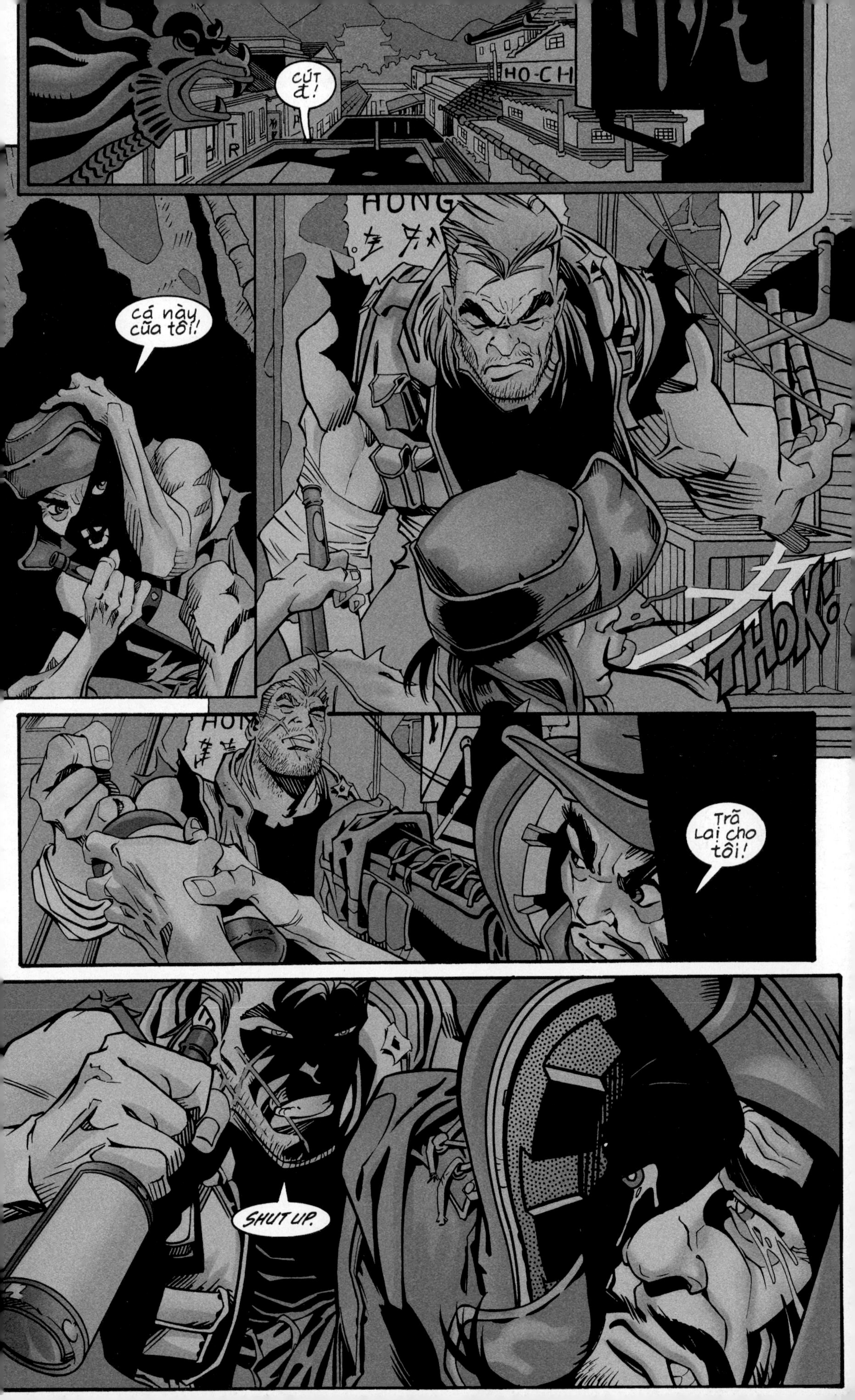
HO-CH
CÚT đi!
HONG
cá này của tôi!
THOK!
Trả lại cho tôi!
SHUT UP.

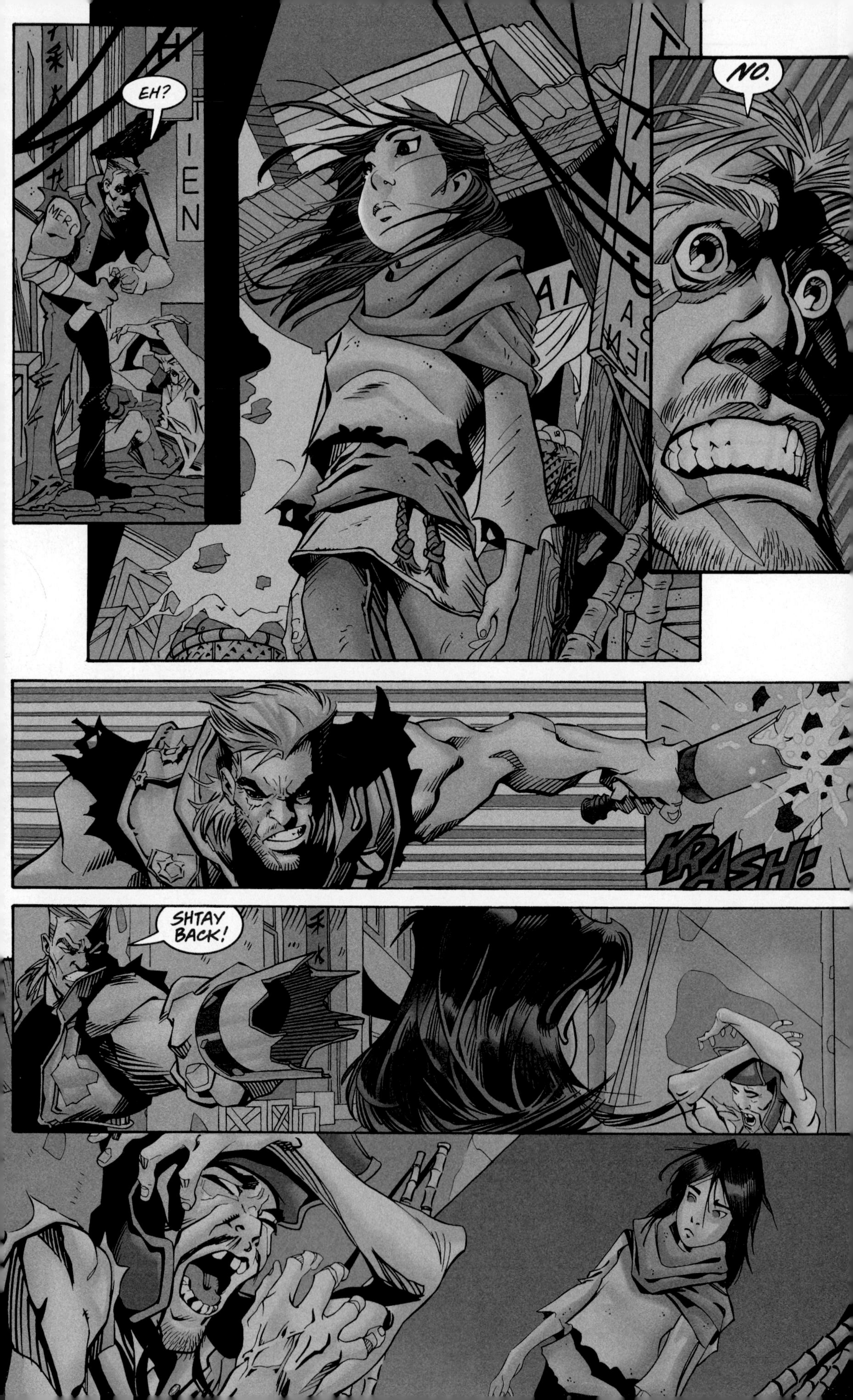

EH?
MERC
IEN
NO.
KRASH!
SHTAY BACK!

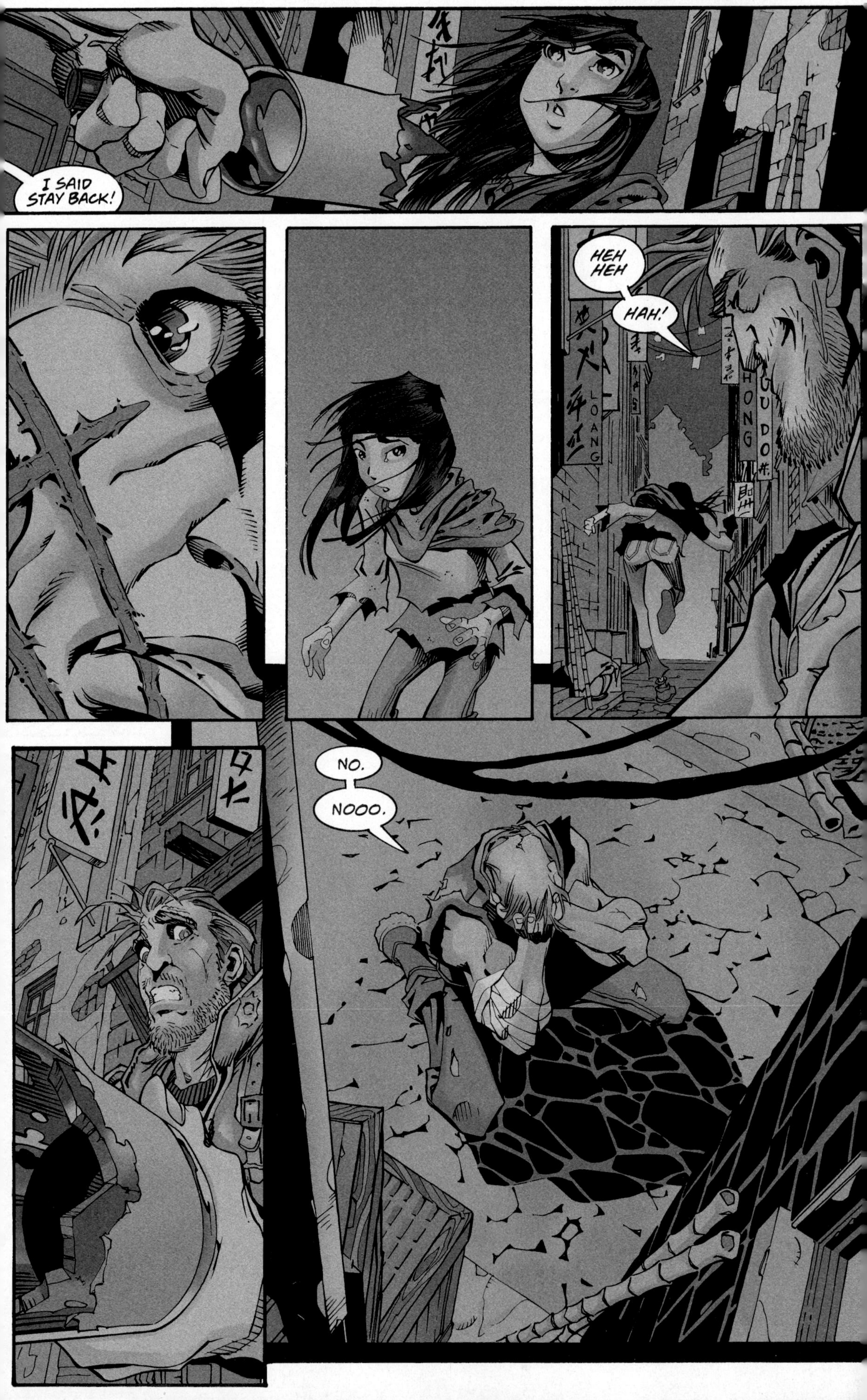
I SAID STAY BACK!
HEH HEH
HAH!
LOANG
HONG
HUDO
NO.
NOOO.

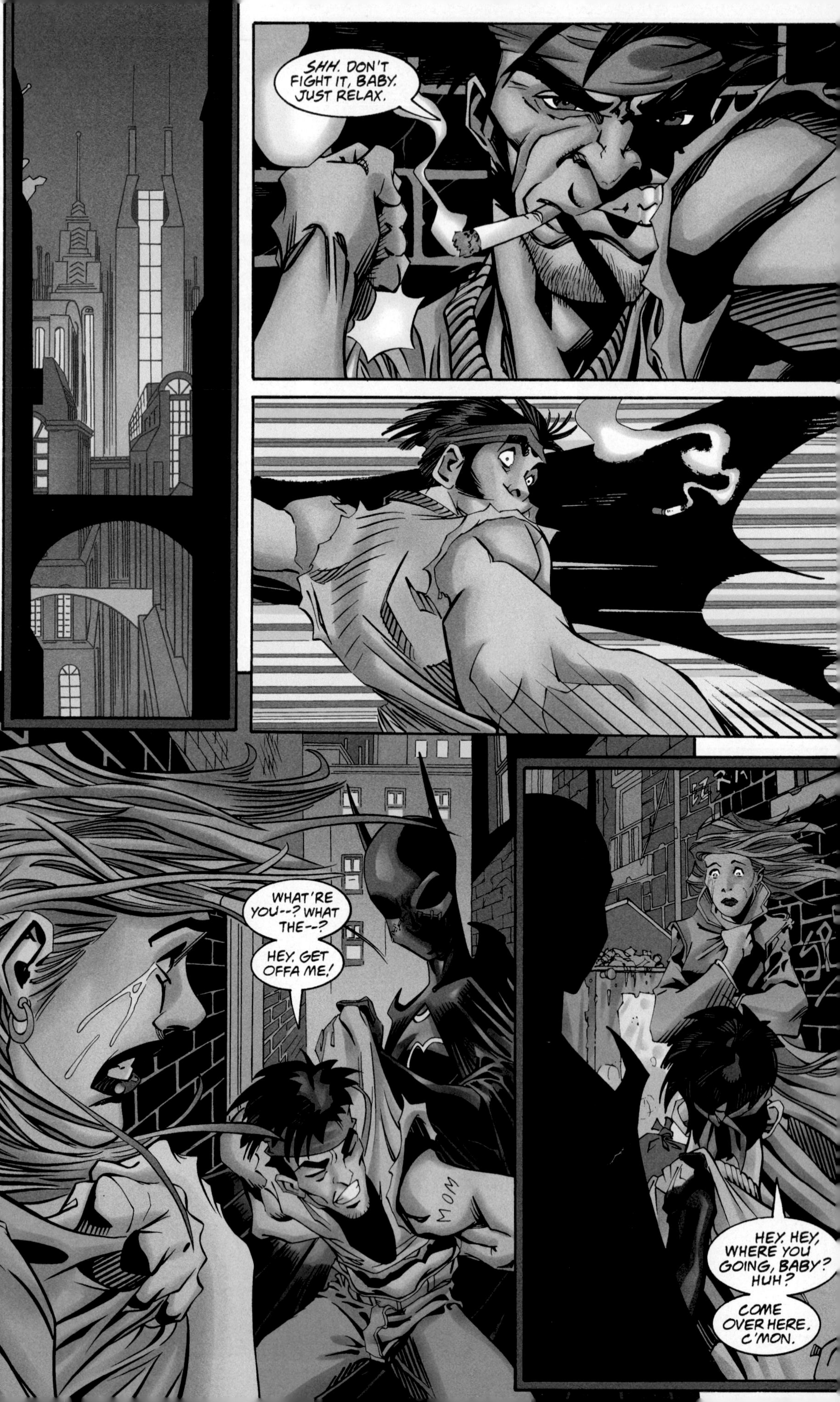
SHH. DON'T FIGHT IT, BABY. JUST RELAX.
WHAT'RE YOU--? WHAT THE--?
HEY, GET OFFA ME!
MOM
HEY. HEY, WHERE YOU GOING, BABY? HUH?
COME OVER HERE. C'MON.

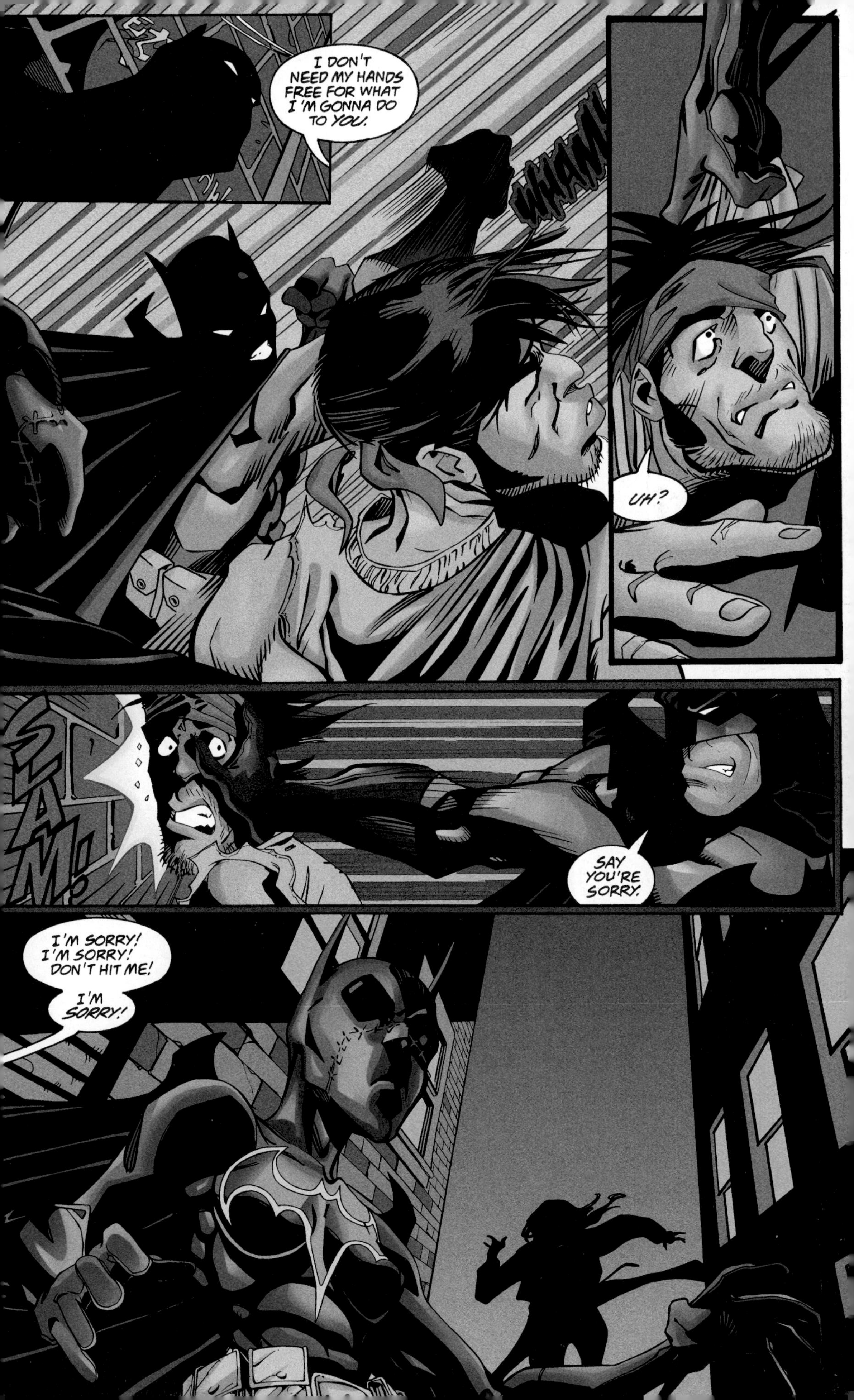
I DON'T NEED MY HANDS FREE FOR WHAT I'M GONNA DO TO YOU.
WHAM!
UH?
SLAM!
SAY YOU'RE SORRY.
I'M SORRY! I'M SORRY! DON'T HIT ME!
I'M SORRY!

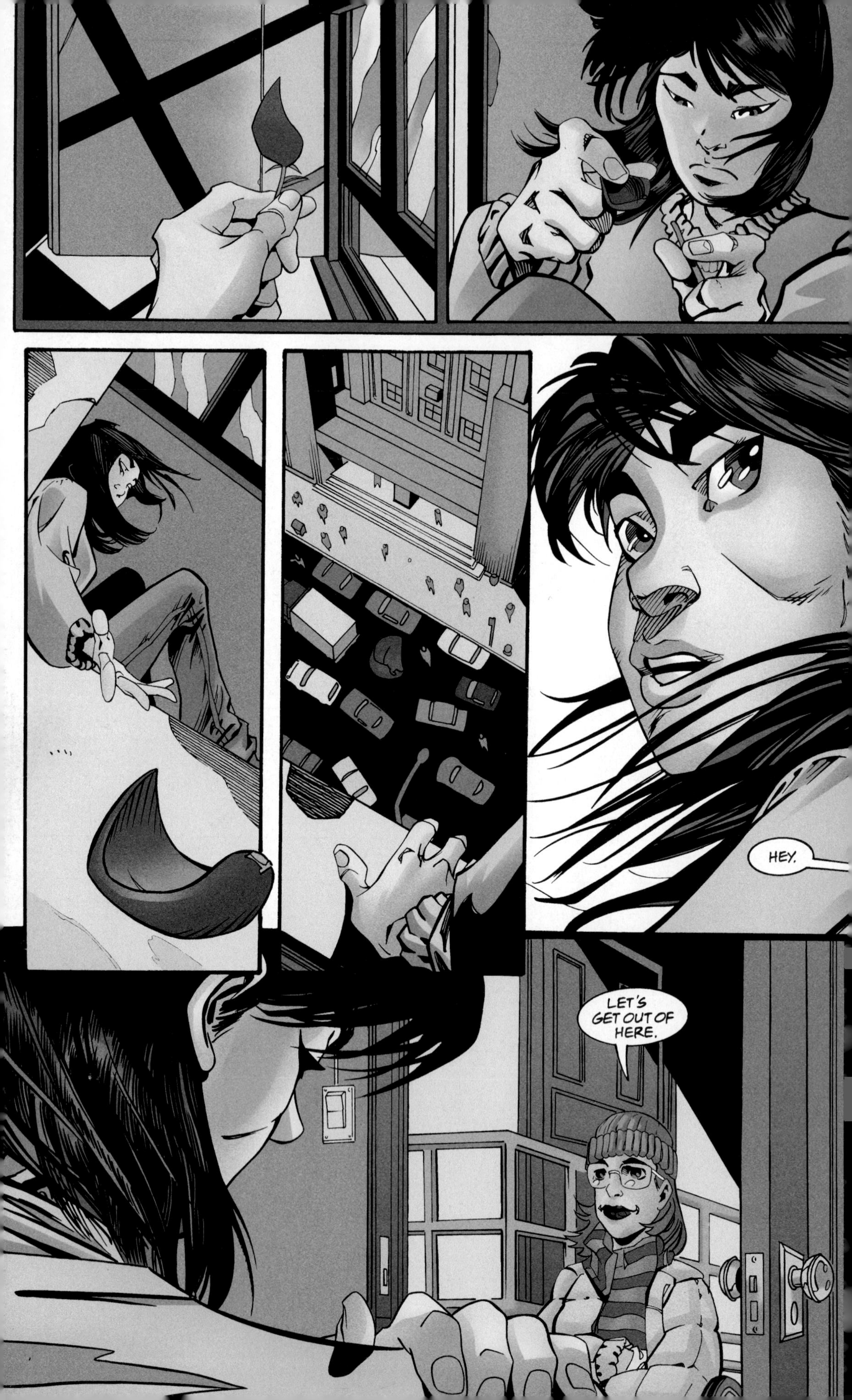
...
HEY.
LET'S GET OUT OF HERE.

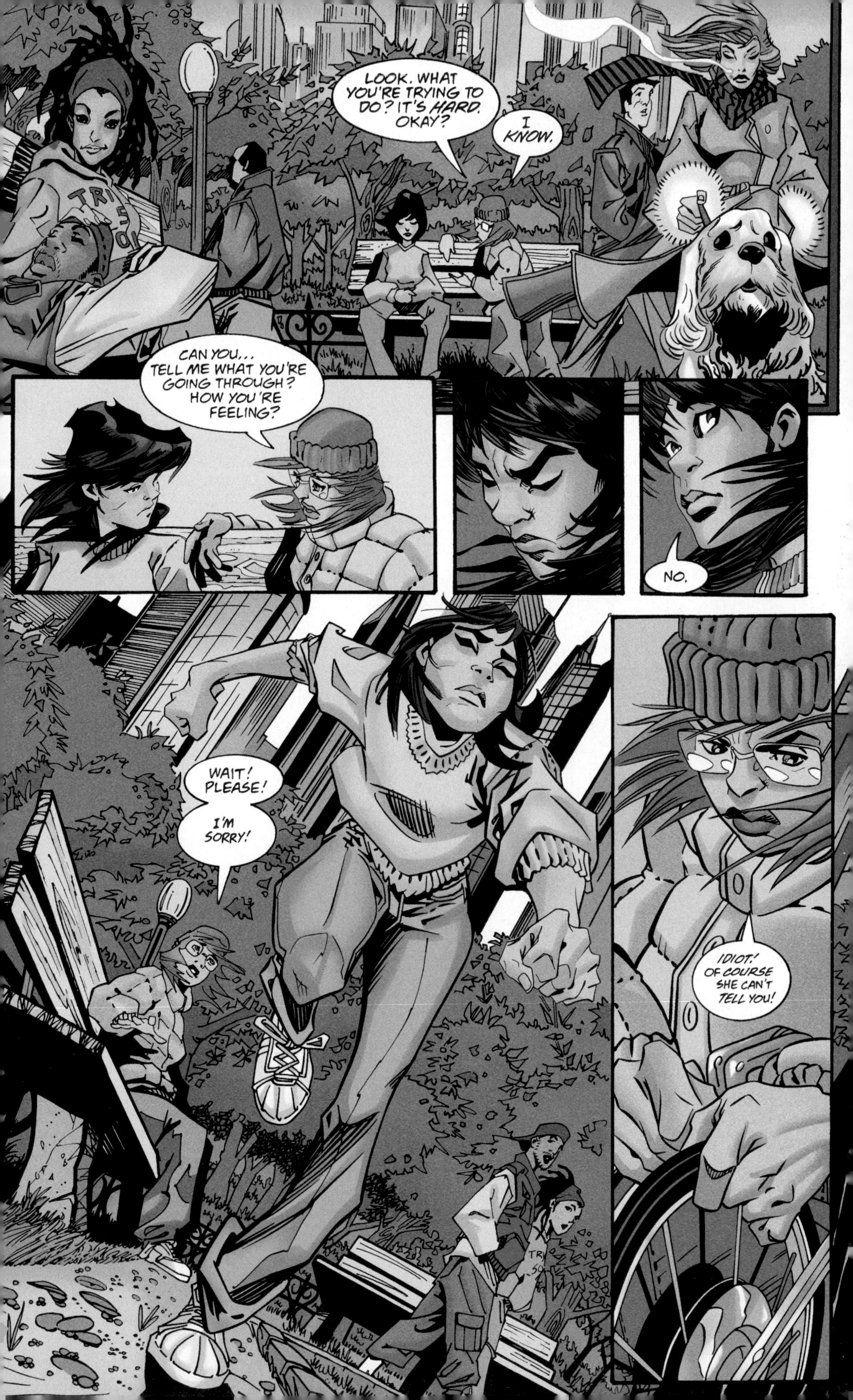
LOOK. WHAT YOU'RE TRYING TO DO? IT'S HARD. OKAY?
I KNOW.
CAN YOU... TELL ME WHAT YOU'RE GOING THROUGH? HOW YOU'RE FEELING?
NO.
WAIT! PLEASE!
I'M SORRY!
IDIOT! OF COURSE SHE CAN'T TELL YOU!

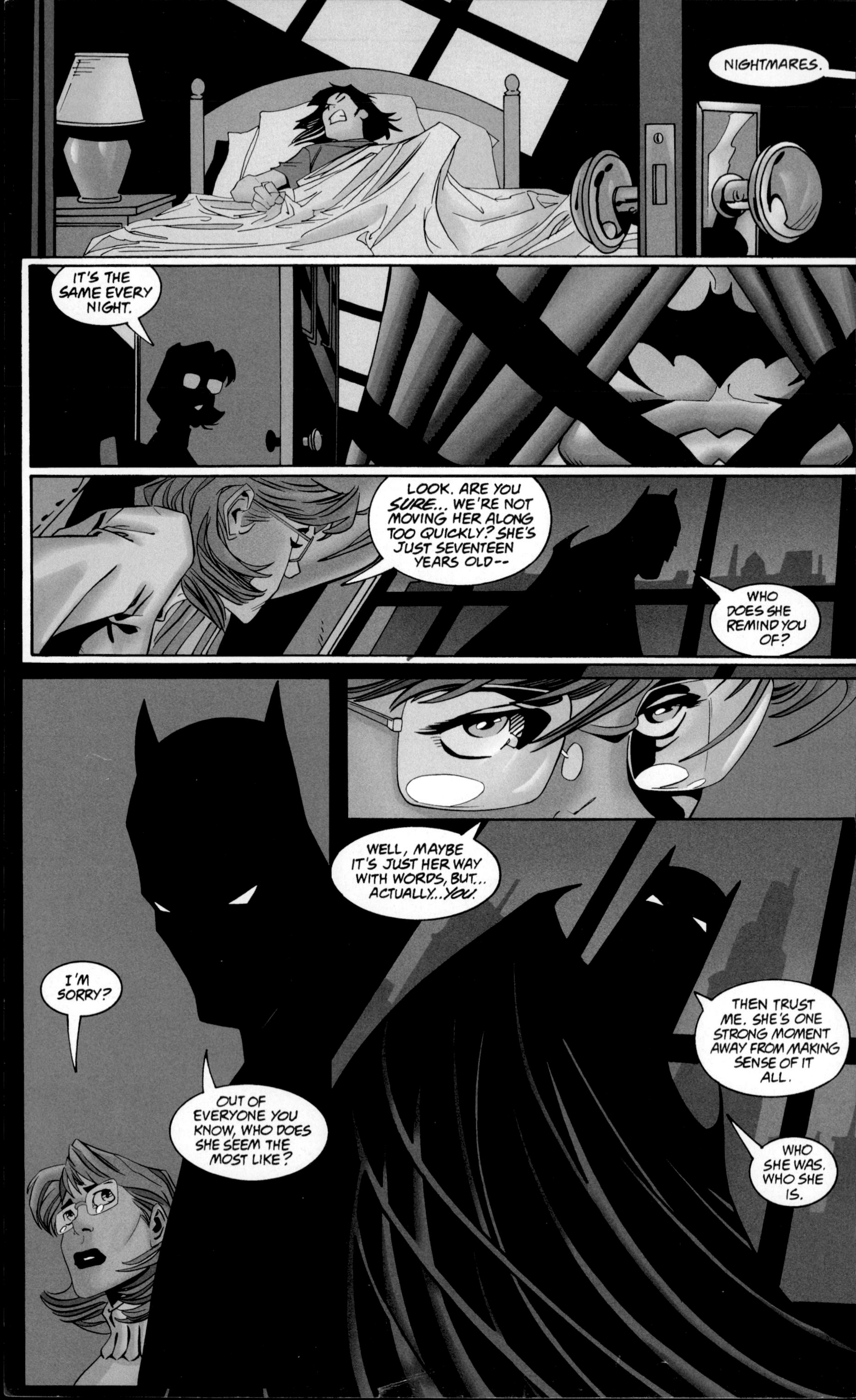
NIGHTMARES.
IT'S THE SAME EVERY NIGHT.
LOOK. ARE YOU SURE... WE'RE NOT MOVING HER ALONG TOO QUICKLY? SHE'S JUST SEVENTEEN YEARS OLD--
WHO DOES SHE REMIND YOU OF?
WELL, MAYBE IT'S JUST HER WAY WITH WORDS, BUT... ACTUALLY... YOU.
I'M SORRY?
OUT OF EVERYONE YOU KNOW, WHO DOES SHE SEEM THE MOST LIKE?
THEN TRUST ME. SHE'S ONE STRONG MOMENT AWAY FROM MAKING SENSE OF IT ALL.
WHO SHE WAS. WHO SHE IS.

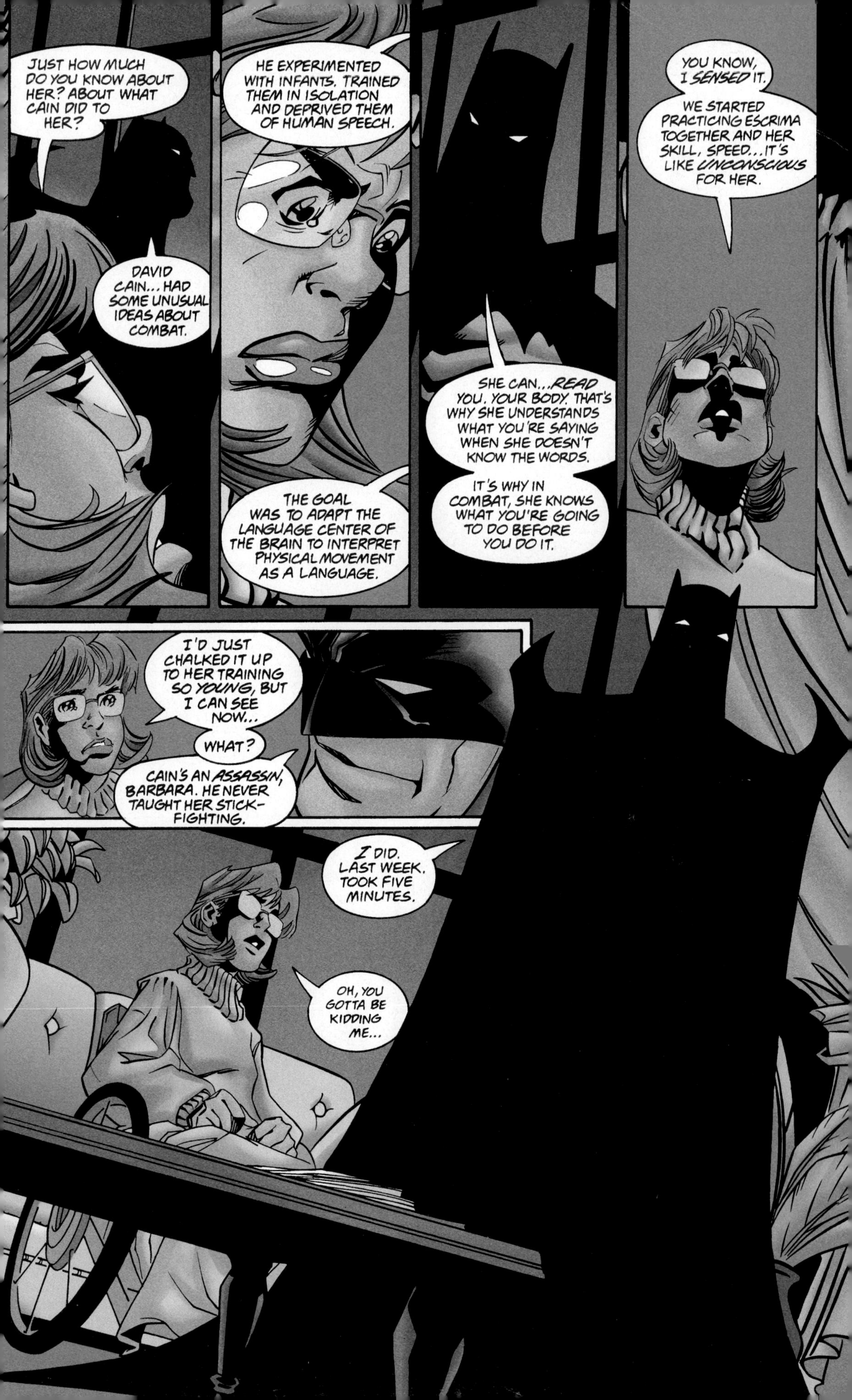
JUST HOW MUCH DO YOU KNOW ABOUT HER? ABOUT WHAT CAIN DID TO HER?
DAVID CAIN... HAD SOME UNUSUAL IDEAS ABOUT COMBAT.
HE EXPERIMENTED WITH INFANTS. TRAINED THEM IN ISOLATION AND DEPRIVED THEM OF HUMAN SPEECH.
THE GOAL WAS TO ADAPT THE LANGUAGE CENTER OF THE BRAIN TO INTERPRET PHYSICAL MOVEMENT AS A LANGUAGE.
SHE CAN... READ YOU. YOUR BODY. THAT'S WHY SHE UNDERSTANDS WHAT YOU'RE SAYING WHEN SHE DOESN'T KNOW THE WORDS.
IT'S WHY IN COMBAT, SHE KNOWS WHAT YOU'RE GOING TO DO BEFORE YOU DO IT.
YOU KNOW, I SENSED IT.
WE STARTED PRACTICING ESCRIMA TOGETHER AND HER SKILL, SPEED... IT'S LIKE UNCONSCIOUS FOR HER.
I'D JUST CHALKED IT UP TO HER TRAINING SO YOUNG, BUT I CAN SEE NOW...
WHAT?
CAIN'S AN ASSASSIN, BARBARA. HE NEVER TAUGHT HER STICK-FIGHTING.
I DID. LAST WEEK. TOOK FIVE MINUTES.
OH, YOU GOTTA BE KIDDING ME...

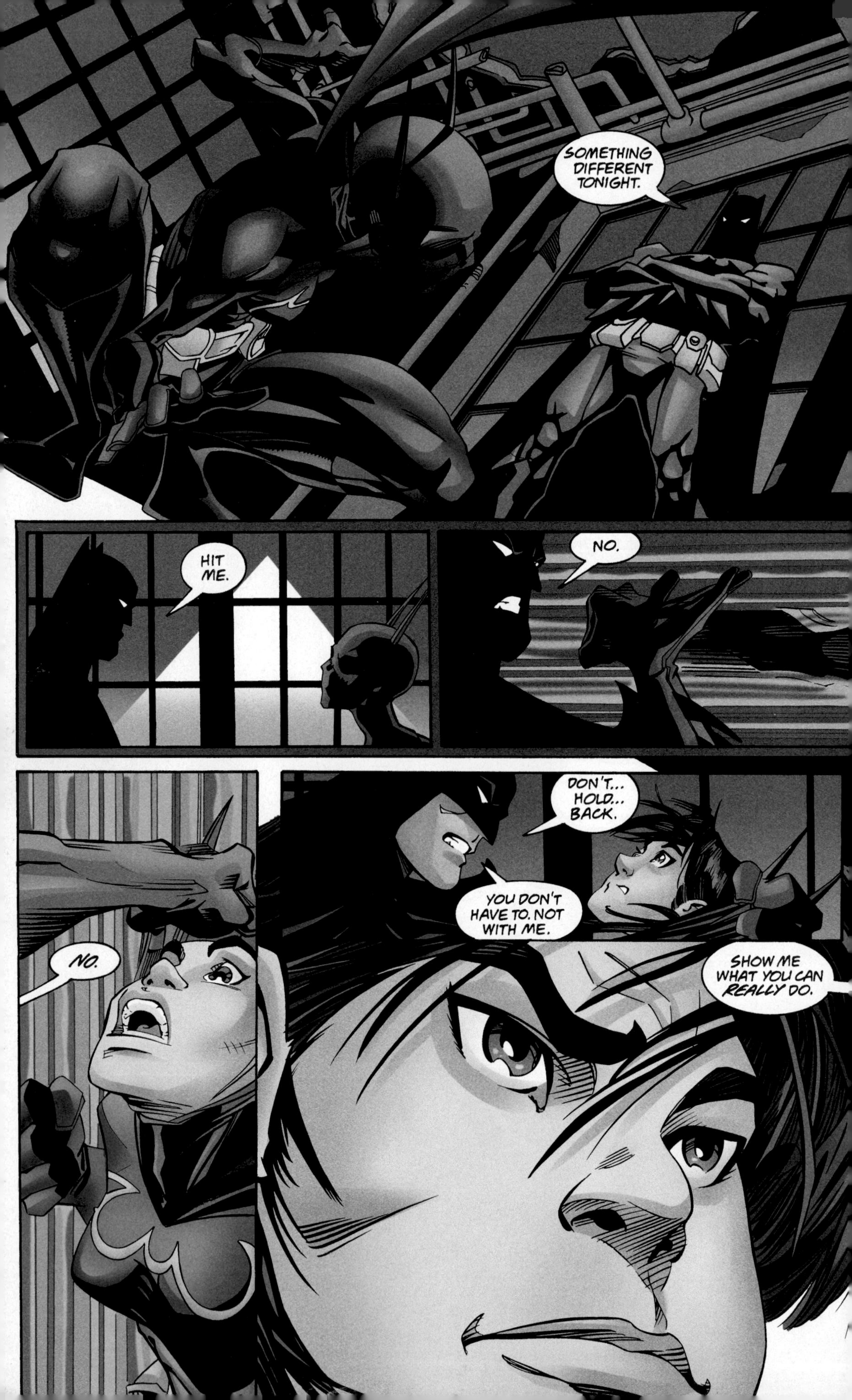
SOMETHING DIFFERENT TONIGHT.
HIT ME.
NO.
DON'T... HOLD... BACK.
YOU DON'T HAVE TO. NOT WITH ME.
NO.
SHOW ME WHAT YOU CAN REALLY DO.

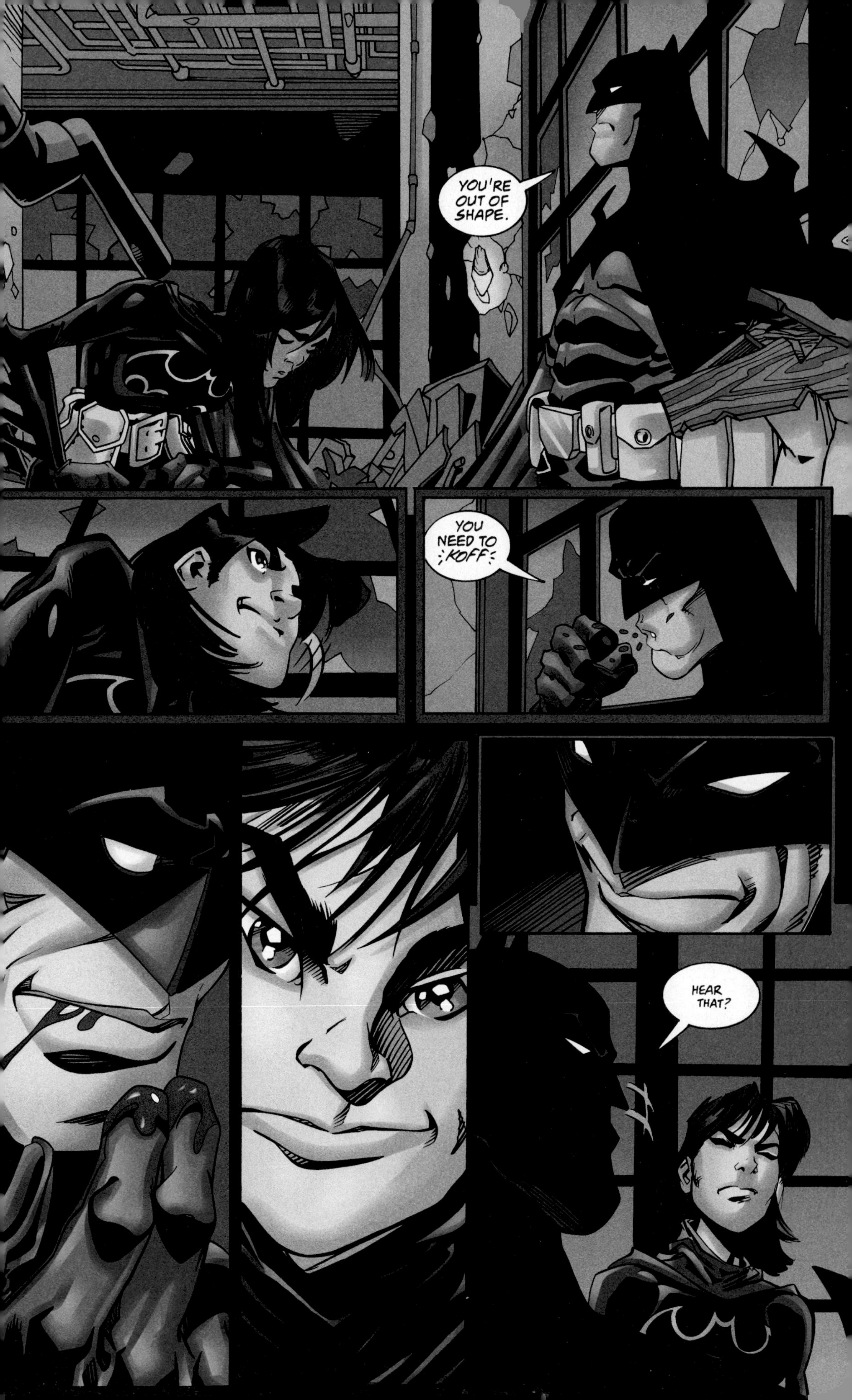
YOU'RE OUT OF SHAPE.
YOU NEED TO KOFF
HEAR THAT?

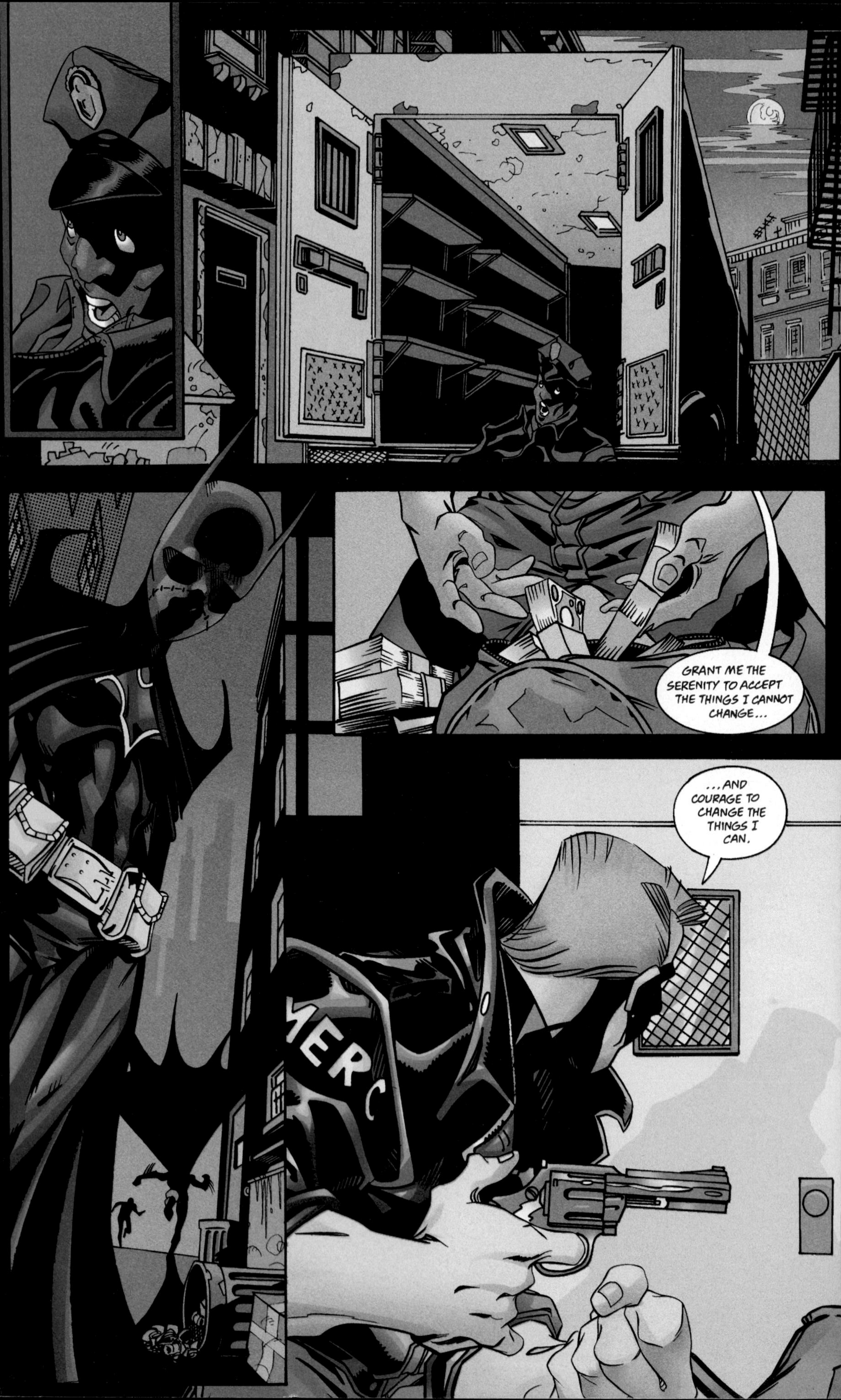
GRANT ME THE SERENITY TO ACCEPT THE THINGS I CANNOT CHANGE...
...AND COURAGE TO CHANGE THE THINGS I CAN.
MERC

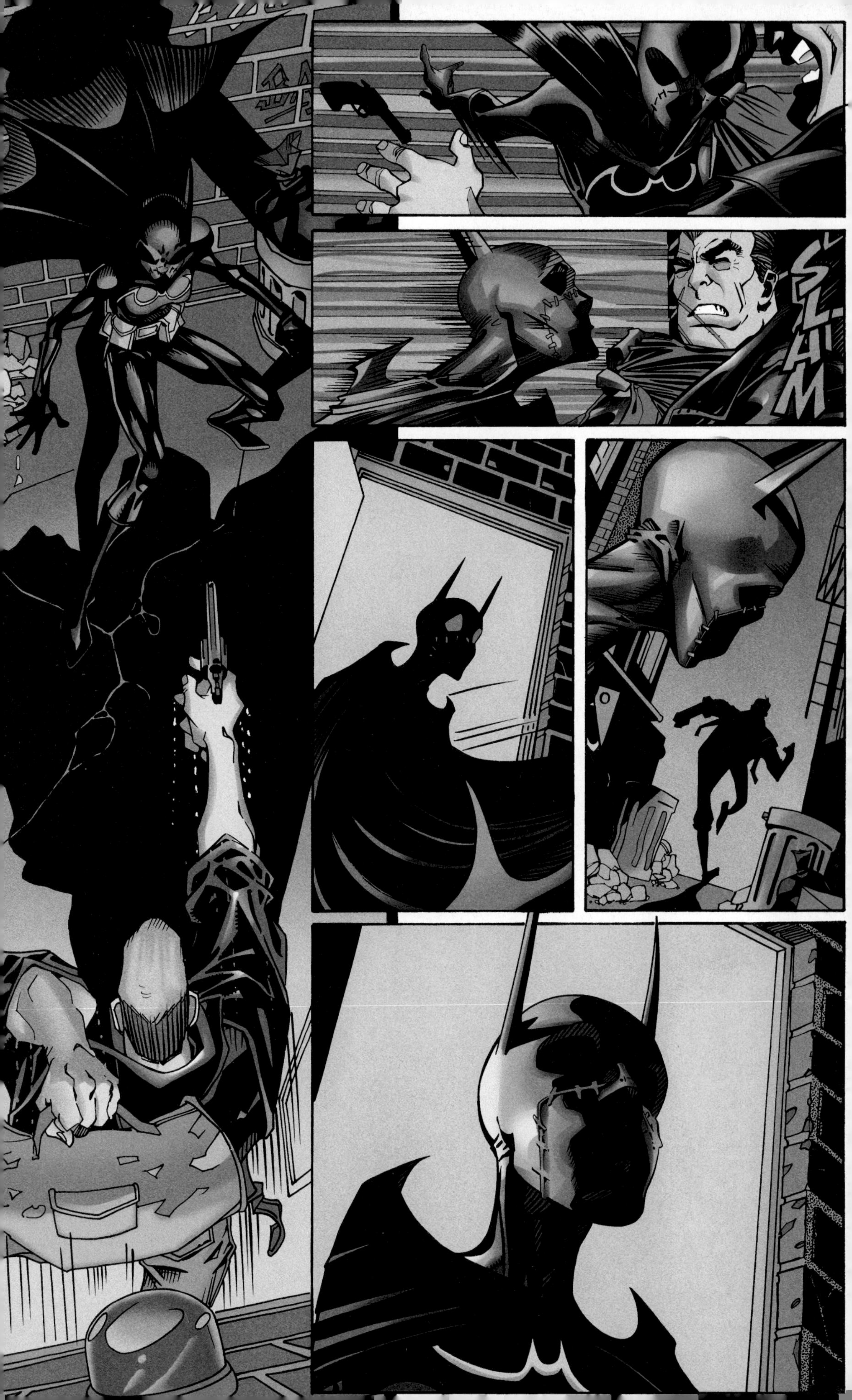
SLAM

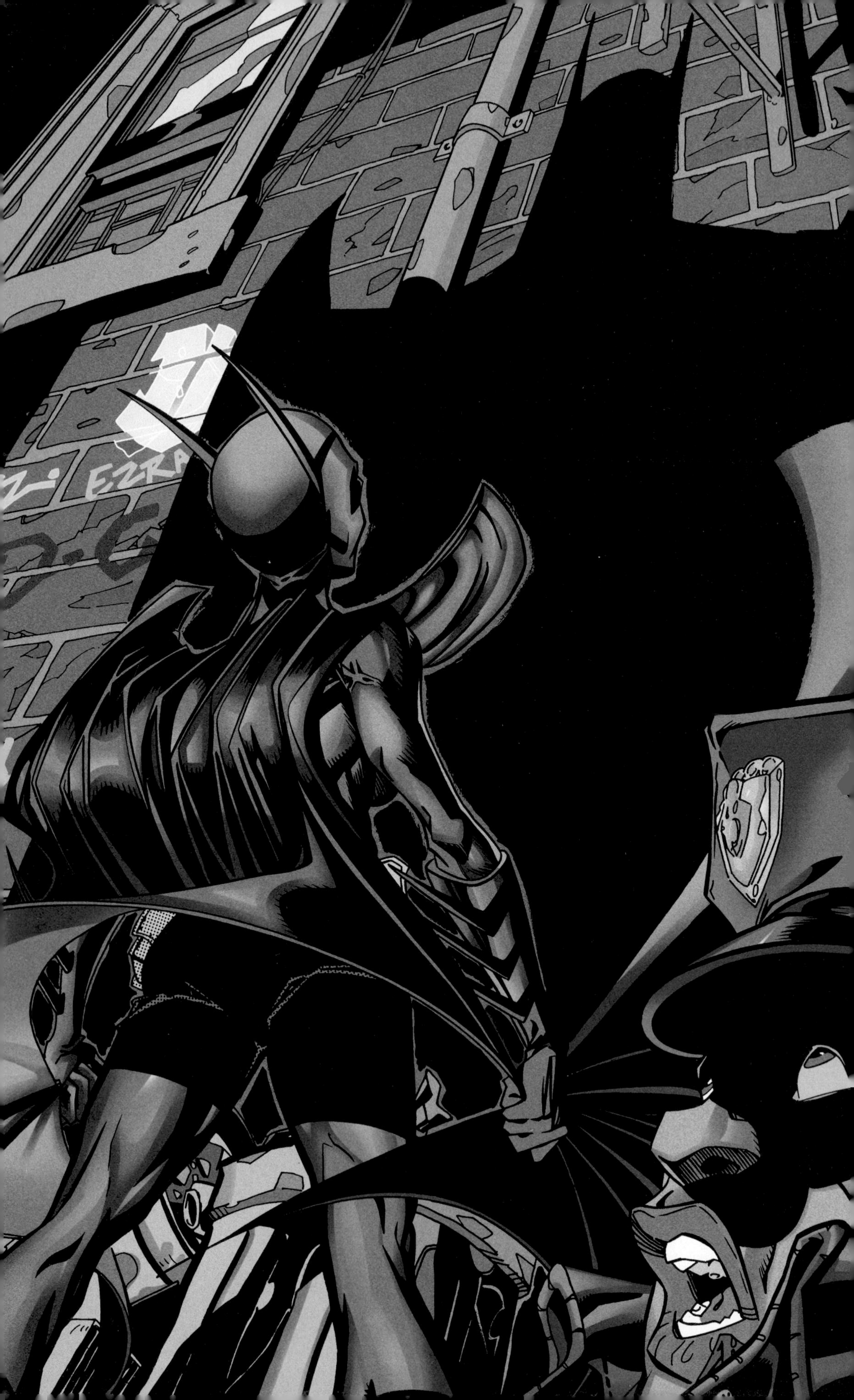
EZRA

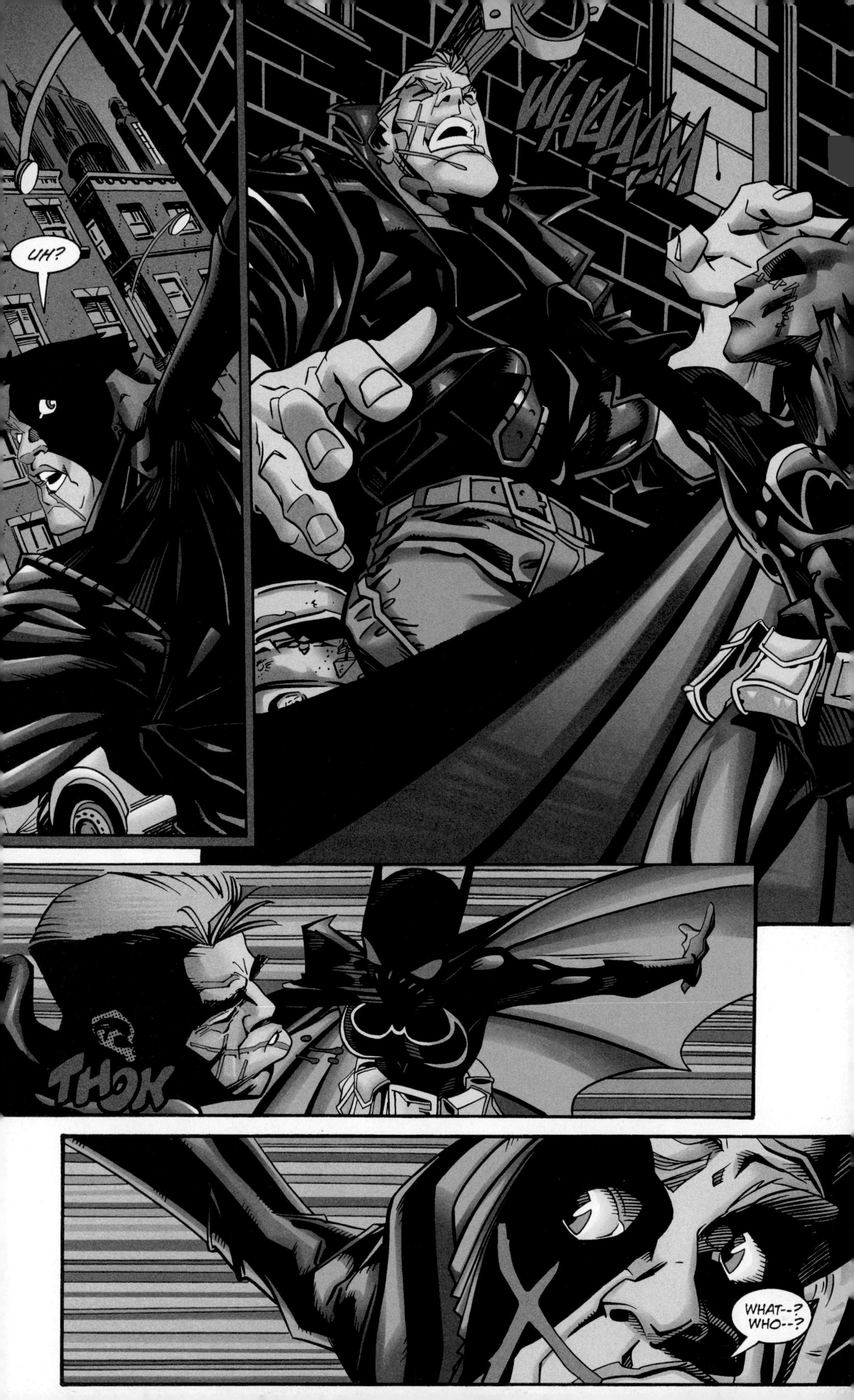
WHAAAM
UH?
THOK
WHAT--? WHO--?

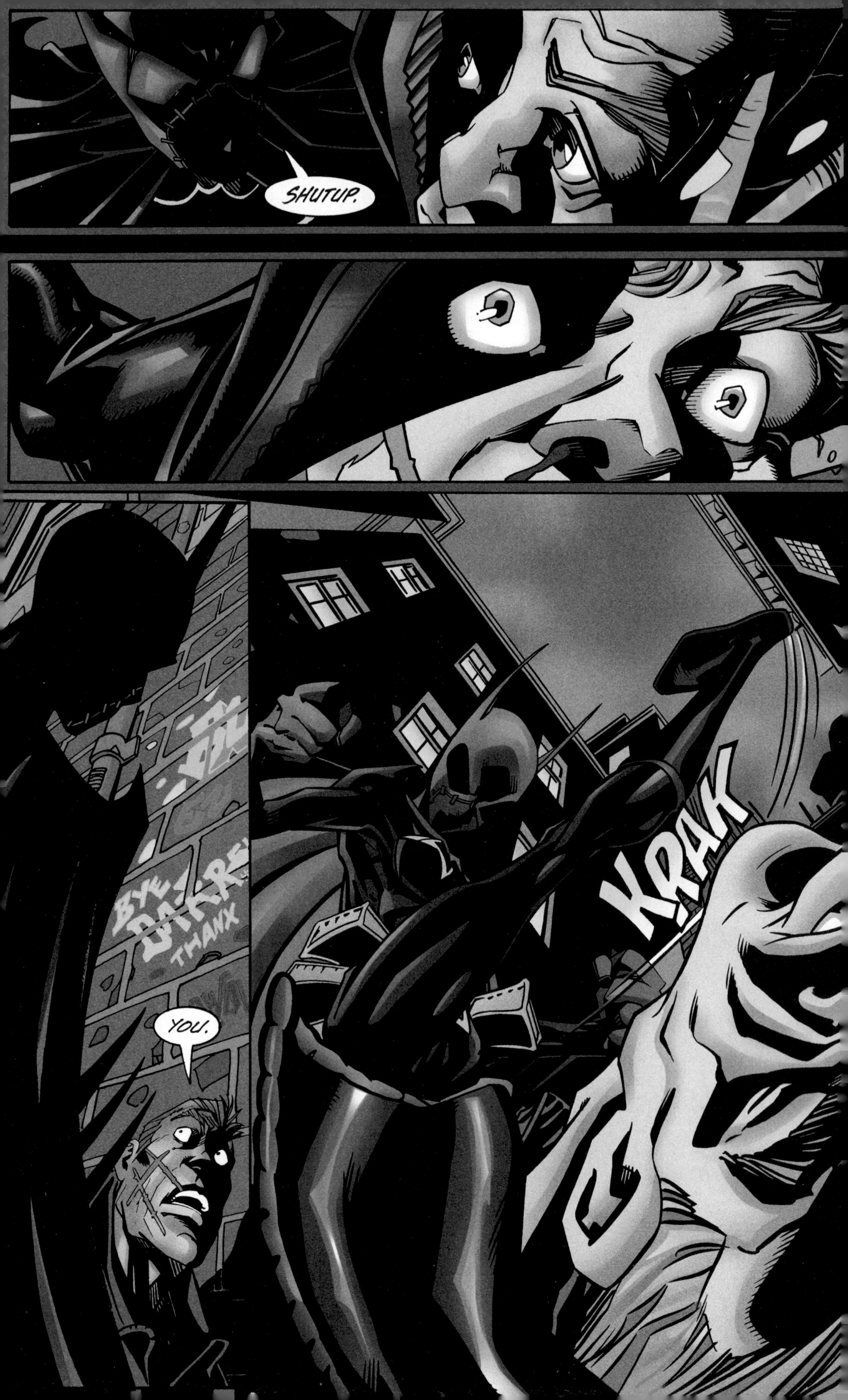
SHUTUP.
BYE
THANX
YOU.
KRAK

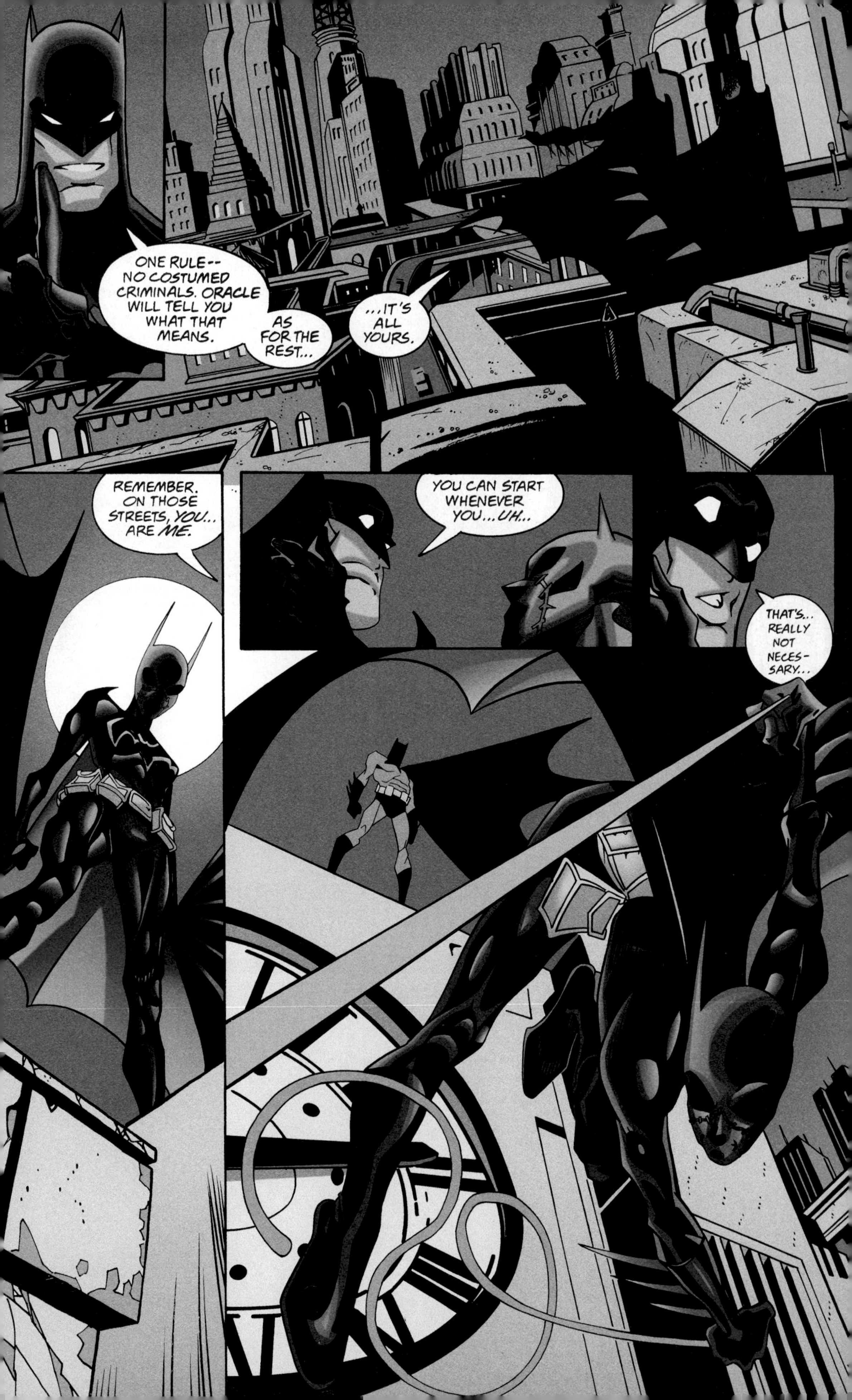
ONE RULE--
NO COSTUMED CRIMINALS. ORACLE WILL TELL YOU WHAT THAT MEANS.
AS FOR THE REST...
...IT'S ALL YOURS.
REMEMBER. ON THOSE STREETS, YOU... ARE ME.
YOU CAN START WHENEVER YOU... UH...
THAT'S... REALLY NOT NECES-SARY...

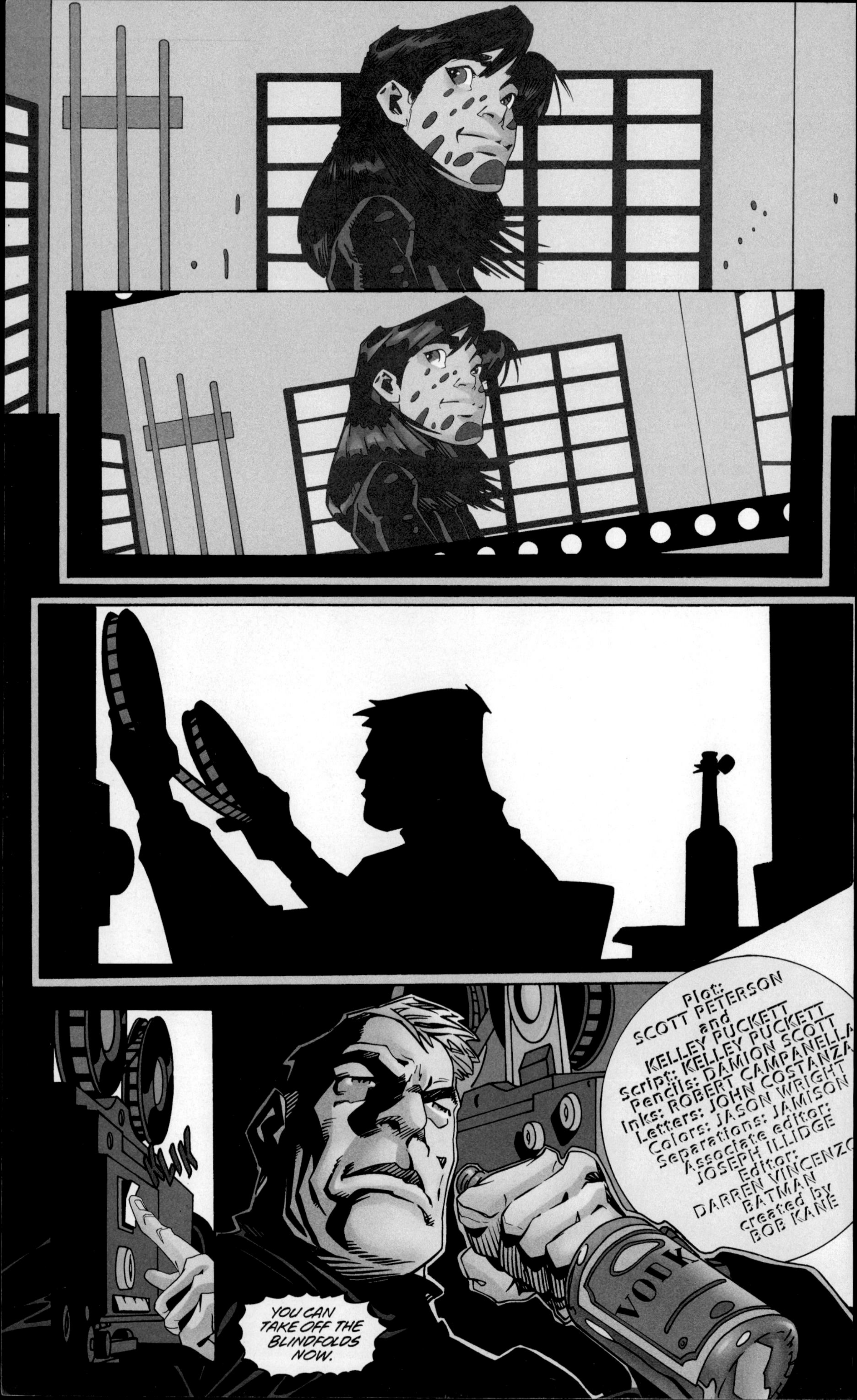
Plot:
SCOTT PETERSON
and
KELLEY PUCKETT
Script: KELLEY PUCKETT
Pencils: DAMION SCOTT
Inks: ROBERT CAMPANELLA
Letters: JOHN COSTANZA
Colors: JASON WRIGHT
Separations: JAMISON
Associate editor:
JOSEPH ILLIDGE
Editor:
DARREN VINCENZO
BATMAN
created by
BOB KANE
KLIK
YOU CAN TAKE OFF THE BLINDFOLDS NOW.

BATGIRL #2 cover by
Damion Scott & Robert Campanella

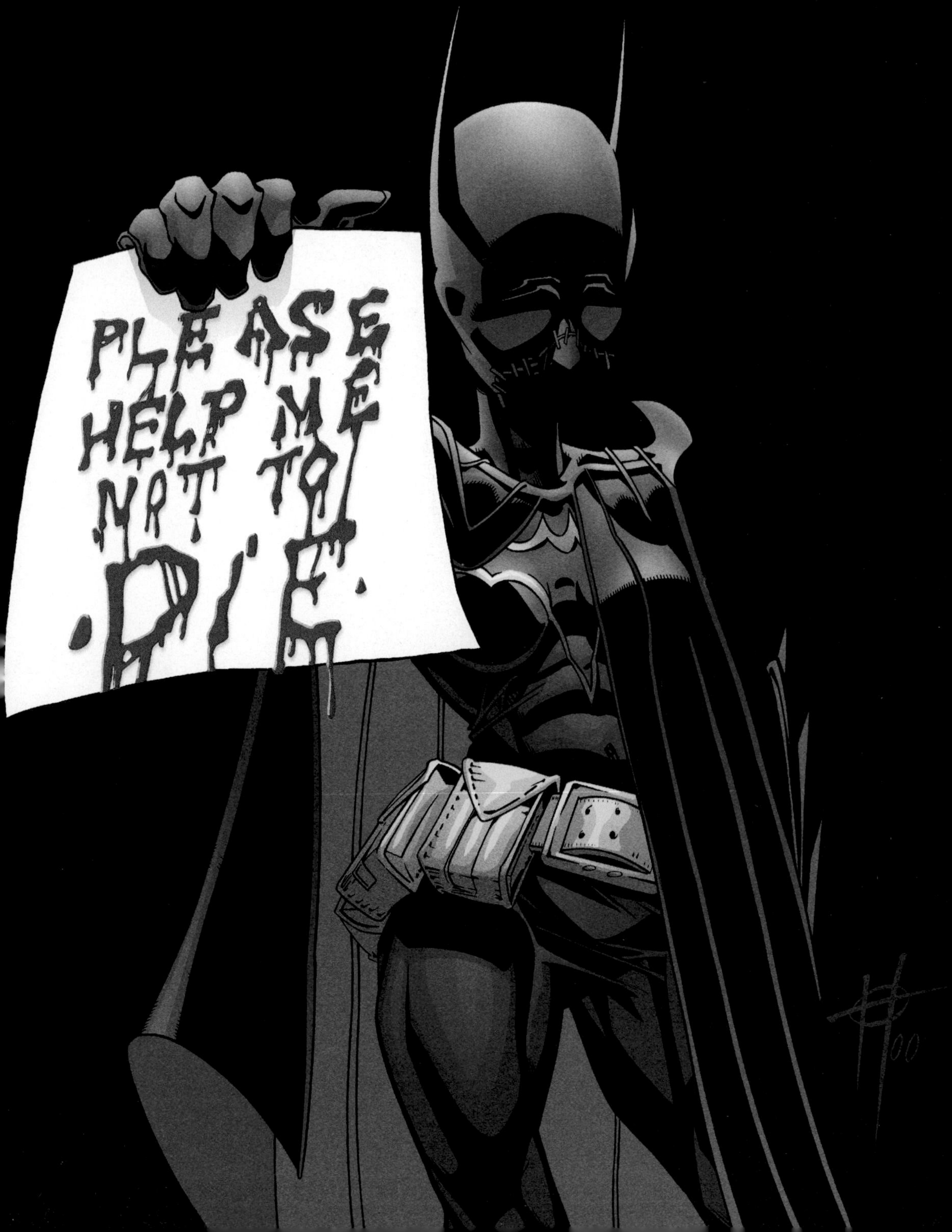
PLEASE HELP ME NOT TO DIE.

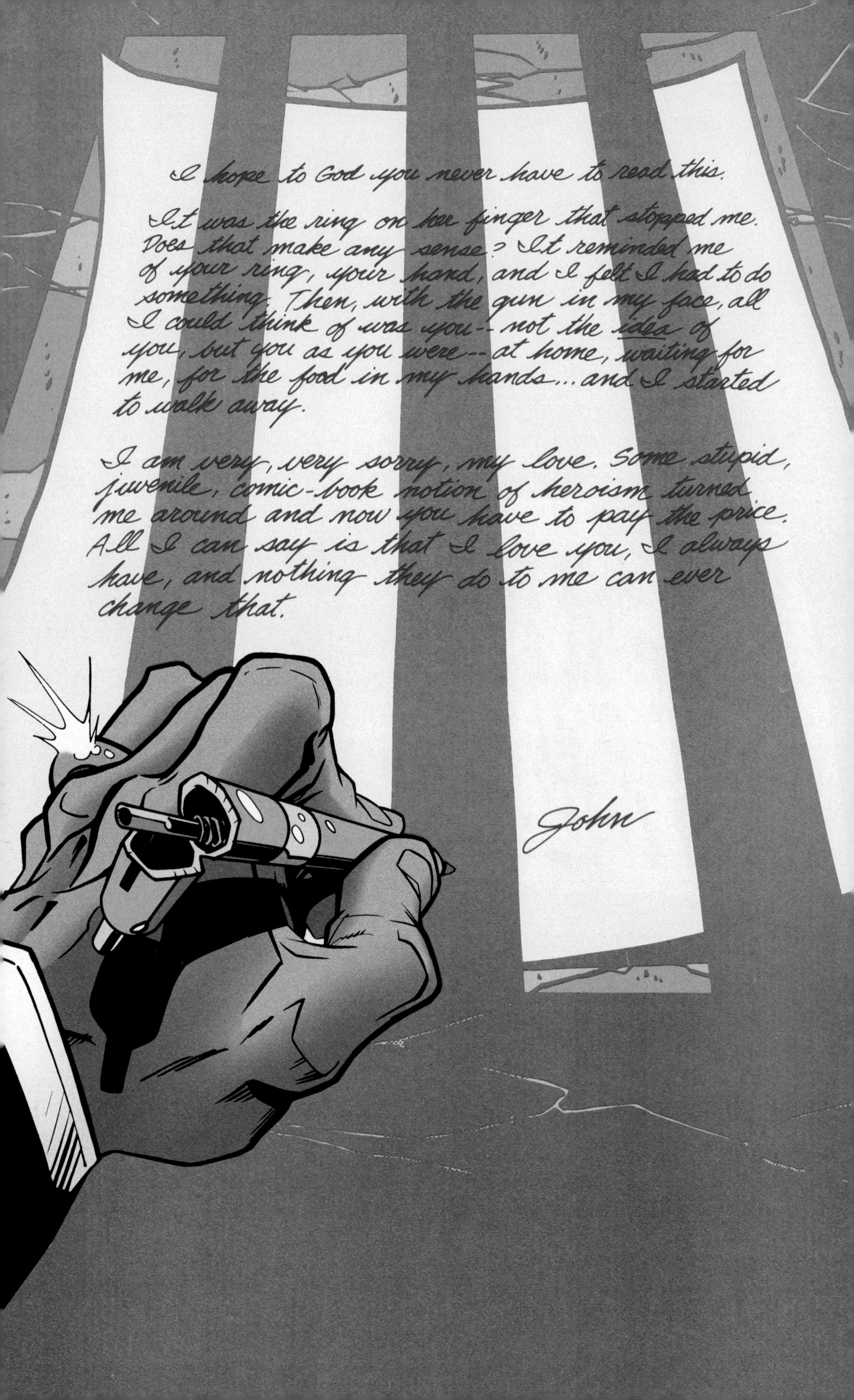
I hope to God you never have to read this.
It was the ring on her finger that stopped me. Does that make any sense? It reminded me of your ring, your hand, and I felt I had to do something. Then, with the gun in my face, all I could think of was you-- not the idea of you, but you as you were-- at home, waiting for me, for the food in my hands... and I started to walk away.
I am very, very sorry, my love. Some stupid, juvenile, comic-book notion of heroism turned me around and now you have to pay the price. All I can say is that I love you, I always have, and nothing they do to me can ever change that.
John

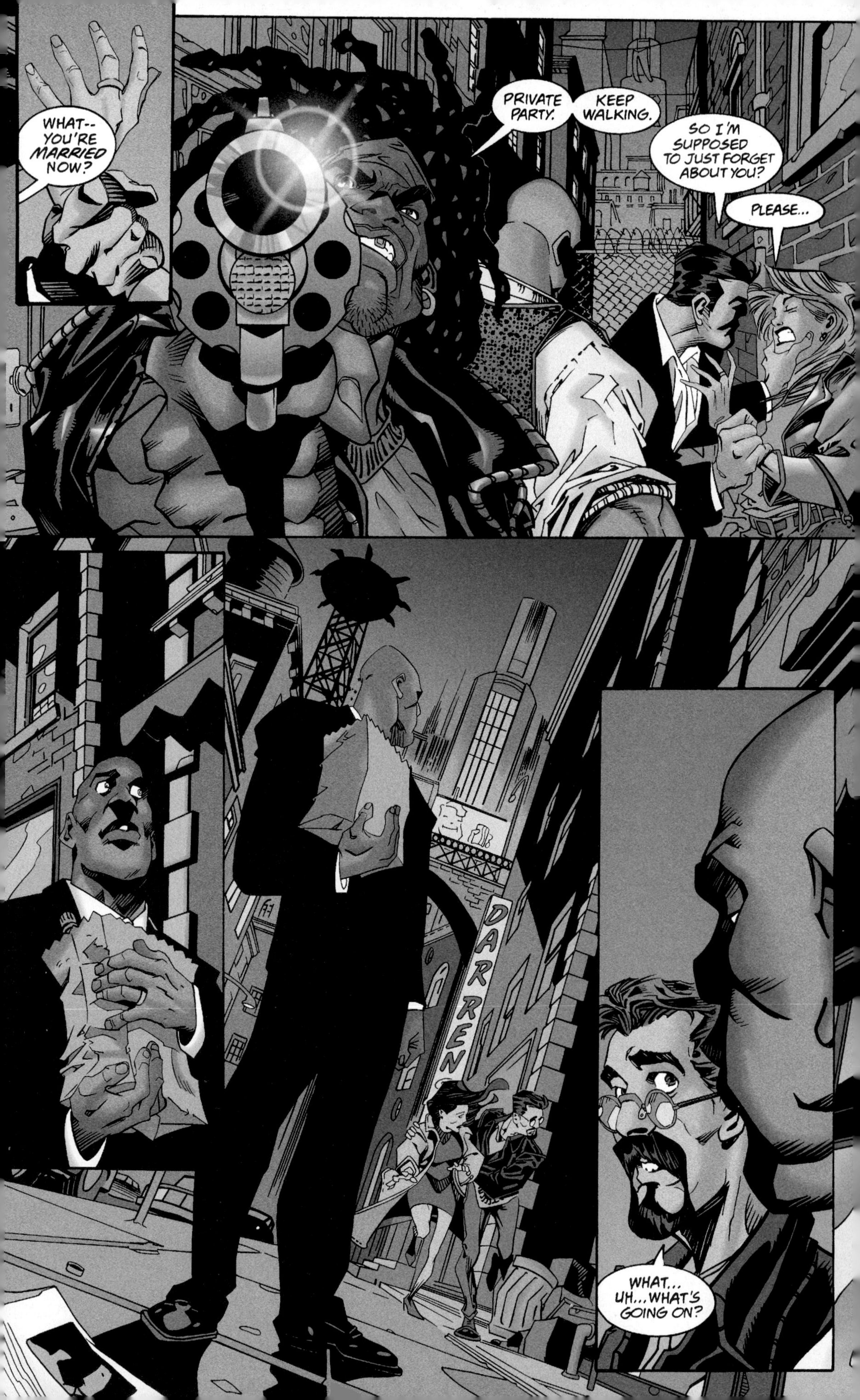

WHAT-- YOU'RE *MARRIED* NOW?
PRIVATE PARTY.
KEEP WALKING.
SO I'M SUPPOSED TO JUST FORGET ABOUT YOU?
PLEASE...
DARREN
WHAT... UH... WHAT'S GOING ON?

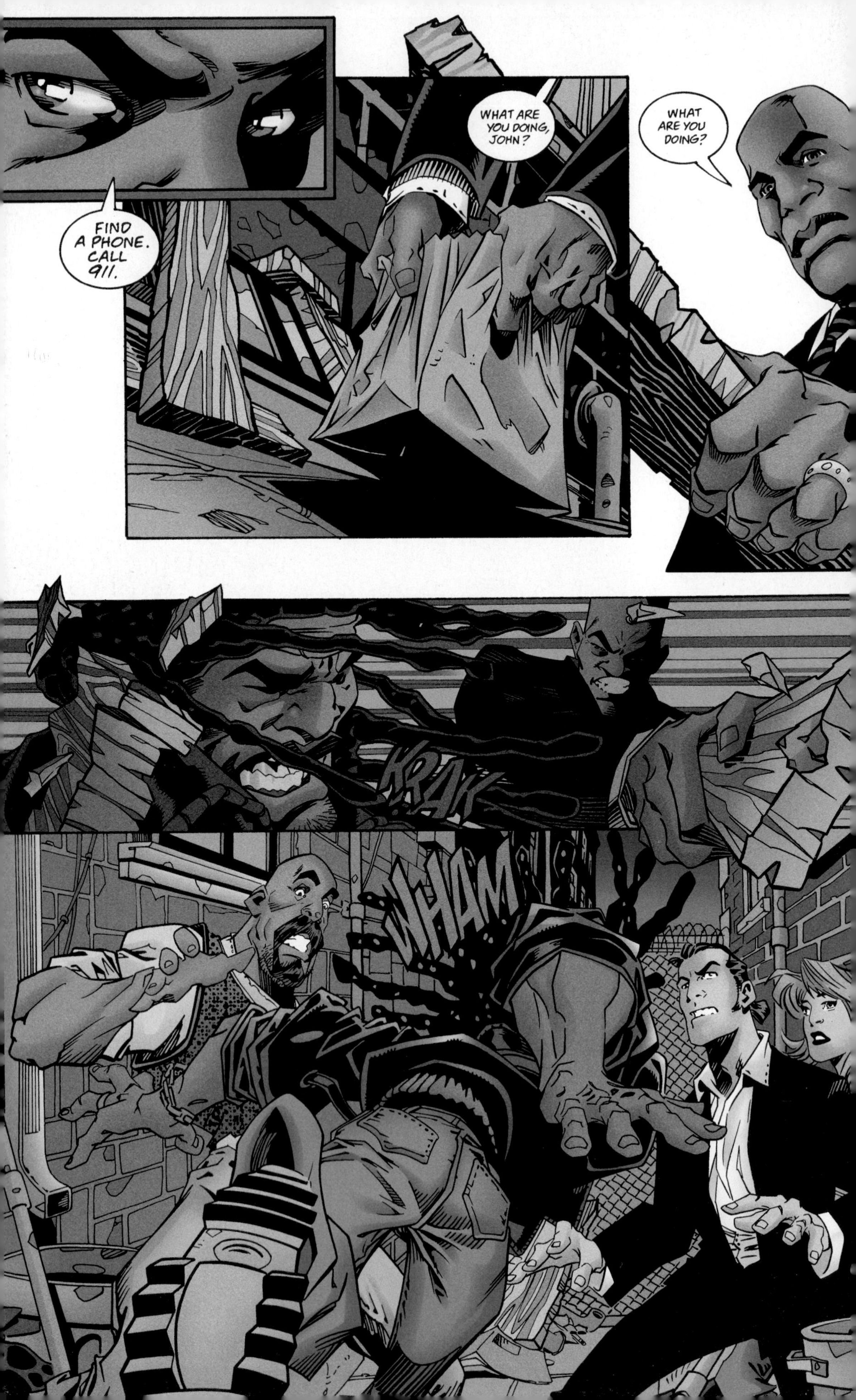
FIND A PHONE. CALL 911.
WHAT ARE YOU DOING, JOHN?
WHAT ARE YOU DOING?
KRAK
WHAM

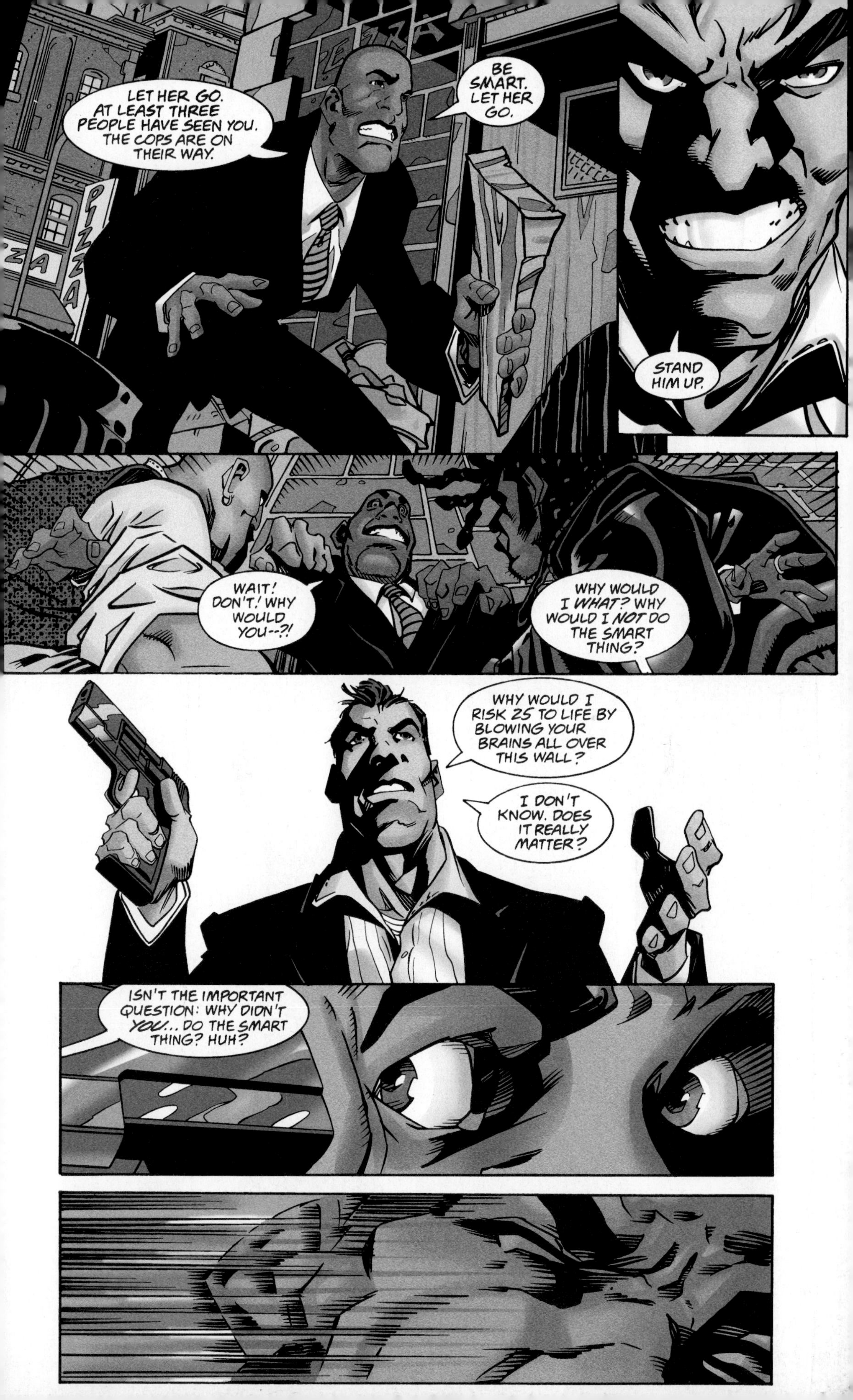
LET HER GO. AT LEAST THREE PEOPLE HAVE SEEN YOU. THE COPS ARE ON THEIR WAY.
BE SMART. LET HER GO.
STAND HIM UP.
WAIT! DON'T! WHY WOULD YOU--?!
WHY WOULD I WHAT? WHY WOULD I NOT DO THE SMART THING?
WHY WOULD I RISK 25 TO LIFE BY BLOWING YOUR BRAINS ALL OVER THIS WALL?
I DON'T KNOW. DOES IT REALLY MATTER?
ISN'T THE IMPORTANT QUESTION: WHY DIDN'T YOU... DO THE SMART THING? HUH?

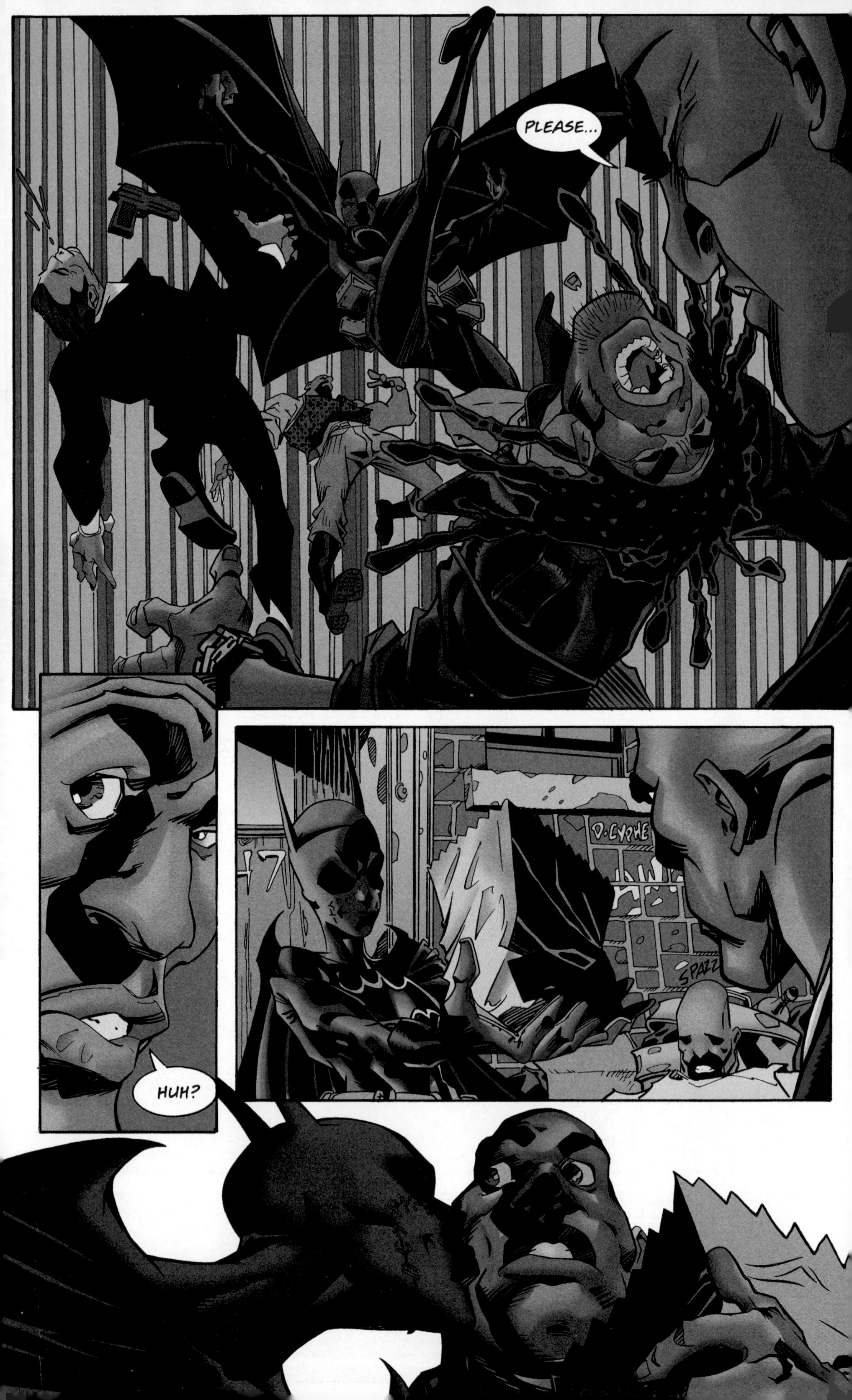
PLEASE...
HUH?

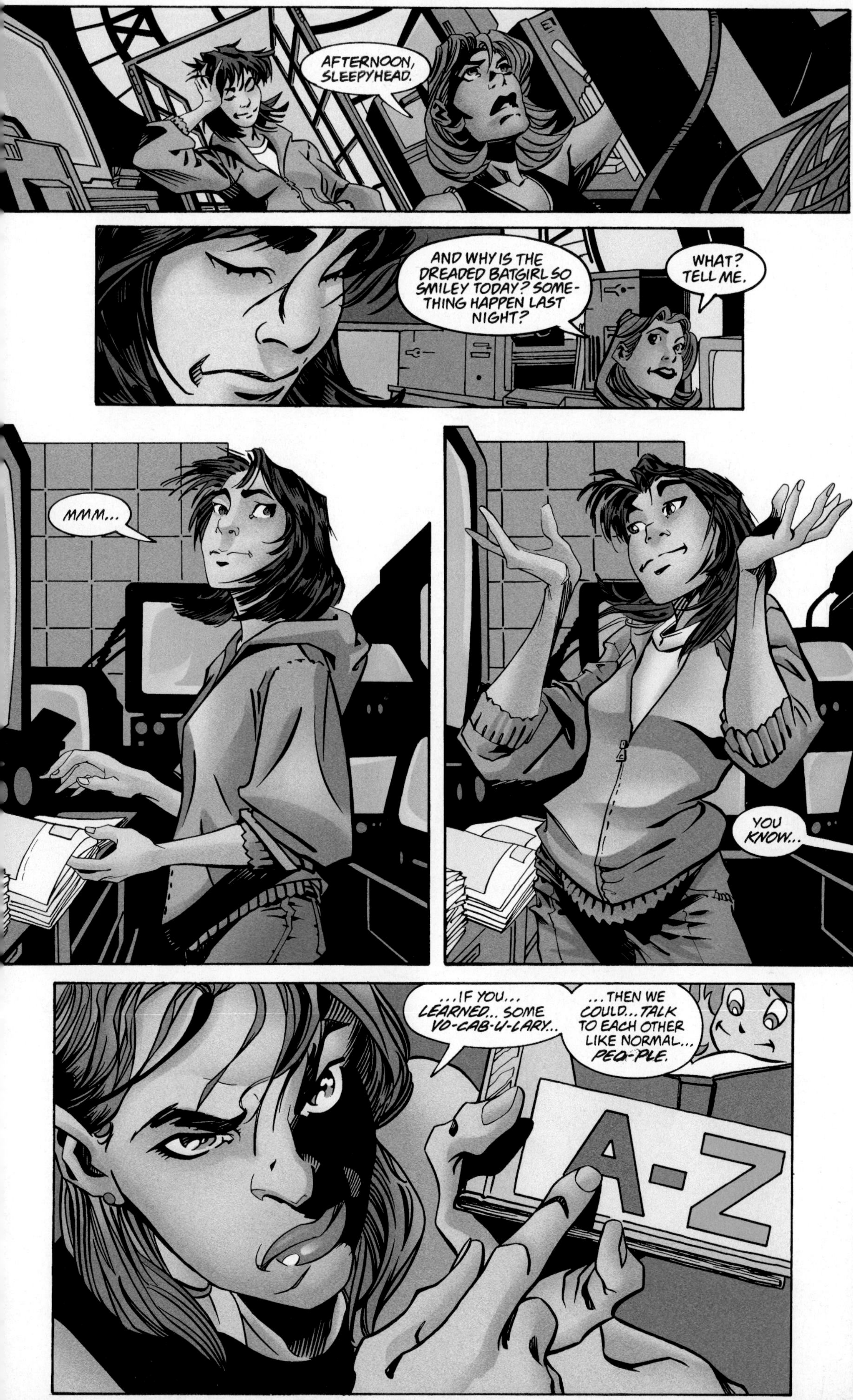
AFTERNOON, SLEEPYHEAD.
AND WHY IS THE DREADED BATGIRL SO SMILEY TODAY? SOMETHING HAPPEN LAST NIGHT?
WHAT? TELL ME.
MMM...
YOU KNOW...
...IF YOU... LEARNED... SOME VO-CAB-U-LARY...
...THEN WE COULD... TALK TO EACH OTHER LIKE NORMAL... PEO-PLE.
A-Z

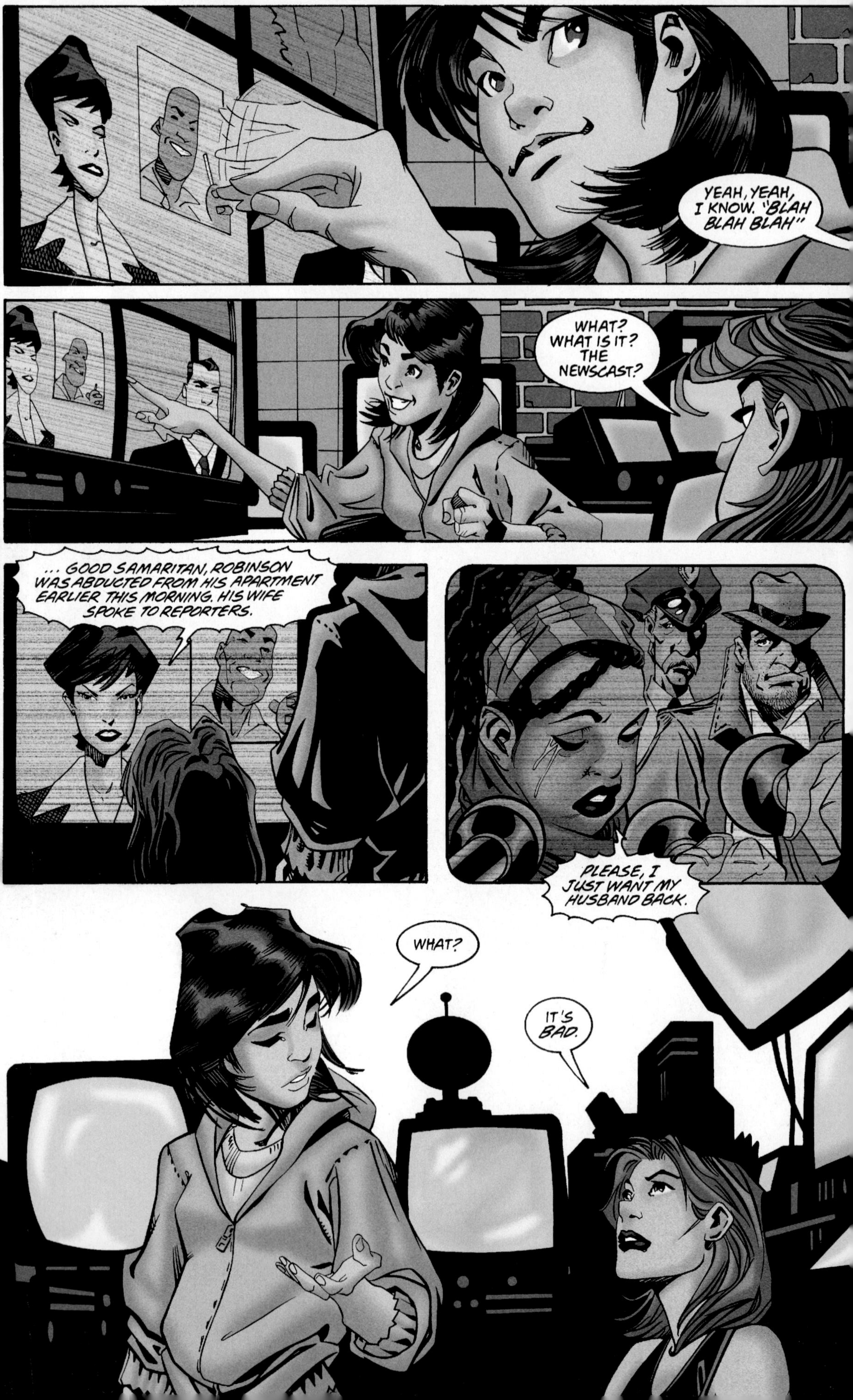
YEAH, YEAH, I KNOW. "BLAH BLAH BLAH"
WHAT? WHAT IS IT? THE NEWSCAST?
... GOOD SAMARITAN, ROBINSON WAS ABDUCTED FROM HIS APARTMENT EARLIER THIS MORNING. HIS WIFE SPOKE TO REPORTERS.
PLEASE, I JUST WANT MY HUSBAND BACK.
WHAT?
IT'S BAD.

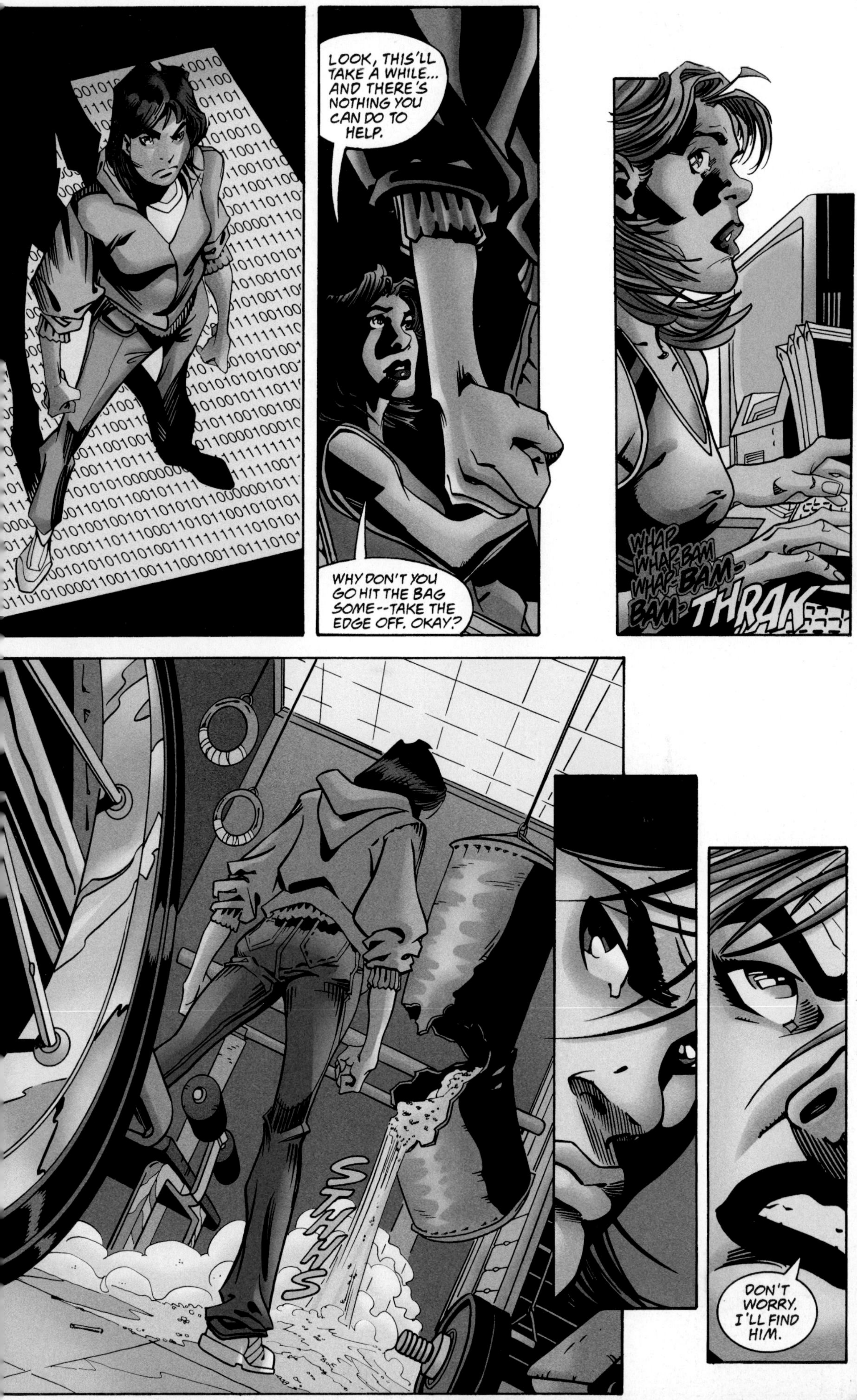
LOOK, THIS'LL TAKE A WHILE... AND THERE'S NOTHING YOU CAN DO TO HELP.
WHY DON'T YOU GO HIT THE BAG SOME--TAKE THE EDGE OFF. OKAY?
WHAP WHAP-BAM WHAP-BAM-BAM-THRAK
STHHHSS
DON'T WORRY. I'LL FIND HIM.

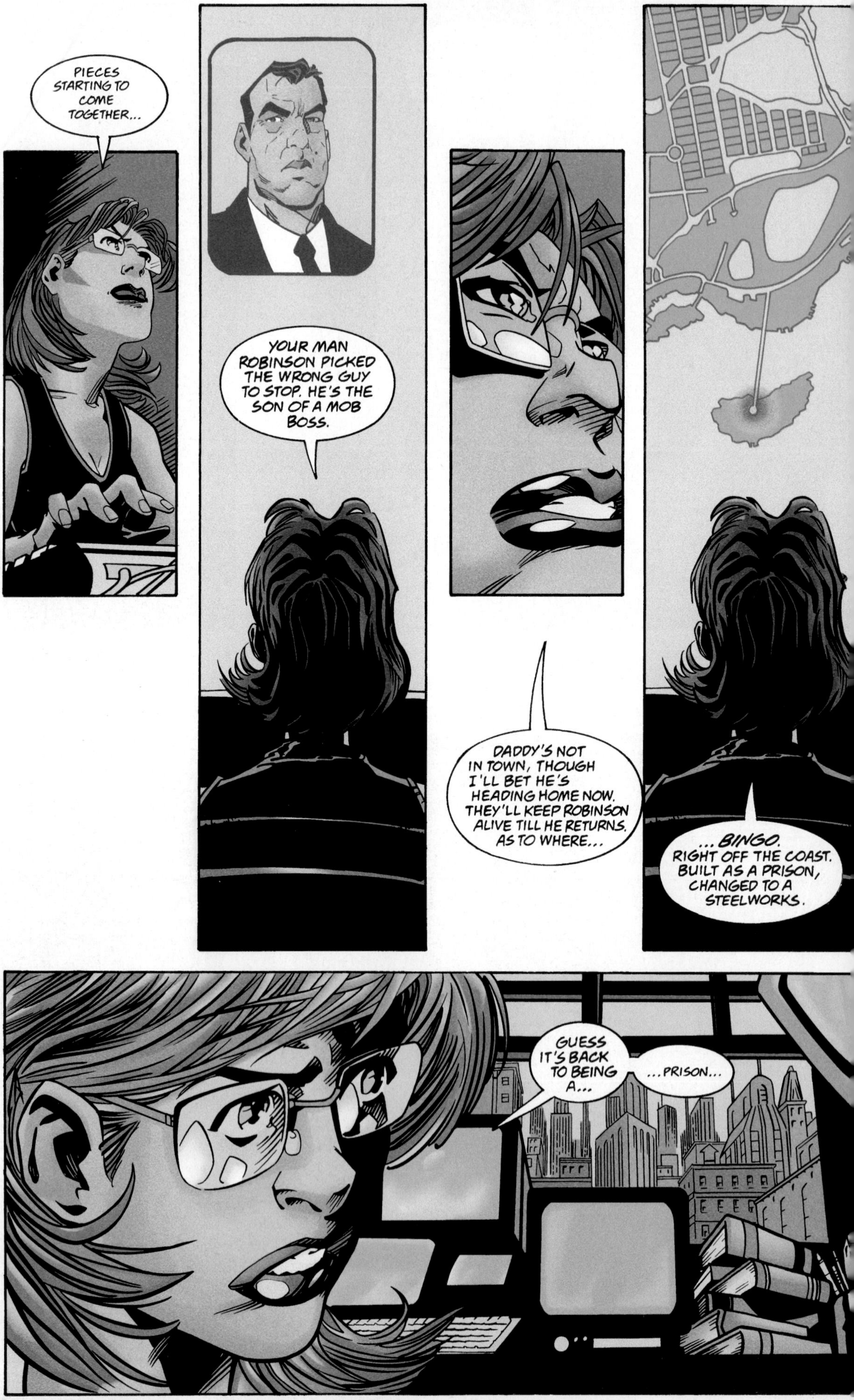
PIECES STARTING TO COME TOGETHER...
YOUR MAN ROBINSON PICKED THE WRONG GUY TO STOP. HE'S THE SON OF A MOB BOSS.
DADDY'S NOT IN TOWN, THOUGH I'LL BET HE'S HEADING HOME NOW. THEY'LL KEEP ROBINSON ALIVE TILL HE RETURNS. AS TO WHERE...
...BINGO. RIGHT OFF THE COAST. BUILT AS A PRISON, CHANGED TO A STEELWORKS.
GUESS IT'S BACK TO BEING A...
...PRISON...

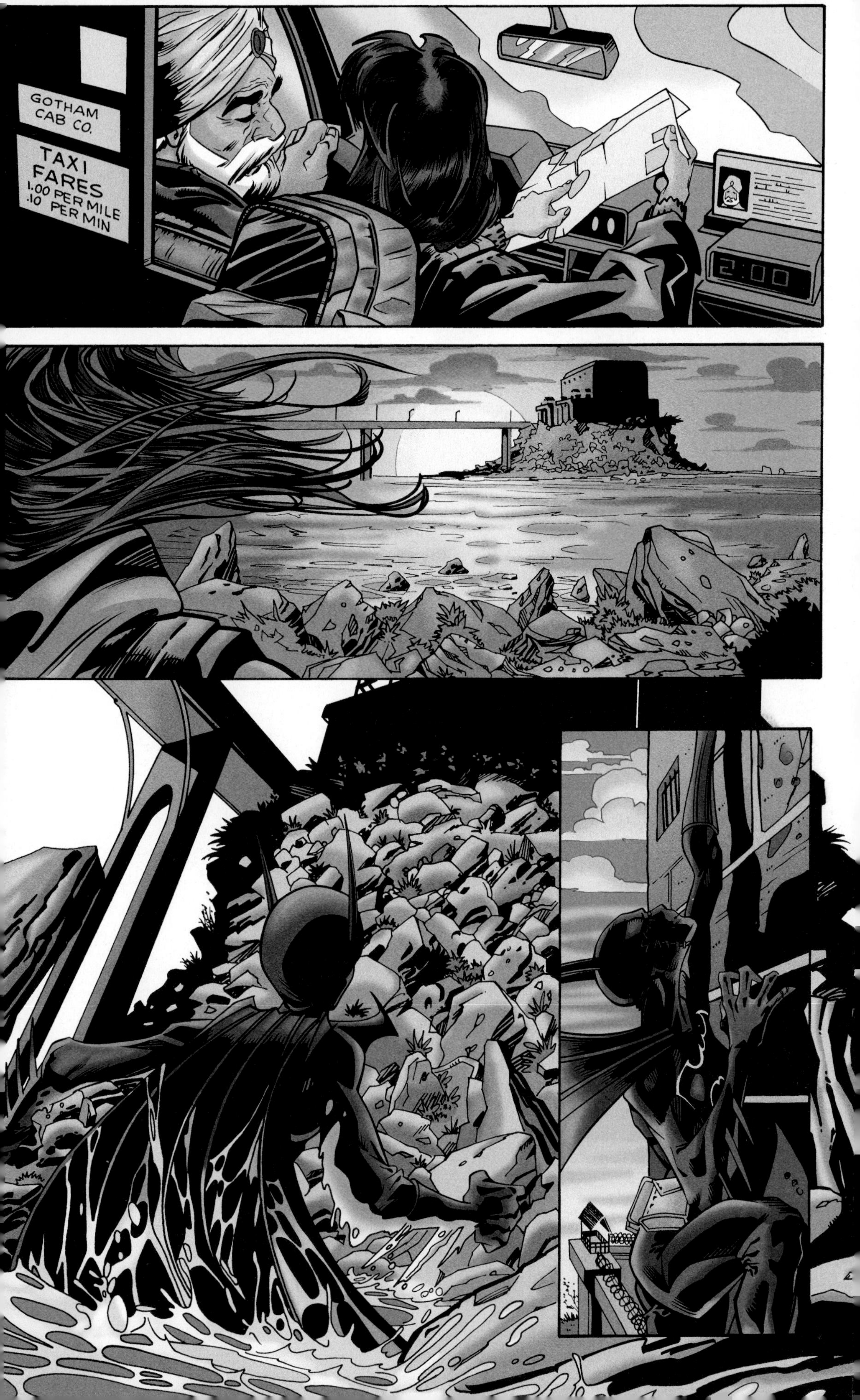
GOTHAM CAB CO.
TAXI FARES
1.00 PER MILE
.10 PER MIN
2:00

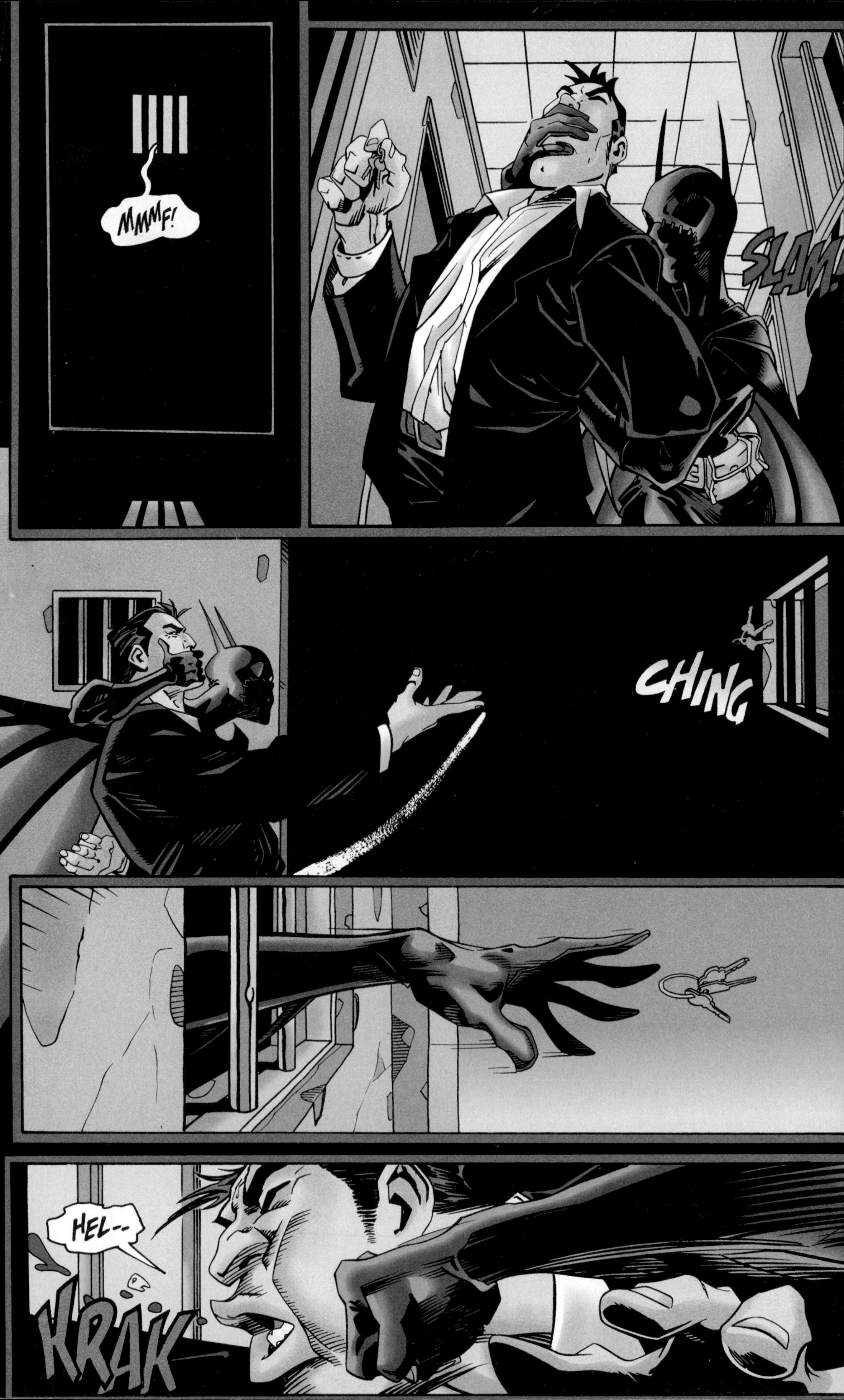
MMMF!
SLAM!
CHING
HEL--
KRAK

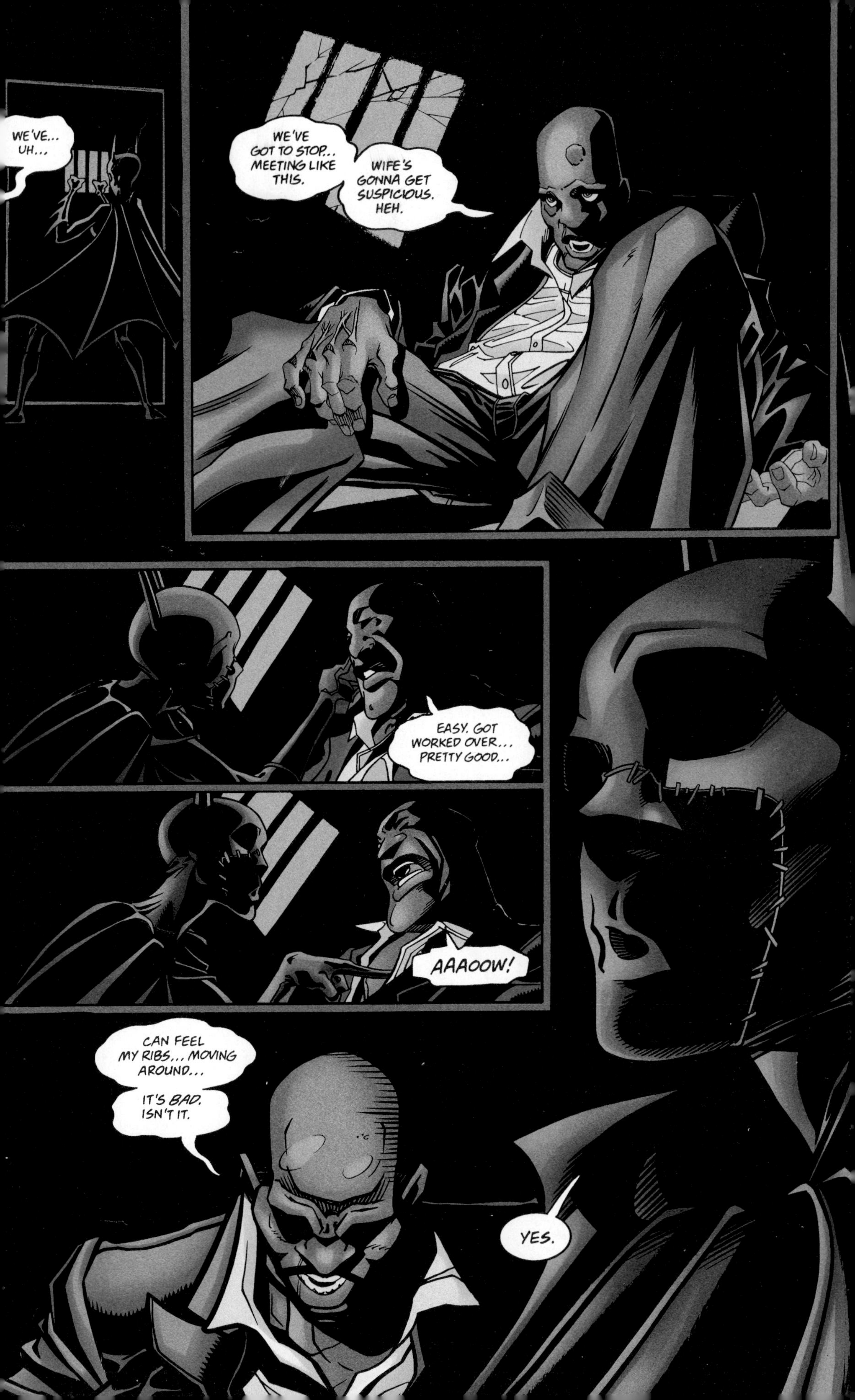
WE'VE... UH...
WE'VE GOT TO STOP... MEETING LIKE THIS.
WIFE'S GONNA GET SUSPICIOUS. HEH.
EASY. GOT WORKED OVER... PRETTY GOOD...
AAAOOW!
CAN FEEL MY RIBS... MOVING AROUND...
IT'S BAD. ISN'T IT.
YES.

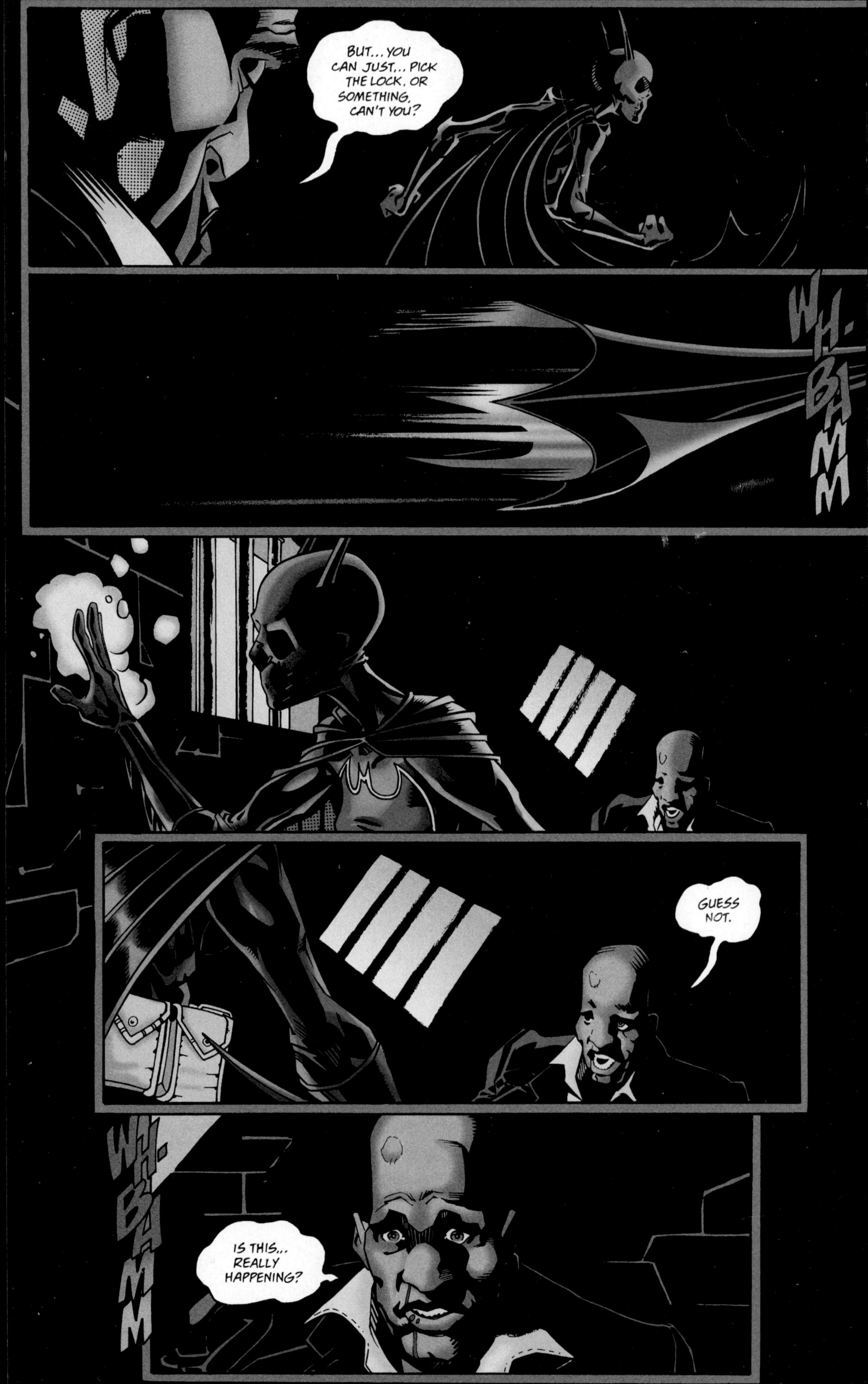
BUT... YOU CAN JUST... PICK THE LOCK, OR SOMETHING, CAN'T YOU?
WH-BAMM
GUESS NOT.
WH-BAMM
IS THIS... REALLY HAPPENING?

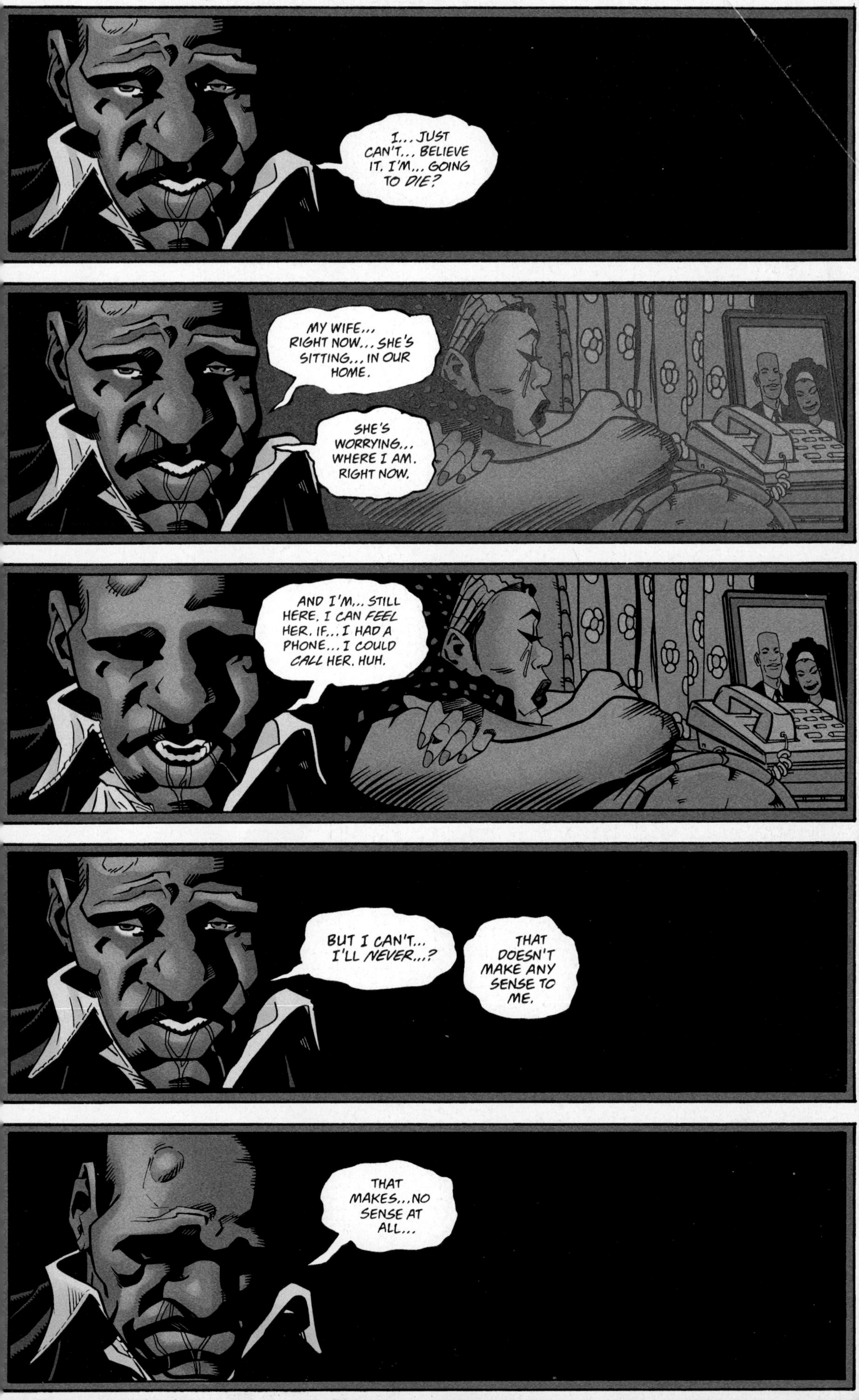

I... JUST CAN'T... BELIEVE IT. I'M... GOING TO *DIE?*
MY WIFE... RIGHT NOW... SHE'S SITTING... IN OUR HOME.
SHE'S WORRYING... WHERE I AM. RIGHT NOW.
AND I'M... STILL HERE. I CAN *FEEL* HER. IF... I HAD A PHONE... I COULD *CALL* HER. HUH.
BUT I CAN'T... I'LL *NEVER*...?
THAT DOESN'T MAKE ANY SENSE TO ME.
THAT MAKES... NO SENSE AT ALL...

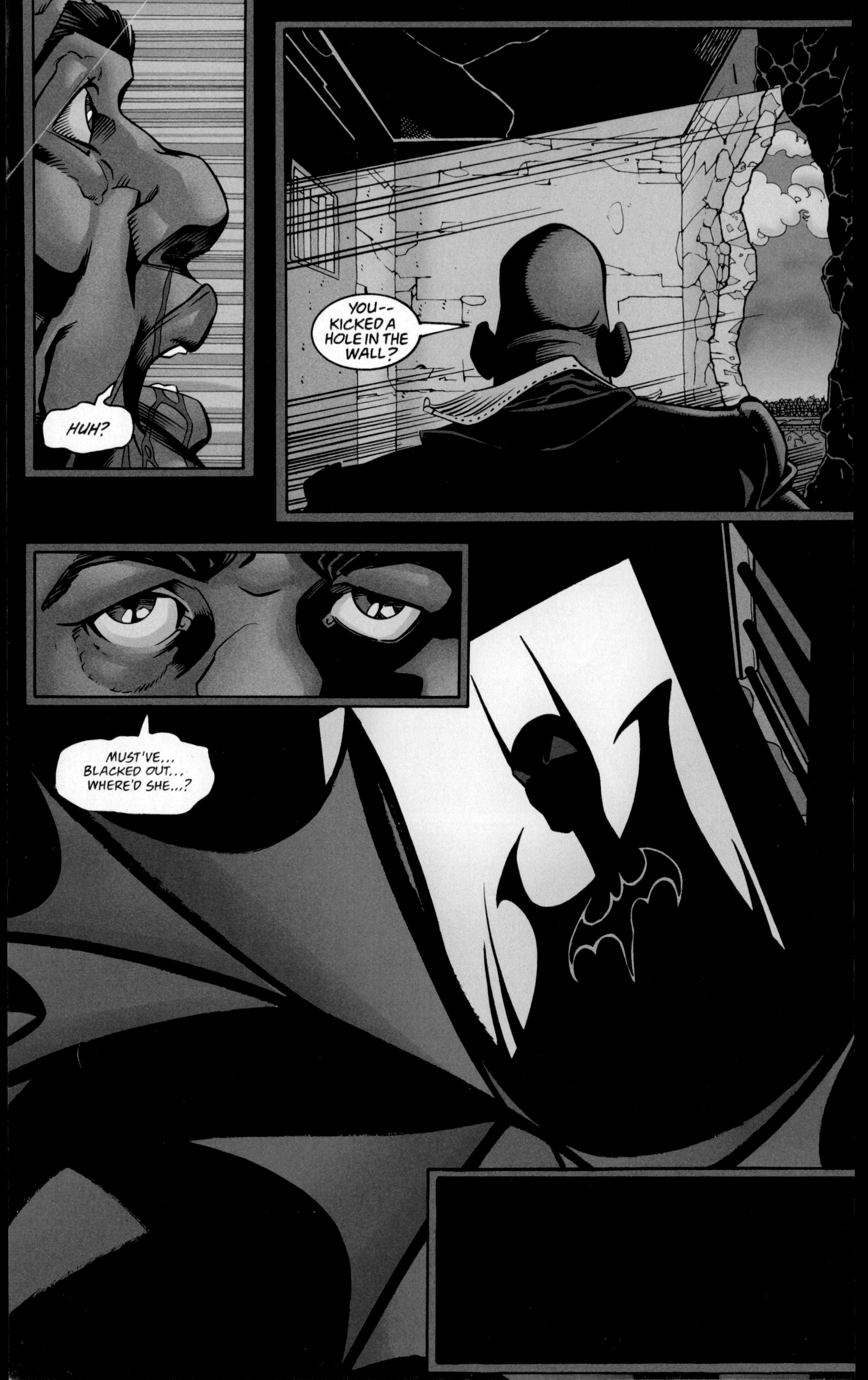
HUH?
YOU--
KICKED A
HOLE IN THE
WALL?
MUST'VE...
BLACKED OUT...
WHERE'D SHE...?

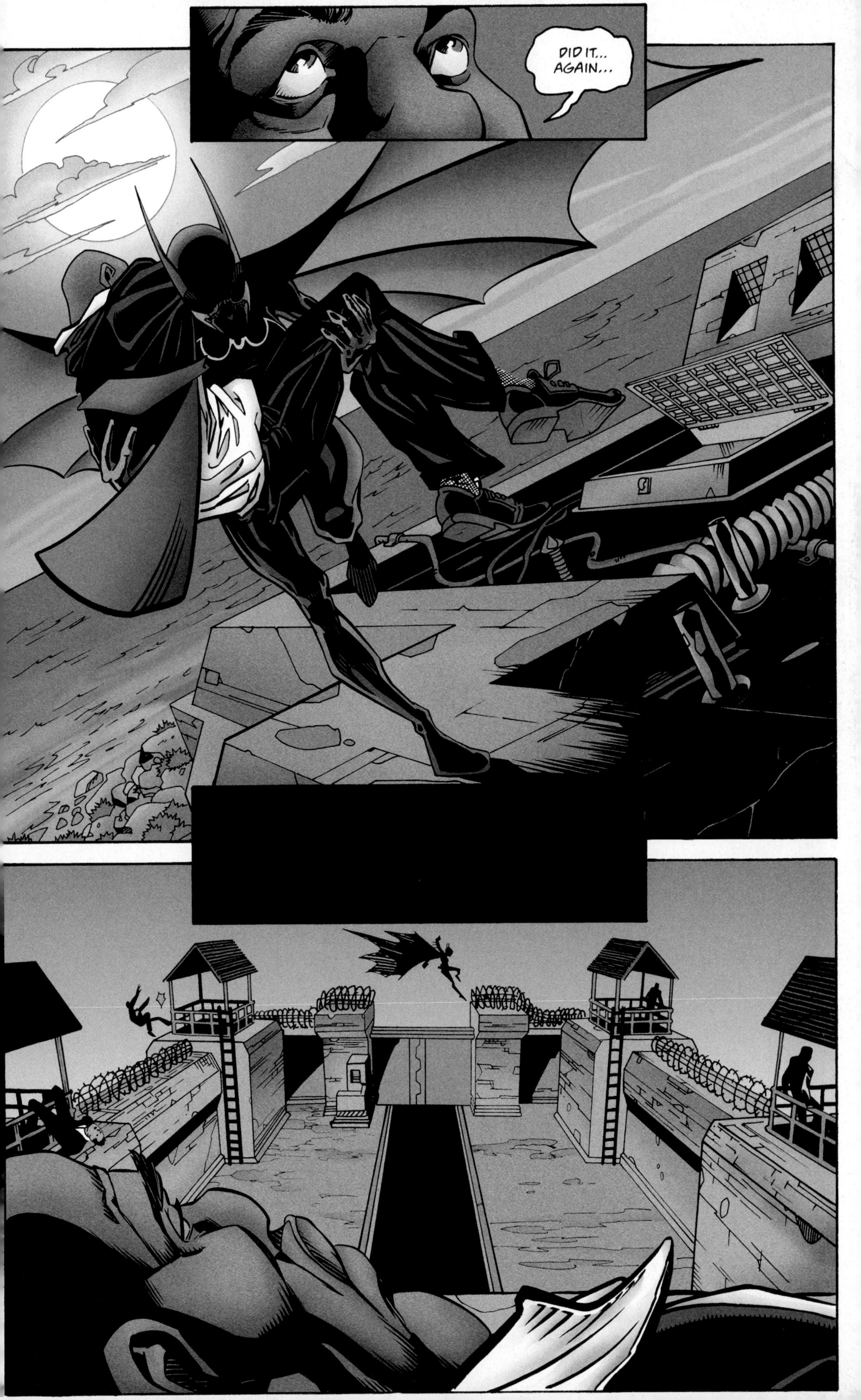
DID IT... AGAIN...
[redacted]

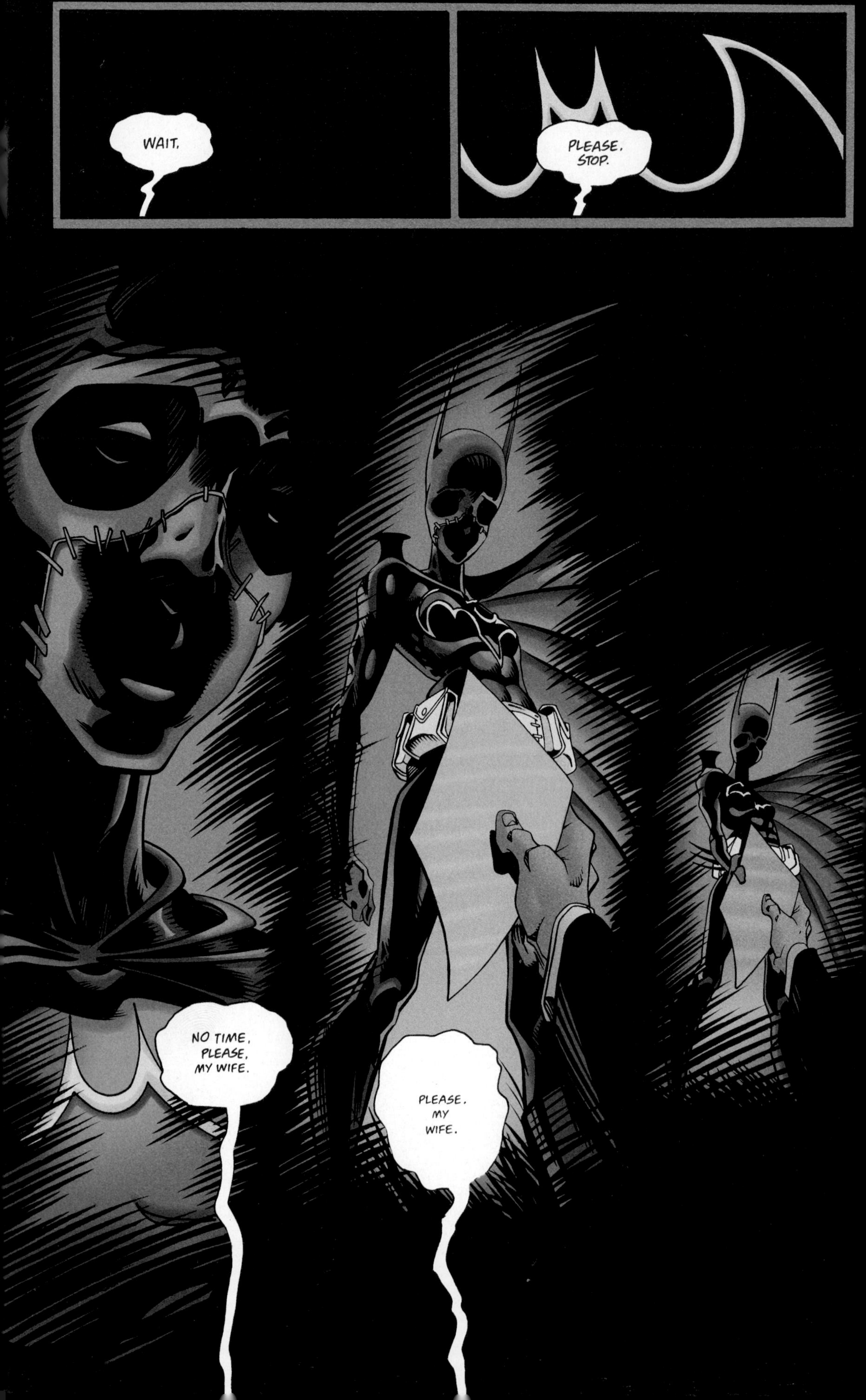
WAIT.
PLEASE. STOP.
NO TIME. PLEASE. MY WIFE.
PLEASE. MY WIFE.

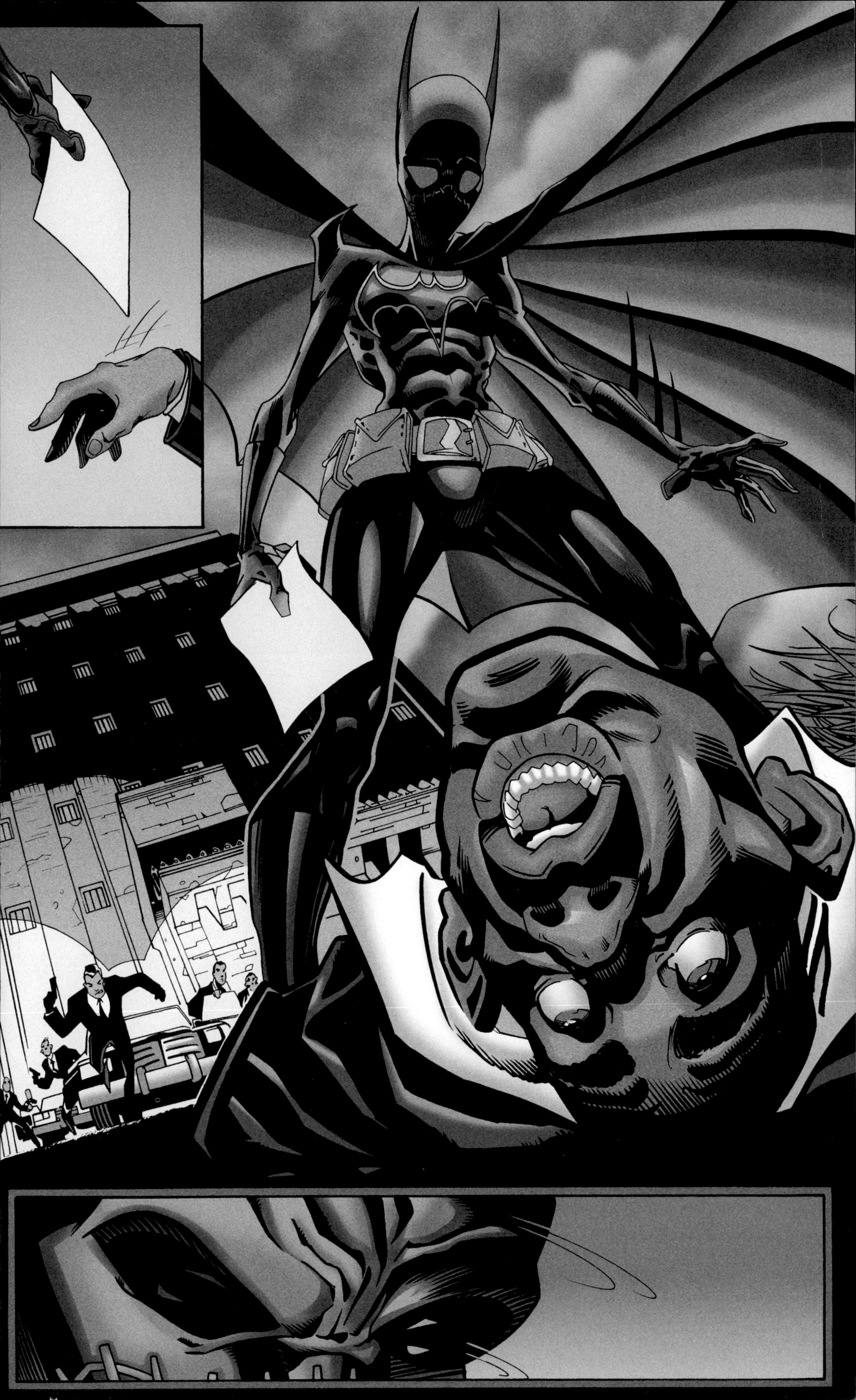

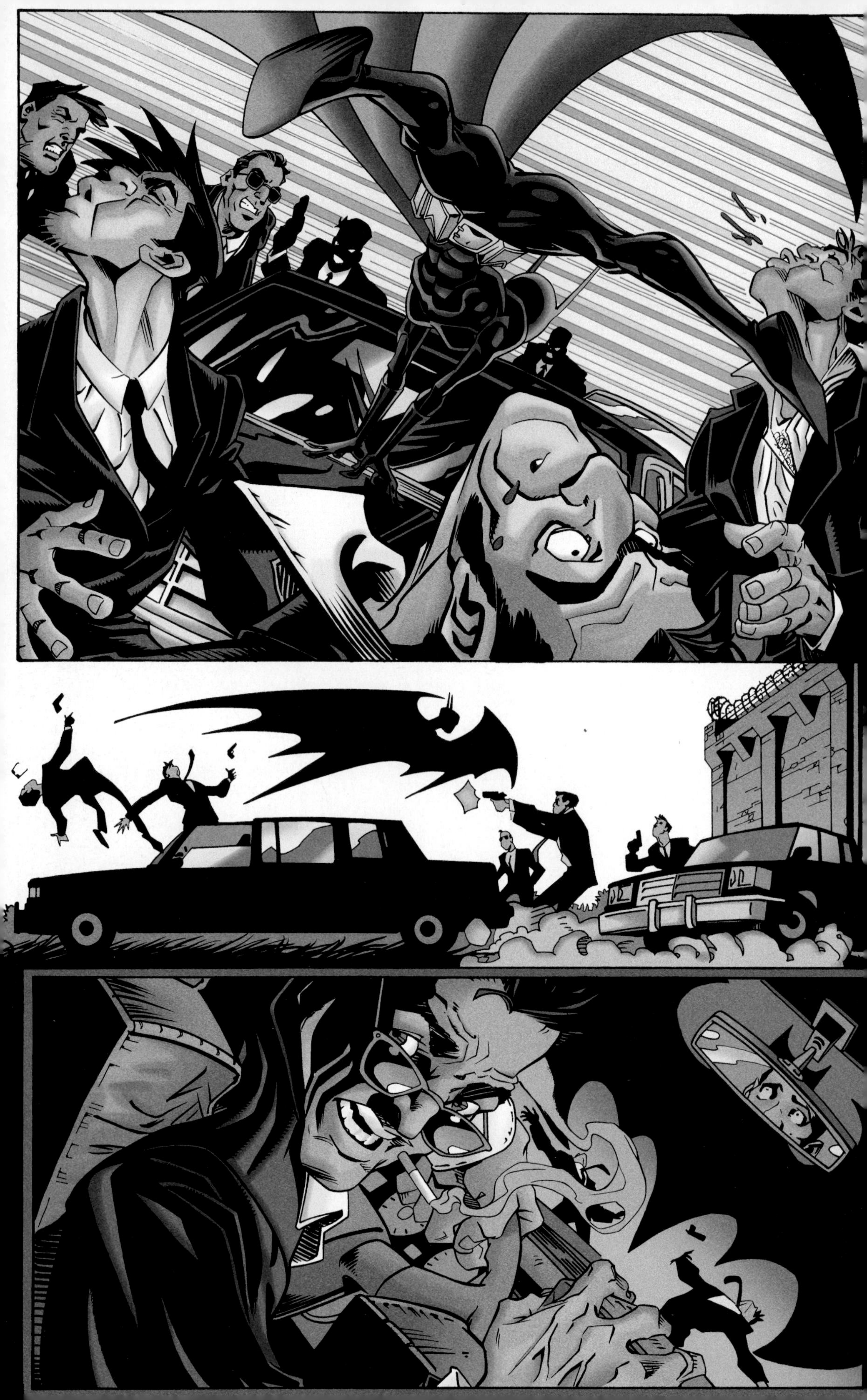

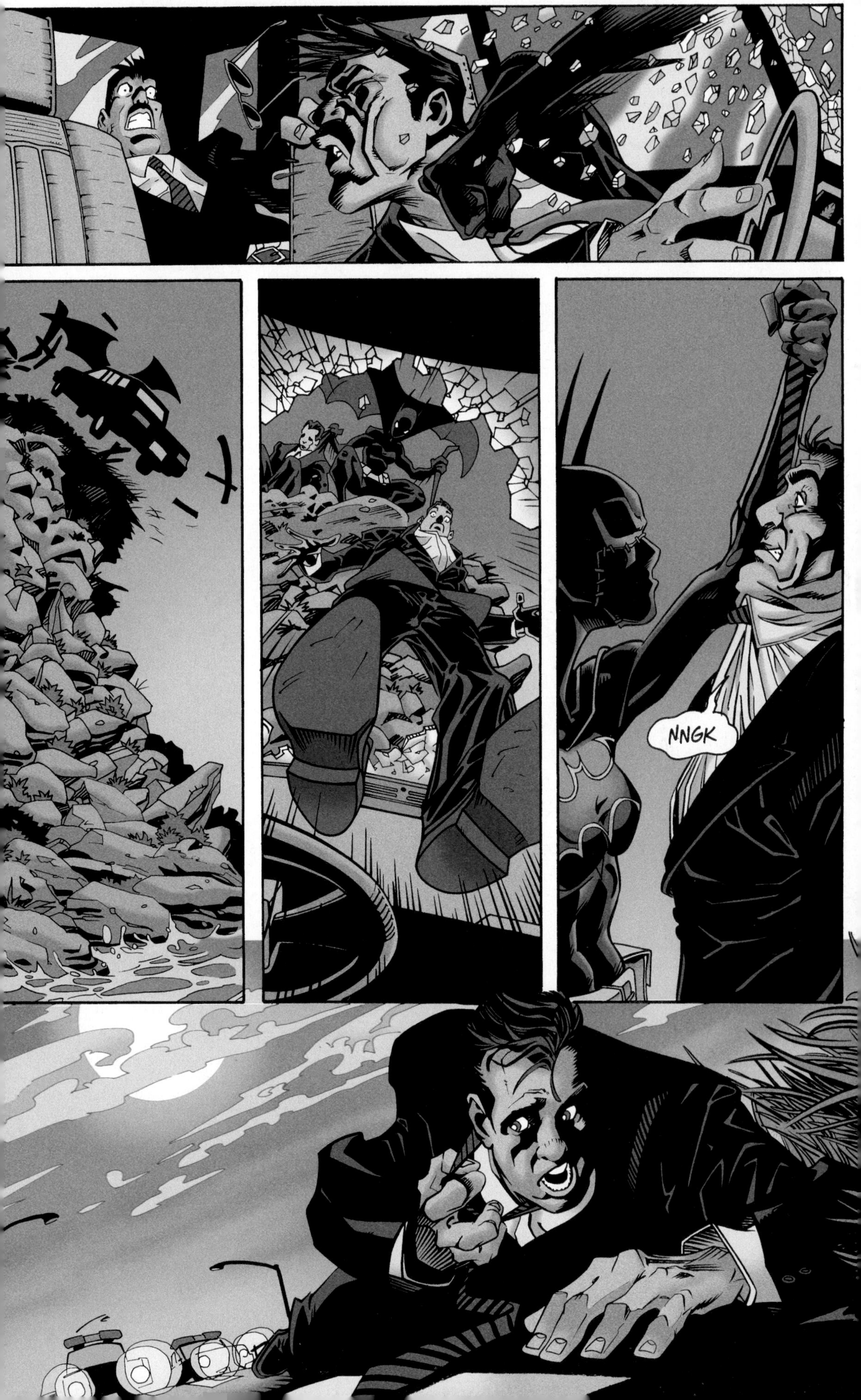
NNGK

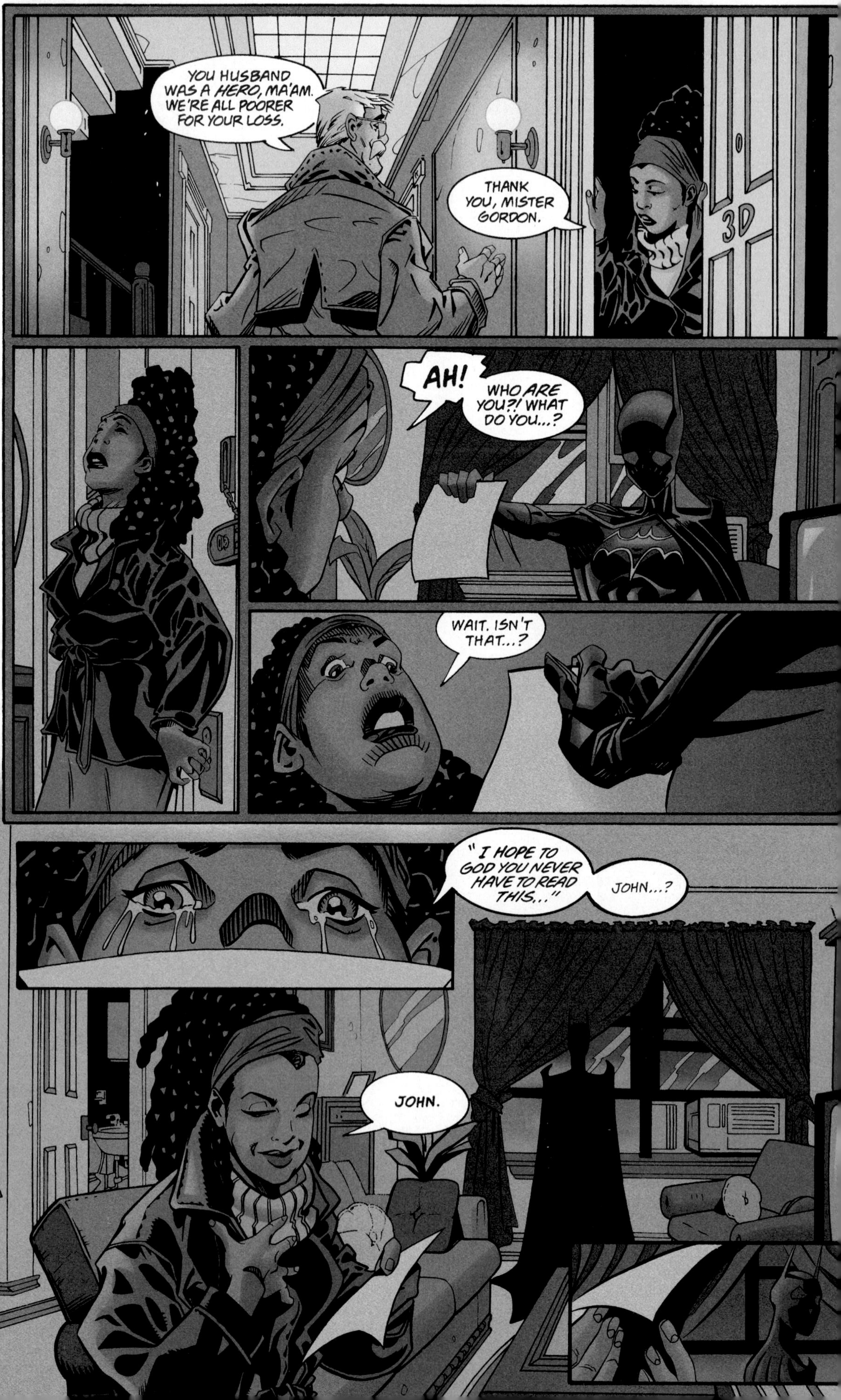
YOU HUSBAND WAS A HERO, MA'AM. WE'RE ALL POORER FOR YOUR LOSS.
THANK YOU, MISTER GORDON.
AH!
WHO ARE YOU?! WHAT DO YOU...?
WAIT. ISN'T THAT...?
"I HOPE TO GOD YOU NEVER HAVE TO READ THIS..."
JOHN...?
JOHN.

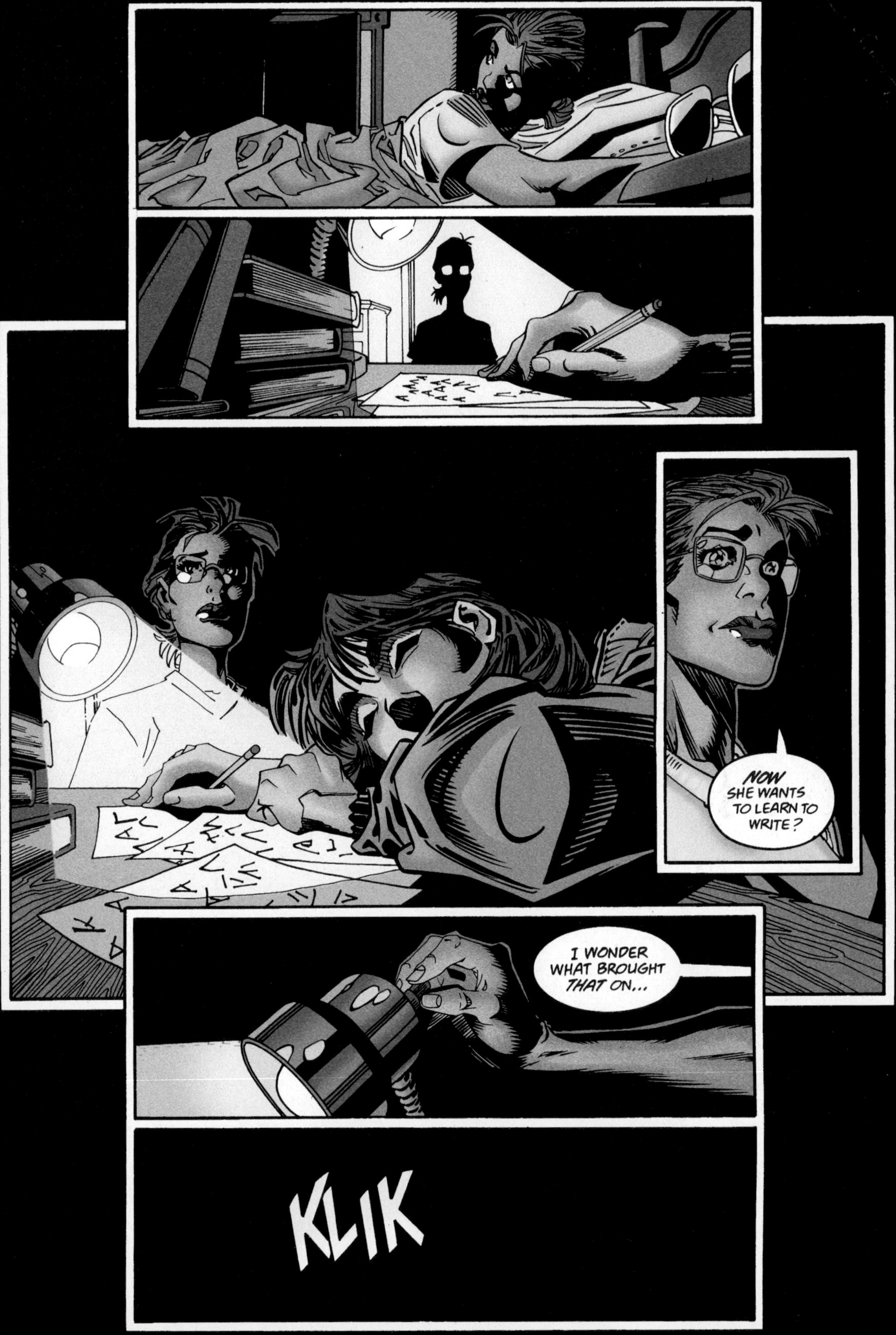
NOW SHE WANTS TO LEARN TO WRITE?
I WONDER WHAT BROUGHT THAT ON...
KLIK

Plot: SCOTT PETERSON and KELLEY PUCKETT
Script: KELLEY PUCKETT Pencils: DAMION SCOTT
Inks: ROBERT CAMPANELLA Letters: JOHN COSTANZA
Colors: JASON WRIGHT Separations: JAMISON
Associate editor: JOSEPH ILLIDGE
Editors: DARREN VINCENZO and DENNIS O'NEIL
BATMAN created by BOB KANE

BATGIRL #3 cover by
Damion Scott & Robert Campanella

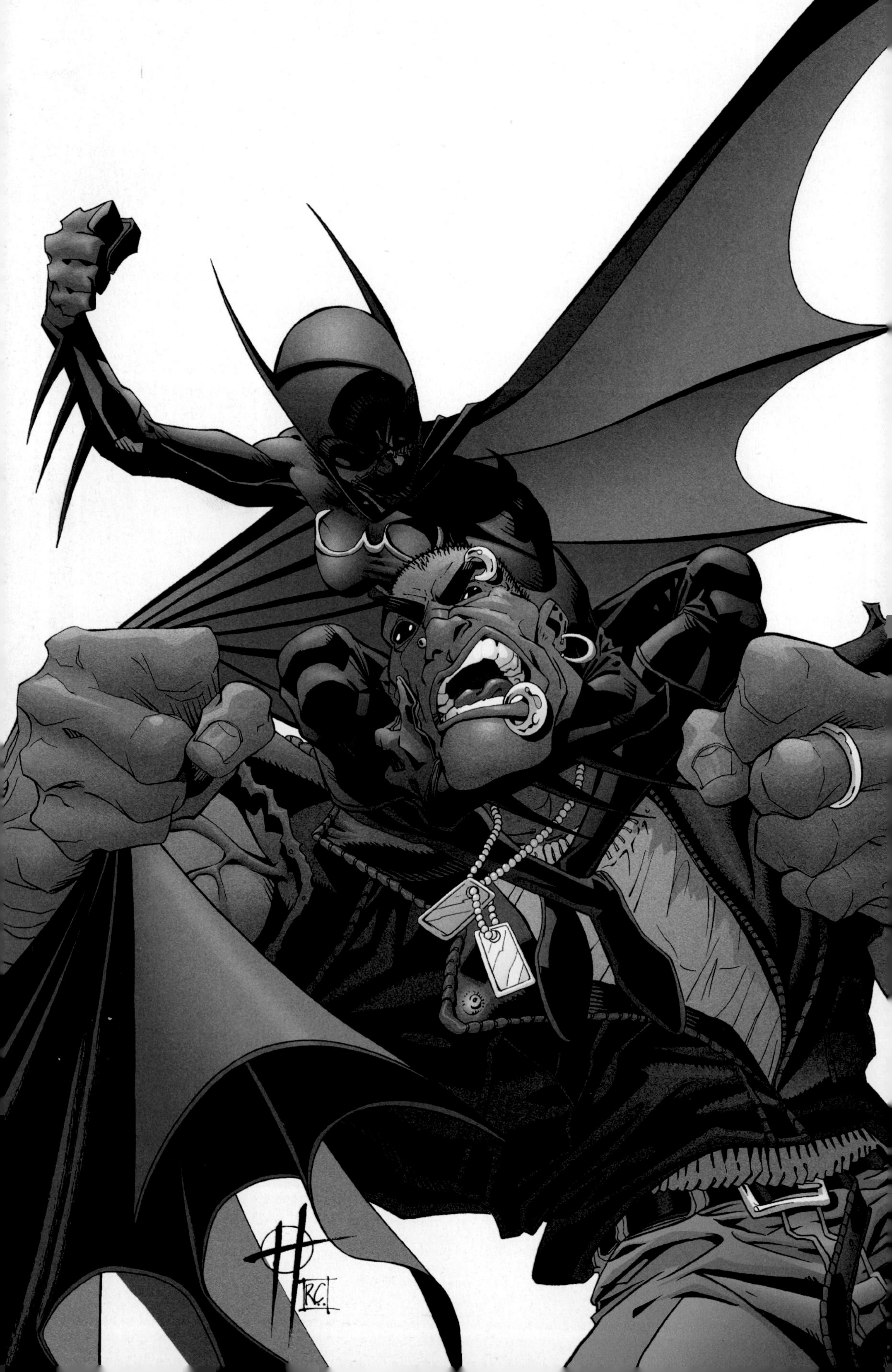

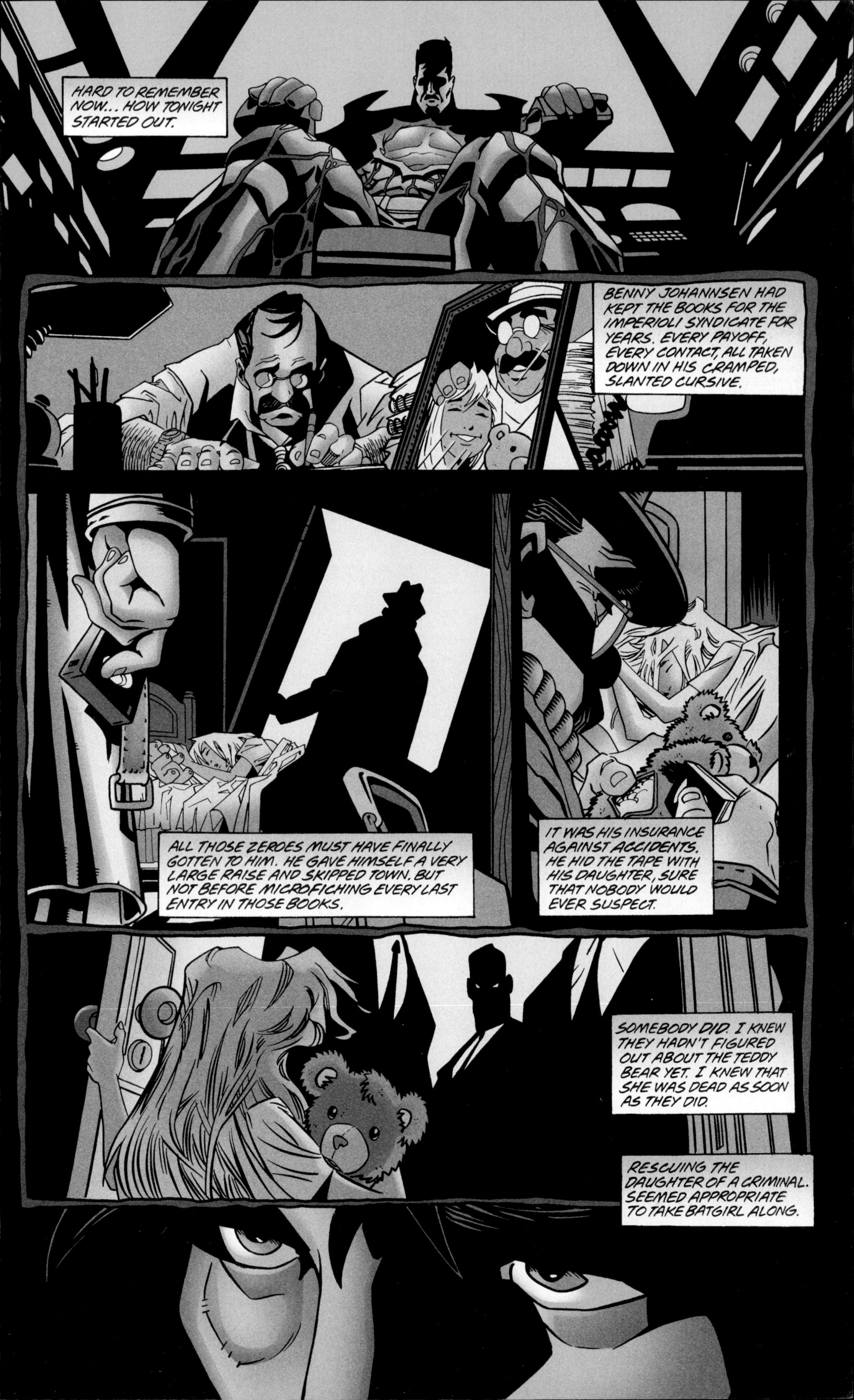
HARD TO REMEMBER NOW... HOW TONIGHT STARTED OUT.
BENNY JOHANNSEN HAD KEPT THE BOOKS FOR THE IMPERIOLI SYNDICATE FOR YEARS. EVERY PAYOFF, EVERY CONTACT, ALL TAKEN DOWN IN HIS CRAMPED, SLANTED CURSIVE.
ALL THOSE ZEROES MUST HAVE FINALLY GOTTEN TO HIM. HE GAVE HIMSELF A VERY LARGE RAISE AND SKIPPED TOWN. BUT NOT BEFORE MICROFICHING EVERY LAST ENTRY IN THOSE BOOKS.
IT WAS HIS INSURANCE AGAINST ACCIDENTS. HE HID THE TAPE WITH HIS DAUGHTER, SURE THAT NOBODY WOULD EVER SUSPECT.
SOMEBODY DID. I KNEW THEY HADN'T FIGURED OUT ABOUT THE TEDDY BEAR YET. I KNEW THAT SHE WAS DEAD AS SOON AS THEY DID.
RESCUING THE DAUGHTER OF A CRIMINAL. SEEMED APPROPRIATE TO TAKE BATGIRL ALONG.

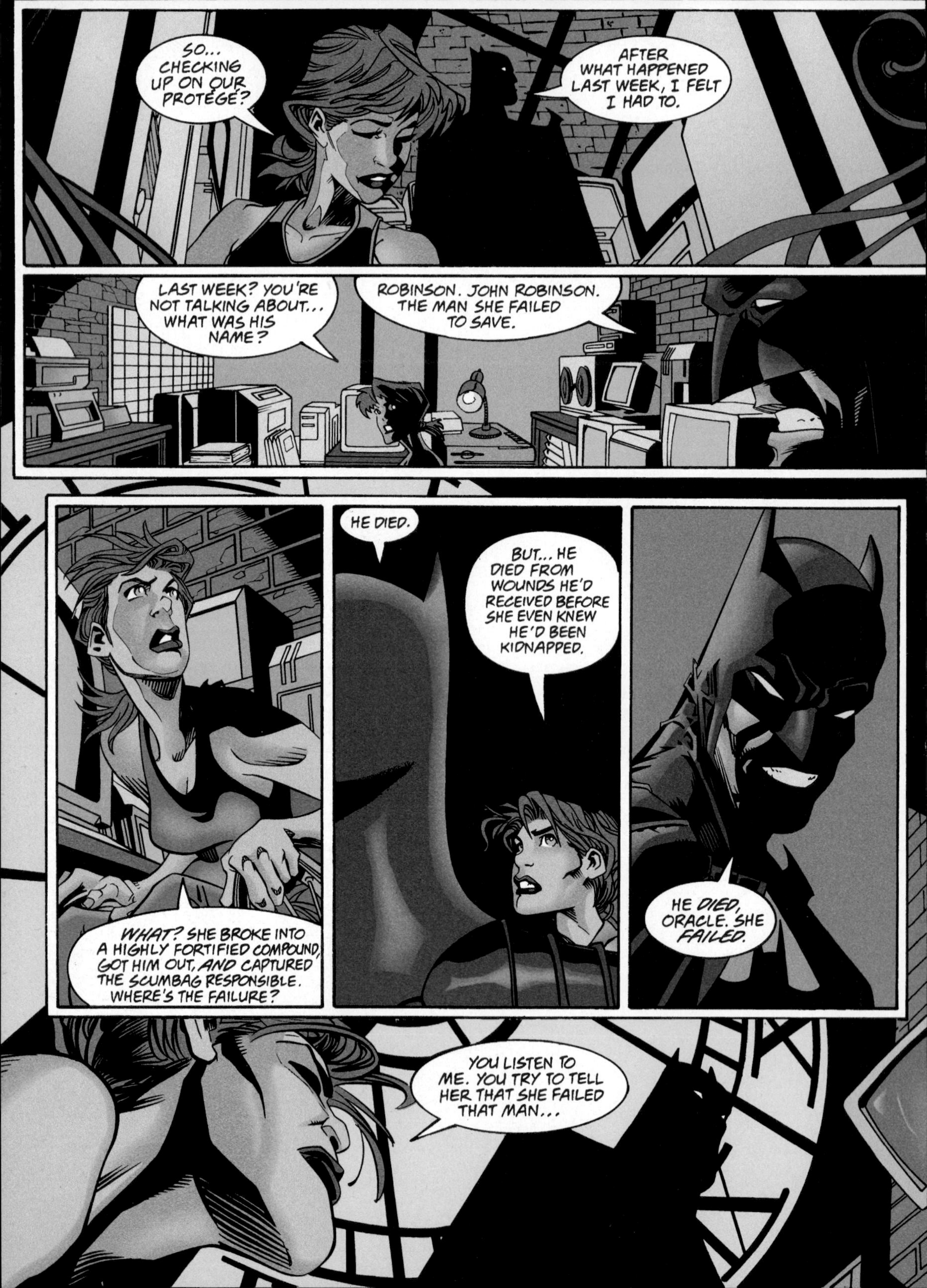
SO... CHECKING UP ON OUR PROTEGE?
AFTER WHAT HAPPENED LAST WEEK, I FELT I HAD TO.
LAST WEEK? YOU'RE NOT TALKING ABOUT... WHAT WAS HIS NAME?
ROBINSON. JOHN ROBINSON. THE MAN SHE FAILED TO SAVE.
WHAT? SHE BROKE INTO A HIGHLY FORTIFIED COMPOUND, GOT HIM OUT, AND CAPTURED THE SCUMBAG RESPONSIBLE. WHERE'S THE FAILURE?
HE DIED.
BUT... HE DIED FROM WOUNDS HE'D RECEIVED BEFORE SHE EVEN KNEW HE'D BEEN KIDNAPPED.
HE DIED, ORACLE. SHE FAILED.
YOU LISTEN TO ME. YOU TRY TO TELL HER THAT SHE FAILED THAT MAN...

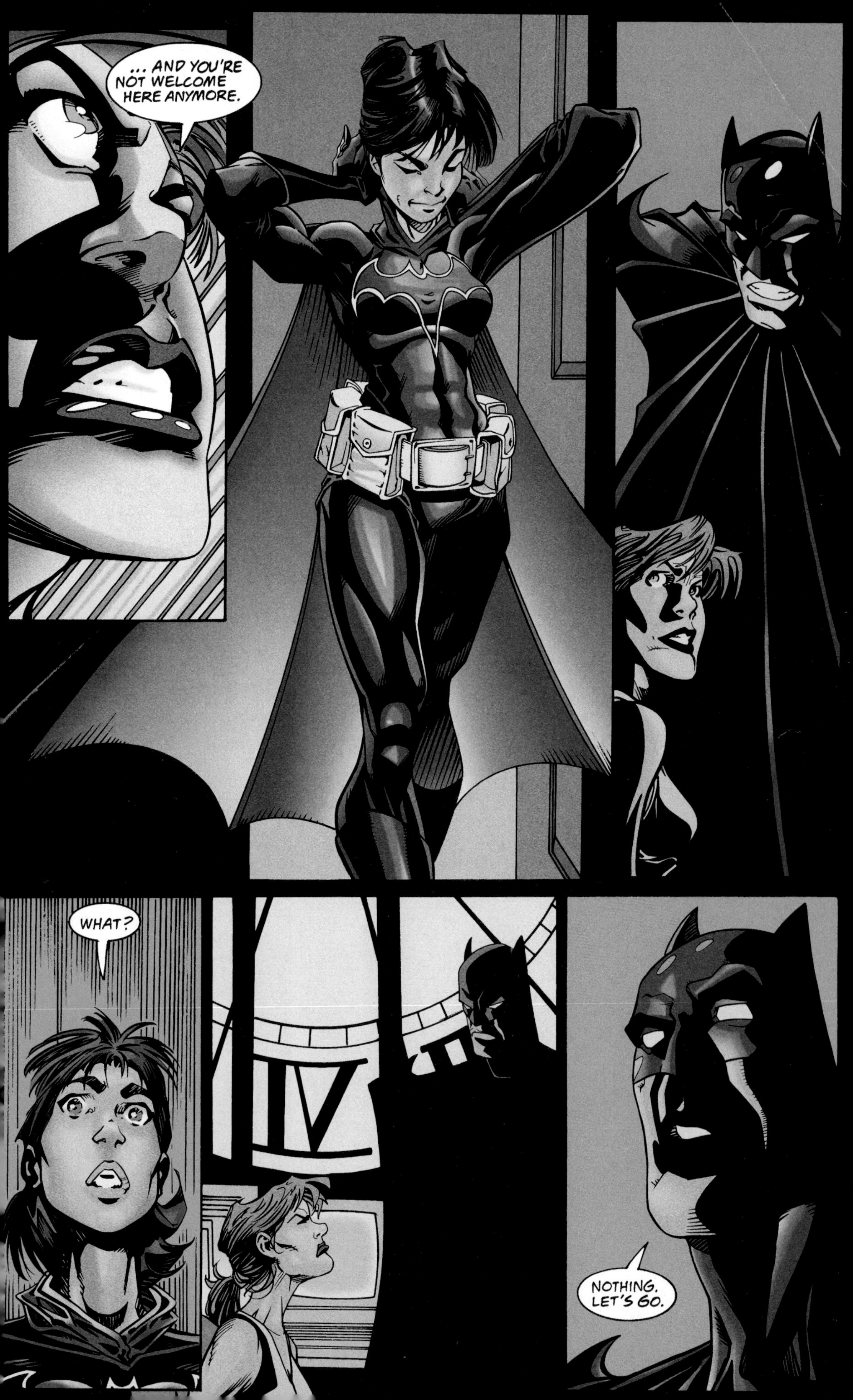
... AND YOU'RE NOT WELCOME HERE ANYMORE.
WHAT?
NOTHING. LET'S GO.

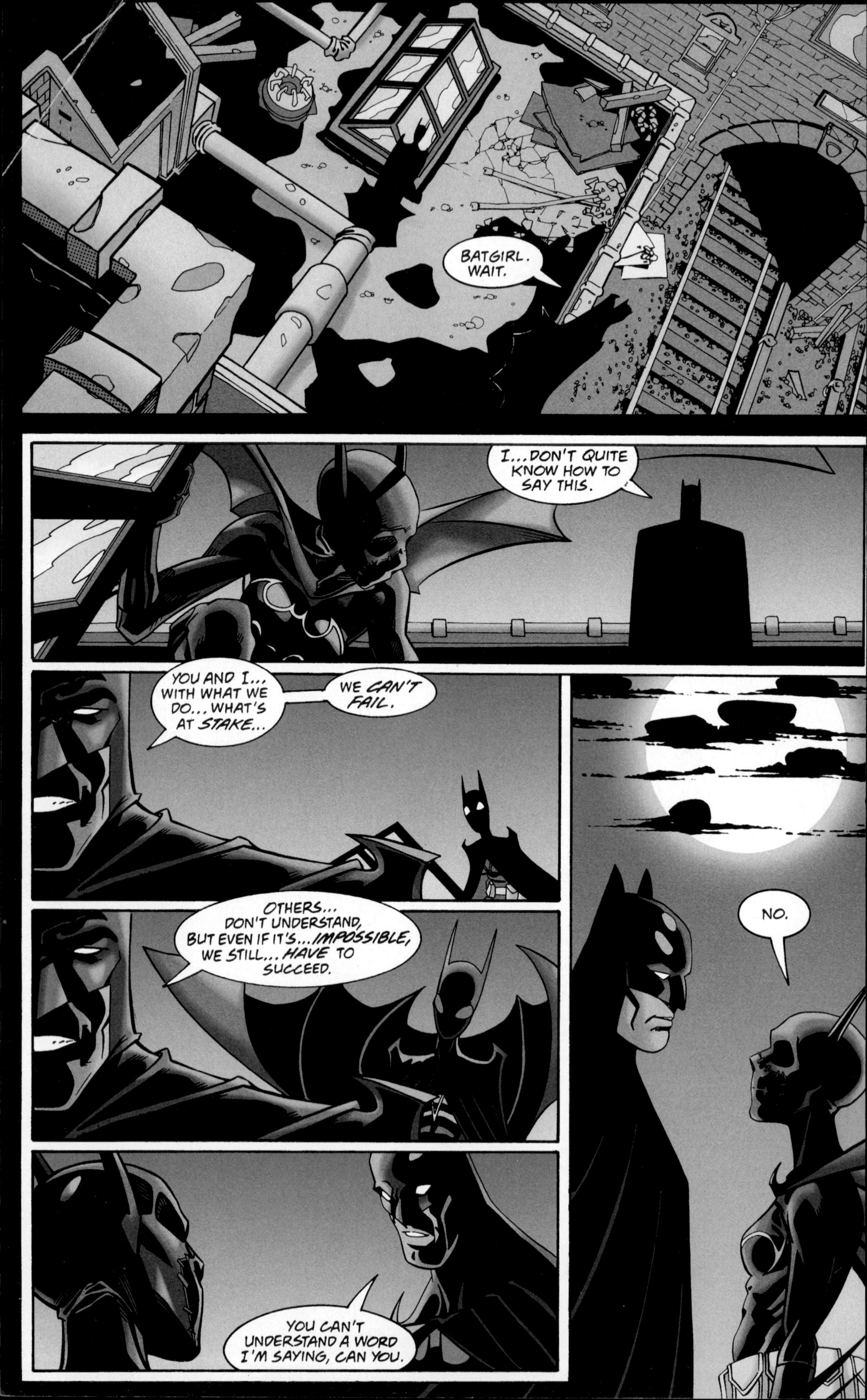
BATGIRL. WAIT.
I...DON'T QUITE KNOW HOW TO SAY THIS.
YOU AND I... WITH WHAT WE DO...WHAT'S AT STAKE...
WE CAN'T FAIL.
OTHERS... DON'T UNDERSTAND, BUT EVEN IF IT'S...IMPOSSIBLE, WE STILL...HAVE TO SUCCEED.
YOU CAN'T UNDERSTAND A WORD I'M SAYING, CAN YOU.
NO.

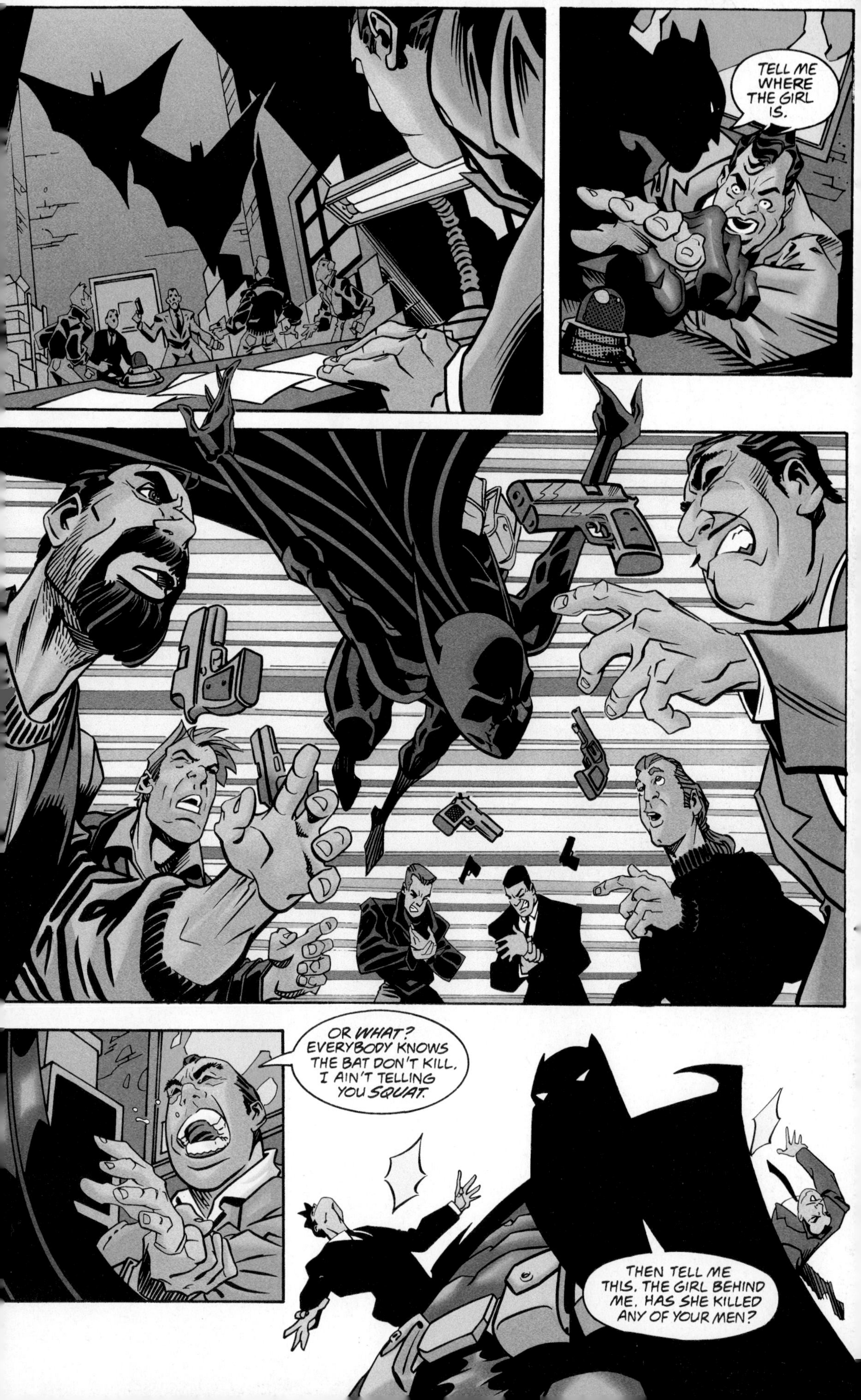
TELL ME WHERE THE GIRL IS.
OR WHAT? EVERYBODY KNOWS THE BAT DON'T KILL. I AIN'T TELLING YOU SQUAT.
THEN TELL ME THIS. THE GIRL BEHIND ME. HAS SHE KILLED ANY OF YOUR MEN?

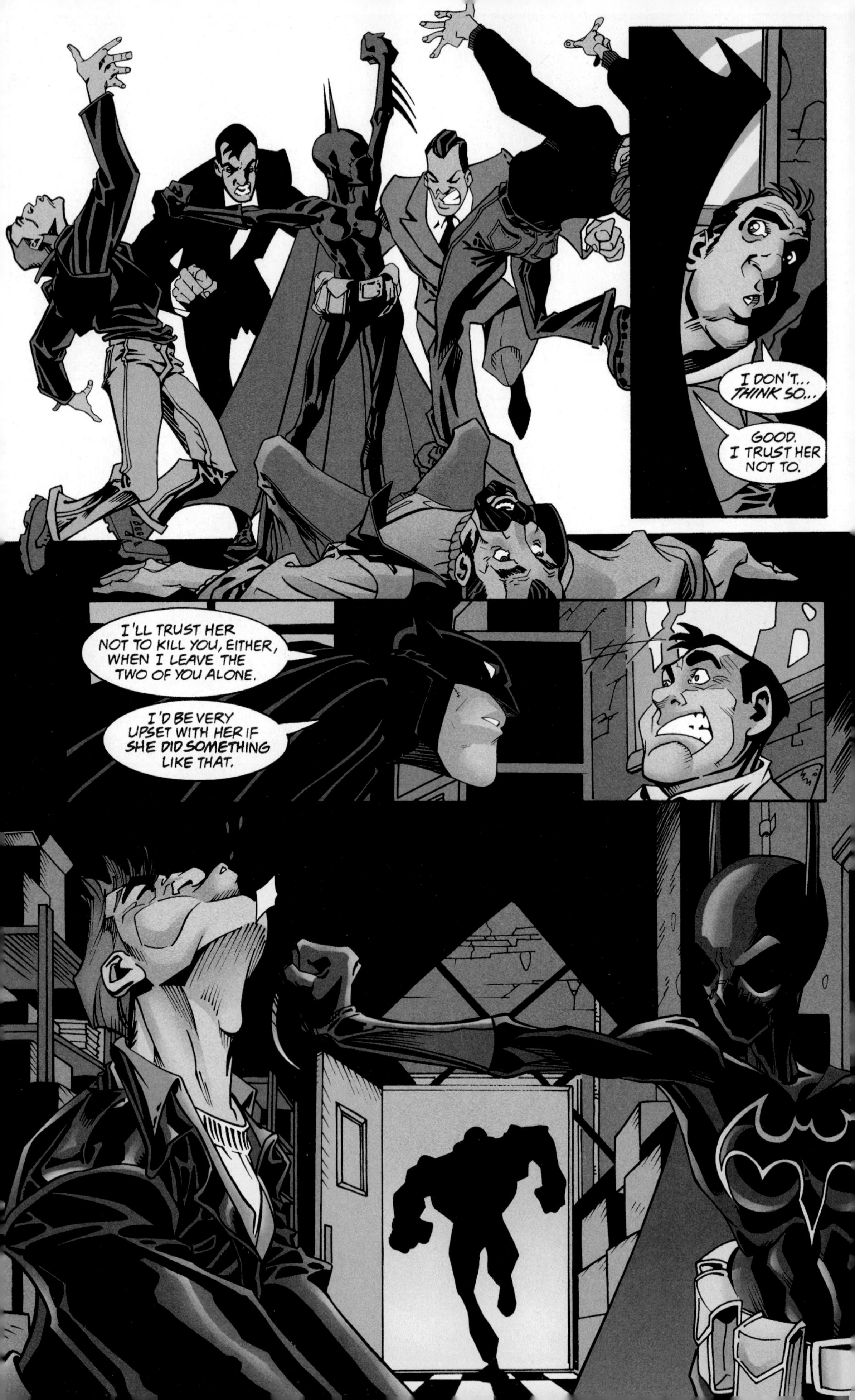
I DON'T... THINK SO...
GOOD. I TRUST HER NOT TO.
I'LL TRUST HER NOT TO KILL YOU, EITHER, WHEN I LEAVE THE TWO OF YOU ALONE.
I'D BE VERY UPSET WITH HER IF SHE DID SOMETHING LIKE THAT.

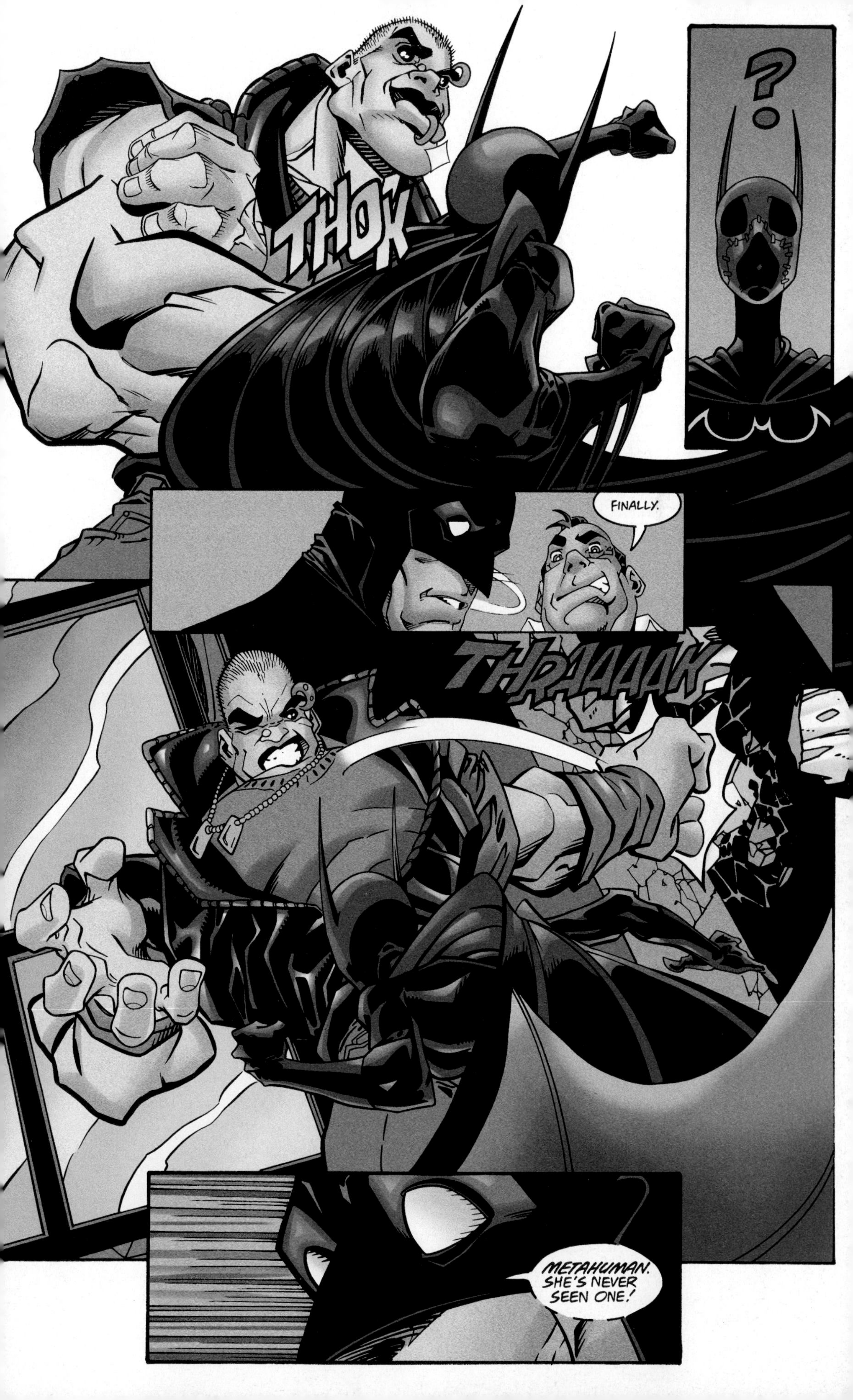
THOK
?
FINALLY.
THRAAAAK
METAHUMAN. SHE'S NEVER SEEN ONE!

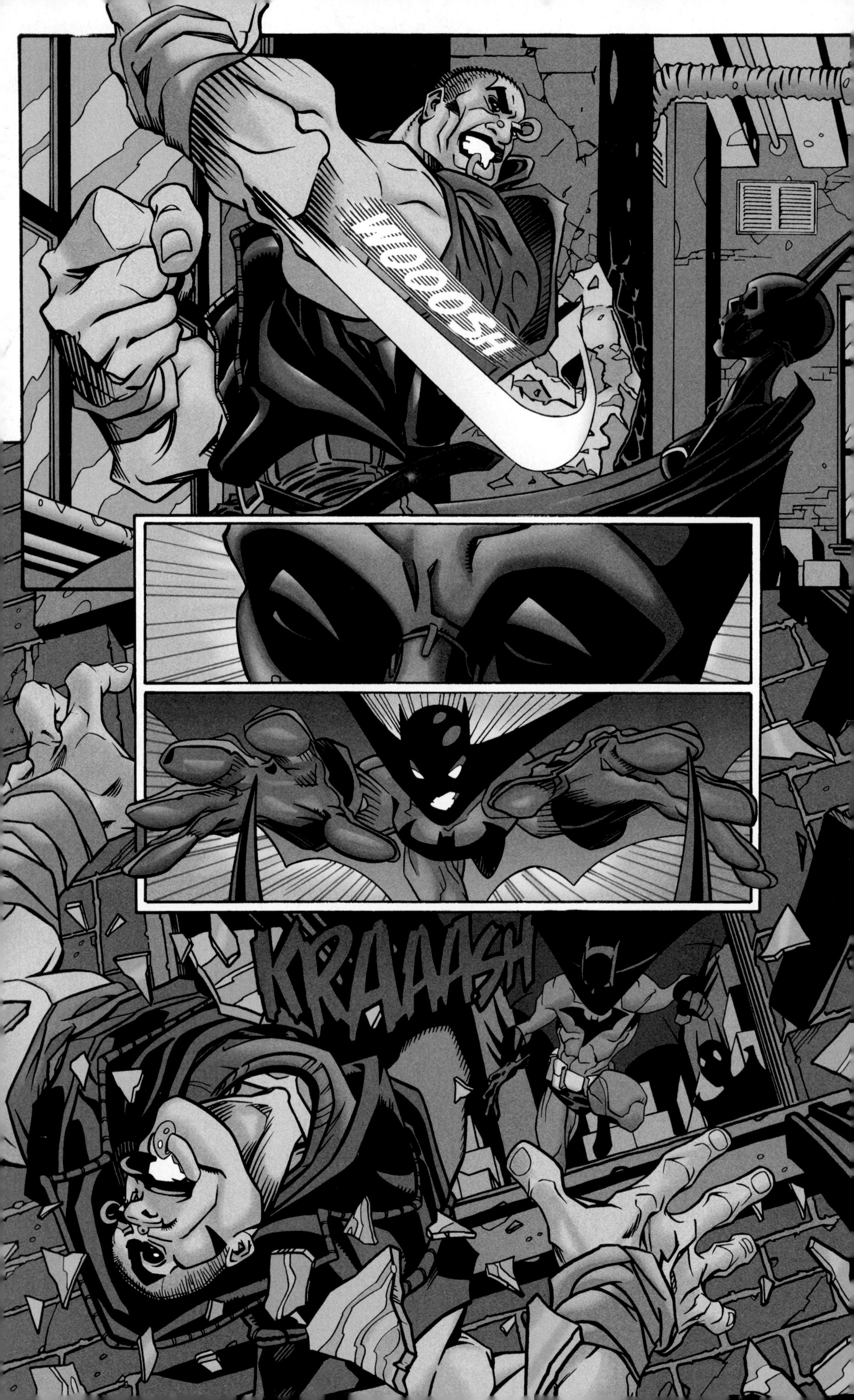
WOOOSH
KRAAASH

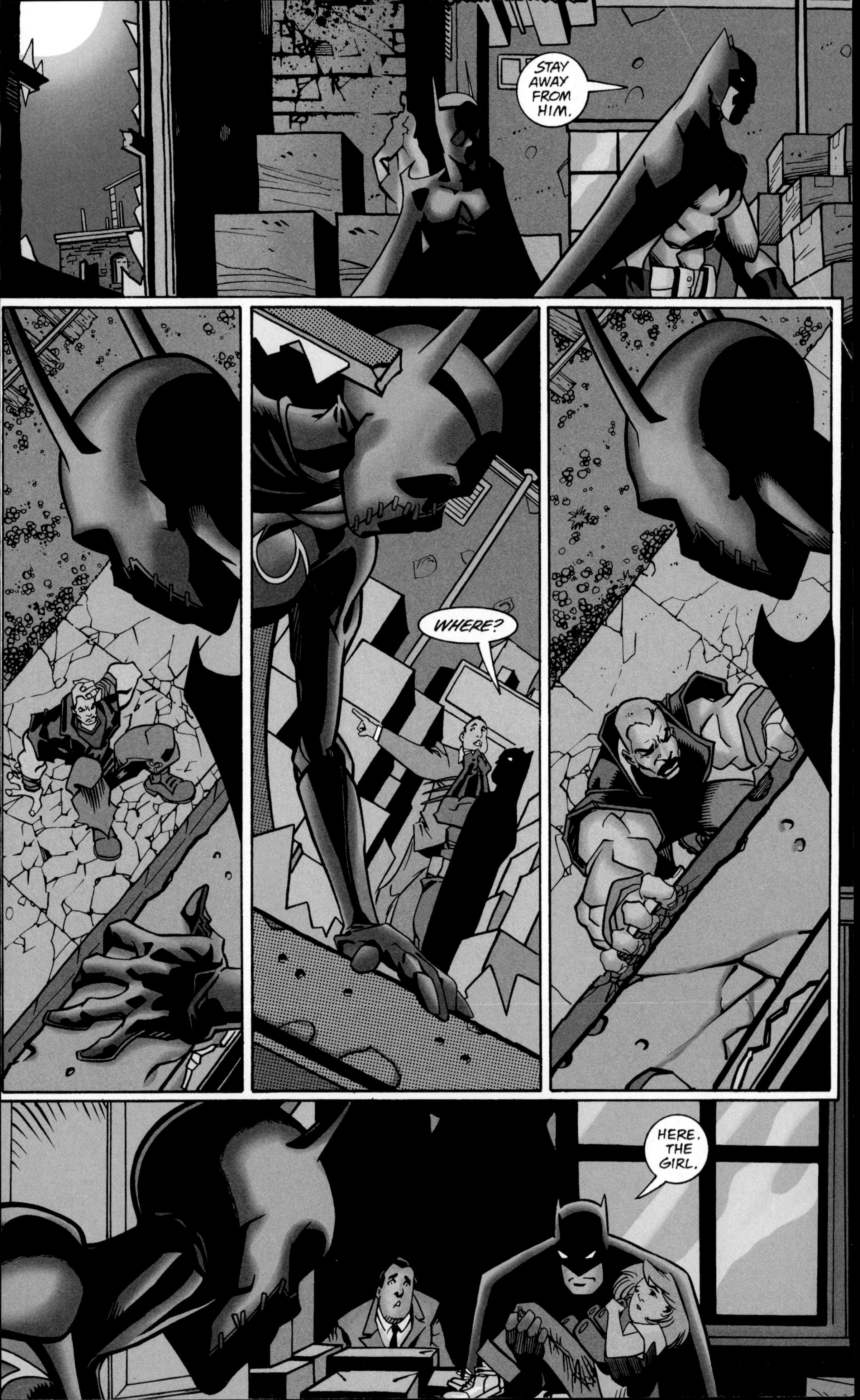
STAY AWAY FROM HIM.
WHERE?
HERE. THE GIRL.

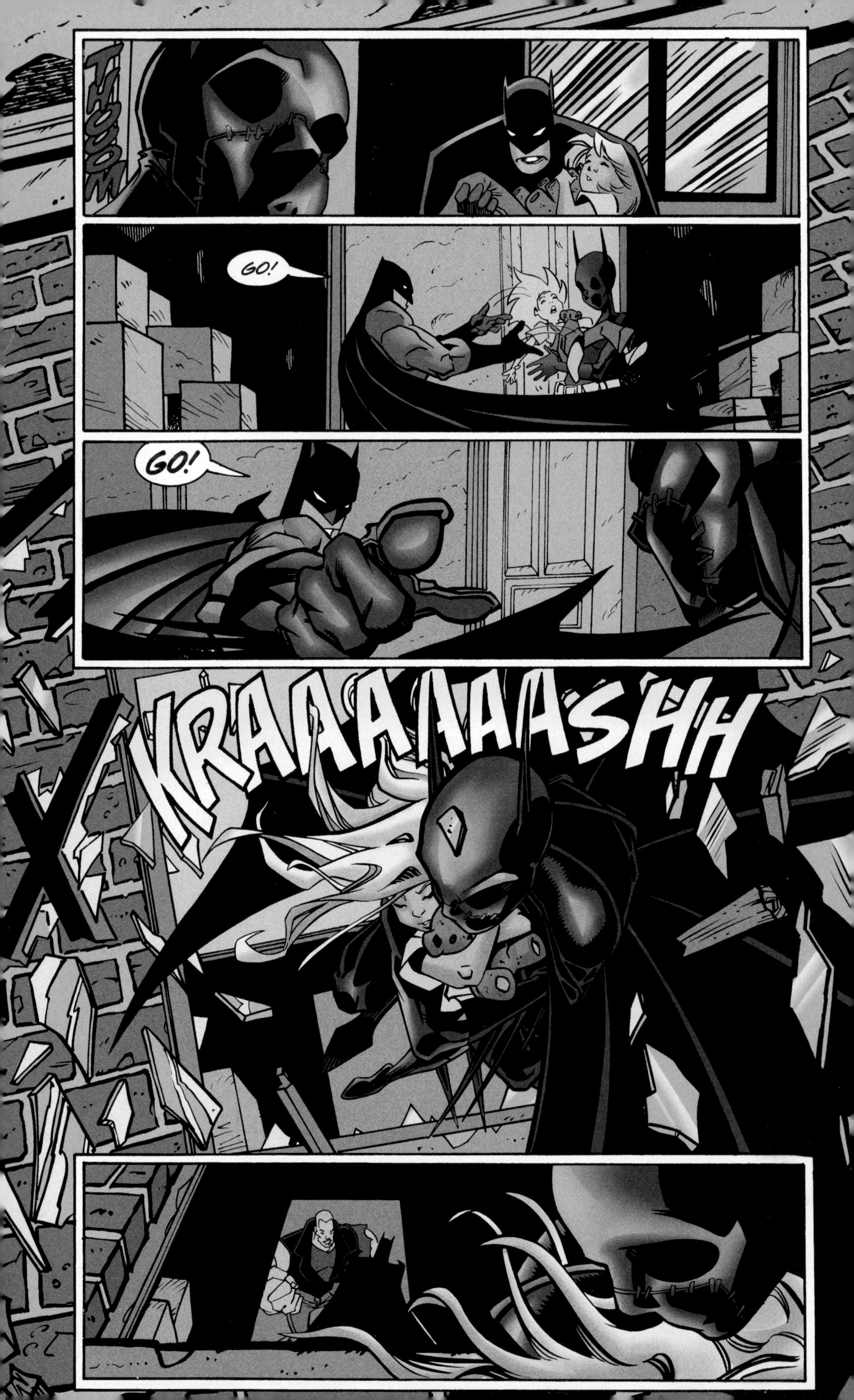

THOOOM
GO!
GO!
KRAAAAAAASHH

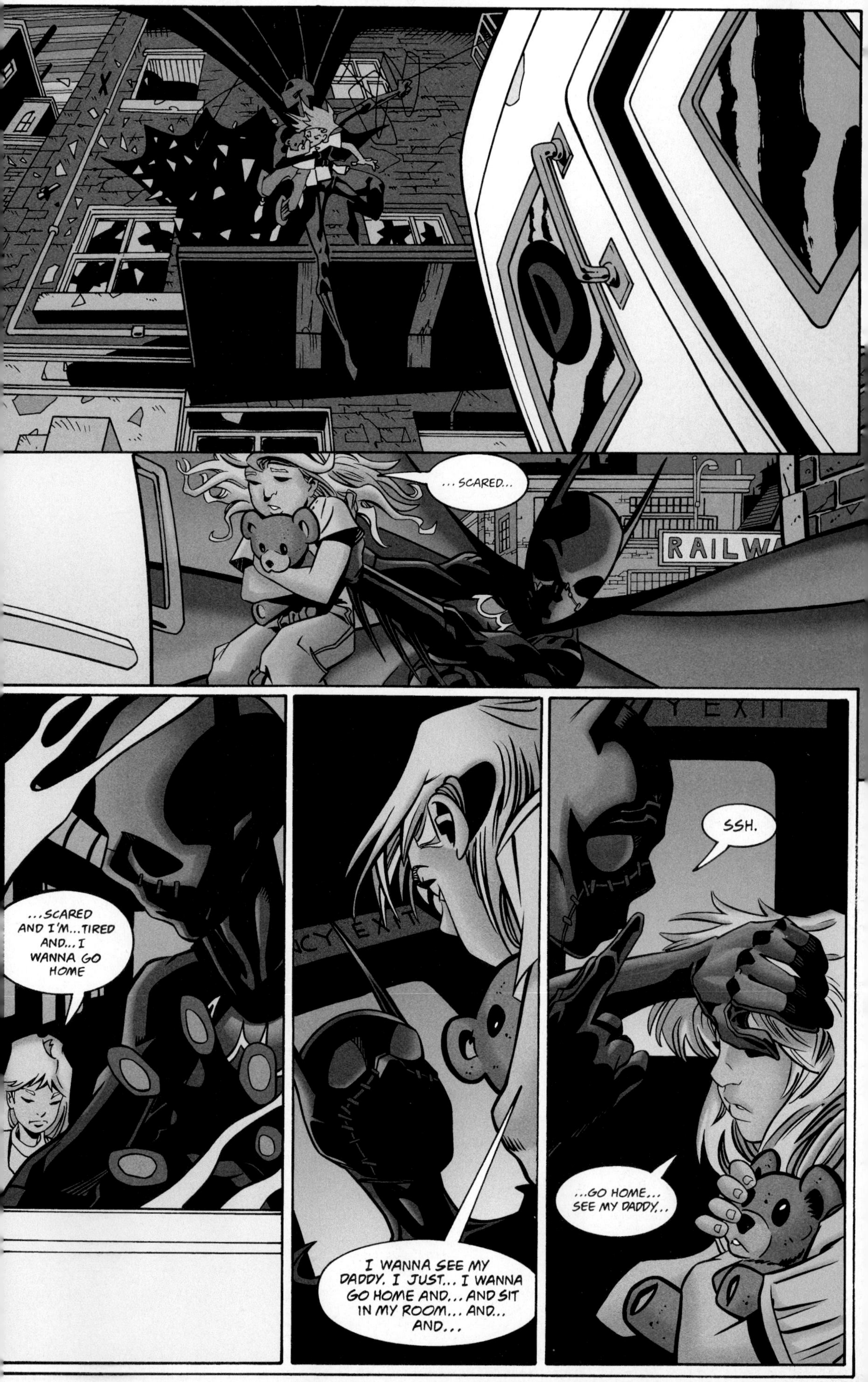
RAILW
...SCARED...
...SCARED AND I'M...TIRED AND...I WANNA GO HOME
I WANNA SEE MY DADDY. I JUST... I WANNA GO HOME AND... AND SIT IN MY ROOM... AND... AND...
SSH.
...GO HOME... SEE MY DADDY...

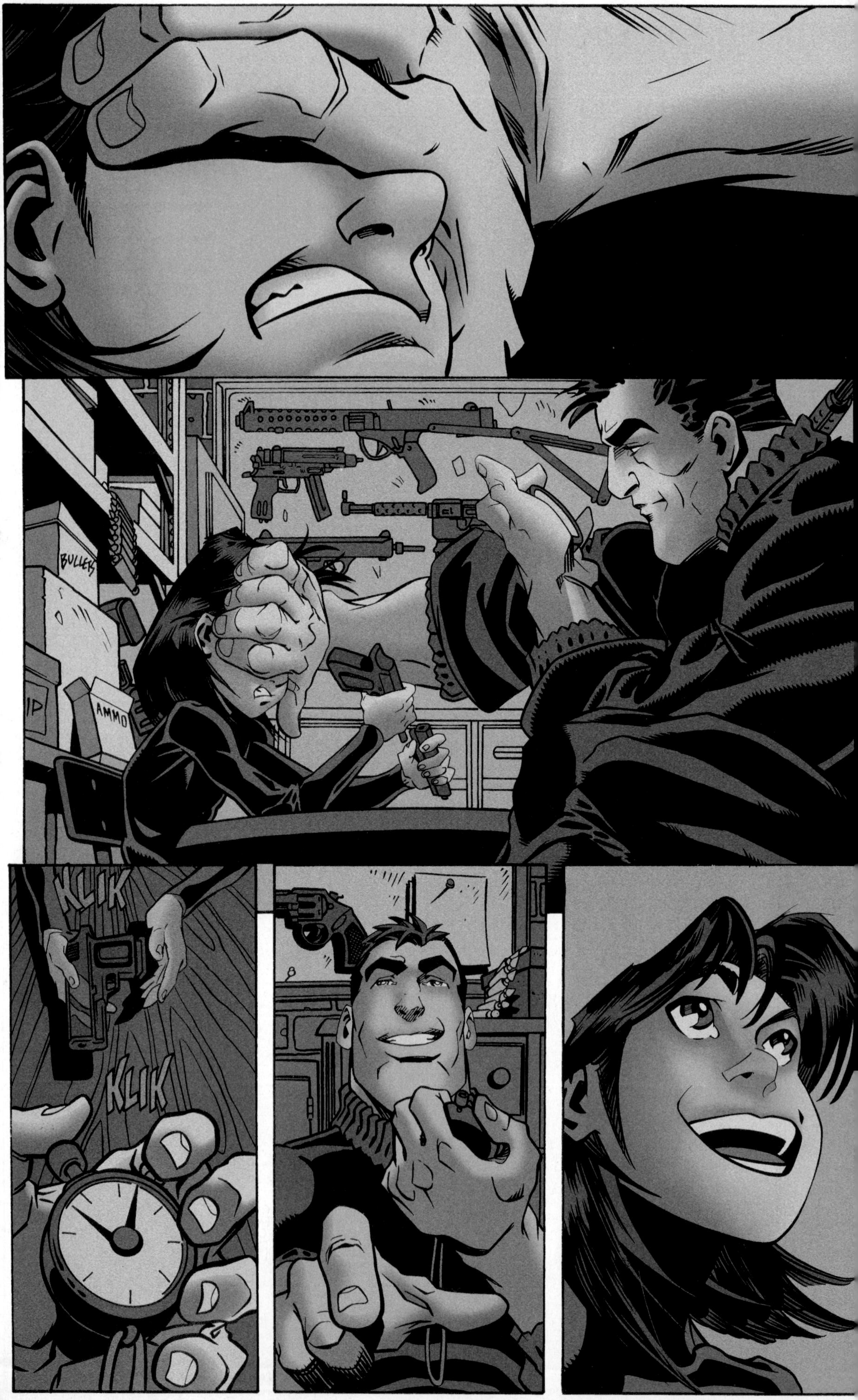
BULLETS
IP
AMMO
KLIK
KLIK

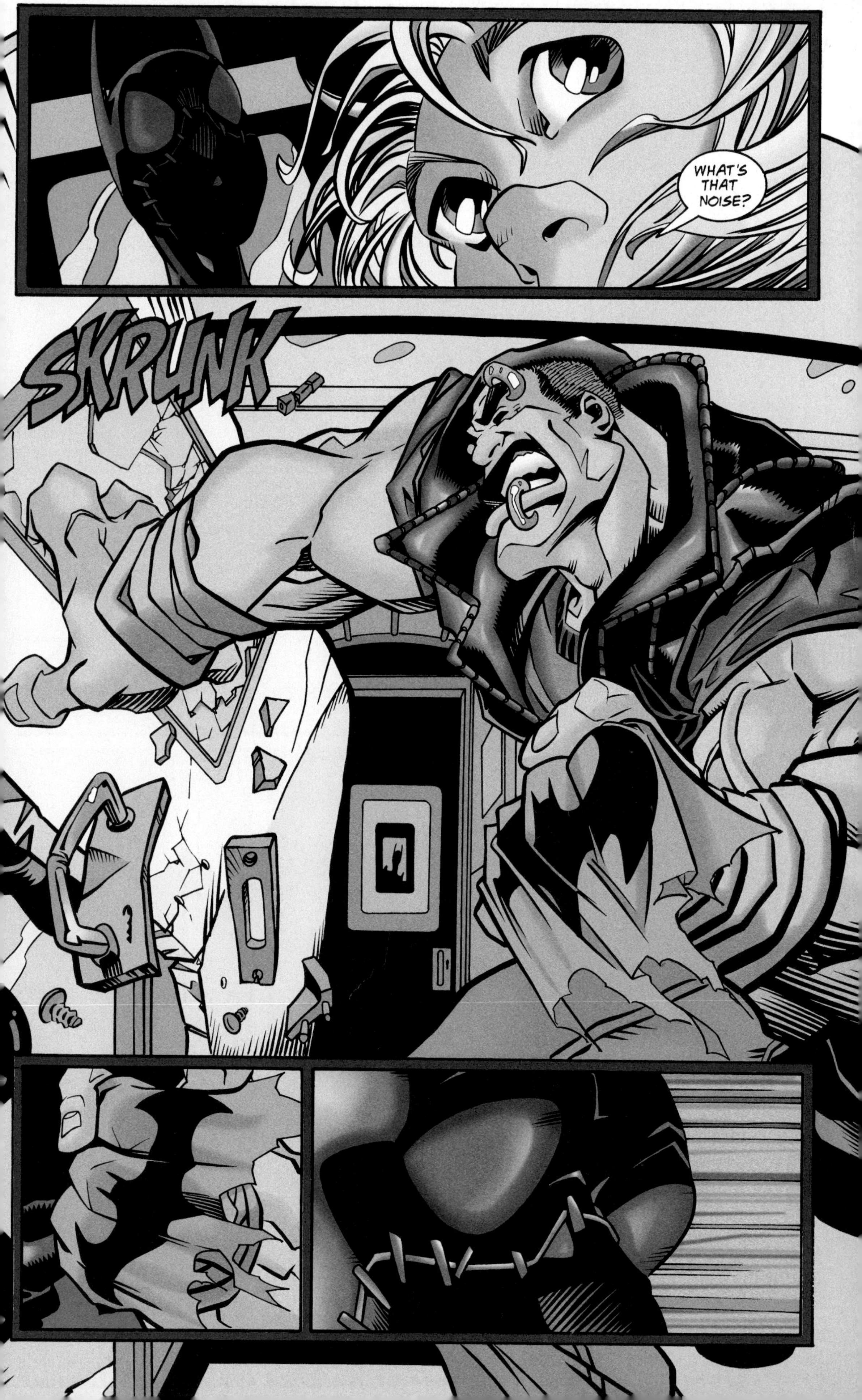
WHAT'S THAT NOISE?
SKRUNK

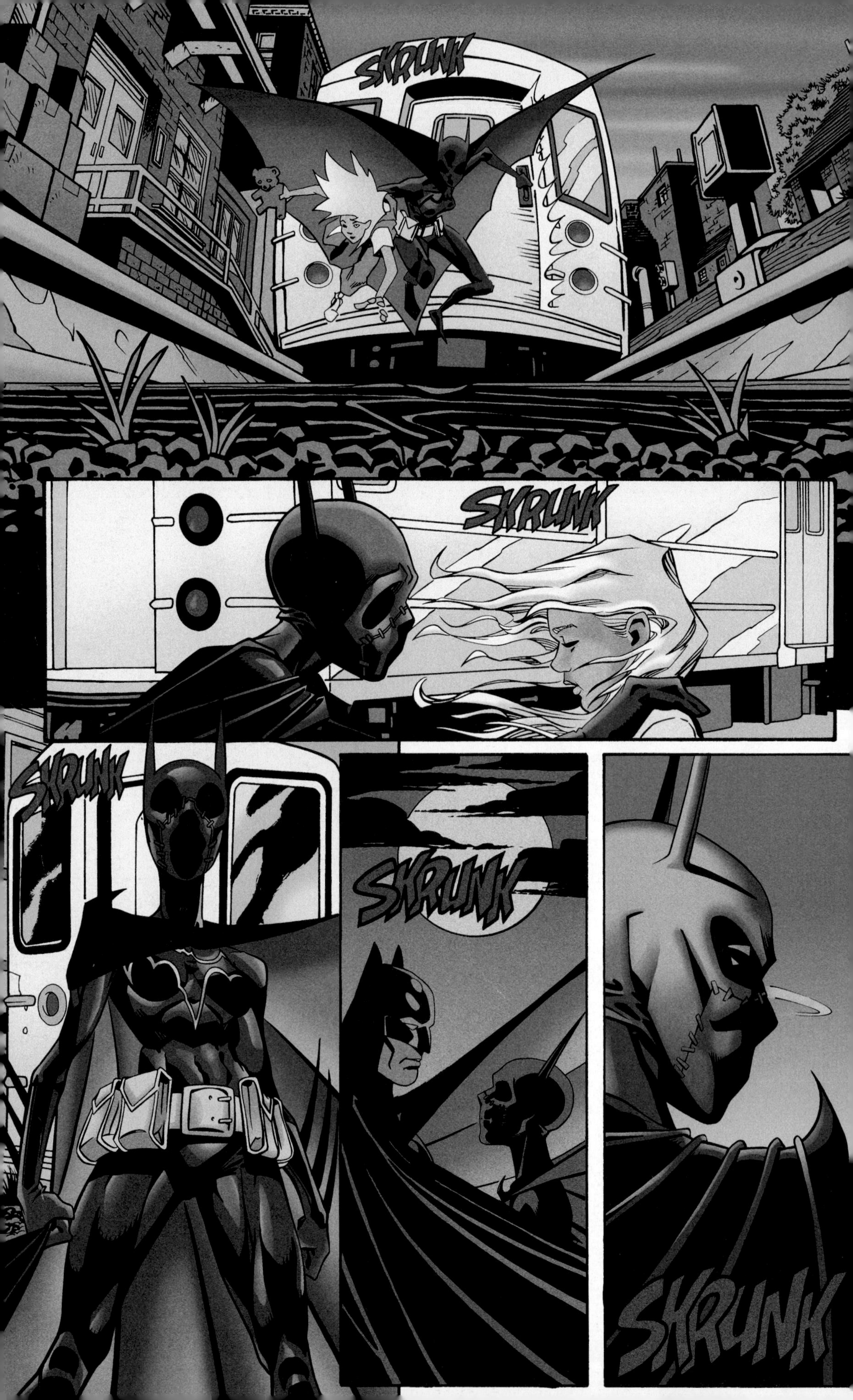
SKRUNK
SKRUNK
SKRUNK
SKRUNK
SKRUNK

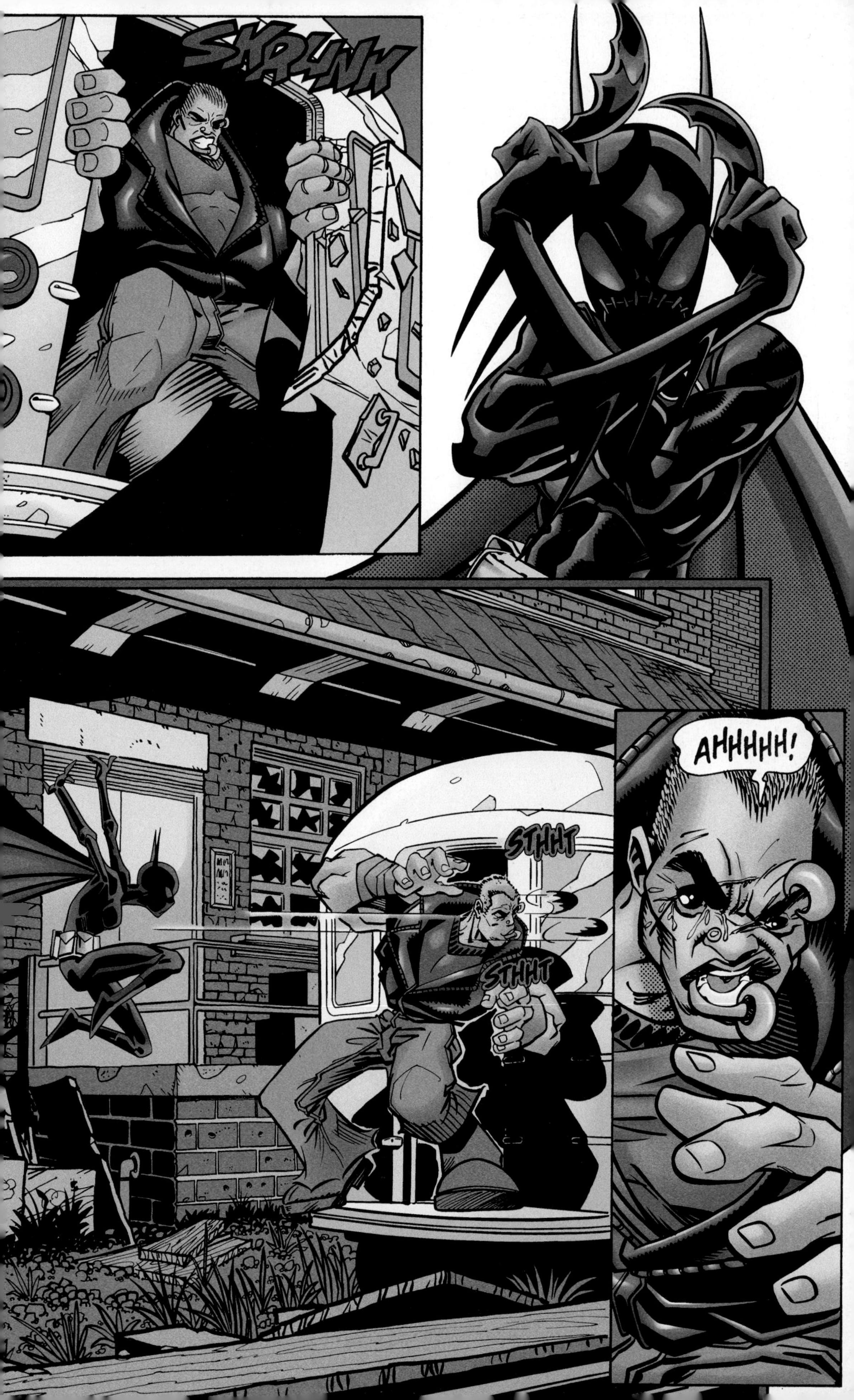
SKRUNK
STHHT
STHHT
AHHHHH!

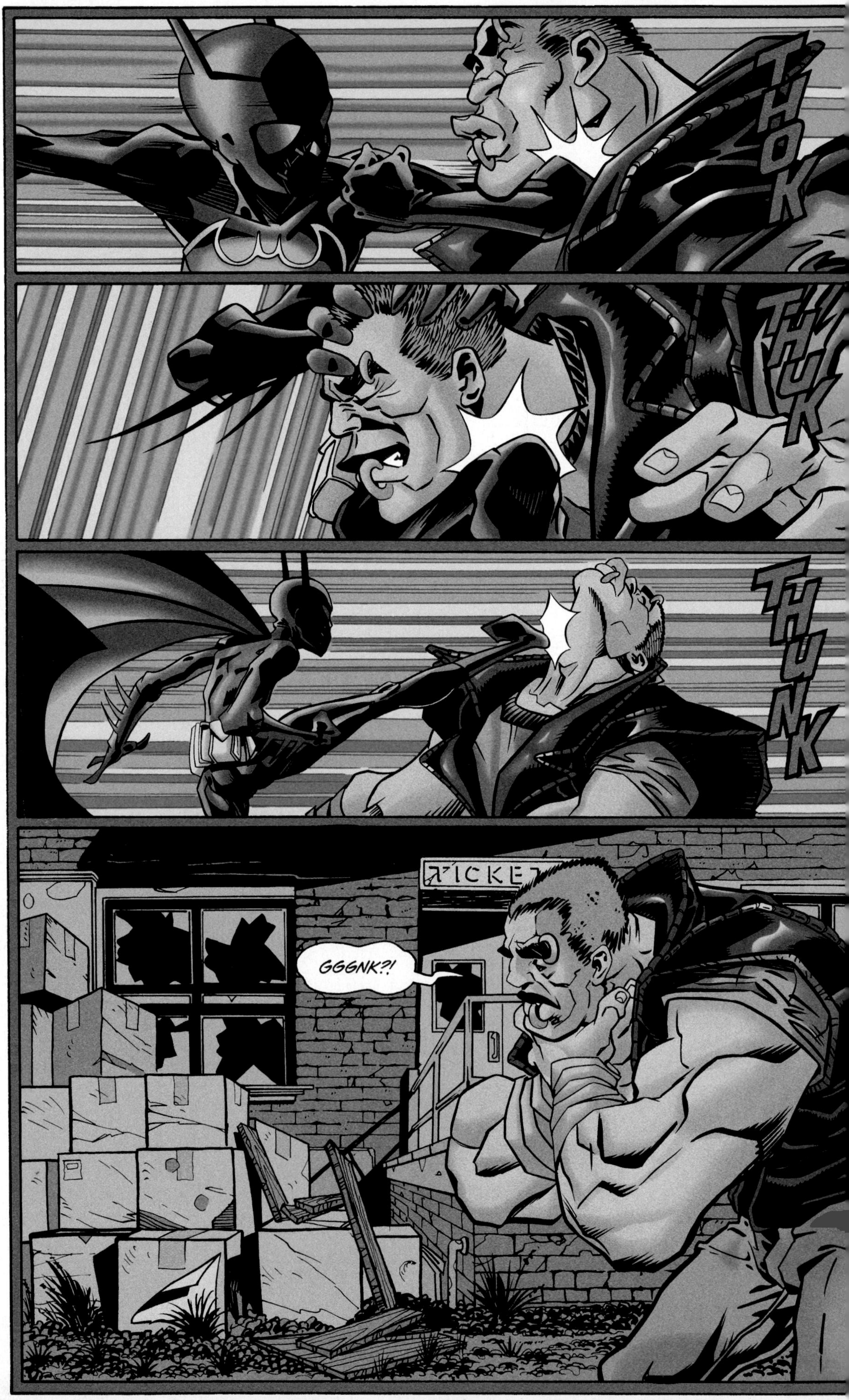
THOK
THUK
THUNK
TICKET
GGGNK?!

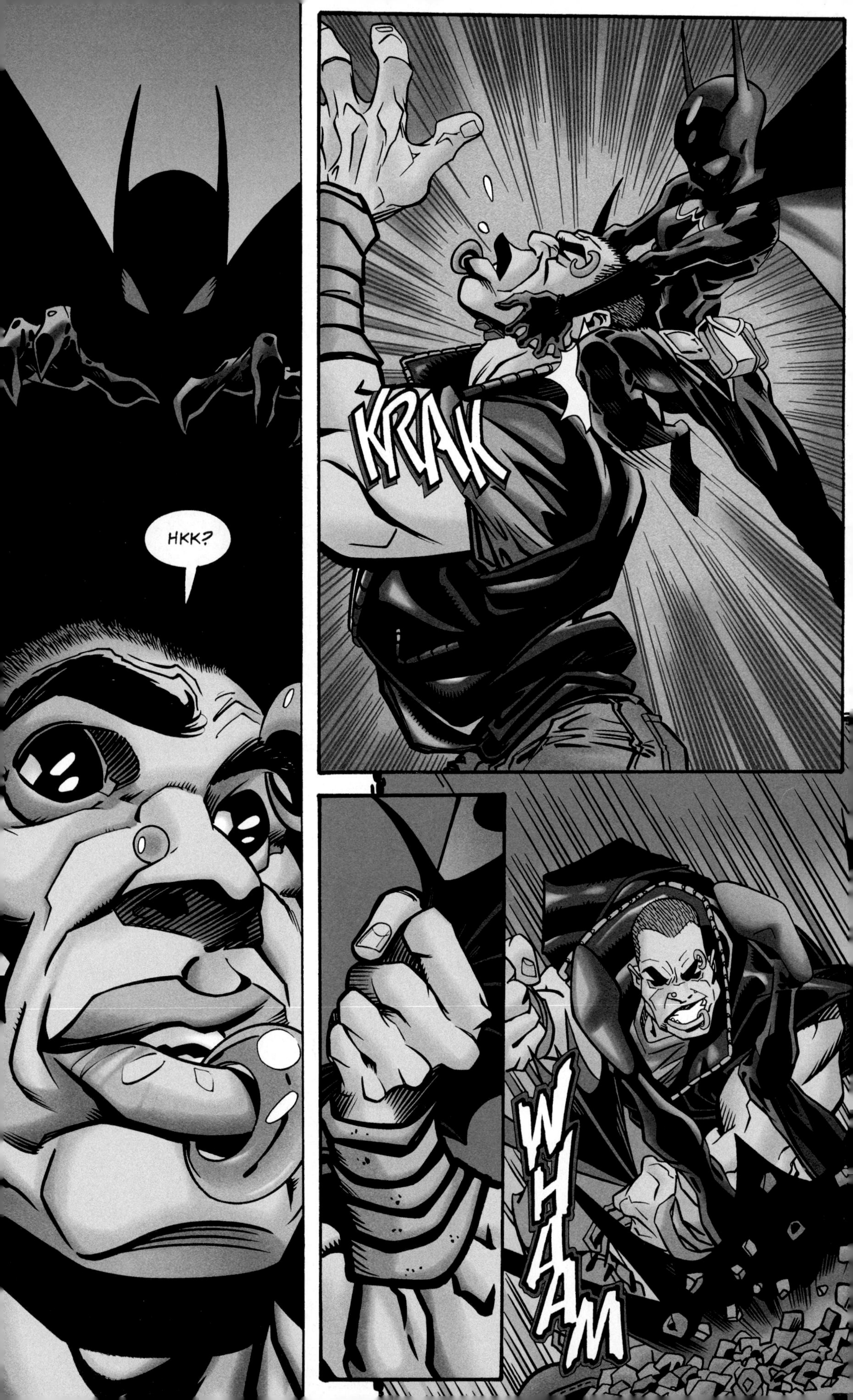
HKK?
KRAK
WHAAM

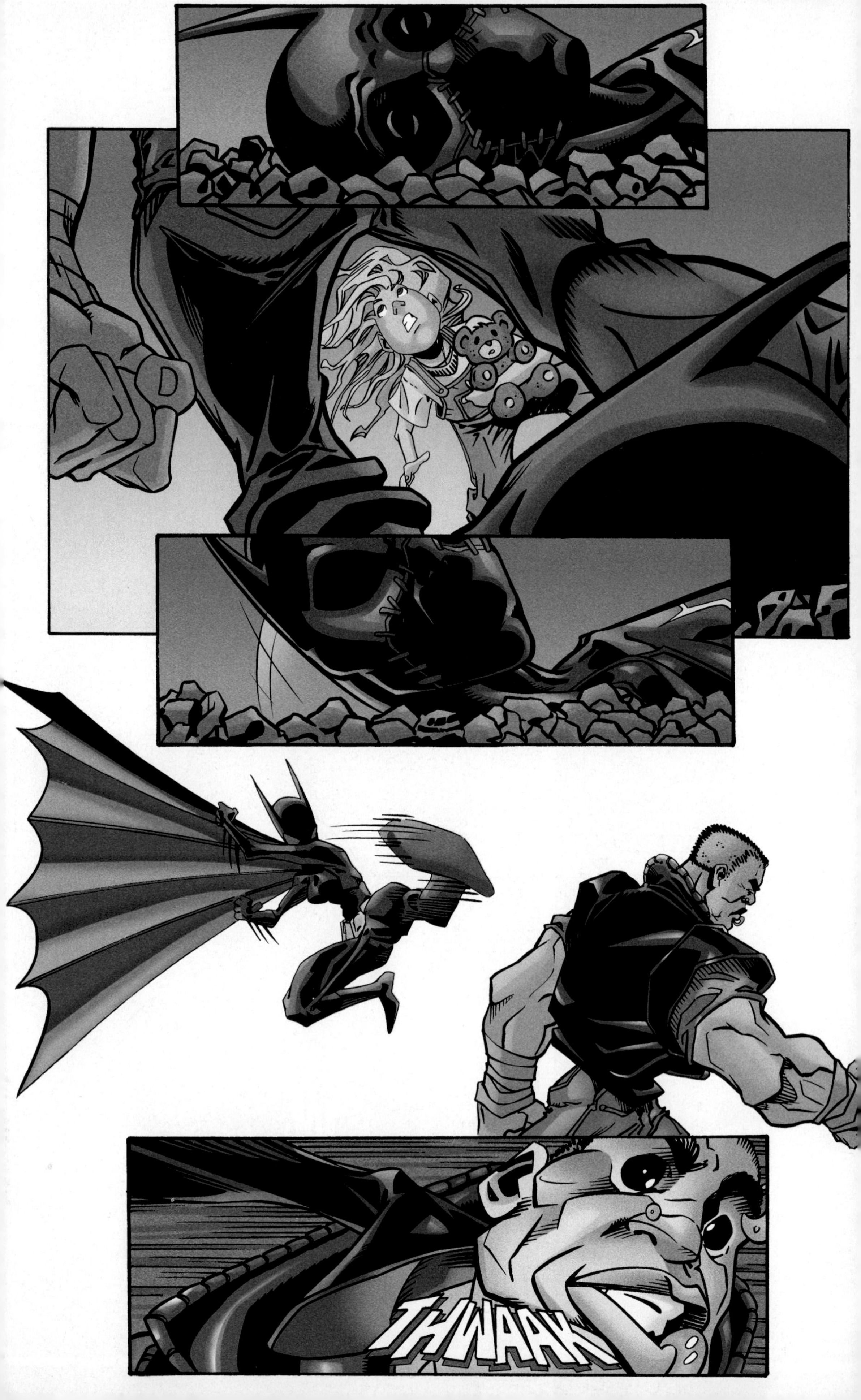
THWAAK

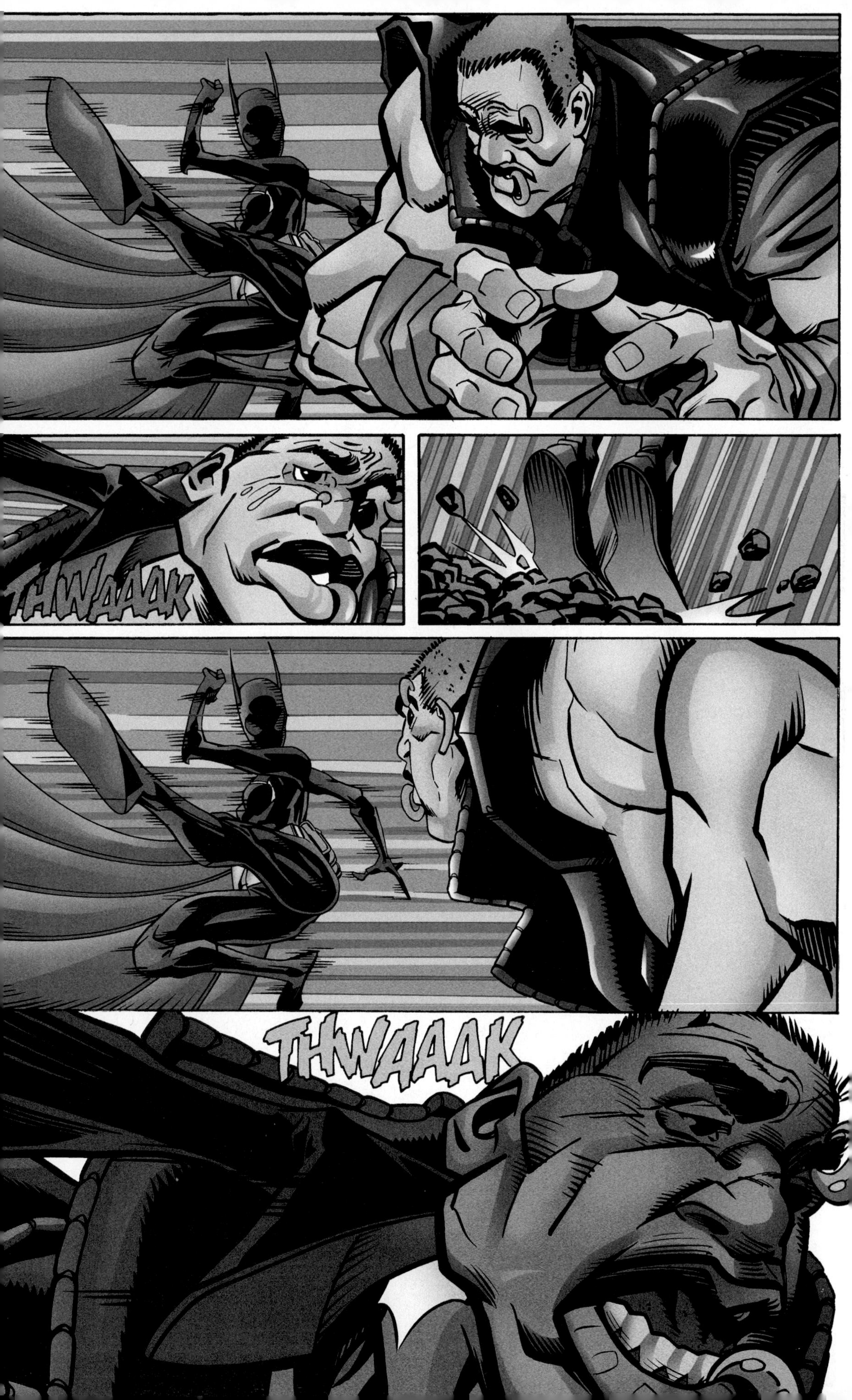
THWAAAK
THWAAAK

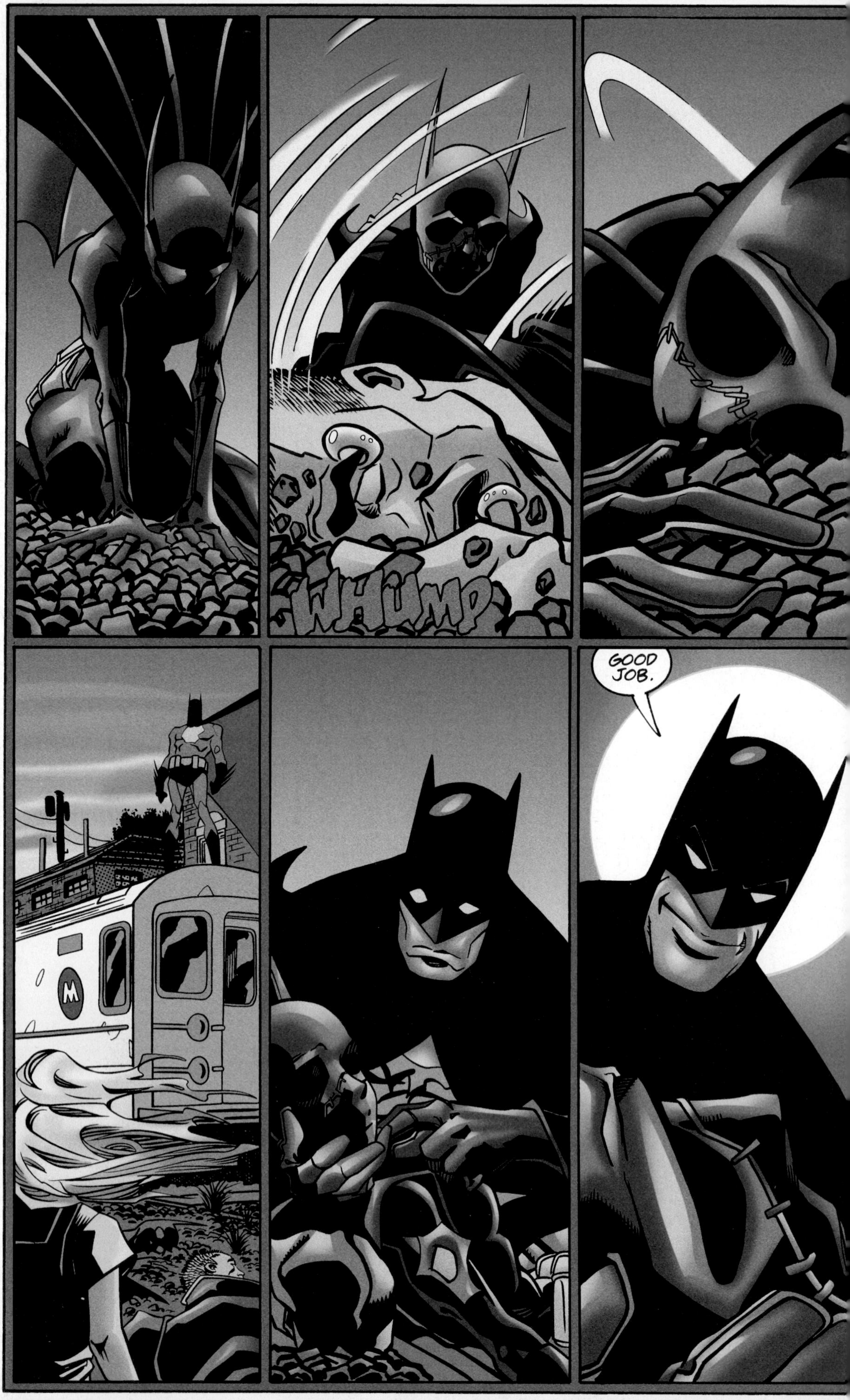
WHUMP
GOOD JOB.

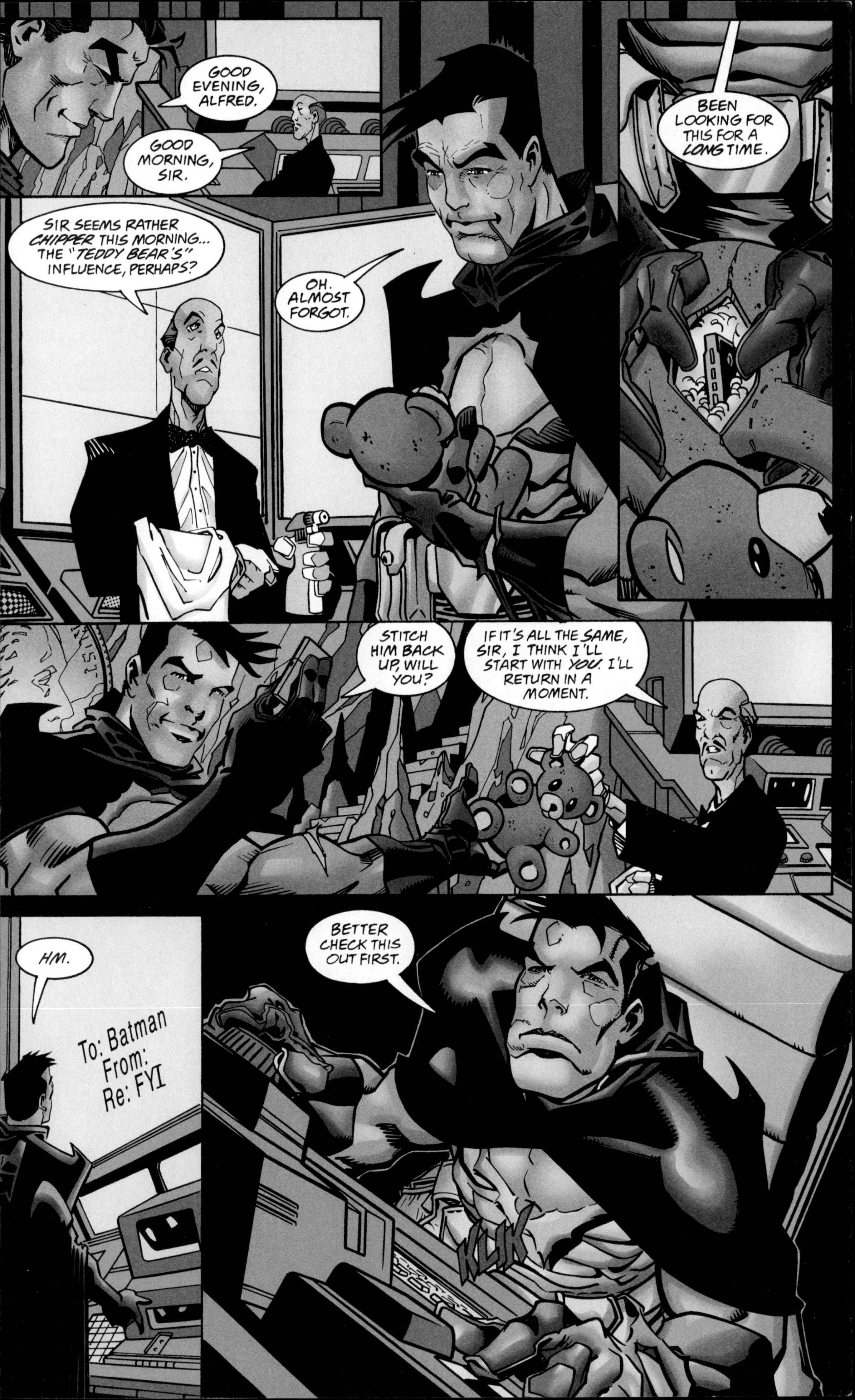
GOOD EVENING, ALFRED.
GOOD MORNING, SIR.
BEEN LOOKING FOR THIS FOR A LONG TIME.
SIR SEEMS RATHER CHIPPER THIS MORNING... THE "TEDDY BEAR'S" INFLUENCE, PERHAPS?
OH. ALMOST FORGOT.
STITCH HIM BACK UP, WILL YOU?
IF IT'S ALL THE SAME, SIR, I THINK I'LL START WITH YOU. I'LL RETURN IN A MOMENT.
HM.
To: Batman
From:
Re: FYI
BETTER CHECK THIS OUT FIRST.
KLIK

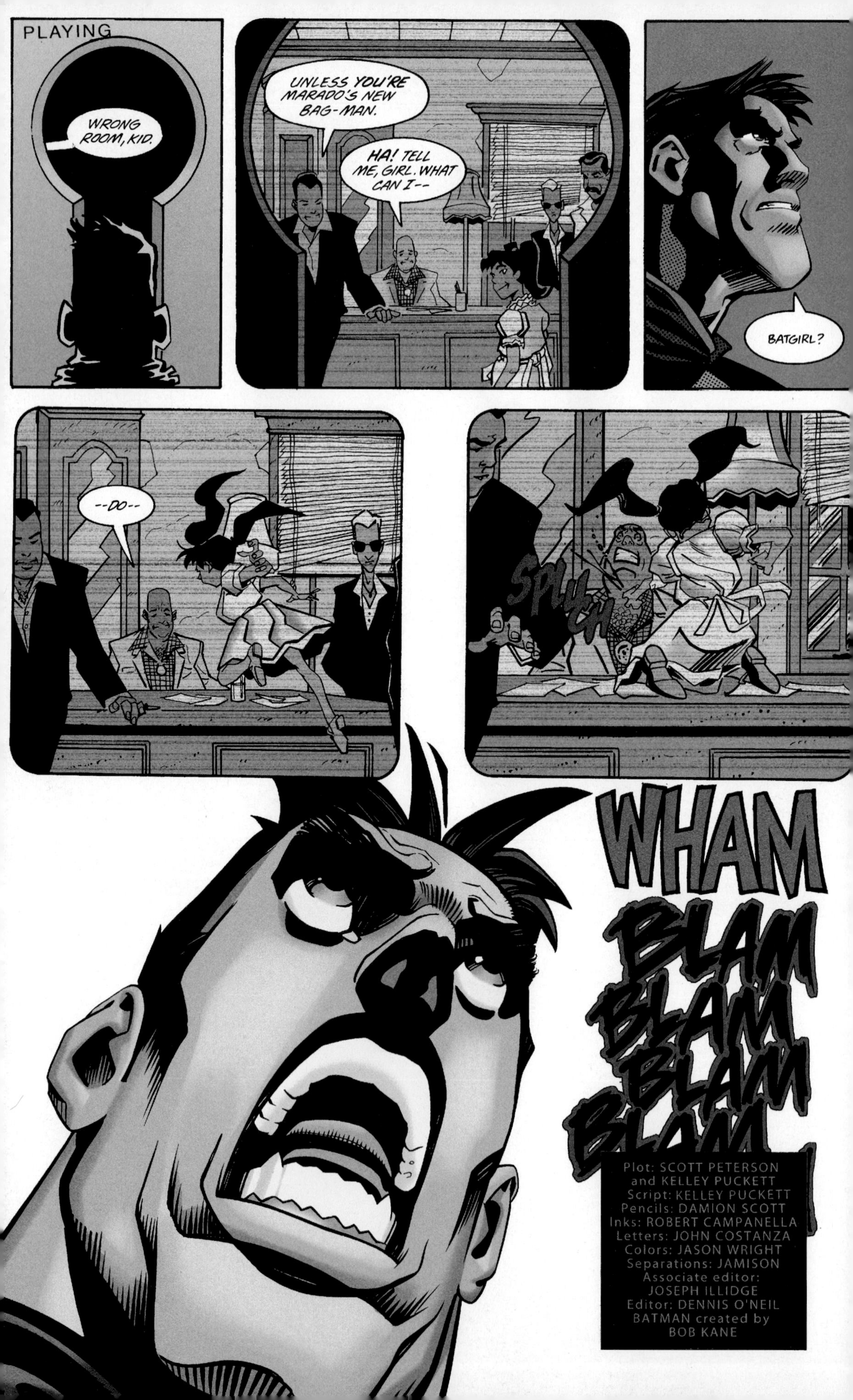
PLAYING
WRONG ROOM, KID.
UNLESS YOU'RE MARADO'S NEW BAG-MAN.
HA! TELL ME, GIRL. WHAT CAN I--
BATGIRL?
--DO--
SPLUTCH
WHAM
BLAM
BLAM
BLAM
Plot: SCOTT PETERSON and KELLEY PUCKETT
Script: KELLEY PUCKETT
Pencils: DAMION SCOTT
Inks: ROBERT CAMPANELLA
Letters: JOHN COSTANZA
Colors: JASON WRIGHT
Separations: JAMISON
Associate editor: JOSEPH ILLIDGE
Editor: DENNIS O'NEIL
BATMAN created by BOB KANE

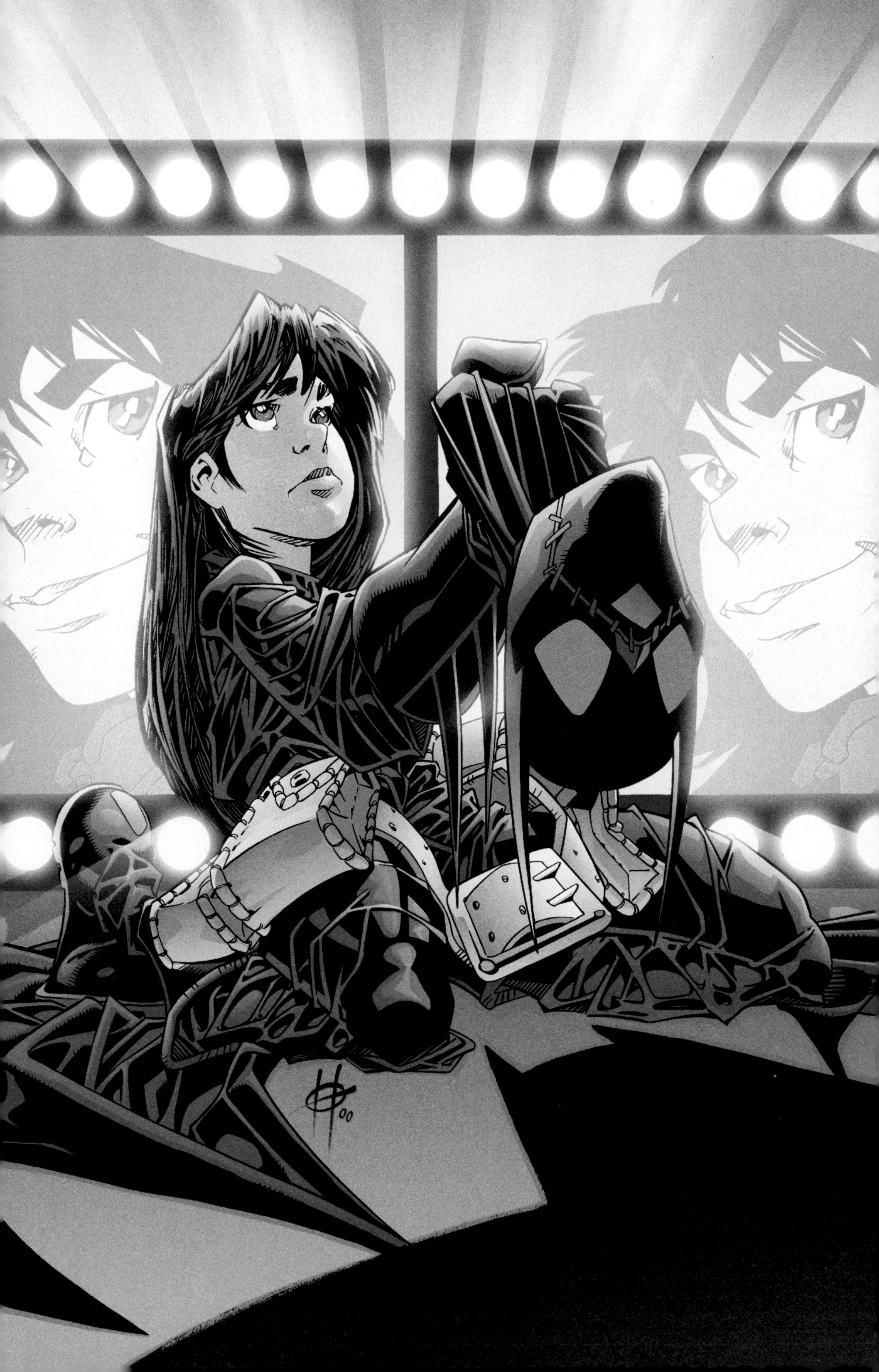

BATGIRL #4 cover by
Damion Scott & Robert Campanella

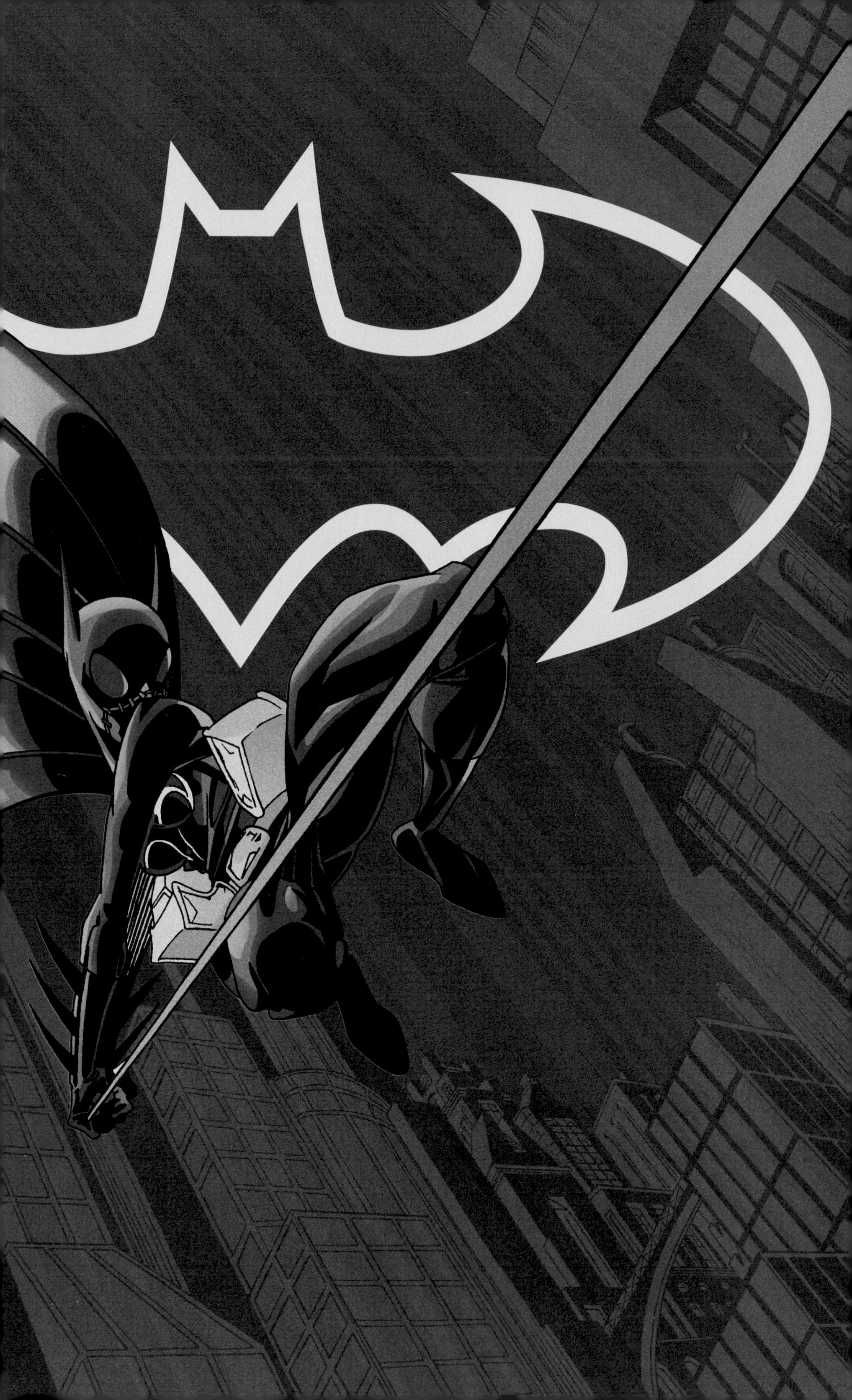

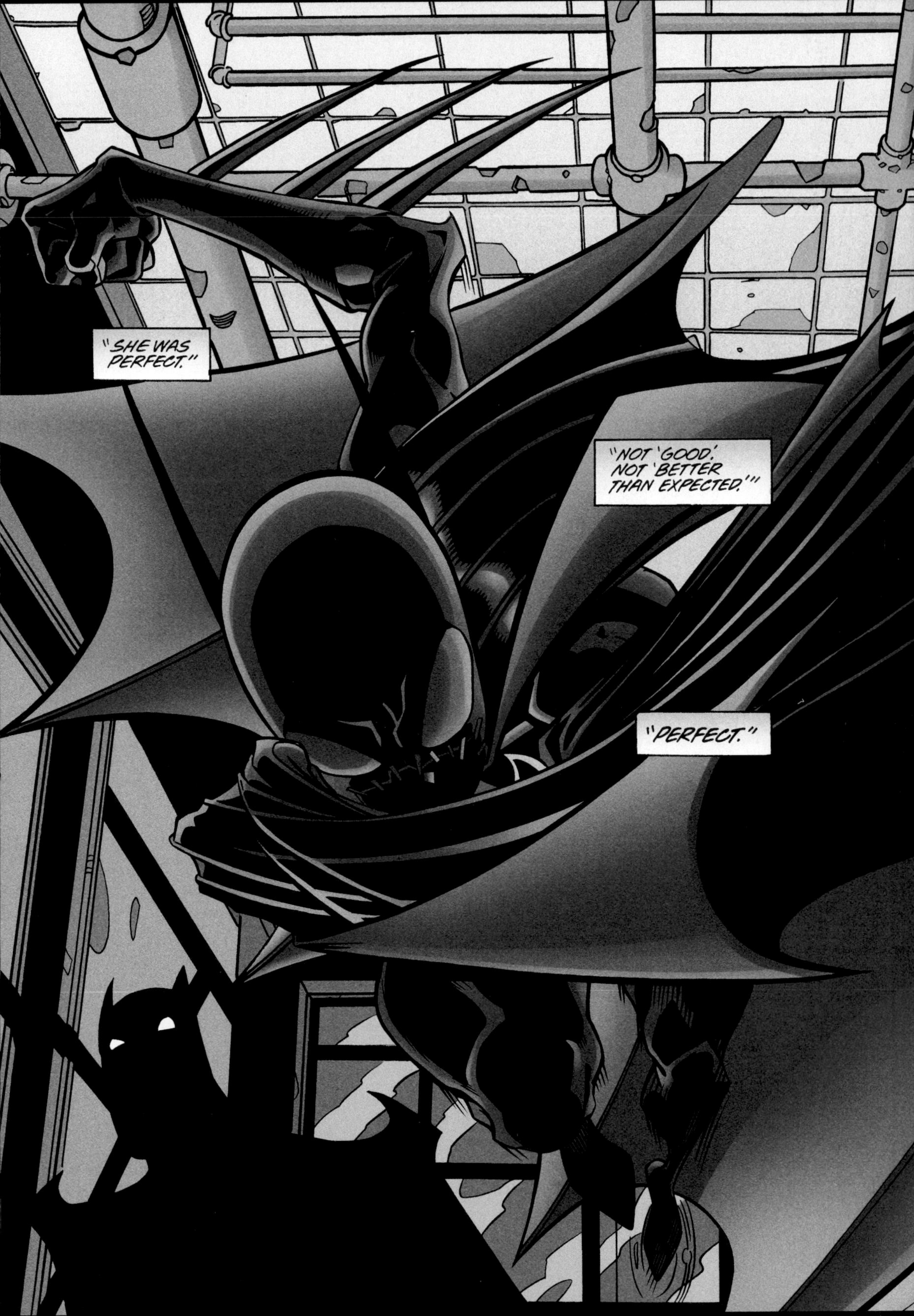
"SHE WAS PERFECT."
"NOT 'GOOD.' NOT 'BETTER THAN EXPECTED.'"
"PERFECT."

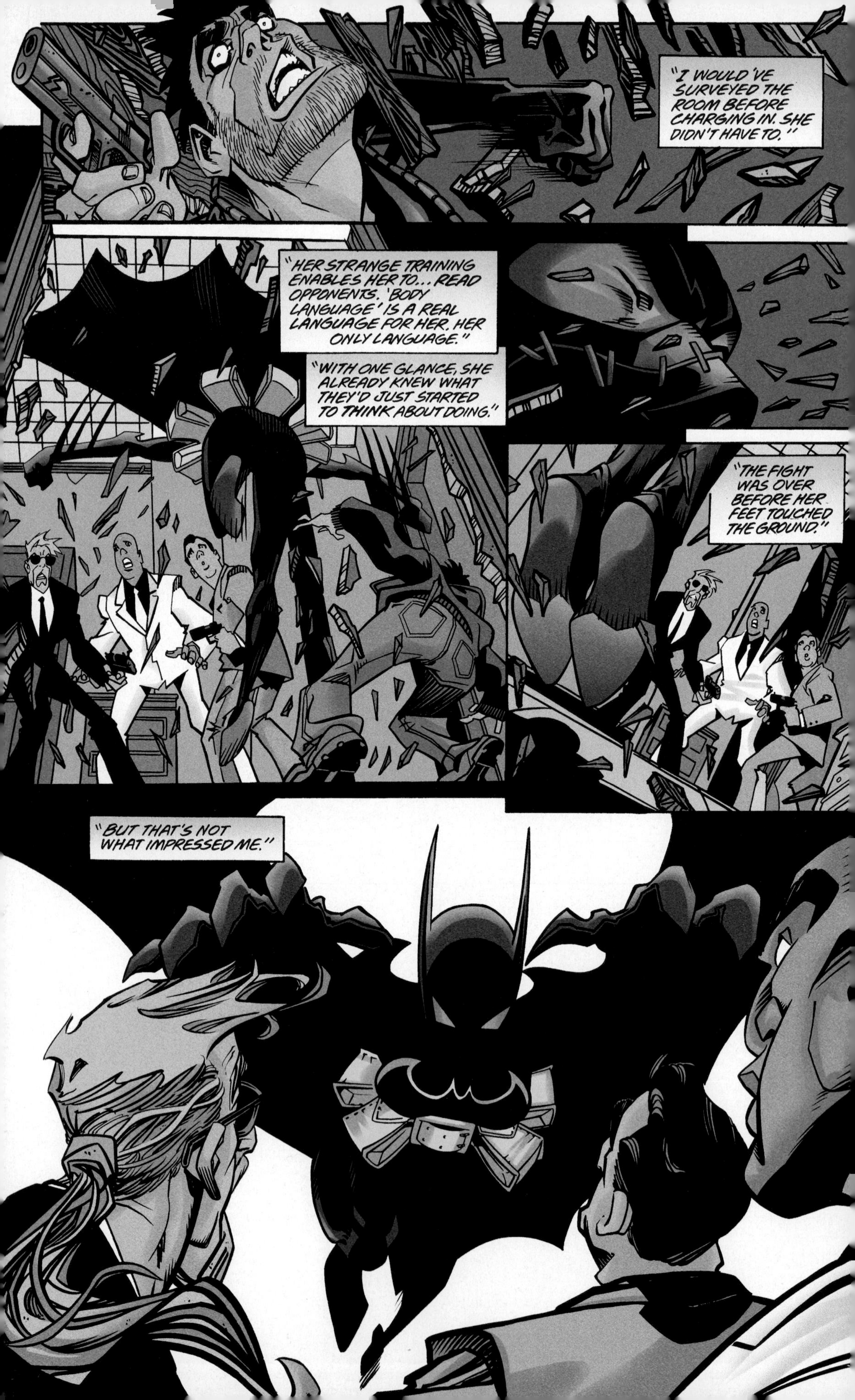
"I WOULD'VE SURVEYED THE ROOM BEFORE CHARGING IN. SHE DIDN'T HAVE TO."
"HER STRANGE TRAINING ENABLES HER TO... READ OPPONENTS. 'BODY LANGUAGE' IS A REAL LANGUAGE FOR HER. HER ONLY LANGUAGE."
"WITH ONE GLANCE, SHE ALREADY KNEW WHAT THEY'D JUST STARTED TO THINK ABOUT DOING."
"THE FIGHT WAS OVER BEFORE HER FEET TOUCHED THE GROUND."
"BUT THAT'S NOT WHAT IMPRESSED ME."

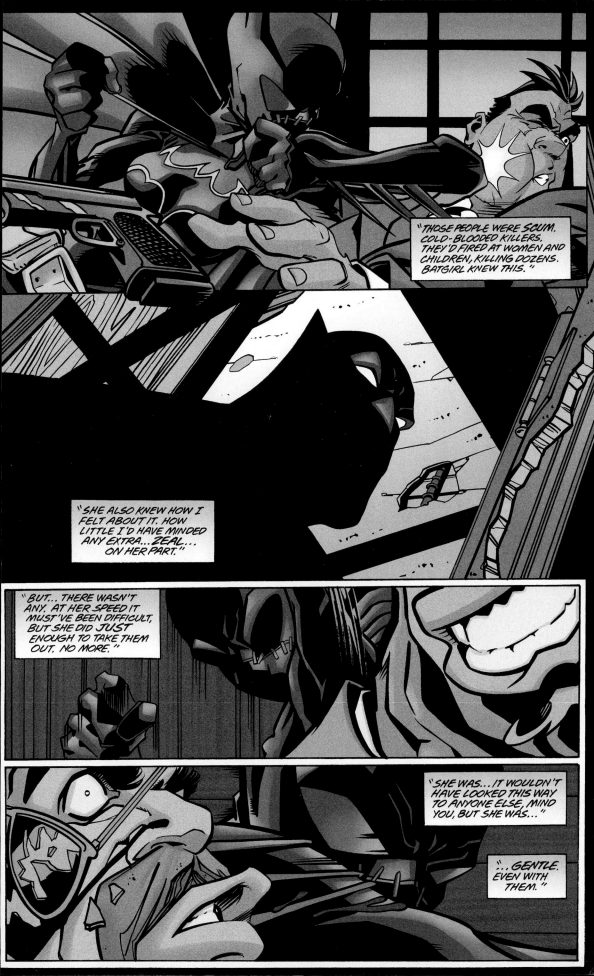

"THOSE PEOPLE WERE SCUM. COLD-BLOODED KILLERS. THEY'D FIRED AT WOMEN AND CHILDREN, KILLING DOZENS. BATGIRL KNEW THIS."

"SHE ALSO KNEW HOW I FELT ABOUT IT. HOW LITTLE I'D HAVE MINDED ANY EXTRA...ZEAL... ON HER PART."

"BUT... THERE WASN'T ANY. AT HER SPEED IT MUST'VE BEEN DIFFICULT, BUT SHE DID JUST ENOUGH TO TAKE THEM OUT. NO MORE."

"SHE WAS... IT WOULDN'T HAVE LOOKED THIS WAY TO ANYONE ELSE, MIND YOU, BUT SHE WAS..."

"...GENTLE, EVEN WITH THEM."

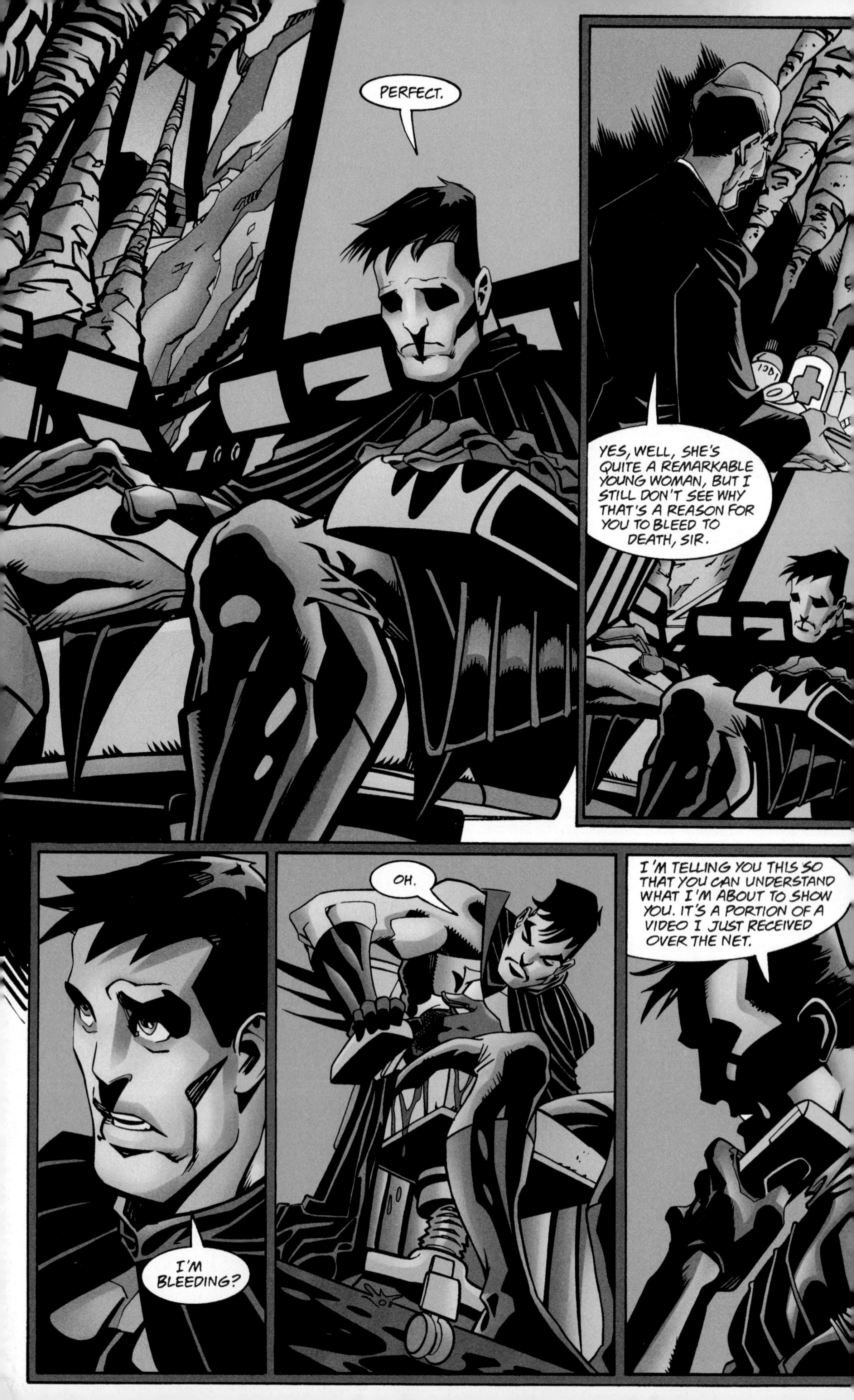
PERFECT.
YES, WELL, SHE'S QUITE A REMARKABLE YOUNG WOMAN, BUT I STILL DON'T SEE WHY THAT'S A REASON FOR YOU TO BLEED TO DEATH, SIR.
I'M BLEEDING?
OH.
I'M TELLING YOU THIS SO THAT YOU CAN UNDERSTAND WHAT I'M ABOUT TO SHOW YOU. IT'S A PORTION OF A VIDEO I JUST RECEIVED OVER THE NET.

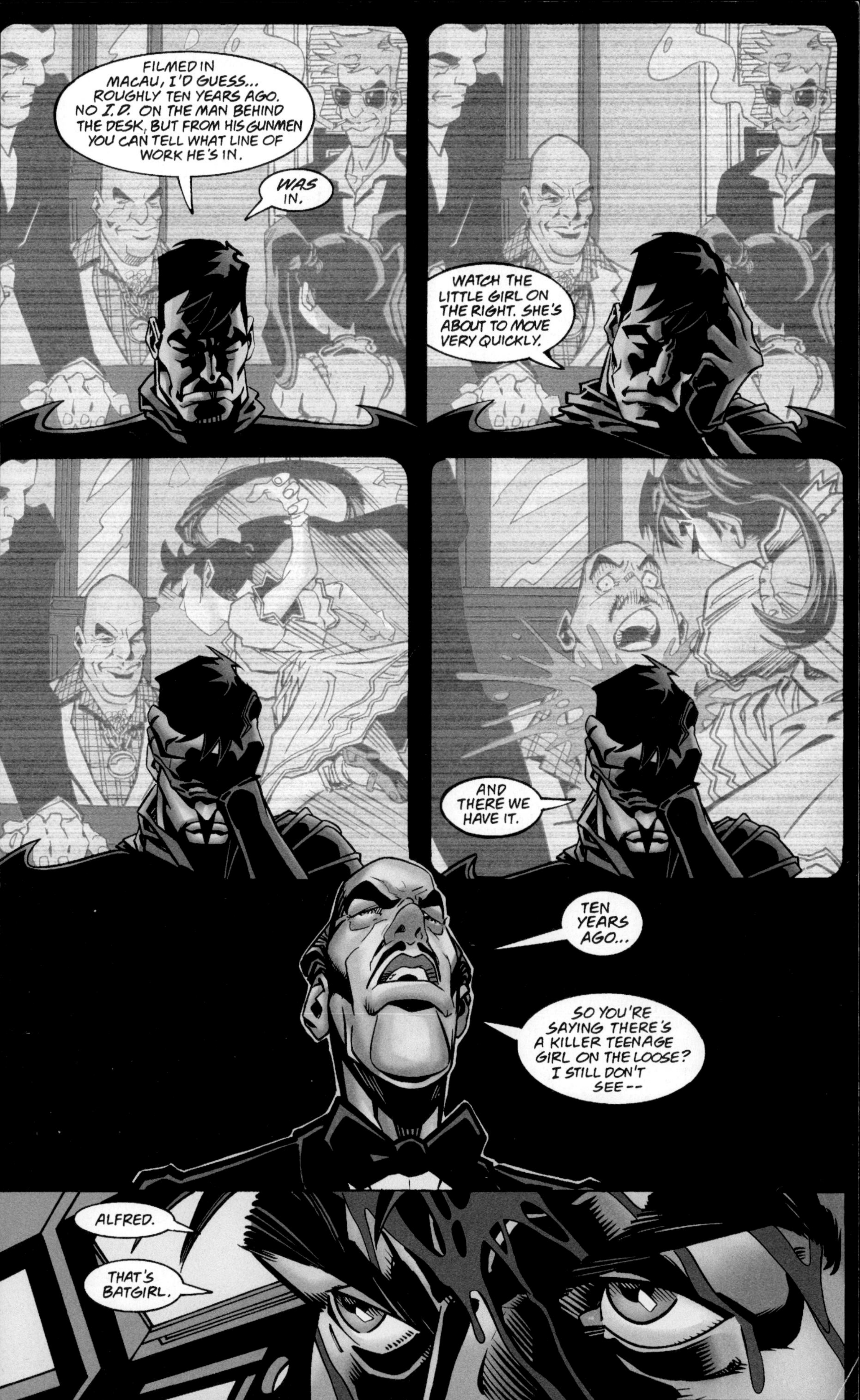
FILMED IN MACAU, I'D GUESS... ROUGHLY TEN YEARS AGO. NO I.D. ON THE MAN BEHIND THE DESK, BUT FROM HIS GUNMEN YOU CAN TELL WHAT LINE OF WORK HE'S IN.
WAS IN.
WATCH THE LITTLE GIRL ON THE RIGHT. SHE'S ABOUT TO MOVE VERY QUICKLY.
AND THERE WE HAVE IT.
TEN YEARS AGO...
SO YOU'RE SAYING THERE'S A KILLER TEENAGE GIRL ON THE LOOSE? I STILL DON'T SEE--
ALFRED.
THAT'S BATGIRL.

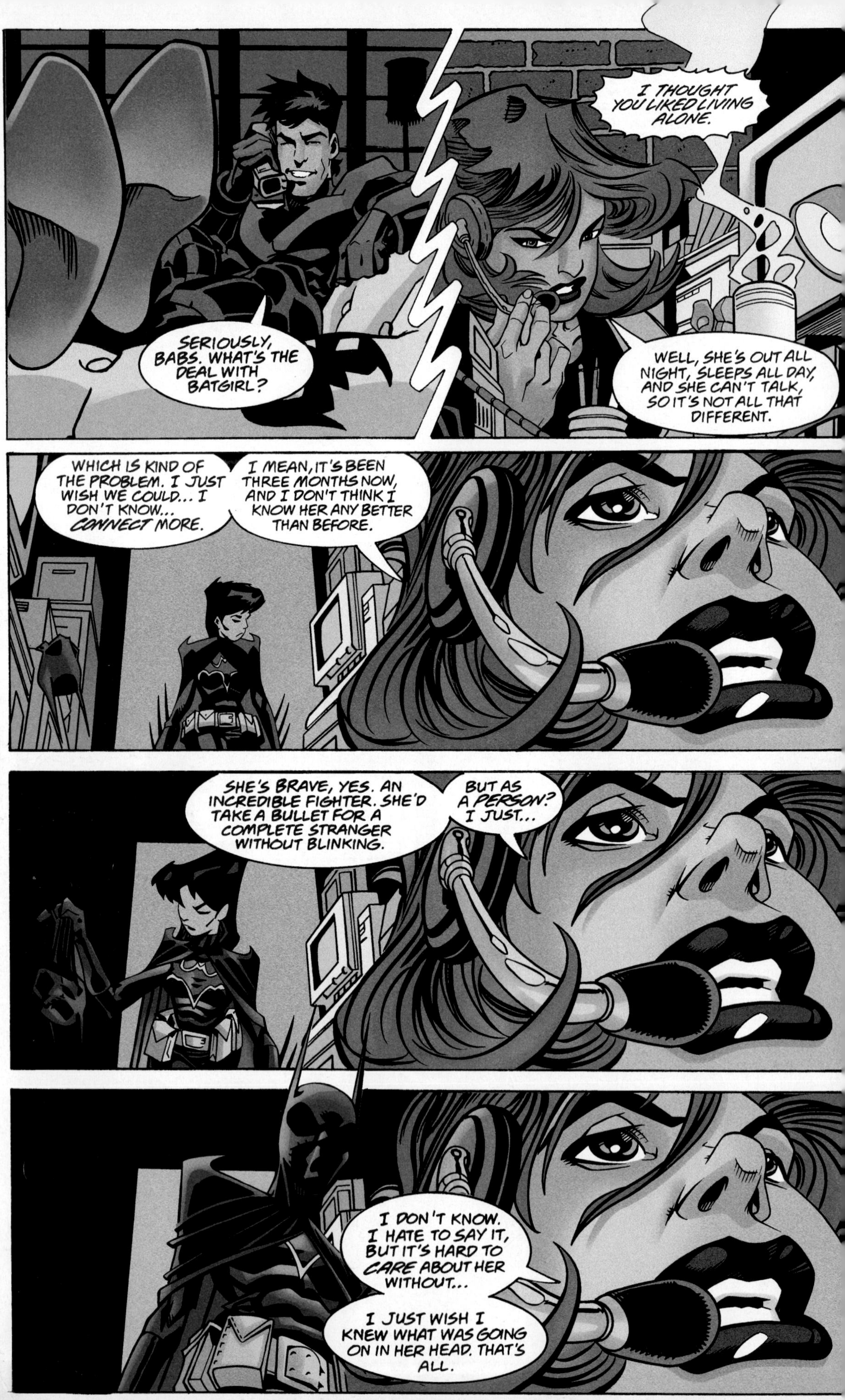
I THOUGHT YOU LIKED LIVING ALONE.
SERIOUSLY, BABS. WHAT'S THE DEAL WITH BATGIRL?
WELL, SHE'S OUT ALL NIGHT, SLEEPS ALL DAY, AND SHE CAN'T TALK, SO IT'S NOT ALL THAT DIFFERENT.
WHICH IS KIND OF THE PROBLEM. I JUST WISH WE COULD... I DON'T KNOW... CONNECT MORE.
I MEAN, IT'S BEEN THREE MONTHS NOW, AND I DON'T THINK I KNOW HER ANY BETTER THAN BEFORE.
SHE'S BRAVE, YES. AN INCREDIBLE FIGHTER. SHE'D TAKE A BULLET FOR A COMPLETE STRANGER WITHOUT BLINKING.
BUT AS A PERSON? I JUST...
I DON'T KNOW. I HATE TO SAY IT, BUT IT'S HARD TO CARE ABOUT HER WITHOUT...
I JUST WISH I KNEW WHAT WAS GOING ON IN HER HEAD. THAT'S ALL.

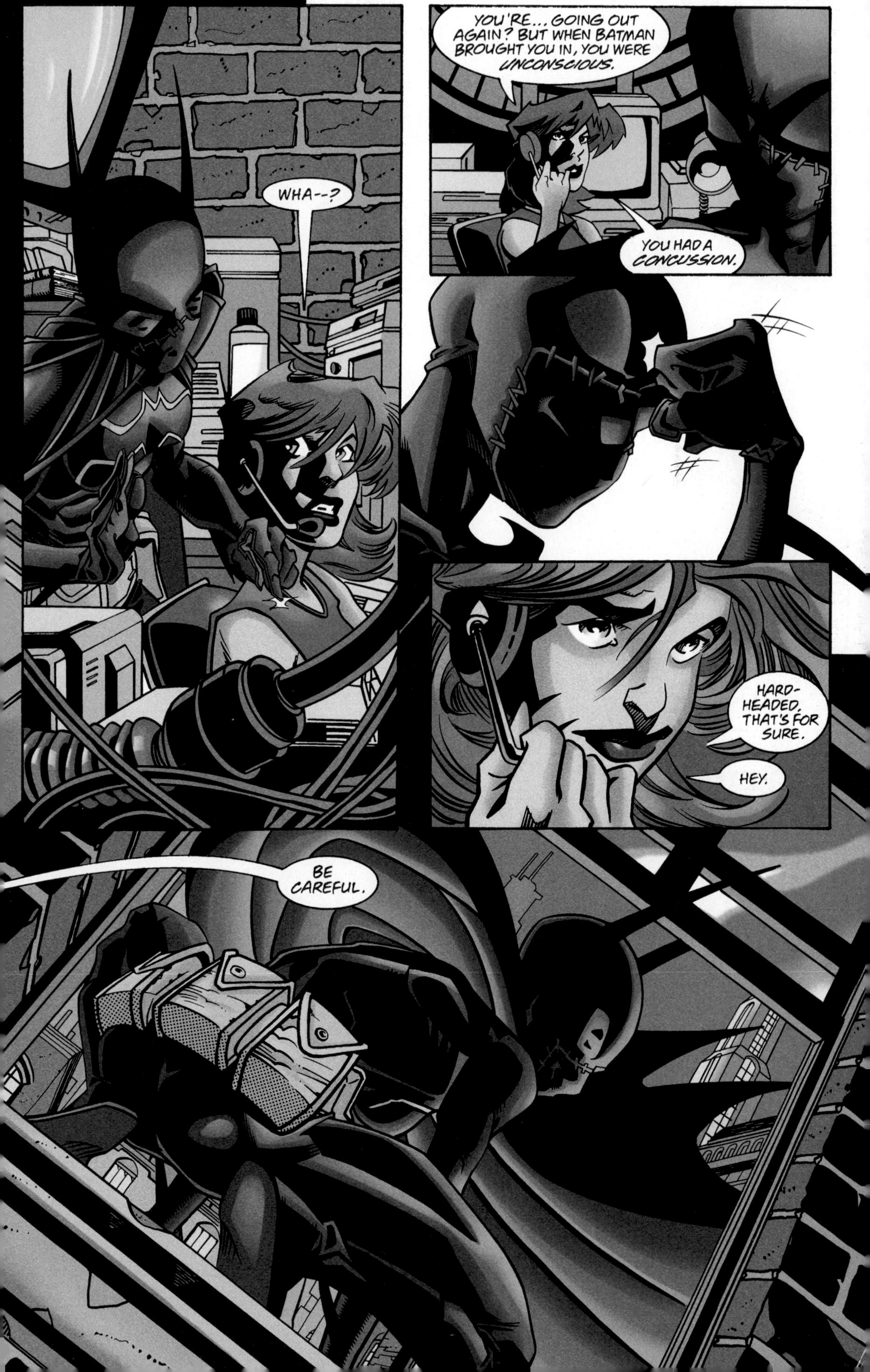
WHA--?
YOU'RE... GOING OUT AGAIN? BUT WHEN BATMAN BROUGHT YOU IN, YOU WERE UNCONSCIOUS.
YOU HAD A CONCUSSION.
HARD-HEADED. THAT'S FOR SURE.
HEY.
BE CAREFUL.

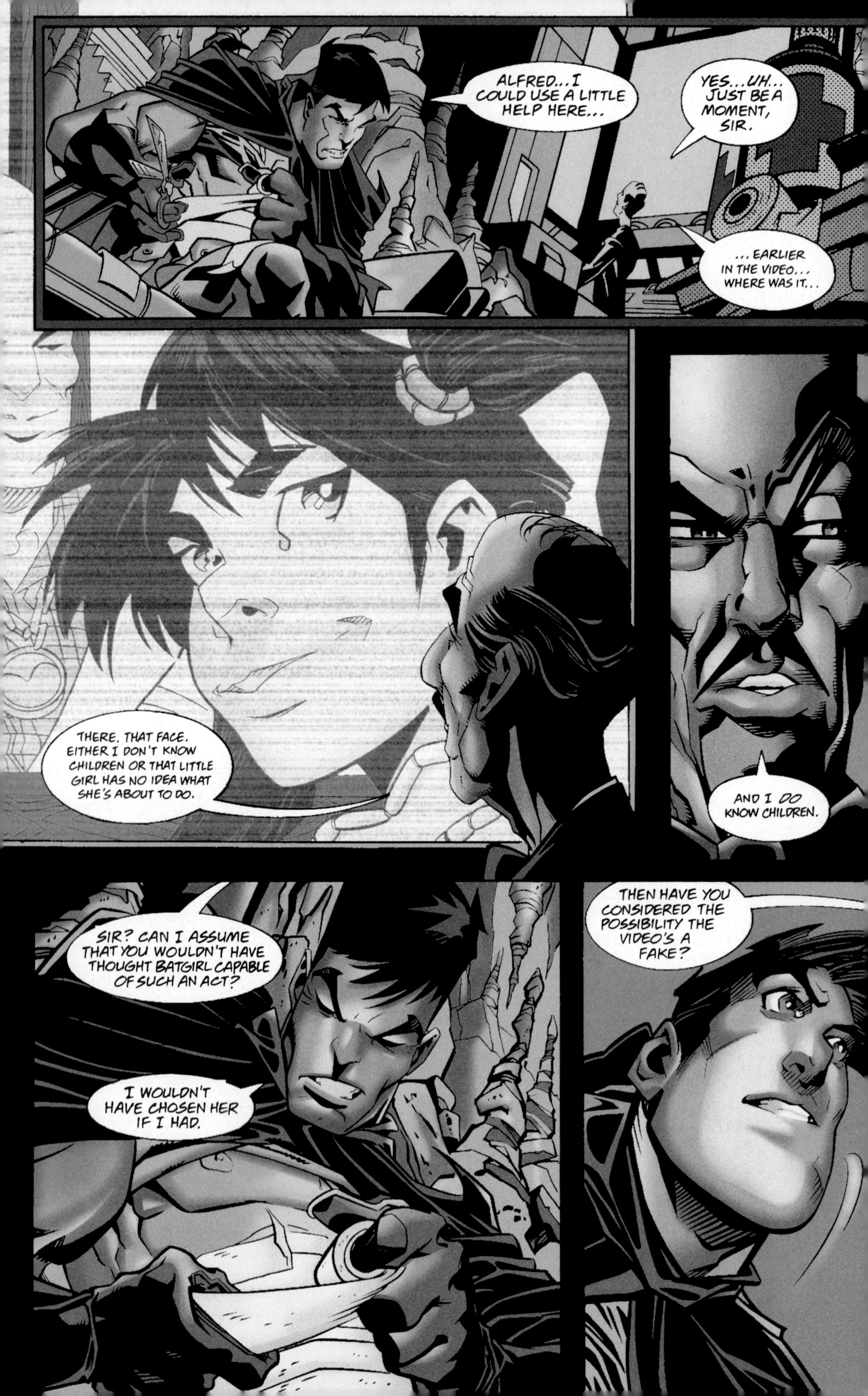
ALFRED... I COULD USE A LITTLE HELP HERE...
YES... UH... JUST BE A MOMENT, SIR.
... EARLIER IN THE VIDEO... WHERE WAS IT...
THERE. THAT FACE. EITHER I DON'T KNOW CHILDREN OR THAT LITTLE GIRL HAS NO IDEA WHAT SHE'S ABOUT TO DO.
AND I DO KNOW CHILDREN.
SIR? CAN I ASSUME THAT YOU WOULDN'T HAVE THOUGHT BATGIRL CAPABLE OF SUCH AN ACT?
I WOULDN'T HAVE CHOSEN HER IF I HAD.
THEN HAVE YOU CONSIDERED THE POSSIBILITY THE VIDEO'S A FAKE?

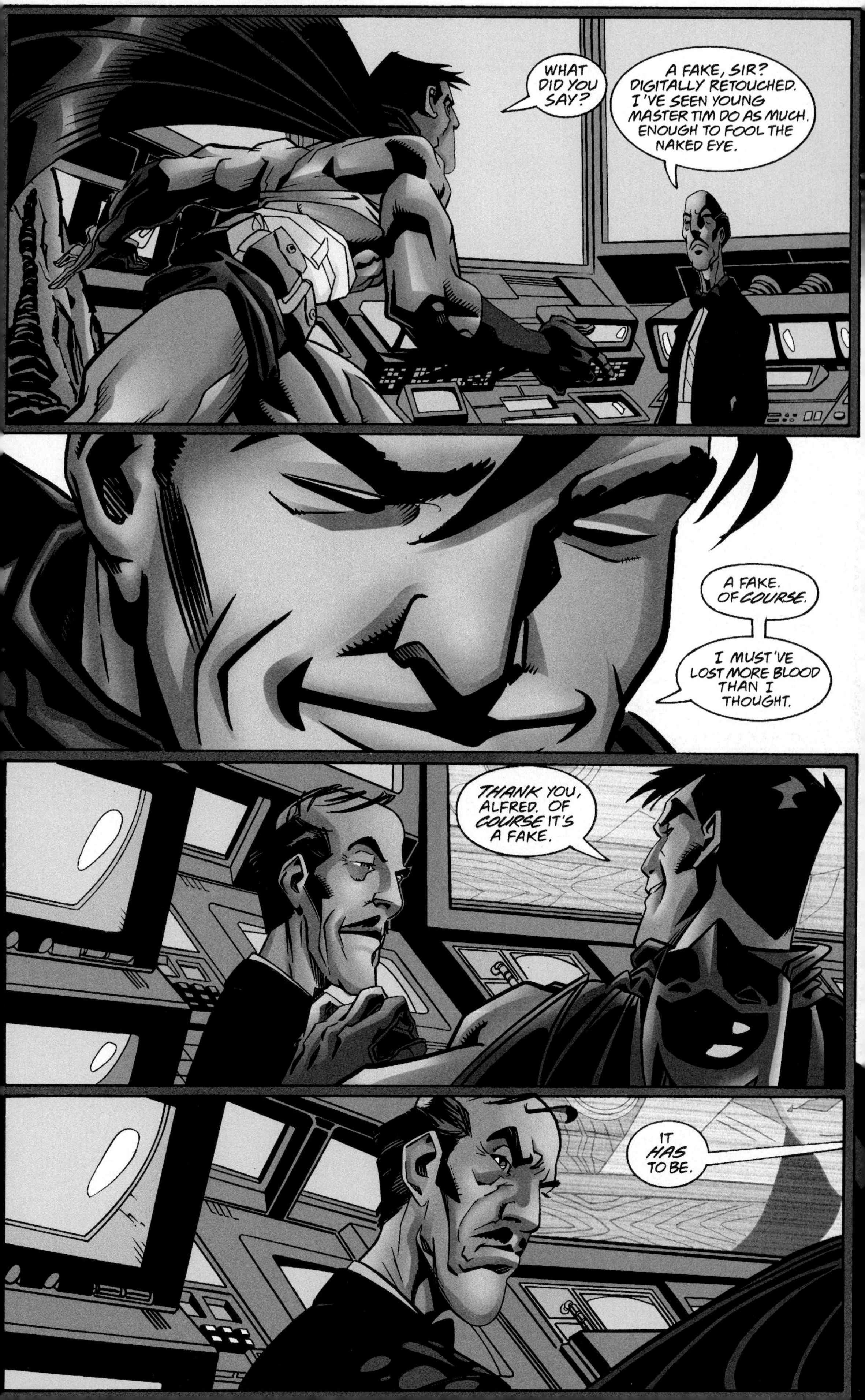
WHAT DID YOU SAY?
A FAKE, SIR? DIGITALLY RETOUCHED. I'VE SEEN YOUNG MASTER TIM DO AS MUCH. ENOUGH TO FOOL THE NAKED EYE.
A FAKE. OF COURSE.
I MUST'VE LOST MORE BLOOD THAN I THOUGHT.
THANK YOU, ALFRED. OF COURSE IT'S A FAKE.
IT HAS TO BE.

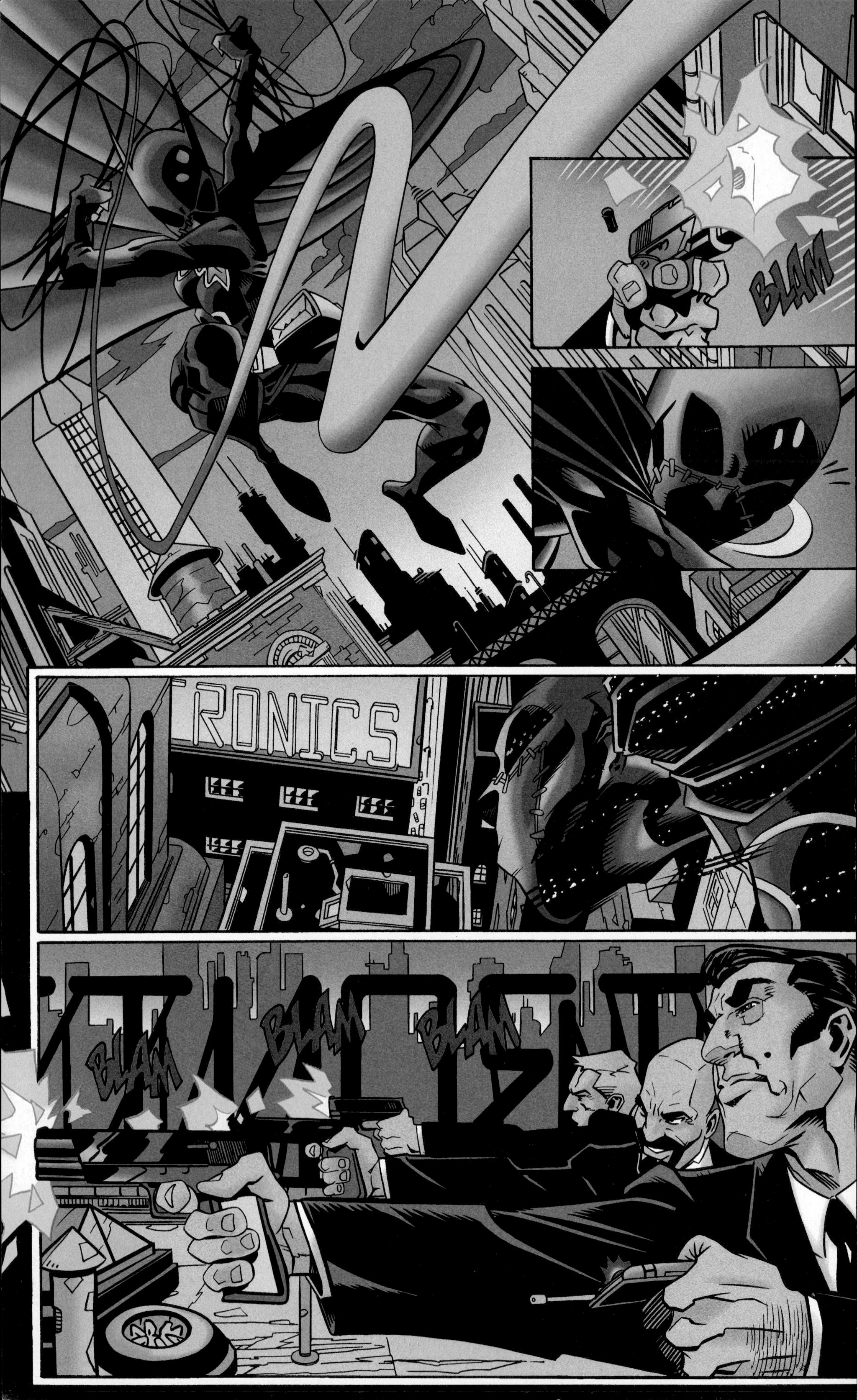
BLAM
TRONICS
BLAM
BLAM
BLAM

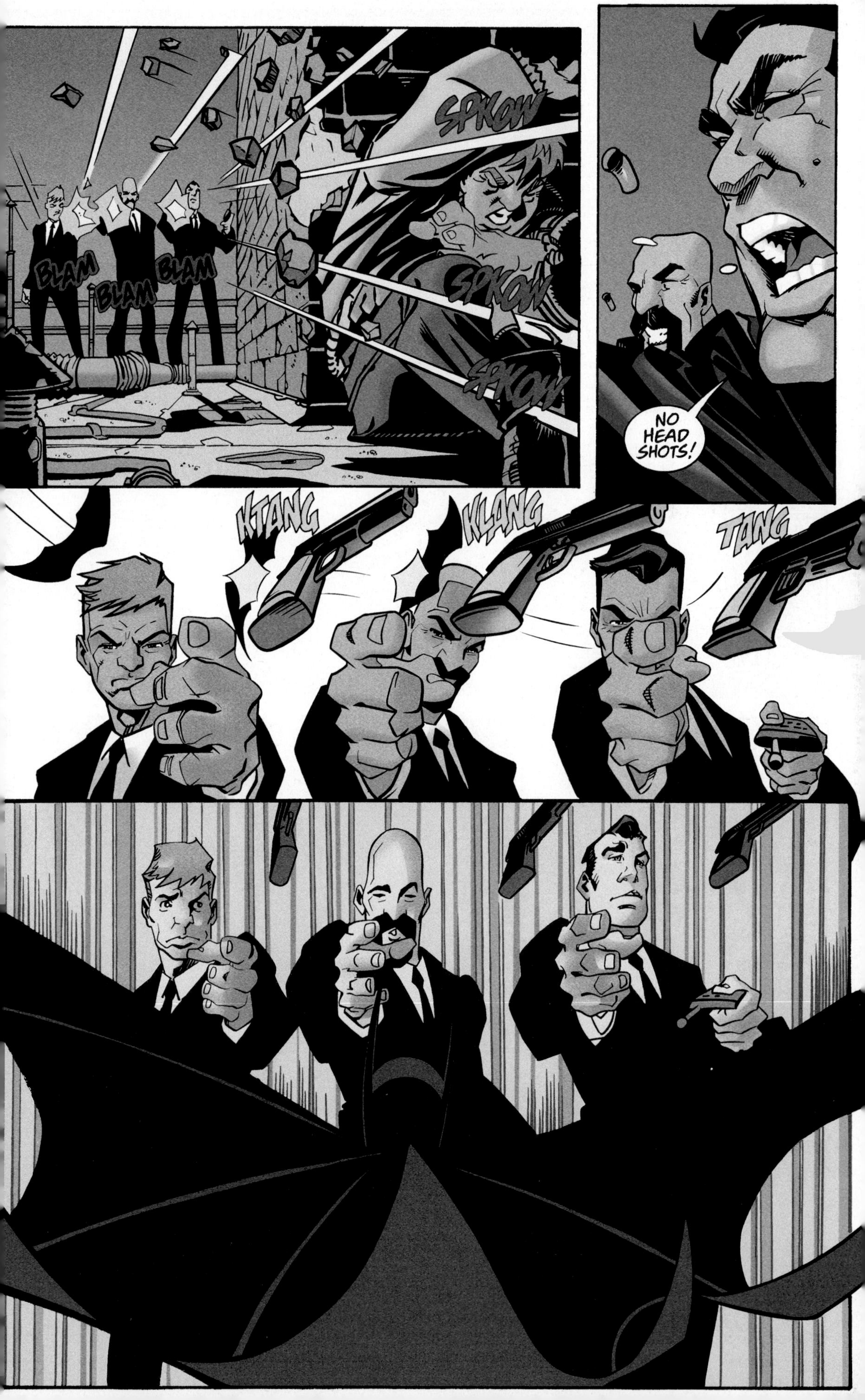
BLAM
BLAM
BLAM
SPKOW
SPKOW
SPKOW
NO HEAD SHOTS!
KTANG
KLANG
TANG

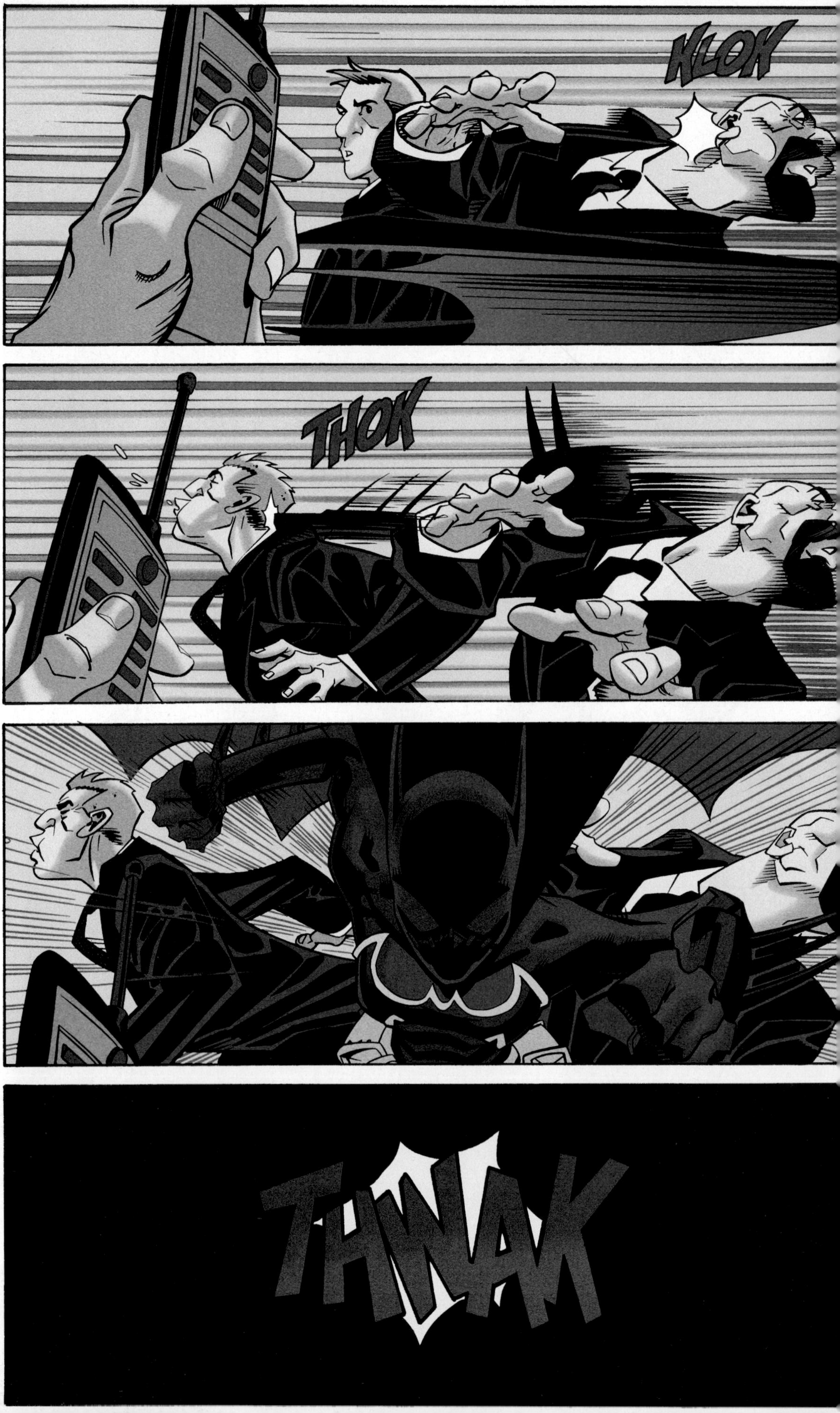
KLOK
THOK
THWAK

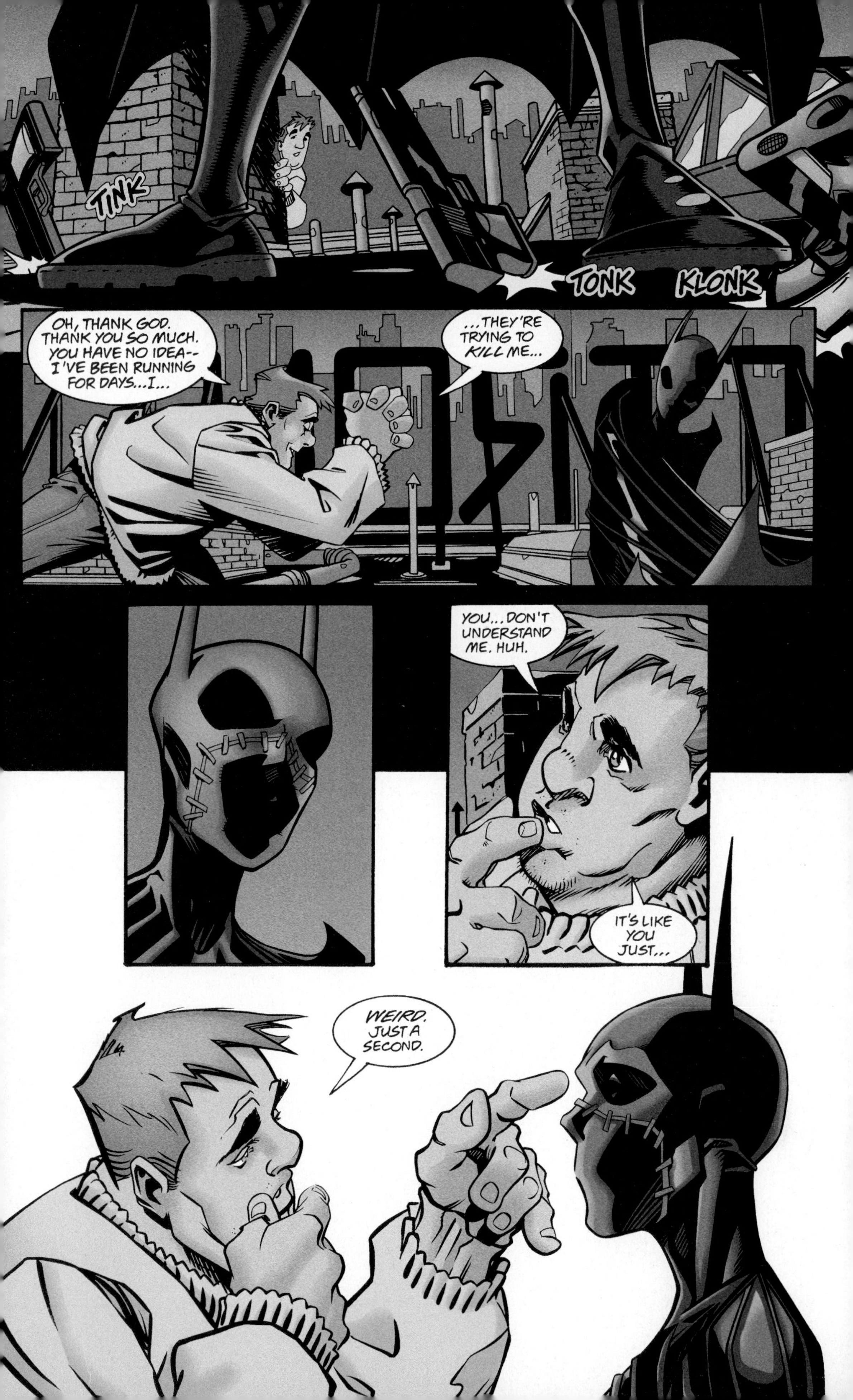
TINK
TONK
KLONK
OH, THANK GOD. THANK YOU SO MUCH. YOU HAVE NO IDEA-- I'VE BEEN RUNNING FOR DAYS...I...
...THEY'RE TRYING TO KILL ME...
YOU...DON'T UNDERSTAND ME. HUH.
IT'S LIKE YOU JUST...
WEIRD. JUST A SECOND.

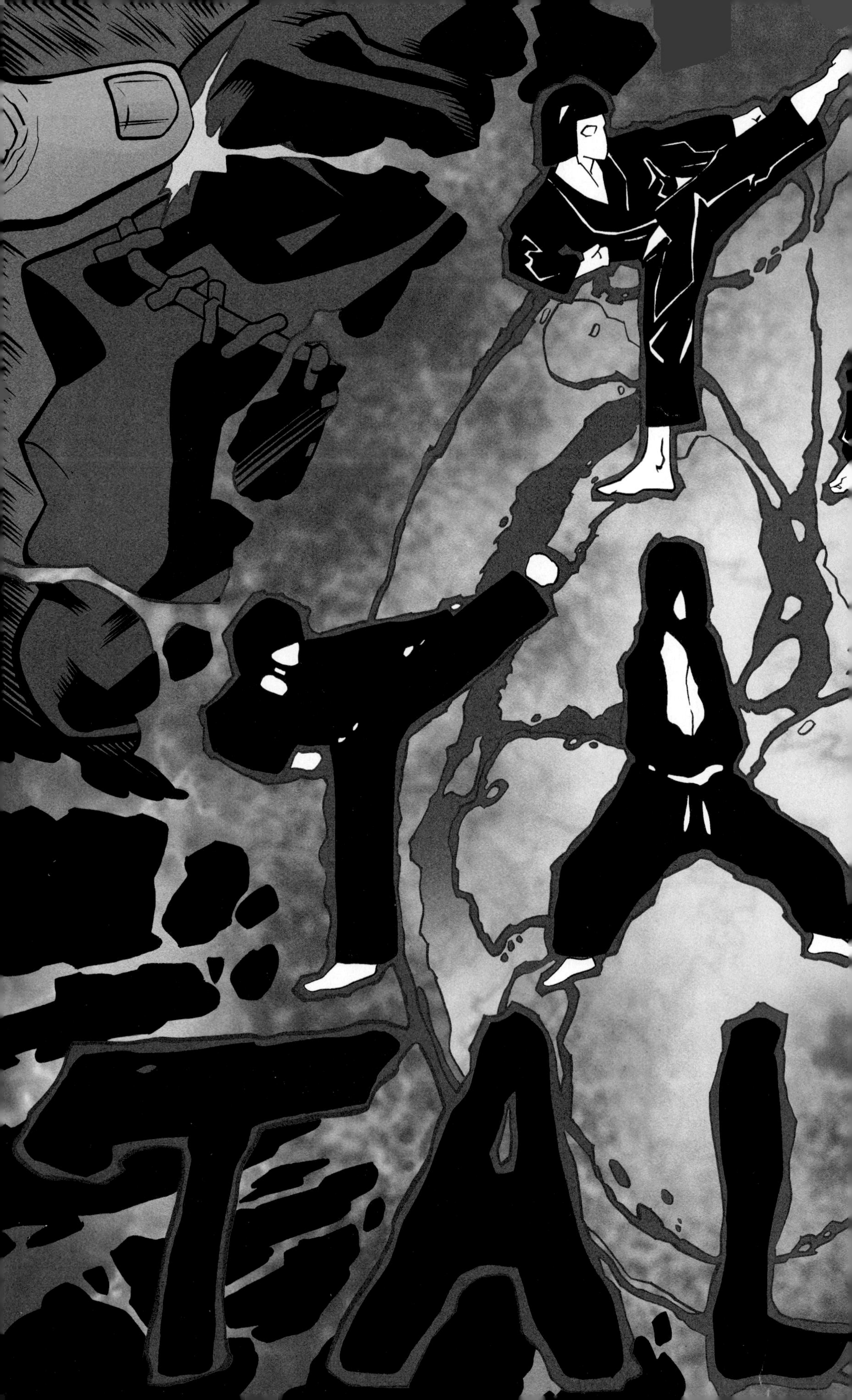
TAI

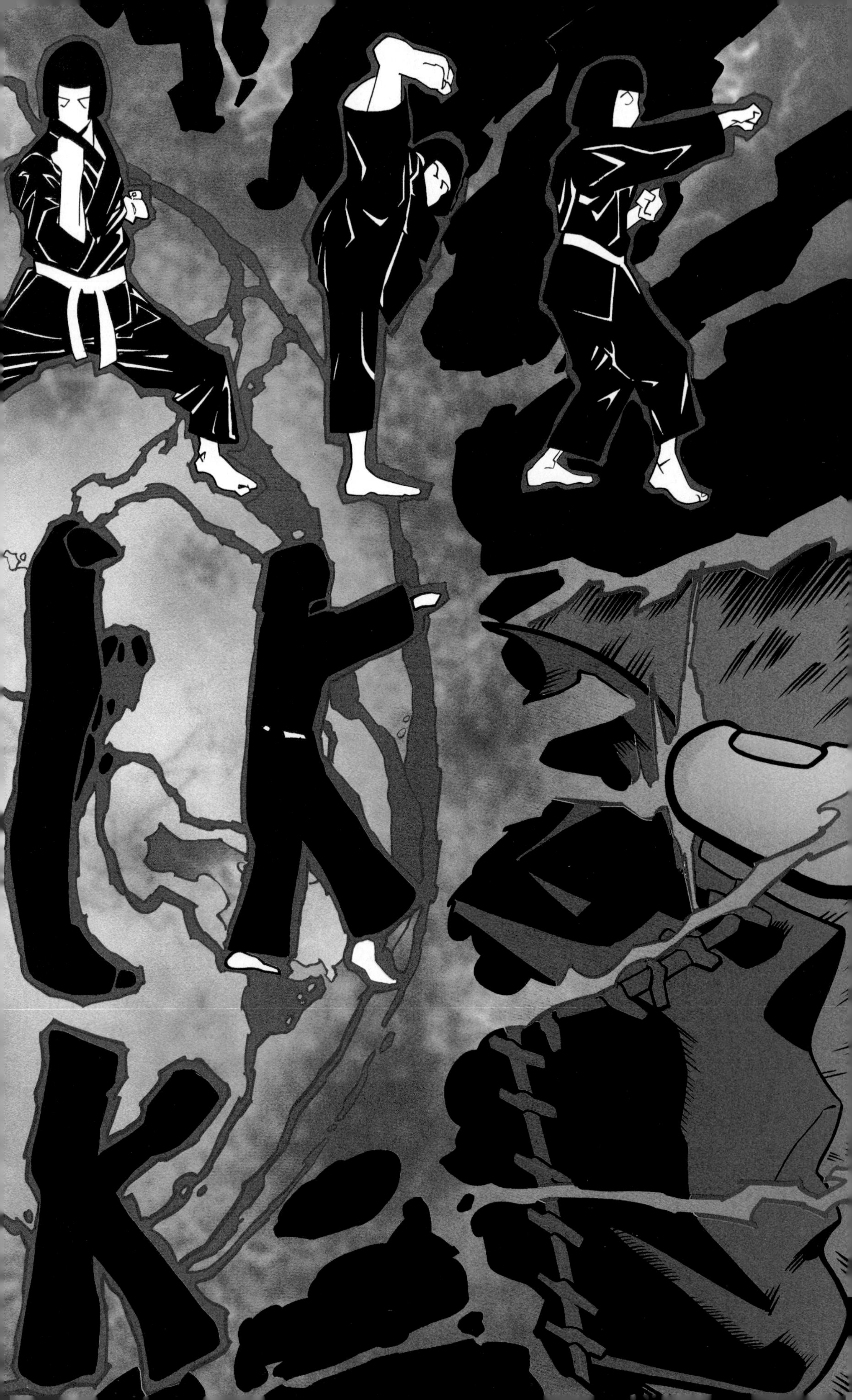

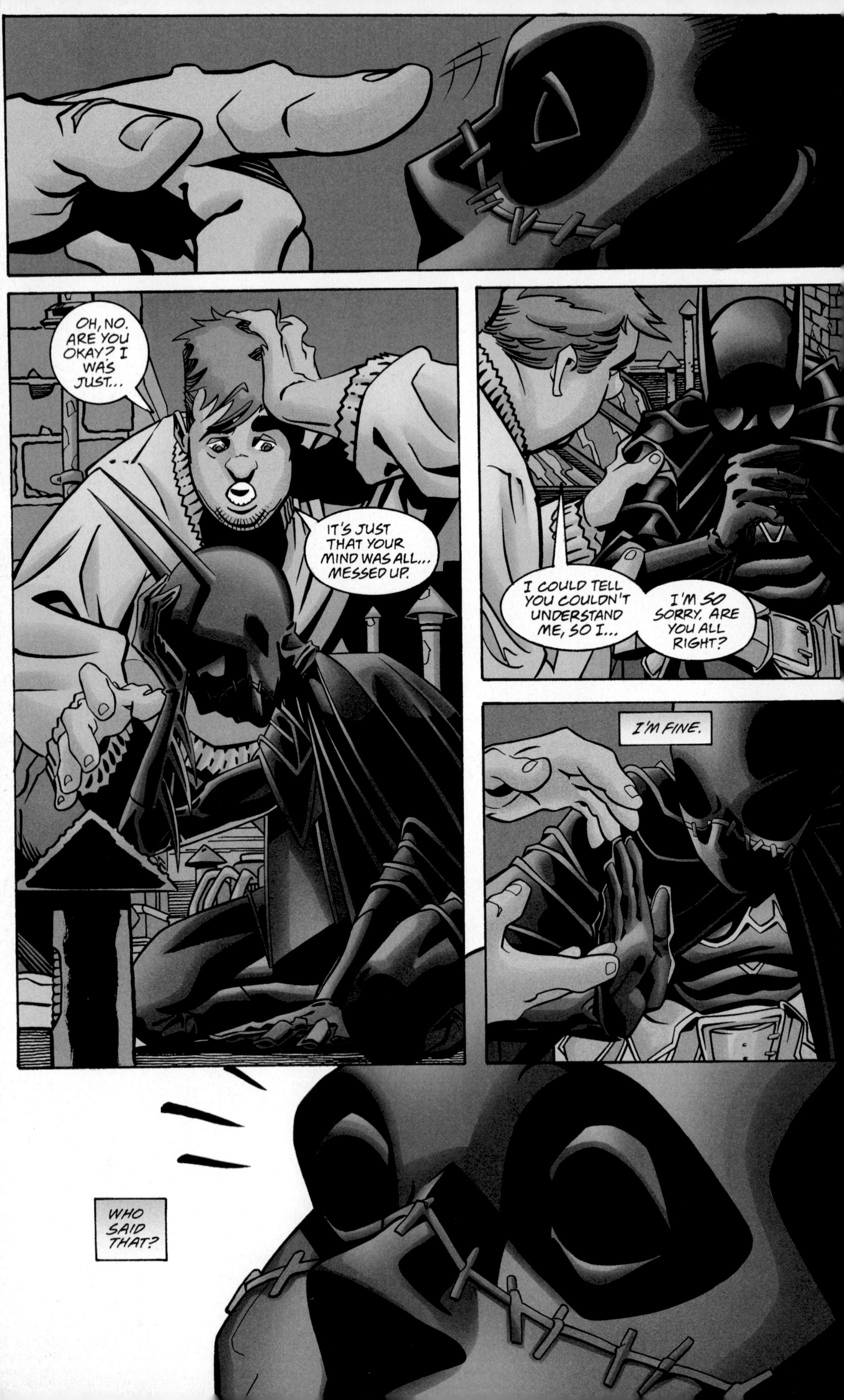
OH, NO. ARE YOU OKAY? I WAS JUST...
IT'S JUST THAT YOUR MIND WAS ALL... MESSED UP.
I COULD TELL YOU COULDN'T UNDERSTAND ME, SO I...
I'M SO SORRY. ARE YOU ALL RIGHT?
I'M FINE.
WHO SAID THAT?

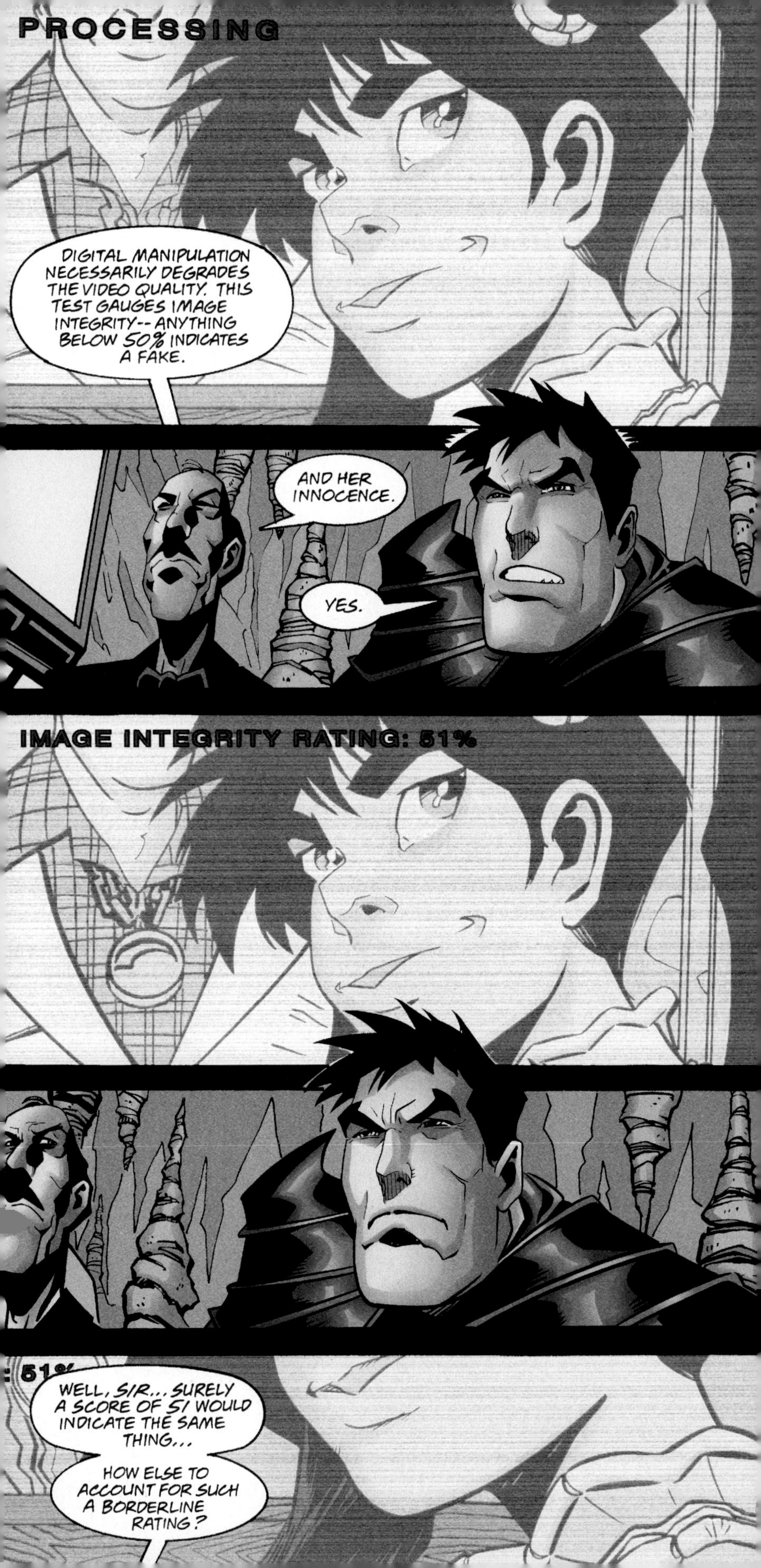
PROCESSING
DIGITAL MANIPULATION NECESSARILY DEGRADES THE VIDEO QUALITY. THIS TEST GAUGES IMAGE INTEGRITY-- ANYTHING BELOW 50% INDICATES A FAKE.
AND HER INNOCENCE.
YES.
IMAGE INTEGRITY RATING: 51%
51%
WELL, SIR... SURELY A SCORE OF 51 WOULD INDICATE THE SAME THING...
HOW ELSE TO ACCOUNT FOR SUCH A BORDERLINE RATING?

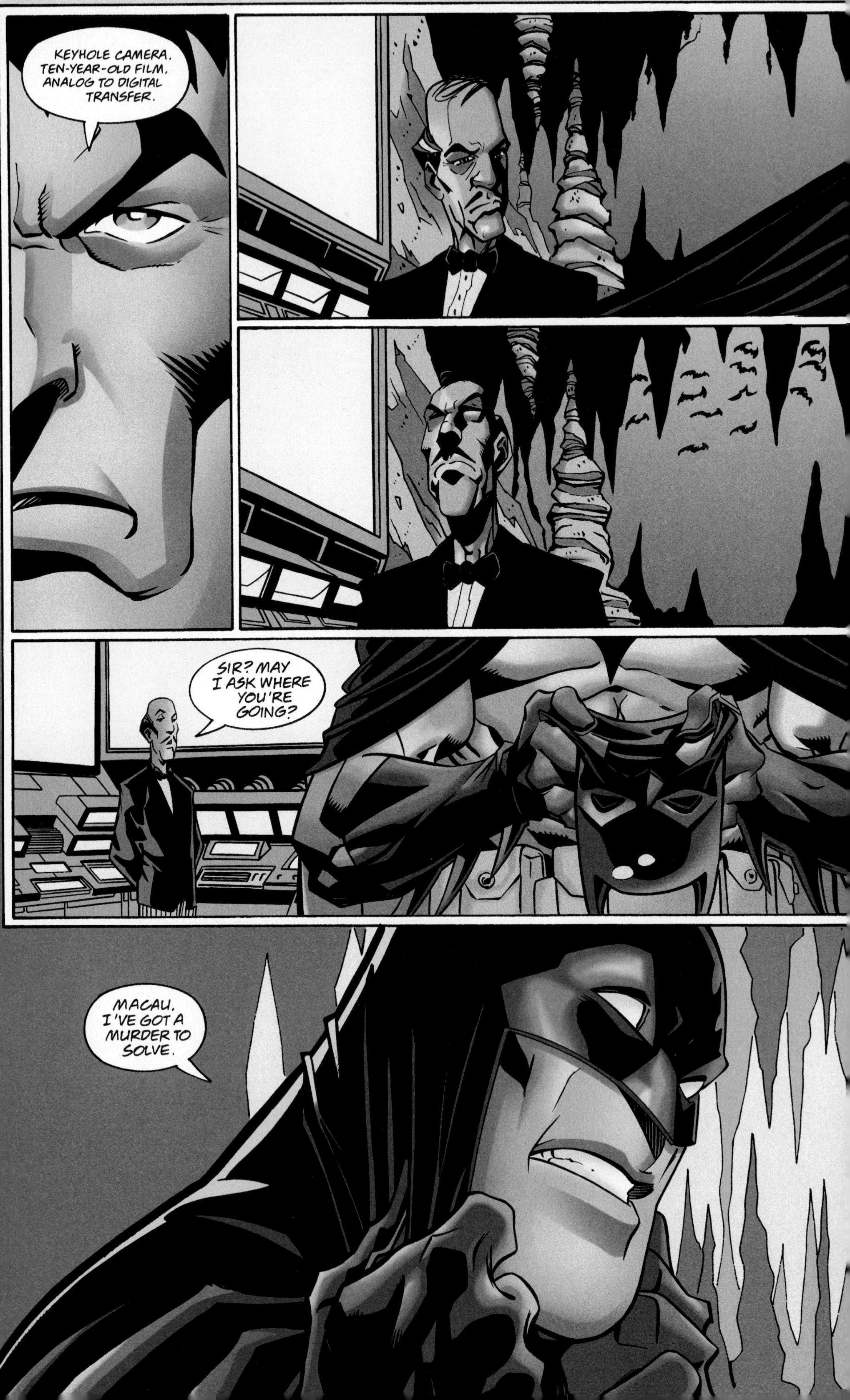
KEYHOLE CAMERA. TEN-YEAR-OLD FILM, ANALOG TO DIGITAL TRANSFER.
SIR? MAY I ASK WHERE YOU'RE GOING?
MACAU. I'VE GOT A MURDER TO SOLVE.

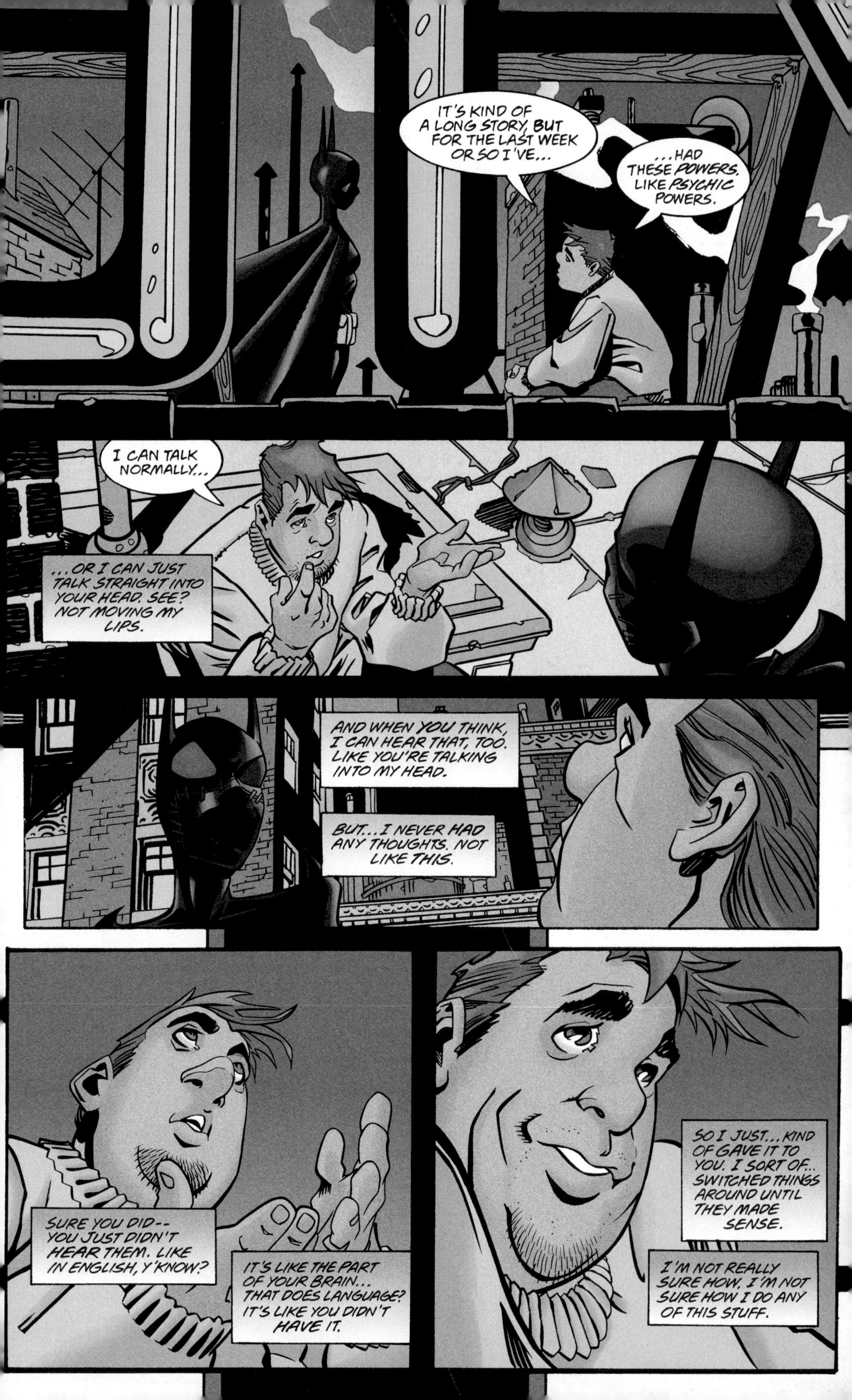

IT'S KIND OF A LONG STORY, BUT FOR THE LAST WEEK OR SO I'VE...
...HAD THESE POWERS. LIKE PSYCHIC POWERS.
I CAN TALK NORMALLY...
...OR I CAN JUST TALK STRAIGHT INTO YOUR HEAD. SEE? NOT MOVING MY LIPS.
AND WHEN YOU THINK, I CAN HEAR THAT, TOO. LIKE YOU'RE TALKING INTO MY HEAD.
BUT...I NEVER HAD ANY THOUGHTS. NOT LIKE THIS.
SURE YOU DID-- YOU JUST DIDN'T HEAR THEM. LIKE IN ENGLISH, Y'KNOW?
IT'S LIKE THE PART OF YOUR BRAIN... THAT DOES LANGUAGE? IT'S LIKE YOU DIDN'T HAVE IT.
SO I JUST... KIND OF GAVE IT TO YOU. I SORT OF... SWITCHED THINGS AROUND UNTIL THEY MADE SENSE.
I'M NOT REALLY SURE HOW. I'M NOT SURE HOW I DO ANY OF THIS STUFF.

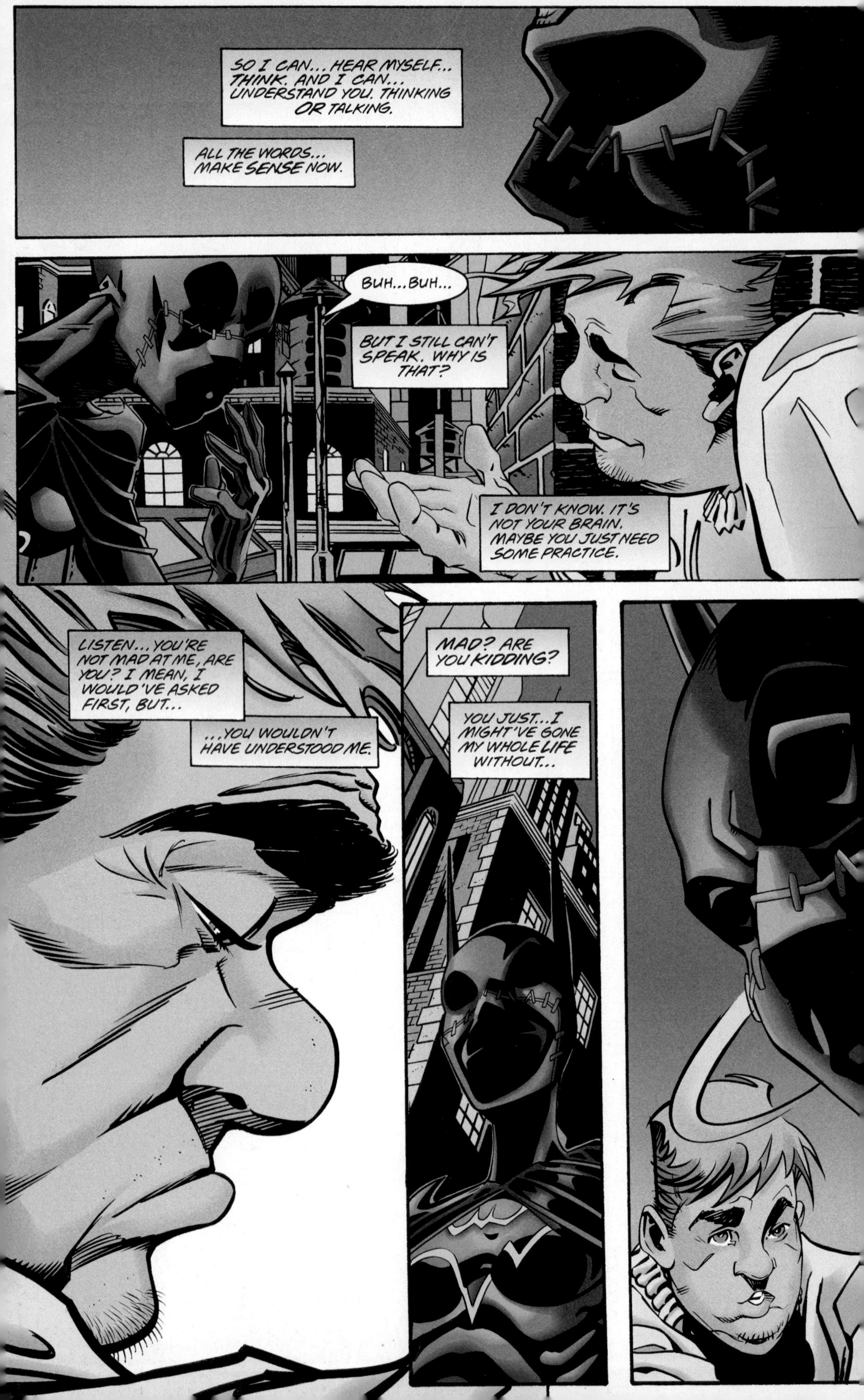
SO I CAN... HEAR MYSELF... THINK. AND I CAN... UNDERSTAND YOU. THINKING OR TALKING.
ALL THE WORDS... MAKE SENSE NOW.
BUH...BUH...
BUT I STILL CAN'T SPEAK. WHY IS THAT?
I DON'T KNOW. IT'S NOT YOUR BRAIN. MAYBE YOU JUST NEED SOME PRACTICE.
LISTEN... YOU'RE NOT MAD AT ME, ARE YOU? I MEAN, I WOULD'VE ASKED FIRST, BUT...
...YOU WOULDN'T HAVE UNDERSTOOD ME.
MAD? ARE YOU KIDDING?
YOU JUST... I MIGHT'VE GONE MY WHOLE LIFE WITHOUT...

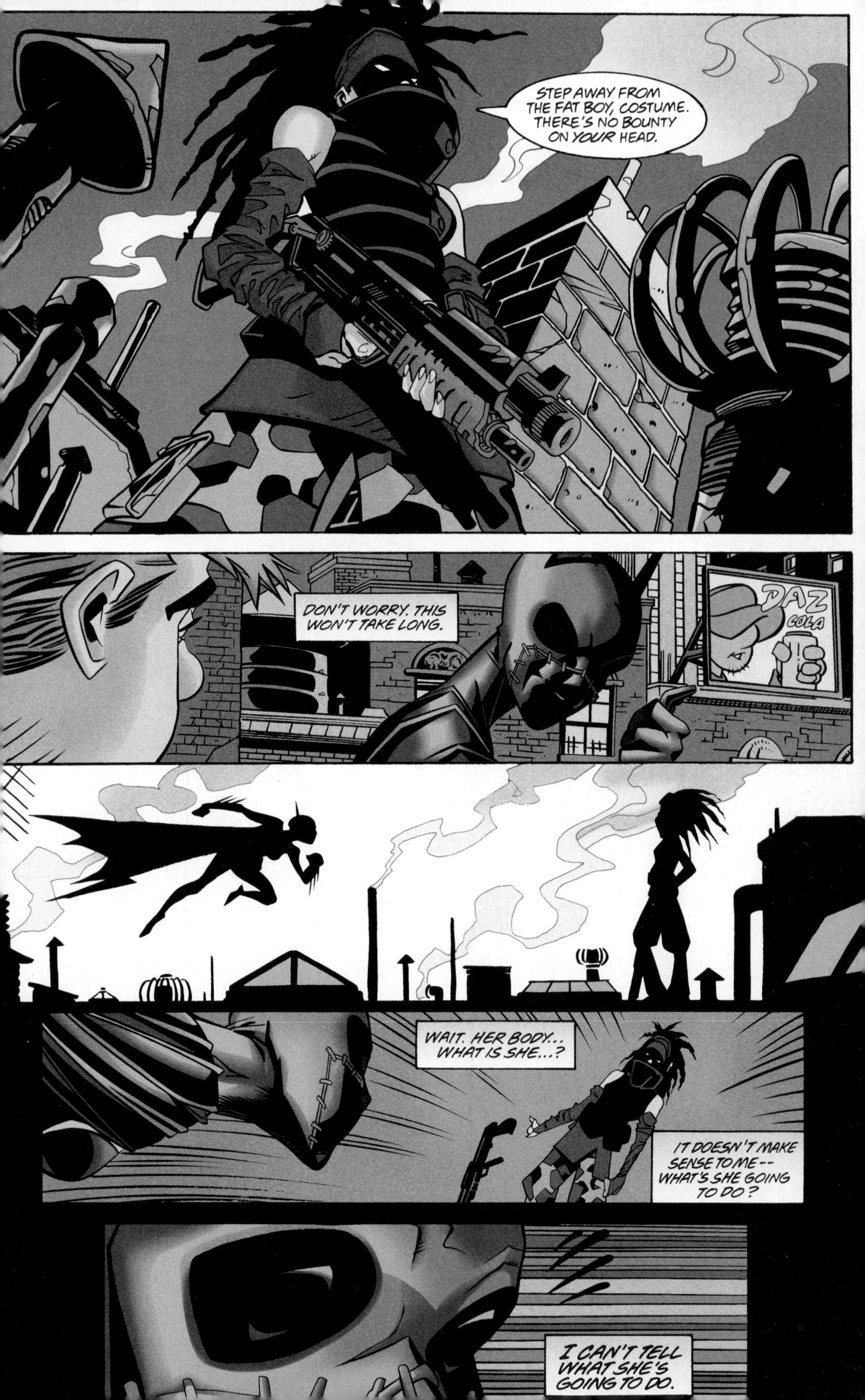
STEP AWAY FROM THE FAT BOY, COSTUME. THERE'S NO BOUNTY ON *YOUR* HEAD.
DON'T WORRY. THIS WON'T TAKE LONG.
DAZ COLA
WAIT. HER BODY.. WHAT IS SHE...?
IT DOESN'T MAKE SENSE TO ME-- WHAT'S SHE GOING TO DO?
I CAN'T TELL WHAT SHE'S GOING TO DO.

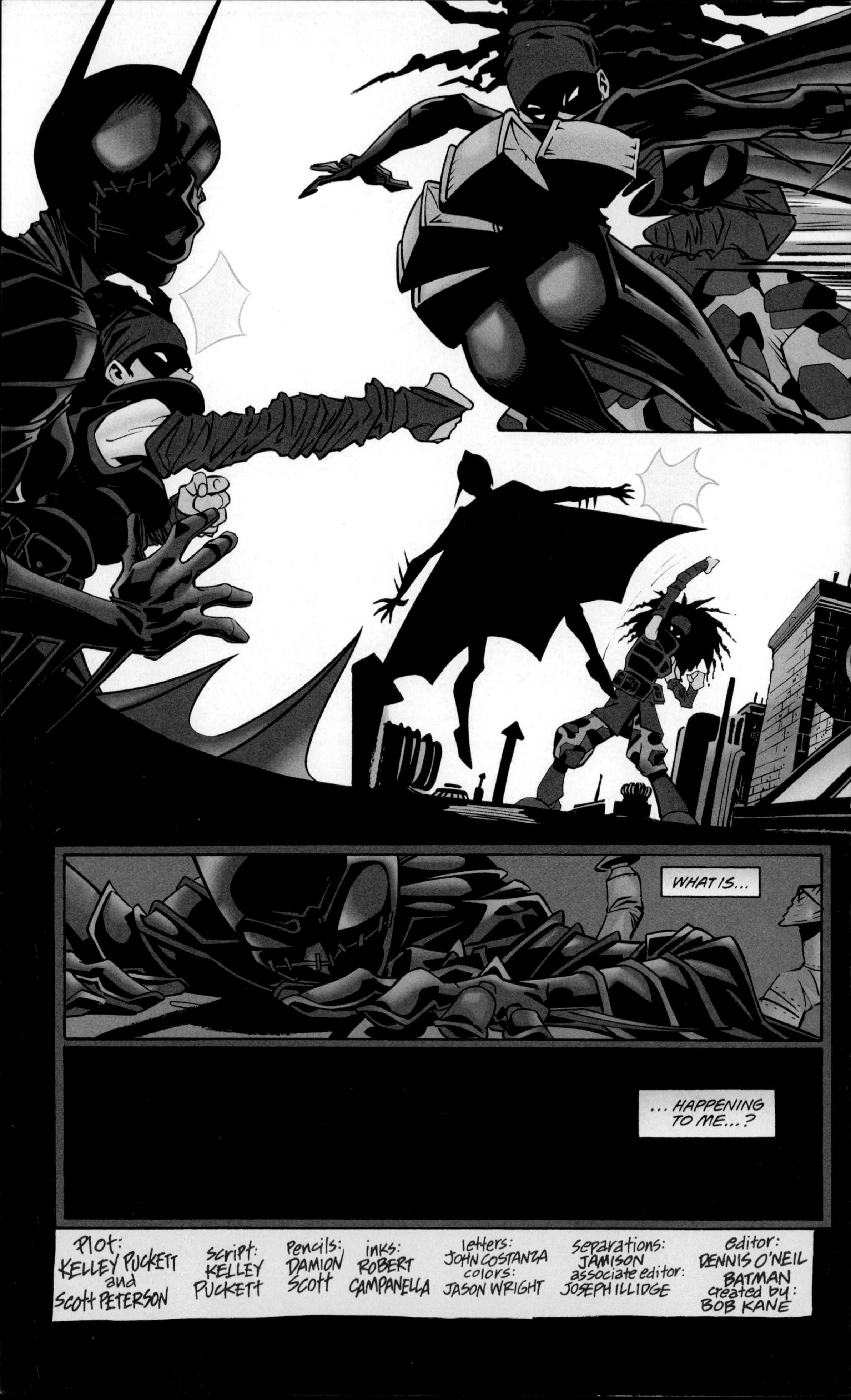
WHAT IS...
... HAPPENING TO ME...?

Plot: KELLEY PUCKETT and SCOTT PETERSON
script: KELLEY PUCKETT
Pencils: DAMION SCOTT
inks: ROBERT CAMPANELLA
letters: JOHN COSTANZA
colors: JASON WRIGHT
Separations: JAMISON
associate editor: JOSEPH ILLIDGE
editor: DENNIS O'NEIL
BATMAN created by: BOB KANE

BATGIRL #5 cover by
Damion Scott & Robert Campanella

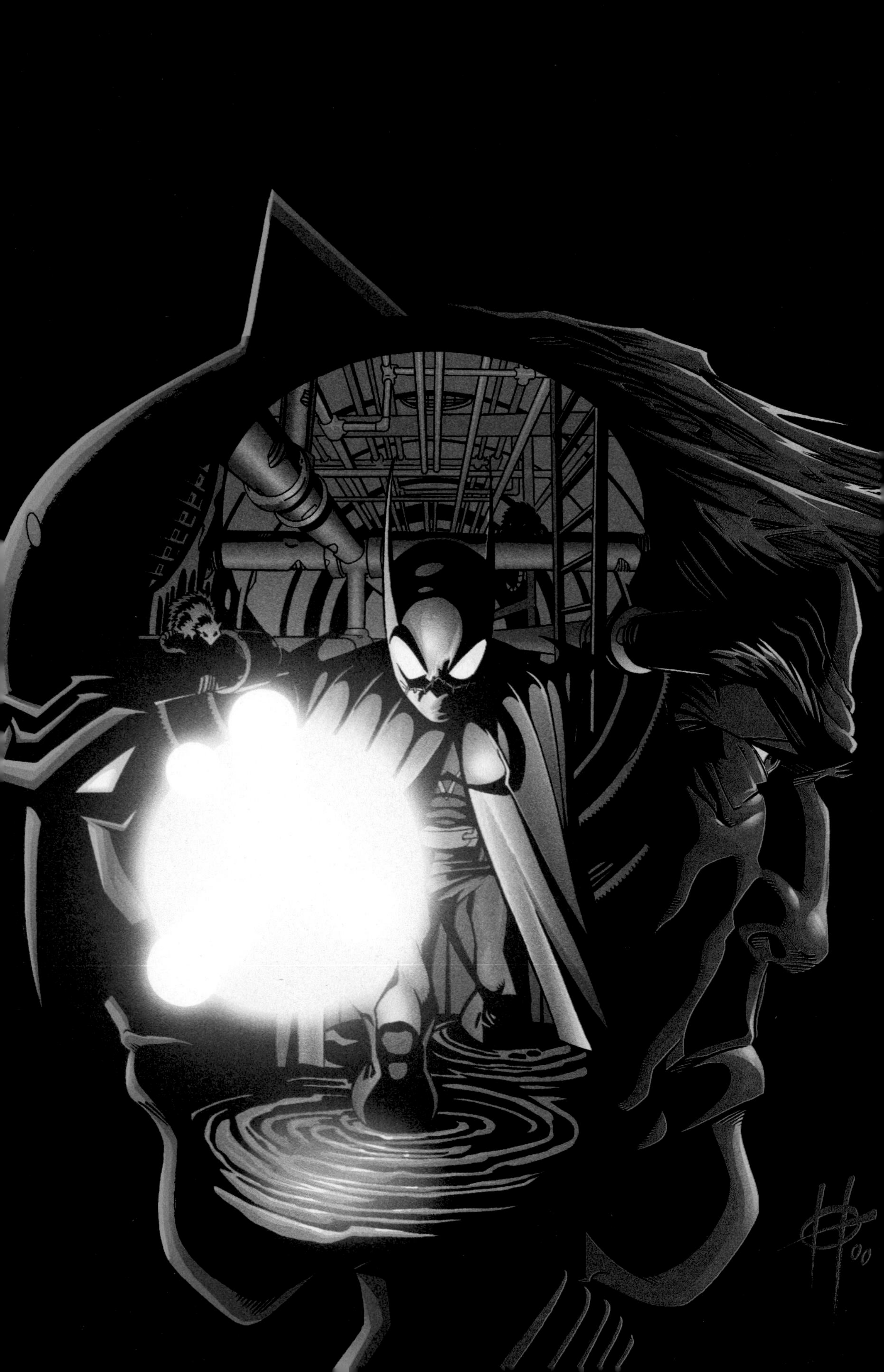

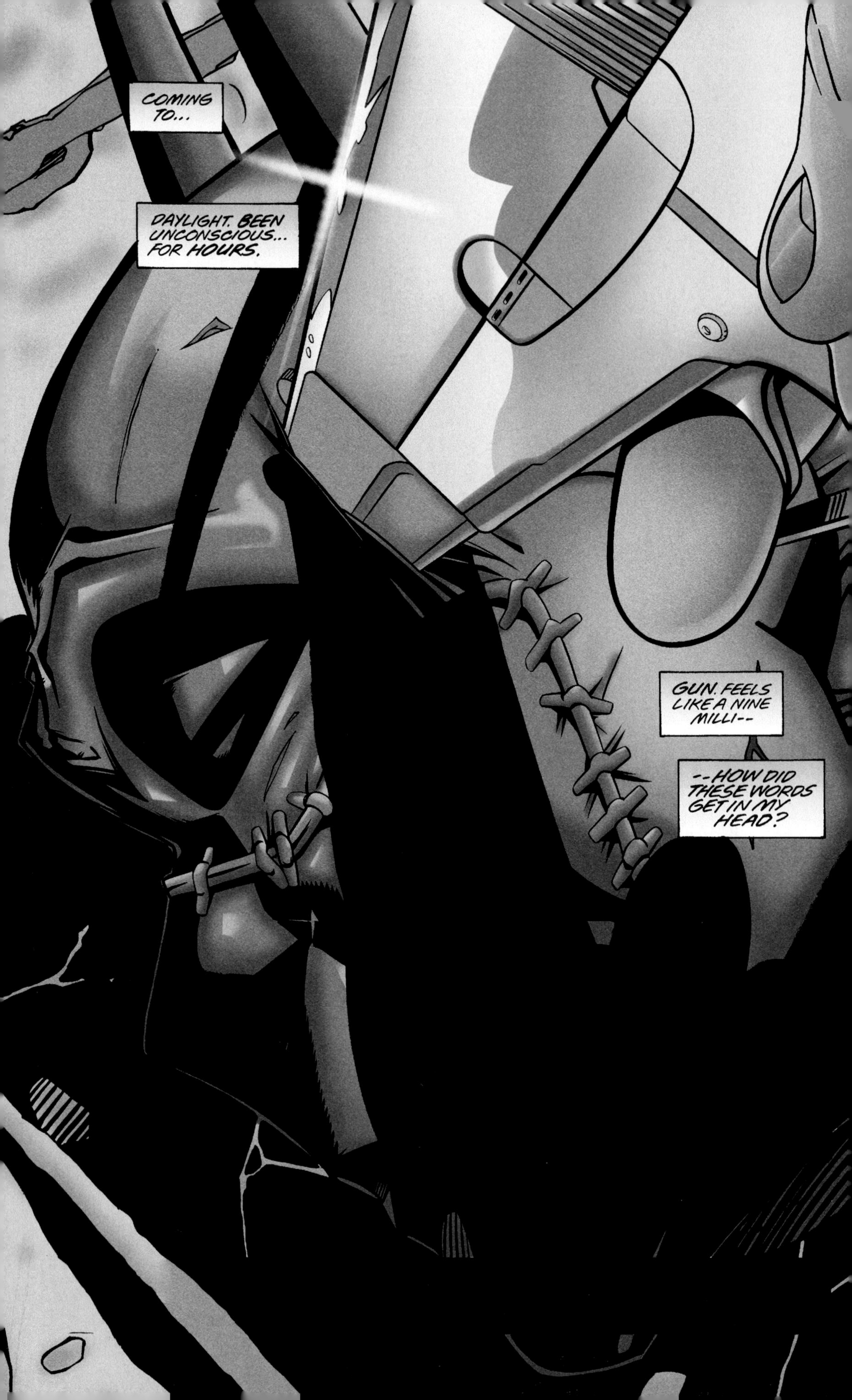
COMING TO...
DAYLIGHT. BEEN UNCONSCIOUS... FOR HOURS.
GUN. FEELS LIKE A NINE MILLI--
--HOW DID THESE WORDS GET IN MY HEAD?

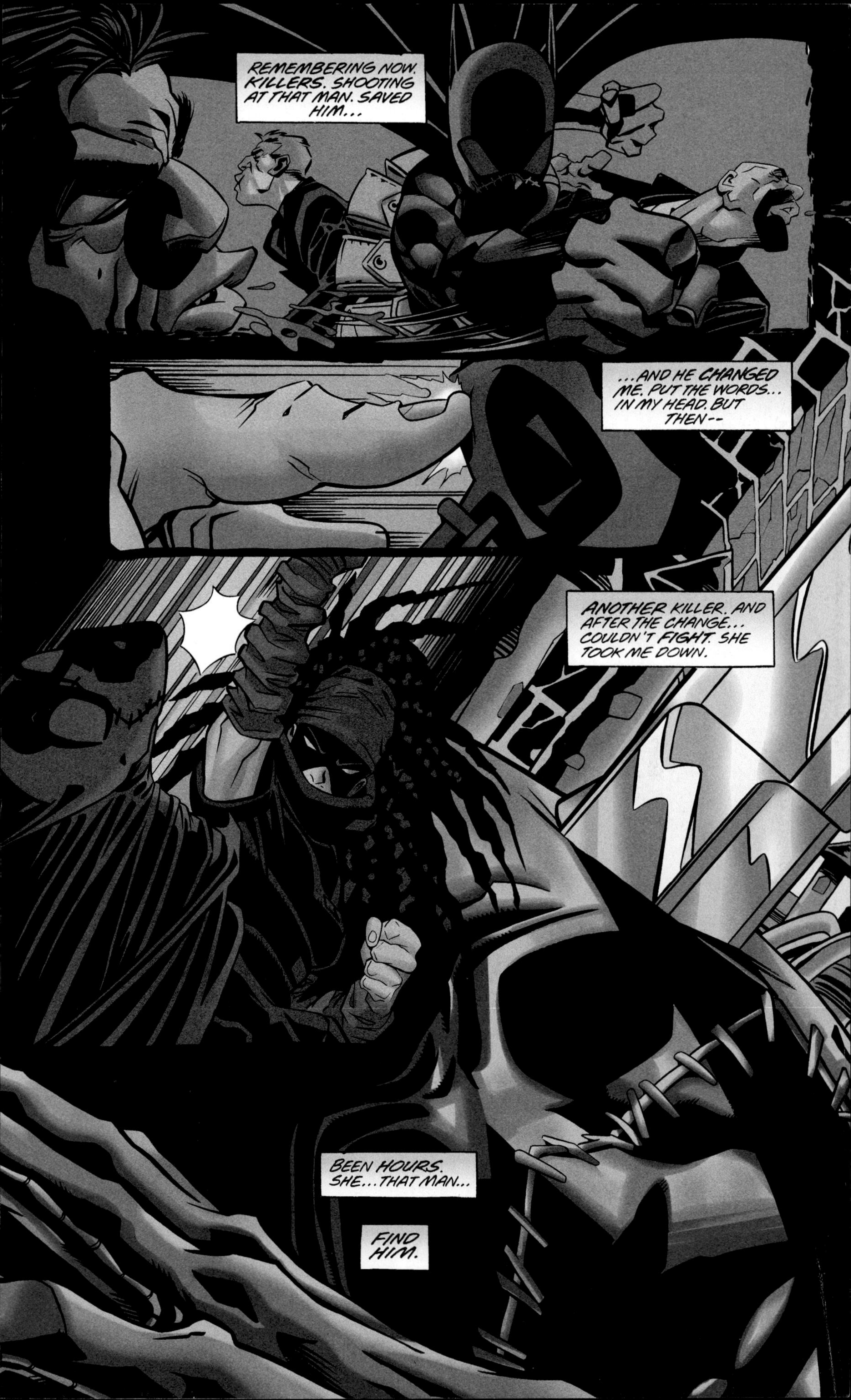

REMEMBERING NOW. KILLERS. SHOOTING AT THAT MAN. SAVED HIM...
...AND HE CHANGED ME. PUT THE WORDS... IN MY HEAD. BUT THEN--
ANOTHER KILLER. AND AFTER THE CHANGE... COULDN'T FIGHT. SHE TOOK ME DOWN.
BEEN HOURS. SHE...THAT MAN...
FIND HIM.

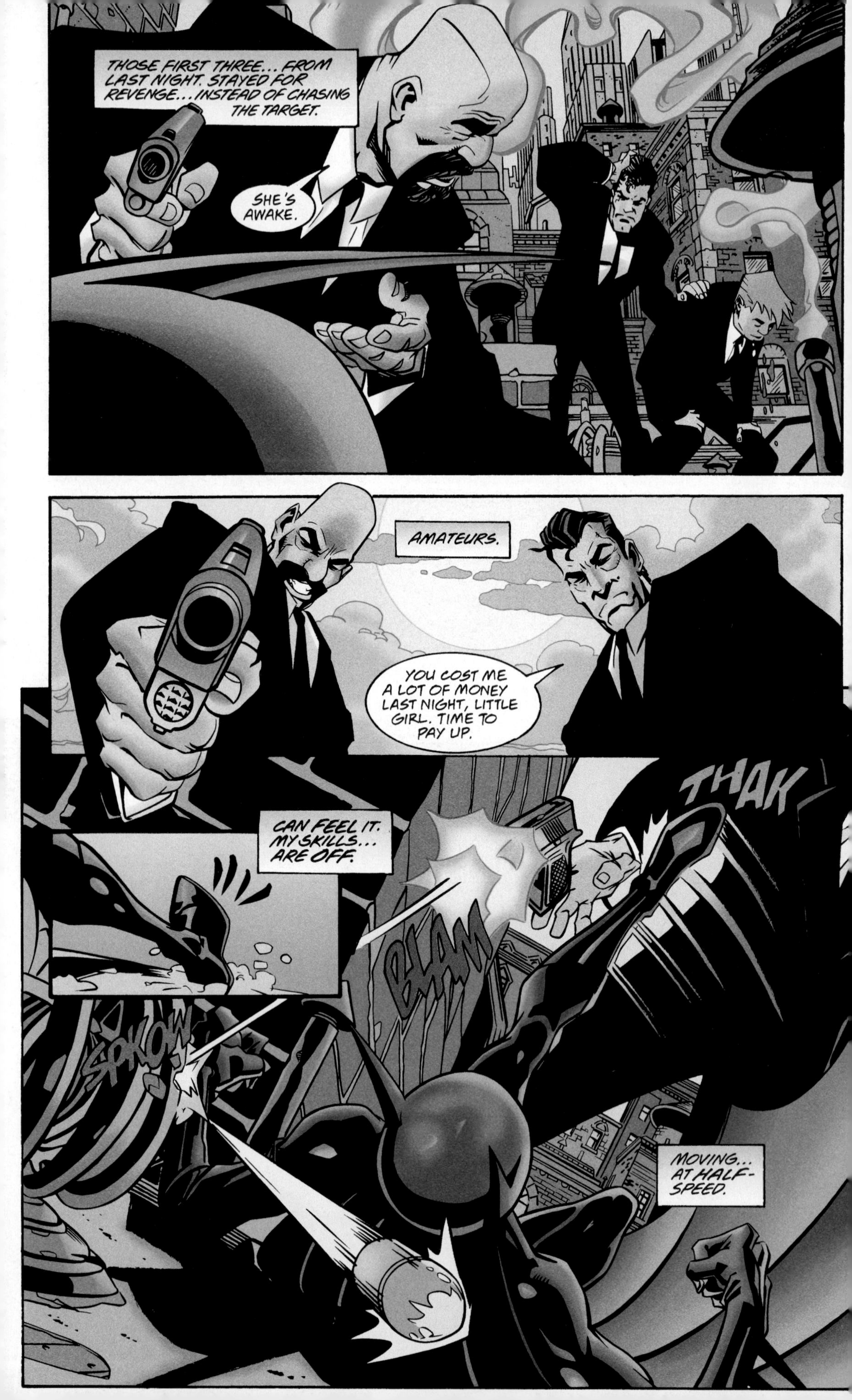
THOSE FIRST THREE... FROM LAST NIGHT. STAYED FOR REVENGE... INSTEAD OF CHASING THE TARGET.
SHE'S AWAKE.
AMATEURS.
YOU COST ME A LOT OF MONEY LAST NIGHT, LITTLE GIRL. TIME TO PAY UP.
THAK
CAN FEEL IT. MY SKILLS... ARE OFF.
BLAM
SPKOW
MOVING... AT HALF-SPEED.

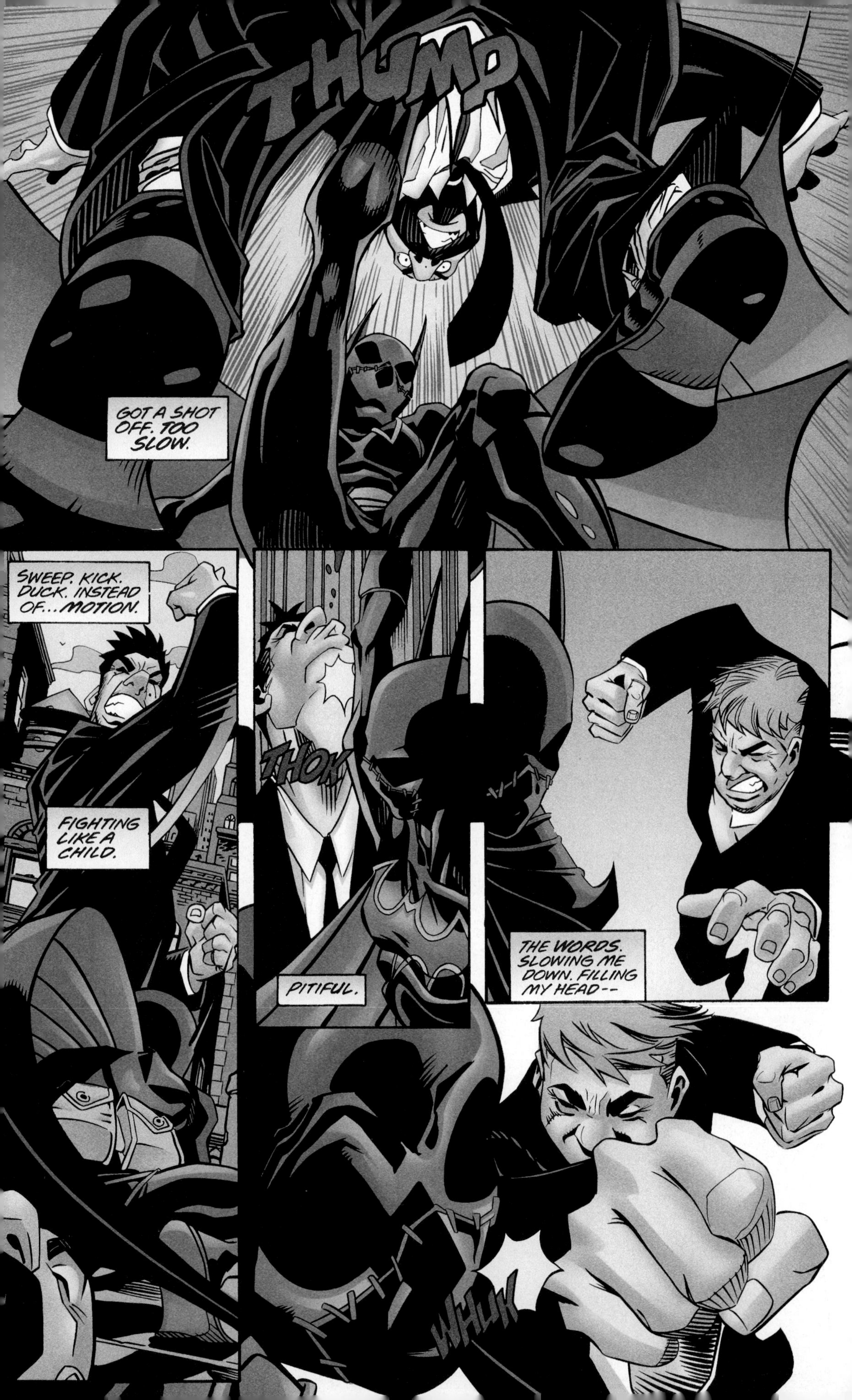
THUMP
GOT A SHOT OFF. TOO SLOW.
SWEEP. KICK. DUCK. INSTEAD OF... MOTION.
FIGHTING LIKE A CHILD.
THOK
PITIFUL.
THE WORDS. SLOWING ME DOWN. FILLING MY HEAD--
WHUK

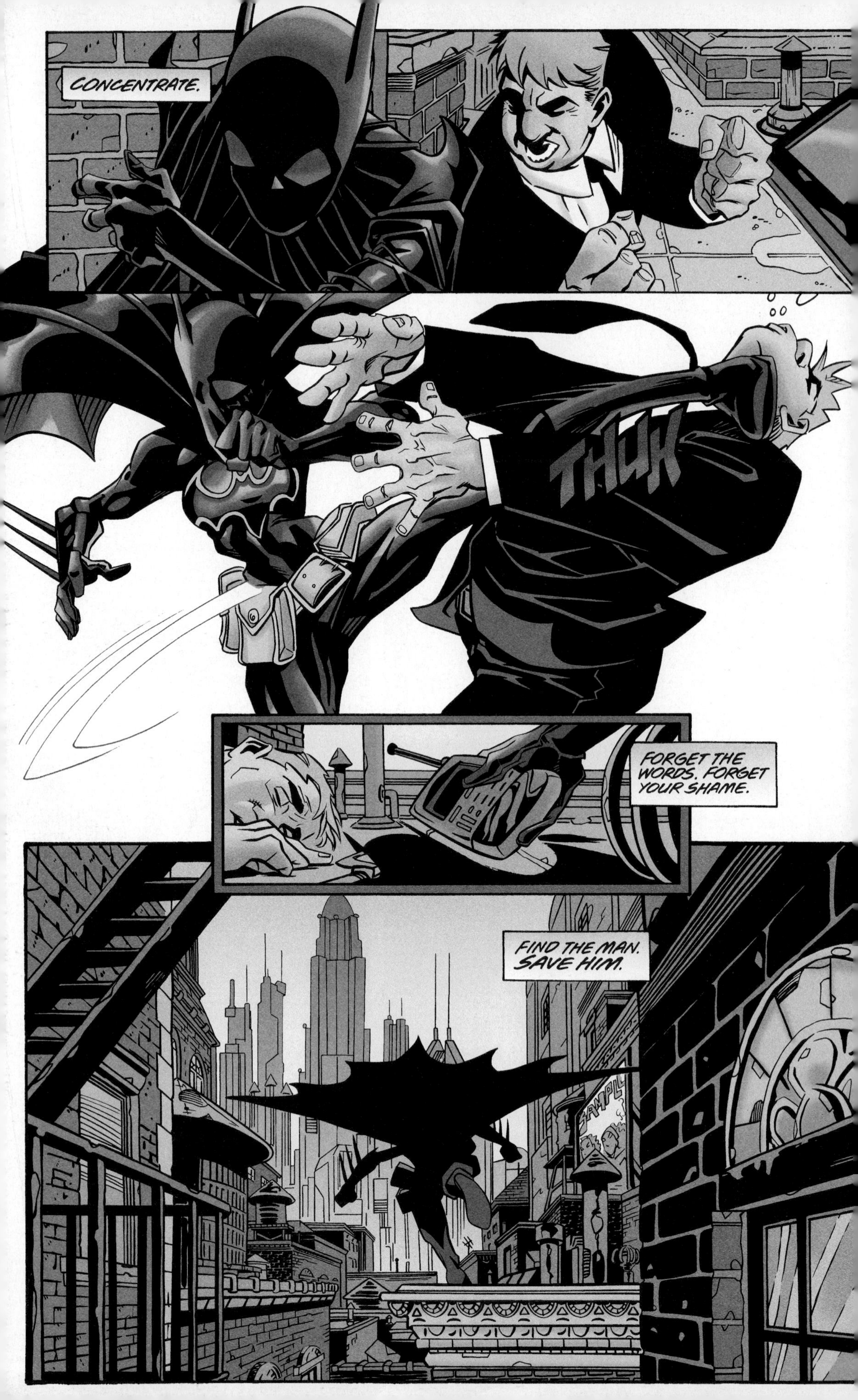
CONCENTRATE.
THUK
FORGET THE WORDS. FORGET YOUR SHAME.
FIND THE MAN. SAVE HIM.

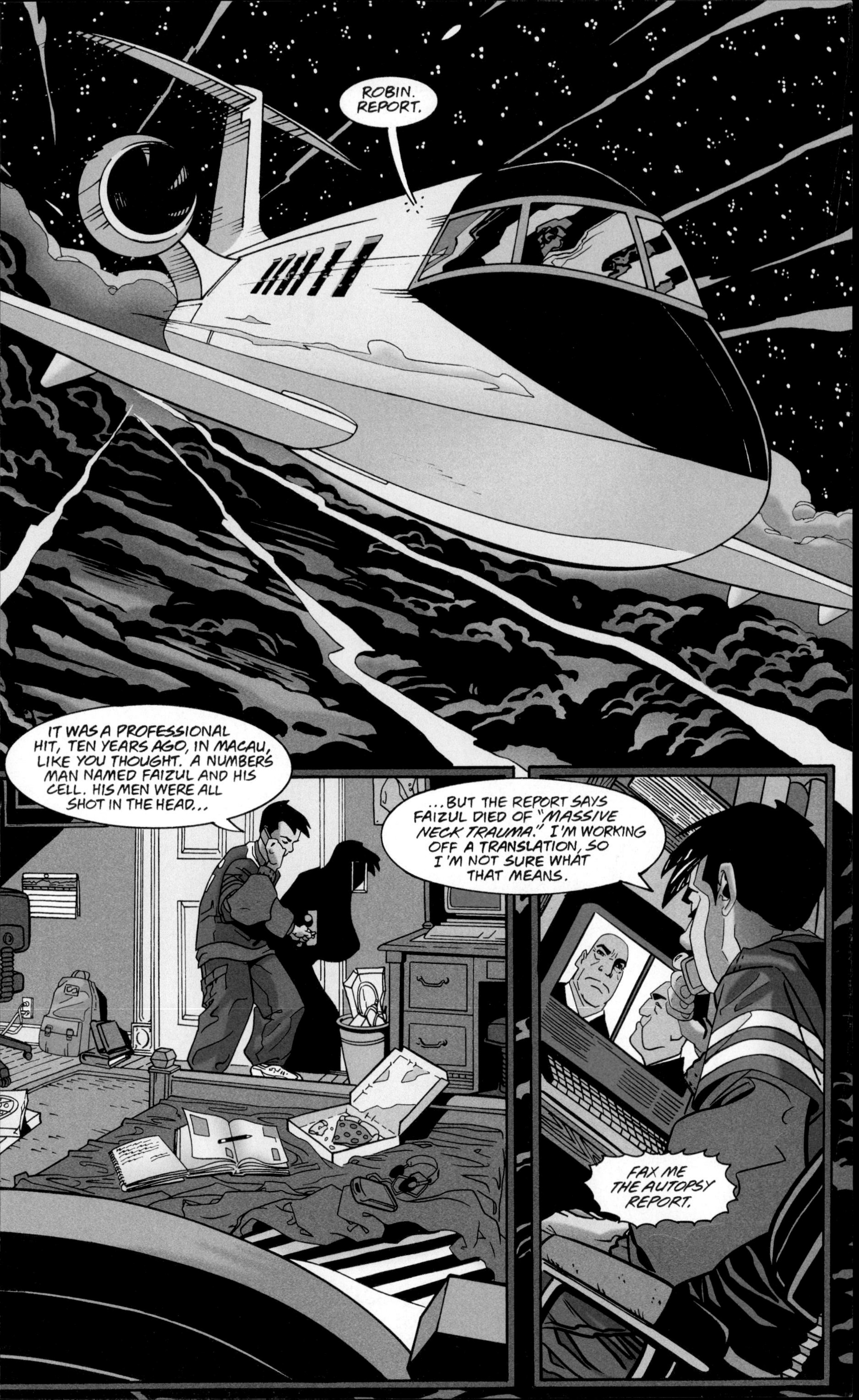
ROBIN. REPORT.
IT WAS A PROFESSIONAL HIT, TEN YEARS AGO, IN MACAU, LIKE YOU THOUGHT. A NUMBERS MAN NAMED FAIZUL AND HIS CELL. HIS MEN WERE ALL SHOT IN THE HEAD...
...BUT THE REPORT SAYS FAIZUL DIED OF "MASSIVE NECK TRAUMA." I'M WORKING OFF A TRANSLATION, SO I'M NOT SURE WHAT THAT MEANS.
FAX ME THE AUTOPSY REPORT.

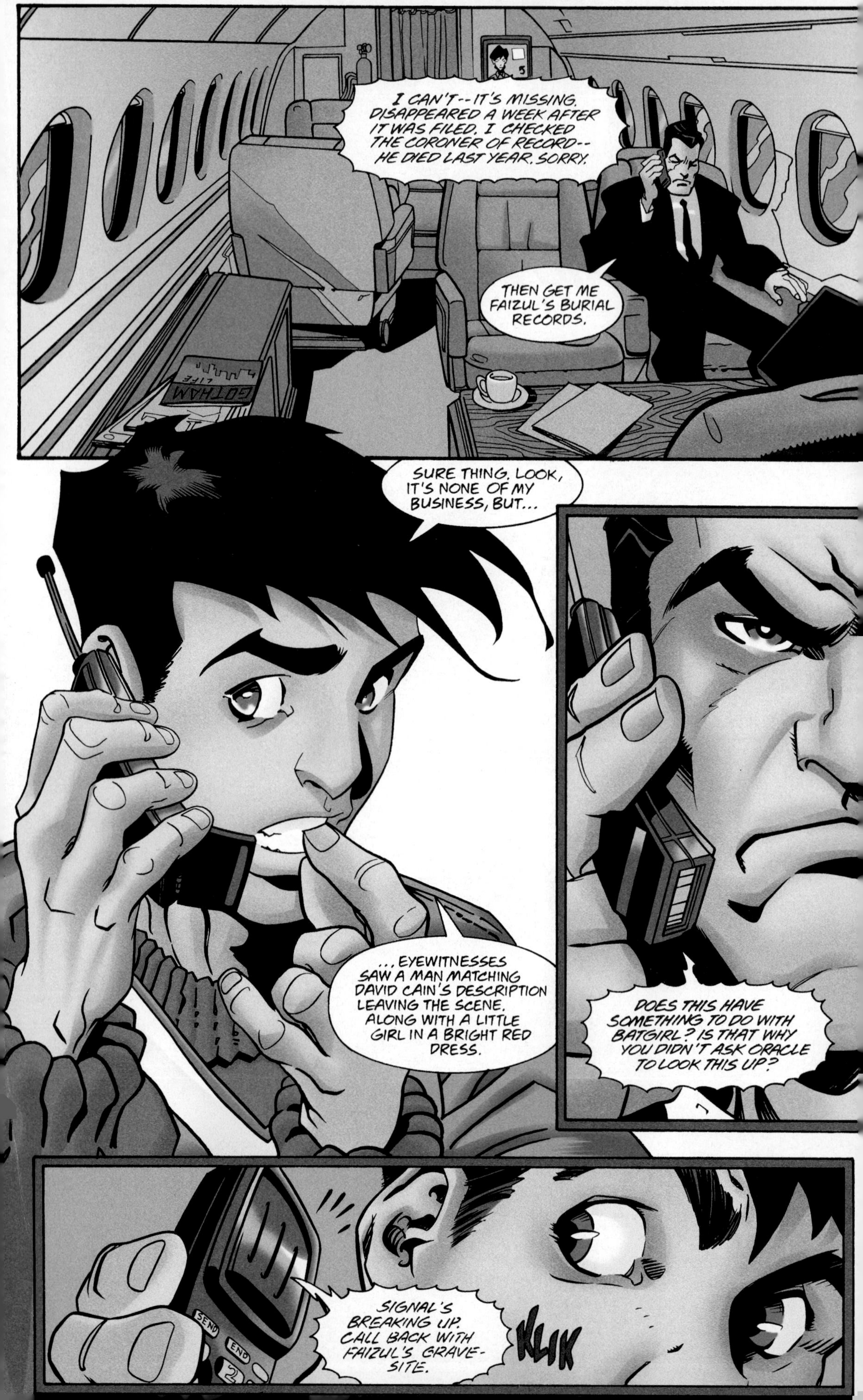
I CAN'T--IT'S MISSING. DISAPPEARED A WEEK AFTER IT WAS FILED. I CHECKED THE CORONER OF RECORD-- HE DIED LAST YEAR. SORRY.
THEN GET ME FAIZUL'S BURIAL RECORDS.
GOTHAM LIFE
SURE THING. LOOK, IT'S NONE OF MY BUSINESS, BUT...
...EYEWITNESSES SAW A MAN MATCHING DAVID CAIN'S DESCRIPTION LEAVING THE SCENE. ALONG WITH A LITTLE GIRL IN A BRIGHT RED DRESS.
DOES THIS HAVE SOMETHING TO DO WITH BATGIRL? IS THAT WHY YOU DIDN'T ASK ORACLE TO LOOK THIS UP?
SIGNAL'S BREAKING UP. CALL BACK WITH FAIZUL'S GRAVE-SITE.
SEND
END
KLIK

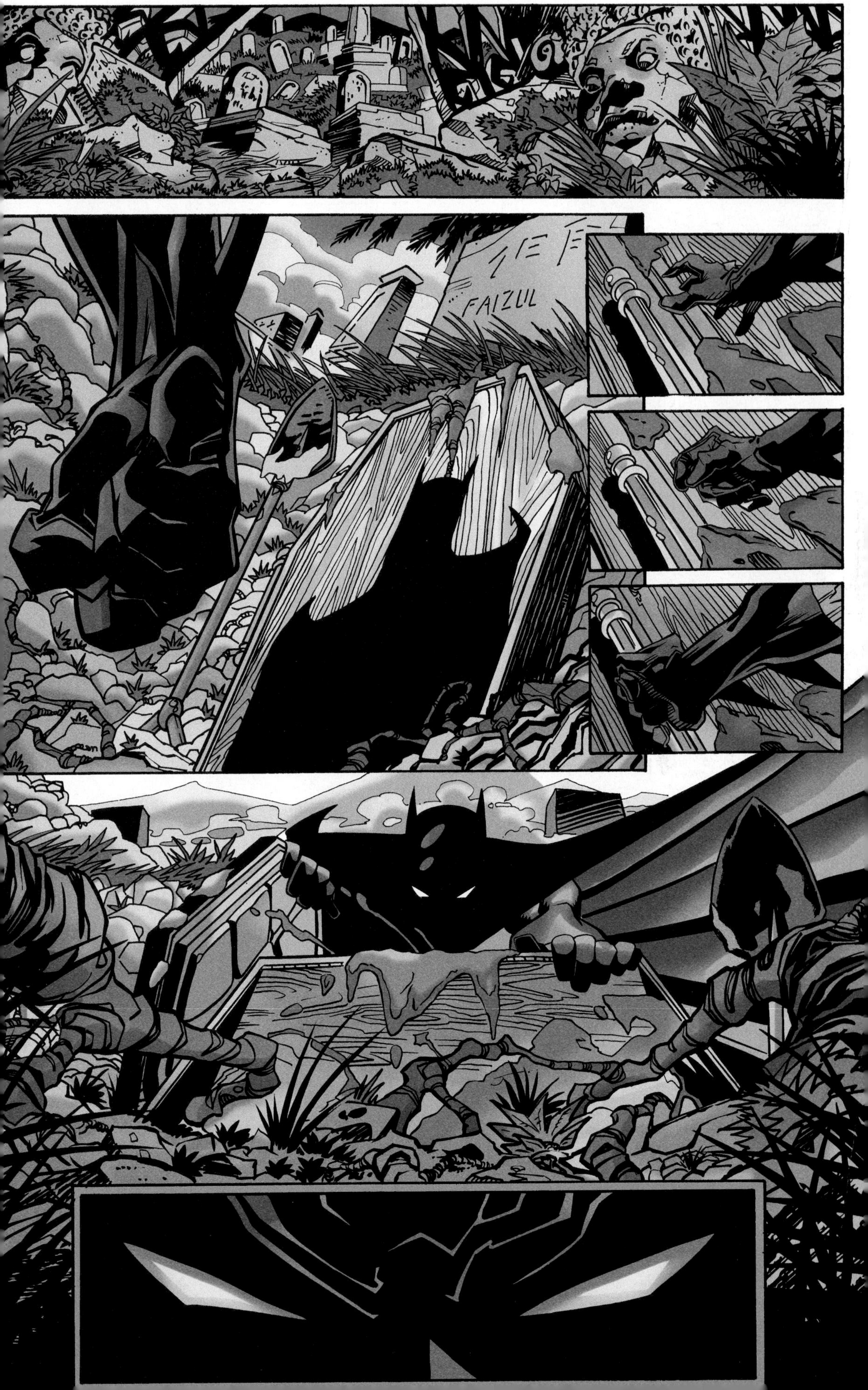
FAIZUL

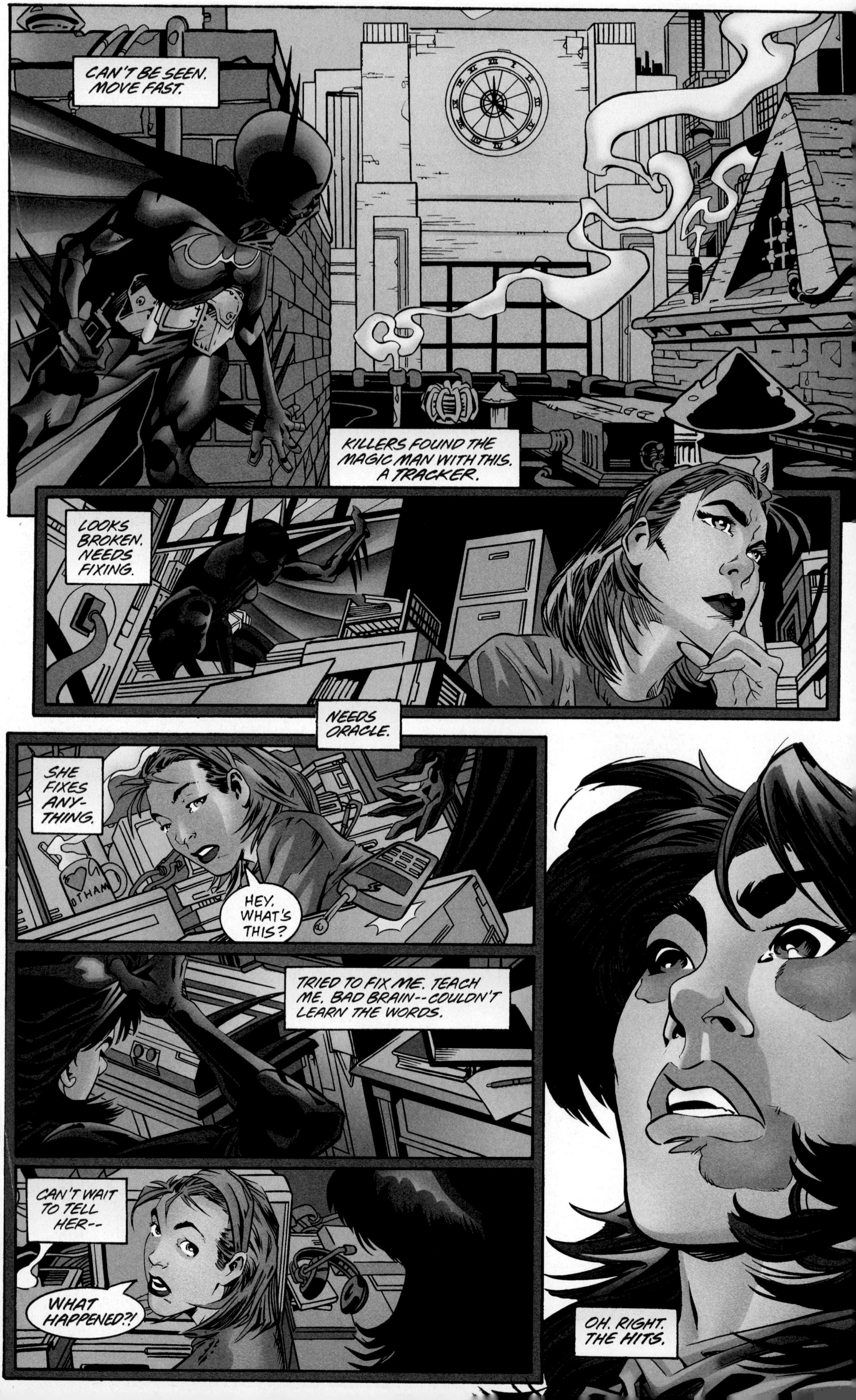
CAN'T BE SEEN. MOVE FAST.
KILLERS FOUND THE MAGIC MAN WITH THIS. A TRACKER.
LOOKS BROKEN. NEEDS FIXING.
NEEDS ORACLE.
SHE FIXES ANY-THING.
HEY. WHAT'S THIS?
TRIED TO FIX ME. TEACH ME. BAD BRAIN--COULDN'T LEARN THE WORDS.
CAN'T WAIT TO TELL HER--
WHAT HAPPENED?!
OH. RIGHT. THE HITS.

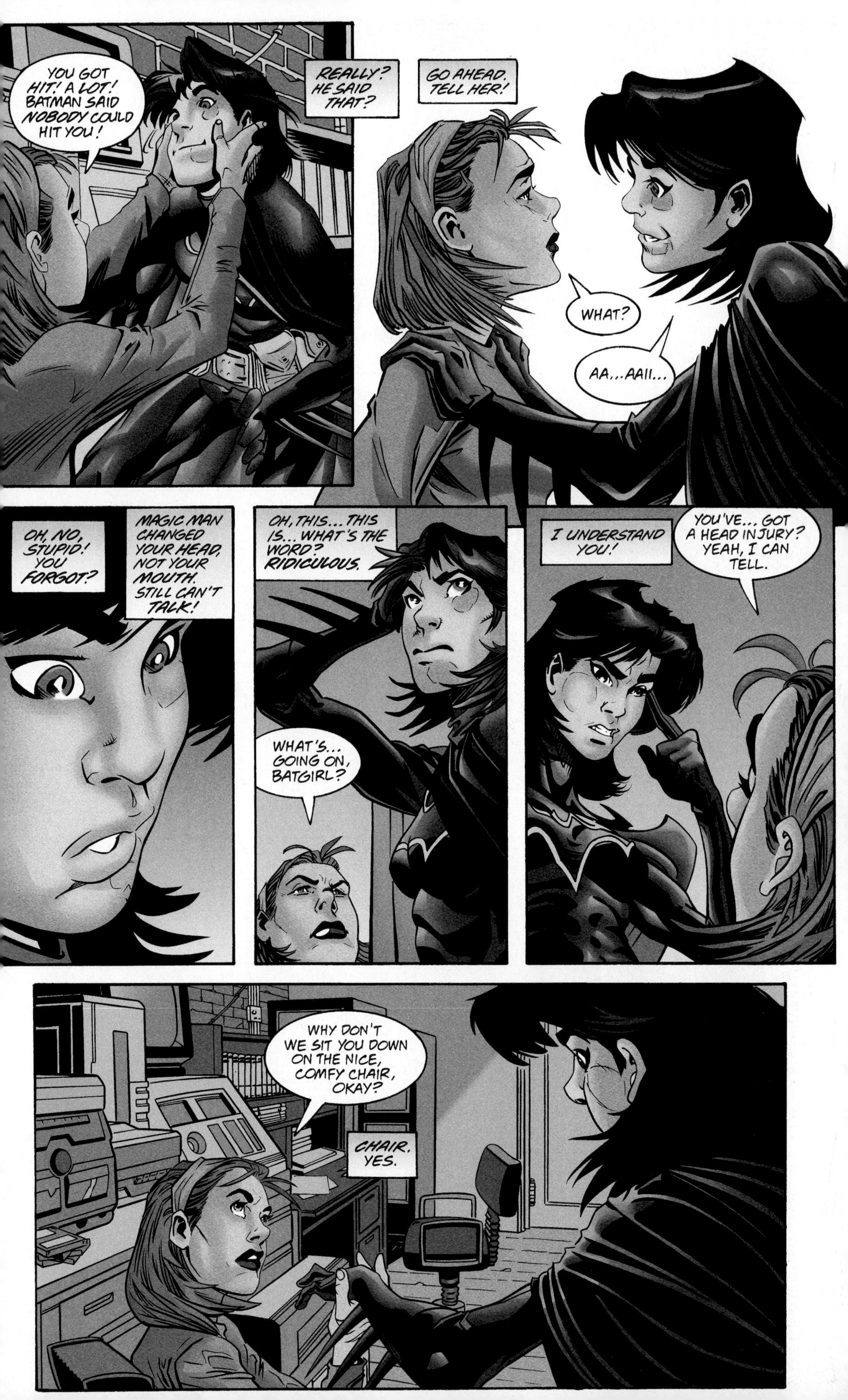
YOU GOT HIT! A LOT! BATMAN SAID NOBODY COULD HIT YOU!
REALLY? HE SAID THAT?
GO AHEAD. TELL HER!
WHAT?
AA...AAII...
OH, NO, STUPID! YOU FORGOT?
MAGIC MAN CHANGED YOUR HEAD, NOT YOUR MOUTH. STILL CAN'T TALK!
OH, THIS... THIS IS... WHAT'S THE WORD? RIDICULOUS.
WHAT'S... GOING ON, BATGIRL?
I UNDERSTAND YOU!
YOU'VE... GOT A HEAD INJURY? YEAH, I CAN TELL.
WHY DON'T WE SIT YOU DOWN ON THE NICE, COMFY CHAIR, OKAY?
CHAIR. YES.

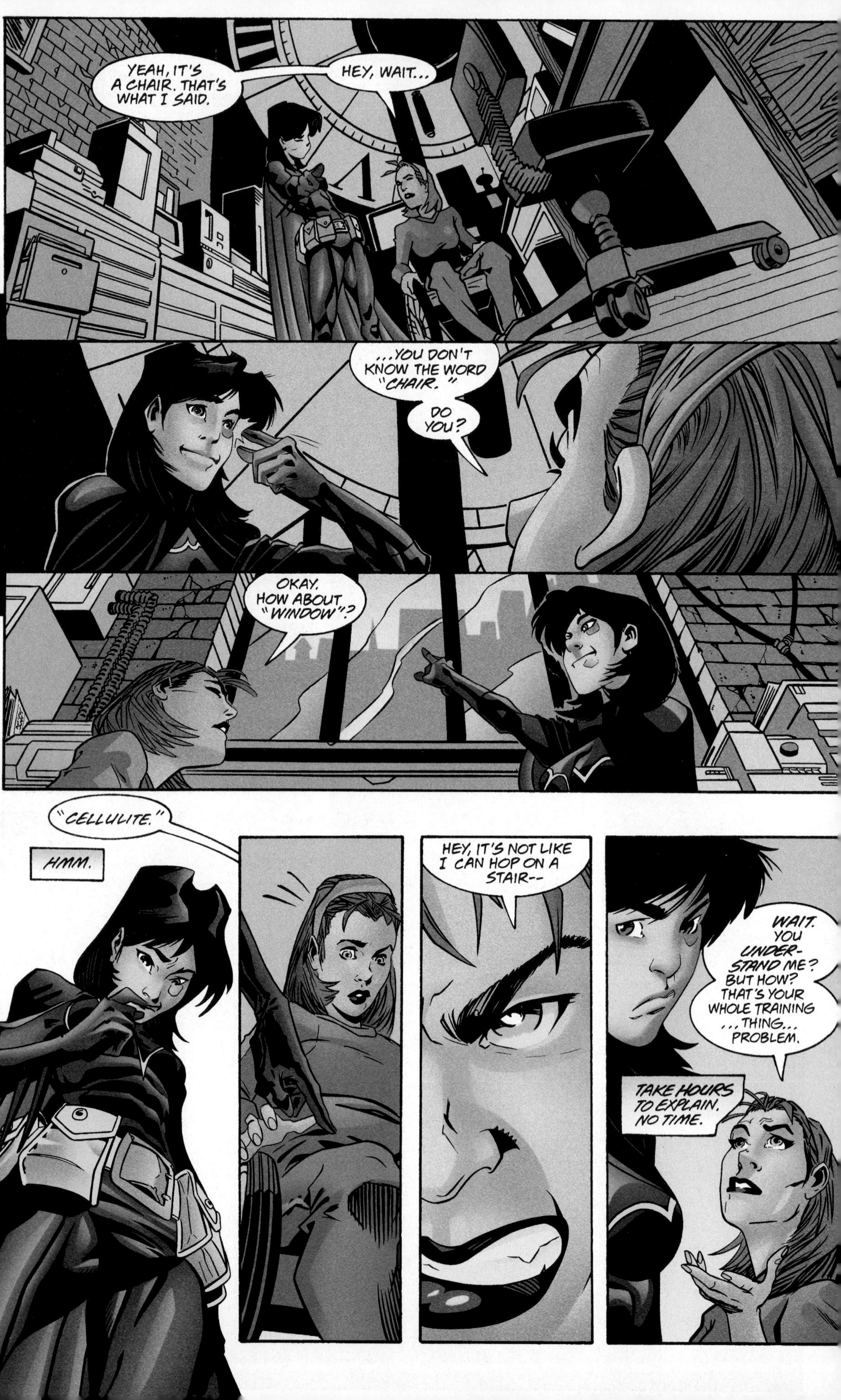
YEAH, IT'S A CHAIR. THAT'S WHAT I SAID.
HEY, WAIT...
...YOU DON'T KNOW THE WORD "CHAIR."
DO YOU?
OKAY. HOW ABOUT "WINDOW"?
"CELLULITE."
HMM.
HEY, IT'S NOT LIKE I CAN HOP ON A STAIR--
WAIT. YOU UNDERSTAND ME? BUT HOW? THAT'S YOUR WHOLE TRAINING ...THING... PROBLEM.
TAKE HOURS TO EXPLAIN. NO TIME.

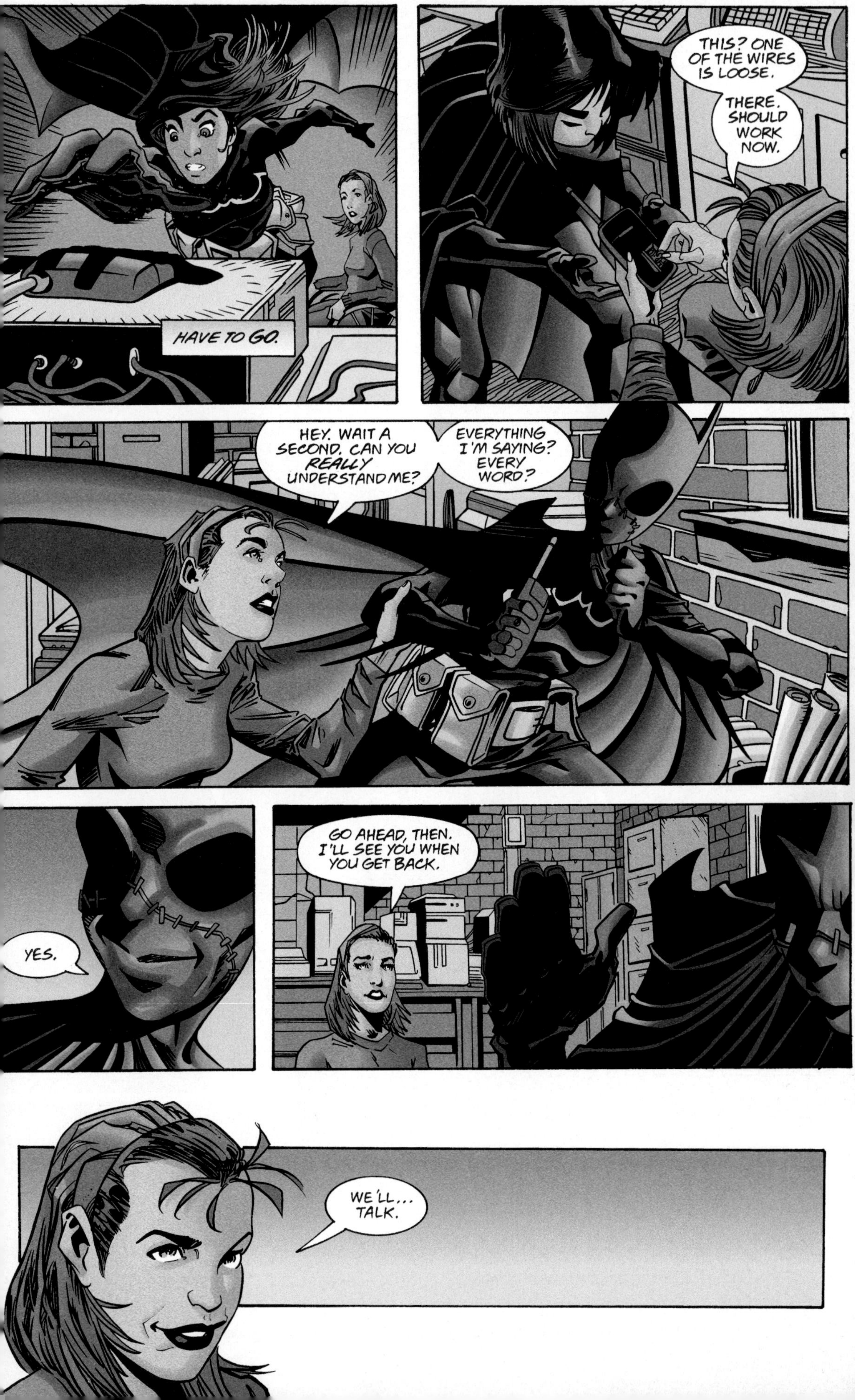
HAVE TO GO.
THIS? ONE OF THE WIRES IS LOOSE.
THERE. SHOULD WORK NOW.
HEY. WAIT A SECOND. CAN YOU REALLY UNDERSTAND ME?
EVERYTHING I'M SAYING? EVERY WORD?
YES.
GO AHEAD, THEN. I'LL SEE YOU WHEN YOU GET BACK.
WE'LL... TALK.

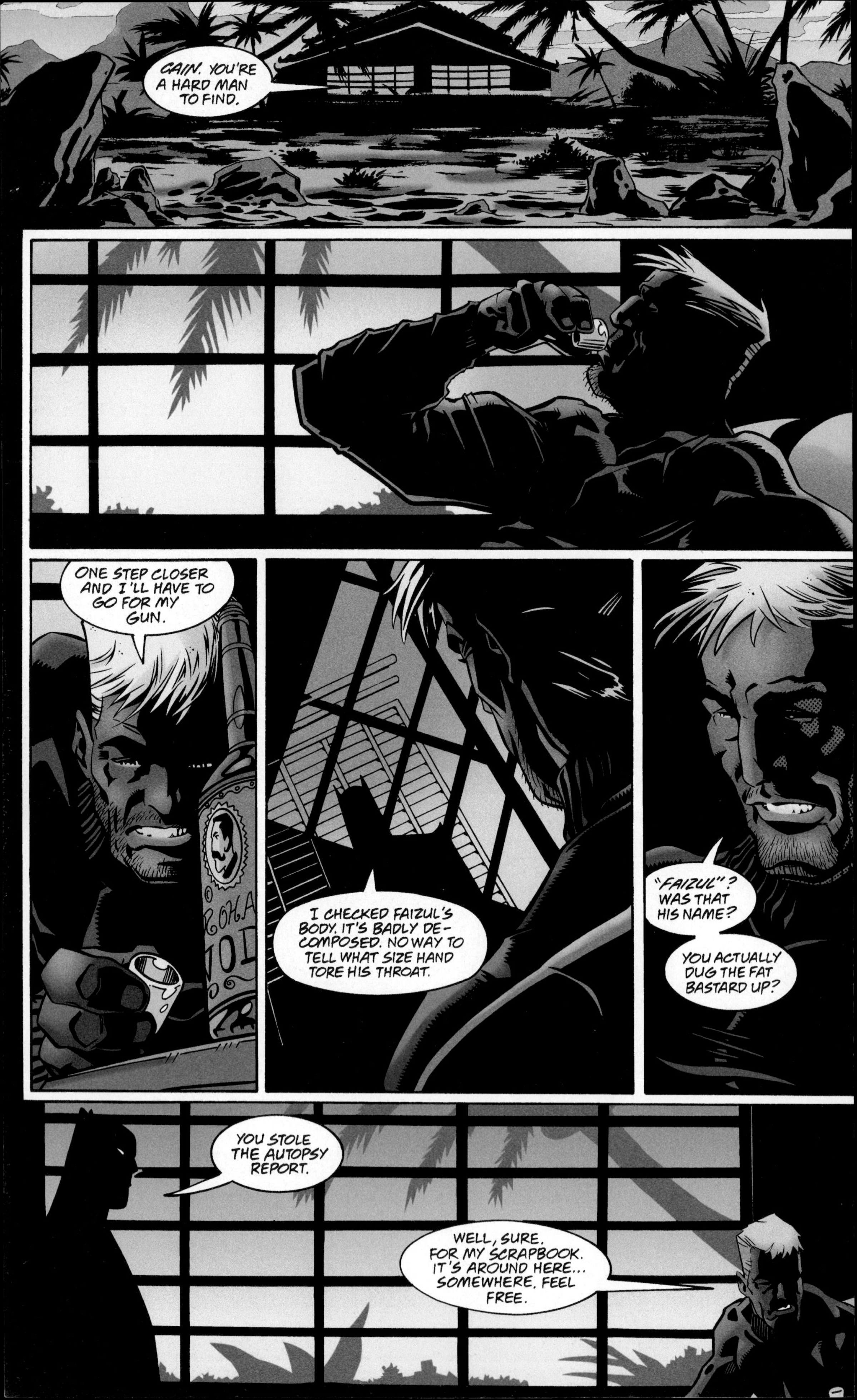
CAIN. YOU'RE A HARD MAN TO FIND.
ONE STEP CLOSER AND I'LL HAVE TO GO FOR MY GUN.
I CHECKED FAIZUL'S BODY. IT'S BADLY DE-COMPOSED. NO WAY TO TELL WHAT SIZE HAND TORE HIS THROAT.
"FAIZUL"? WAS THAT HIS NAME?
YOU ACTUALLY DUG THE FAT BASTARD UP?
YOU STOLE THE AUTOPSY REPORT.
WELL, SURE. FOR MY SCRAPBOOK. IT'S AROUND HERE... SOMEWHERE. FEEL FREE.

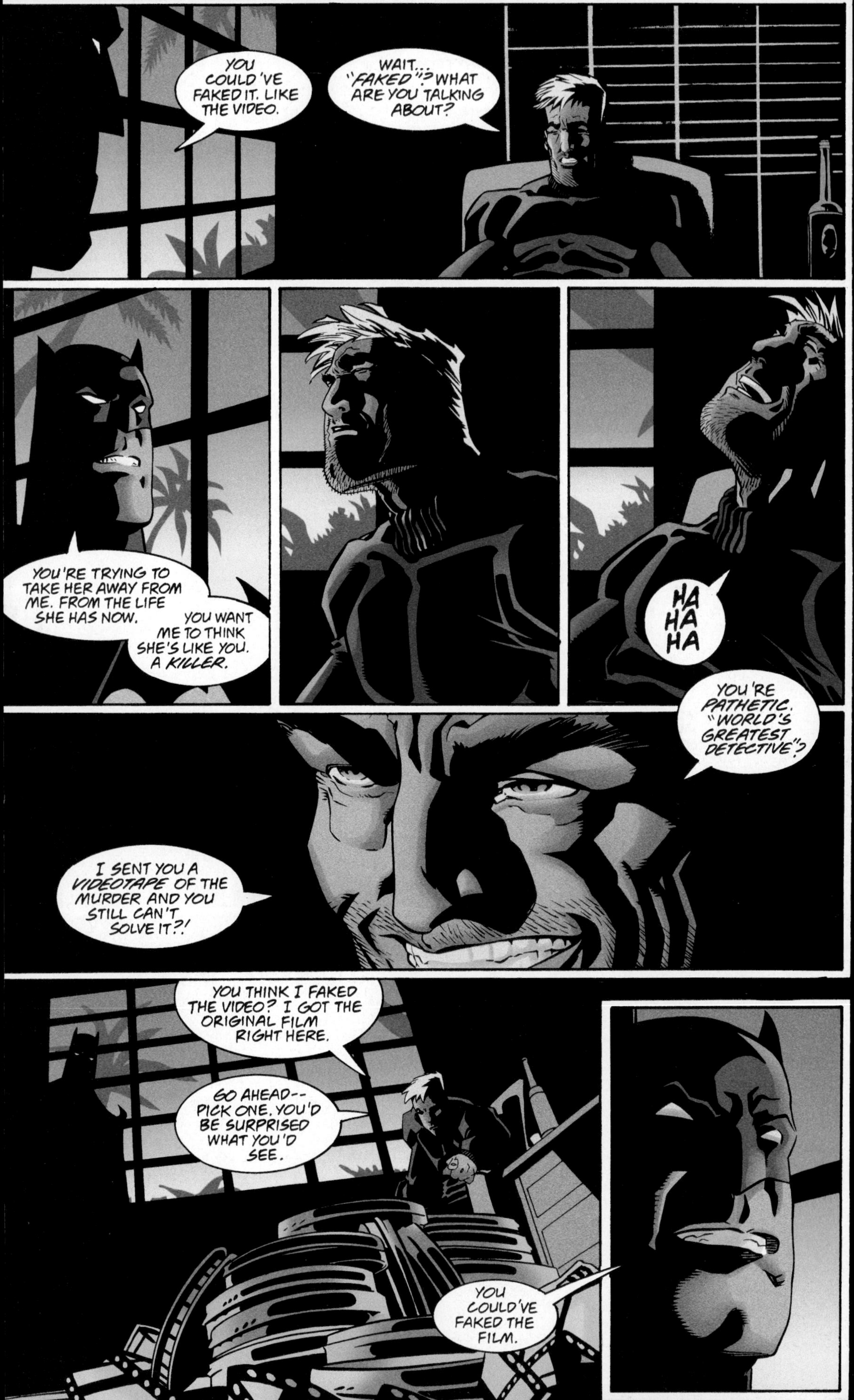
YOU COULD'VE FAKED IT. LIKE THE VIDEO.
WAIT... "FAKED"? WHAT ARE YOU TALKING ABOUT?
YOU'RE TRYING TO TAKE HER AWAY FROM ME. FROM THE LIFE SHE HAS NOW.
YOU WANT ME TO THINK SHE'S LIKE YOU. A KILLER.
HA HA HA
YOU'RE PATHETIC. "WORLD'S GREATEST DETECTIVE"?
I SENT YOU A VIDEOTAPE OF THE MURDER AND YOU STILL CAN'T SOLVE IT?!
YOU THINK I FAKED THE VIDEO? I GOT THE ORIGINAL FILM RIGHT HERE.
GO AHEAD-- PICK ONE. YOU'D BE SURPRISED WHAT YOU'D SEE.
YOU COULD'VE FAKED THE FILM.

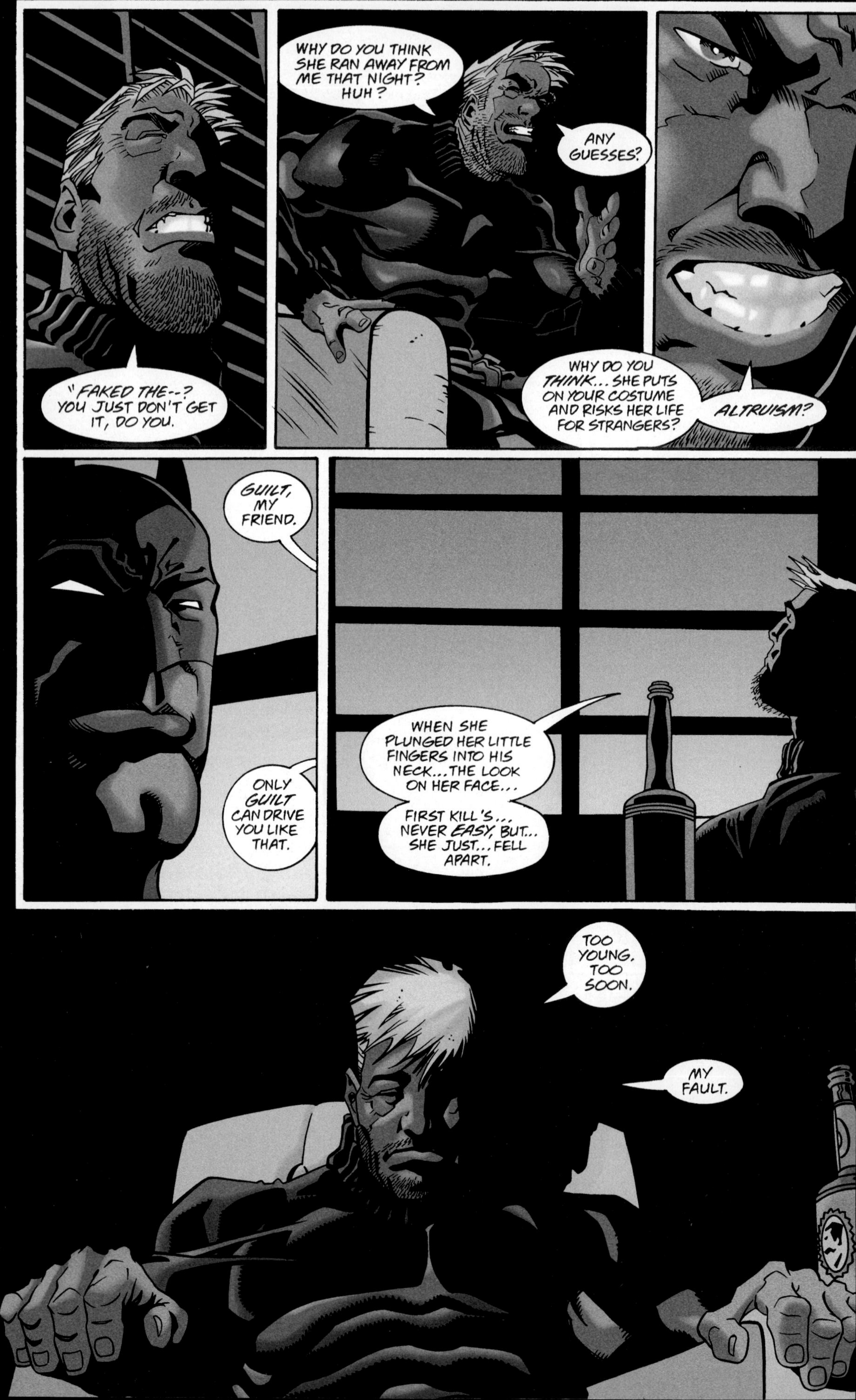

"FAKED THE--? YOU JUST DON'T GET IT, DO YOU.
WHY DO YOU THINK SHE RAN AWAY FROM ME THAT NIGHT? HUH?
ANY GUESSES?
WHY DO YOU THINK... SHE PUTS ON YOUR COSTUME AND RISKS HER LIFE FOR STRANGERS?
ALTRUISM?
GUILT, MY FRIEND.
ONLY GUILT CAN DRIVE YOU LIKE THAT.
WHEN SHE PLUNGED HER LITTLE FINGERS INTO HIS NECK... THE LOOK ON HER FACE...
FIRST KILL'S... NEVER EASY, BUT... SHE JUST... FELL APART.
TOO YOUNG, TOO SOON.
MY FAULT.

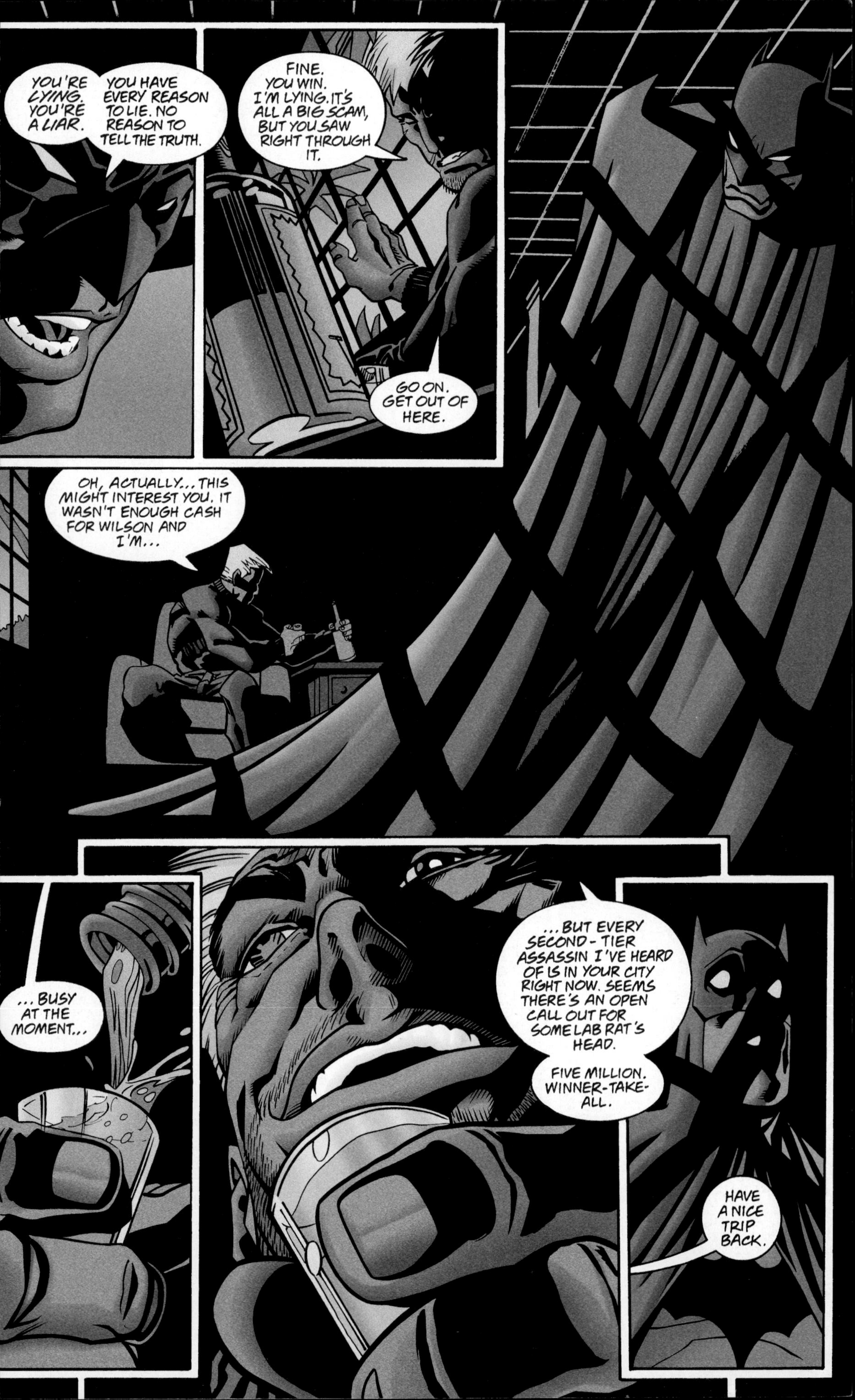
YOU'RE LYING. YOU'RE A LIAR.
YOU HAVE EVERY REASON TO LIE. NO REASON TO TELL THE TRUTH.
FINE. YOU WIN. I'M LYING. IT'S ALL A BIG SCAM, BUT YOU SAW RIGHT THROUGH IT.
GO ON. GET OUT OF HERE.
OH, ACTUALLY... THIS MIGHT INTEREST YOU. IT WASN'T ENOUGH CASH FOR WILSON AND I'M...
...BUSY AT THE MOMENT...
...BUT EVERY SECOND-TIER ASSASSIN I'VE HEARD OF IS IN YOUR CITY RIGHT NOW. SEEMS THERE'S AN OPEN CALL OUT FOR SOME LAB RAT'S HEAD.
FIVE MILLION. WINNER-TAKE-ALL.
HAVE A NICE TRIP BACK.

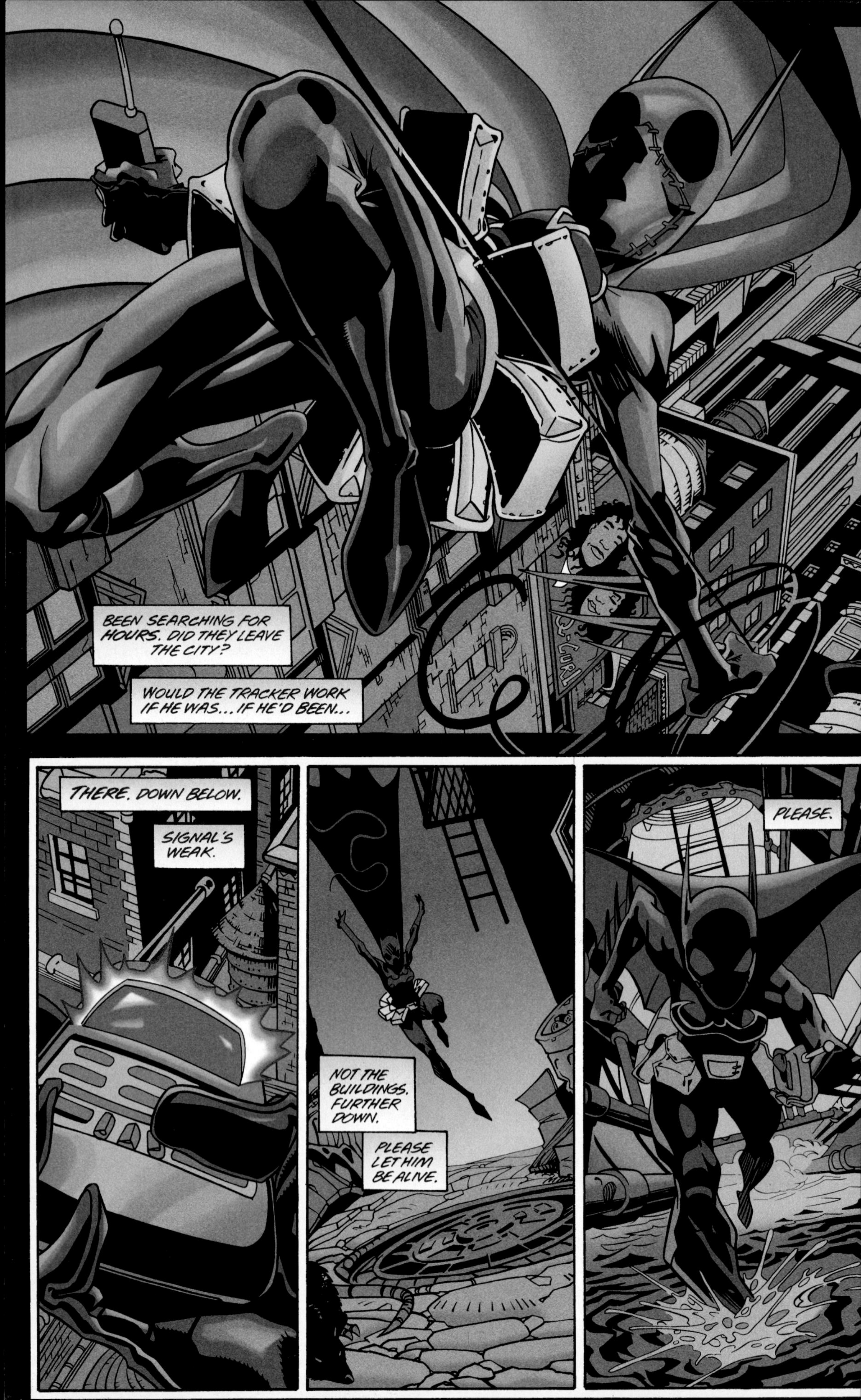
BEEN SEARCHING FOR HOURS. DID THEY LEAVE THE CITY?
WOULD THE TRACKER WORK IF HE WAS... IF HE'D BEEN...
THERE. DOWN BELOW.
SIGNAL'S WEAK.
NOT THE BUILDINGS. FURTHER DOWN.
PLEASE LET HIM BE ALIVE.
PLEASE.

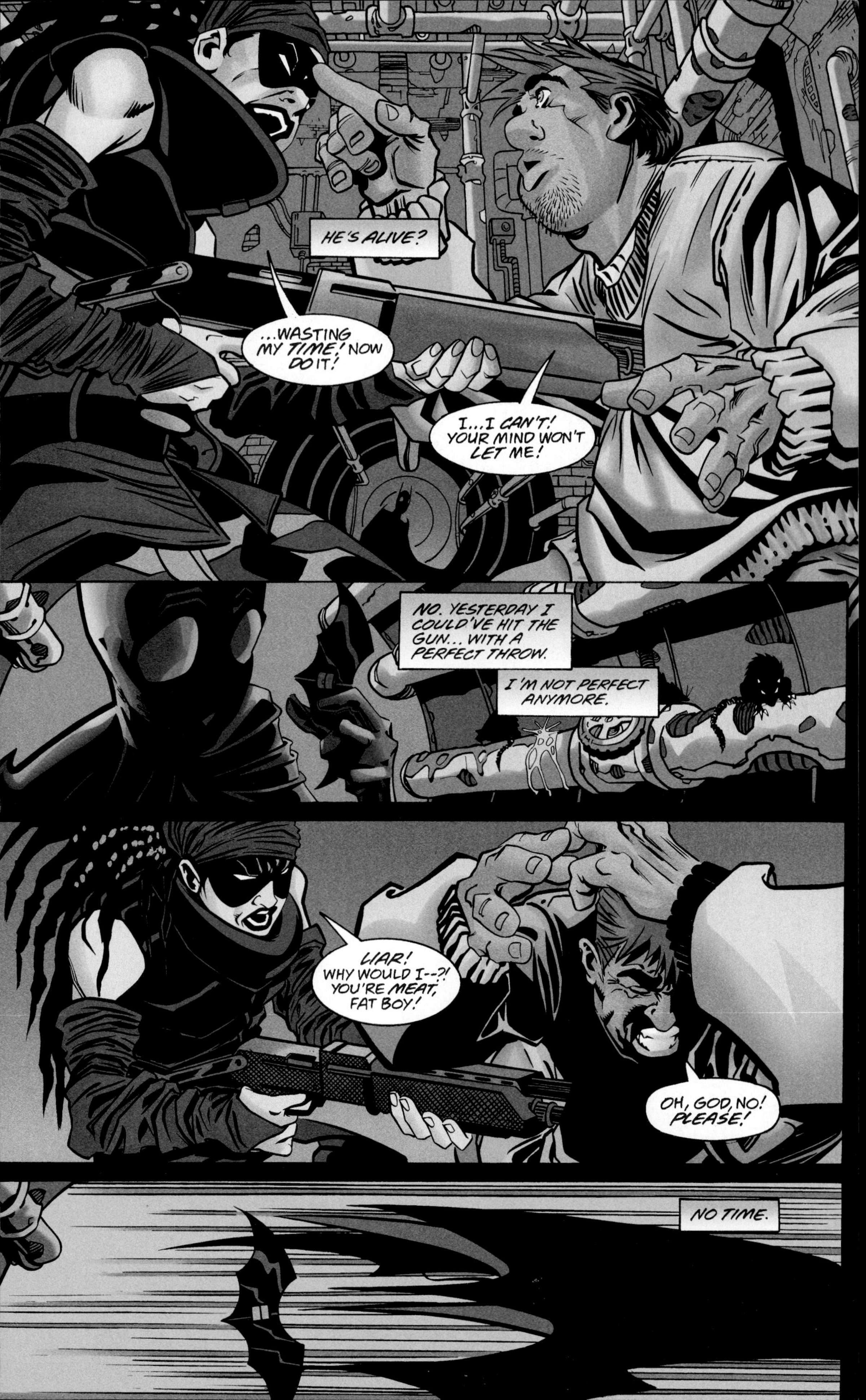
HE'S ALIVE?
...WASTING MY TIME! NOW DO IT!
I...I CAN'T! YOUR MIND WON'T LET ME!
NO. YESTERDAY I COULD'VE HIT THE GUN... WITH A PERFECT THROW.
I'M NOT PERFECT ANYMORE.
LIAR! WHY WOULD I--?! YOU'RE MEAT, FAT BOY!
OH, GOD, NO! PLEASE!
NO TIME.

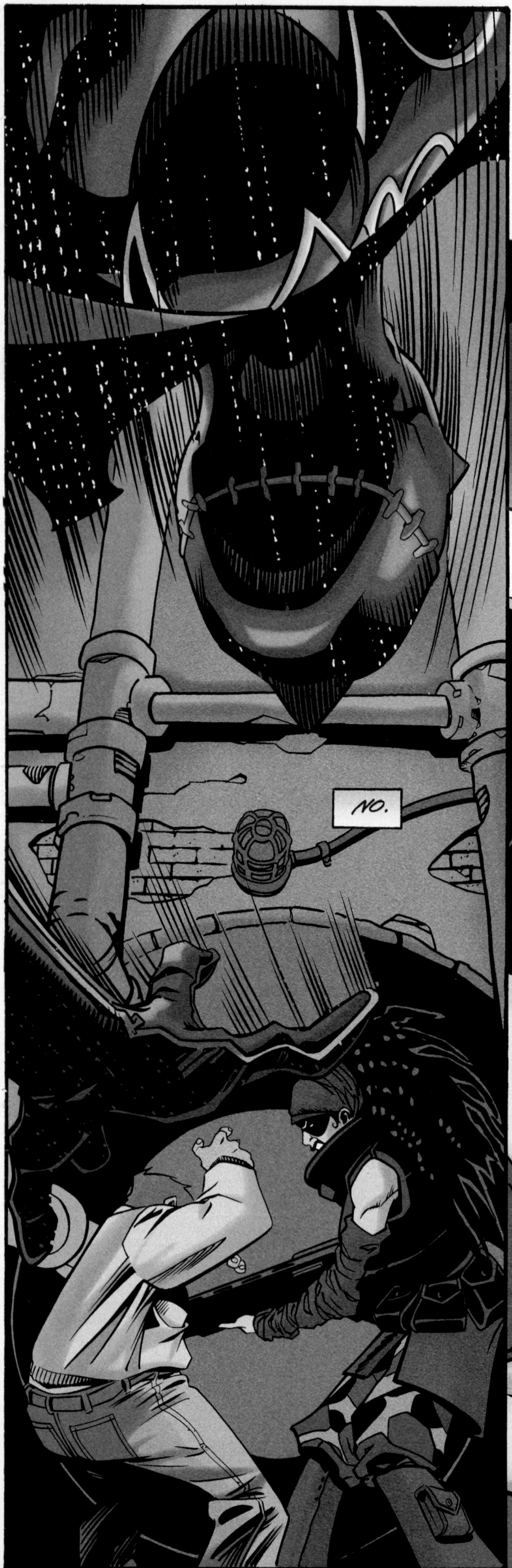
NO.

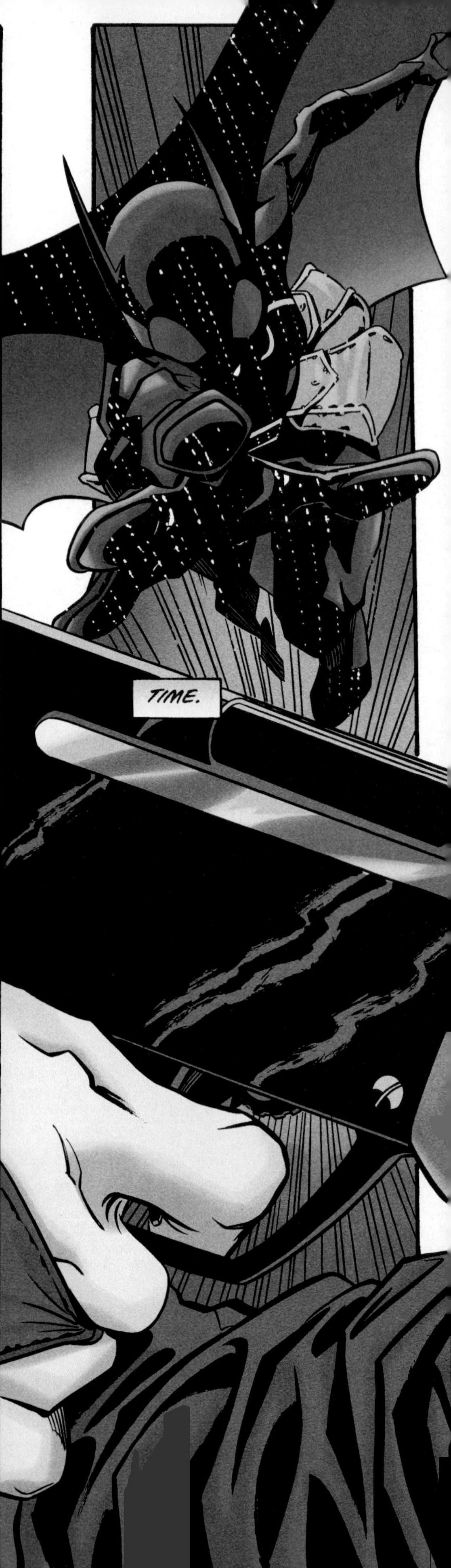
TIME.

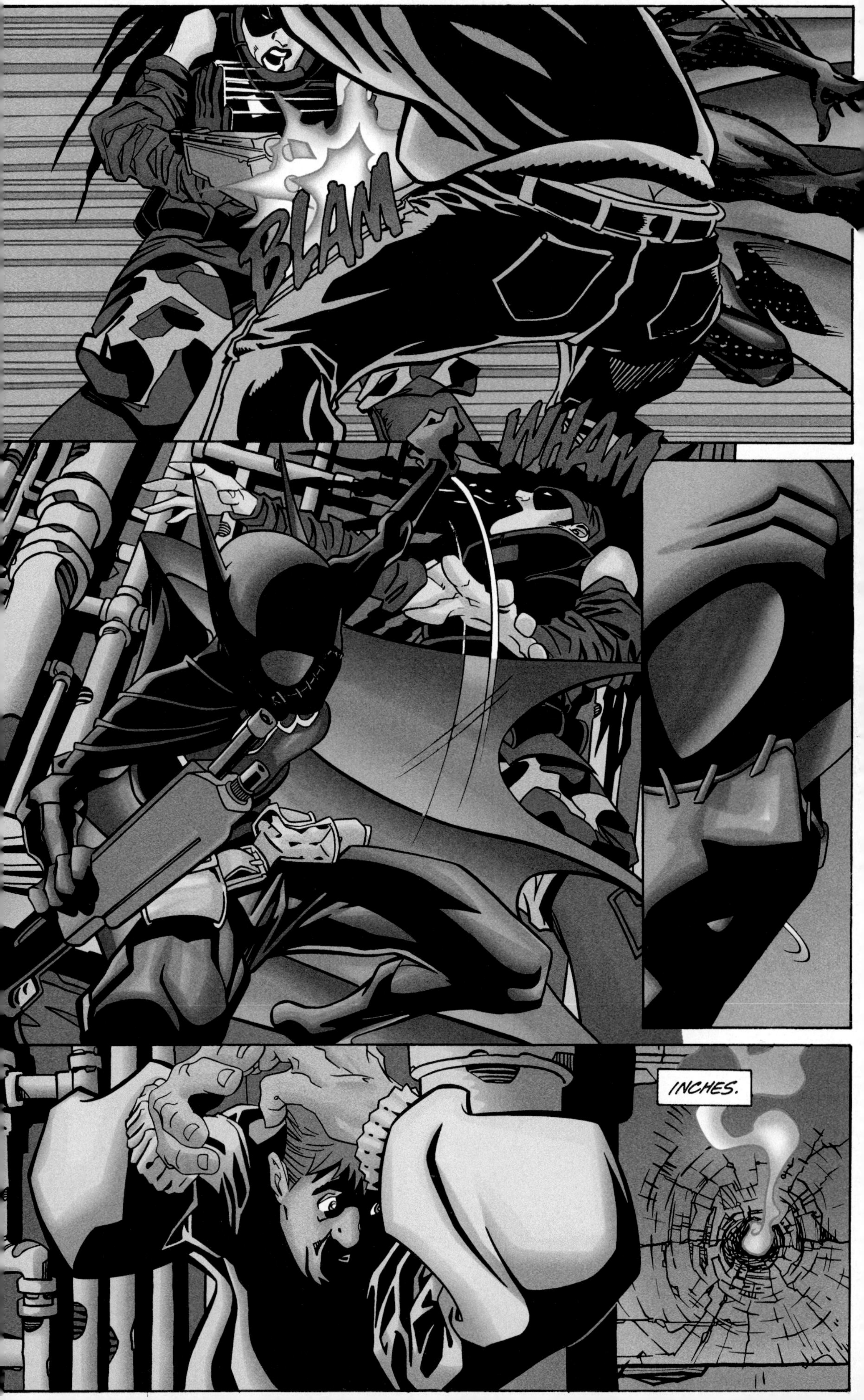
BLAM
WHAM
INCHES.

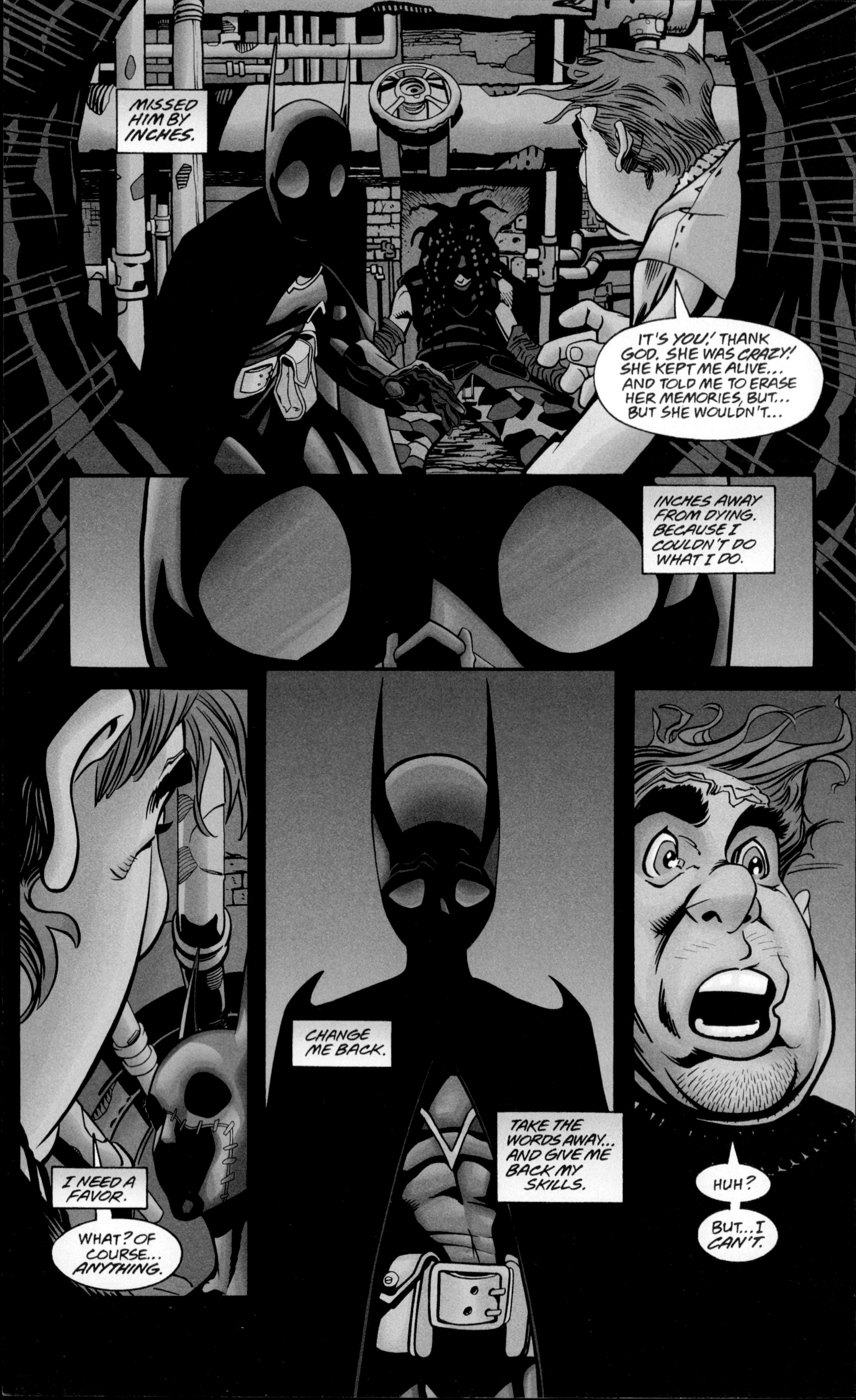

MISSED HIM BY INCHES.
IT'S YOU! THANK GOD. SHE WAS CRAZY! SHE KEPT ME ALIVE... AND TOLD ME TO ERASE HER MEMORIES, BUT... BUT SHE WOULDN'T...
INCHES AWAY FROM DYING. BECAUSE I COULDN'T DO WHAT I DO.
I NEED A FAVOR.
WHAT? OF COURSE... ANYTHING.
CHANGE ME BACK.
TAKE THE WORDS AWAY... AND GIVE ME BACK MY SKILLS.
HUH?
BUT... I CAN'T.

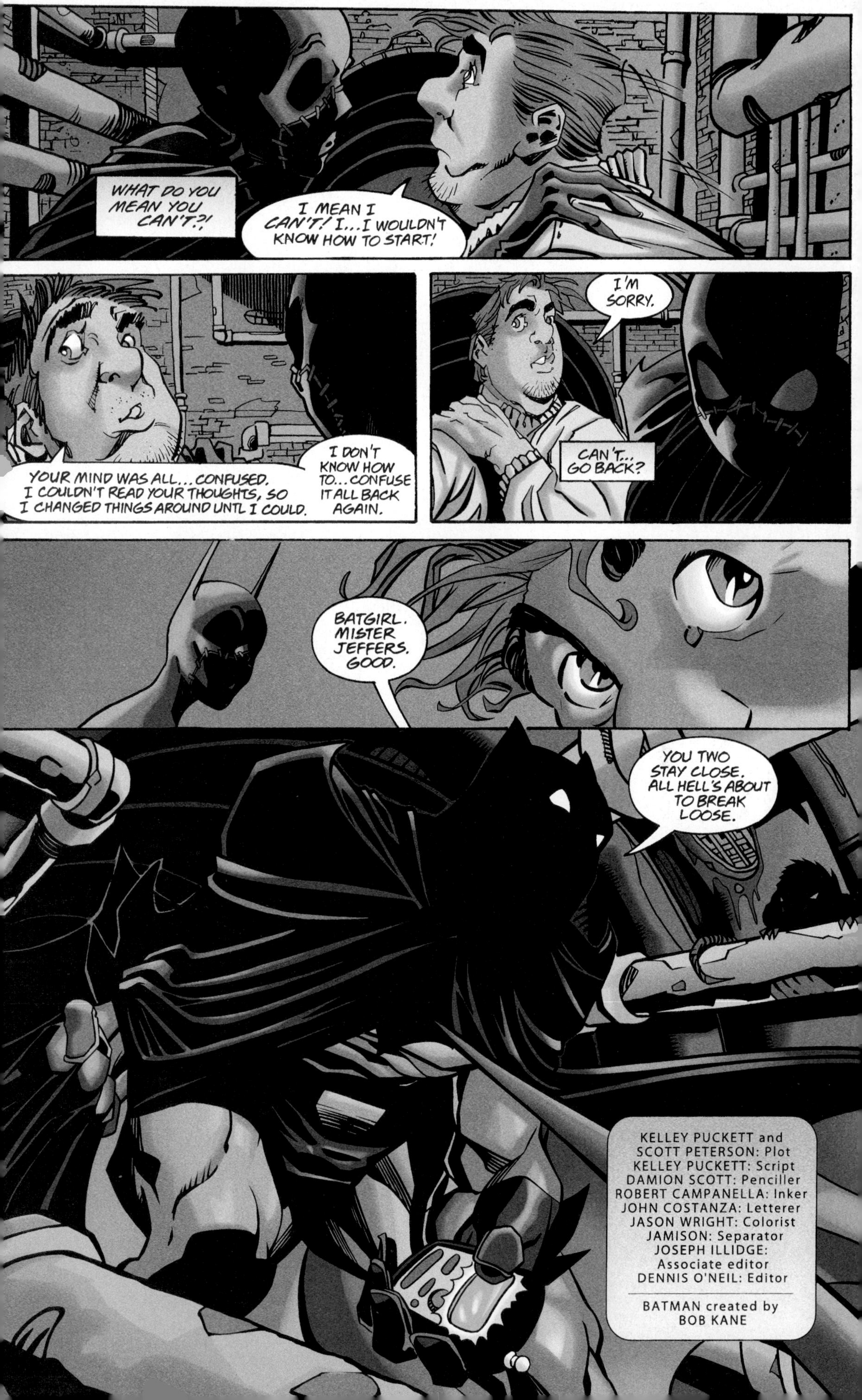
WHAT DO YOU MEAN YOU CAN'T?!
I MEAN I CAN'T! I...I WOULDN'T KNOW HOW TO START!
YOUR MIND WAS ALL...CONFUSED. I COULDN'T READ YOUR THOUGHTS, SO I CHANGED THINGS AROUND UNTL I COULD.
I DON'T KNOW HOW TO...CONFUSE IT ALL BACK AGAIN.
I'M SORRY.
CAN'T... GO BACK?
BATGIRL. MISTER JEFFERS. GOOD.
YOU TWO STAY CLOSE. ALL HELL'S ABOUT TO BREAK LOOSE.
KELLEY PUCKETT and SCOTT PETERSON: Plot
KELLEY PUCKETT: Script
DAMION SCOTT: Penciller
ROBERT CAMPANELLA: Inker
JOHN COSTANZA: Letterer
JASON WRIGHT: Colorist
JAMISON: Separator
JOSEPH ILLIDGE: Associate editor
DENNIS O'NEIL: Editor
BATMAN created by BOB KANE

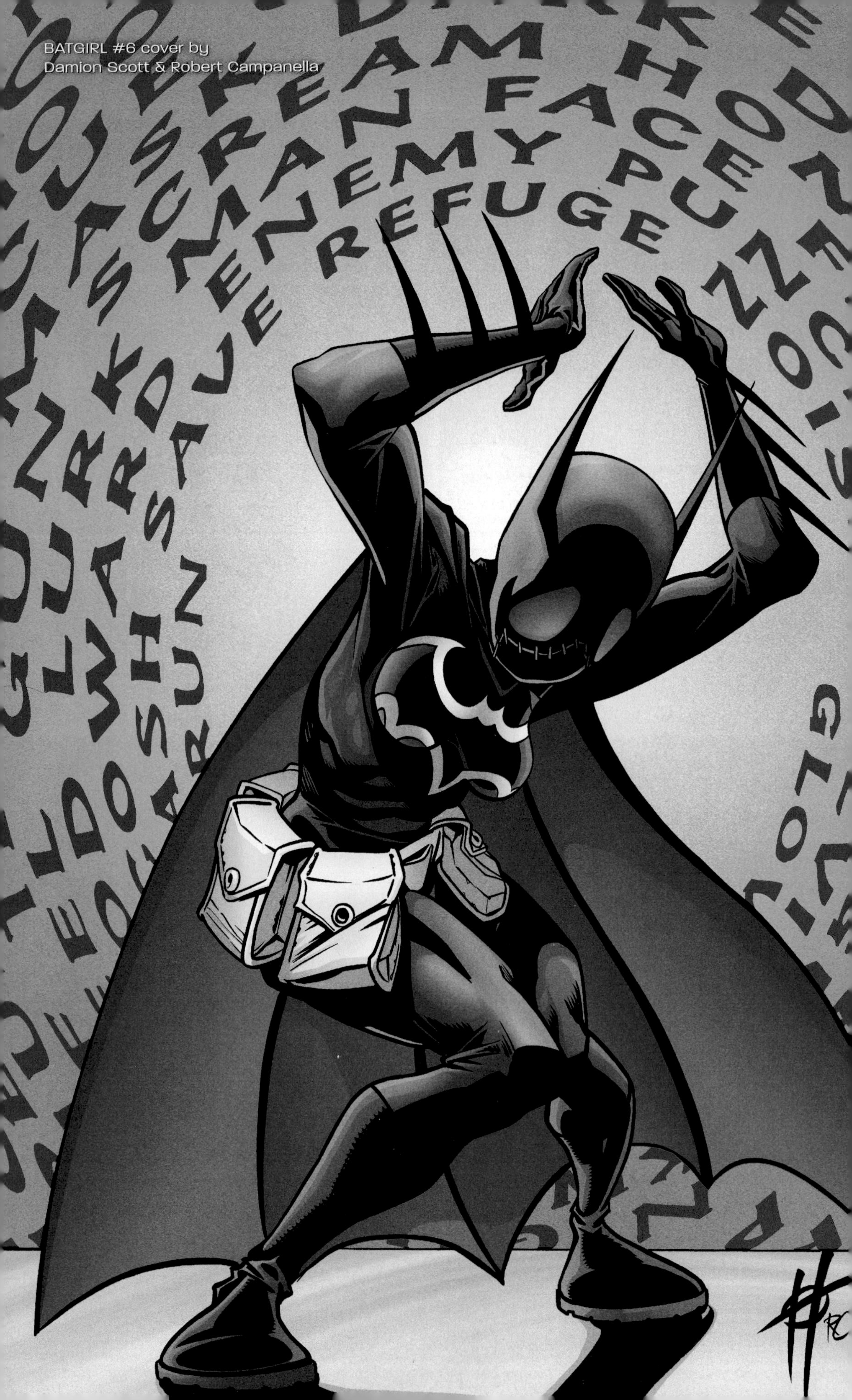
REFUGE
ENEMY
BATGIRL #6 cover by
Damion Scott & Robert Campanella

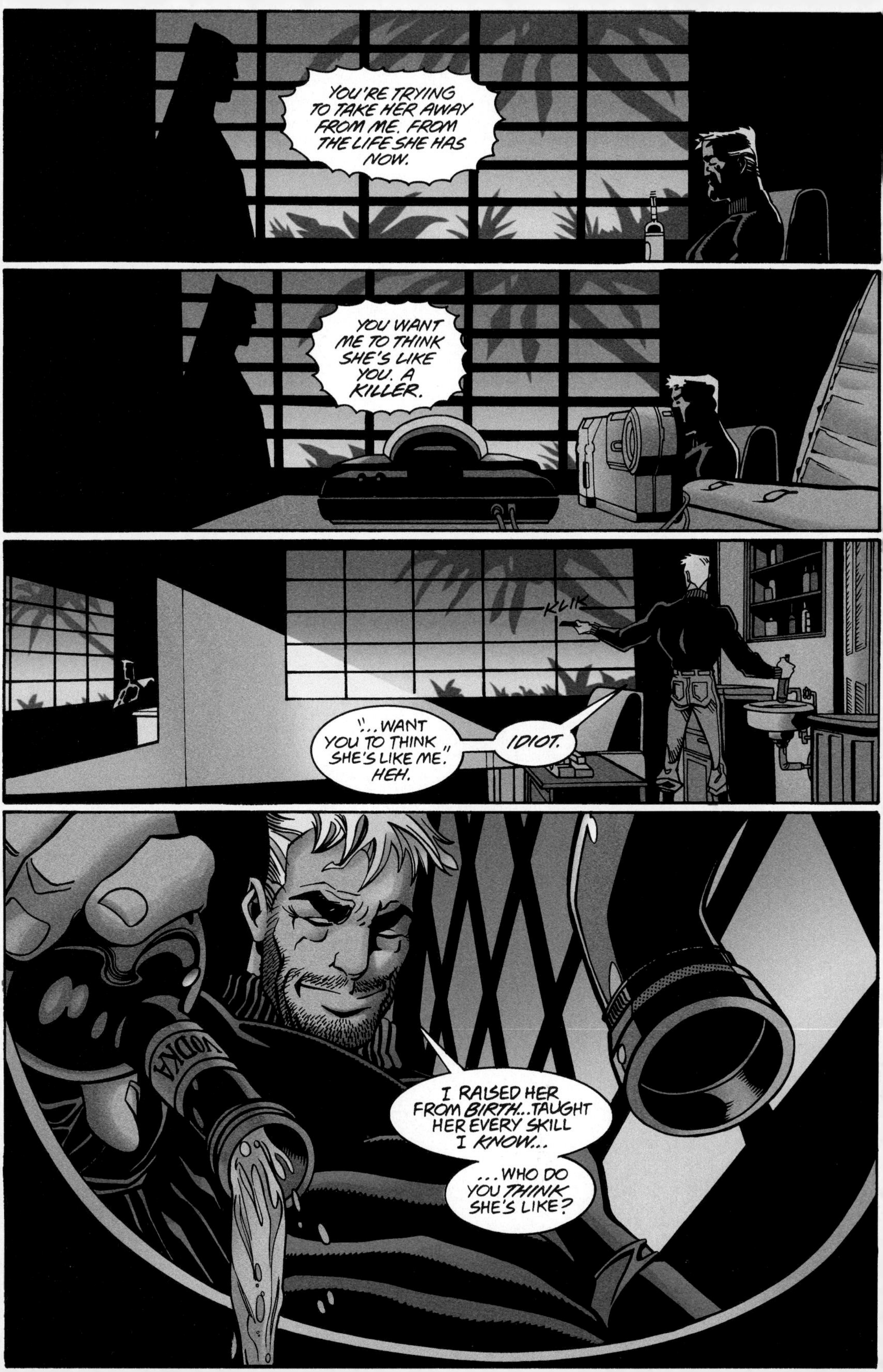

YOU'RE TRYING TO TAKE HER AWAY FROM ME. FROM THE LIFE SHE HAS NOW.
YOU WANT ME TO THINK SHE'S LIKE YOU. A KILLER.
KLIK
"...WANT YOU TO THINK SHE'S LIKE ME." HEH.
IDIOT.
VODKA
I RAISED HER FROM BIRTH...TAUGHT HER EVERY SKILL I KNOW...
...WHO DO YOU THINK SHE'S LIKE?

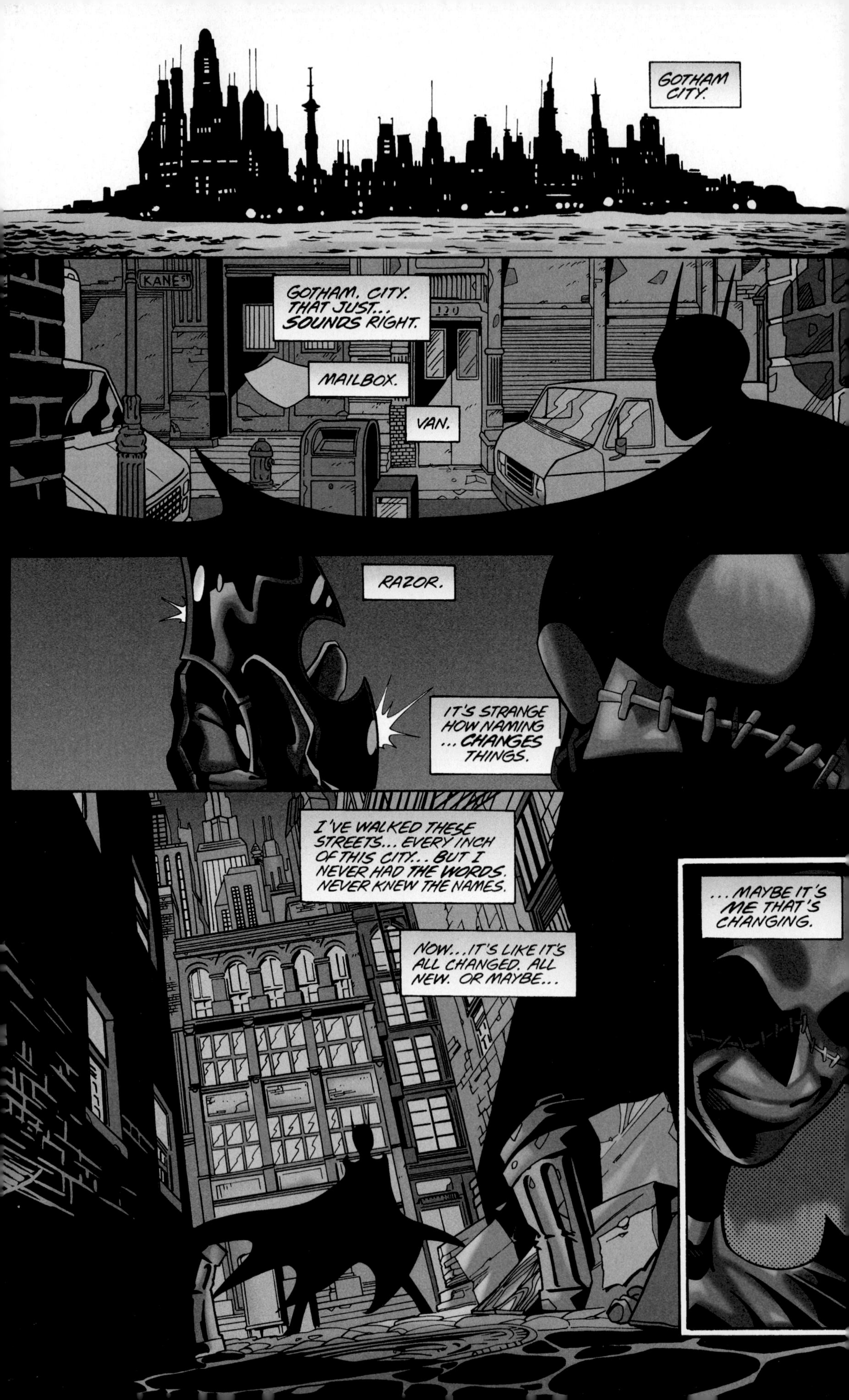
GOTHAM CITY.
KANE ST
GOTHAM. CITY. THAT JUST... SOUNDS RIGHT.
120
MAILBOX.
VAN.
RAZOR.
IT'S STRANGE HOW NAMING ...CHANGES THINGS.
I'VE WALKED THESE STREETS... EVERY INCH OF THIS CITY... BUT I NEVER HAD THE WORDS. NEVER KNEW THE NAMES.
NOW...IT'S LIKE IT'S ALL CHANGED. ALL NEW. OR MAYBE...
...MAYBE IT'S ME THAT'S CHANGING.

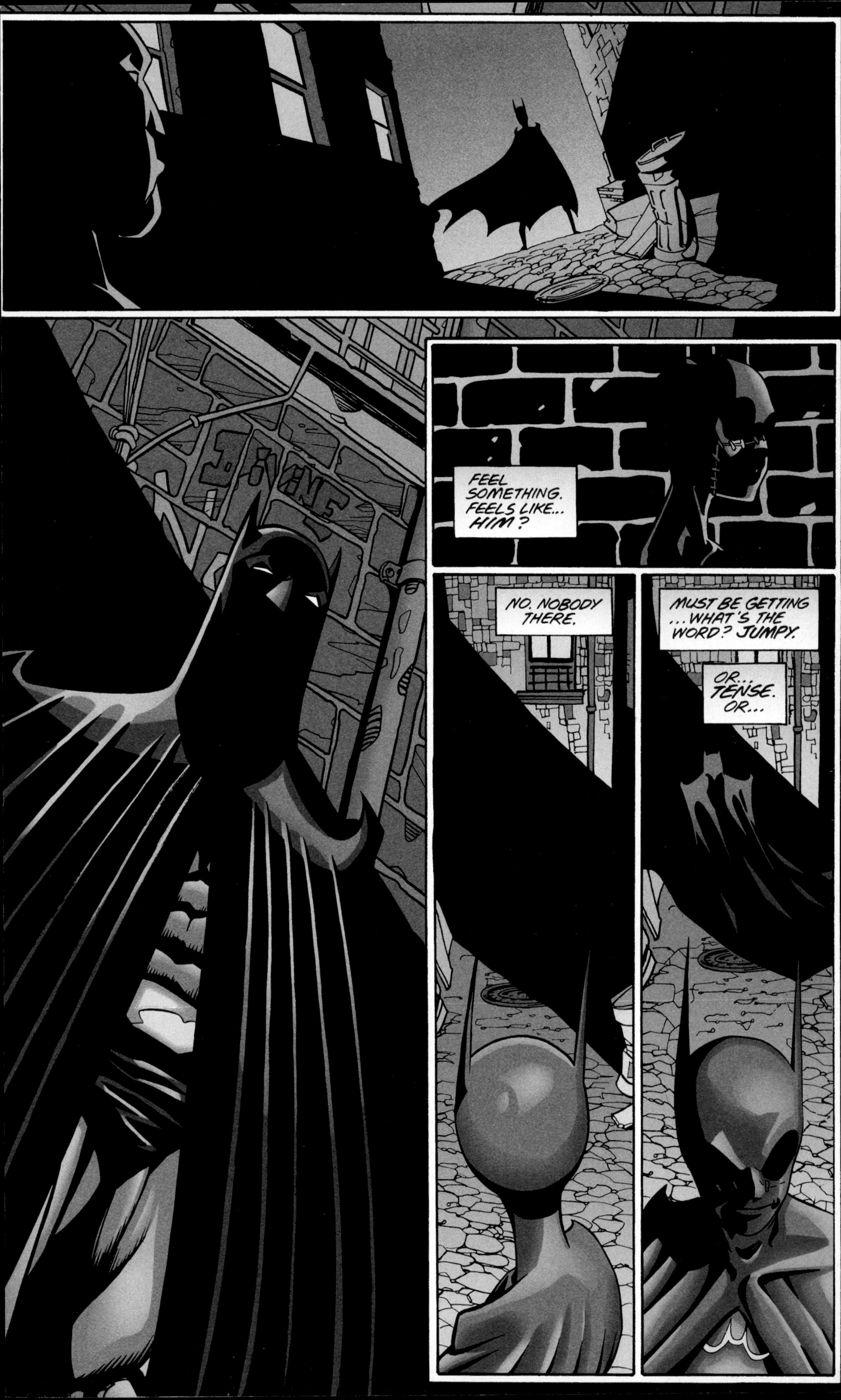
FEEL SOMETHING. FEELS LIKE... HIM?
NO. NOBODY THERE.
MUST BE GETTING ...WHAT'S THE WORD? JUMPY.
OR... TENSE. OR...

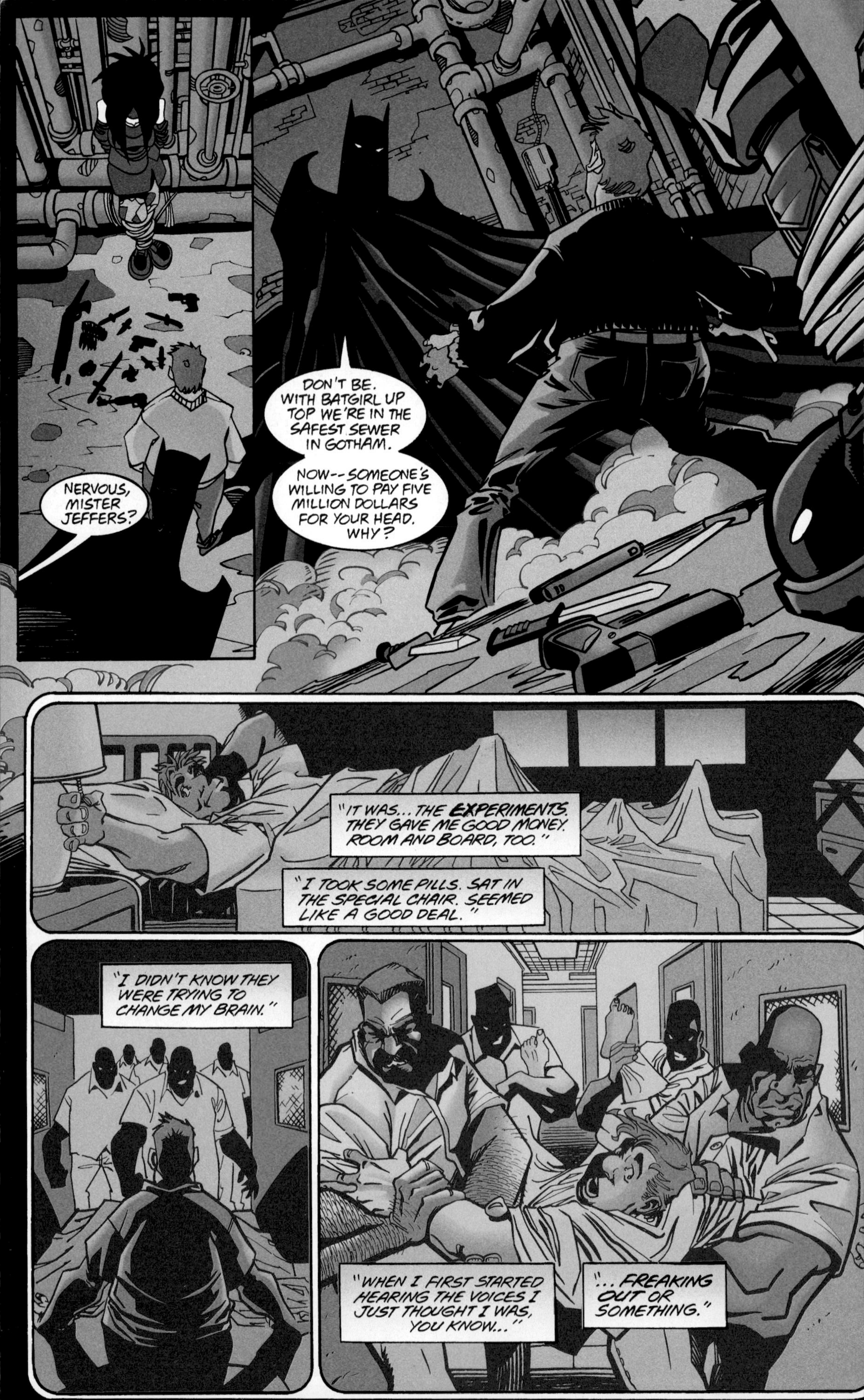
NERVOUS, MISTER JEFFERS?
DON'T BE. WITH BATGIRL UP TOP WE'RE IN THE SAFEST SEWER IN GOTHAM.
NOW--SOMEONE'S WILLING TO PAY FIVE MILLION DOLLARS FOR YOUR HEAD. WHY?
"IT WAS... THE EXPERIMENTS. THEY GAVE ME GOOD MONEY. ROOM AND BOARD, TOO."
"I TOOK SOME PILLS. SAT IN THE SPECIAL CHAIR. SEEMED LIKE A GOOD DEAL."
"I DIDN'T KNOW THEY WERE TRYING TO CHANGE MY BRAIN."
"WHEN I FIRST STARTED HEARING THE VOICES I JUST THOUGHT I WAS, YOU KNOW..."
"...FREAKING OUT OR SOMETHING."

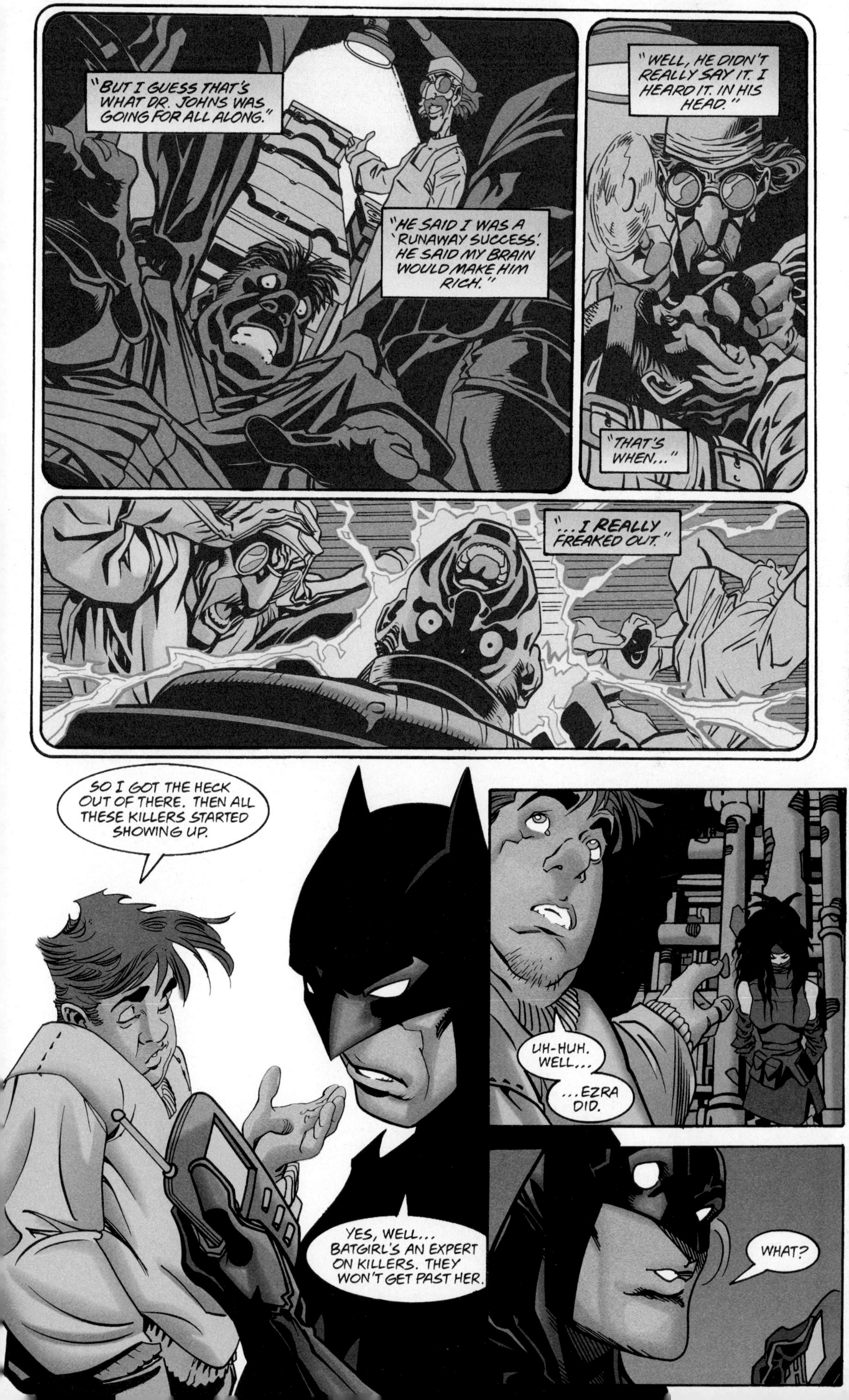
"BUT I GUESS THAT'S WHAT DR. JOHNS WAS GOING FOR ALL ALONG."
"HE SAID I WAS A 'RUNAWAY SUCCESS'. HE SAID MY BRAIN WOULD MAKE HIM RICH."
"WELL, HE DIDN'T REALLY SAY IT. I HEARD IT. IN HIS HEAD."
"THAT'S WHEN..."
"...I REALLY FREAKED OUT."
SO I GOT THE HECK OUT OF THERE. THEN ALL THESE KILLERS STARTED SHOWING UP.
YES, WELL... BATGIRL'S AN EXPERT ON KILLERS. THEY WON'T GET PAST HER.
UH-HUH. WELL...
...EZRA DID.
WHAT?

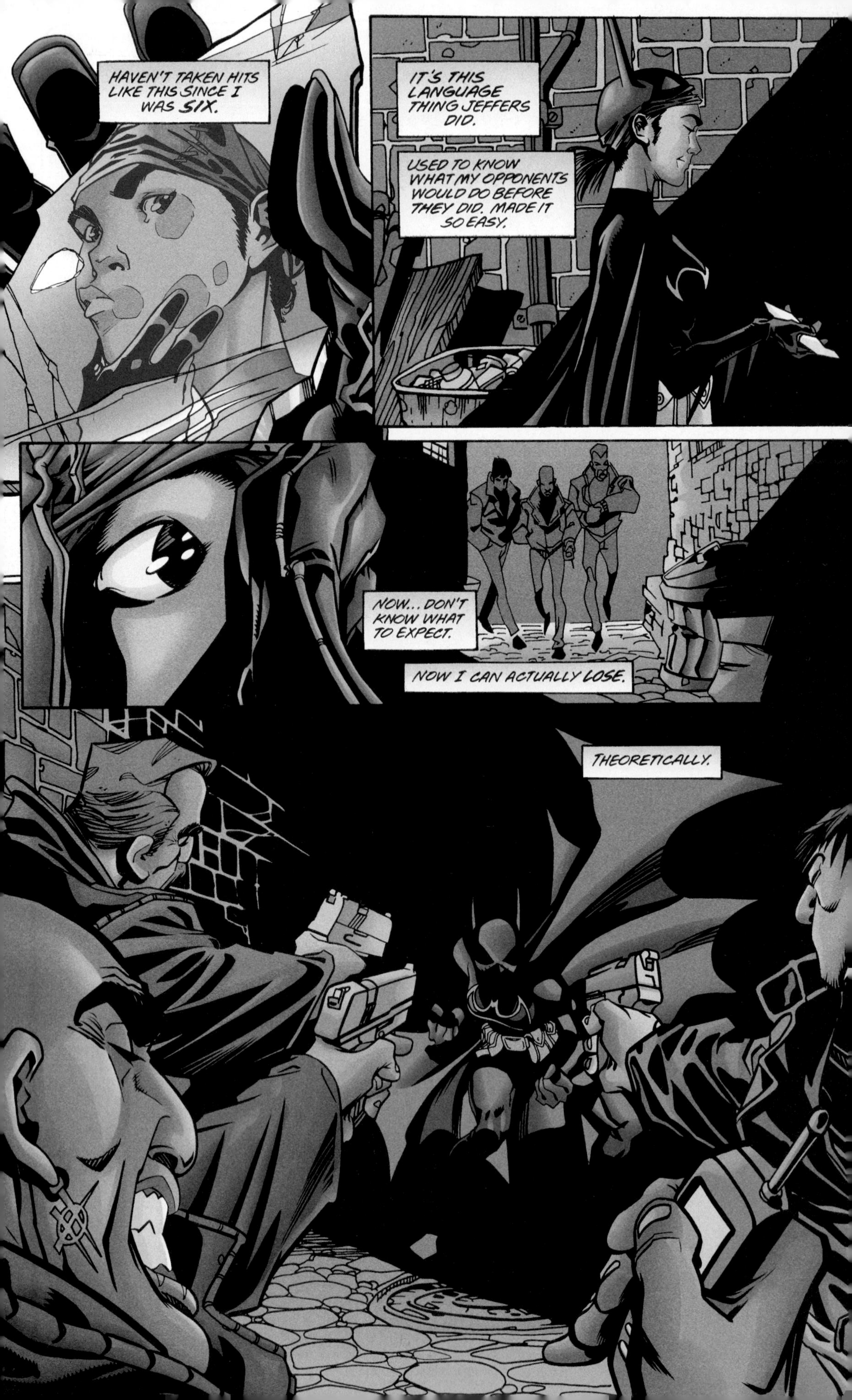
HAVEN'T TAKEN HITS LIKE THIS SINCE I WAS SIX.
IT'S THIS LANGUAGE THING JEFFERS DID.
USED TO KNOW WHAT MY OPPONENTS WOULD DO BEFORE THEY DID. MADE IT SO EASY.
NOW... DON'T KNOW WHAT TO EXPECT.
NOW I CAN ACTUALLY LOSE.
THEORETICALLY.

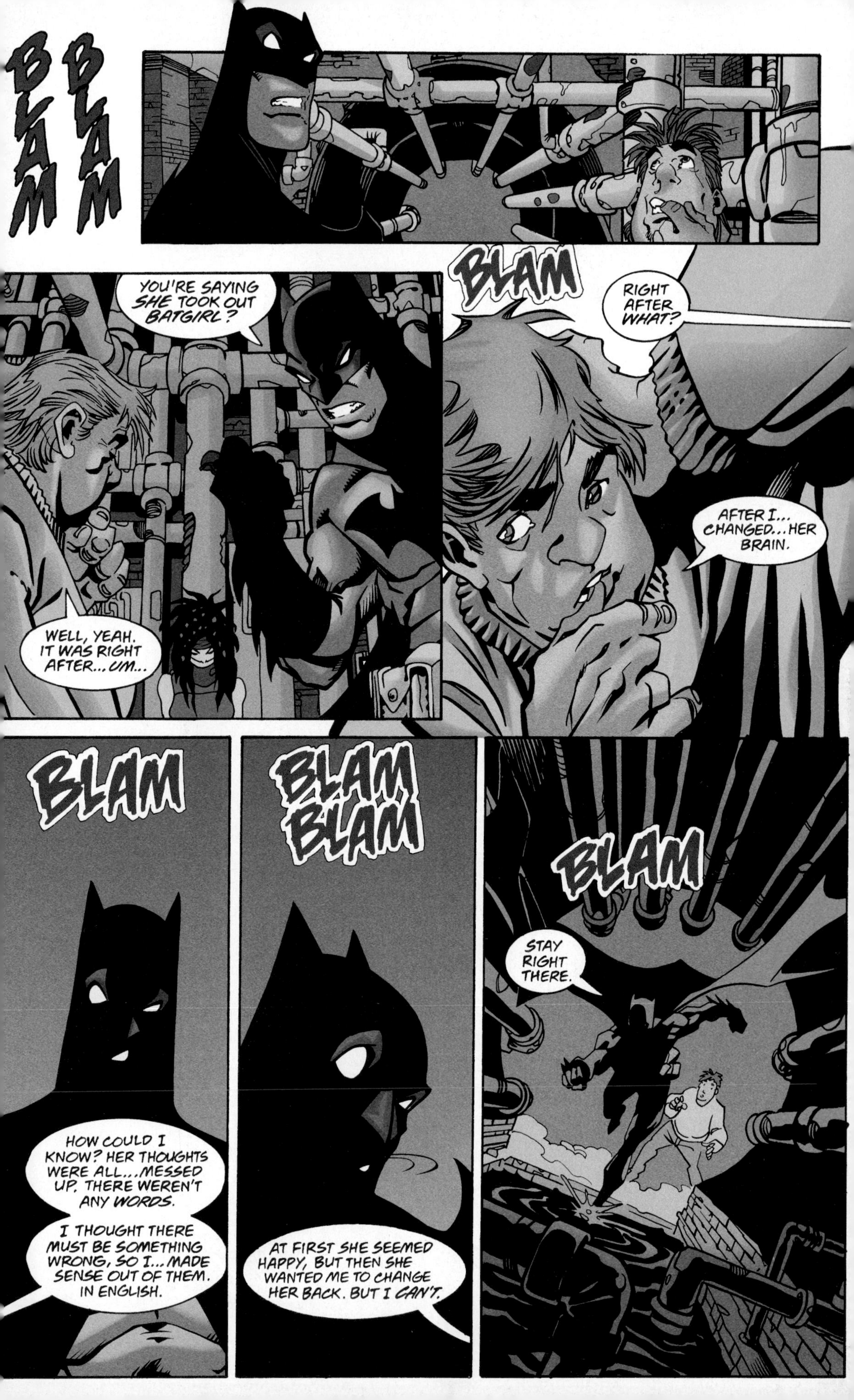
BLAM BLAM
YOU'RE SAYING SHE TOOK OUT BATGIRL?
WELL, YEAH. IT WAS RIGHT AFTER... UM...
BLAM
RIGHT AFTER WHAT?
AFTER I... CHANGED... HER BRAIN.
BLAM
HOW COULD I KNOW? HER THOUGHTS WERE ALL... MESSED UP. THERE WEREN'T ANY WORDS.
I THOUGHT THERE MUST BE SOMETHING WRONG, SO I... MADE SENSE OUT OF THEM. IN ENGLISH.
BLAM BLAM
AT FIRST SHE SEEMED HAPPY, BUT THEN SHE WANTED ME TO CHANGE HER BACK. BUT I CAN'T.
BLAM
STAY RIGHT THERE.

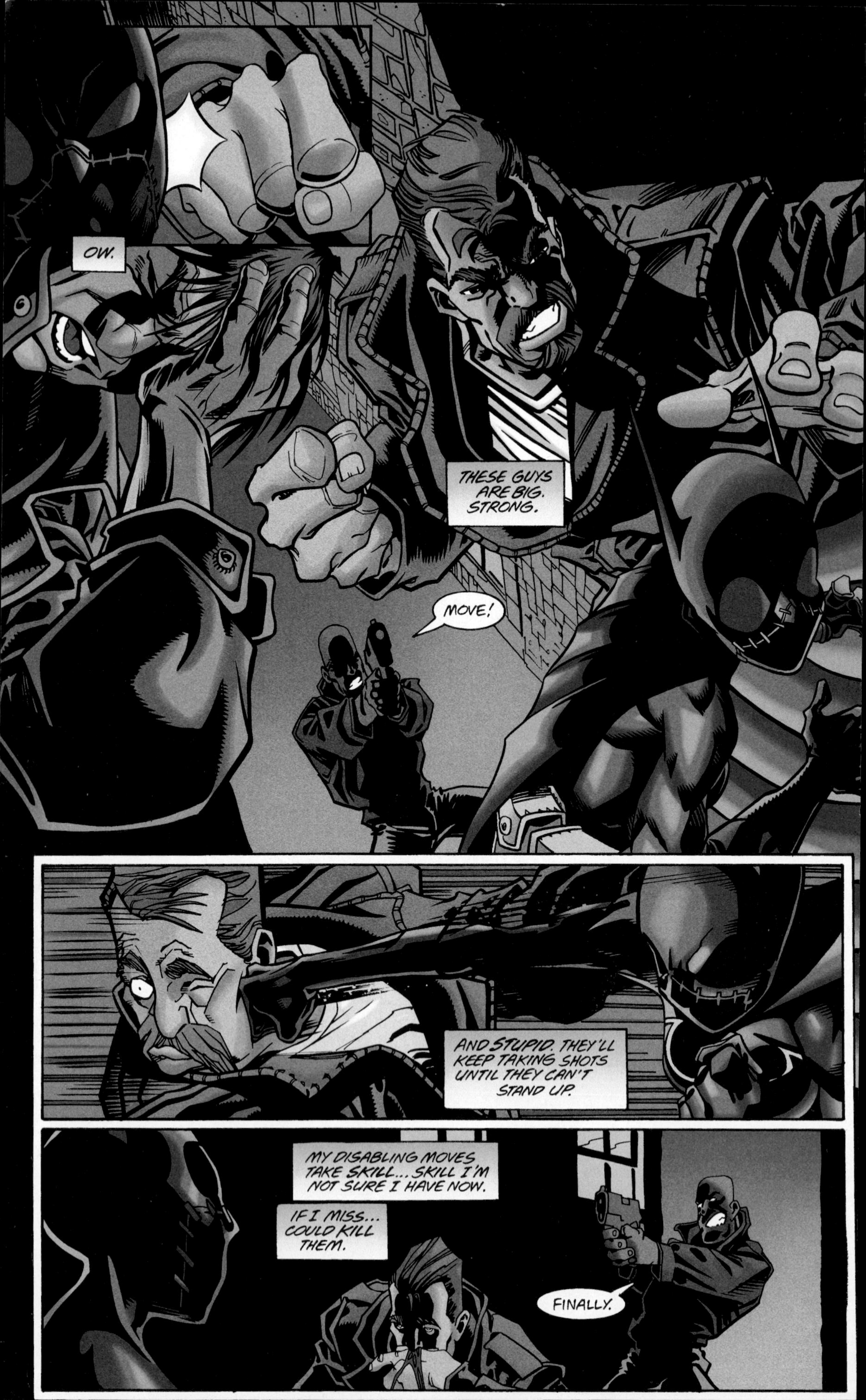
OW.
THESE GUYS ARE BIG. STRONG.
MOVE!
AND STUPID. THEY'LL KEEP TAKING SHOTS UNTIL THEY CAN'T STAND UP.
MY DISABLING MOVES TAKE SKILL... SKILL I'M NOT SURE I HAVE NOW.
IF I MISS... COULD KILL THEM.
FINALLY.

NO! YOU STUPID--
I DON'T WANT TO START CRUSHING BONES.
WHY DON'T YOU JUST STAY DOWN?
BLAM
URK?

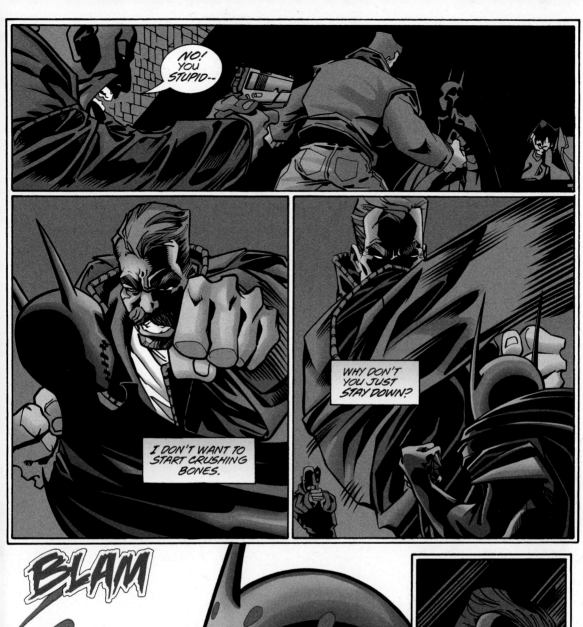

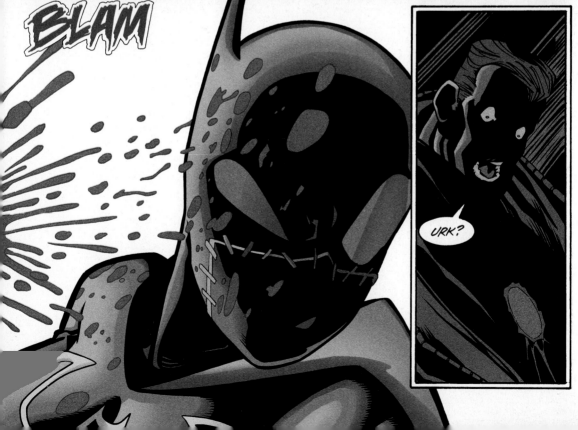

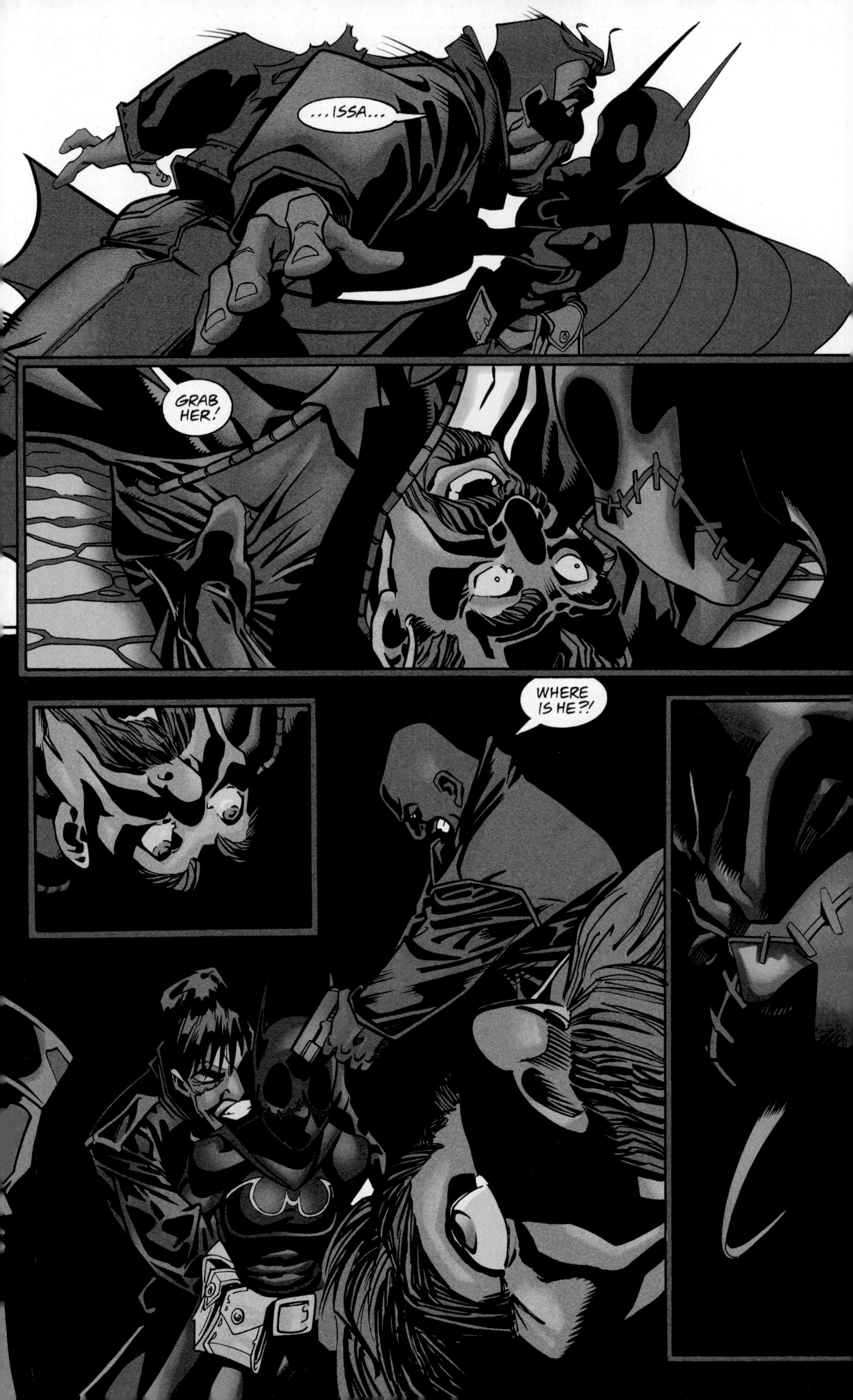
...ISSA...
GRAB HER!
WHERE IS HE?!

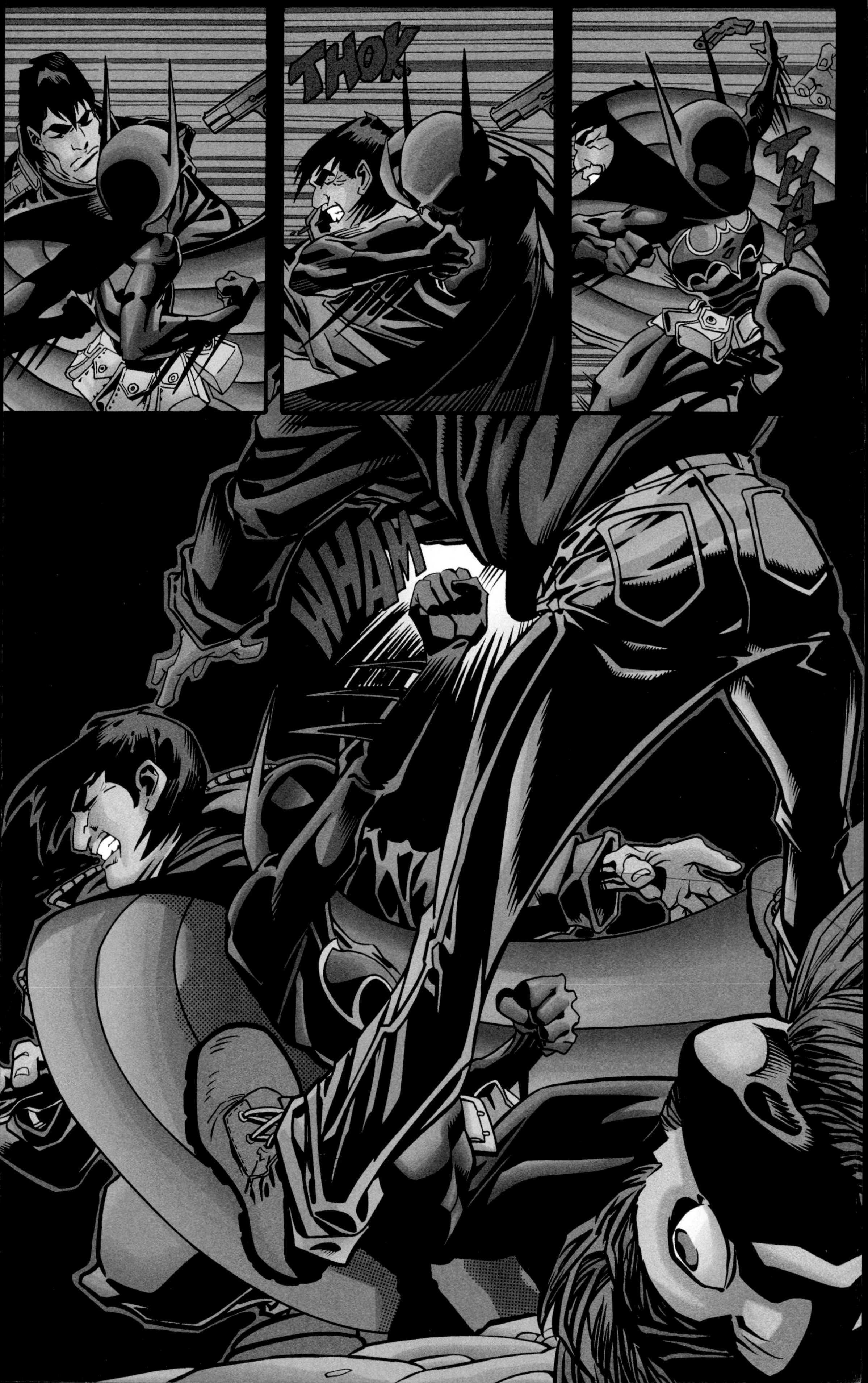
THOK
THAP
WHAM

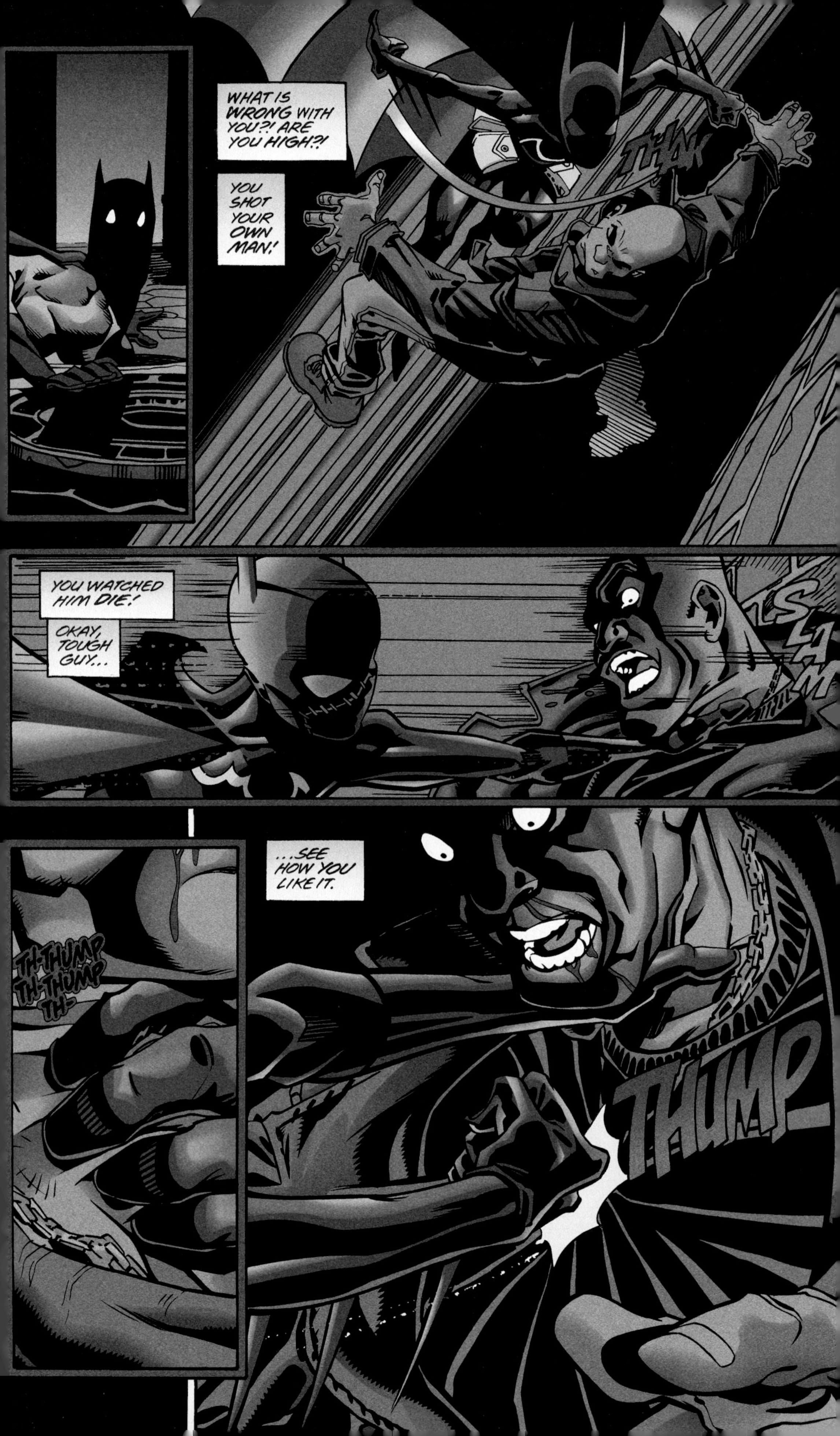

WHAT IS WRONG WITH YOU?! ARE YOU HIGH?!
YOU SHOT YOUR OWN MAN!
THAK
YOU WATCHED HIM DIE!
OKAY, TOUGH GUY...
SLAM
...SEE HOW YOU LIKE IT.
TH-THUMP TH-THUMP TH-
THUMP

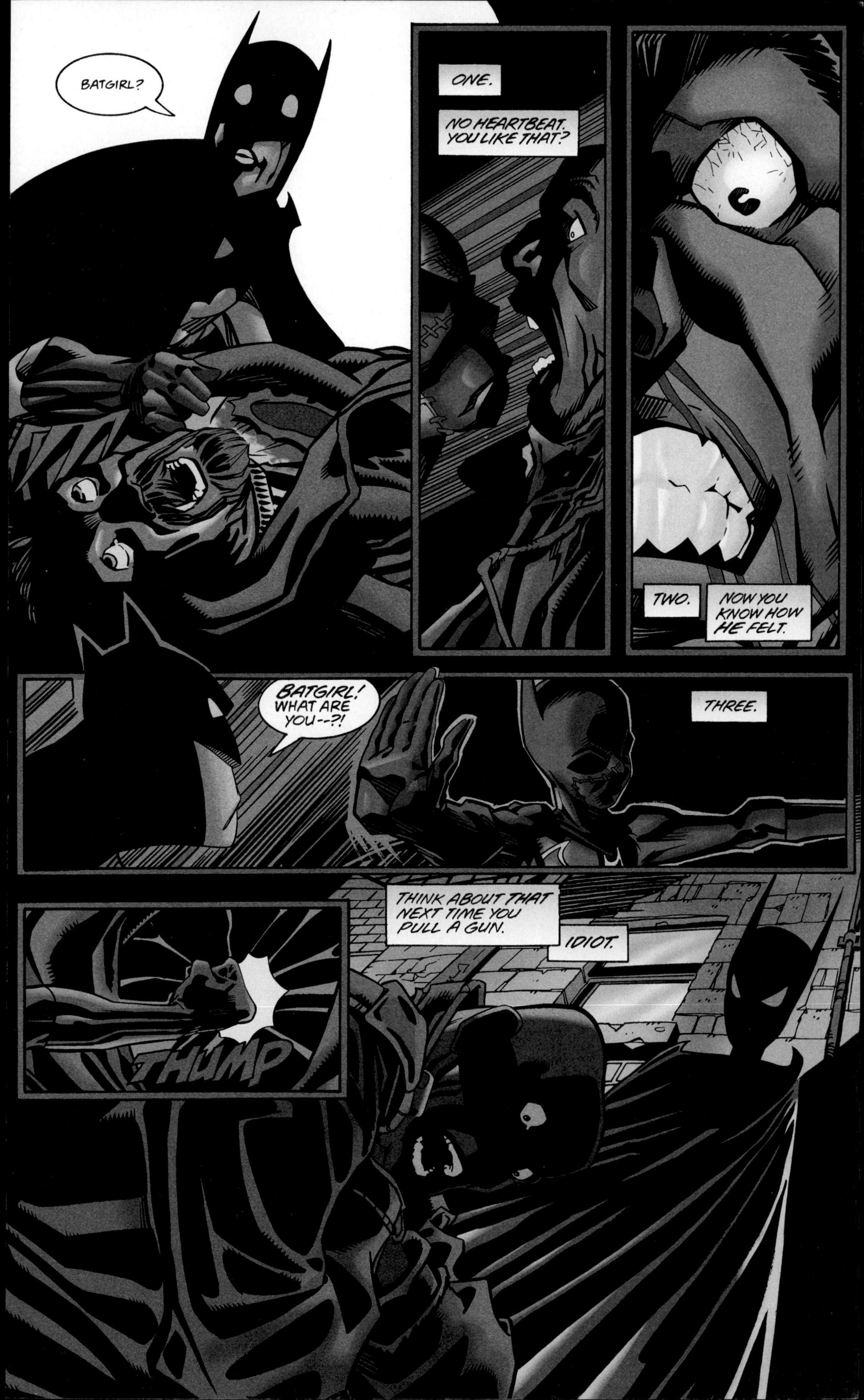
BATGIRL?
ONE.
NO HEARTBEAT. YOU LIKE THAT?
TWO.
NOW YOU KNOW HOW HE FELT.
BATGIRL! WHAT ARE YOU--?!
THREE.
THINK ABOUT THAT NEXT TIME YOU PULL A GUN.
IDIOT.
THUMP

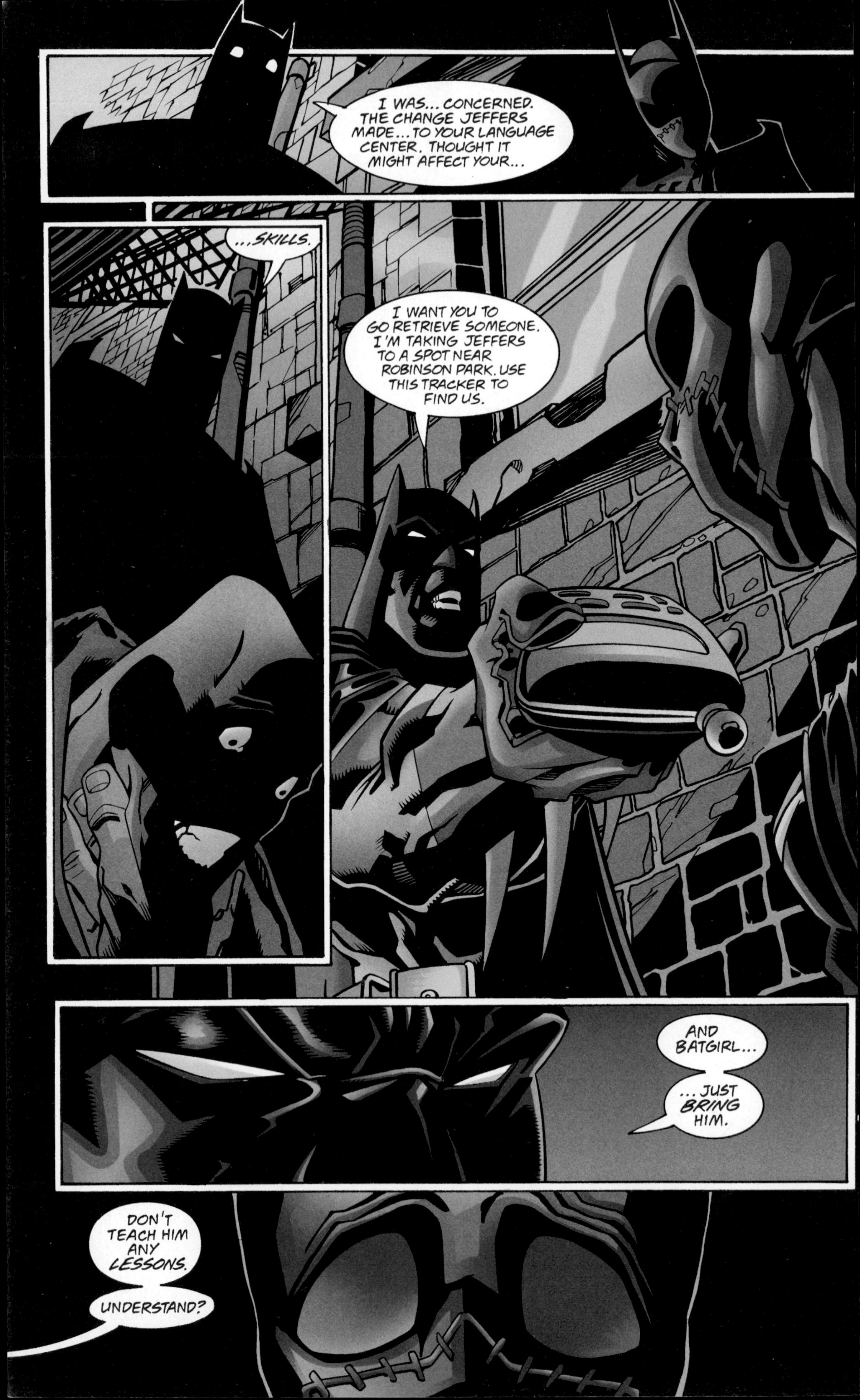
I WAS... CONCERNED. THE CHANGE JEFFERS MADE... TO YOUR LANGUAGE CENTER. THOUGHT IT MIGHT AFFECT YOUR...
...SKILLS.
I WANT YOU TO GO RETRIEVE SOMEONE. I'M TAKING JEFFERS TO A SPOT NEAR ROBINSON PARK. USE THIS TRACKER TO FIND US.
AND BATGIRL...
...JUST *BRING* HIM.
DON'T TEACH HIM ANY *LESSONS*.
UNDERSTAND?

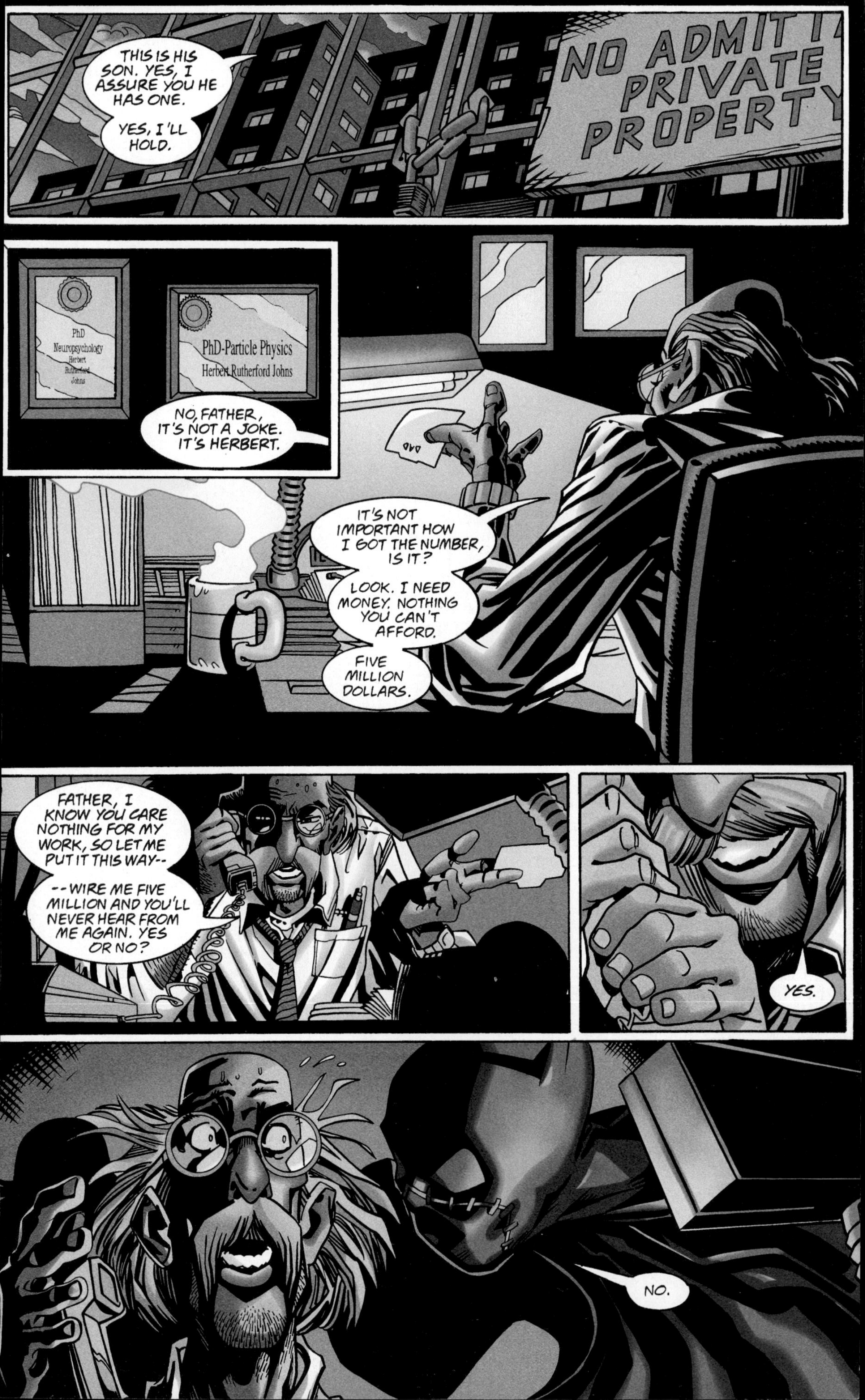

THIS IS HIS SON. YES, I ASSURE YOU HE HAS ONE.
YES, I'LL HOLD.
NO ADMIT
PRIVATE PROPERTY
PhD Neuropsychology Herbert Rutherford Johns
PhD-Particle Physics Herbert Rutherford Johns
NO, FATHER, IT'S NOT A JOKE. IT'S HERBERT.
IT'S NOT IMPORTANT HOW I GOT THE NUMBER, IS IT?
LOOK. I NEED MONEY. NOTHING YOU CAN'T AFFORD.
FIVE MILLION DOLLARS.
FATHER, I KNOW YOU CARE NOTHING FOR MY WORK, SO LET ME PUT IT THIS WAY--
--WIRE ME FIVE MILLION AND YOU'LL NEVER HEAR FROM ME AGAIN. YES OR NO?
YES.
NO.

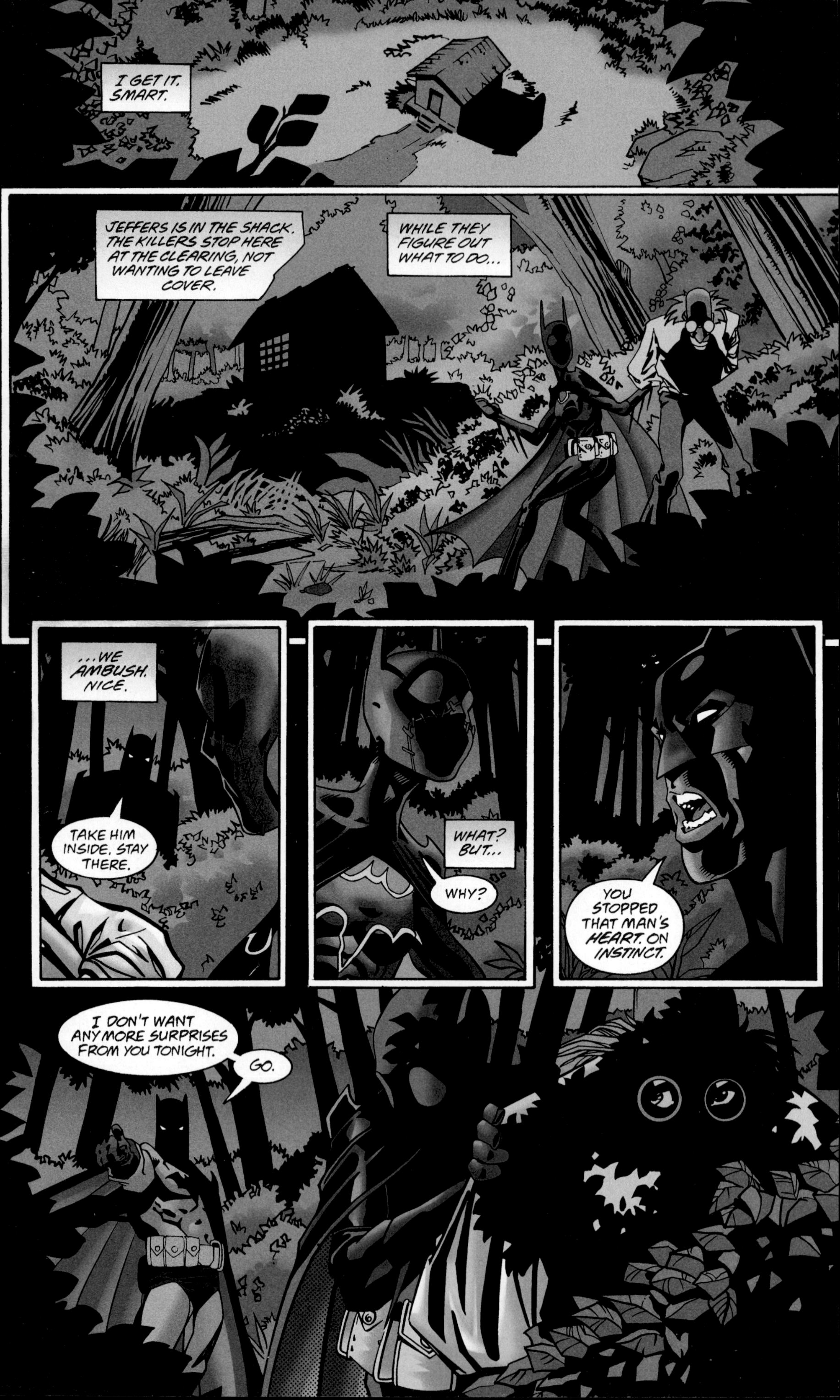
I GET IT. SMART.
JEFFERS IS IN THE SHACK. THE KILLERS STOP HERE AT THE CLEARING, NOT WANTING TO LEAVE COVER.
WHILE THEY FIGURE OUT WHAT TO DO...
...WE AMBUSH. NICE.
TAKE HIM INSIDE, STAY THERE.
WHAT? BUT...
WHY?
YOU STOPPED THAT MAN'S HEART. ON INSTINCT.
I DON'T WANT ANY MORE SURPRISES FROM YOU TONIGHT.
GO.

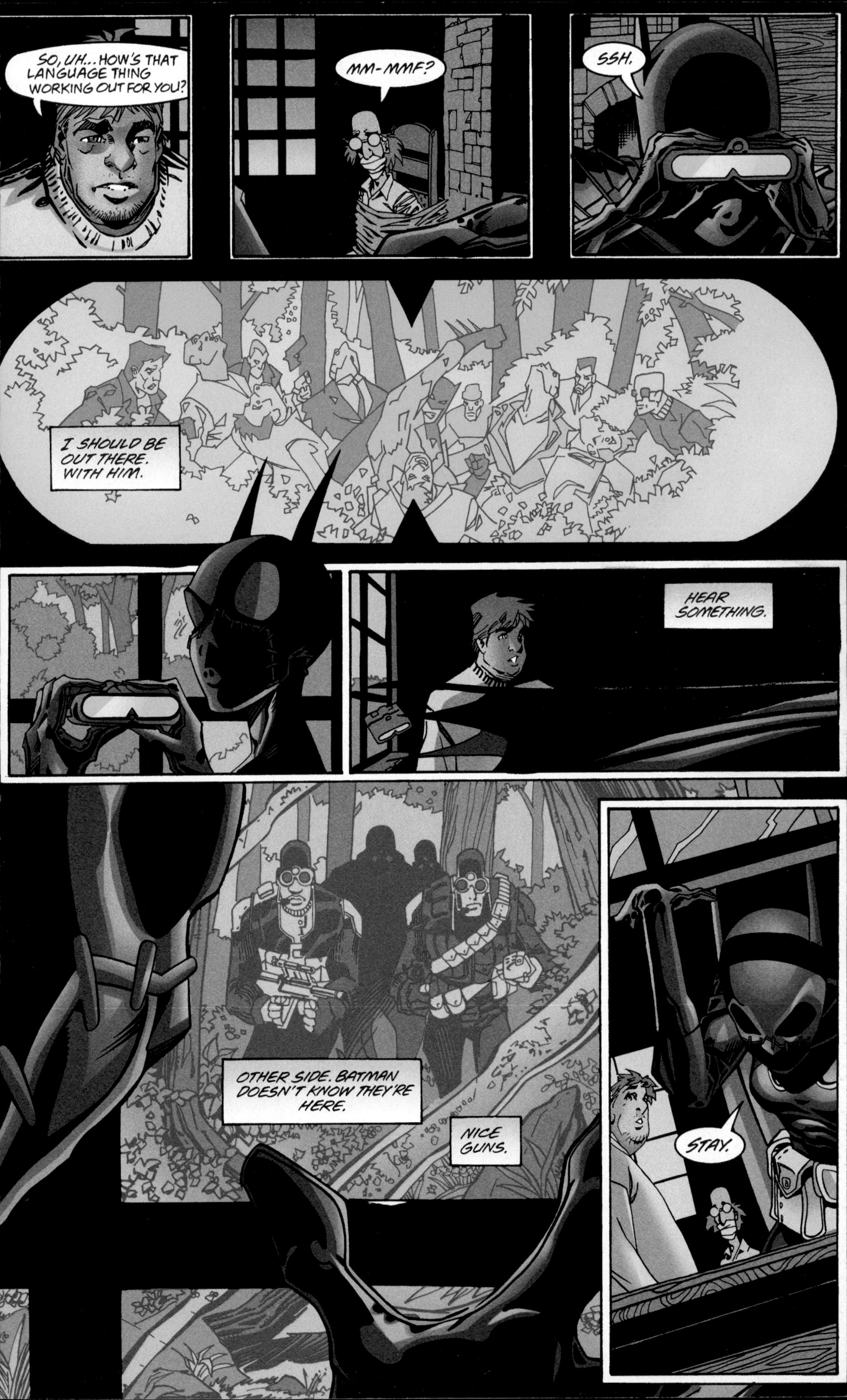
SO, UH... HOW'S THAT LANGUAGE THING WORKING OUT FOR YOU?
MM-MMF?
SSH.
I SHOULD BE OUT THERE. WITH HIM.
HEAR SOMETHING.
OTHER SIDE. BATMAN DOESN'T KNOW THEY'RE HERE.
NICE GUNS.
STAY.

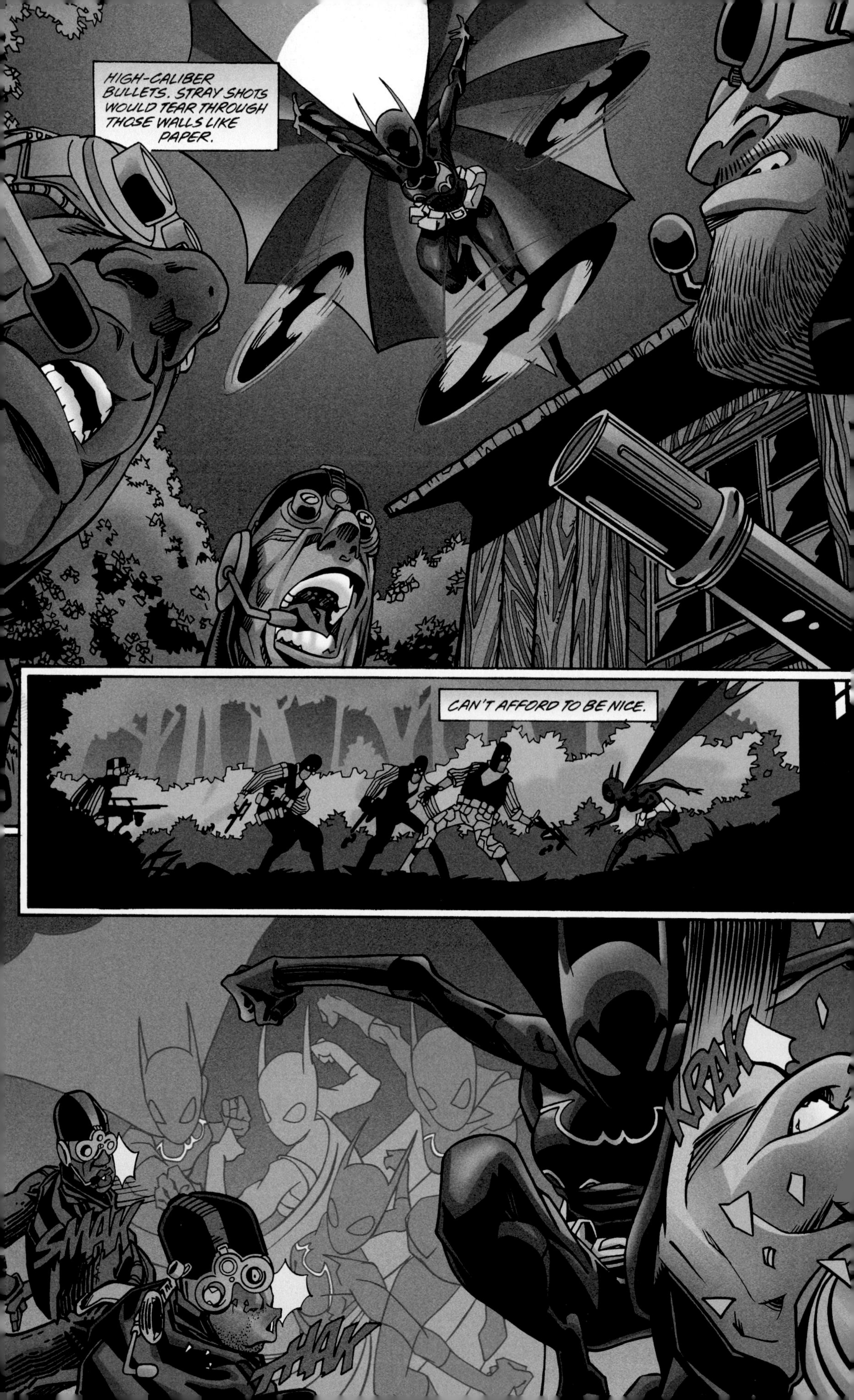

HIGH-CALIBER BULLETS. STRAY SHOTS WOULD TEAR THROUGH THOSE WALLS LIKE PAPER.
CAN'T AFFORD TO BE NICE.
KRAK
SMAK
THAK

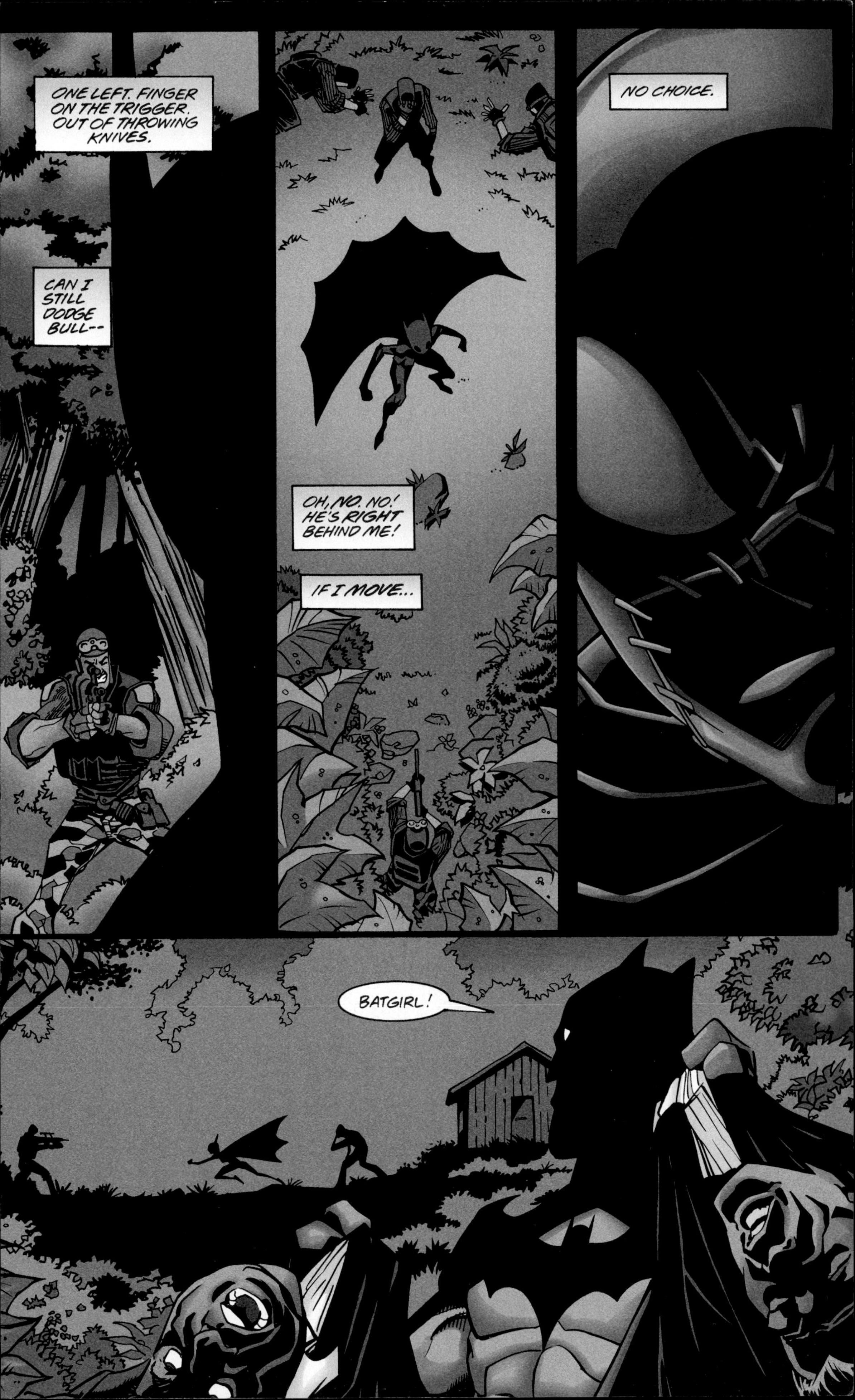
ONE LEFT. FINGER ON THE TRIGGER. OUT OF THROWING KNIVES.
CAN I STILL DODGE BULL--
OH, NO. NO! HE'S RIGHT BEHIND ME!
IF I MOVE...
NO CHOICE.
BATGIRL!

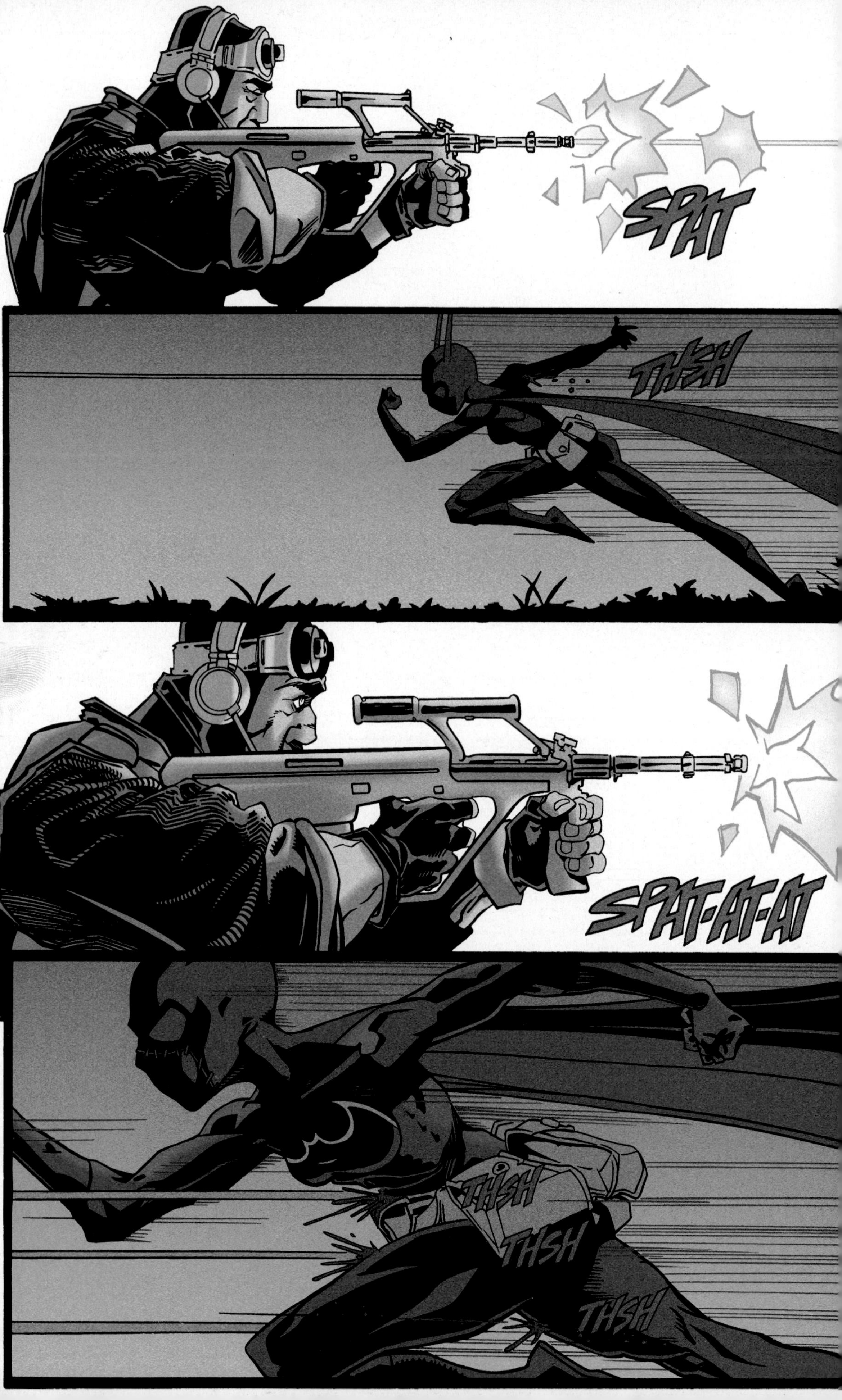
SPAT
THSH
SPAT-AT-AT
THSH
THSH
THSH

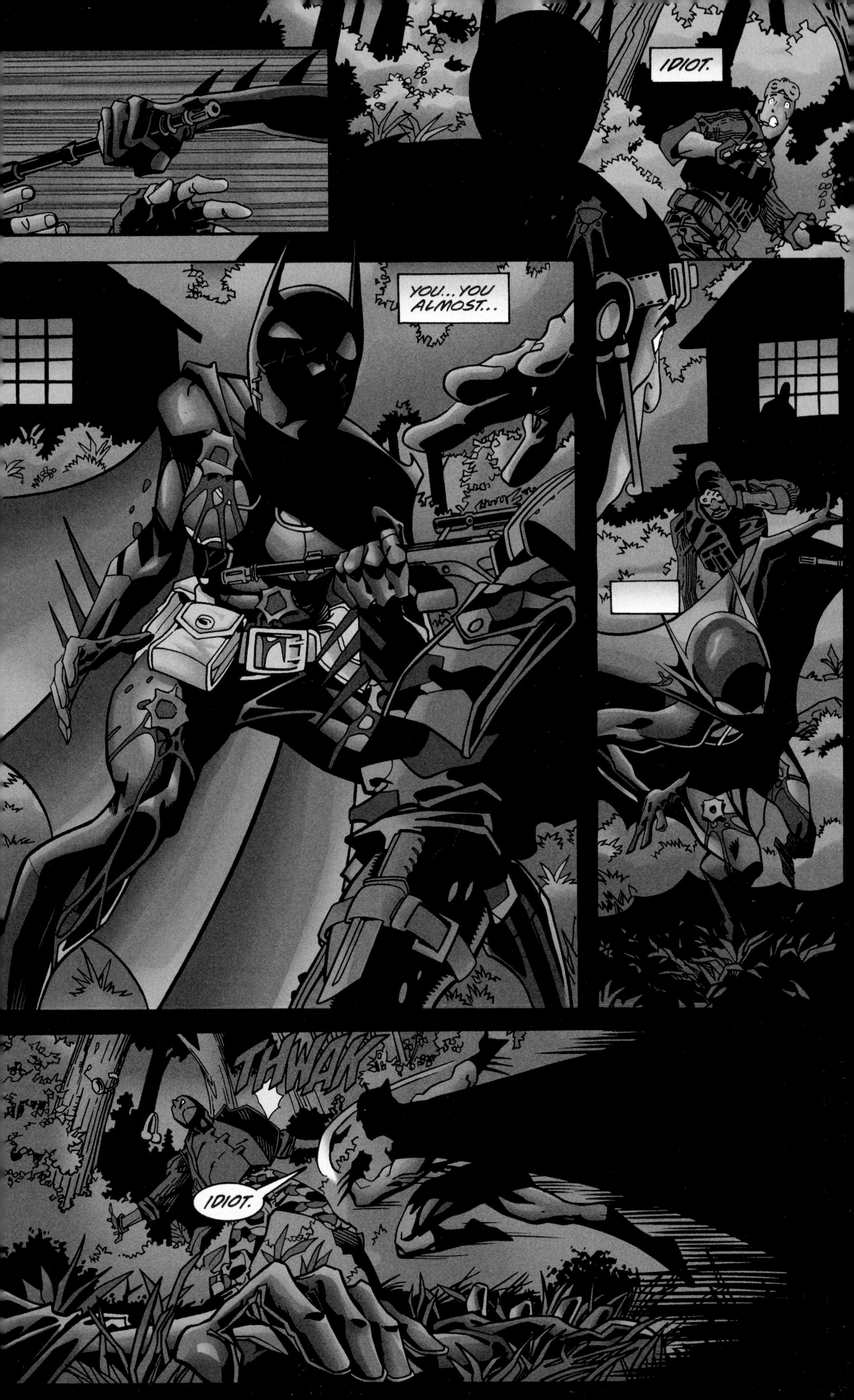
IDIOT.
YOU...YOU ALMOST...
THWAK
IDIOT.

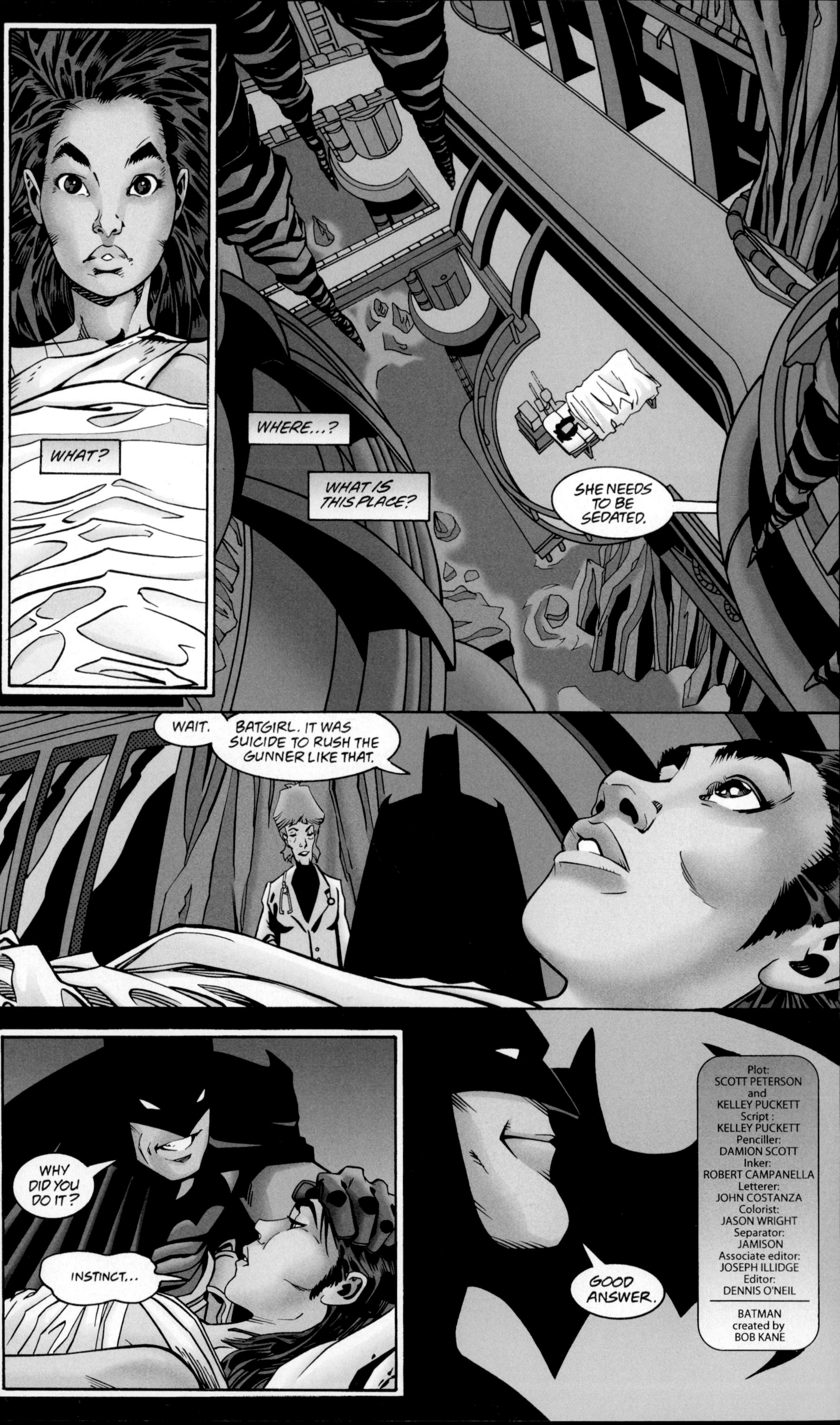
WHAT?
WHERE...?
WHAT IS THIS PLACE?
SHE NEEDS TO BE SEDATED.
WAIT.
BATGIRL. IT WAS SUICIDE TO RUSH THE GUNNER LIKE THAT.
WHY DID YOU DO IT?
INSTINCT...
GOOD ANSWER.
Plot: SCOTT PETERSON and KELLEY PUCKETT Script : KELLEY PUCKETT Penciller: DAMION SCOTT Inker: ROBERT CAMPANELLA Letterer: JOHN COSTANZA Colorist: JASON WRIGHT Separator: JAMISON Associate editor: JOSEPH ILLIDGE Editor: DENNIS O'NEIL
BATMAN created by BOB KANE

BATGIRL #7 cover by
Damion Scott & Robert Campanella

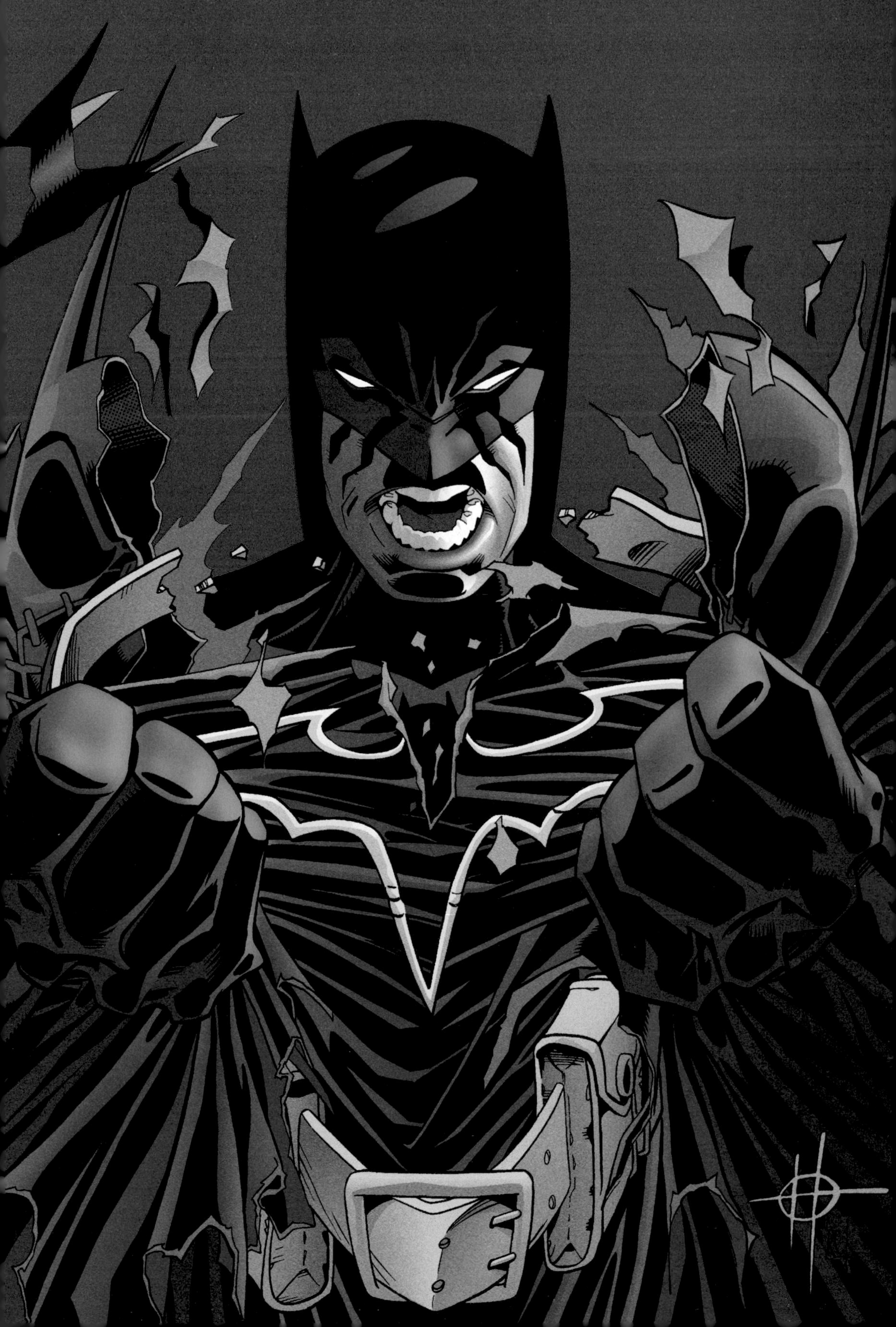

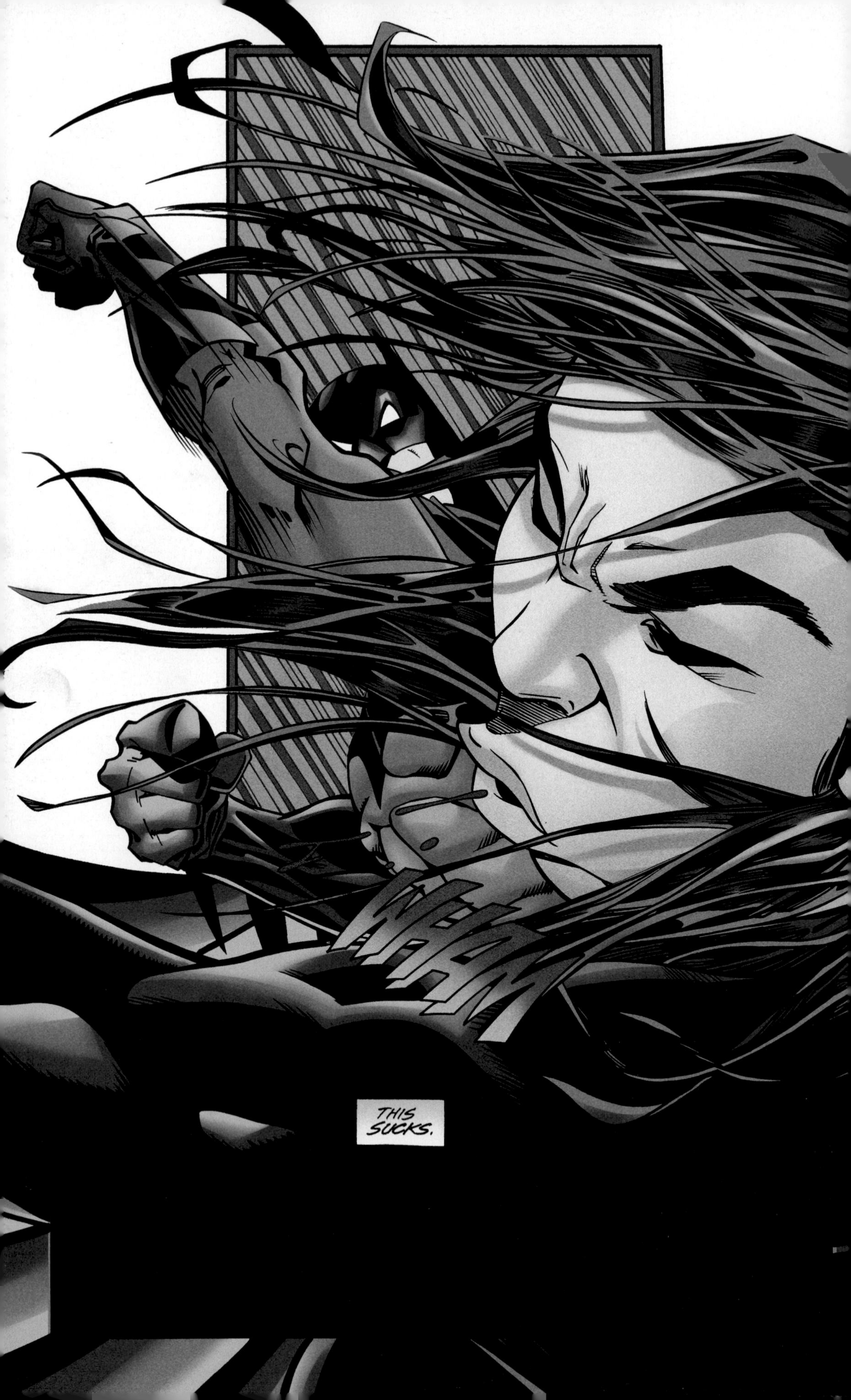
WHAM
THIS SUCKS.

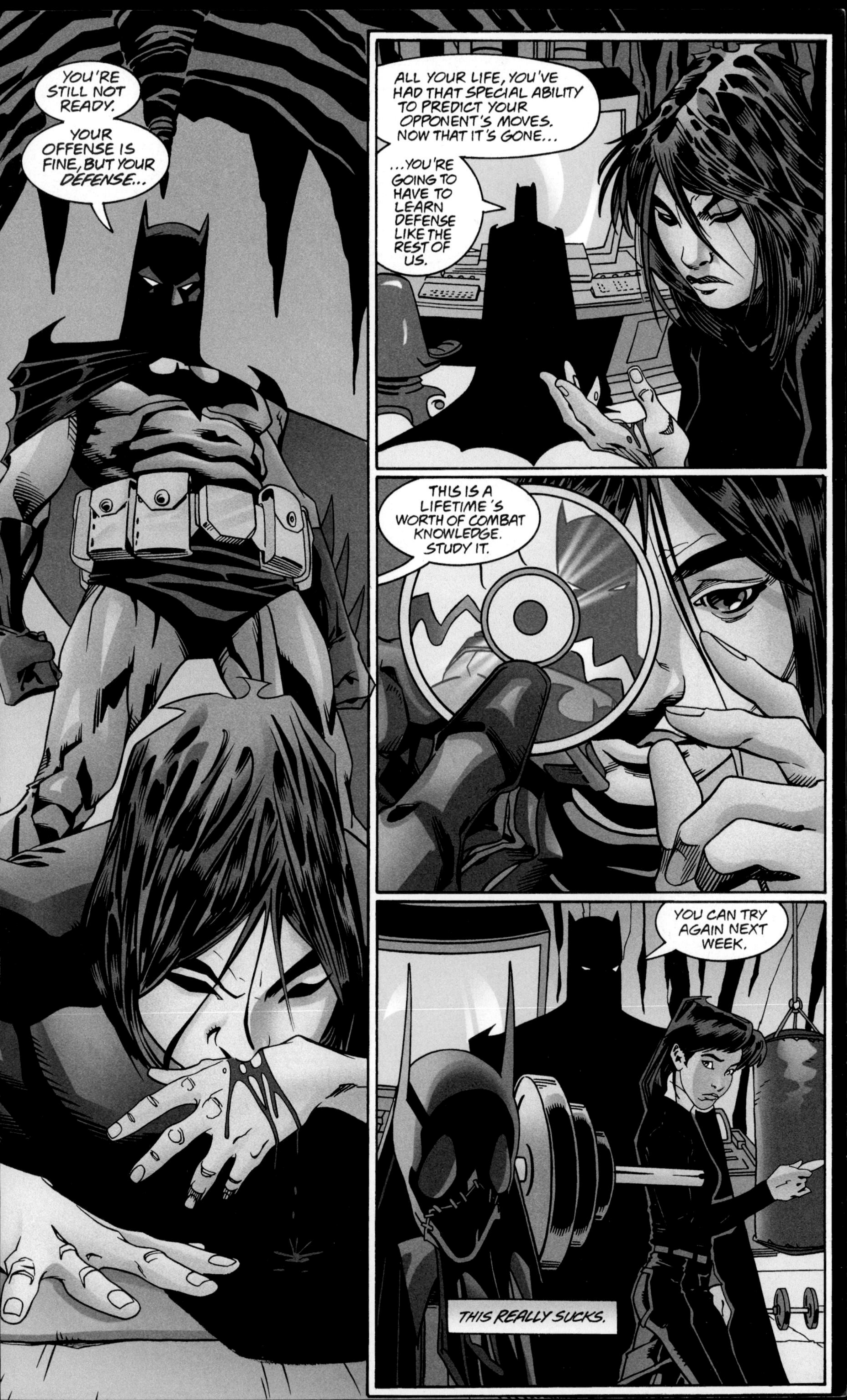
YOU'RE STILL NOT READY.
YOUR OFFENSE IS FINE, BUT YOUR DEFENSE...
ALL YOUR LIFE, YOU'VE HAD THAT SPECIAL ABILITY TO PREDICT YOUR OPPONENT'S MOVES. NOW THAT IT'S GONE...
...YOU'RE GOING TO HAVE TO LEARN DEFENSE LIKE THE REST OF US.
THIS IS A LIFETIME'S WORTH OF COMBAT KNOWLEDGE. STUDY IT.
YOU CAN TRY AGAIN NEXT WEEK.
THIS REALLY SUCKS.

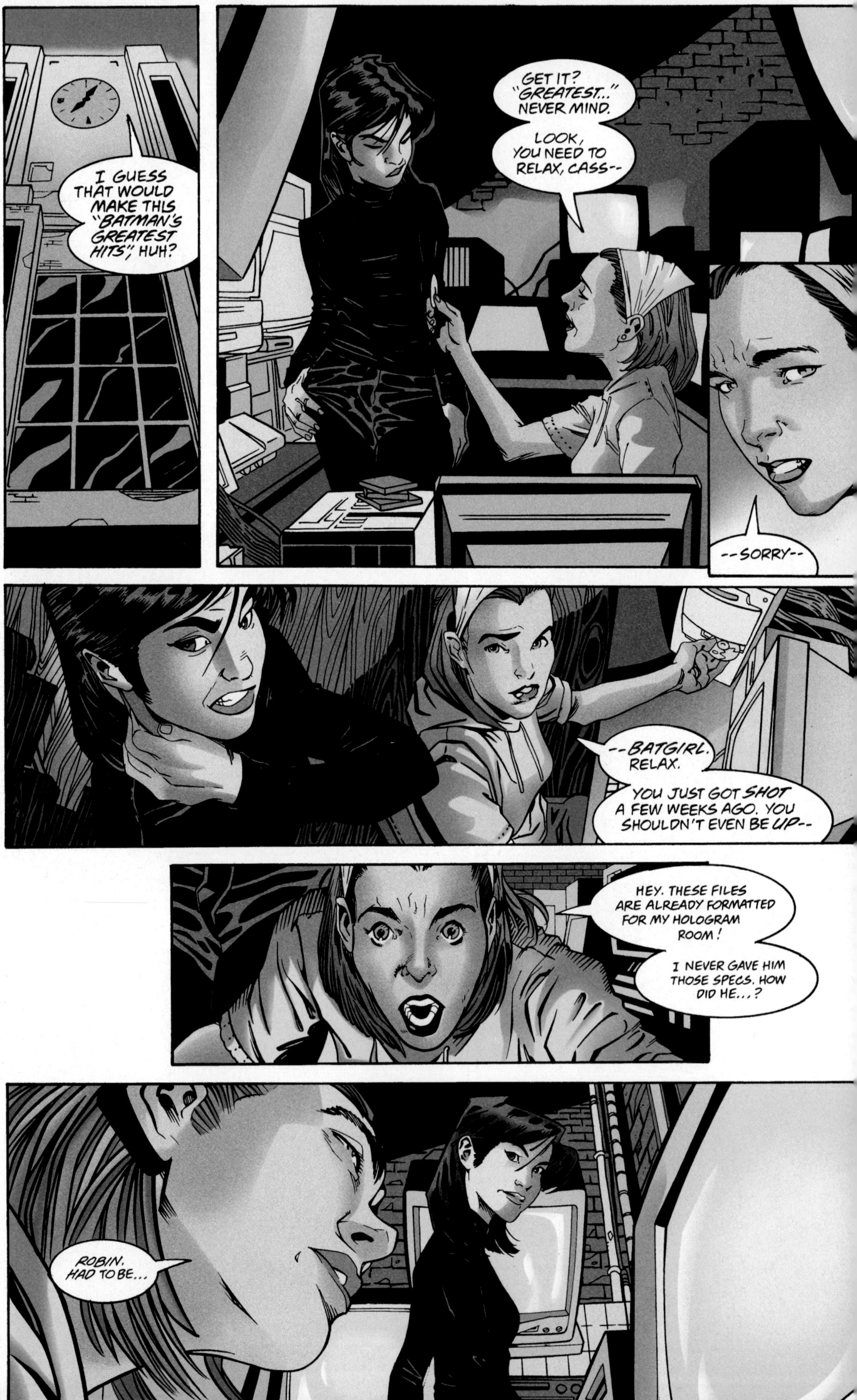
I GUESS THAT WOULD MAKE THIS "BATMAN'S GREATEST HITS," HUH?
GET IT? "GREATEST..." NEVER MIND.
LOOK, YOU NEED TO RELAX, CASS--
--SORRY--
--BATGIRL. RELAX.
YOU JUST GOT SHOT A FEW WEEKS AGO. YOU SHOULDN'T EVEN BE UP--
HEY. THESE FILES ARE ALREADY FORMATTED FOR MY HOLOGRAM ROOM!
I NEVER GAVE HIM THOSE SPECS. HOW DID HE...?
ROBIN. HAD TO BE...

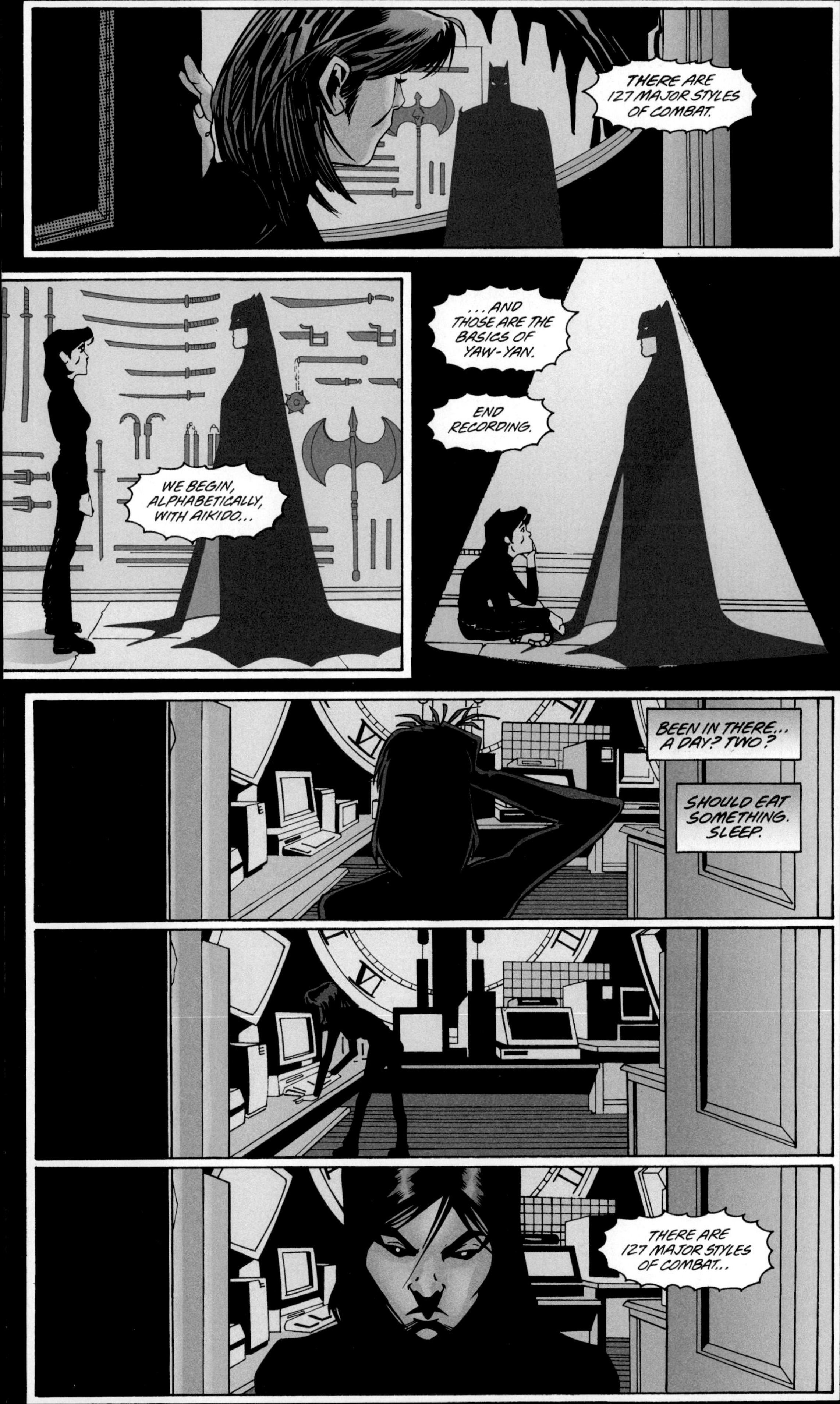
THERE ARE 127 MAJOR STYLES OF COMBAT.
WE BEGIN, ALPHABETICALLY, WITH AIKIDO...
...AND THOSE ARE THE BASICS OF YAW-YAN.
END RECORDING.
BEEN IN THERE... A DAY? TWO?
SHOULD EAT SOMETHING. SLEEP.
THERE ARE 127 MAJOR STYLES OF COMBAT...

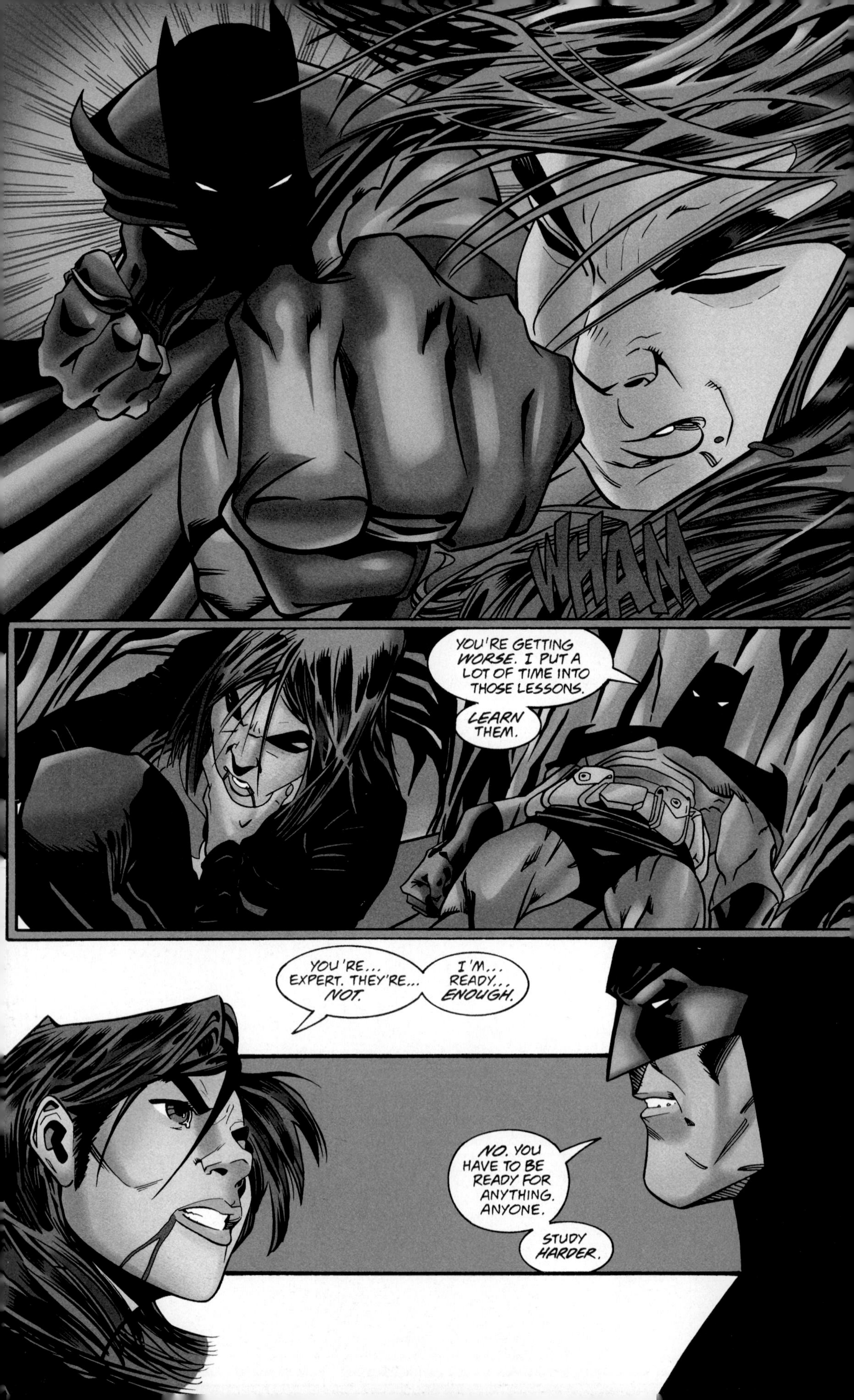
WHAM
YOU'RE GETTING WORSE. I PUT A LOT OF TIME INTO THOSE LESSONS.
LEARN THEM.
YOU'RE... EXPERT. THEY'RE... NOT.
I'M... READY... ENOUGH.
NO. YOU HAVE TO BE READY FOR ANYTHING. ANYONE.
STUDY HARDER.

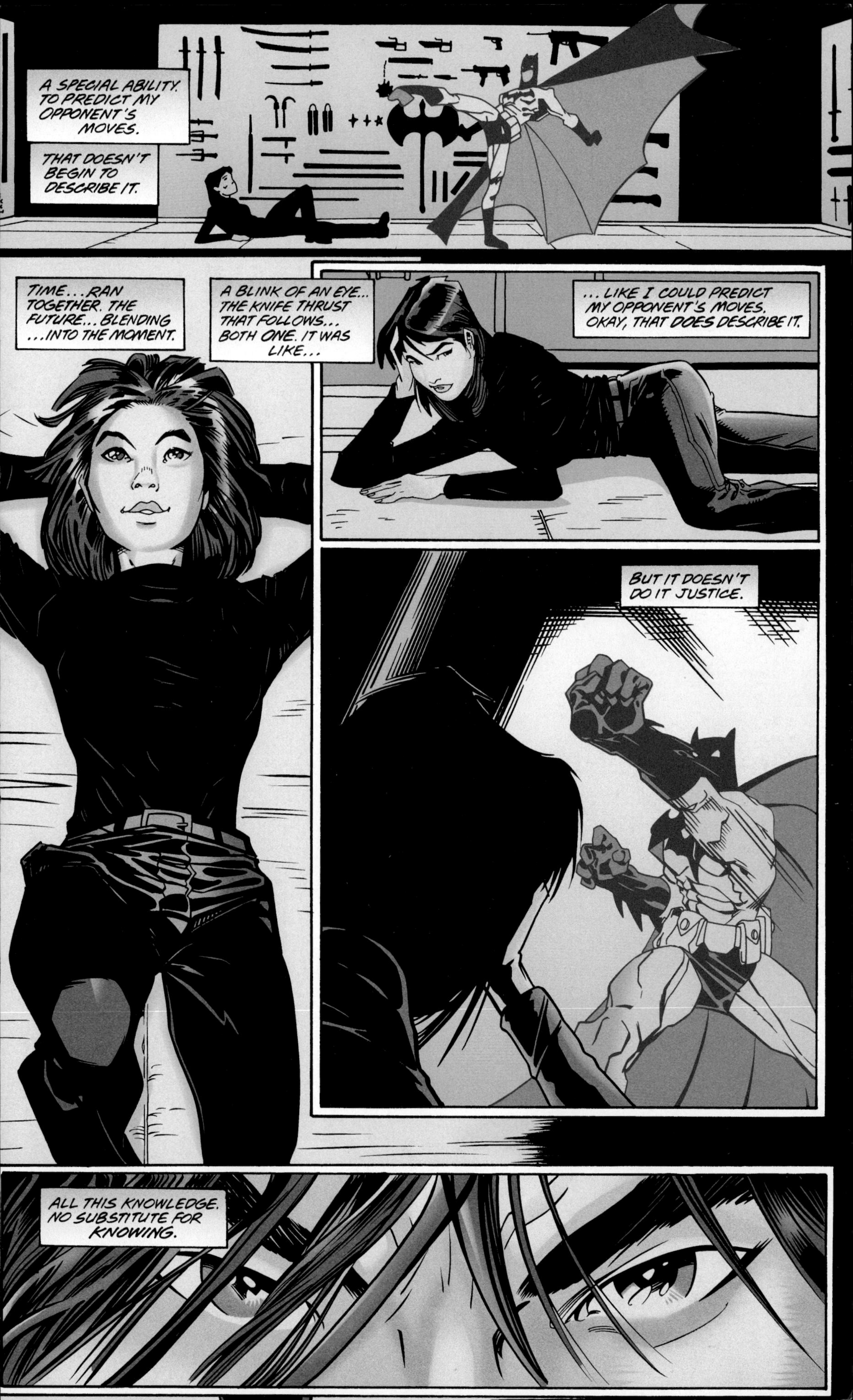
A SPECIAL ABILITY. TO PREDICT MY OPPONENT'S MOVES.
THAT DOESN'T BEGIN TO DESCRIBE IT.
TIME... RAN TOGETHER. THE FUTURE... BLENDING ...INTO THE MOMENT.
A BLINK OF AN EYE... THE KNIFE THRUST THAT FOLLOWS... BOTH ONE. IT WAS LIKE...
...LIKE I COULD PREDICT MY OPPONENT'S MOVES. OKAY, THAT DOES DESCRIBE IT.
BUT IT DOESN'T DO IT JUSTICE.
ALL THIS KNOWLEDGE. NO SUBSTITUTE FOR KNOWING.

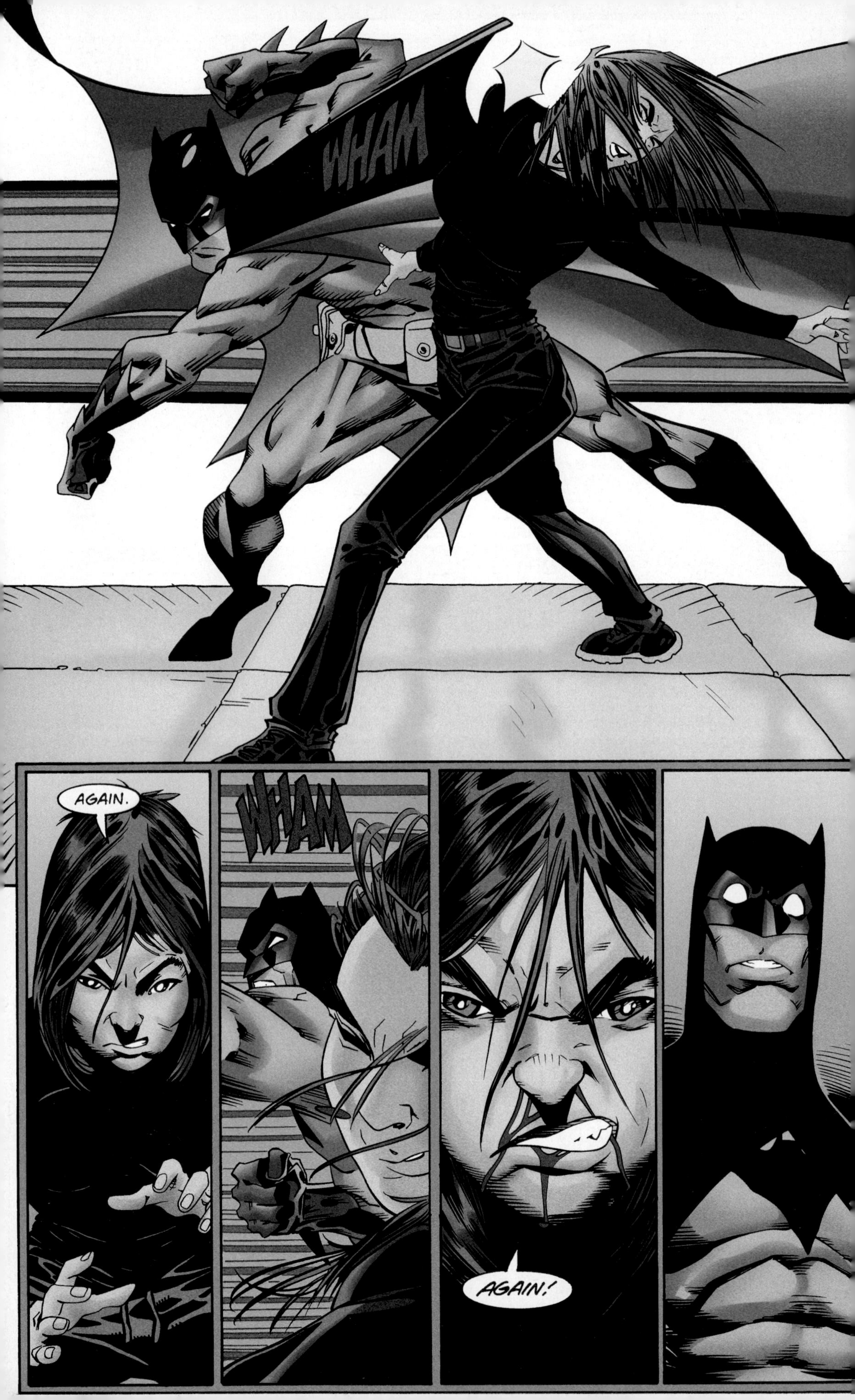
WHAM
AGAIN.
WHAM
AGAIN!

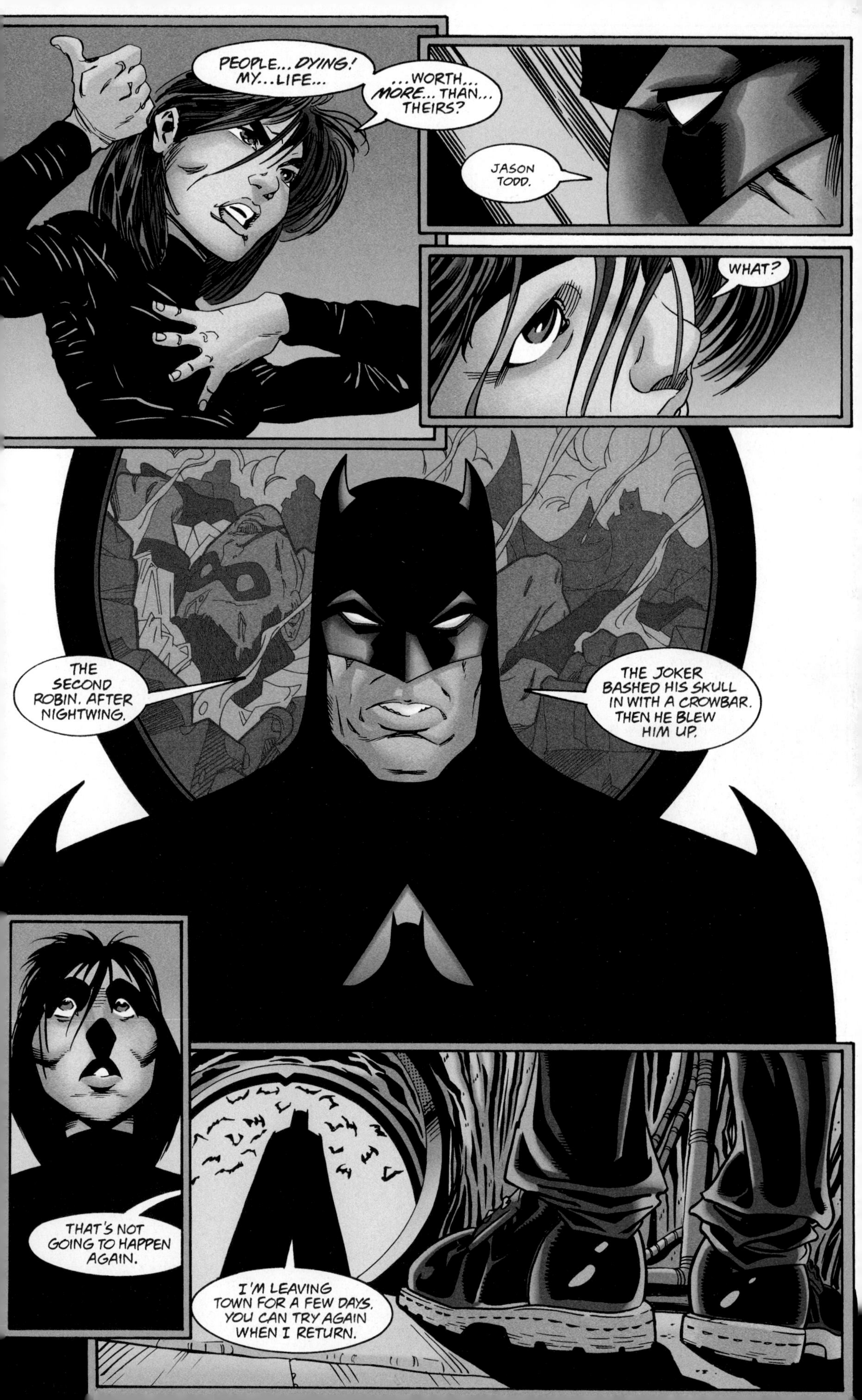
PEOPLE... DYING! MY... LIFE...
...WORTH... MORE... THAN... THEIRS?
JASON TODD.
WHAT?
THE SECOND ROBIN. AFTER NIGHTWING.
THE JOKER BASHED HIS SKULL IN WITH A CROWBAR. THEN HE BLEW HIM UP.
THAT'S NOT GOING TO HAPPEN AGAIN.
I'M LEAVING TOWN FOR A FEW DAYS. YOU CAN TRY AGAIN WHEN I RETURN.

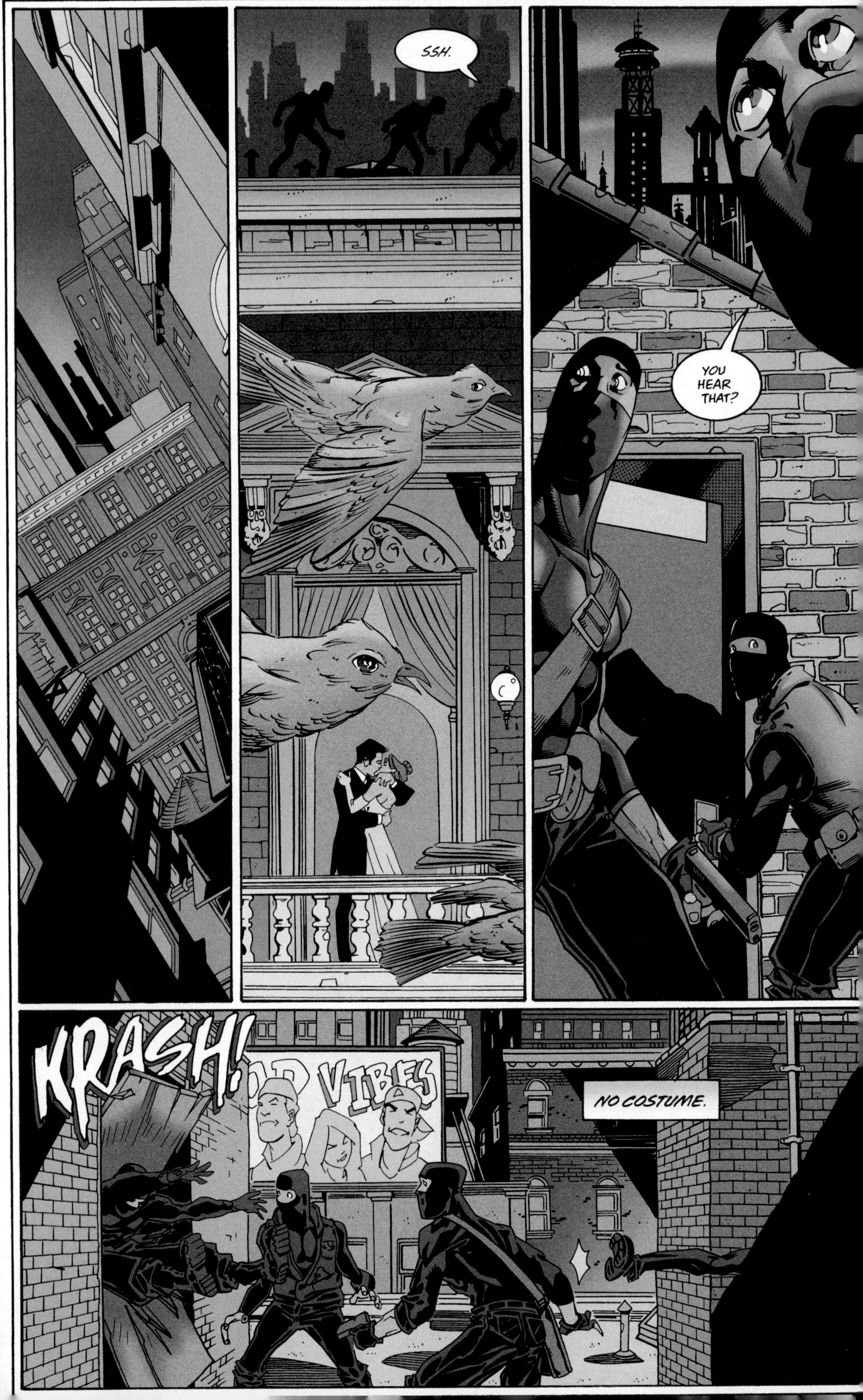
SSH.
YOU HEAR THAT?
KRASH!
NO COSTUME.

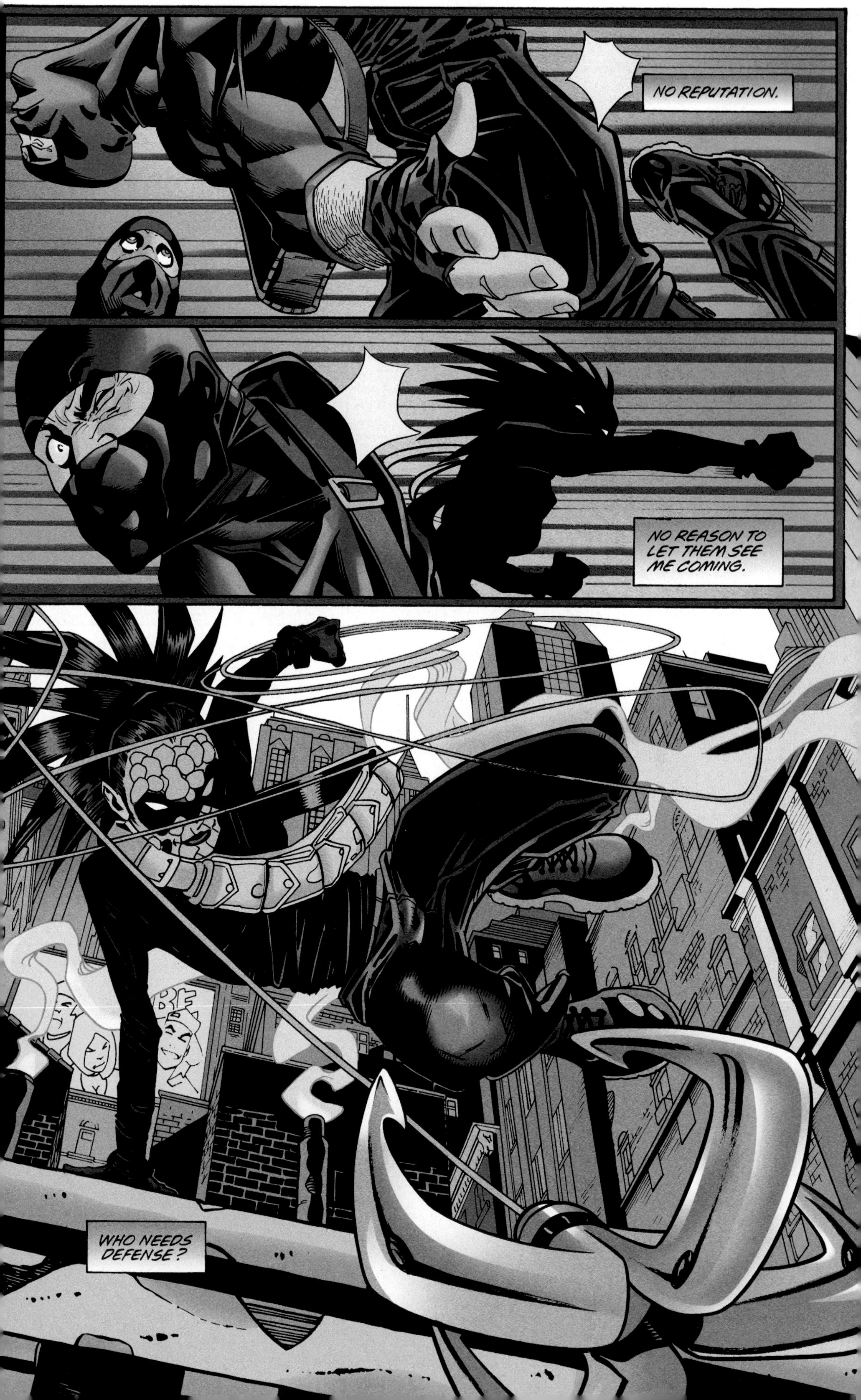
NO REPUTATION.
NO REASON TO LET THEM SEE ME COMING.
WHO NEEDS DEFENSE?

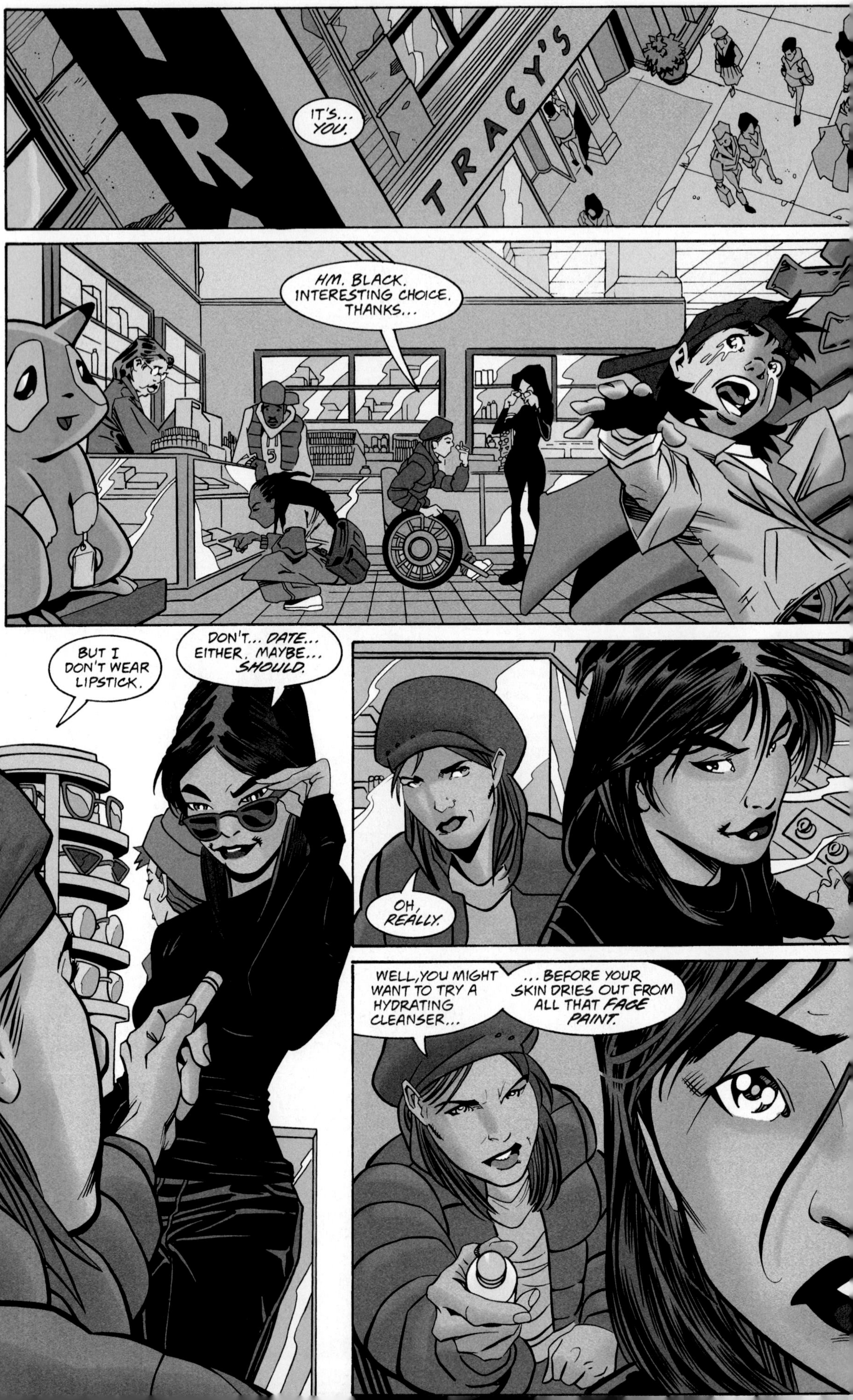
TRACY'S
IT'S... YOU.
HM. BLACK. INTERESTING CHOICE. THANKS...
BUT I DON'T WEAR LIPSTICK.
DON'T... DATE... EITHER. MAYBE... SHOULD.
OH, REALLY.
WELL, YOU MIGHT WANT TO TRY A HYDRATING CLEANSER...
... BEFORE YOUR SKIN DRIES OUT FROM ALL THAT FACE PAINT.

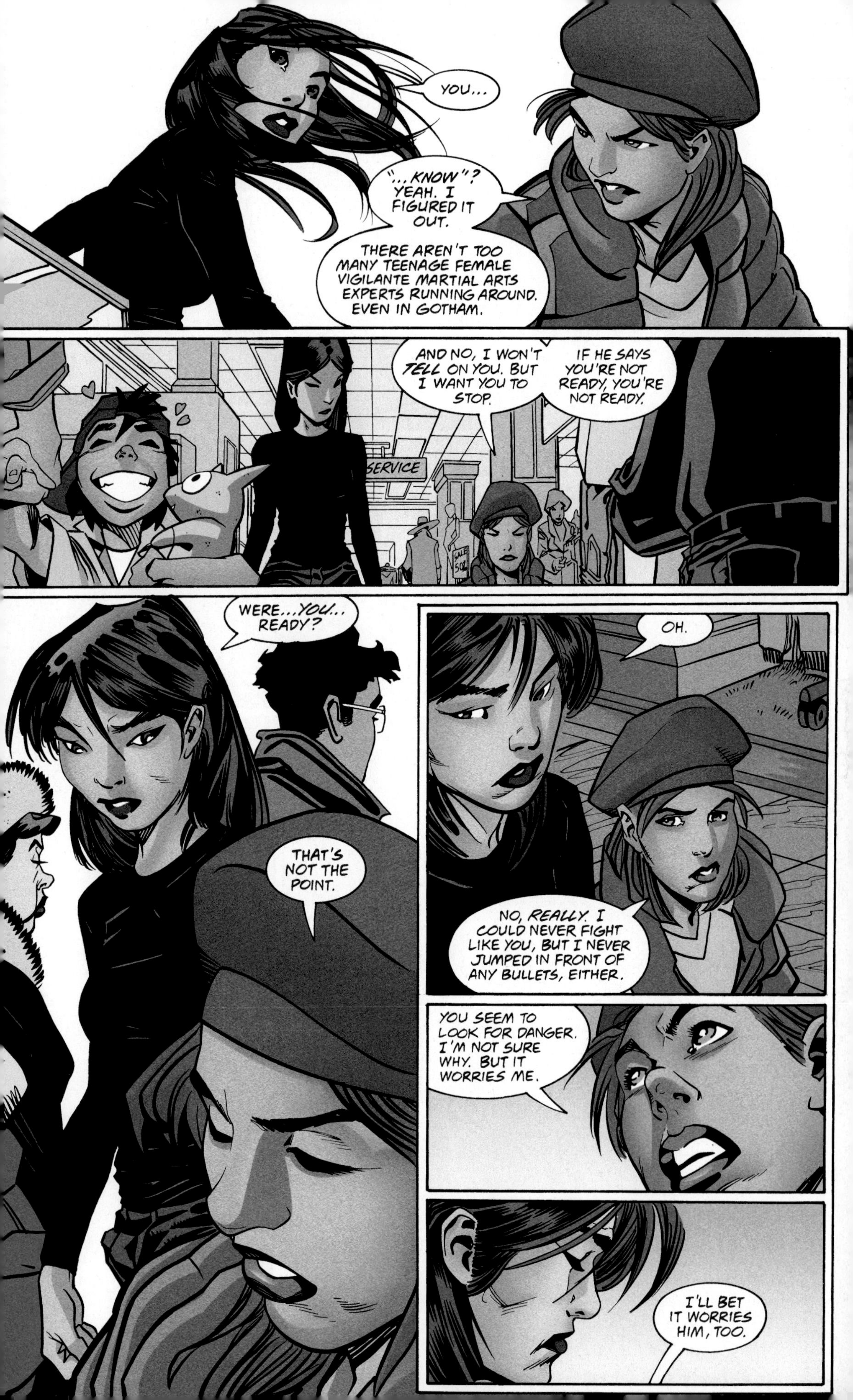
YOU...
"...KNOW"? YEAH. I FIGURED IT OUT.
THERE AREN'T TOO MANY TEENAGE FEMALE VIGILANTE MARTIAL ARTS EXPERTS RUNNING AROUND. EVEN IN GOTHAM.
AND NO, I WON'T TELL ON YOU. BUT I WANT YOU TO STOP.
IF HE SAYS YOU'RE NOT READY, YOU'RE NOT READY.
SERVICE
SALE 50%
WERE...YOU... READY?
THAT'S NOT THE POINT.
OH.
NO, REALLY. I COULD NEVER FIGHT LIKE YOU, BUT I NEVER JUMPED IN FRONT OF ANY BULLETS, EITHER.
YOU SEEM TO LOOK FOR DANGER. I'M NOT SURE WHY. BUT IT WORRIES ME.
I'LL BET IT WORRIES HIM, TOO.

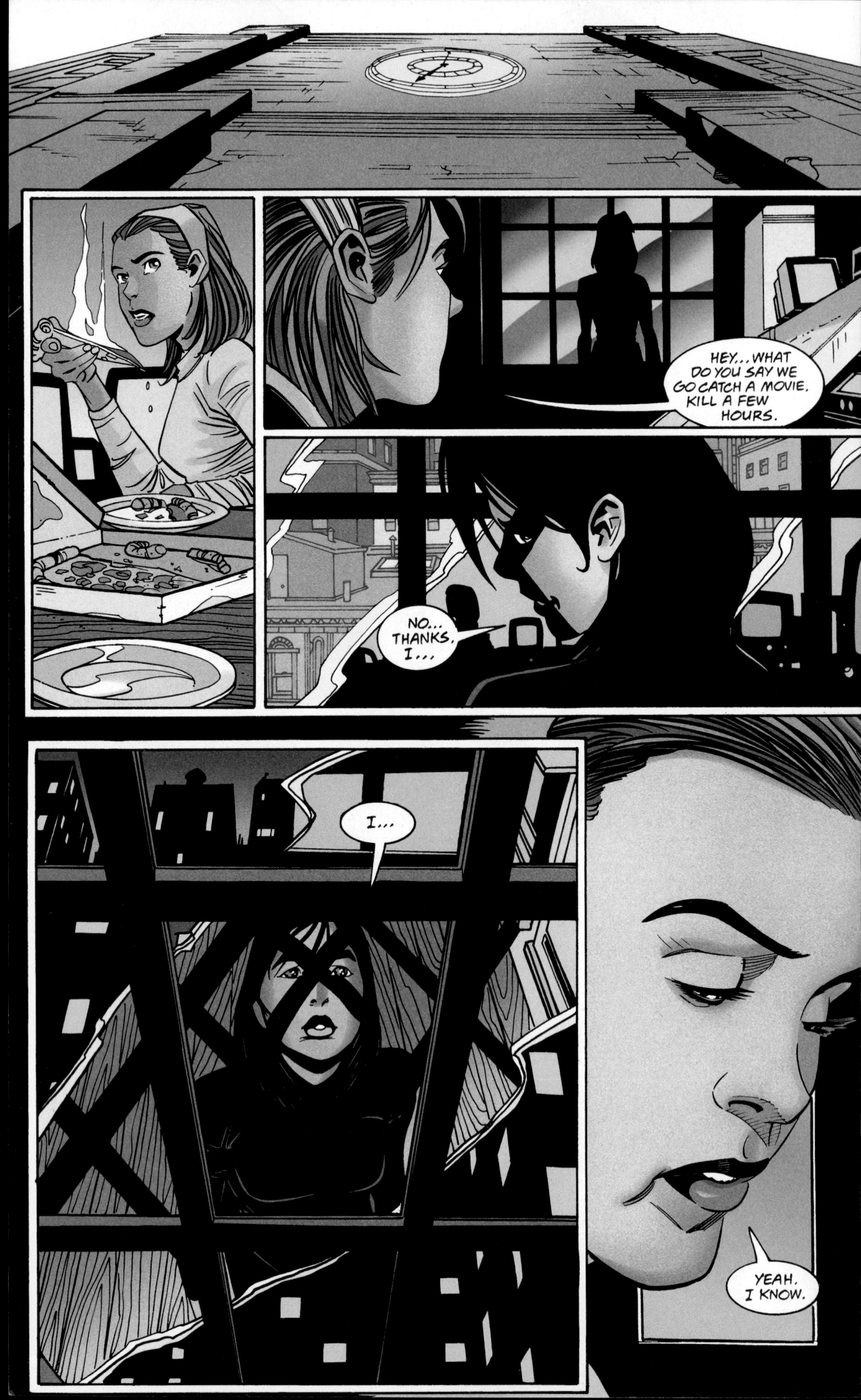
HEY... WHAT DO YOU SAY WE GO CATCH A MOVIE. KILL A FEW HOURS.
NO... THANKS. I...
I...
YEAH. I KNOW.

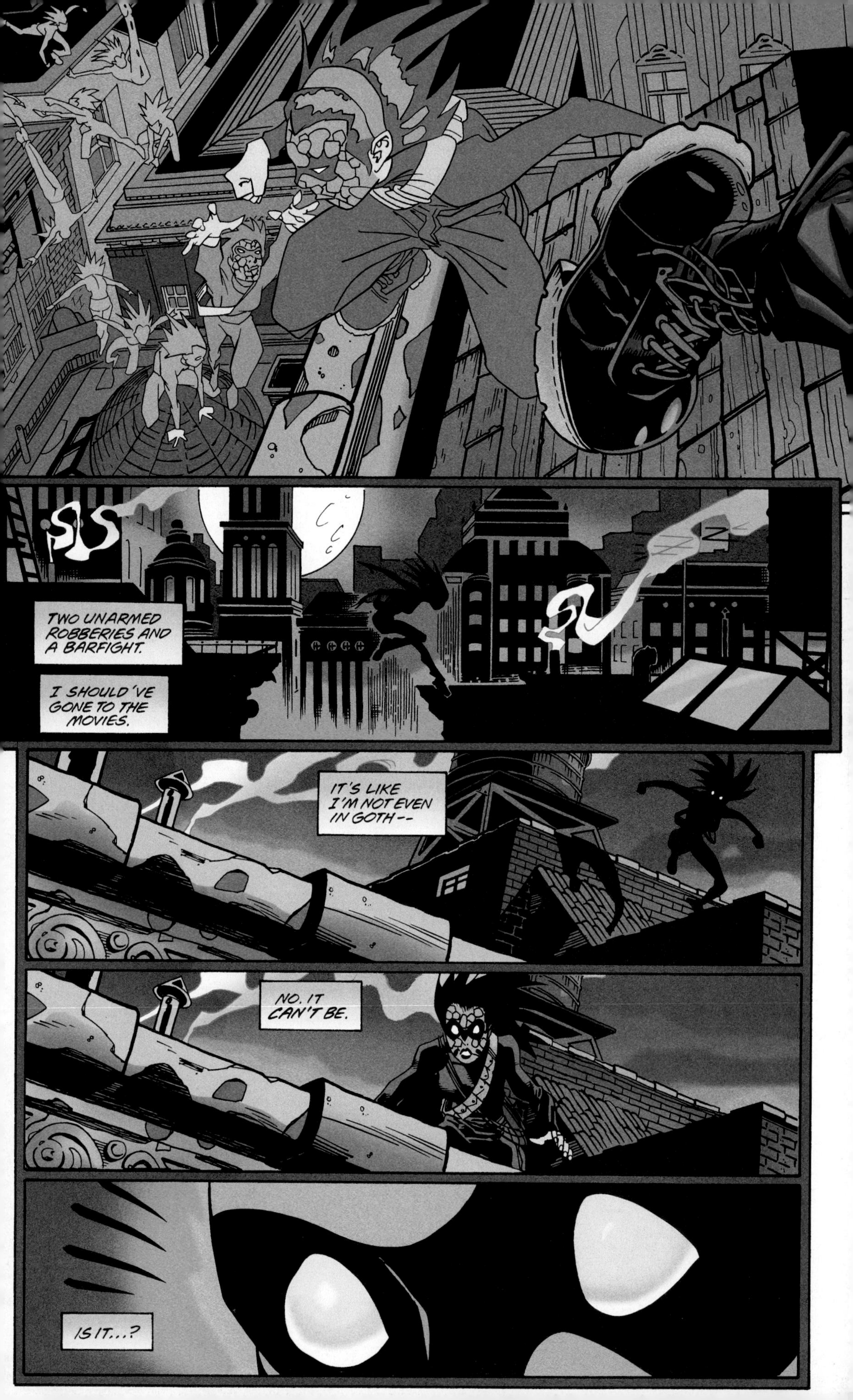

TWO UNARMED ROBBERIES AND A BARFIGHT.
I SHOULD'VE GONE TO THE MOVIES.
IT'S LIKE I'M NOT EVEN IN GOTH--
NO. IT CAN'T BE.
IS IT...?

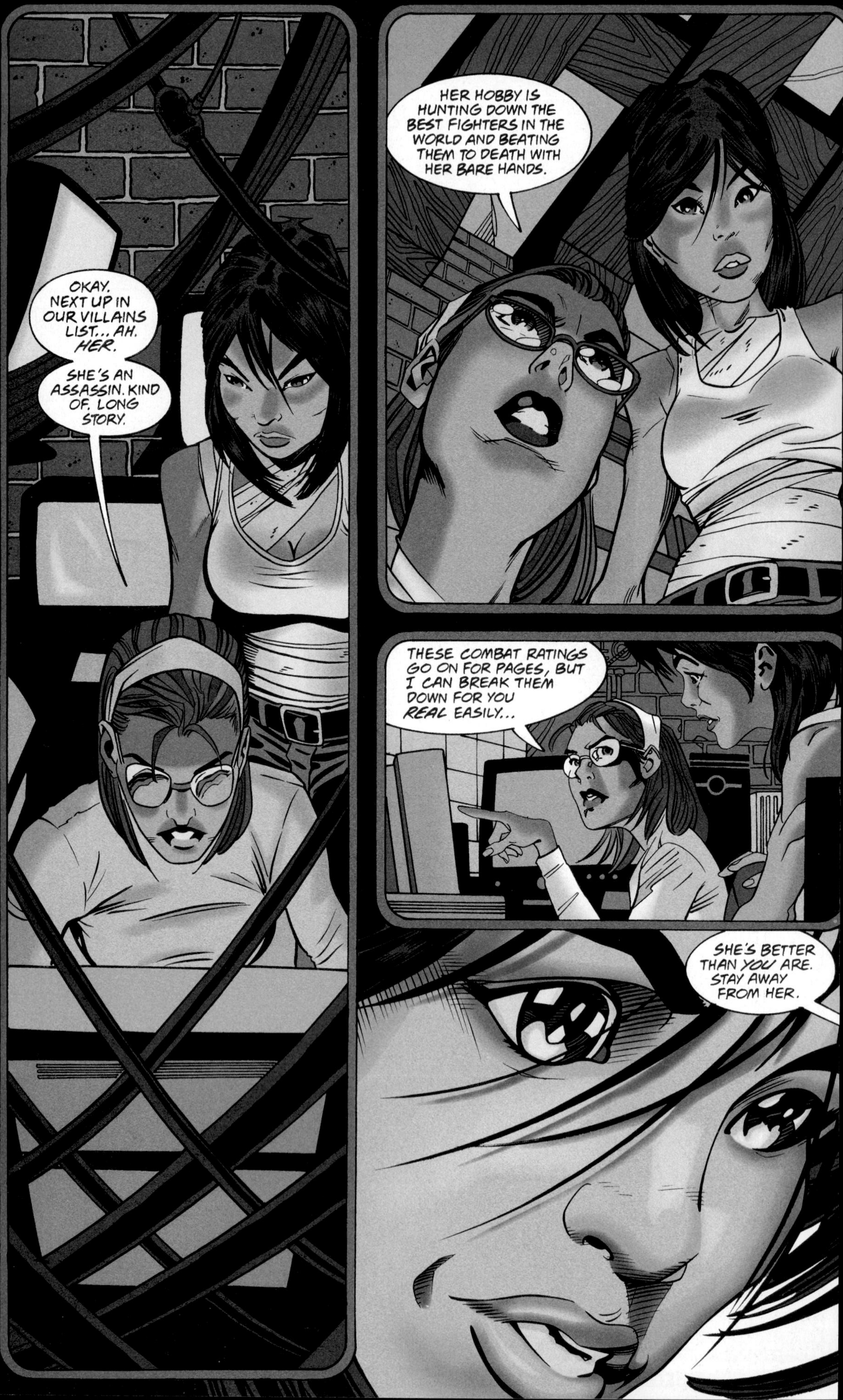
OKAY. NEXT UP IN OUR VILLAINS LIST... AH. *HER*.
SHE'S AN ASSASSIN. KIND OF. LONG STORY.
HER HOBBY IS HUNTING DOWN THE BEST FIGHTERS IN THE WORLD AND BEATING THEM TO DEATH WITH HER BARE HANDS.
THESE COMBAT RATINGS GO ON FOR PAGES, BUT I CAN BREAK THEM DOWN FOR YOU *REAL* EASILY...
SHE'S BETTER THAN *YOU* ARE. STAY AWAY FROM HER.

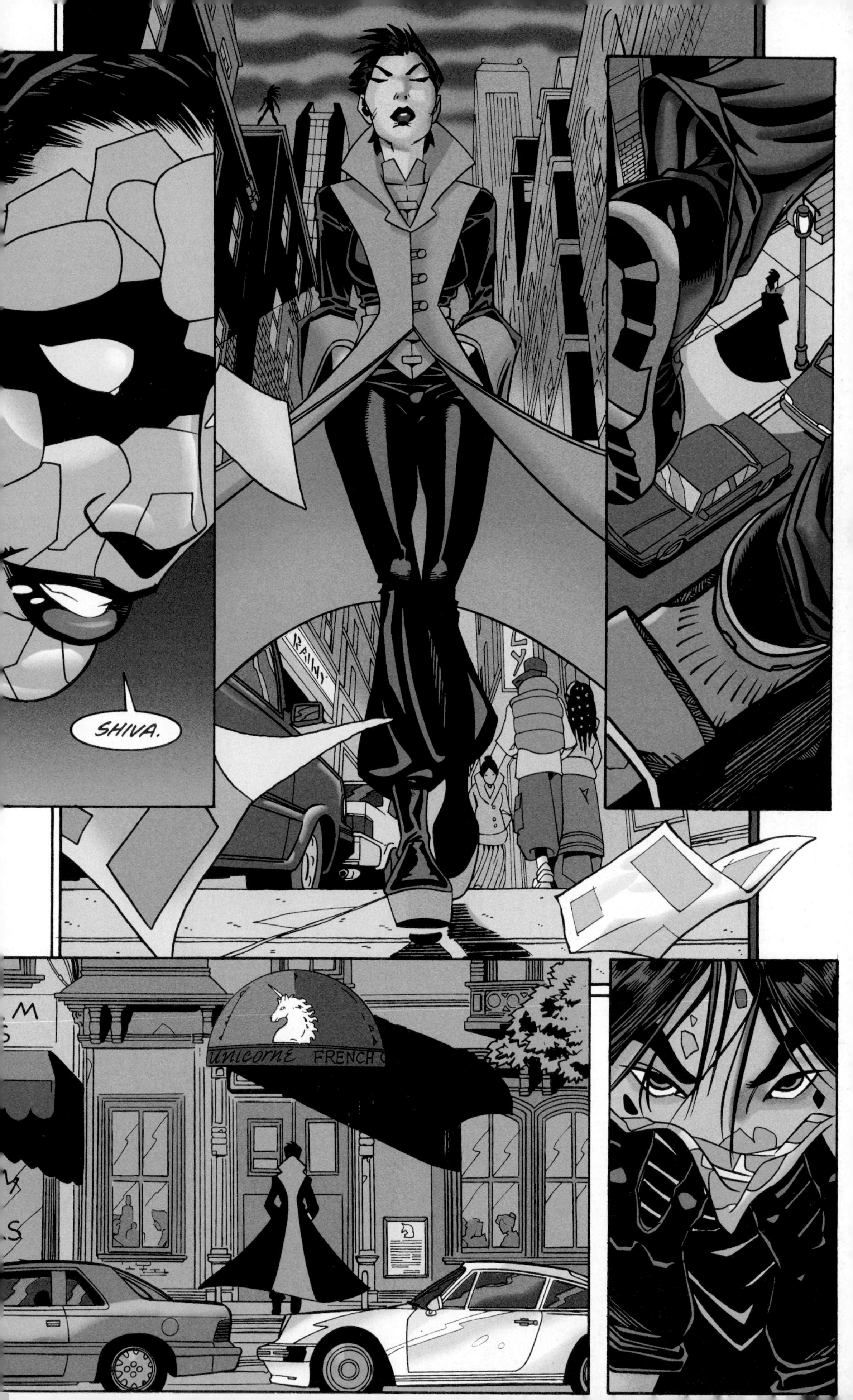
SHIVA.
unicorne FRENCH C

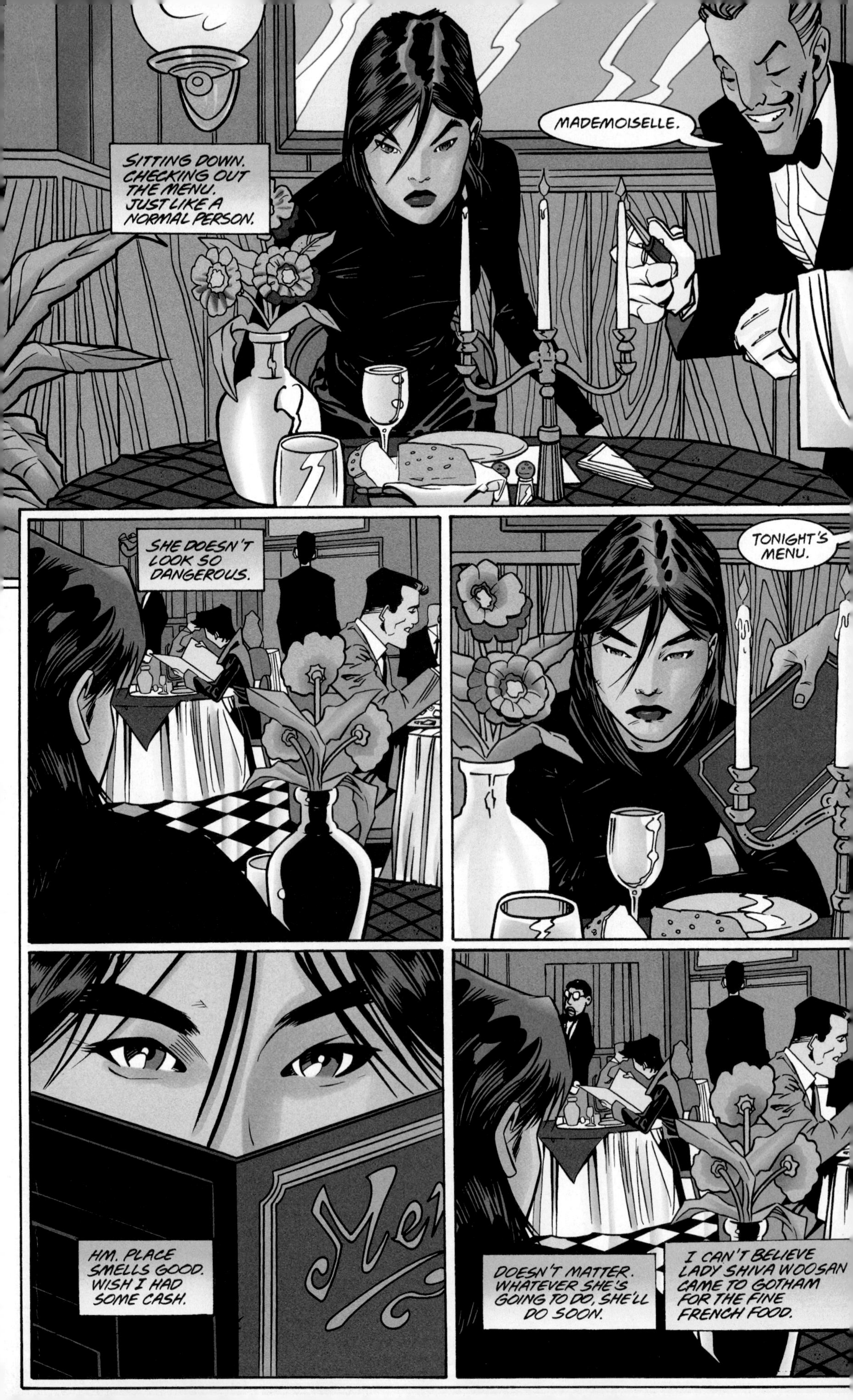
SITTING DOWN. CHECKING OUT THE MENU. JUST LIKE A NORMAL PERSON.
MADEMOISELLE.
SHE DOESN'T LOOK SO DANGEROUS.
TONIGHT'S MENU.
HM. PLACE SMELLS GOOD. WISH I HAD SOME CASH.
DOESN'T MATTER. WHATEVER SHE'S GOING TO DO, SHE'LL DO SOON.
I CAN'T BELIEVE LADY SHIVA WOOSAN CAME TO GOTHAM FOR THE FINE FRENCH FOOD.

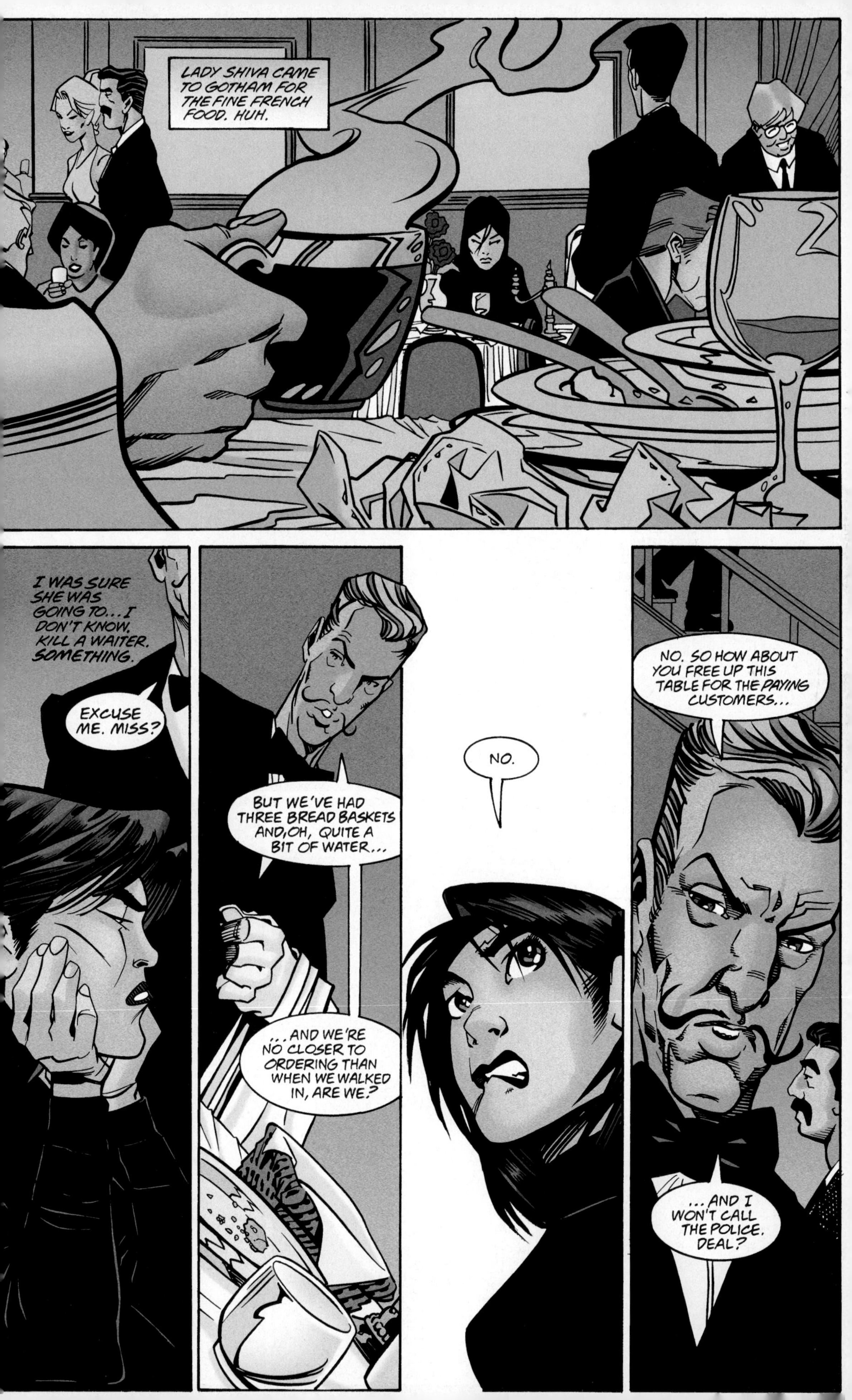
LADY SHIVA CAME TO GOTHAM FOR THE FINE FRENCH FOOD. HUH.
I WAS SURE SHE WAS GOING TO... I DON'T KNOW. KILL A WAITER. SOMETHING.
EXCUSE ME. MISS?
BUT WE'VE HAD THREE BREAD BASKETS AND, OH, QUITE A BIT OF WATER...
...AND WE'RE NO CLOSER TO ORDERING THAN WHEN WE WALKED IN, ARE WE?
NO.
NO. SO HOW ABOUT YOU FREE UP THIS TABLE FOR THE PAYING CUSTOMERS...
...AND I WON'T CALL THE POLICE. DEAL?

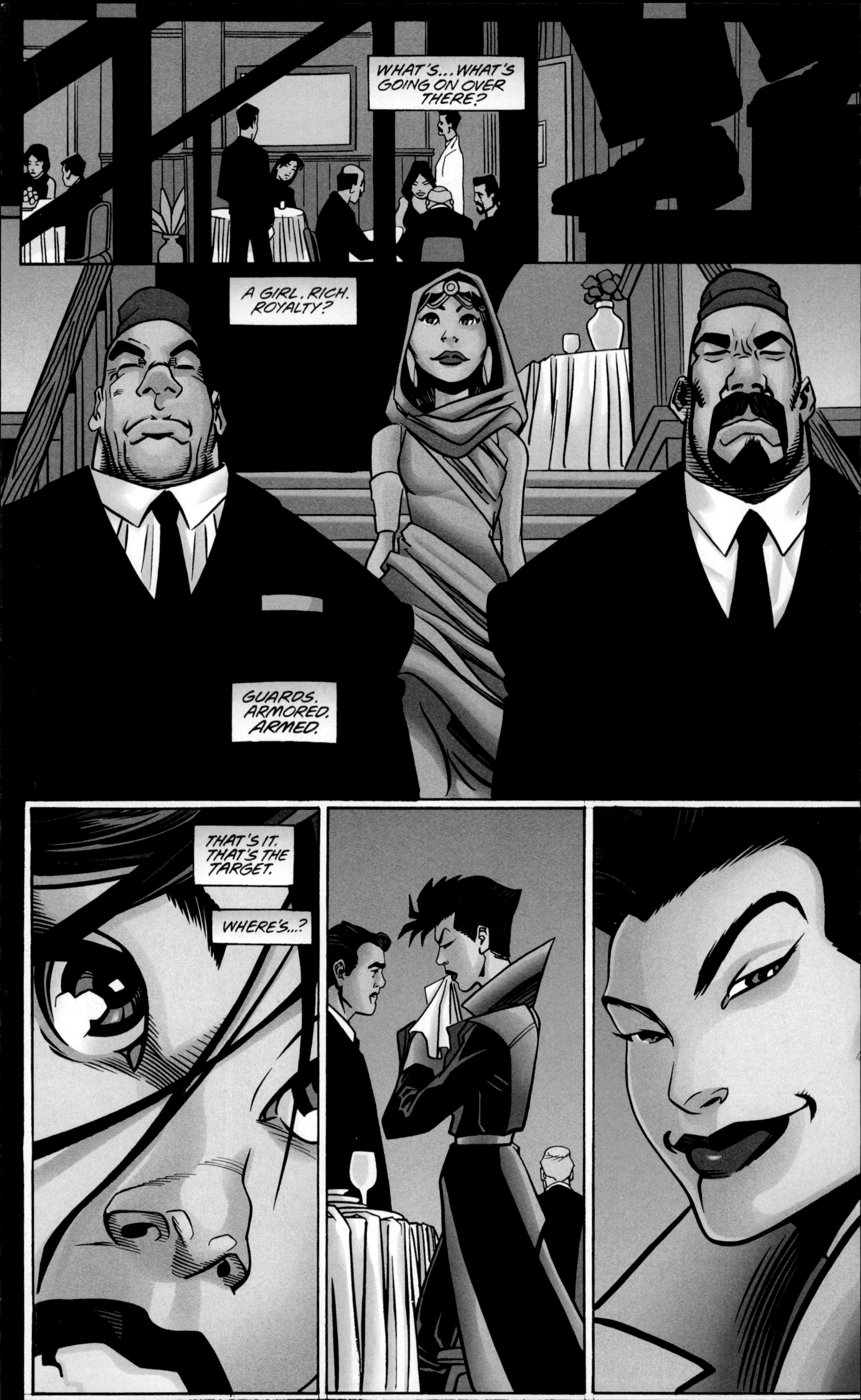
WHAT'S... WHAT'S GOING ON OVER THERE?
A GIRL. RICH. ROYALTY?
GUARDS. ARMORED. ARMED.
THAT'S IT. THAT'S THE TARGET.
WHERE'S...?

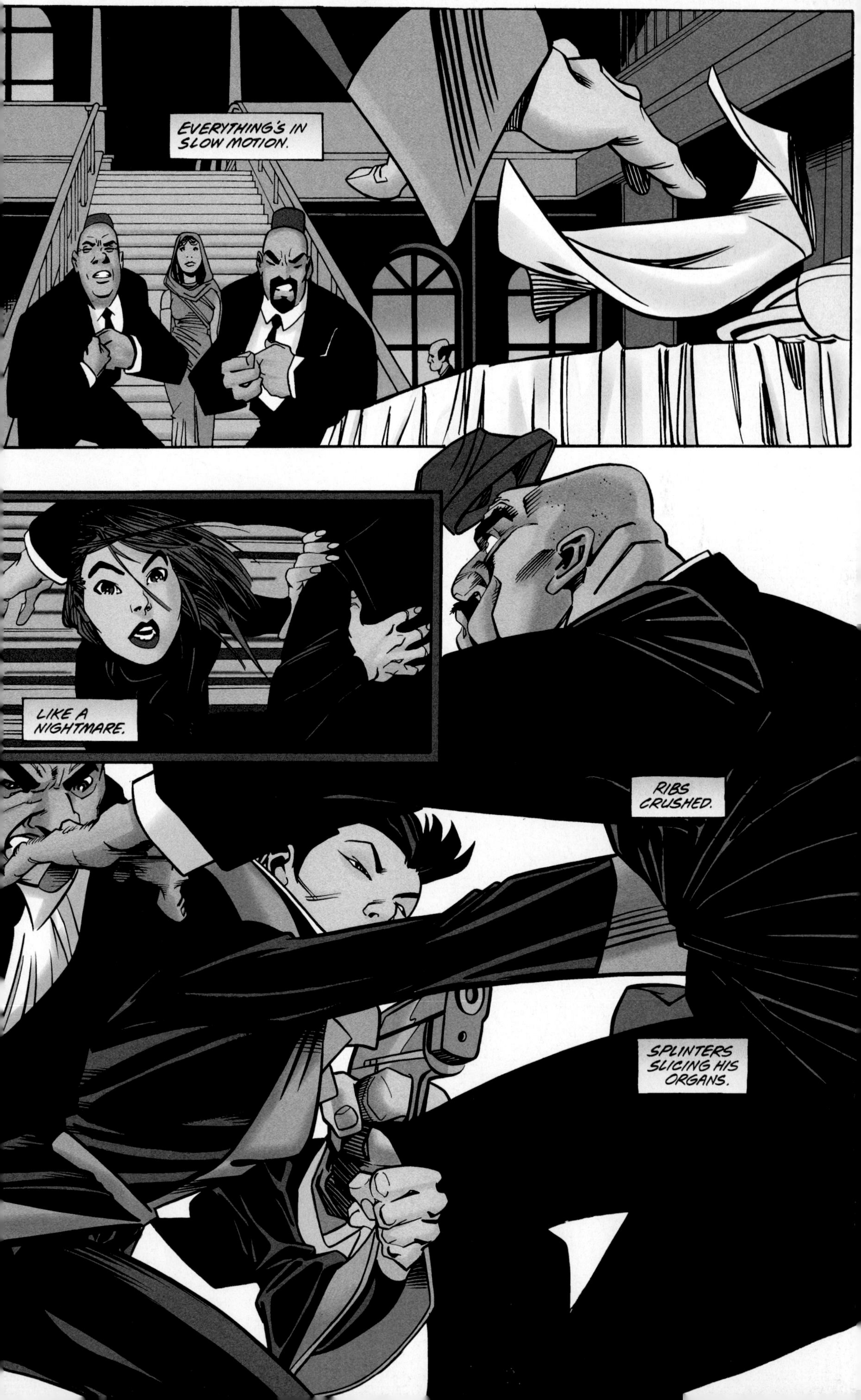
EVERYTHING'S IN SLOW MOTION.
LIKE A NIGHTMARE.
RIBS CRUSHED.
SPLINTERS SLICING HIS ORGANS.

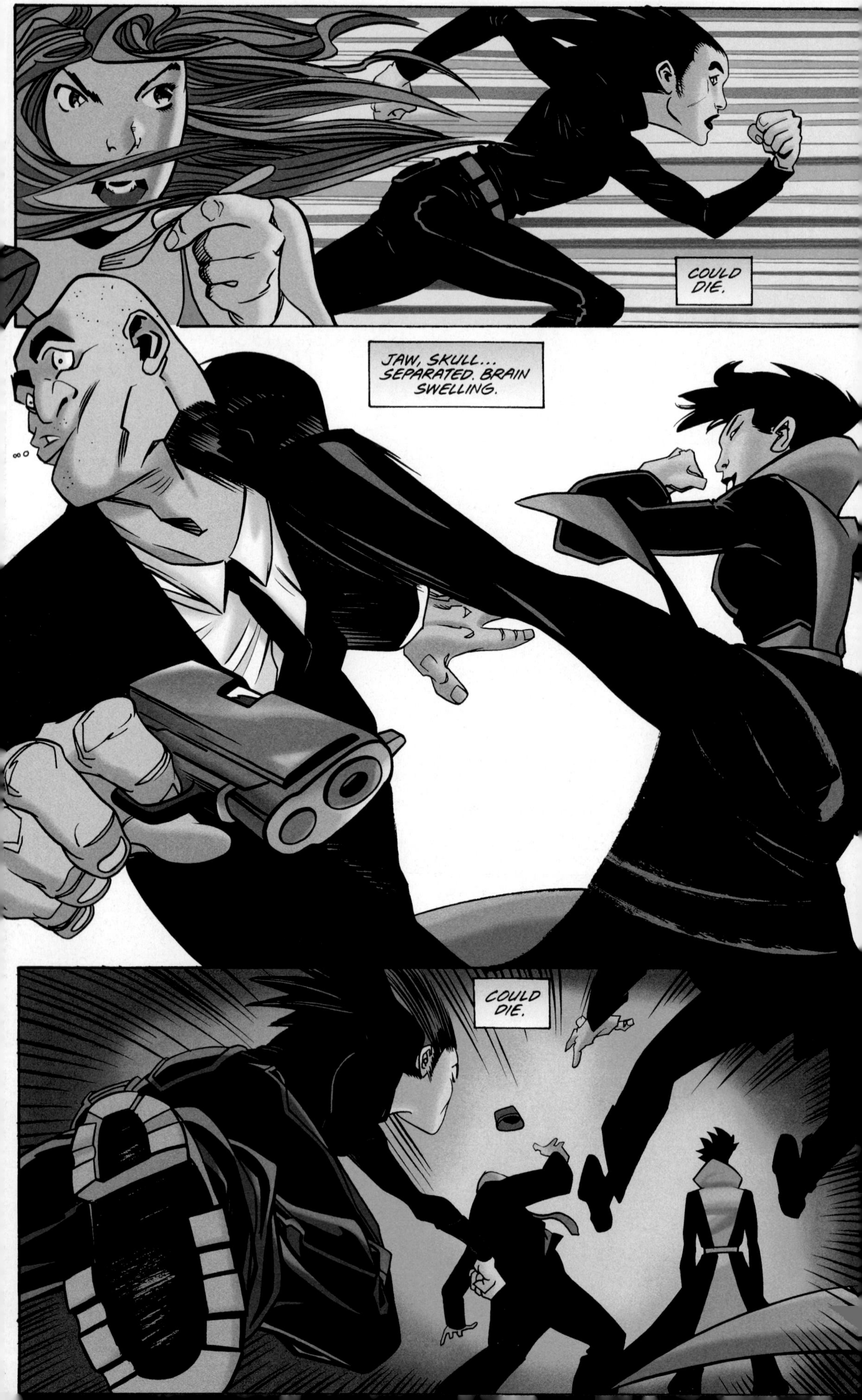
COULD DIE.
JAW, SKULL... SEPARATED. BRAIN SWELLING.
COULD DIE.

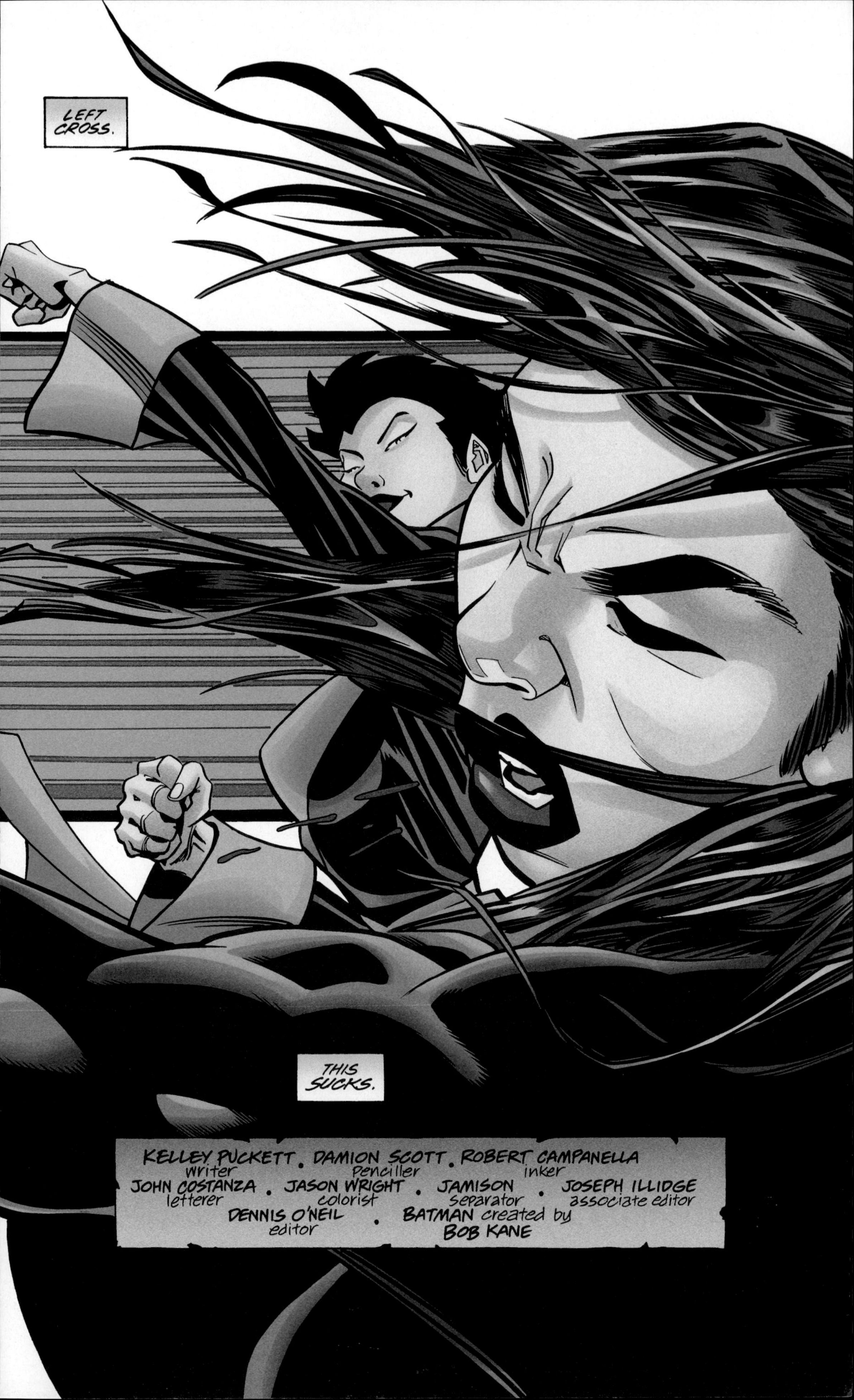
LEFT CROSS.
THIS SUCKS.
KELLEY PUCKETT writer . DAMION SCOTT penciller . ROBERT CAMPANELLA inker
JOHN COSTANZA letterer . JASON WRIGHT colorist . JAMISON separator . JOSEPH ILLIDGE associate editor
DENNIS O'NEIL editor . BATMAN created by BOB KANE

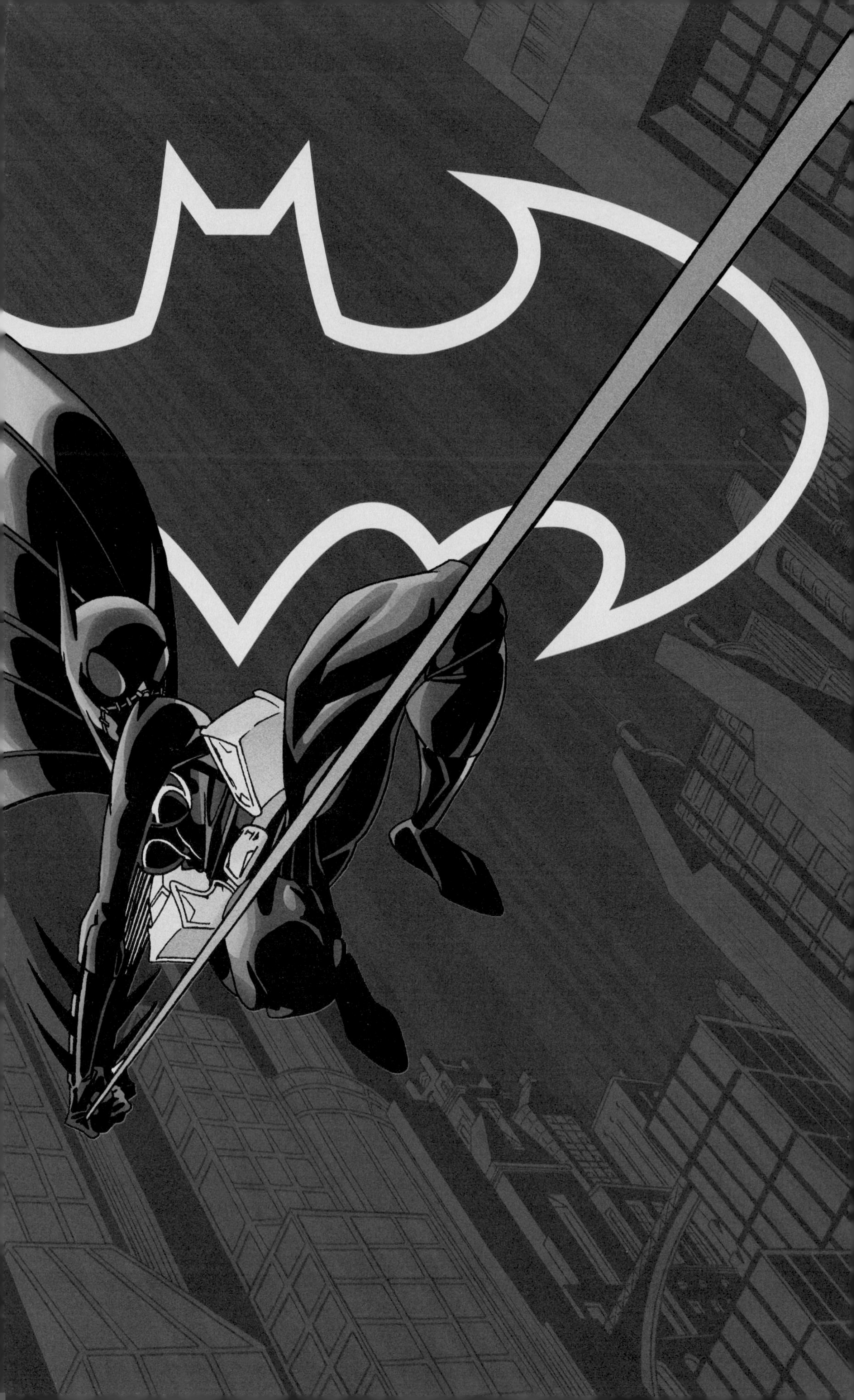

BATGIRL #8 cover by
Damion Scott & Robert Campanella

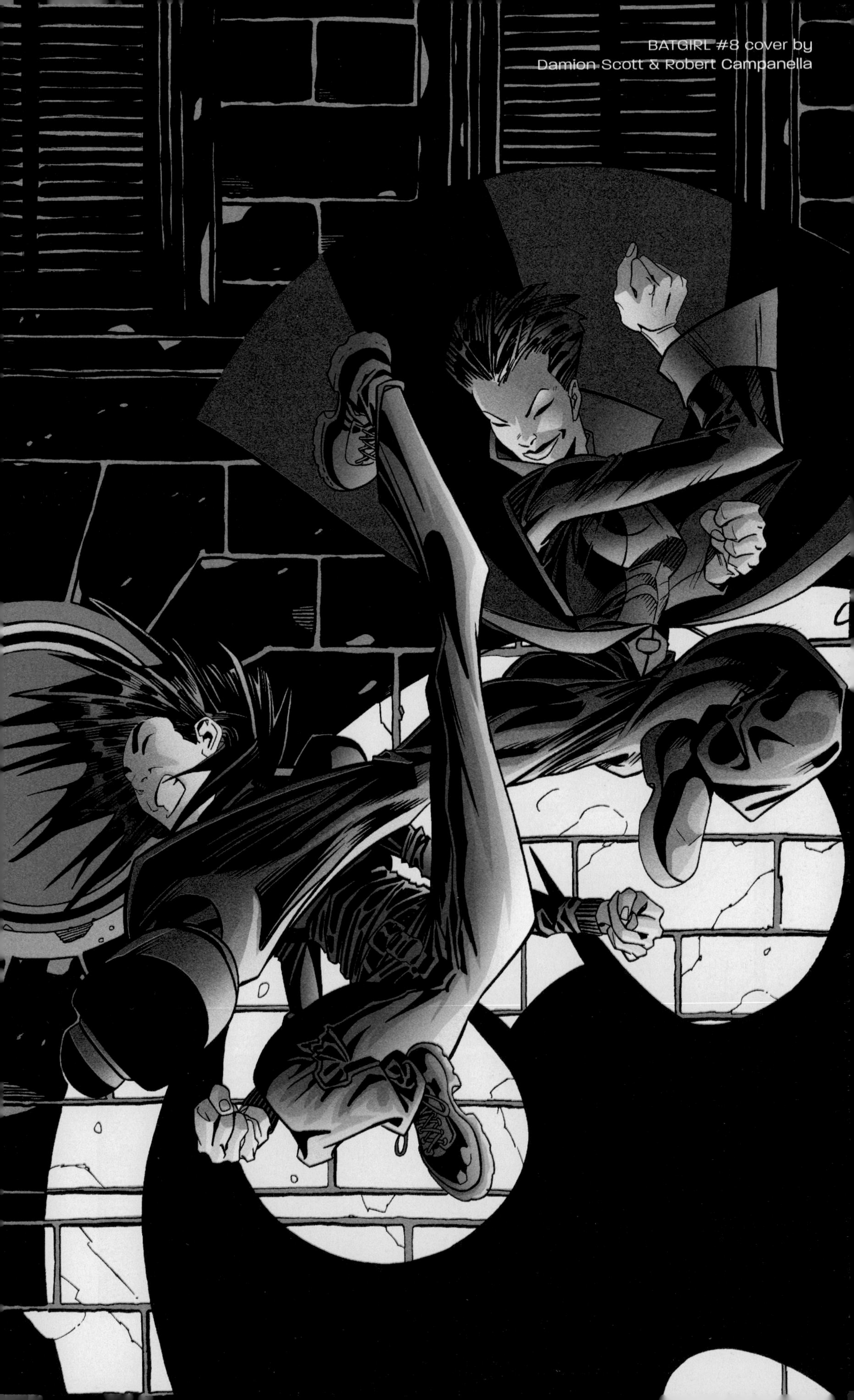

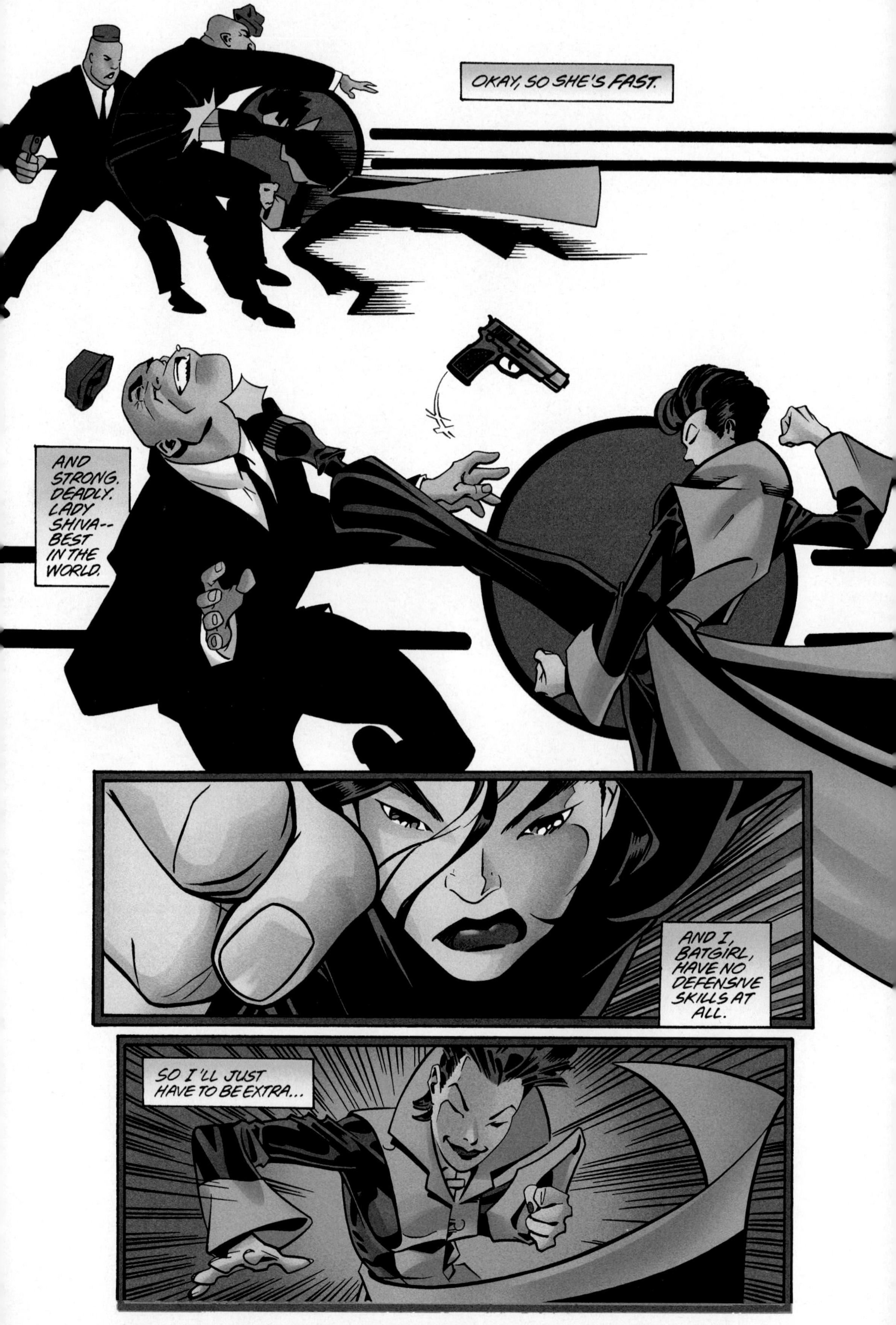
OKAY, SO SHE'S FAST.
AND STRONG. DEADLY. LADY SHIVA-- BEST IN THE WORLD.
AND I, BATGIRL, HAVE NO DEFENSIVE SKILLS AT ALL.
SO I'LL JUST HAVE TO BE EXTRA...

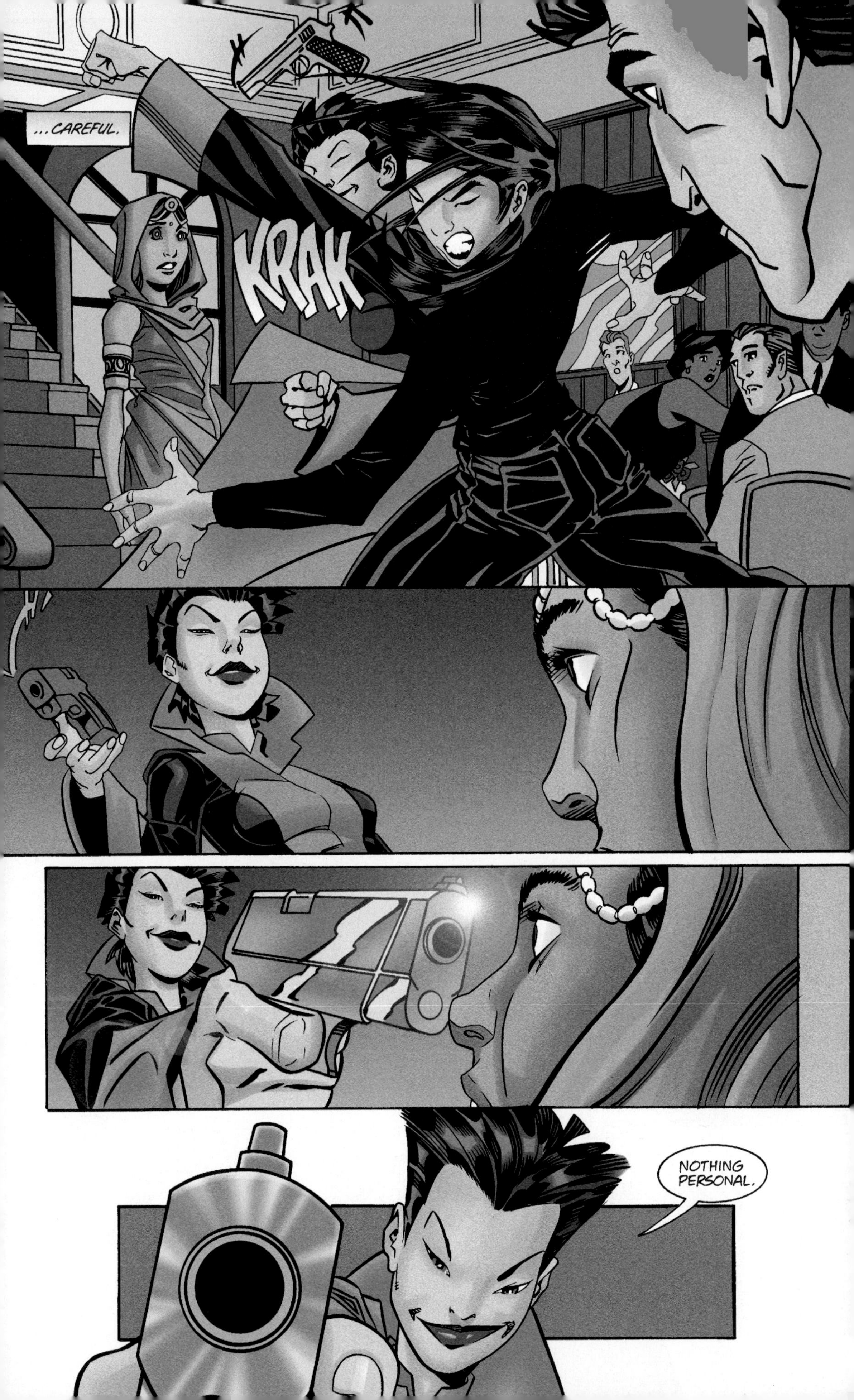
...CAREFUL.
KRAK
NOTHING PERSONAL.

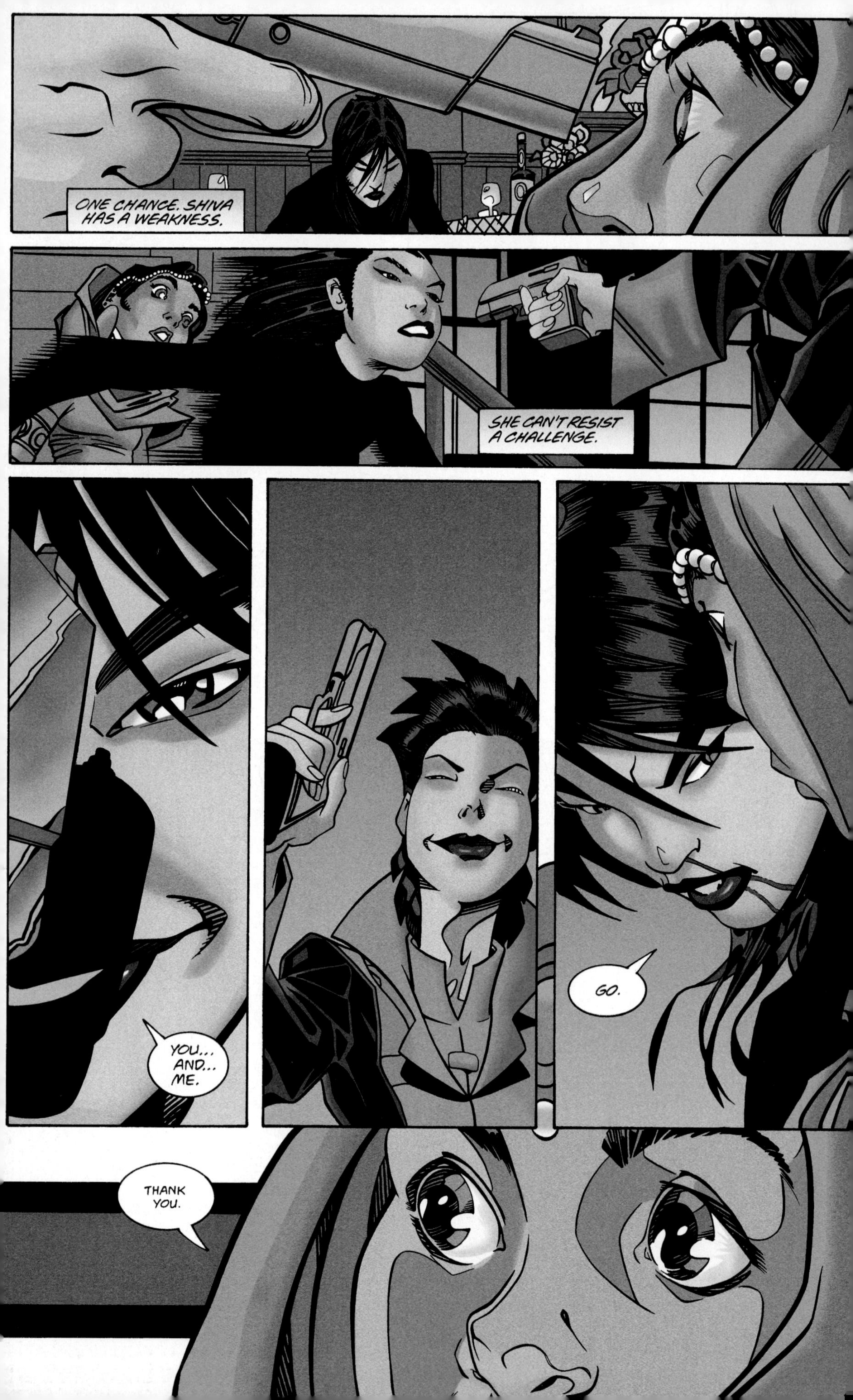
ONE CHANCE. SHIVA HAS A WEAKNESS.
SHE CAN'T RESIST A CHALLENGE.
YOU... AND... ME.
GO.
THANK YOU.

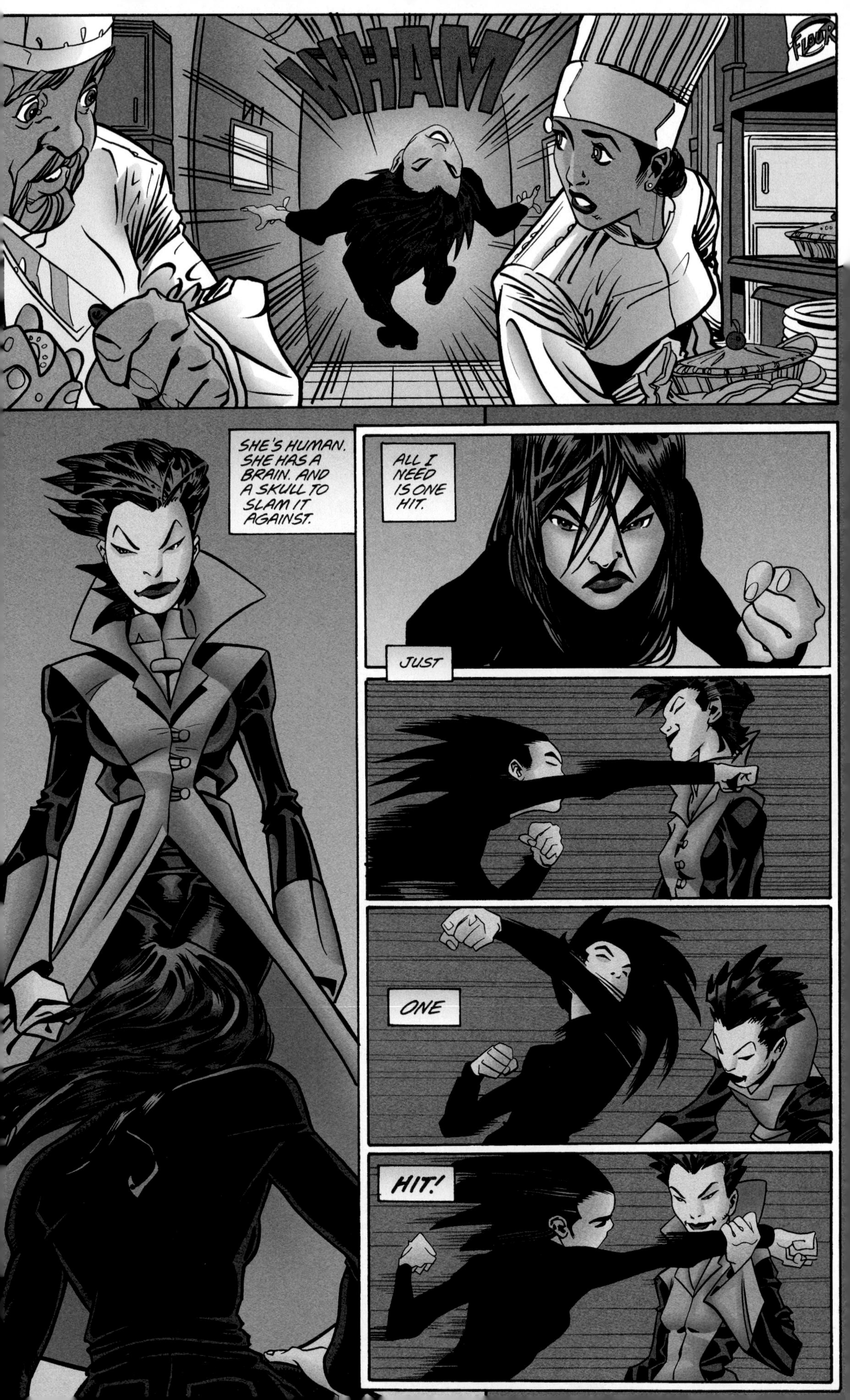
WHAM
FLOUR
SHE'S HUMAN. SHE HAS A BRAIN. AND A SKULL TO SLAM IT AGAINST.
ALL I NEED IS ONE HIT.
JUST
ONE
HIT!

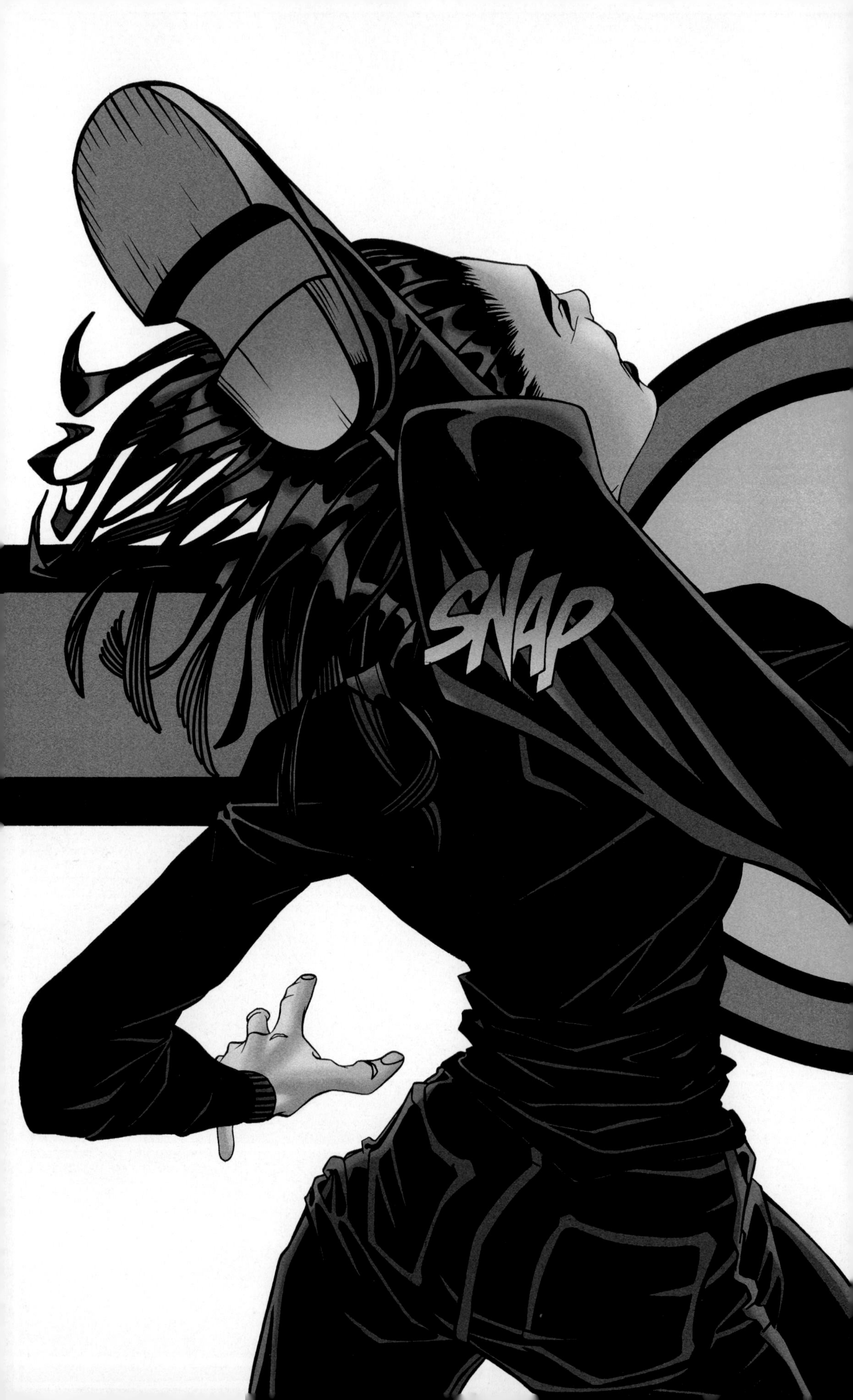
SNAP

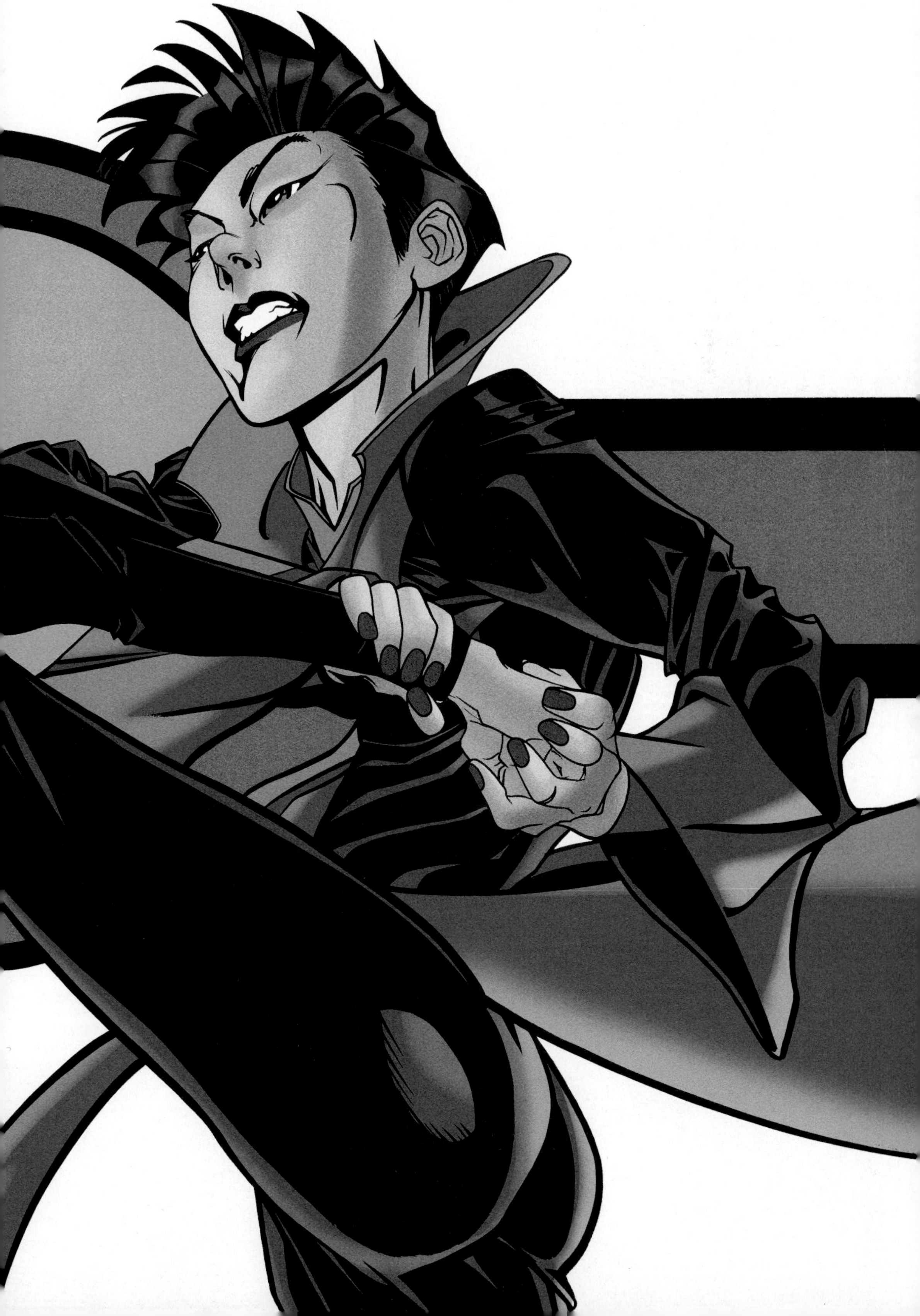

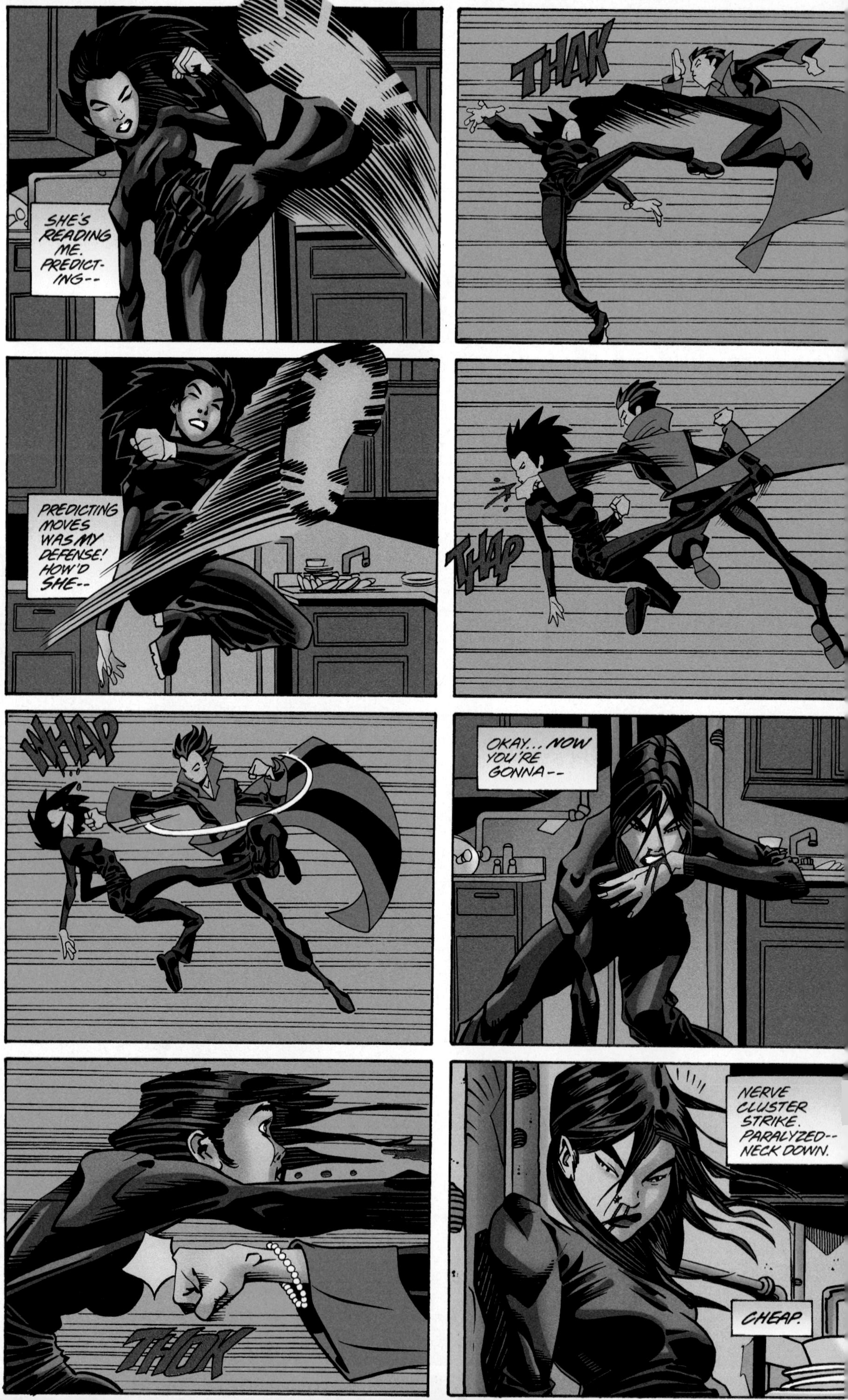
SHE'S READING ME. PREDICT-ING--
THAK
PREDICTING MOVES WAS MY DEFENSE! HOW'D SHE--
THAP
WHAP
OKAY... NOW YOU'RE GONNA--
THOK
NERVE CLUSTER STRIKE. PARALYZED-- NECK DOWN.
CHEAP.

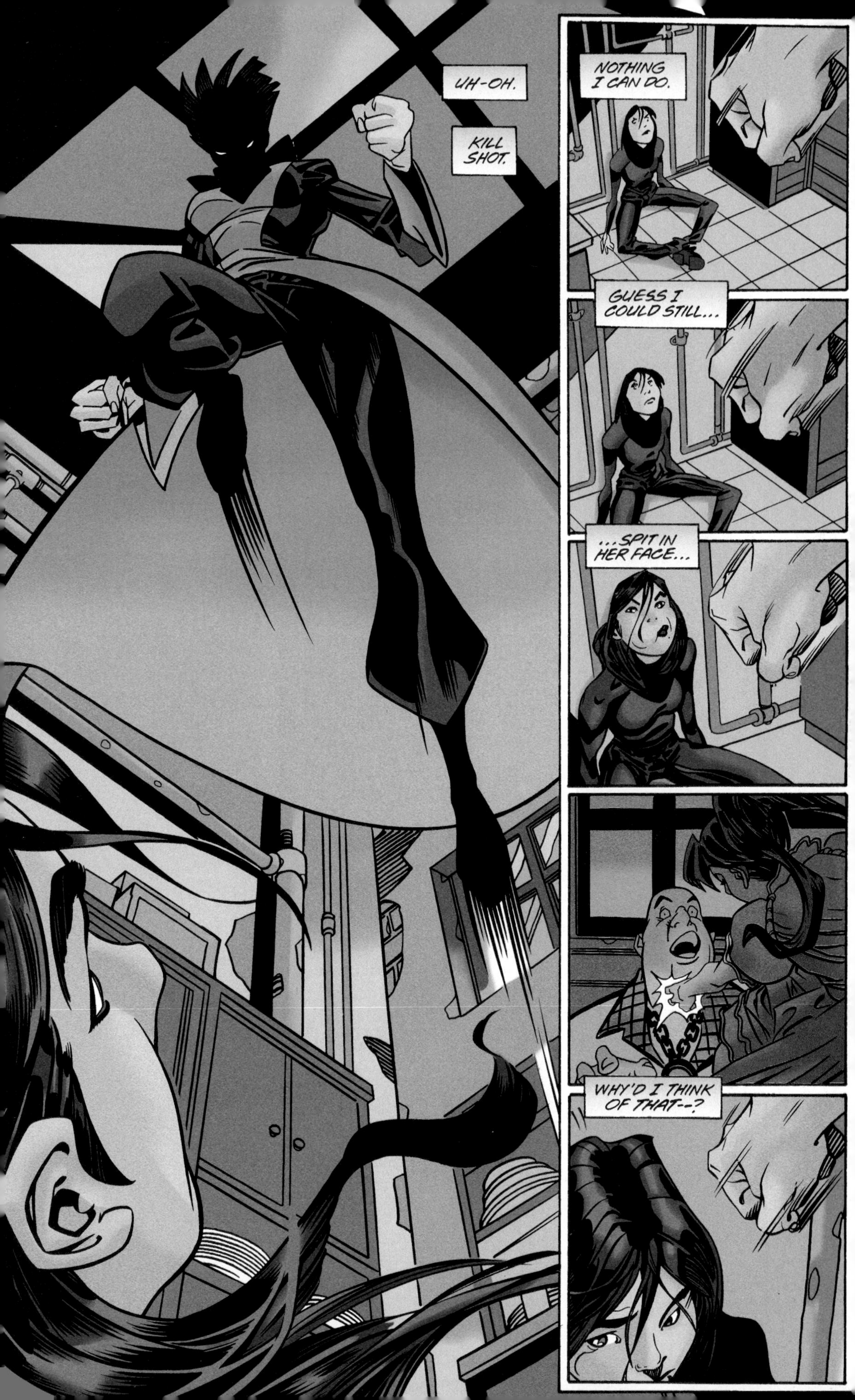
UH-OH.
KILL SHOT.
NOTHING I CAN DO.
GUESS I COULD STILL...
...SPIT IN HER FACE...
WHY'D I THINK OF THAT--?

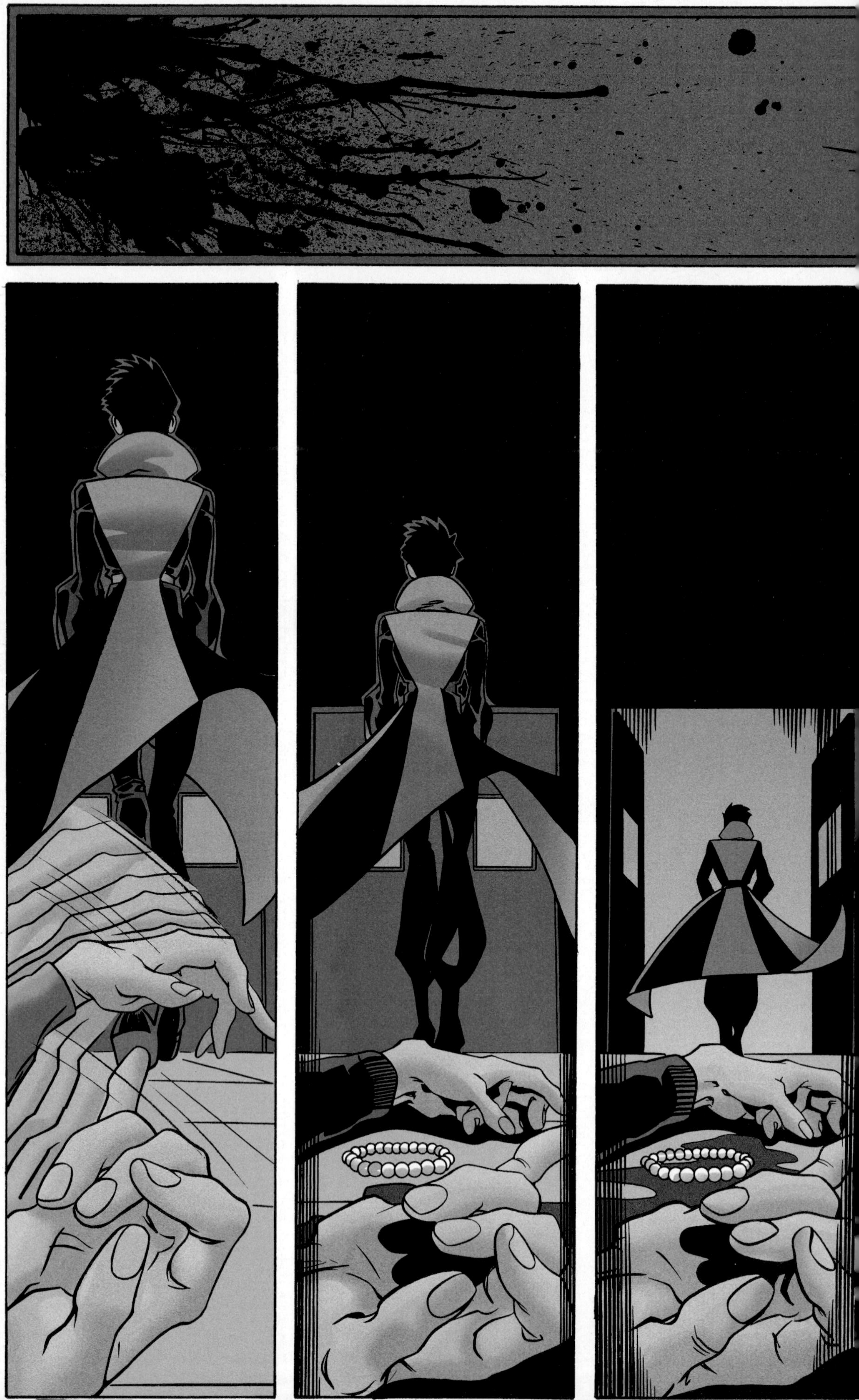

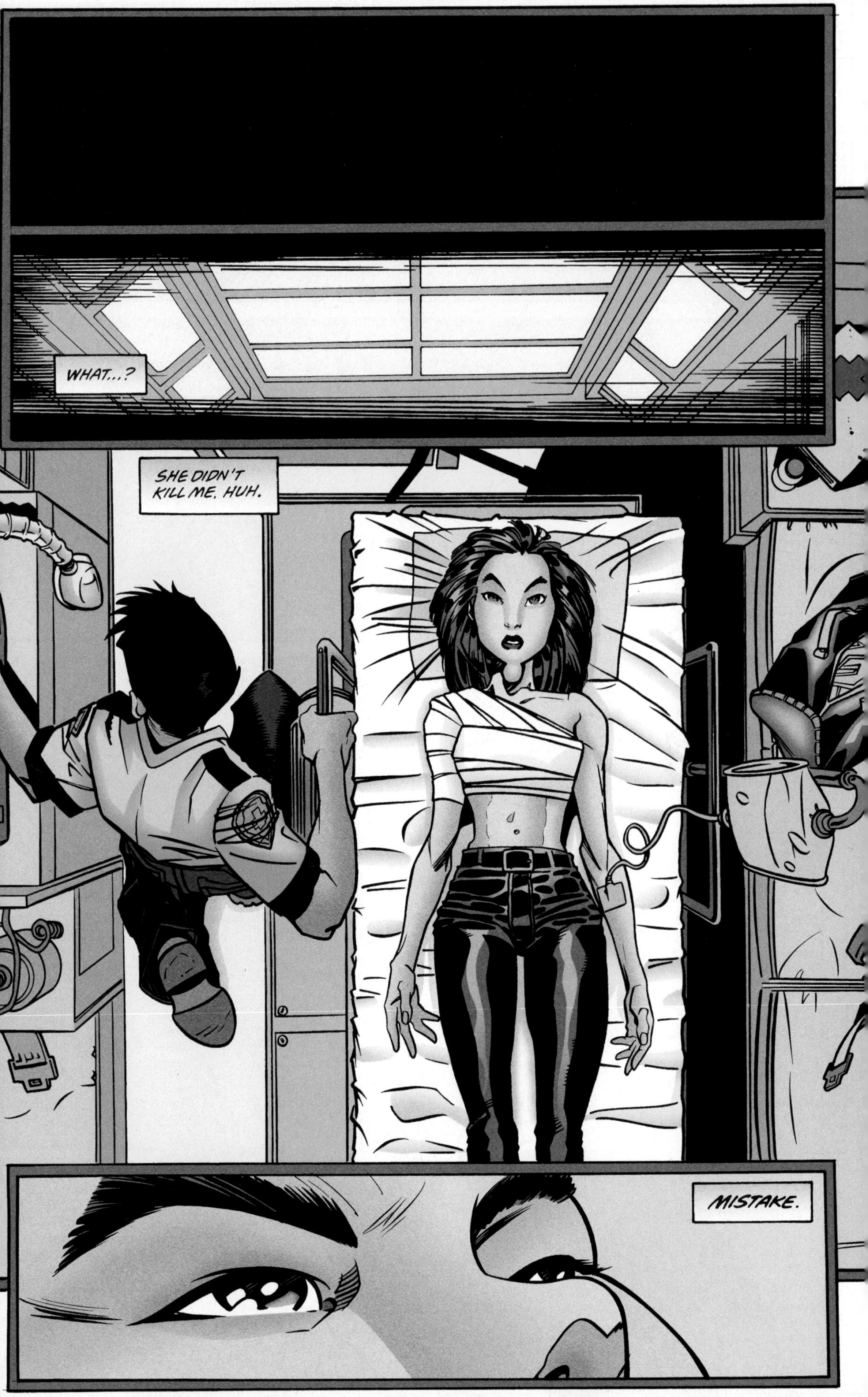
WHAT...?
SHE DIDN'T KILL ME. HUH.
MISTAKE.

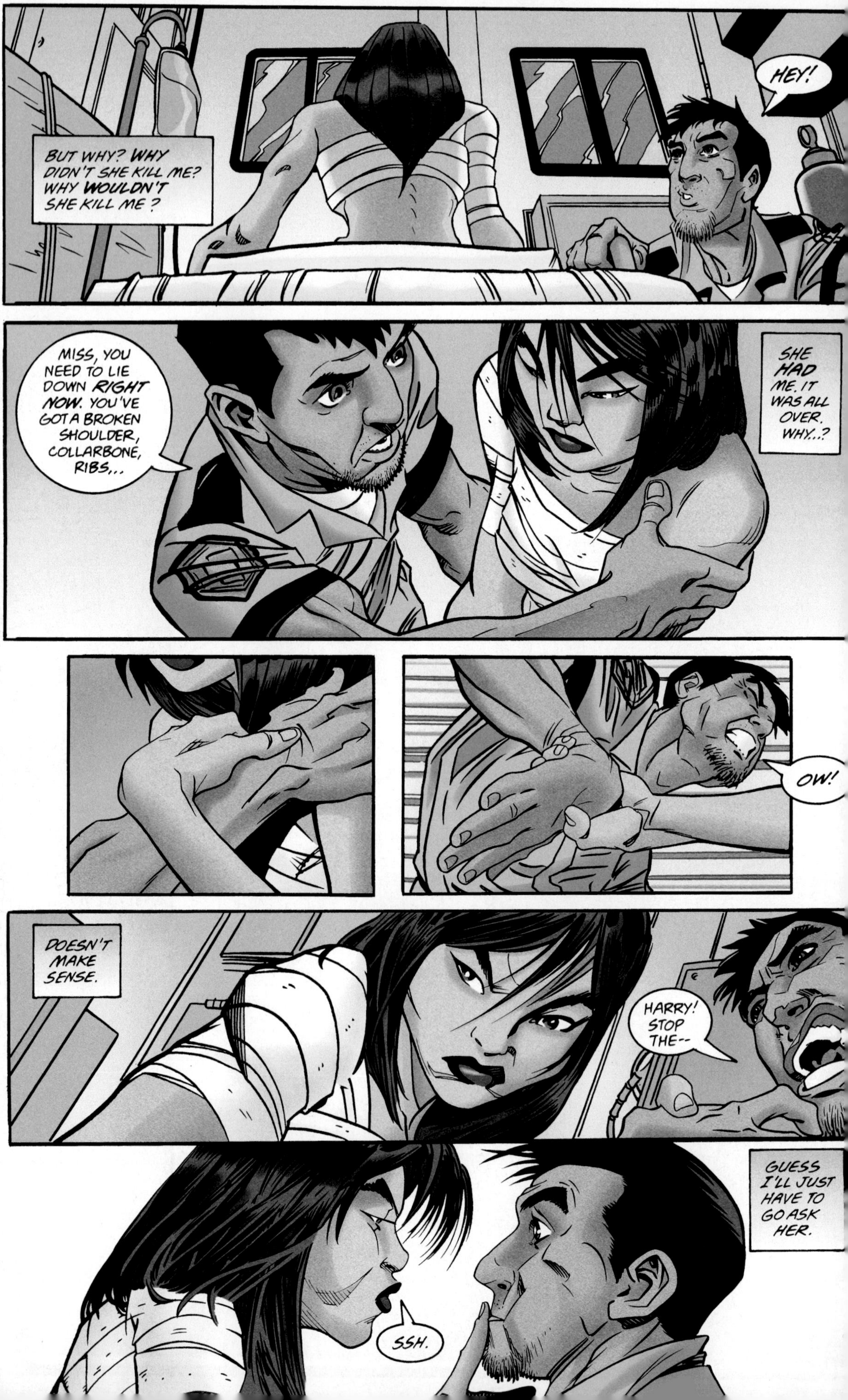
HEY!
BUT WHY? WHY DIDN'T SHE KILL ME? WHY WOULDN'T SHE KILL ME?
MISS, YOU NEED TO LIE DOWN RIGHT NOW. YOU'VE GOT A BROKEN SHOULDER, COLLARBONE, RIBS...
SHE HAD ME. IT WAS ALL OVER. WHY...?
OW!
DOESN'T MAKE SENSE.
HARRY! STOP THE--
GUESS I'LL JUST HAVE TO GO ASK HER.
SSH.

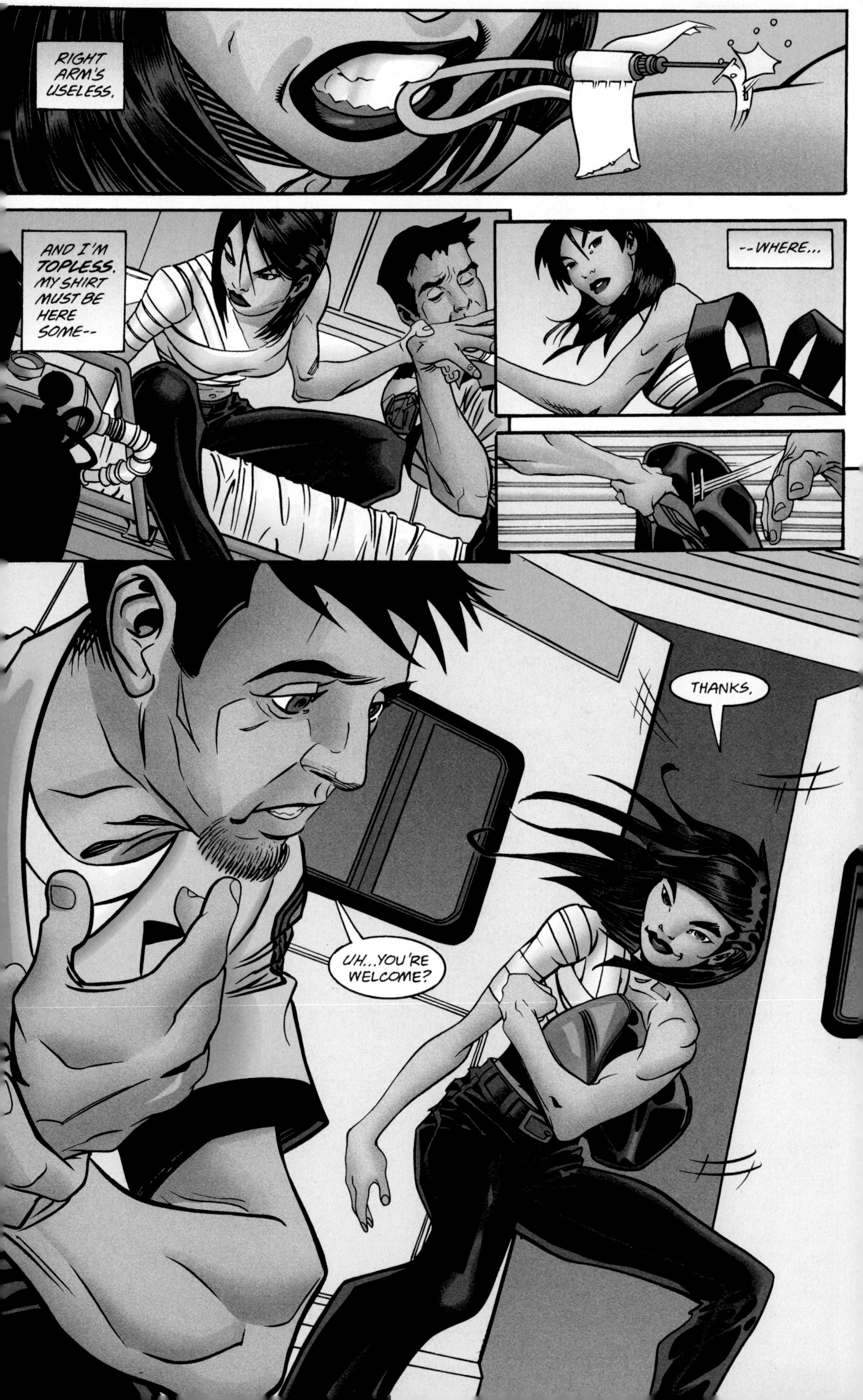
RIGHT ARM'S USELESS.
AND I'M TOPLESS. MY SHIRT MUST BE HERE SOME--
--WHERE...
THANKS.
UH...YOU'RE WELCOME?

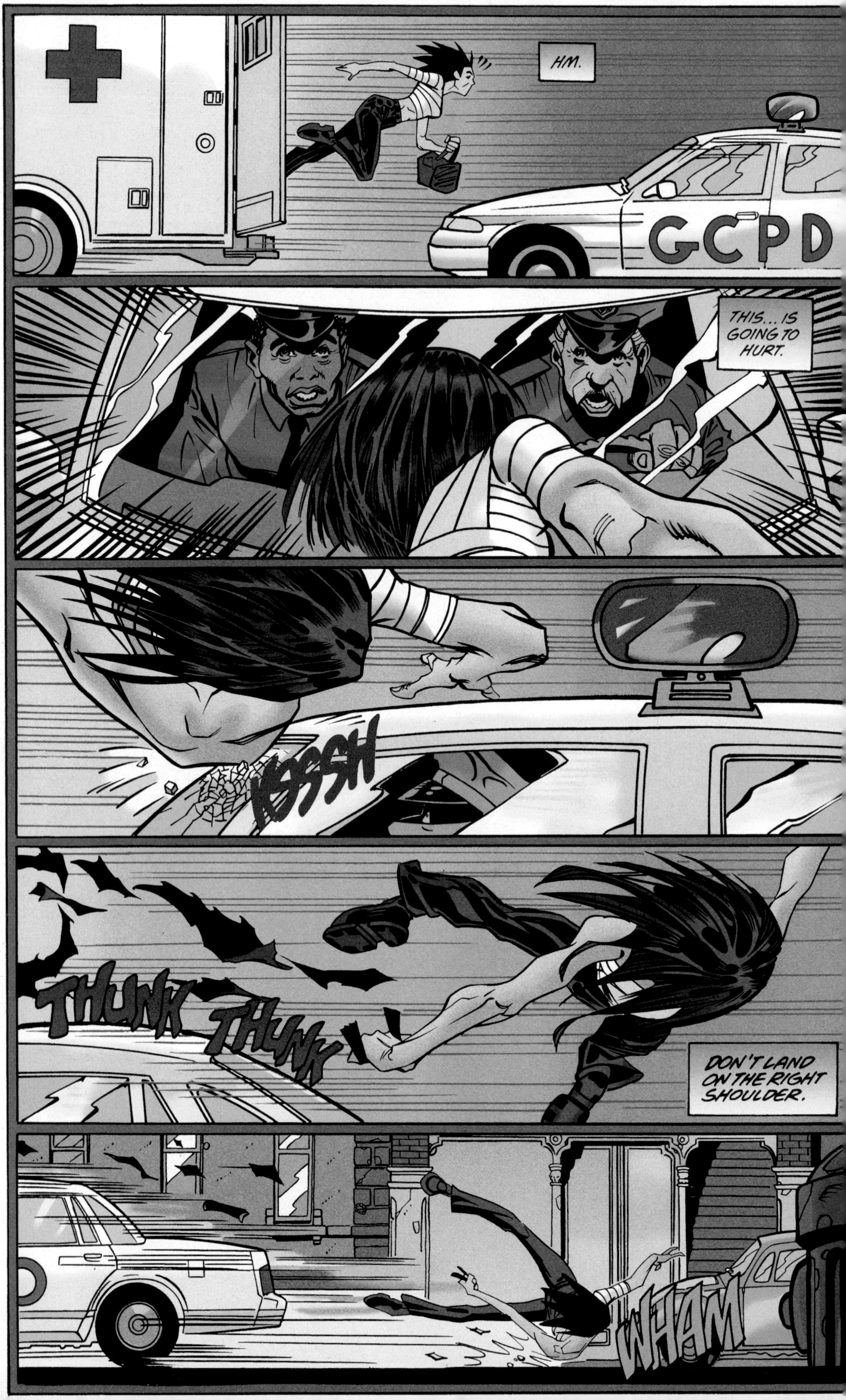

HM.
GCPD
THIS... IS GOING TO HURT.
KSSSH
THUNK
THUNK
DON'T LAND ON THE RIGHT SHOULDER.
WHAM

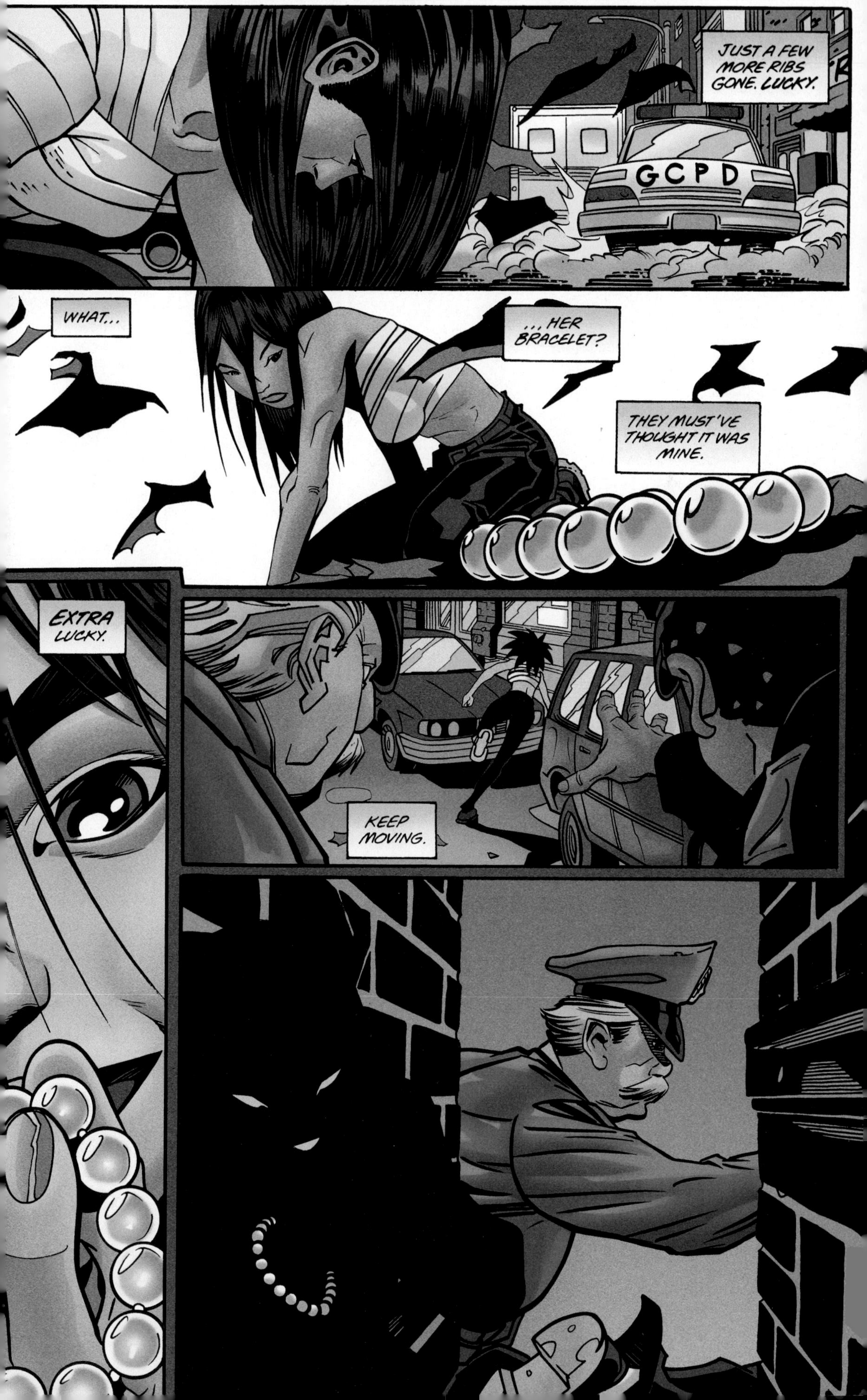
JUST A FEW MORE RIBS GONE. LUCKY.
GCPD
WHAT...
...HER BRACELET?
THEY MUST'VE THOUGHT IT WAS MINE.
EXTRA LUCKY.
KEEP MOVING.

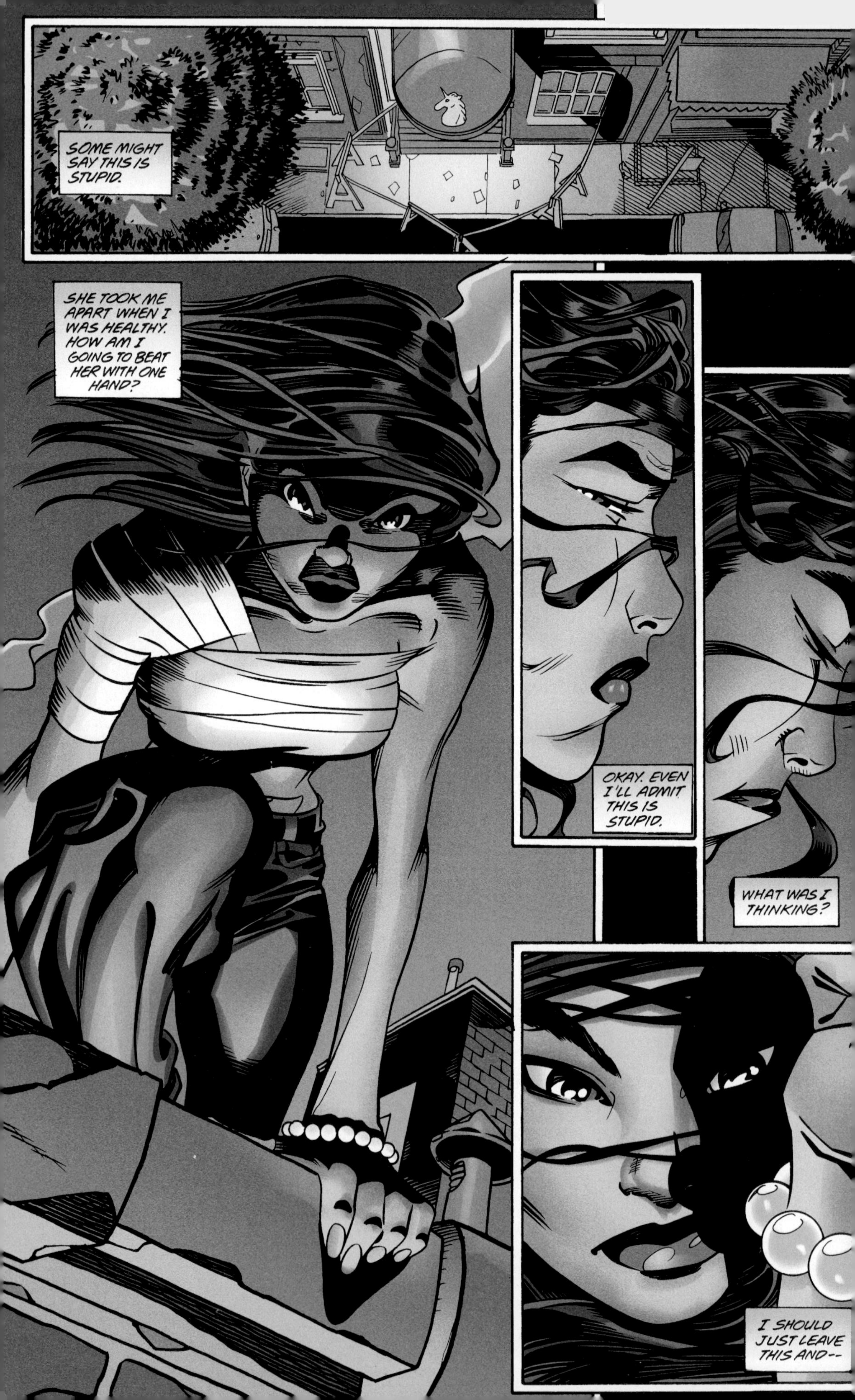
SOME MIGHT SAY THIS IS STUPID.
SHE TOOK ME APART WHEN I WAS HEALTHY. HOW AM I GOING TO BEAT HER WITH ONE HAND?
OKAY. EVEN I'LL ADMIT THIS IS STUPID.
WHAT WAS I THINKING?
I SHOULD JUST LEAVE THIS AND--

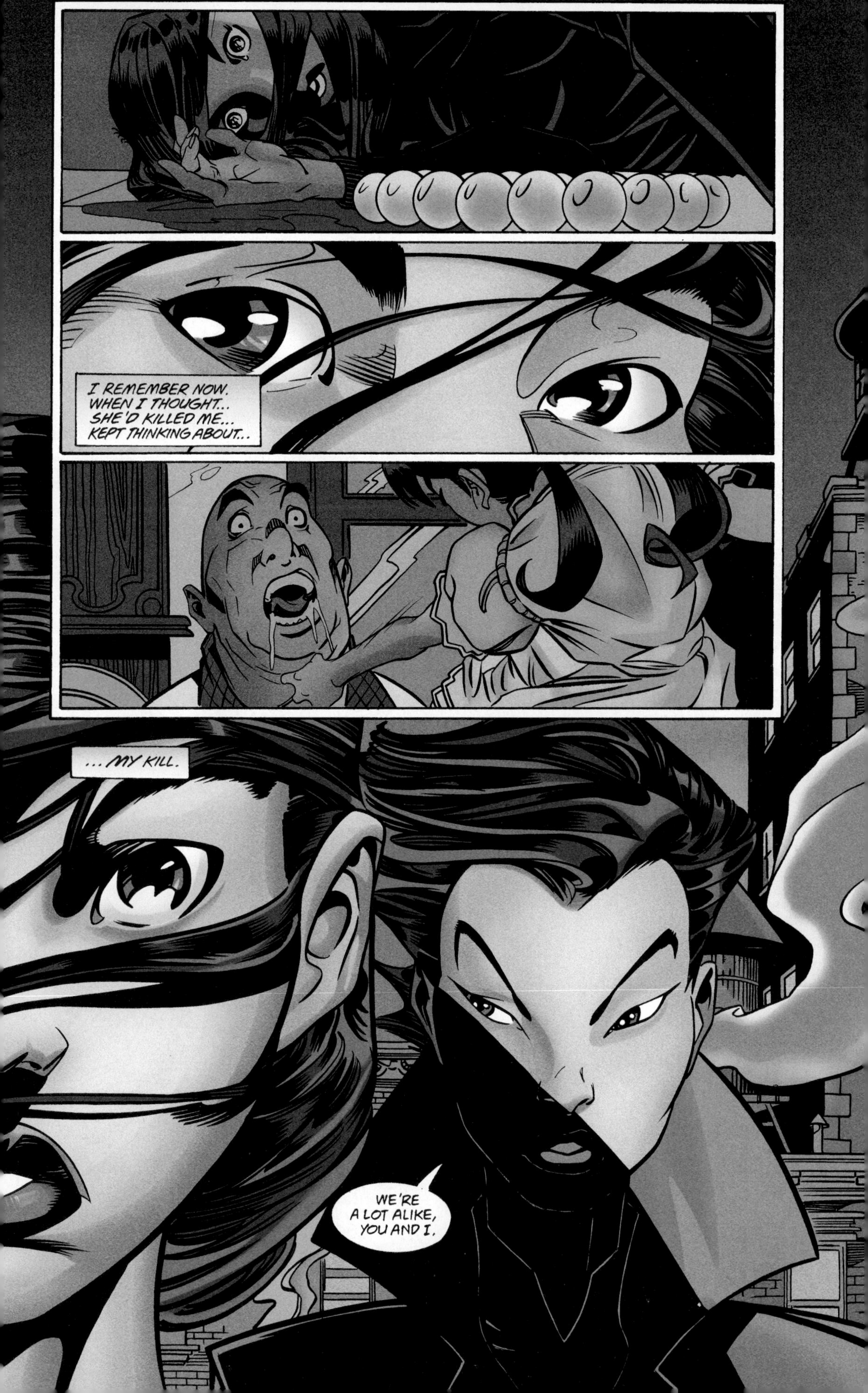
I REMEMBER NOW. WHEN I THOUGHT... SHE'D KILLED ME... KEPT THINKING ABOUT...
...MY KILL.
WE'RE A LOT ALIKE, YOU AND I.

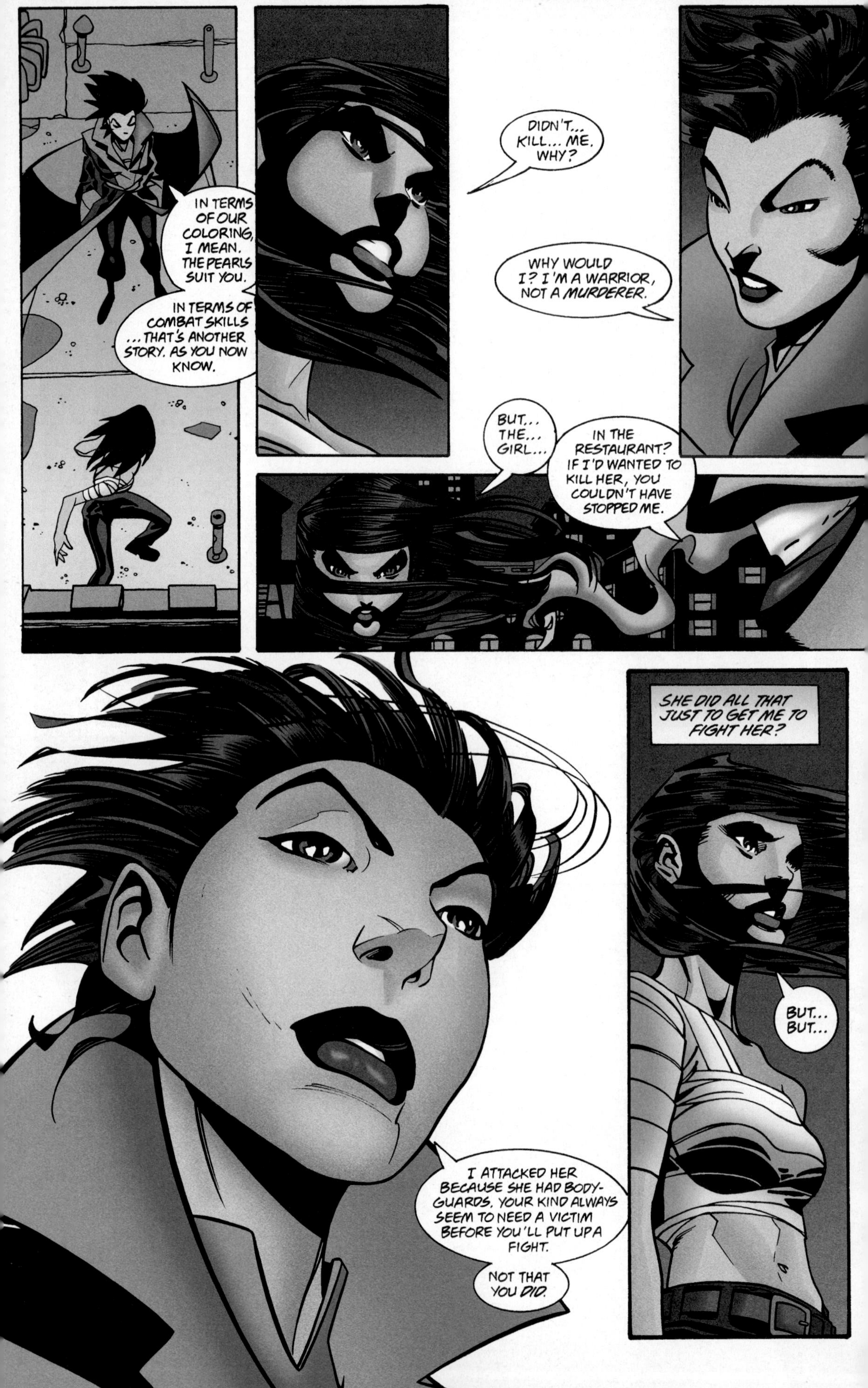
IN TERMS OF OUR COLORING, I MEAN. THE PEARLS SUIT YOU.
IN TERMS OF COMBAT SKILLS ...THAT'S ANOTHER STORY. AS YOU NOW KNOW.
DIDN'T... KILL... ME. WHY?
WHY WOULD I? I'M A WARRIOR, NOT A *MURDERER*.
BUT... THE... GIRL...
IN THE RESTAURANT? IF I'D WANTED TO KILL HER, YOU COULDN'T HAVE STOPPED ME.
SHE DID ALL THAT JUST TO GET ME TO FIGHT HER?
BUT... BUT...
I ATTACKED HER BECAUSE SHE HAD BODY-GUARDS. YOUR KIND ALWAYS SEEM TO NEED A VICTIM BEFORE YOU'LL PUT UP A FIGHT.
NOT THAT YOU *DID*.

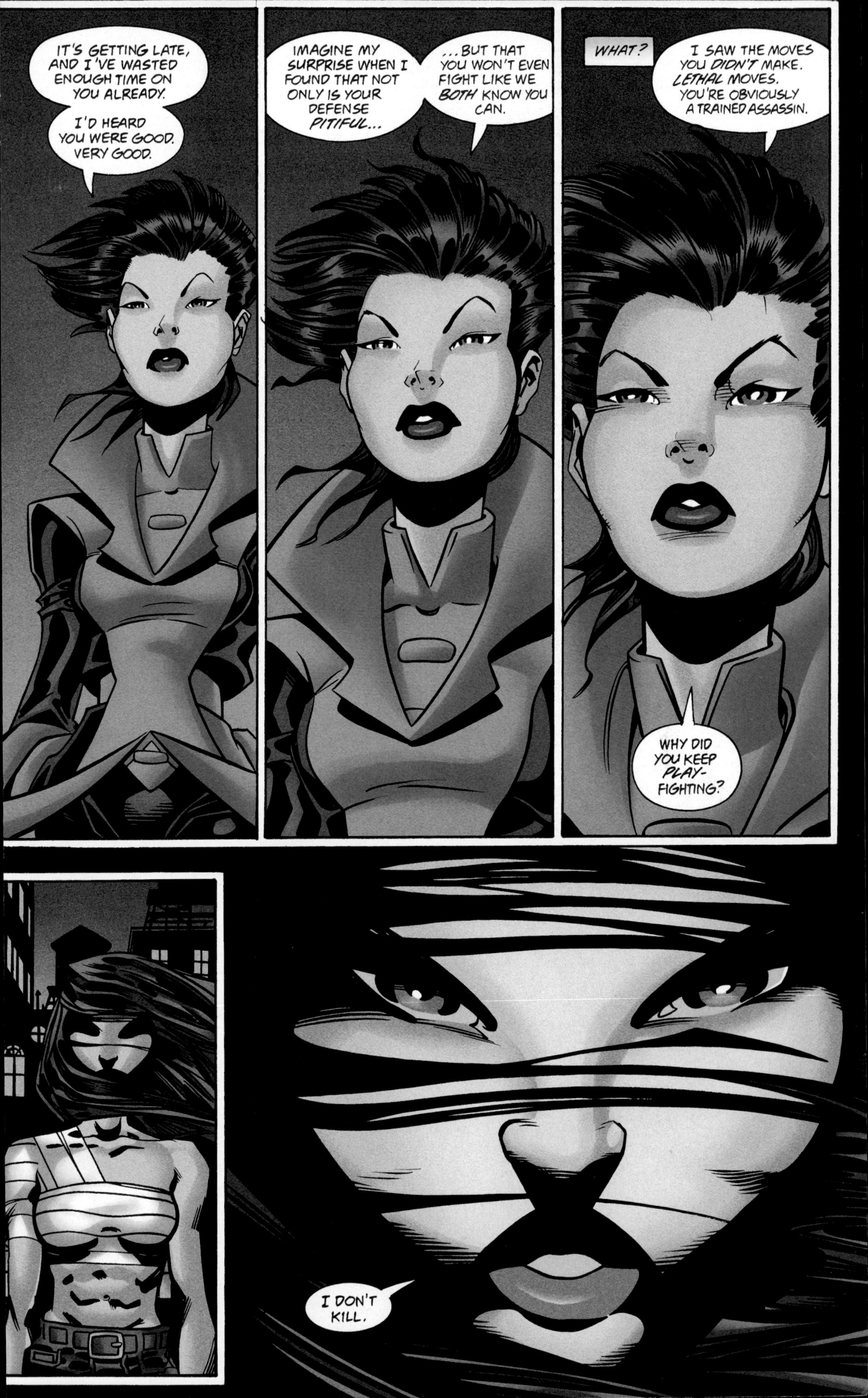
IT'S GETTING LATE, AND I'VE WASTED ENOUGH TIME ON YOU ALREADY.
I'D HEARD YOU WERE GOOD. VERY GOOD.
IMAGINE MY SURPRISE WHEN I FOUND THAT NOT ONLY IS YOUR DEFENSE PITIFUL...
...BUT THAT YOU WON'T EVEN FIGHT LIKE WE BOTH KNOW YOU CAN.
WHAT?
I SAW THE MOVES YOU DIDN'T MAKE. LETHAL MOVES. YOU'RE OBVIOUSLY A TRAINED ASSASSIN.
WHY DID YOU KEEP PLAY-FIGHTING?
I DON'T KILL.

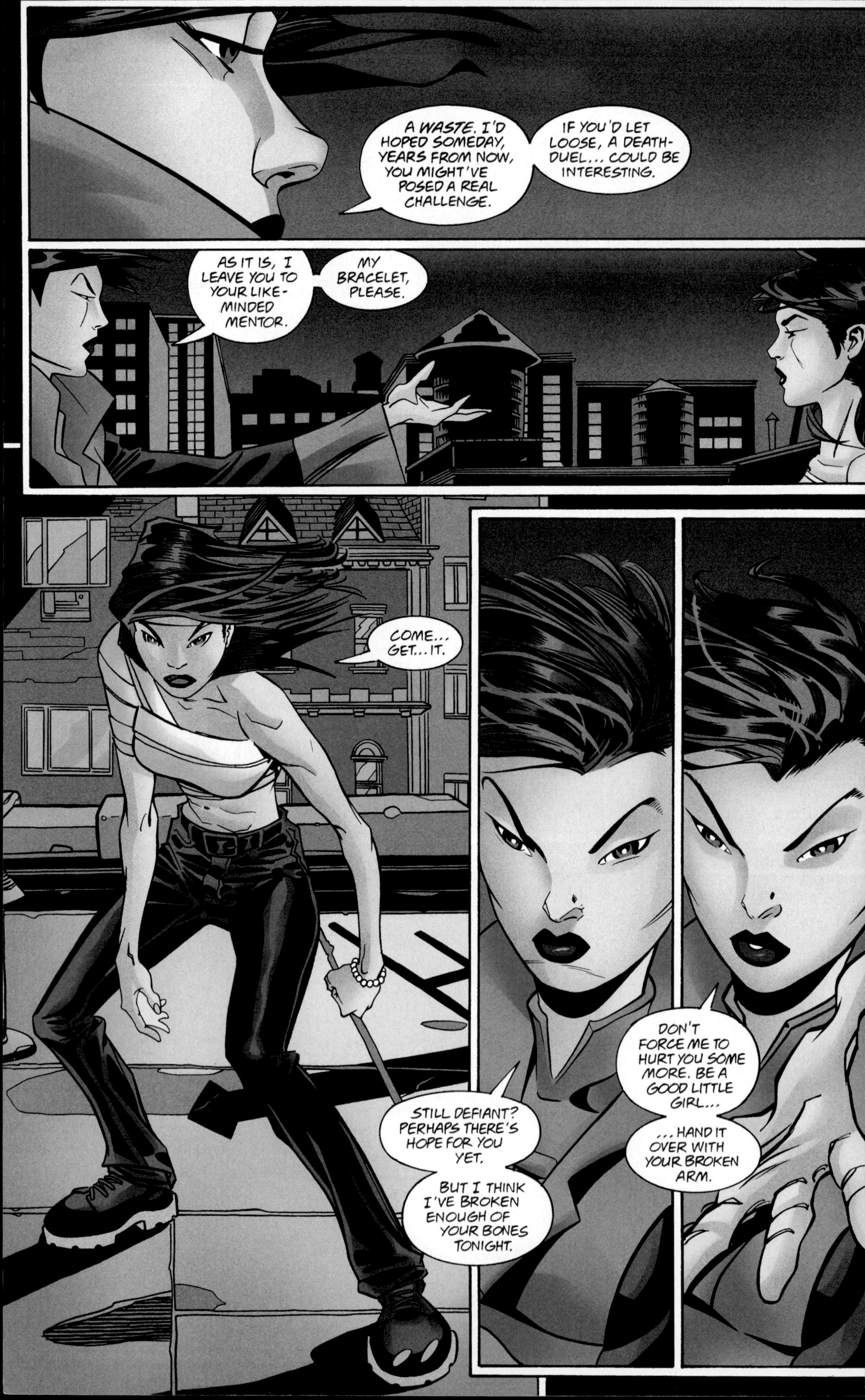
A WASTE. I'D HOPED SOMEDAY, YEARS FROM NOW, YOU MIGHT'VE POSED A REAL CHALLENGE.
IF YOU'D LET LOOSE, A DEATH-DUEL... COULD BE INTERESTING.
AS IT IS, I LEAVE YOU TO YOUR LIKE-MINDED MENTOR.
MY BRACELET, PLEASE.
COME... GET... IT.
STILL DEFIANT? PERHAPS THERE'S HOPE FOR YOU YET.
BUT I THINK I'VE BROKEN ENOUGH OF YOUR BONES TONIGHT.
DON'T FORCE ME TO HURT YOU SOME MORE. BE A GOOD LITTLE GIRL...
...HAND IT OVER WITH YOUR BROKEN ARM.

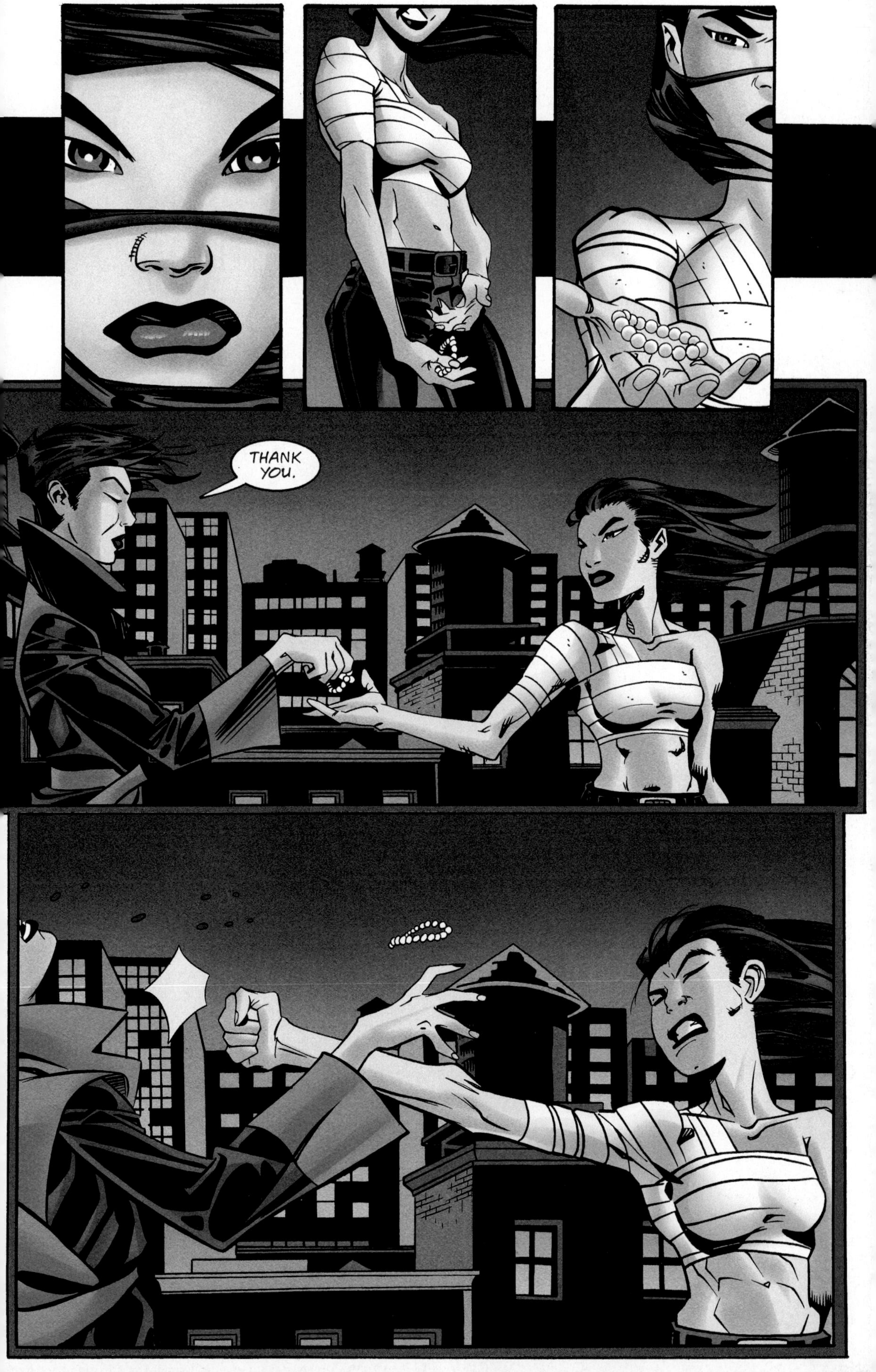
THANK YOU.

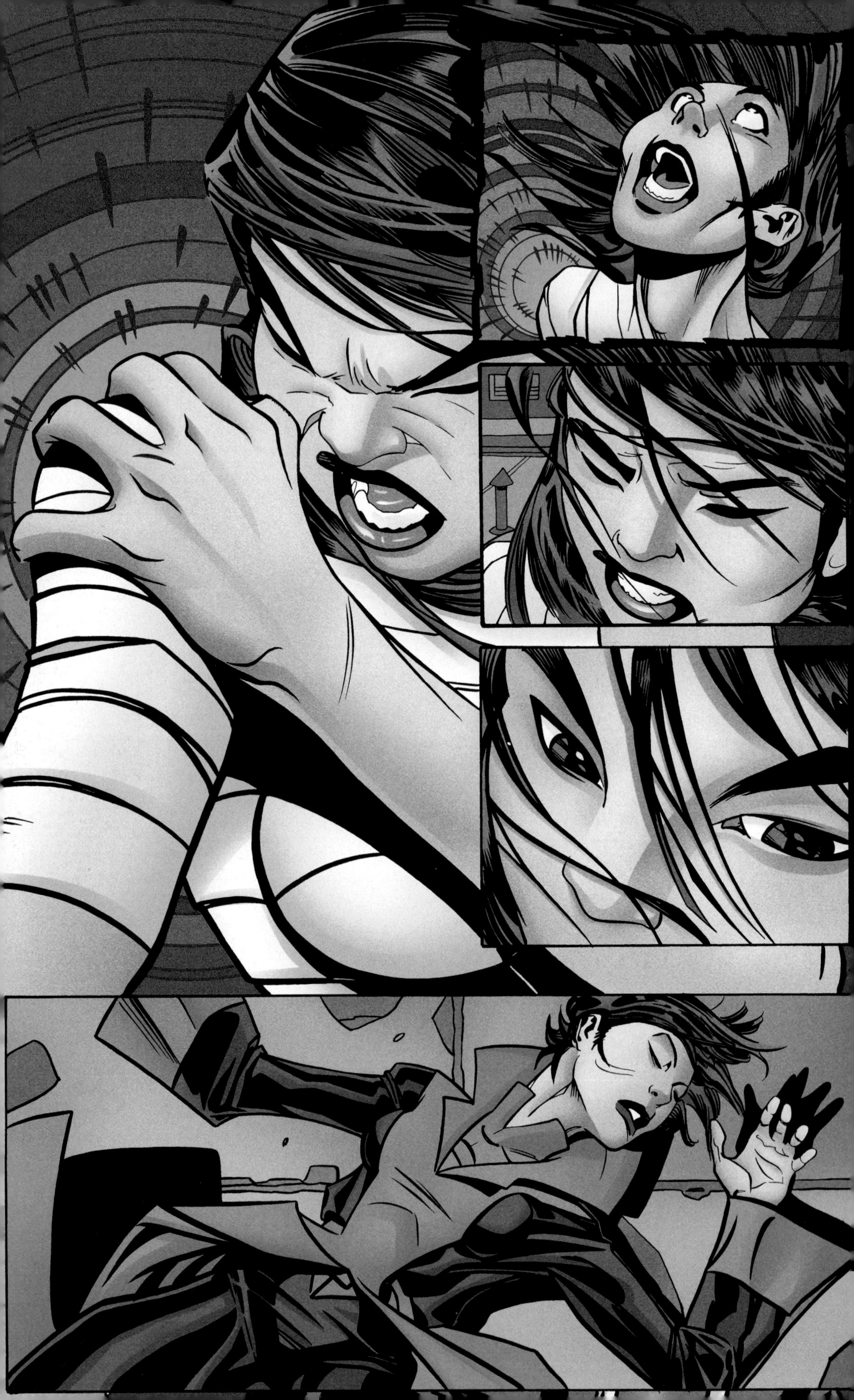

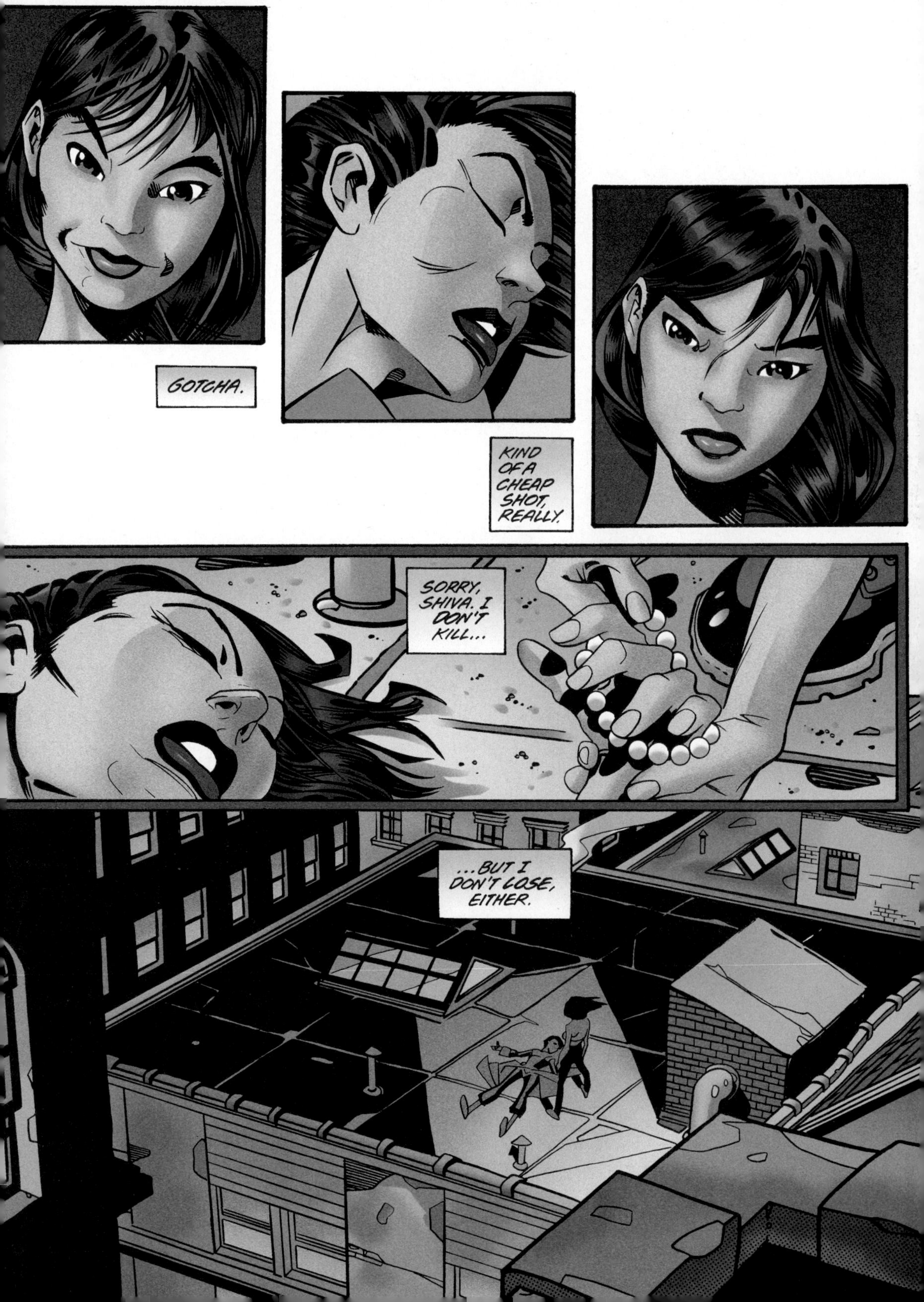
GOTCHA.
KIND OF A CHEAP SHOT, REALLY.
SORRY, SHIVA. I DON'T KILL...
...BUT I DON'T LOSE, EITHER.

BATGIRL #9 cover by
Damion Scott & Robert Campanella

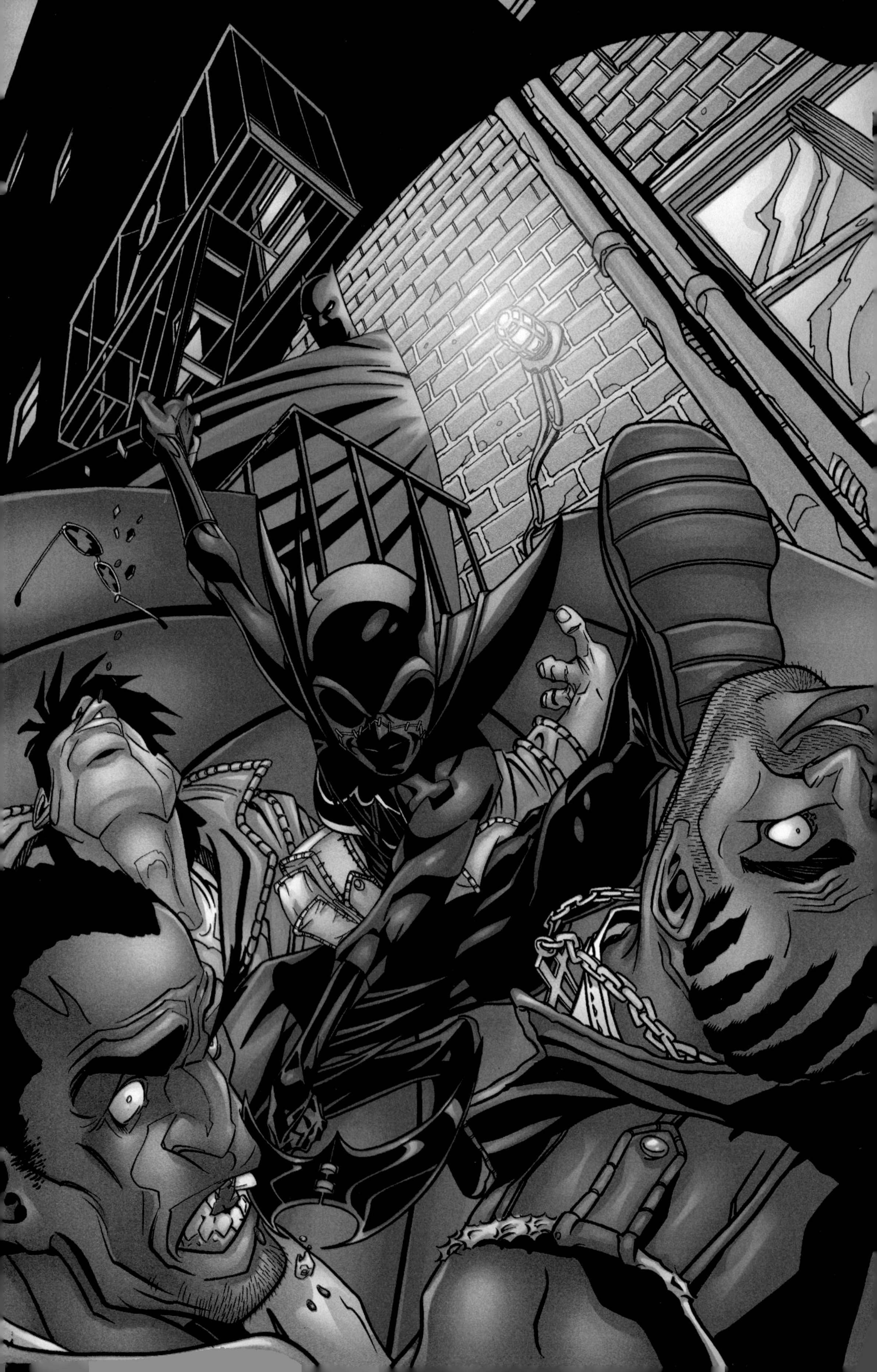

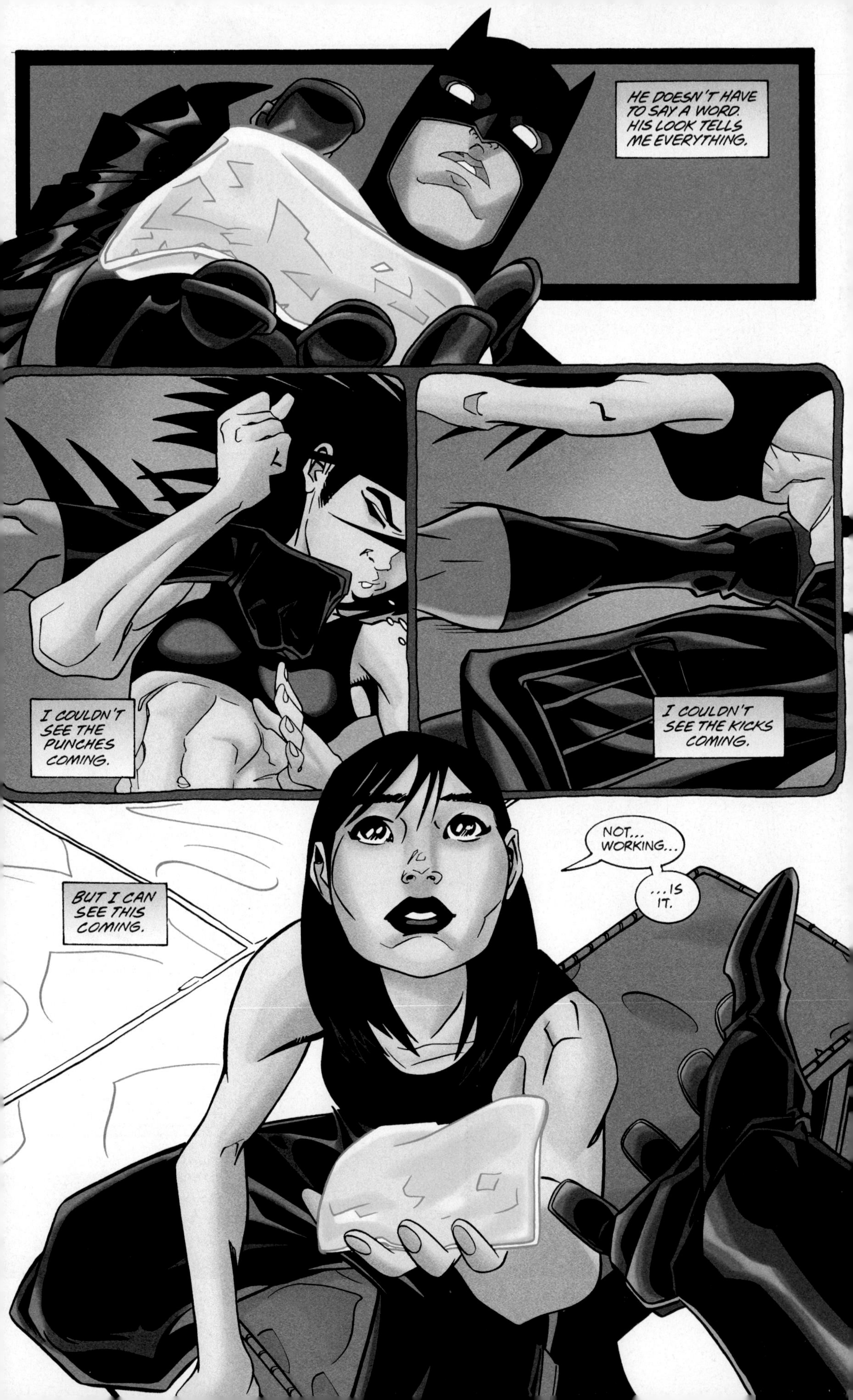
HE DOESN'T HAVE TO SAY A WORD. HIS LOOK TELLS ME EVERYTHING.
I COULDN'T SEE THE PUNCHES COMING.
I COULDN'T SEE THE KICKS COMING.
BUT I CAN SEE THIS COMING.
NOT... WORKING...
...IS IT.

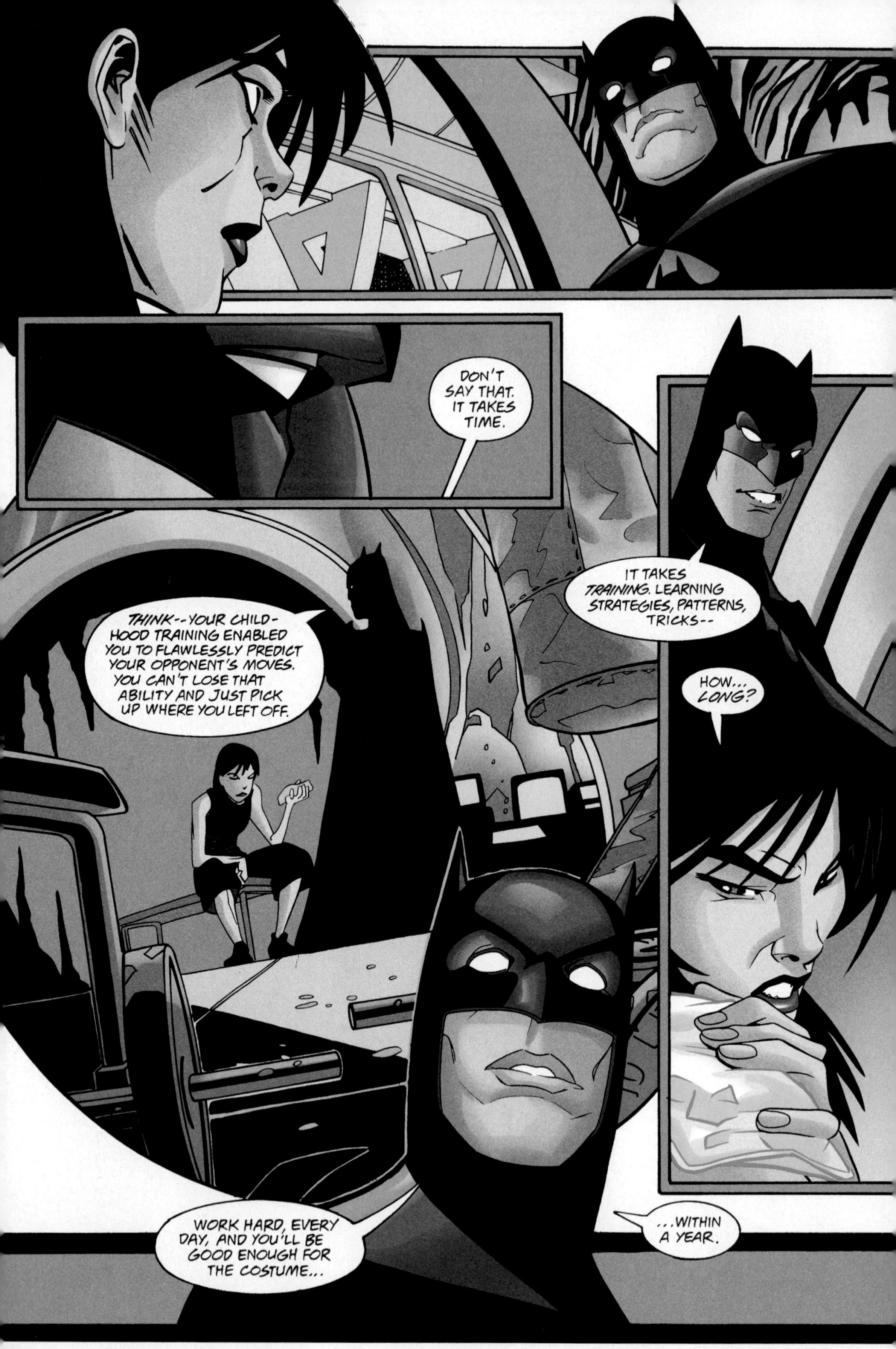
DON'T SAY THAT. IT TAKES TIME.
IT TAKES TRAINING. LEARNING STRATEGIES, PATTERNS, TRICKS--
THINK--YOUR CHILDHOOD TRAINING ENABLED YOU TO FLAWLESSLY PREDICT YOUR OPPONENT'S MOVES. YOU CAN'T LOSE THAT ABILITY AND JUST PICK UP WHERE YOU LEFT OFF.
HOW... LONG?
WORK HARD, EVERY DAY, AND YOU'LL BE GOOD ENOUGH FOR THE COSTUME...
...WITHIN A YEAR.

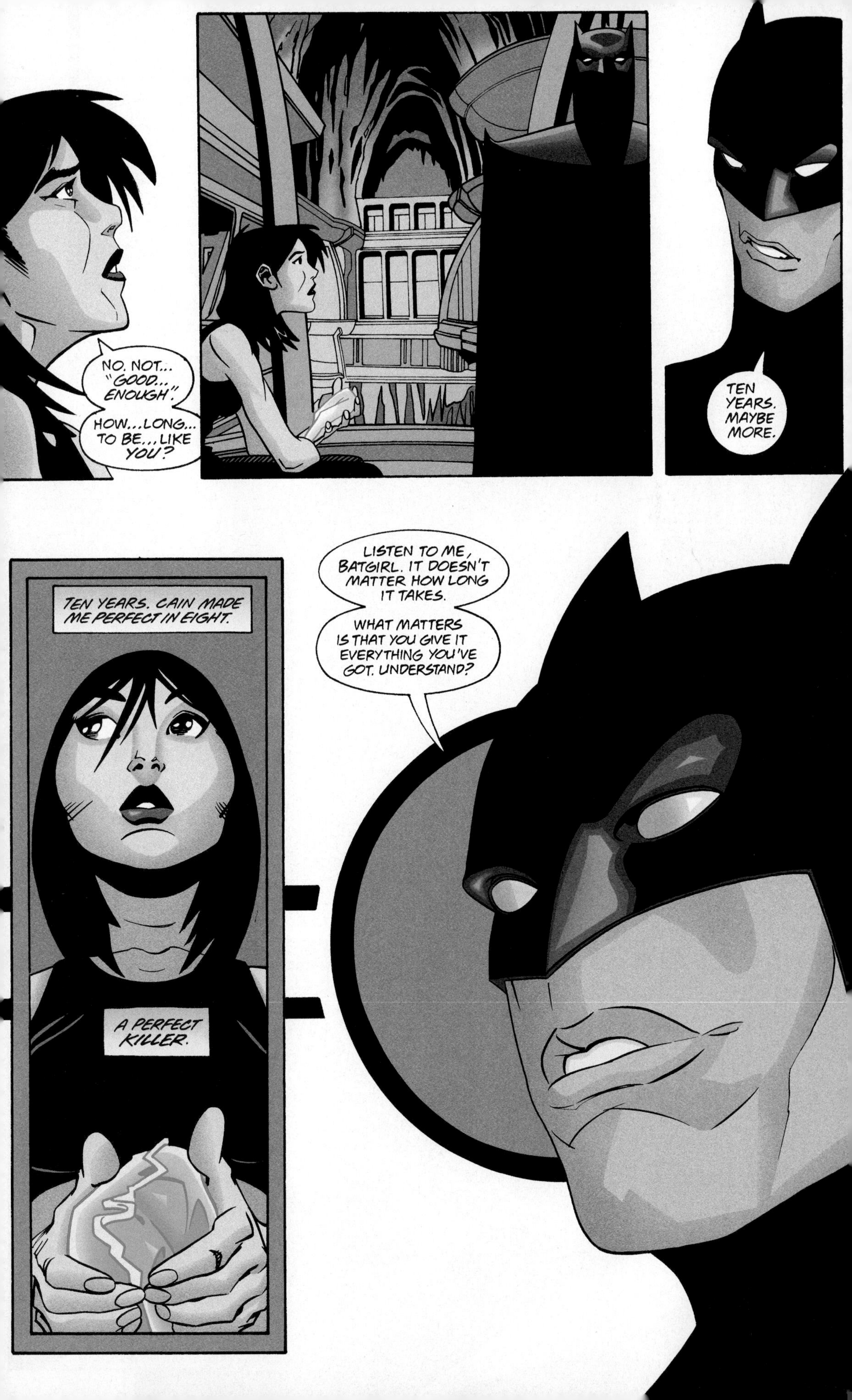
NO. NOT... "GOOD... ENOUGH".
HOW...LONG... TO BE...LIKE YOU?
TEN YEARS. MAYBE MORE.
TEN YEARS. CAIN MADE ME PERFECT IN EIGHT.
A PERFECT KILLER.
LISTEN TO ME, BATGIRL. IT DOESN'T MATTER HOW LONG IT TAKES.
WHAT MATTERS IS THAT YOU GIVE IT EVERYTHING YOU'VE GOT. UNDERSTAND?

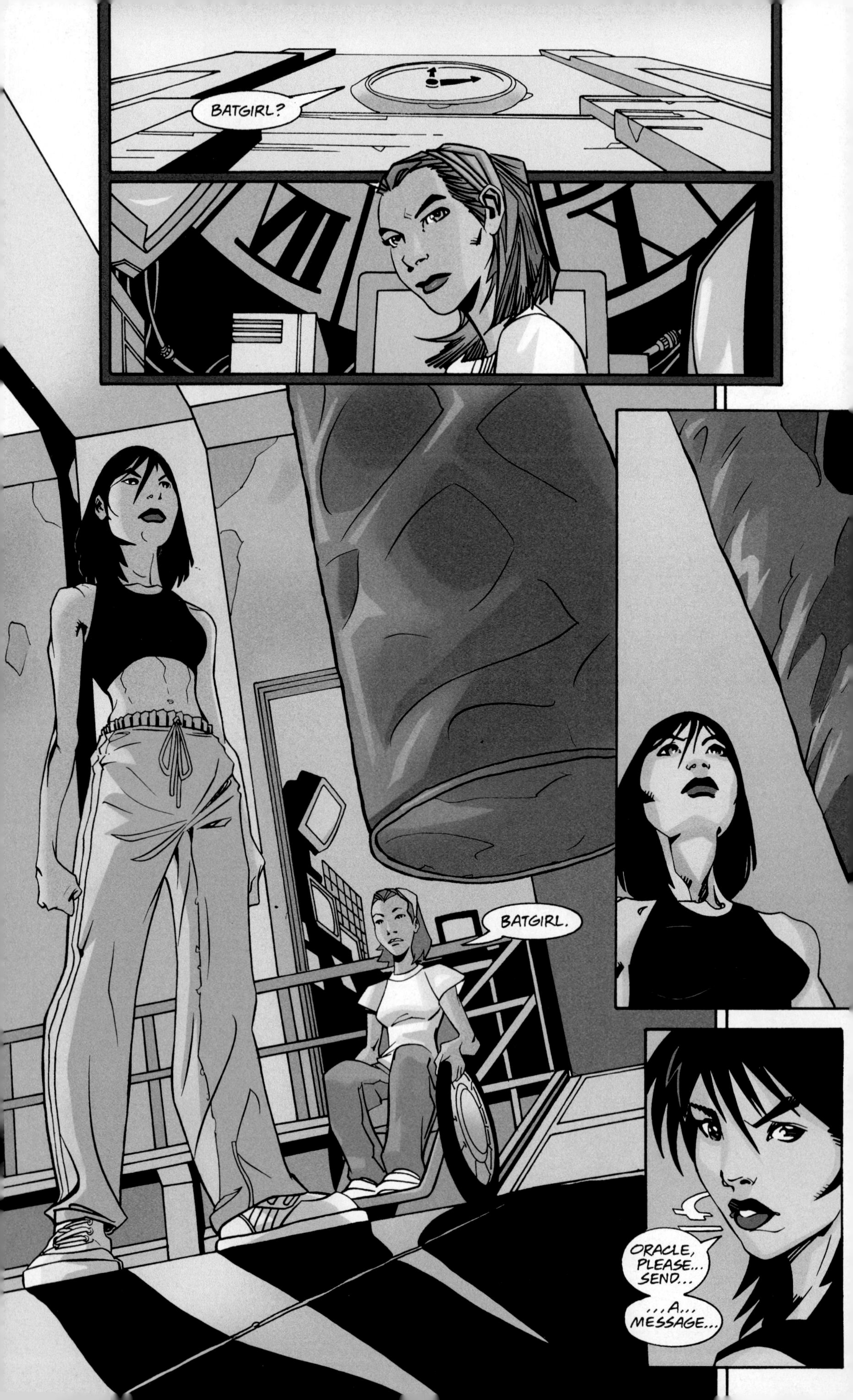
BATGIRL?
BATGIRL.
ORACLE, PLEASE... SEND...
...A... MESSAGE...

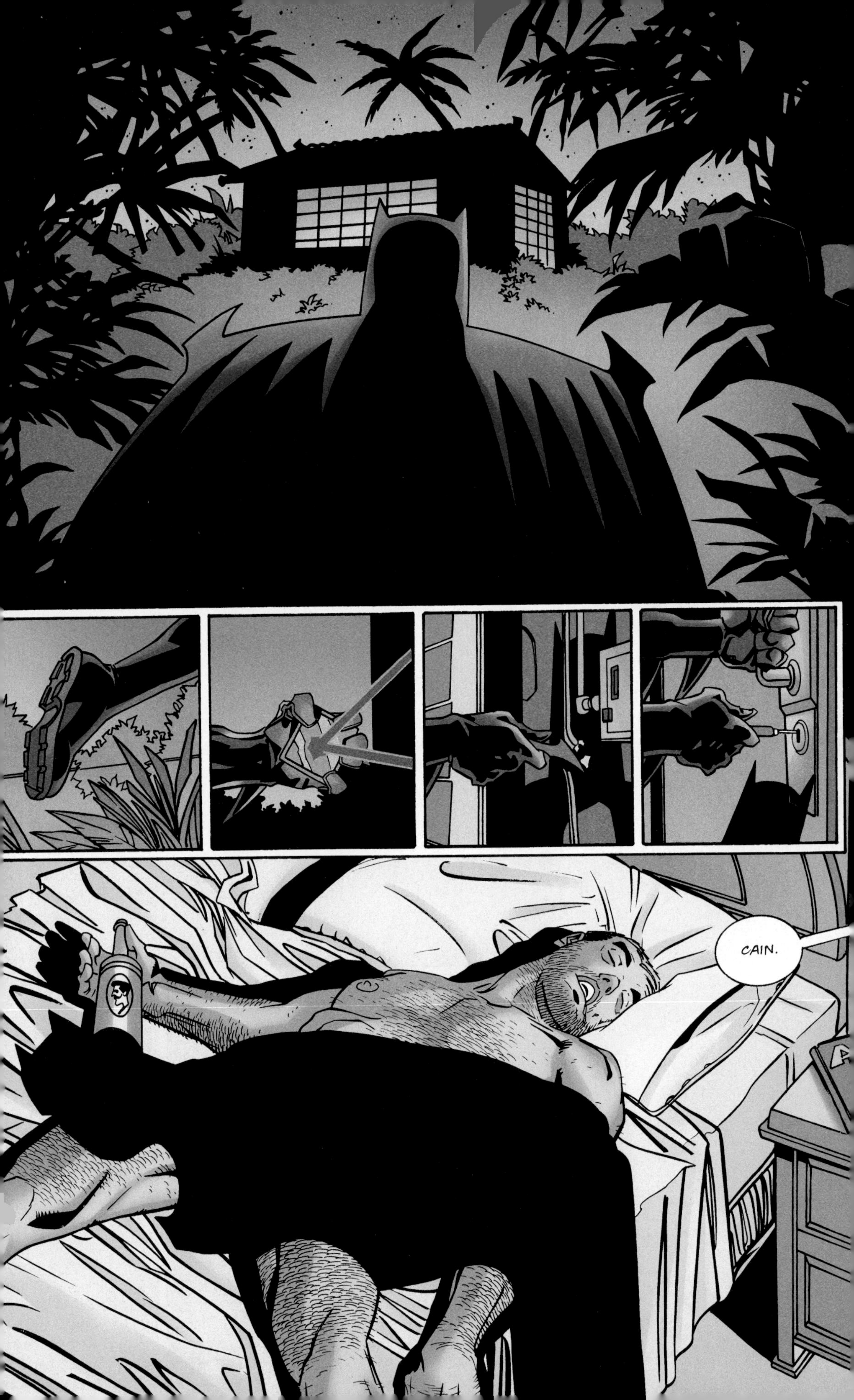
CAIN.

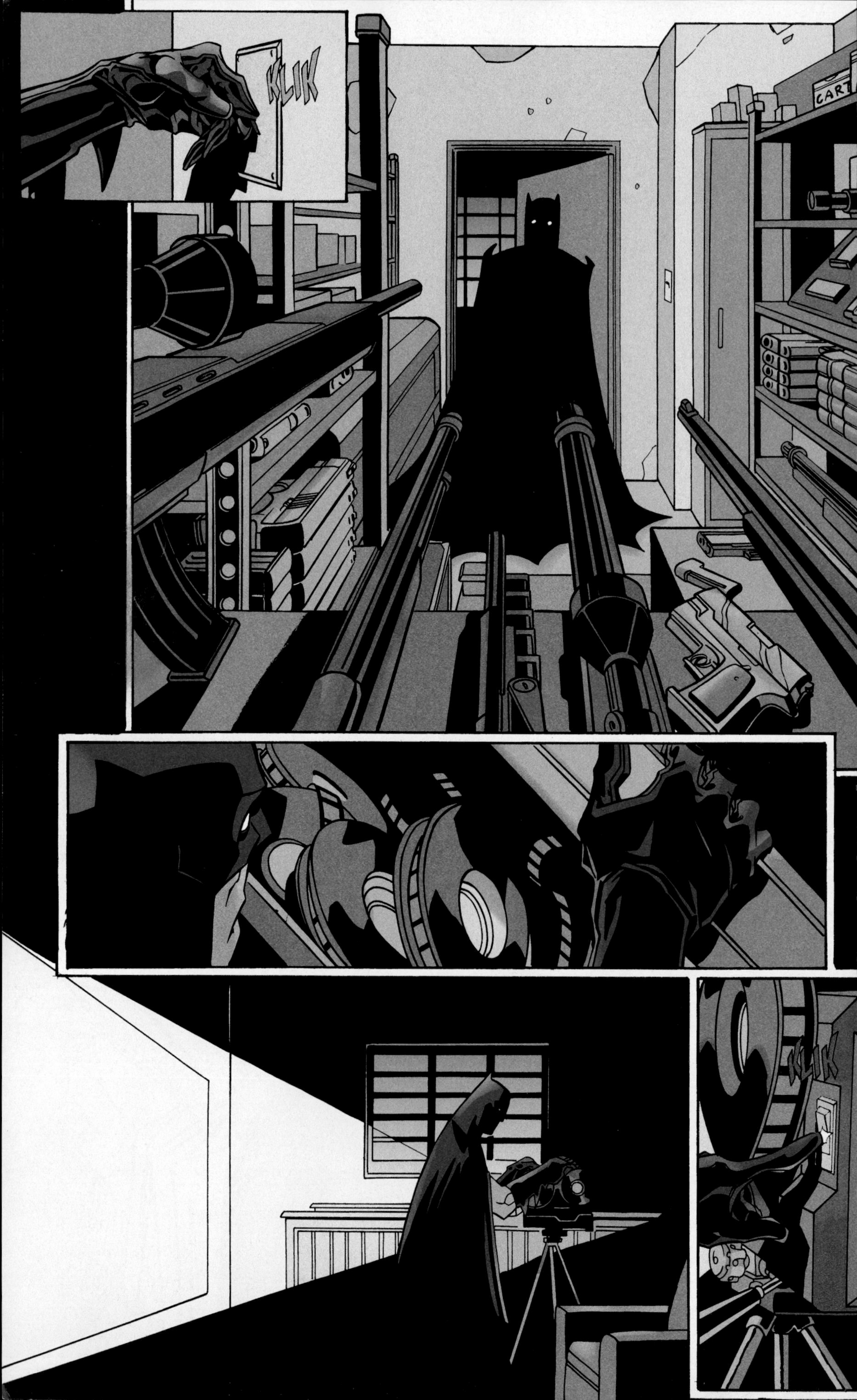
KLIK
KLIK

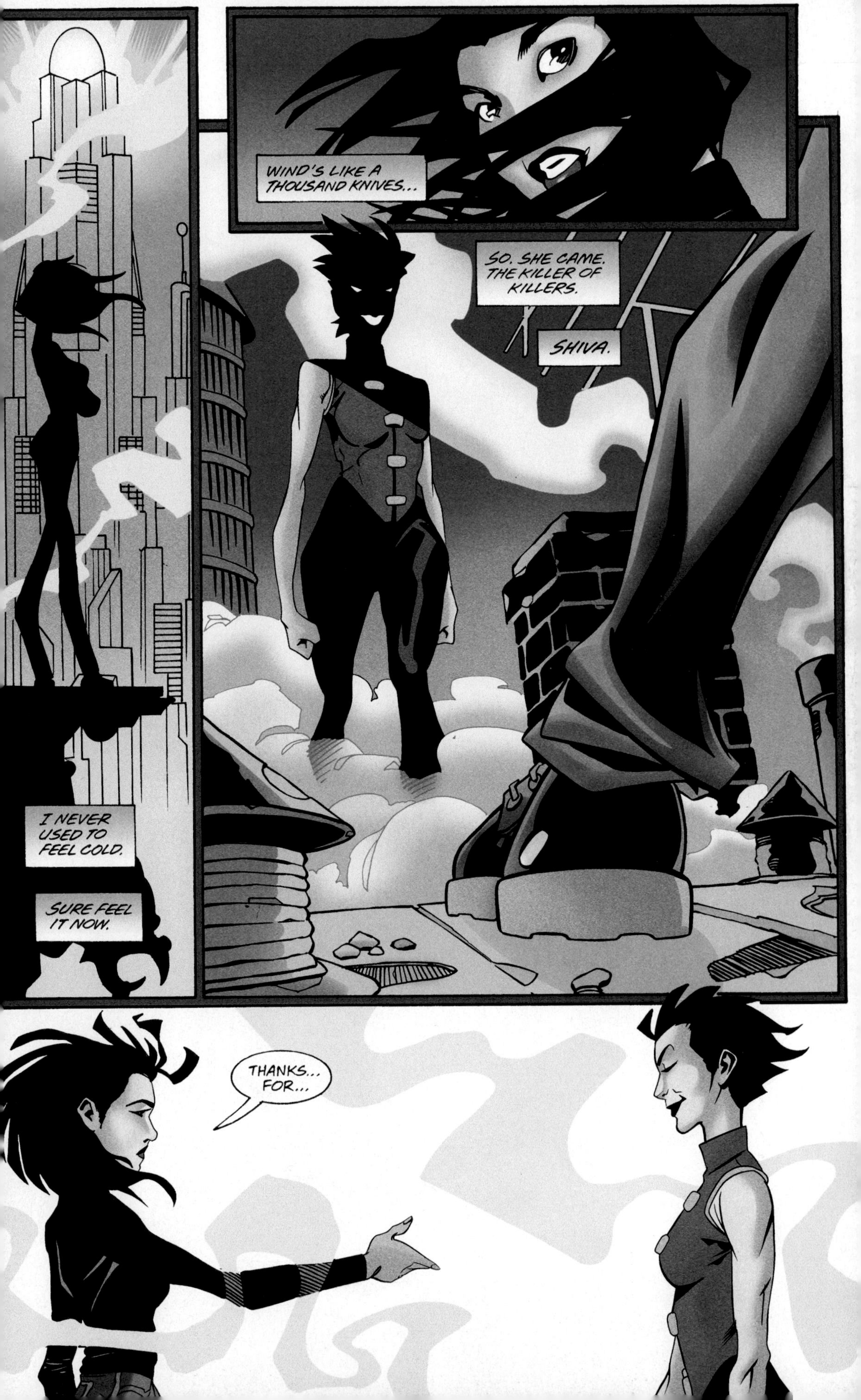
WIND'S LIKE A THOUSAND KNIVES...
I NEVER USED TO FEEL COLD.
SURE FEEL IT NOW.
SO. SHE CAME. THE KILLER OF KILLERS.
SHIVA.
THANKS... FOR...

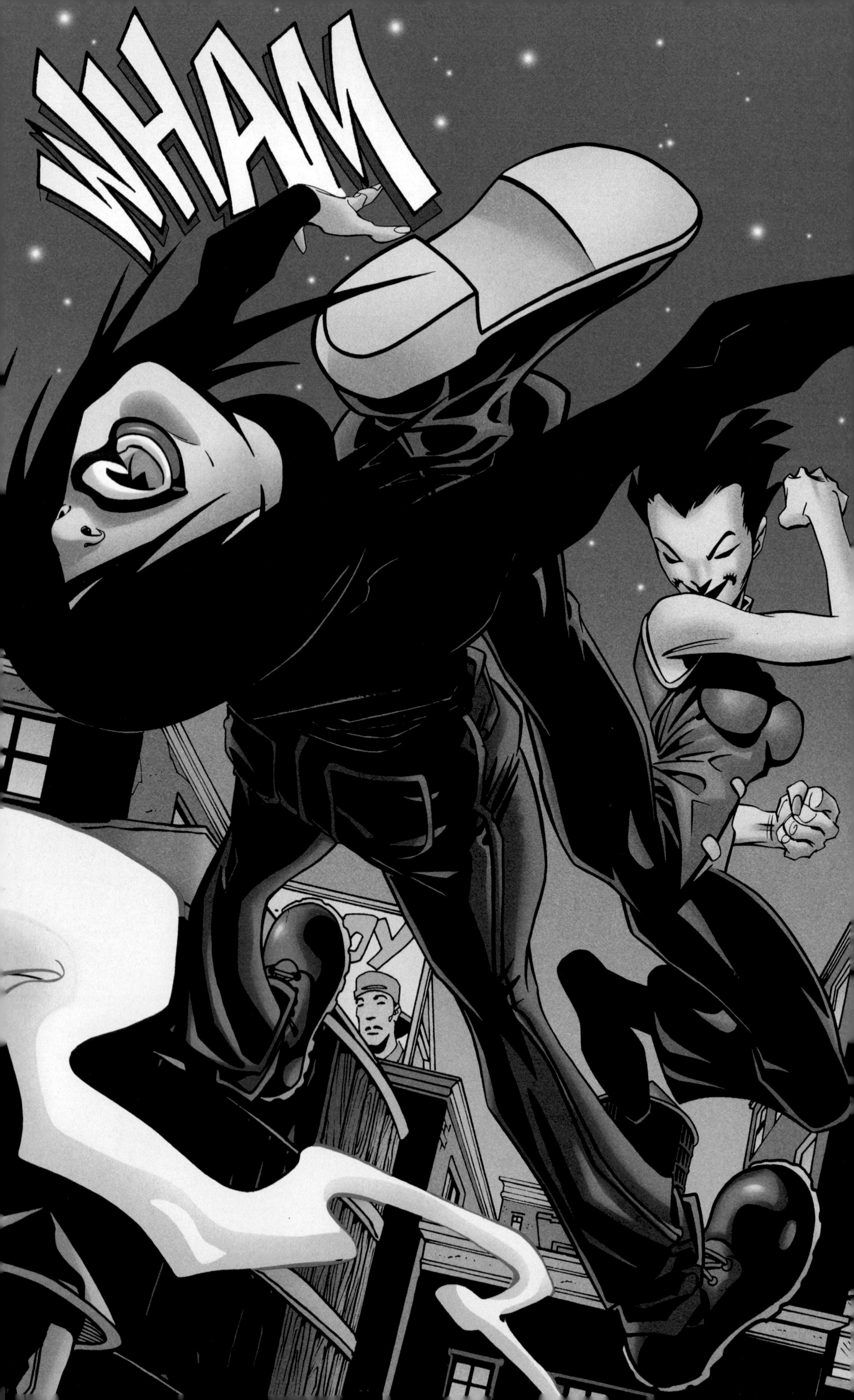
WHAM

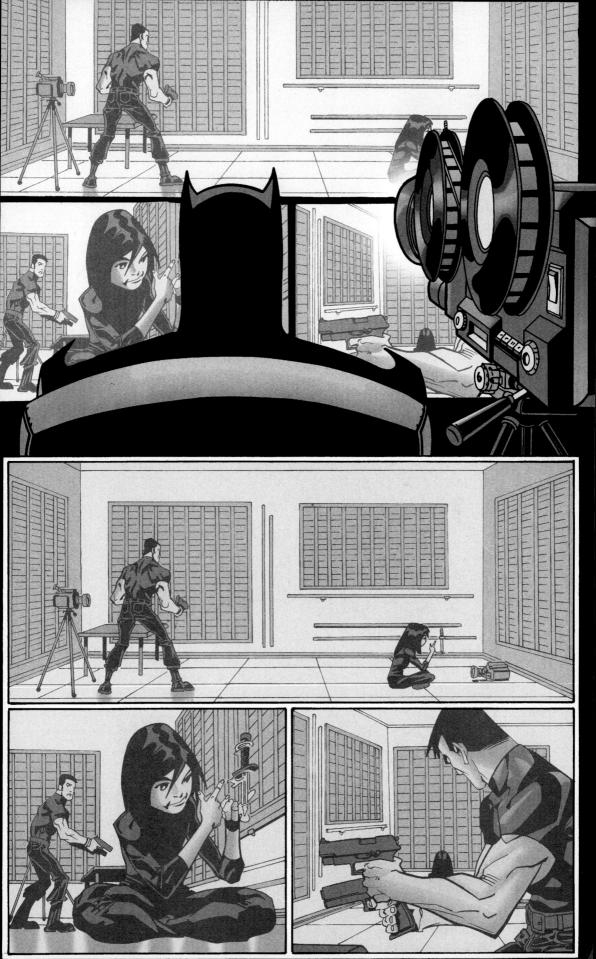

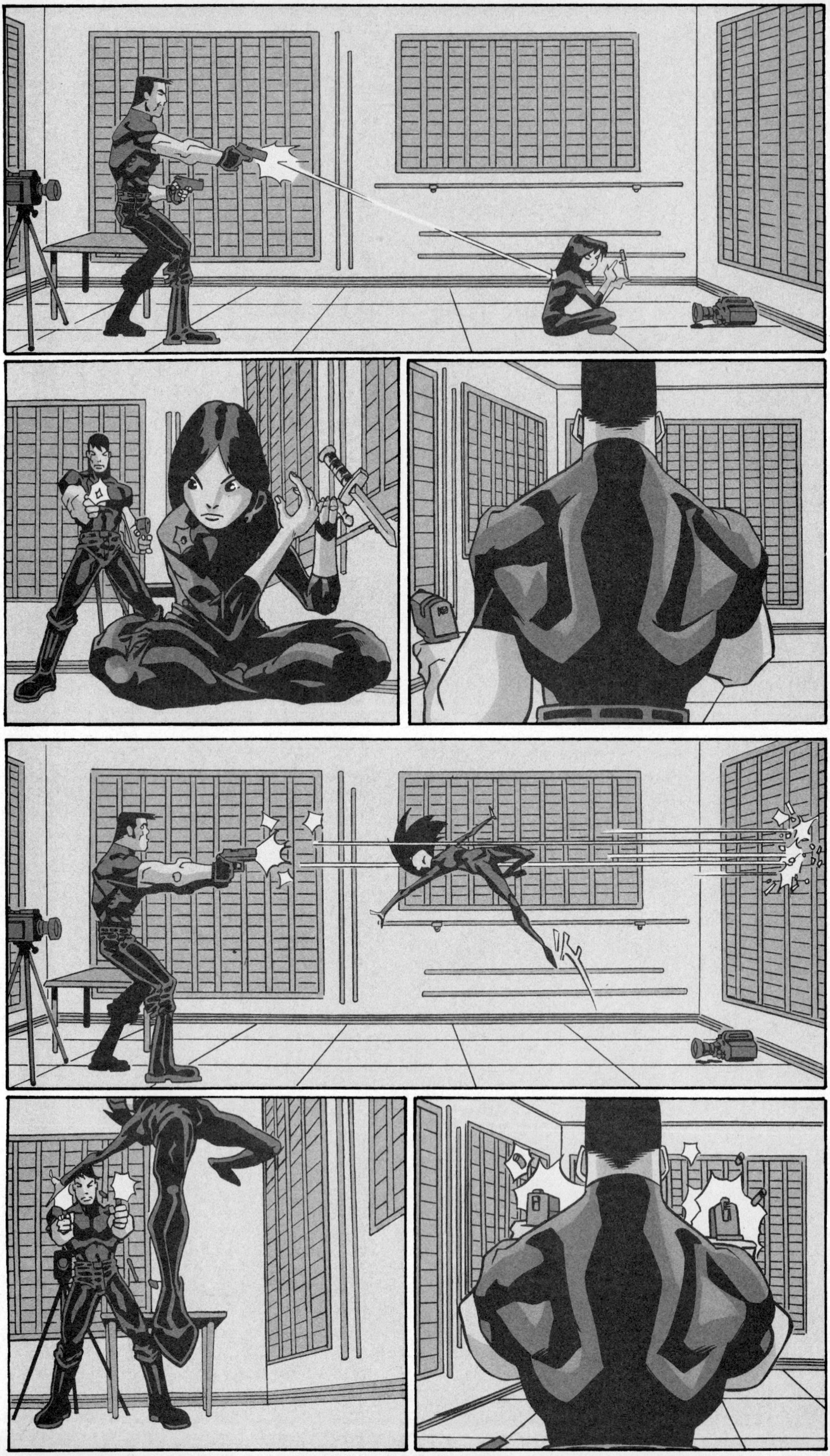

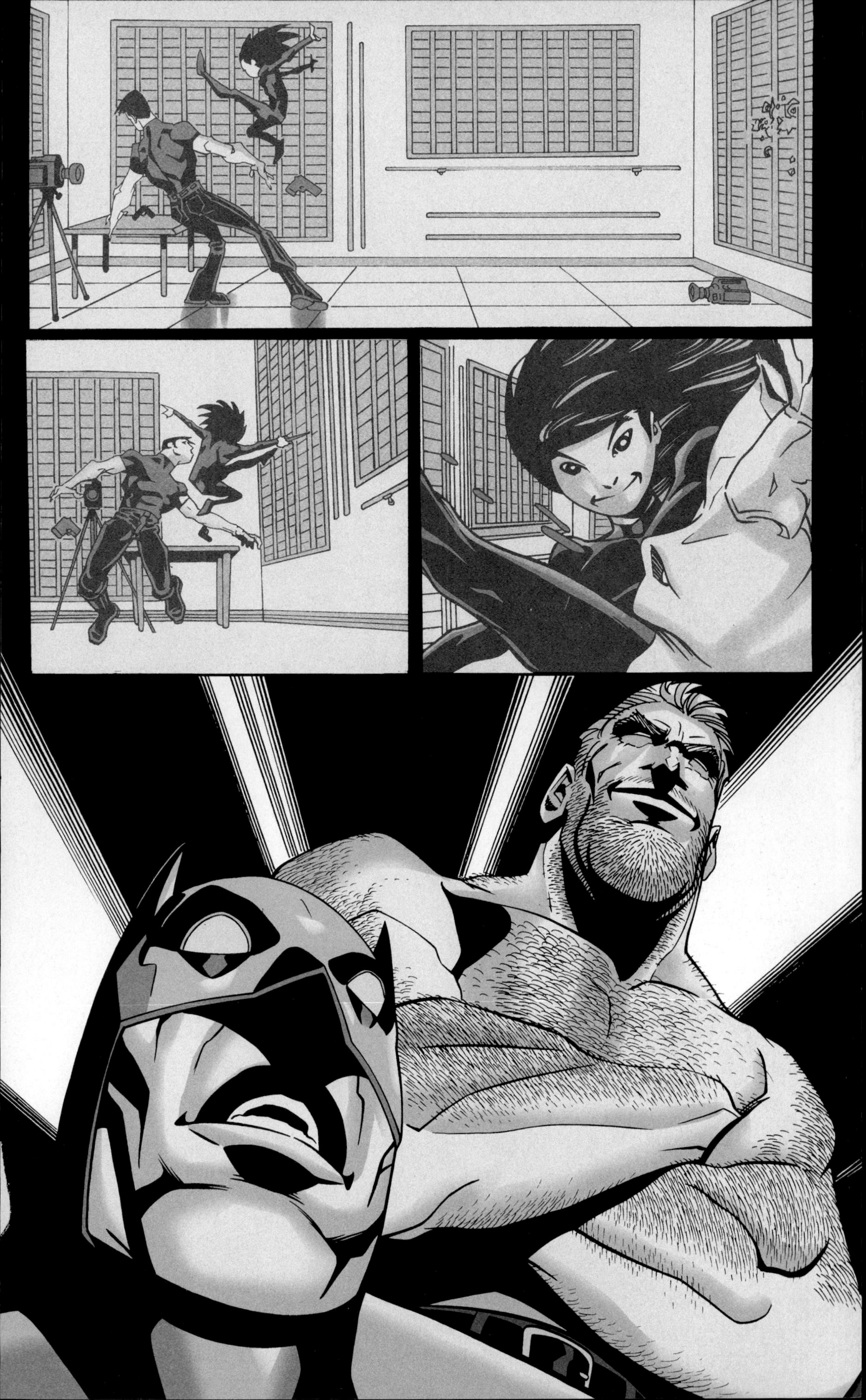

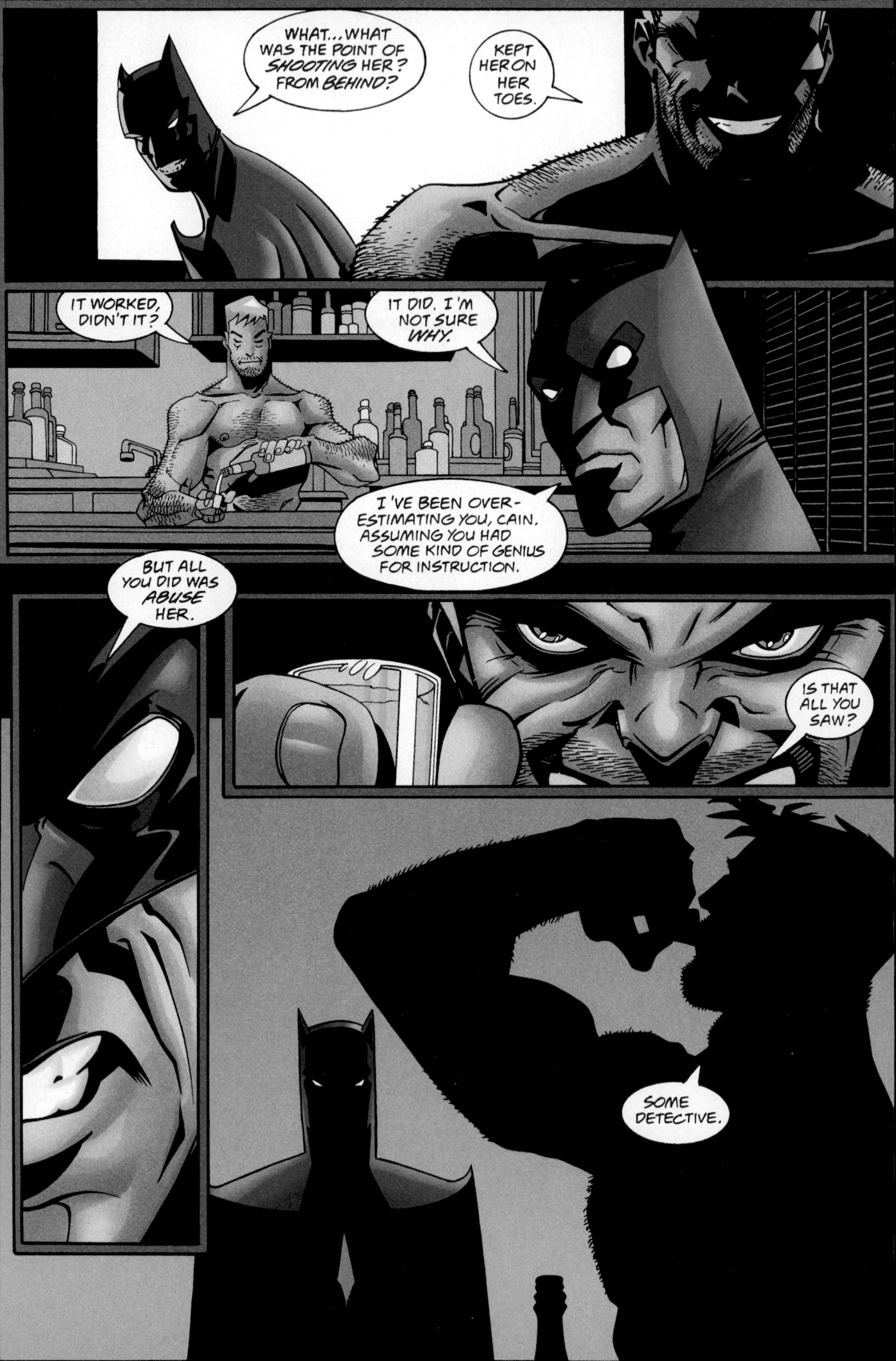
WHAT... WHAT WAS THE POINT OF SHOOTING HER? FROM BEHIND?
KEPT HER ON HER TOES.
IT WORKED, DIDN'T IT?
IT DID. I'M NOT SURE WHY.
I'VE BEEN OVER-ESTIMATING YOU, CAIN, ASSUMING YOU HAD SOME KIND OF GENIUS FOR INSTRUCTION.
BUT ALL YOU DID WAS ABUSE HER.
IS THAT ALL YOU SAW?
SOME DETECTIVE.

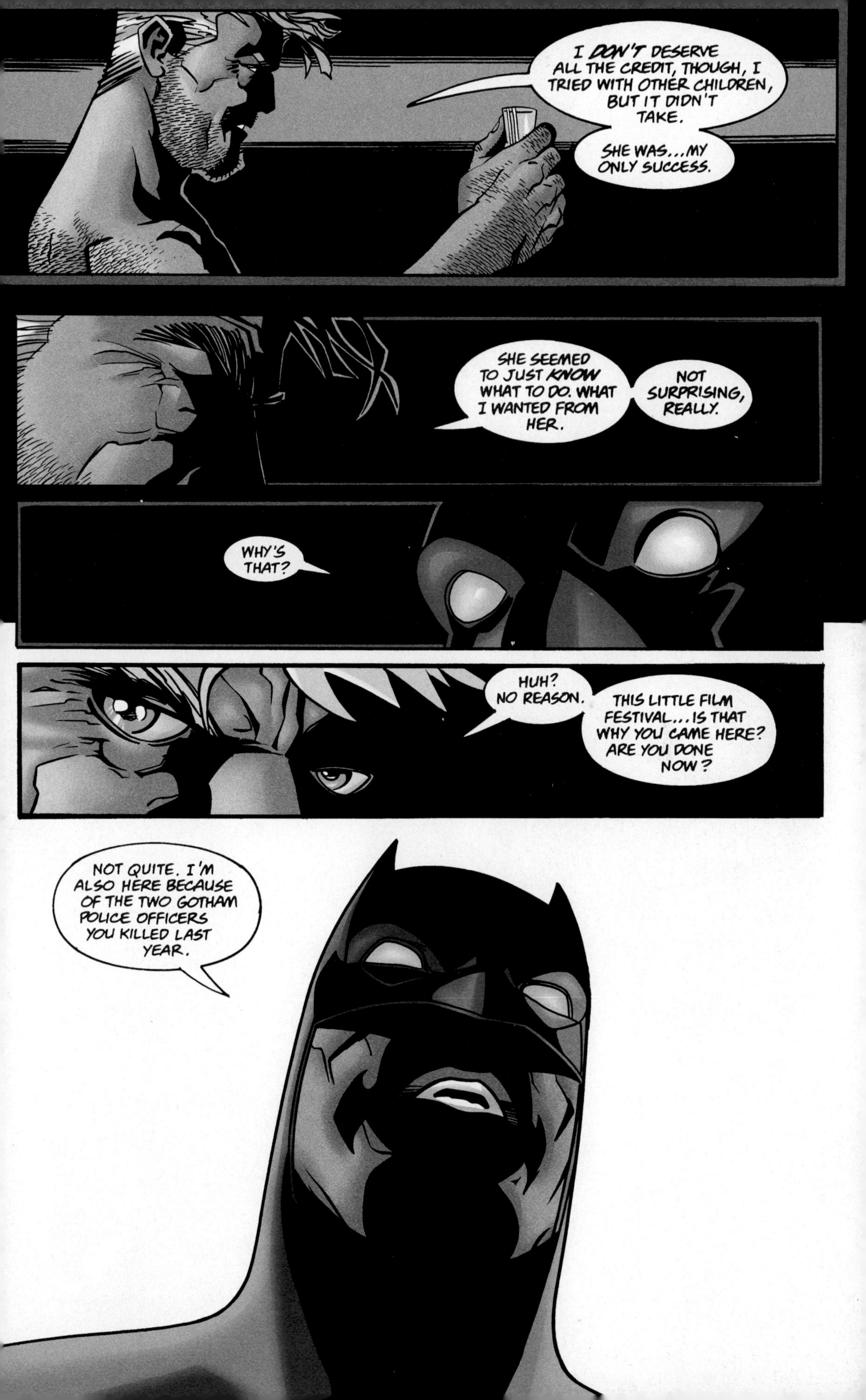

I DON'T DESERVE ALL THE CREDIT, THOUGH, I TRIED WITH OTHER CHILDREN, BUT IT DIDN'T TAKE.
SHE WAS... MY ONLY SUCCESS.
SHE SEEMED TO JUST KNOW WHAT TO DO. WHAT I WANTED FROM HER.
NOT SURPRISING, REALLY.
WHY'S THAT?
HUH? NO REASON.
THIS LITTLE FILM FESTIVAL... IS THAT WHY YOU CAME HERE? ARE YOU DONE NOW?
NOT QUITE. I'M ALSO HERE BECAUSE OF THE TWO GOTHAM POLICE OFFICERS YOU KILLED LAST YEAR.

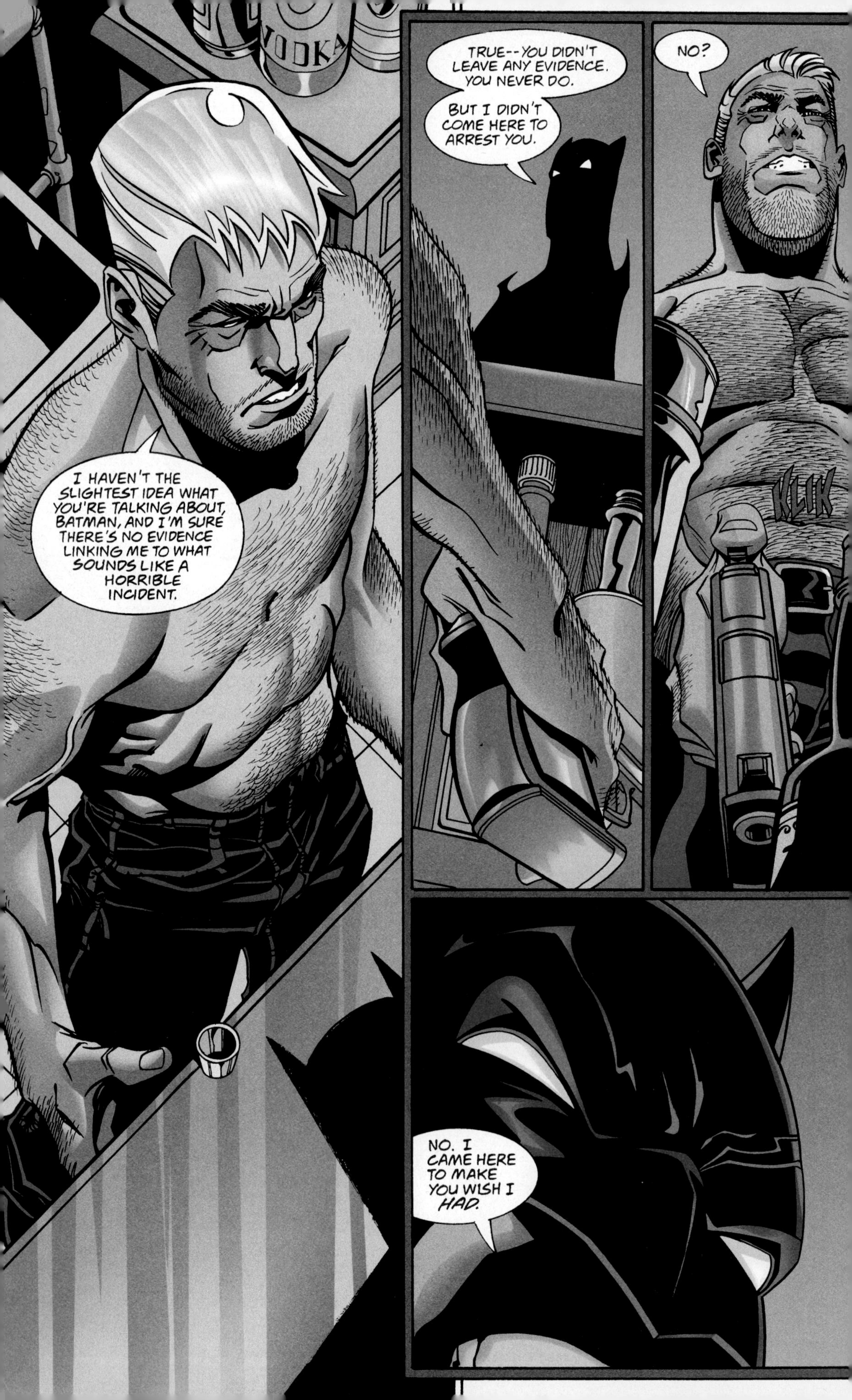
VODKA
I HAVEN'T THE SLIGHTEST IDEA WHAT YOU'RE TALKING ABOUT, BATMAN, AND I'M SURE THERE'S NO EVIDENCE LINKING ME TO WHAT SOUNDS LIKE A HORRIBLE INCIDENT.
TRUE--YOU DIDN'T LEAVE ANY EVIDENCE. YOU NEVER DO.
BUT I DIDN'T COME HERE TO ARREST YOU.
NO?
KLIK
NO. I CAME HERE TO MAKE YOU WISH I *HAD*.

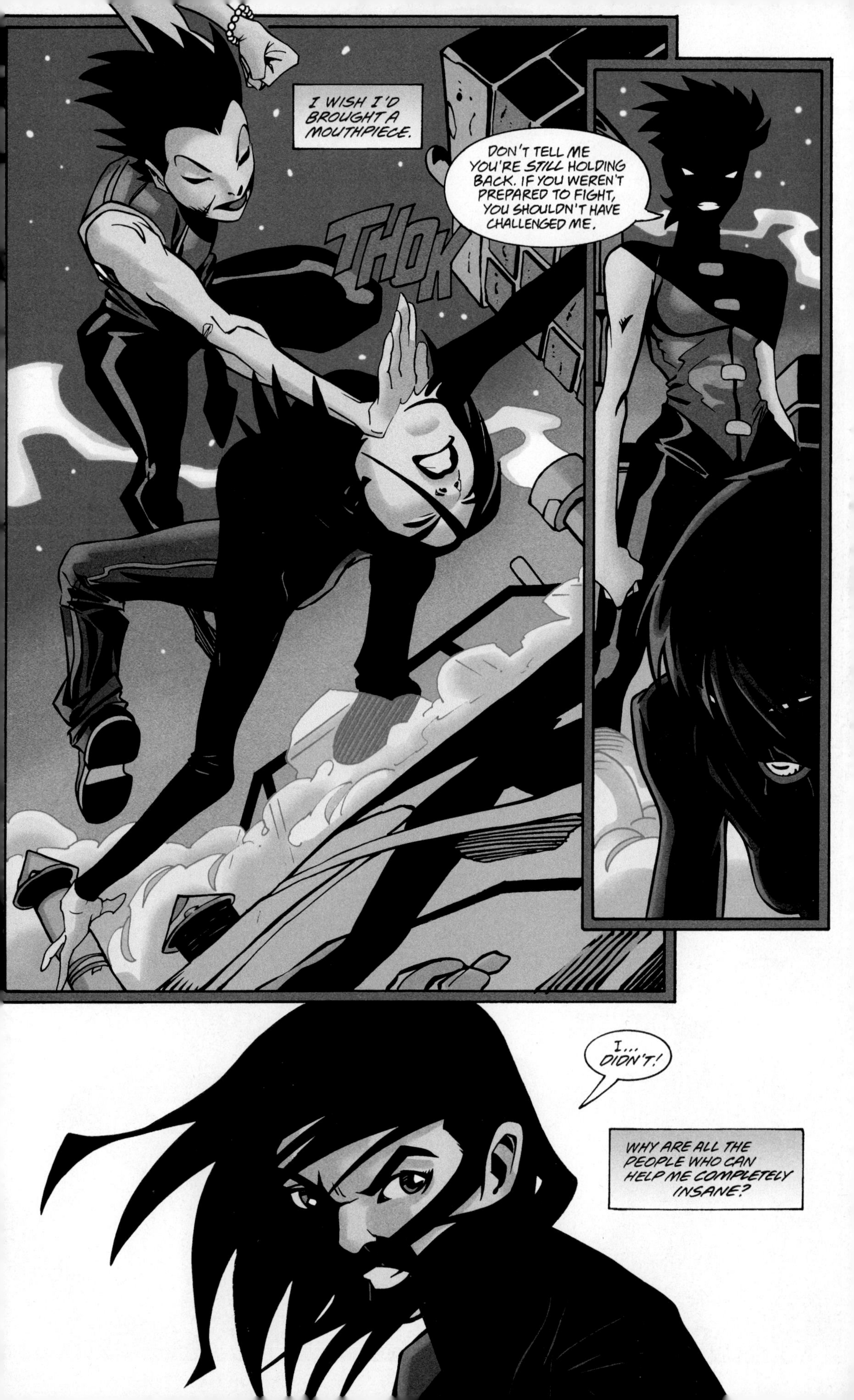

I WISH I'D BROUGHT A MOUTHPIECE.
DON'T TELL ME YOU'RE STILL HOLDING BACK. IF YOU WEREN'T PREPARED TO FIGHT, YOU SHOULDN'T HAVE CHALLENGED ME.
THOK
I... DIDN'T!
WHY ARE ALL THE PEOPLE WHO CAN HELP ME COMPLETELY INSANE?

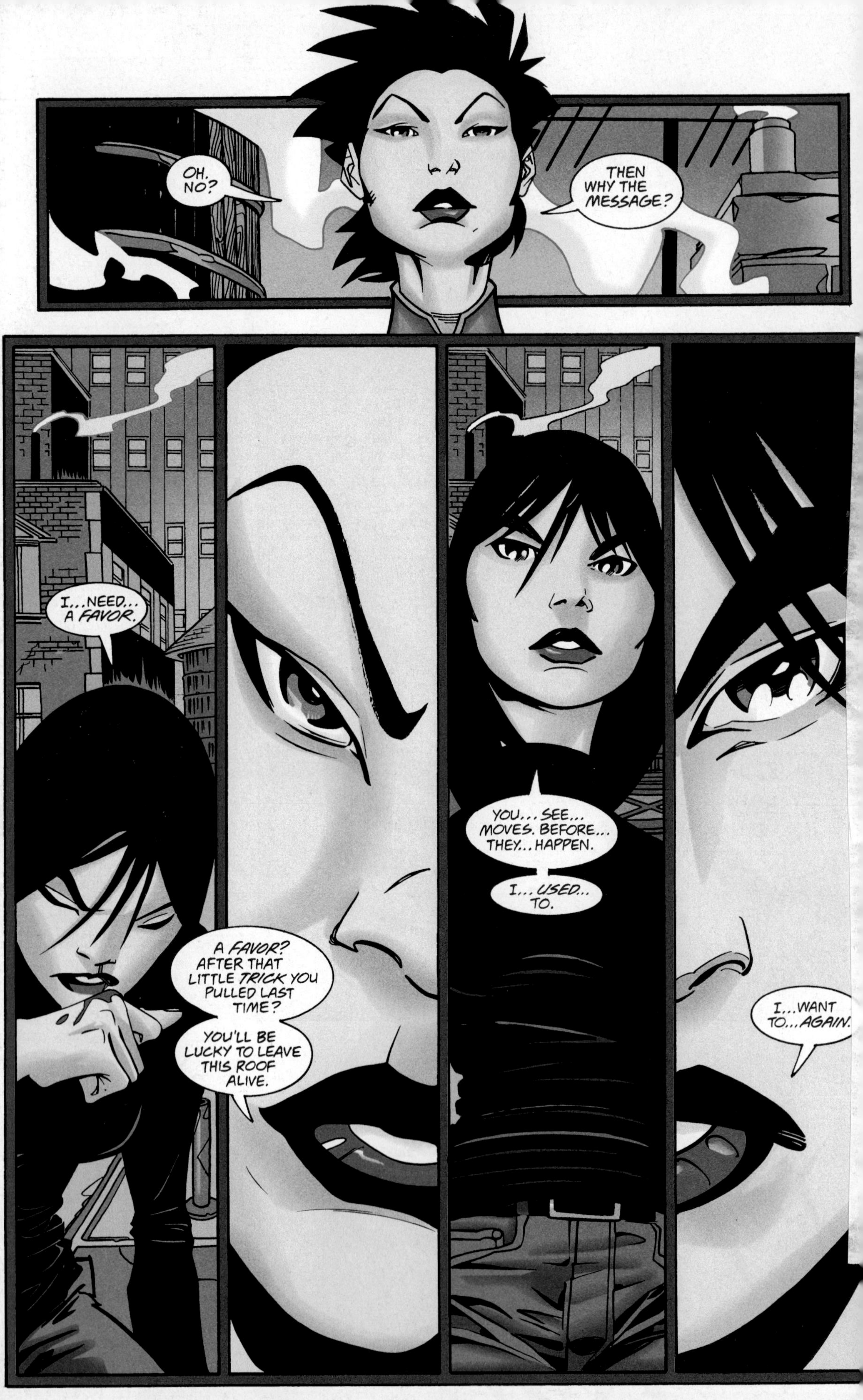
OH. NO?
THEN WHY THE MESSAGE?
I...NEED... A FAVOR.
A FAVOR? AFTER THAT LITTLE TRICK YOU PULLED LAST TIME?
YOU'LL BE LUCKY TO LEAVE THIS ROOF ALIVE.
YOU... SEE... MOVES. BEFORE... THEY... HAPPEN.
I... USED... TO.
I...WANT TO...AGAIN.

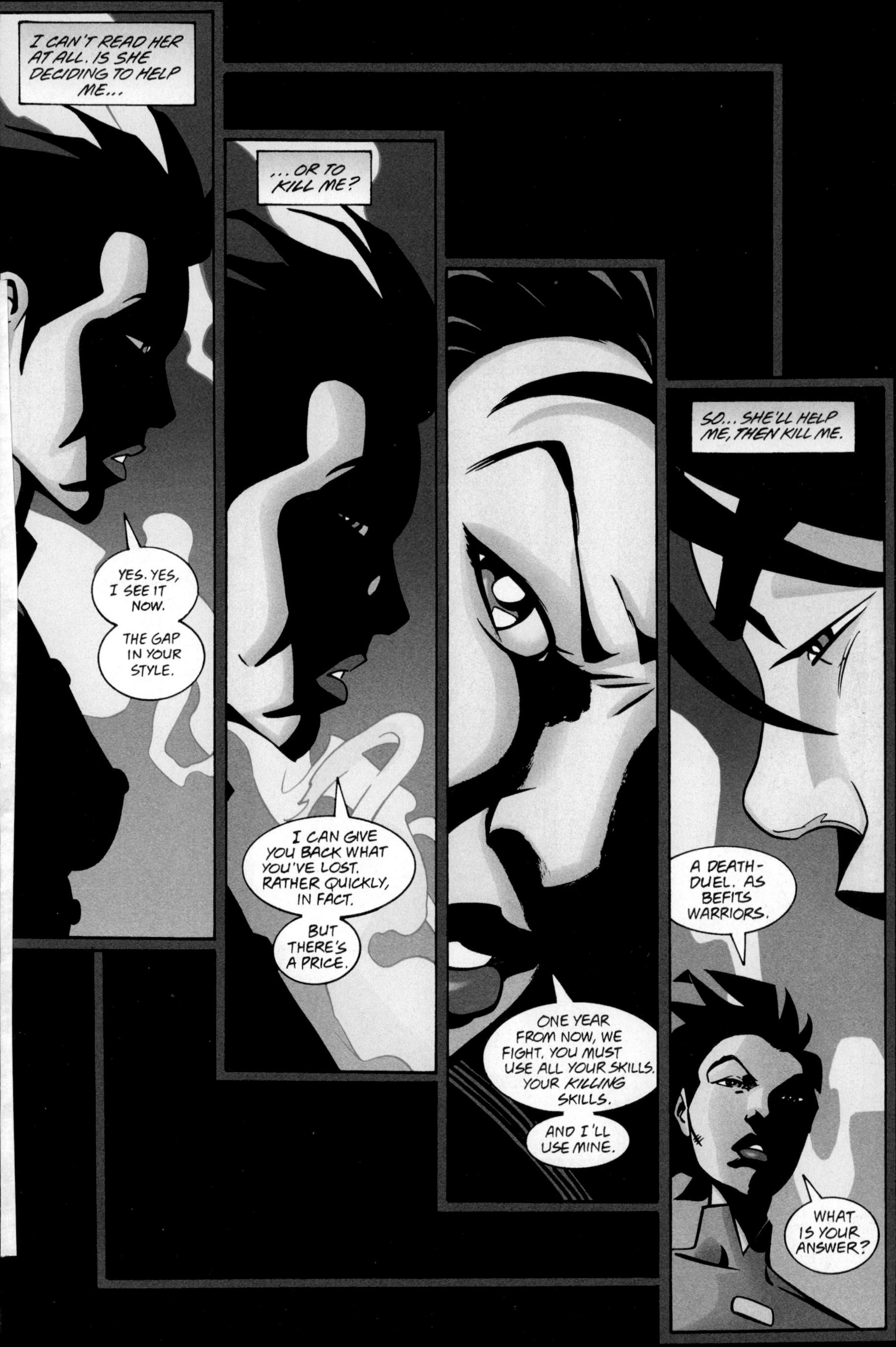
I CAN'T READ HER AT ALL. IS SHE DECIDING TO HELP ME...
YES. YES, I SEE IT NOW.
THE GAP IN YOUR STYLE.
...OR TO KILL ME?
I CAN GIVE YOU BACK WHAT YOU'VE LOST. RATHER QUICKLY, IN FACT.
BUT THERE'S A PRICE.
ONE YEAR FROM NOW, WE FIGHT. YOU MUST USE ALL YOUR SKILLS. YOUR *KILLING* SKILLS.
AND I'LL USE MINE.
SO... SHE'LL HELP ME, THEN KILL ME.
A DEATH-DUEL. AS BEFITS WARRIORS.
WHAT IS YOUR ANSWER?

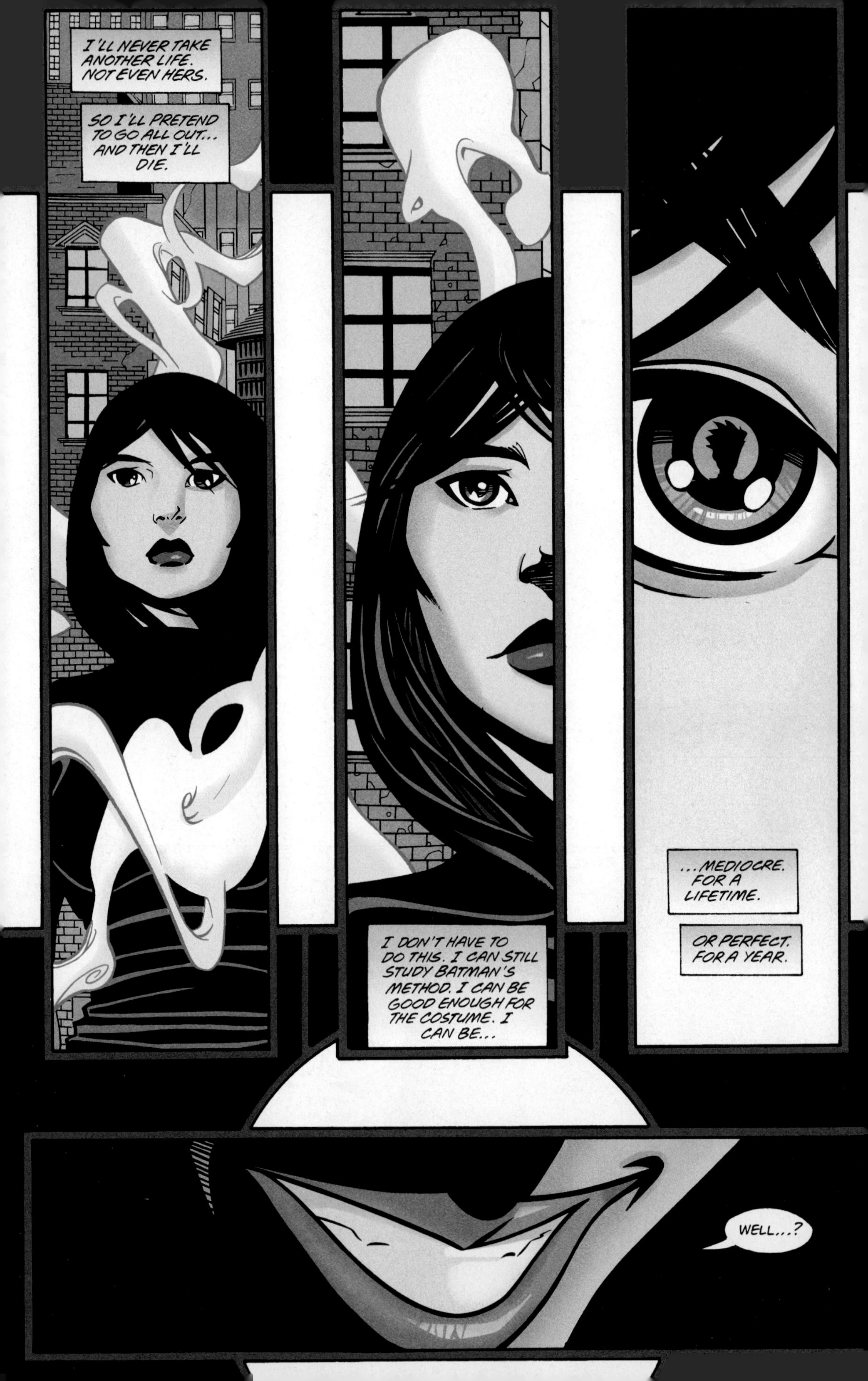
I'LL NEVER TAKE ANOTHER LIFE. NOT EVEN HERS.
SO I'LL PRETEND TO GO ALL OUT... AND THEN I'LL DIE.
I DON'T HAVE TO DO THIS. I CAN STILL STUDY BATMAN'S METHOD. I CAN BE GOOD ENOUGH FOR THE COSTUME. I CAN BE...
...MEDIOCRE. FOR A LIFETIME.
OR PERFECT. FOR A YEAR.
WELL...?

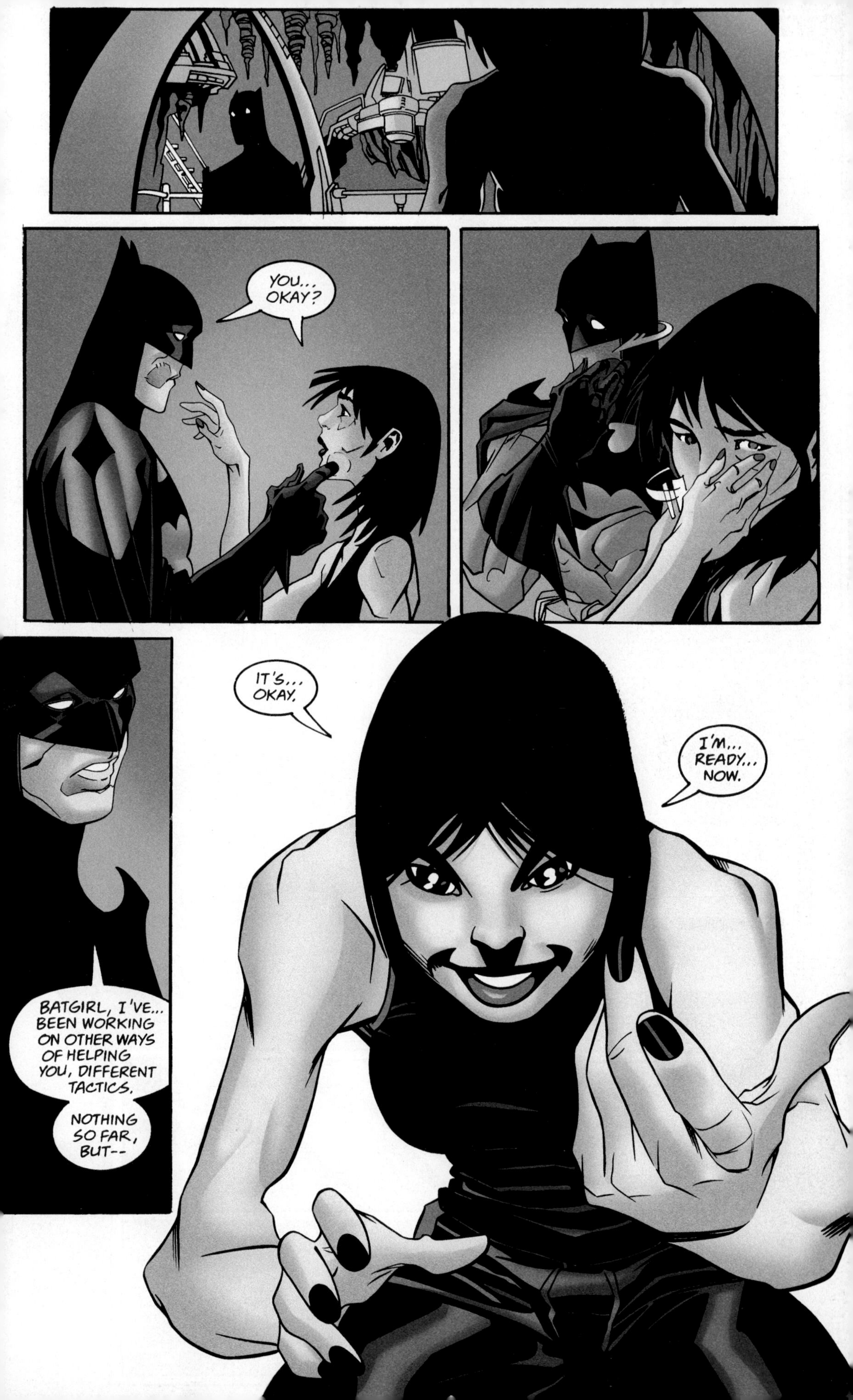
YOU... OKAY?
IT'S... OKAY.
I'M... READY... NOW.
BATGIRL, I'VE... BEEN WORKING ON OTHER WAYS OF HELPING YOU, DIFFERENT TACTICS.
NOTHING SO FAR, BUT--

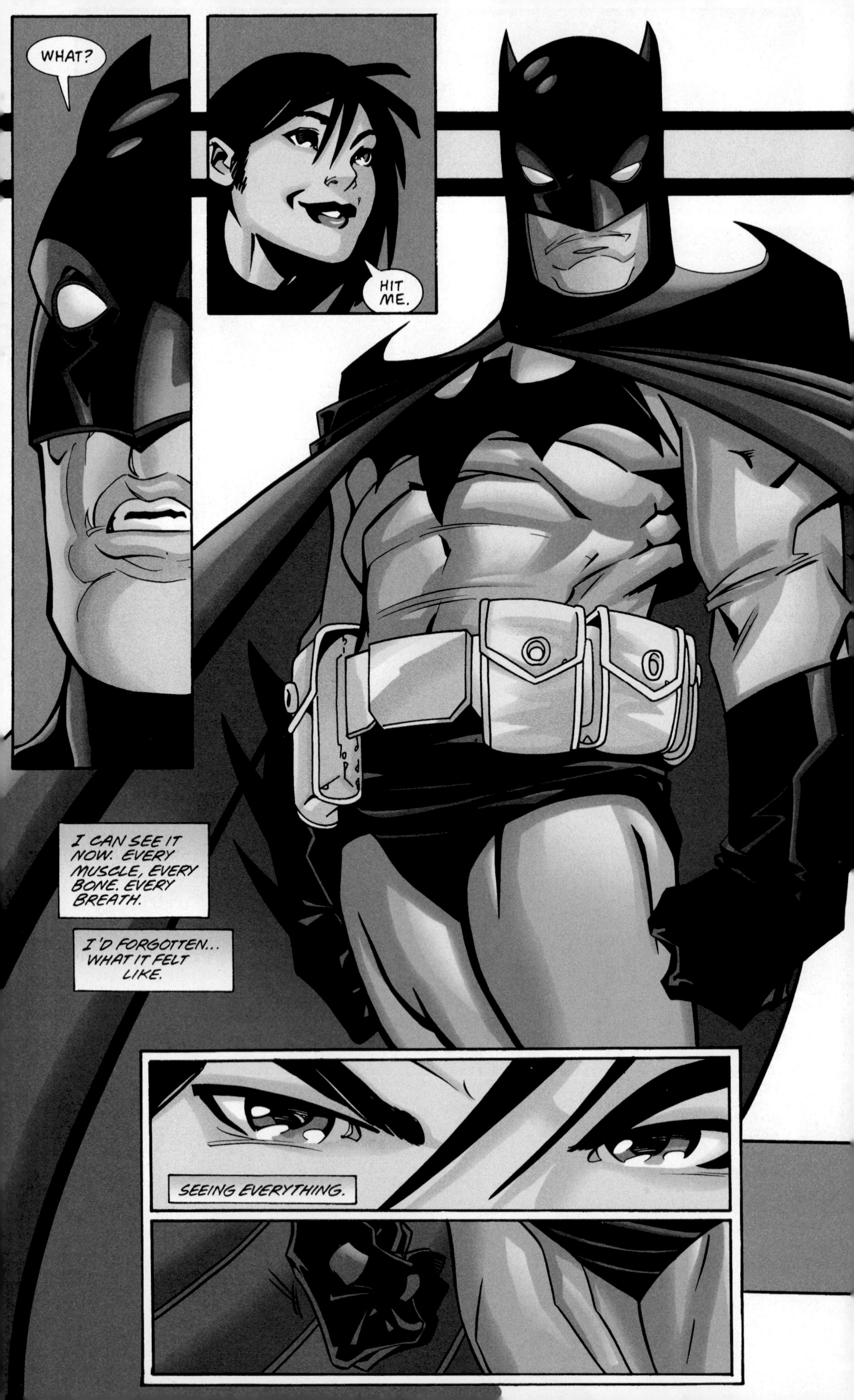
WHAT?
HIT ME.
I CAN SEE IT NOW. EVERY MUSCLE, EVERY BONE. EVERY BREATH.
I'D FORGOTTEN... WHAT IT FELT LIKE.
SEEING EVERYTHING.

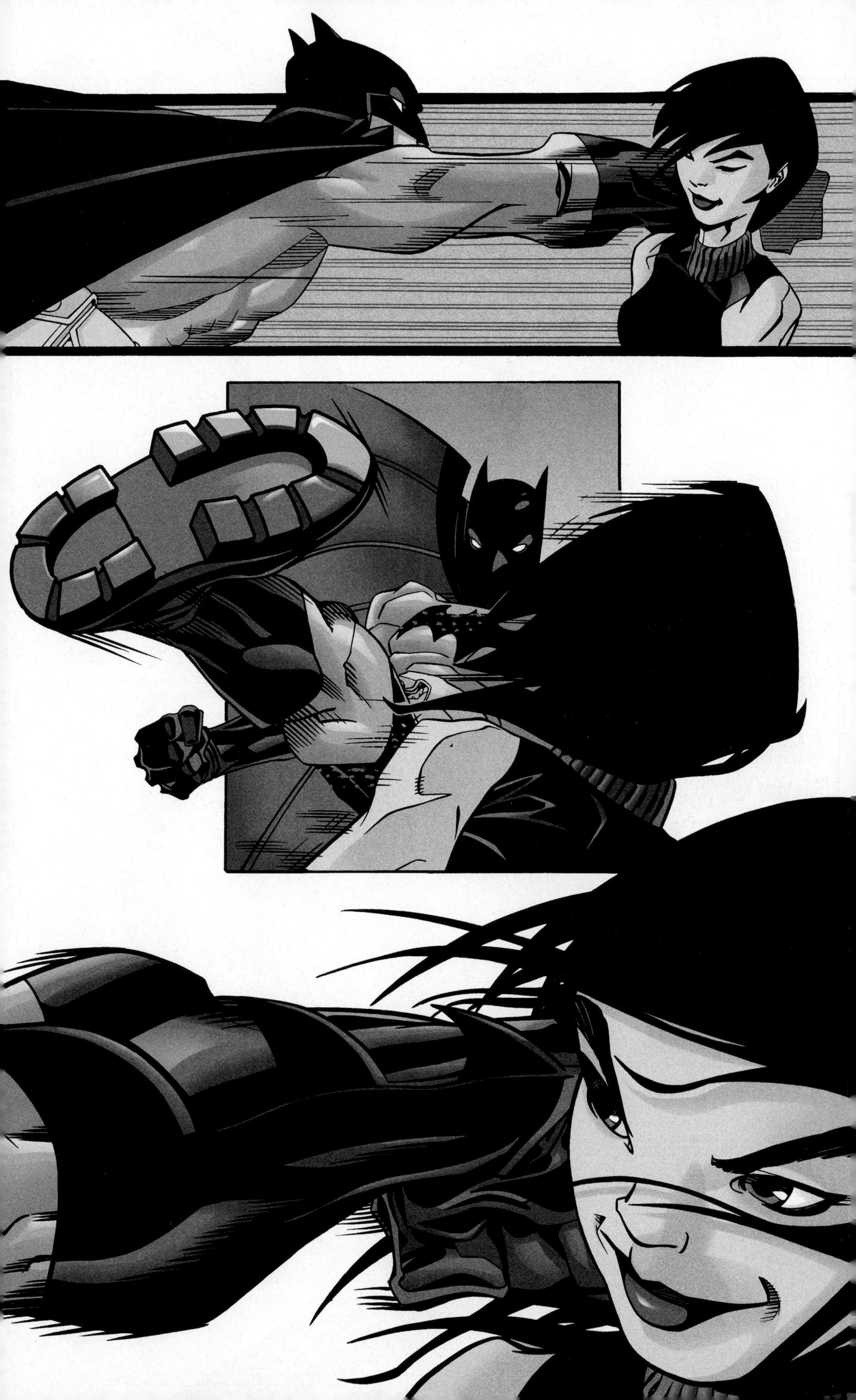

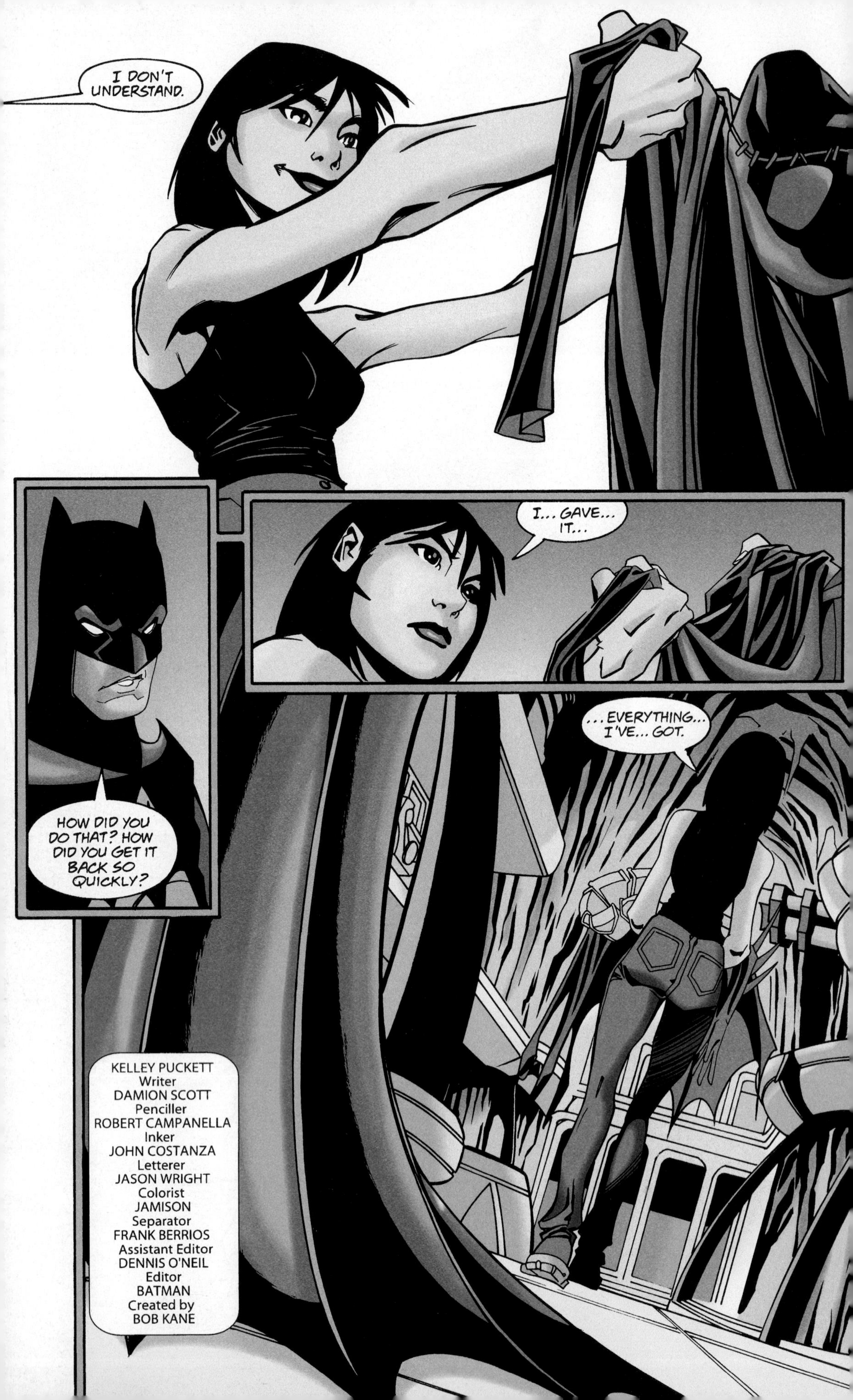

I DON'T UNDERSTAND.
I... GAVE... IT...
...EVERYTHING... I'VE... GOT.
HOW DID YOU DO THAT? HOW DID YOU GET IT BACK SO QUICKLY?
KELLEY PUCKETT Writer
DAMION SCOTT Penciller
ROBERT CAMPANELLA Inker
JOHN COSTANZA Letterer
JASON WRIGHT Colorist
JAMISON Separator
FRANK BERRIOS Assistant Editor
DENNIS O'NEIL Editor
BATMAN Created by BOB KANE

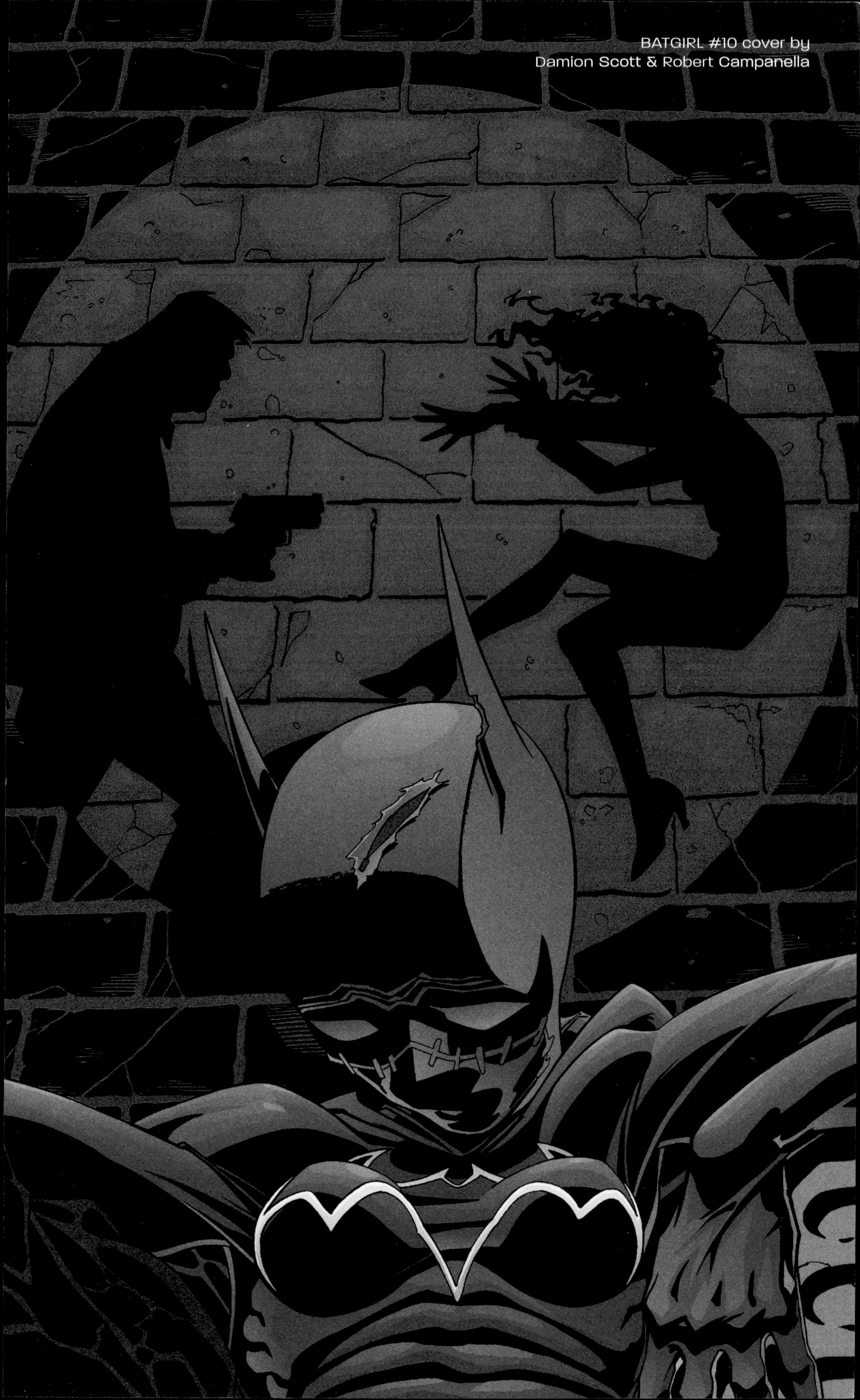

BATGIRL #10 cover by
Damion Scott & Robert Campanella

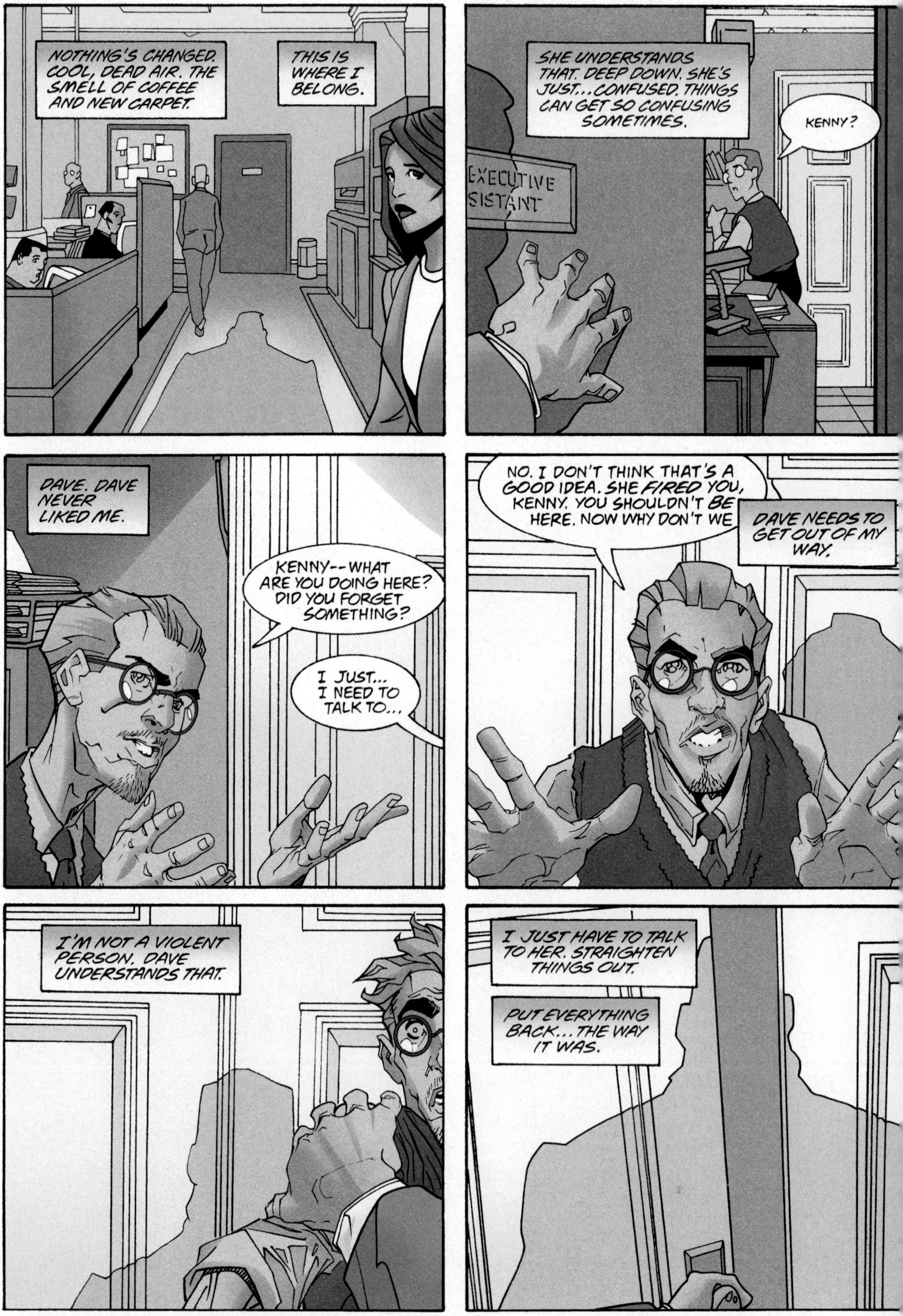
NOTHING'S CHANGED. COOL, DEAD AIR. THE SMELL OF COFFEE AND NEW CARPET.
THIS IS WHERE I BELONG.
SHE UNDERSTANDS THAT. DEEP DOWN. SHE'S JUST...CONFUSED. THINGS CAN GET SO CONFUSING SOMETIMES.
EXECUTIVE
SISTANT
KENNY?
DAVE. DAVE NEVER LIKED ME.
KENNY--WHAT ARE YOU DOING HERE? DID YOU FORGET SOMETHING?
I JUST... I NEED TO TALK TO...
NO. I DON'T THINK THAT'S A GOOD IDEA. SHE FIRED YOU, KENNY. YOU SHOULDN'T BE HERE. NOW WHY DON'T WE
DAVE NEEDS TO GET OUT OF MY WAY.
I'M NOT A VIOLENT PERSON. DAVE UNDERSTANDS THAT.
I JUST HAVE TO TALK TO HER. STRAIGHTEN THINGS OUT.
PUT EVERYTHING BACK...THE WAY IT WAS.

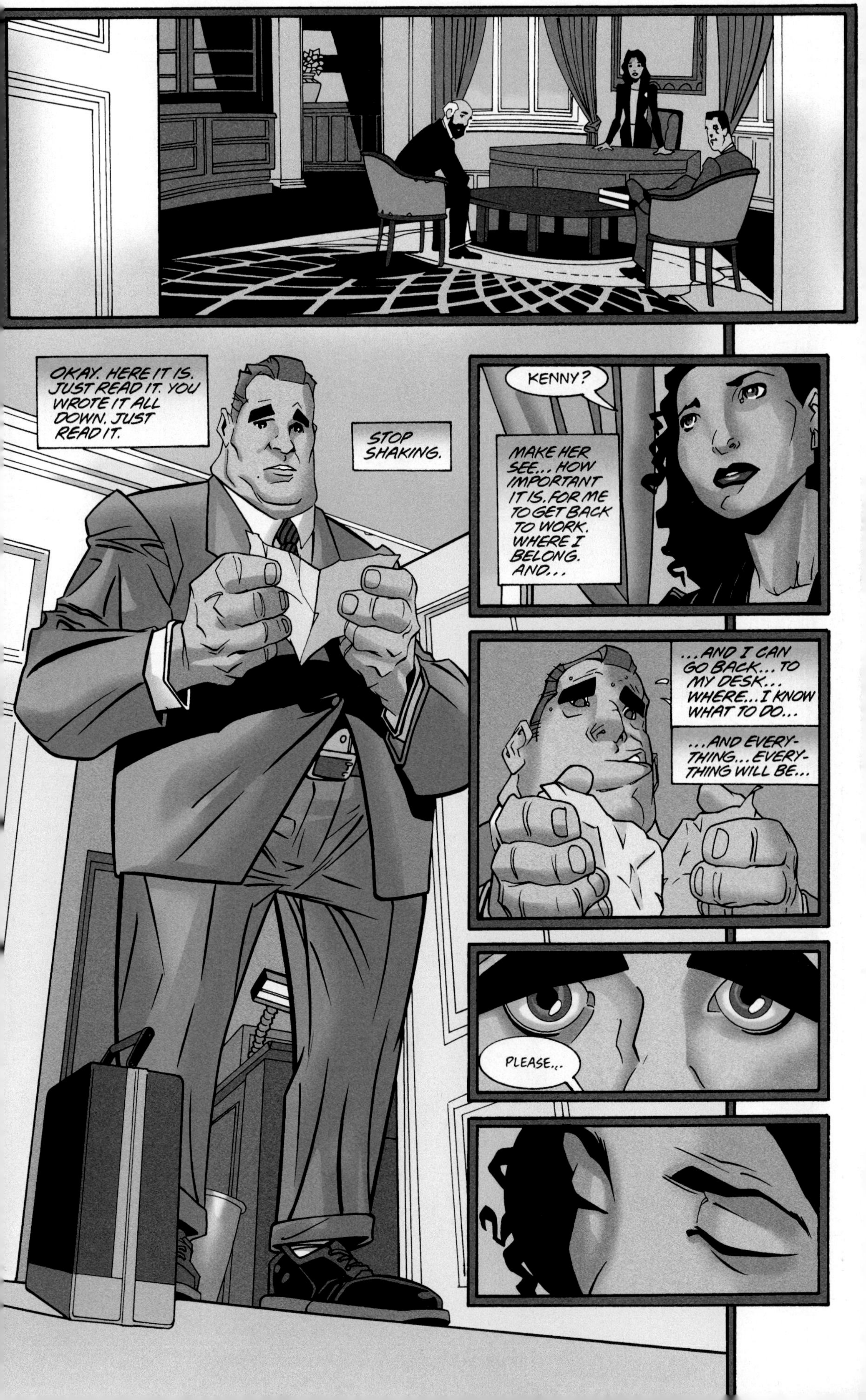

OKAY. HERE IT IS. JUST READ IT. YOU WROTE IT ALL DOWN. JUST READ IT.
STOP SHAKING.
KENNY?
MAKE HER SEE... HOW IMPORTANT IT IS. FOR ME TO GET BACK TO WORK. WHERE I BELONG. AND...
...AND I CAN GO BACK... TO MY DESK... WHERE... I KNOW WHAT TO DO...
...AND EVERYTHING... EVERYTHING WILL BE...
PLEASE...

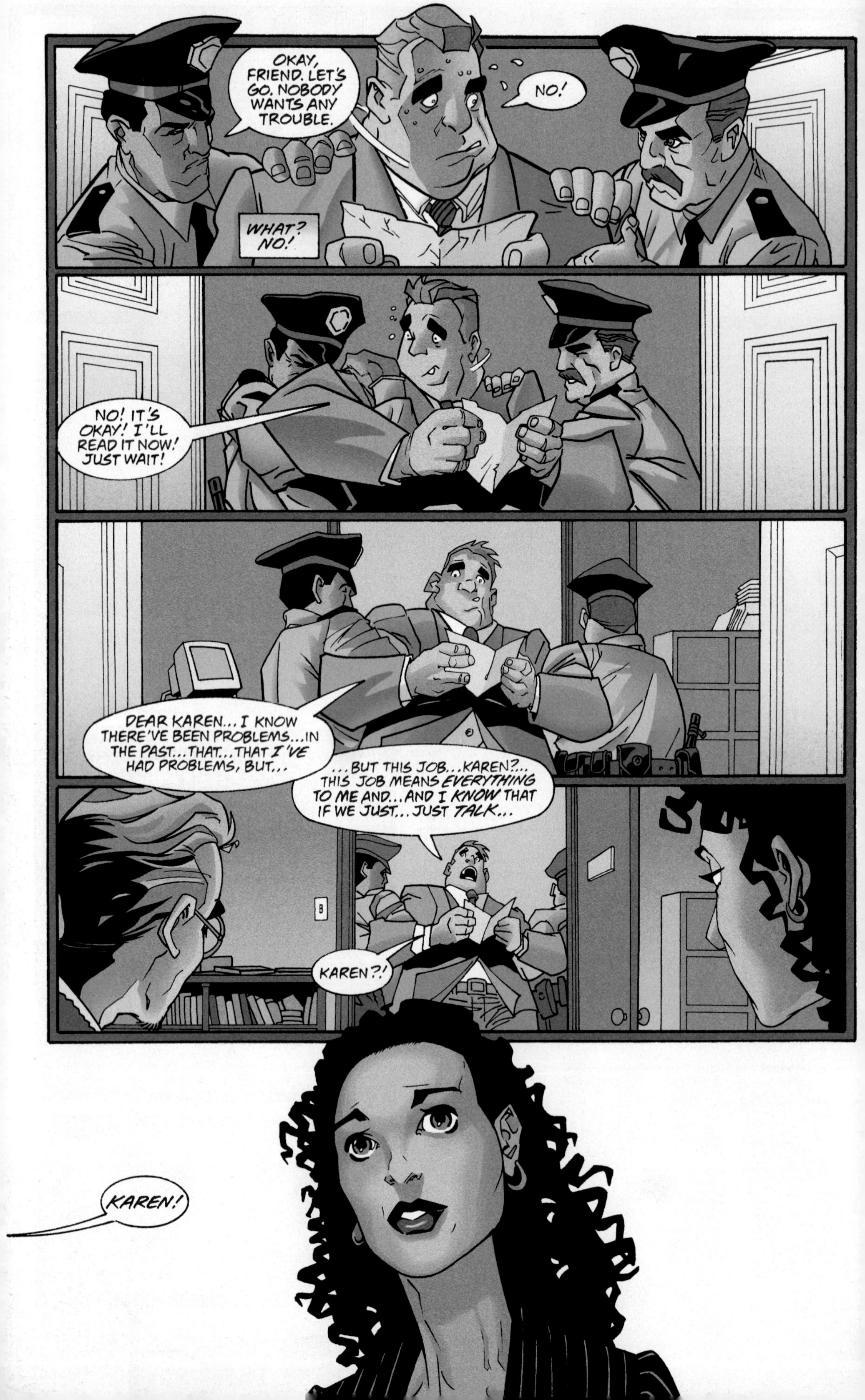
OKAY, FRIEND. LET'S GO. NOBODY WANTS ANY TROUBLE.
NO!
WHAT? NO!
NO! IT'S OKAY! I'LL READ IT NOW! JUST WAIT!
DEAR KAREN... I KNOW THERE'VE BEEN PROBLEMS... IN THE PAST... THAT... THAT I'VE HAD PROBLEMS, BUT...
...BUT THIS JOB... KAREN?... THIS JOB MEANS EVERYTHING TO ME AND... AND I KNOW THAT IF WE JUST... JUST TALK...
KAREN?!
KAREN!

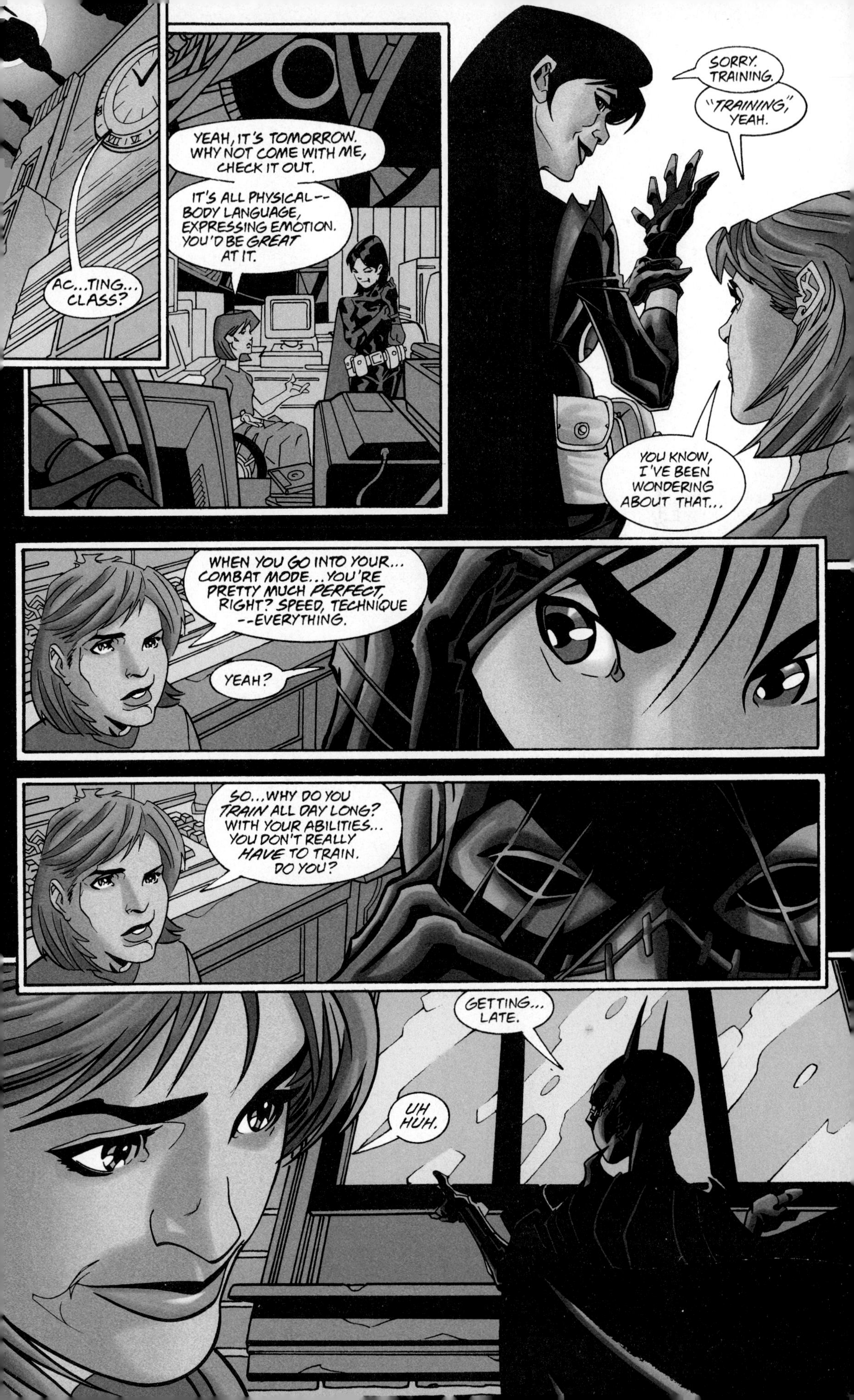
AC...TING... CLASS?
YEAH, IT'S TOMORROW. WHY NOT COME WITH ME, CHECK IT OUT.
IT'S ALL PHYSICAL-- BODY LANGUAGE, EXPRESSING EMOTION. YOU'D BE GREAT AT IT.
SORRY. TRAINING.
"TRAINING," YEAH.
YOU KNOW, I'VE BEEN WONDERING ABOUT THAT...
WHEN YOU GO INTO YOUR... COMBAT MODE... YOU'RE PRETTY MUCH PERFECT, RIGHT? SPEED, TECHNIQUE --EVERYTHING.
YEAH?
SO... WHY DO YOU TRAIN ALL DAY LONG? WITH YOUR ABILITIES... YOU DON'T REALLY HAVE TO TRAIN. DO YOU?
GETTING... LATE.
UH HUH.

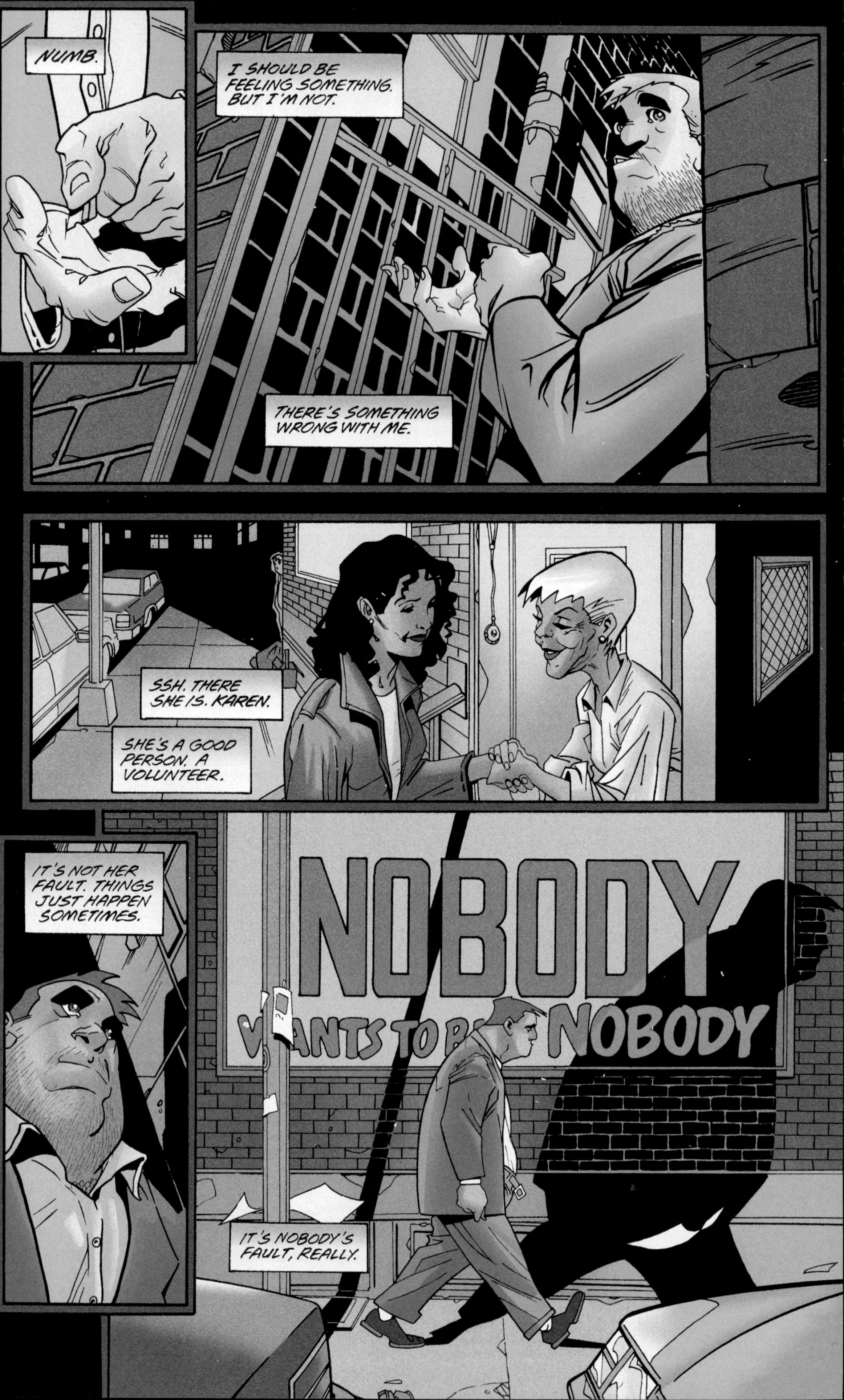
NUMB.
I SHOULD BE FEELING SOMETHING. BUT I'M NOT.
THERE'S SOMETHING WRONG WITH ME.
SSH. THERE SHE IS. KAREN.
SHE'S A GOOD PERSON. A VOLUNTEER.
IT'S NOT HER FAULT. THINGS JUST HAPPEN SOMETIMES.
NOBODY
NOBODY
IT'S NOBODY'S FAULT, REALLY.

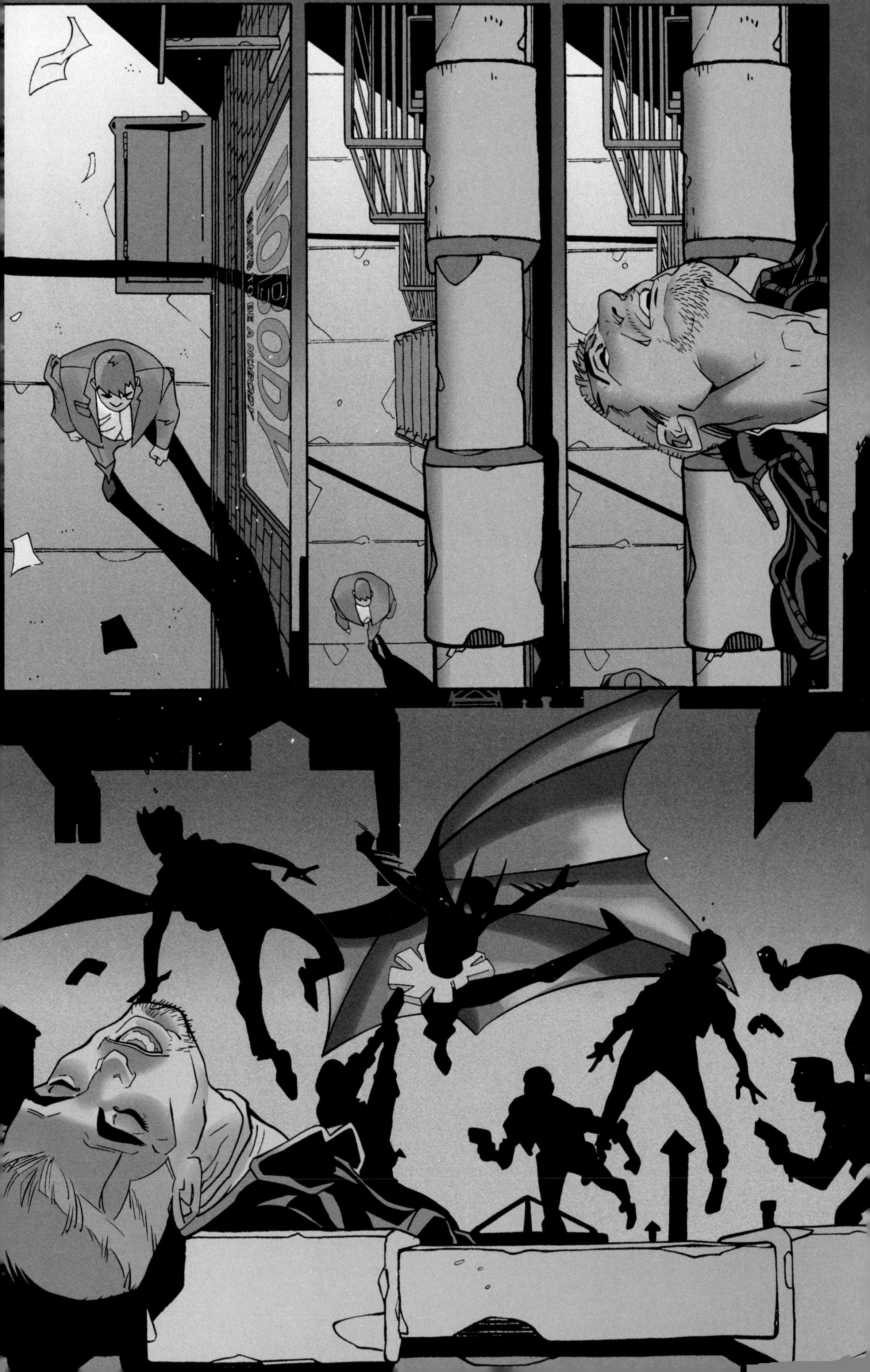
NOBODY
WANTS TO BE A NOBODY

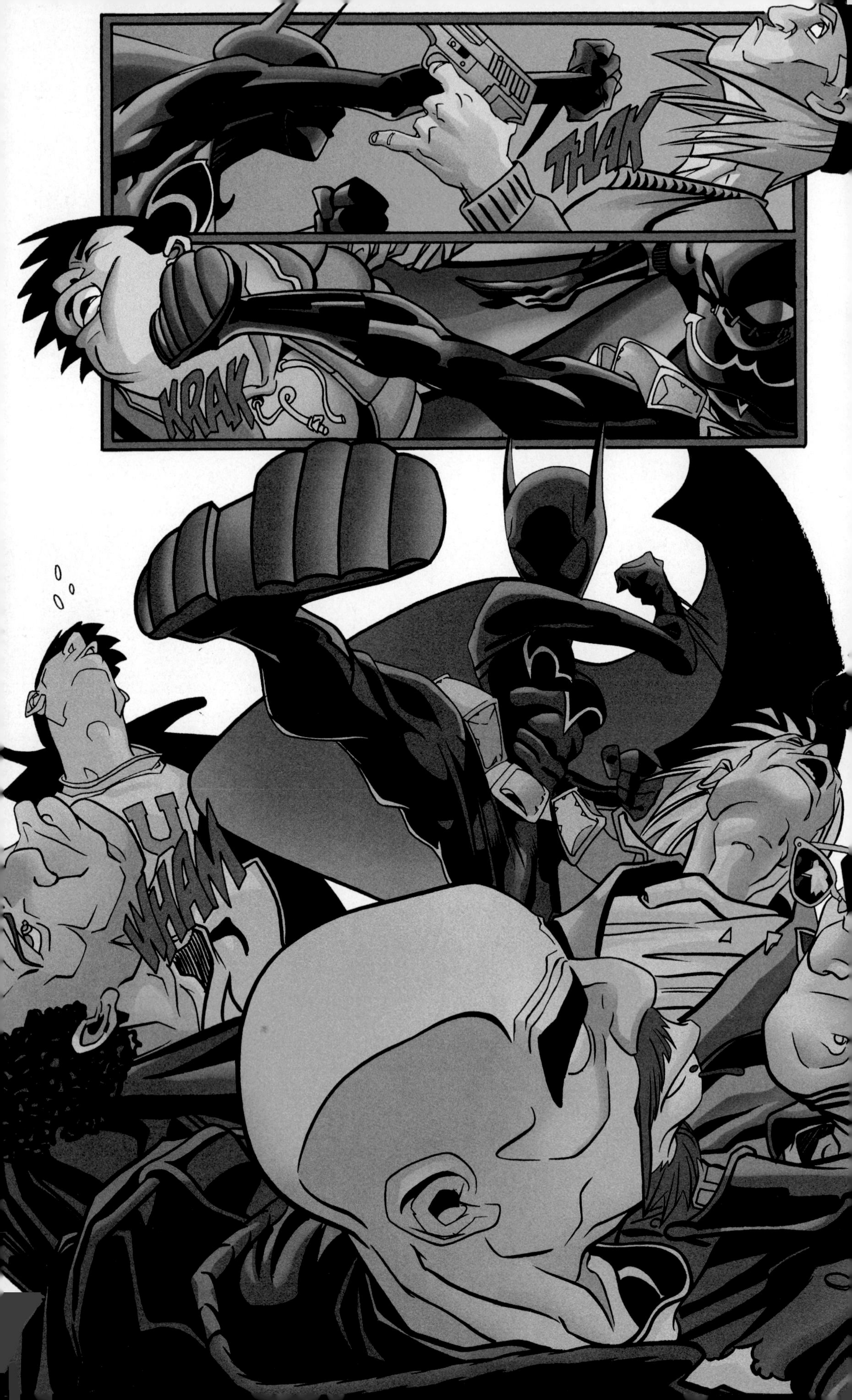
THAK
KRAK
WHAM

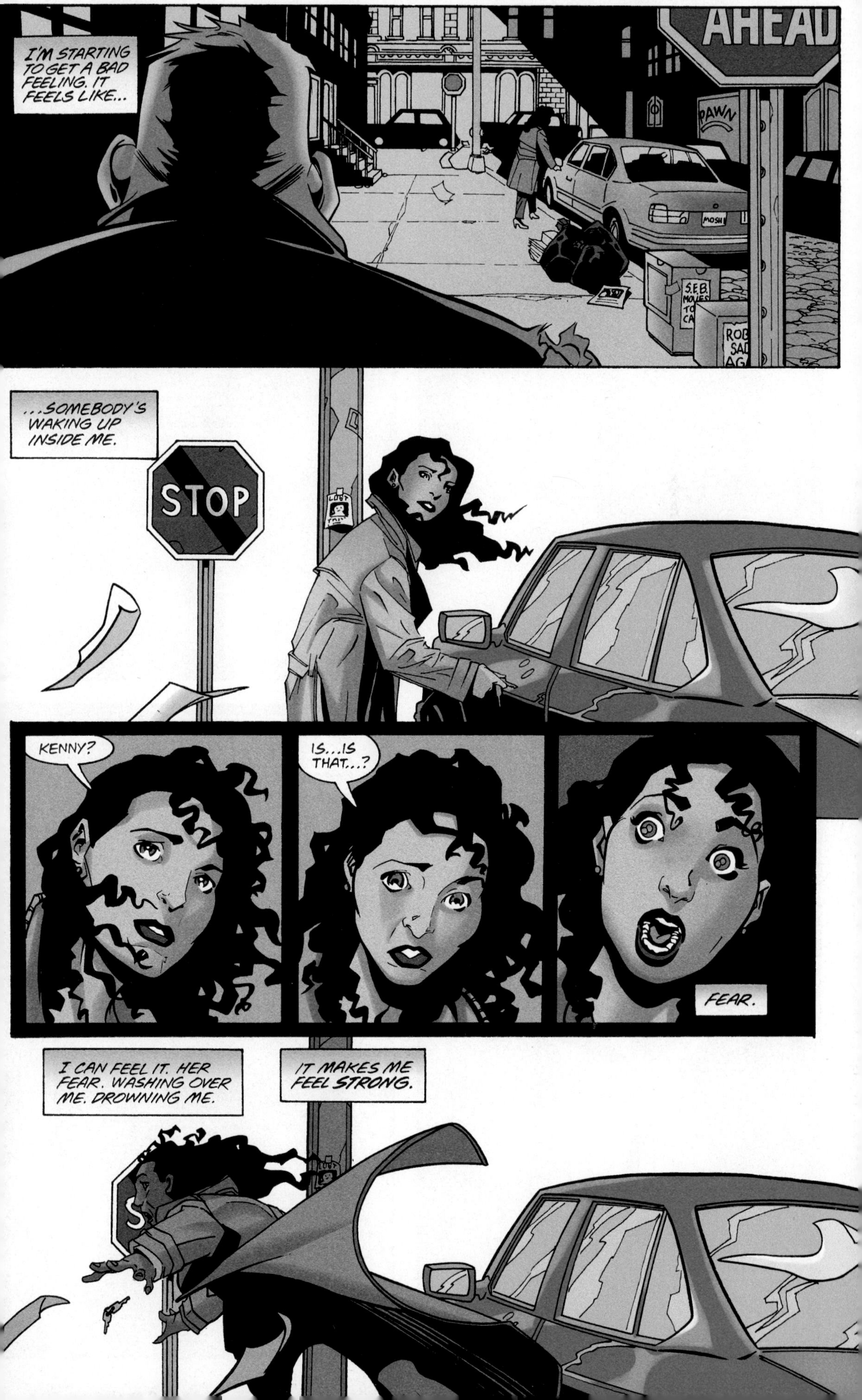

I'M STARTING TO GET A BAD FEELING. IT FEELS LIKE...
AHEAD
PAWN
...SOMEBODY'S WAKING UP INSIDE ME.
STOP
KENNY?
IS...IS THAT...?
FEAR.
I CAN FEEL IT. HER FEAR. WASHING OVER ME. DROWNING ME.
IT MAKES ME FEEL STRONG.

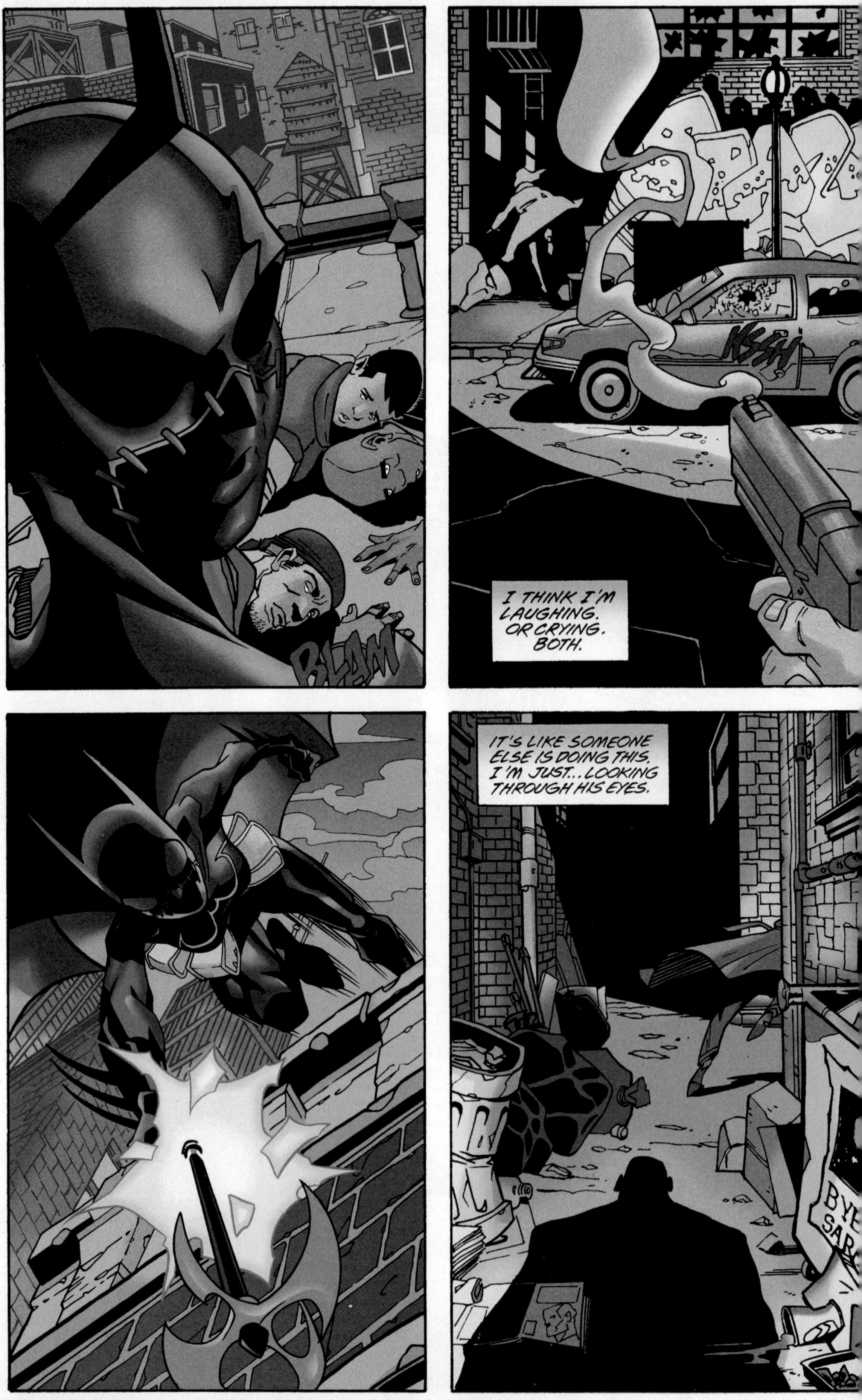
BLAM
KSSH
I THINK I'M LAUGHING. OR CRYING. BOTH.
IT'S LIKE SOMEONE ELSE IS DOING THIS. I'M JUST... LOOKING THROUGH HIS EYES.

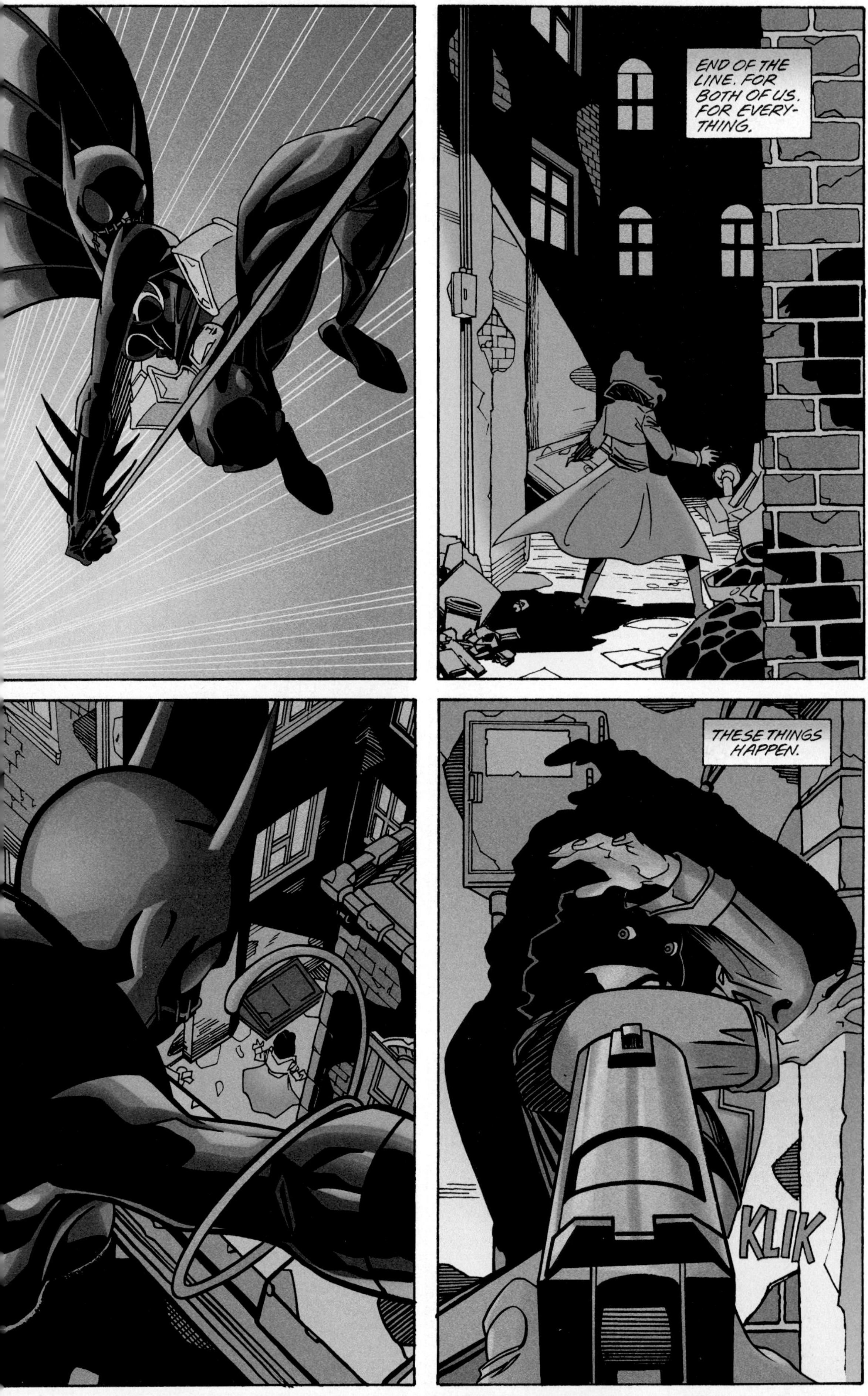
END OF THE LINE. FOR BOTH OF US. FOR EVERY-THING.
THESE THINGS HAPPEN.
KLIK

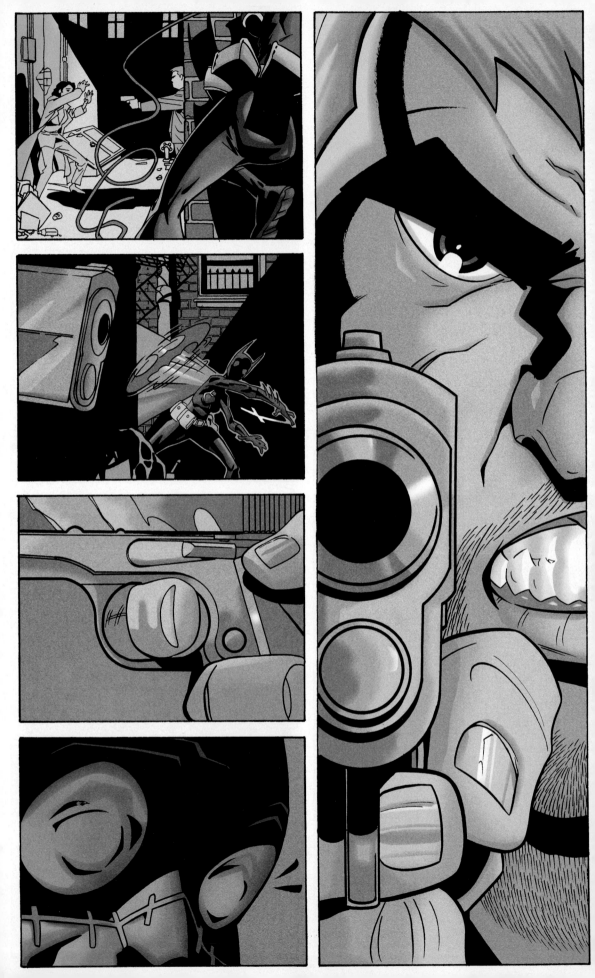

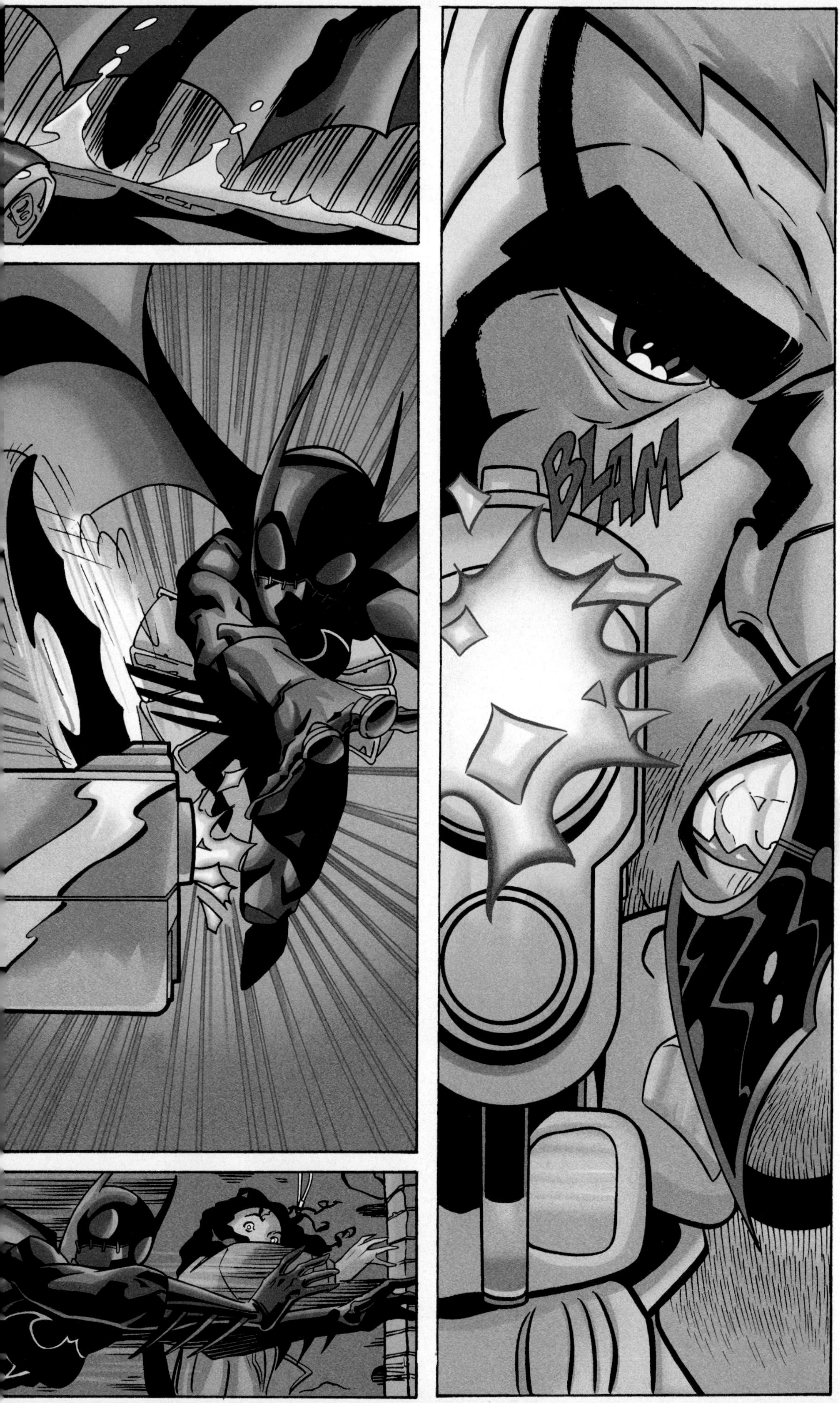
BLAM

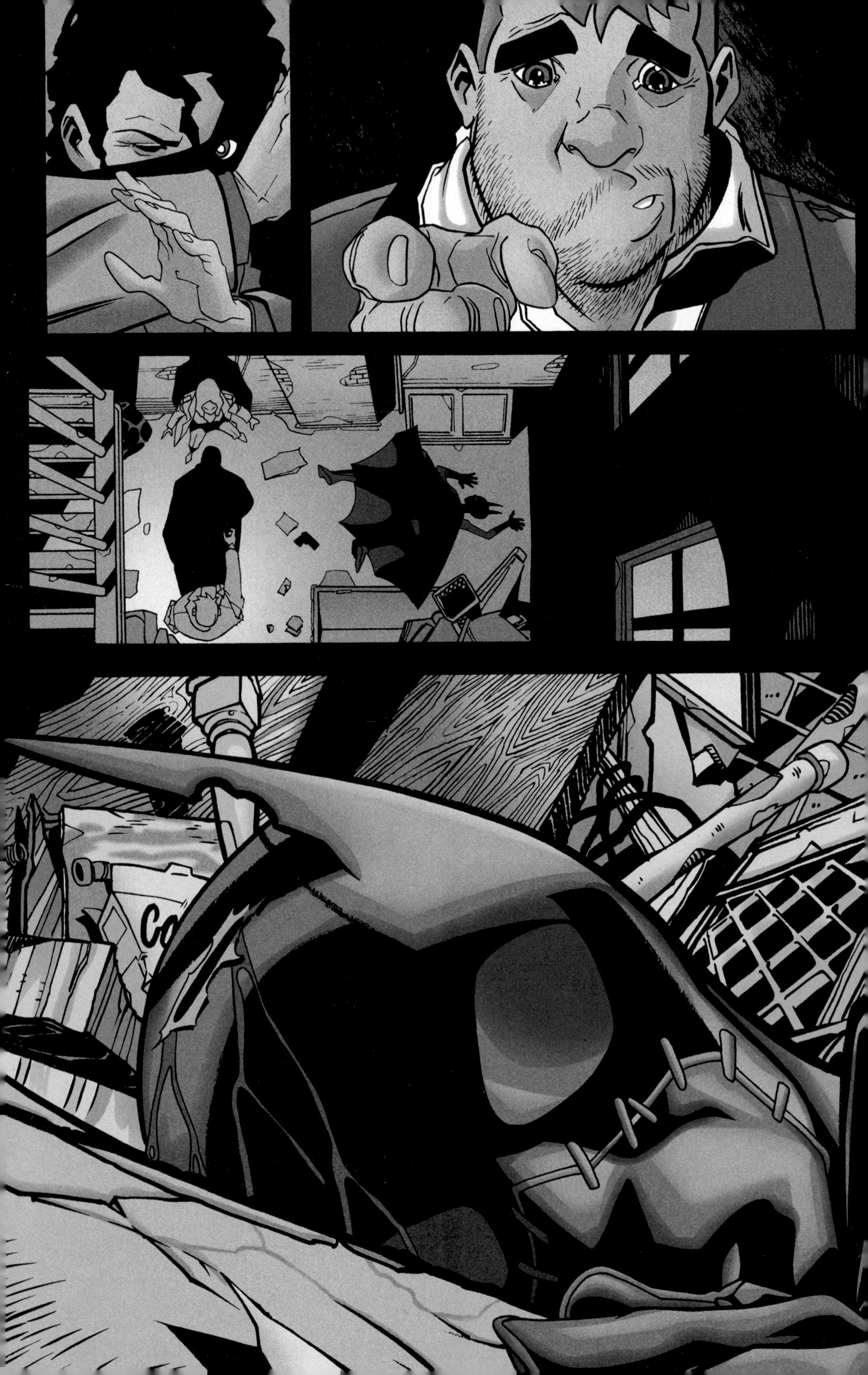

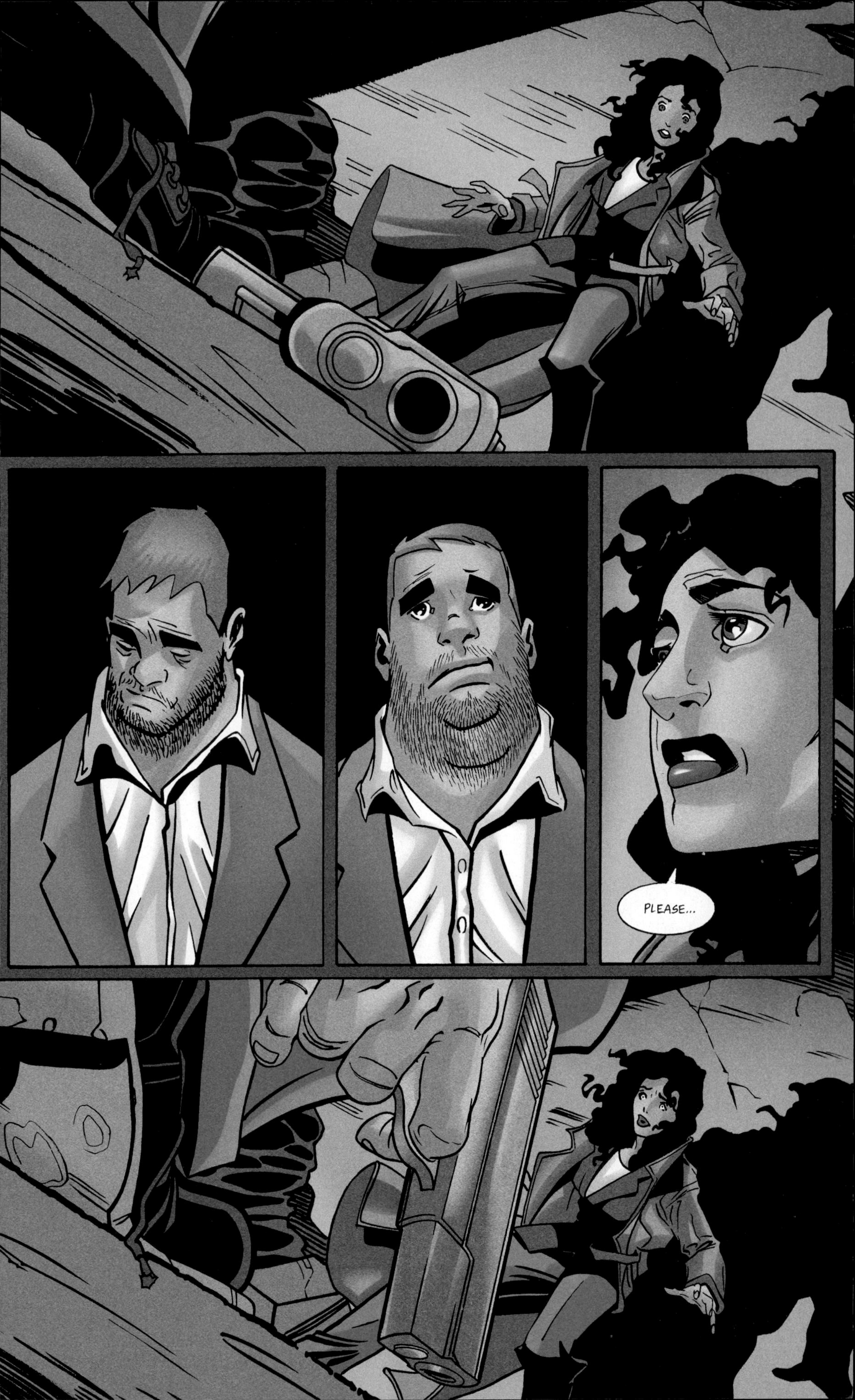
PLEASE...

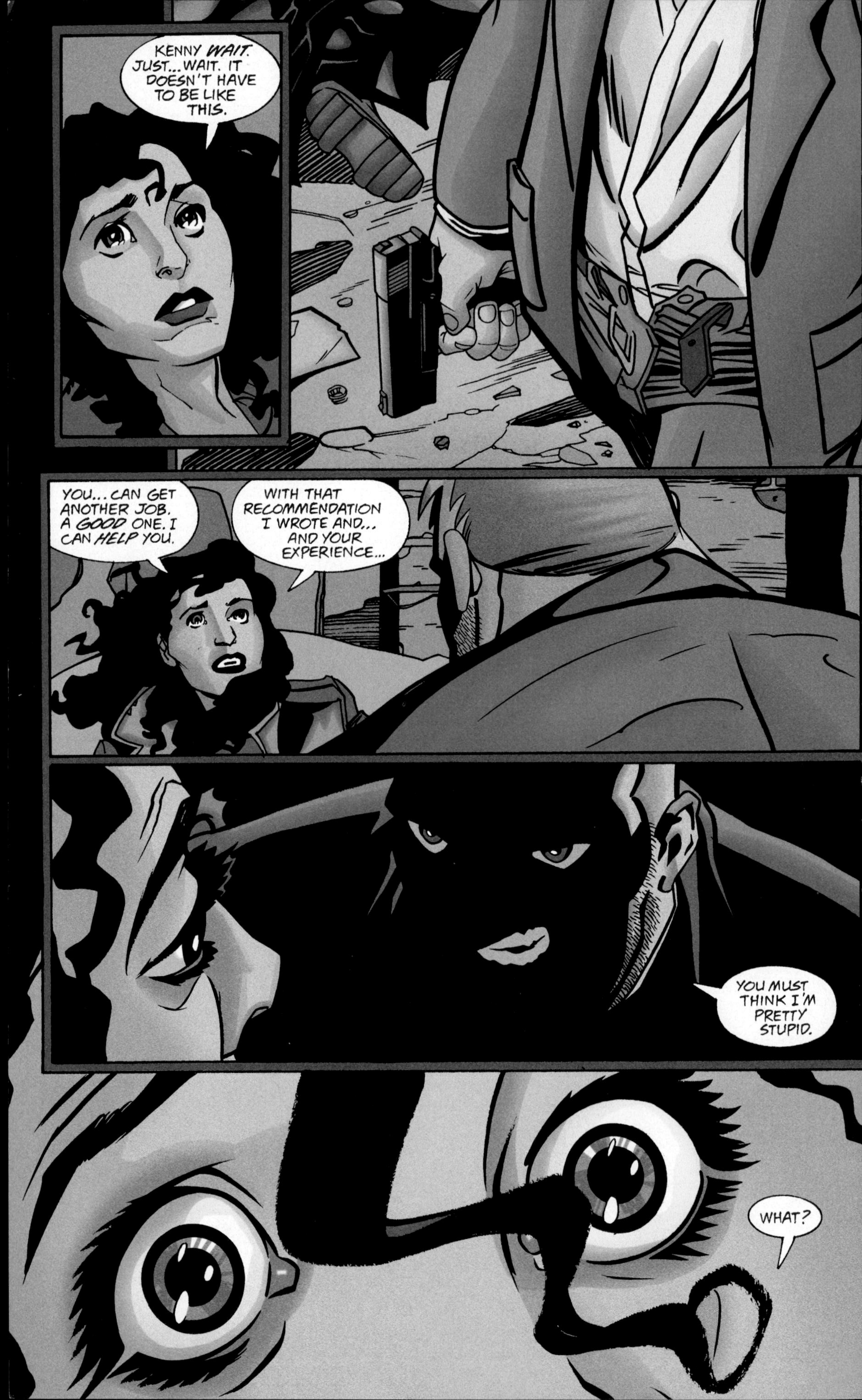
KENNY *WAIT*. JUST...WAIT. IT DOESN'T HAVE TO BE LIKE THIS.
YOU...CAN GET ANOTHER JOB. A *GOOD* ONE. I CAN *HELP* YOU.
WITH THAT RECOMMENDATION I WROTE AND... AND YOUR EXPERIENCE...
YOU MUST THINK I'M PRETTY STUPID.
WHAT?

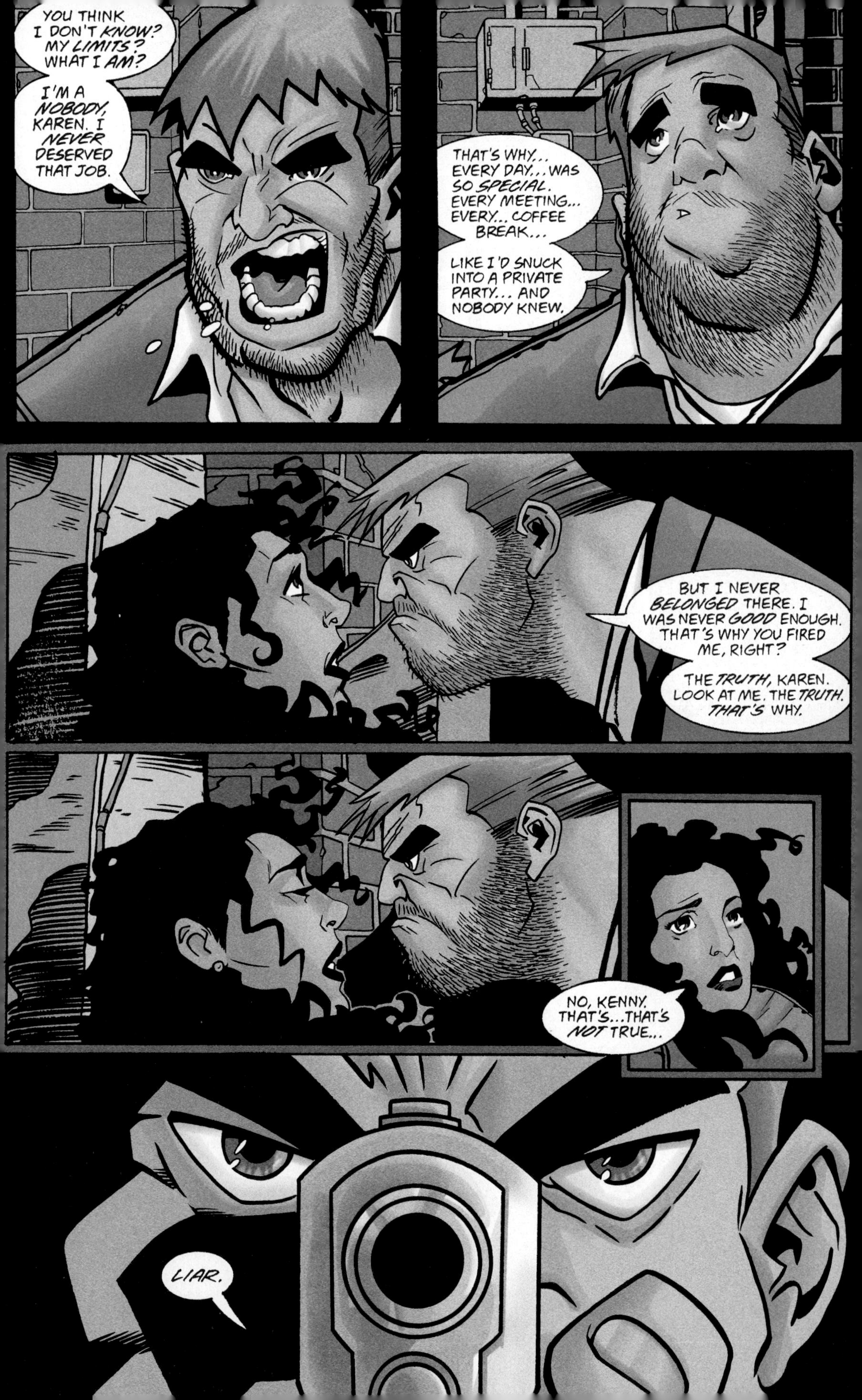
YOU THINK I DON'T KNOW? MY LIMITS? WHAT I AM?
I'M A NOBODY, KAREN. I NEVER DESERVED THAT JOB.
THAT'S WHY... EVERY DAY... WAS SO SPECIAL. EVERY MEETING... EVERY... COFFEE BREAK...
LIKE I'D SNUCK INTO A PRIVATE PARTY... AND NOBODY KNEW.
BUT I NEVER BELONGED THERE. I WAS NEVER GOOD ENOUGH. THAT'S WHY YOU FIRED ME, RIGHT?
THE TRUTH, KAREN. LOOK AT ME. THE TRUTH. THAT'S WHY.
NO, KENNY. THAT'S... THAT'S NOT TRUE...
LIAR.

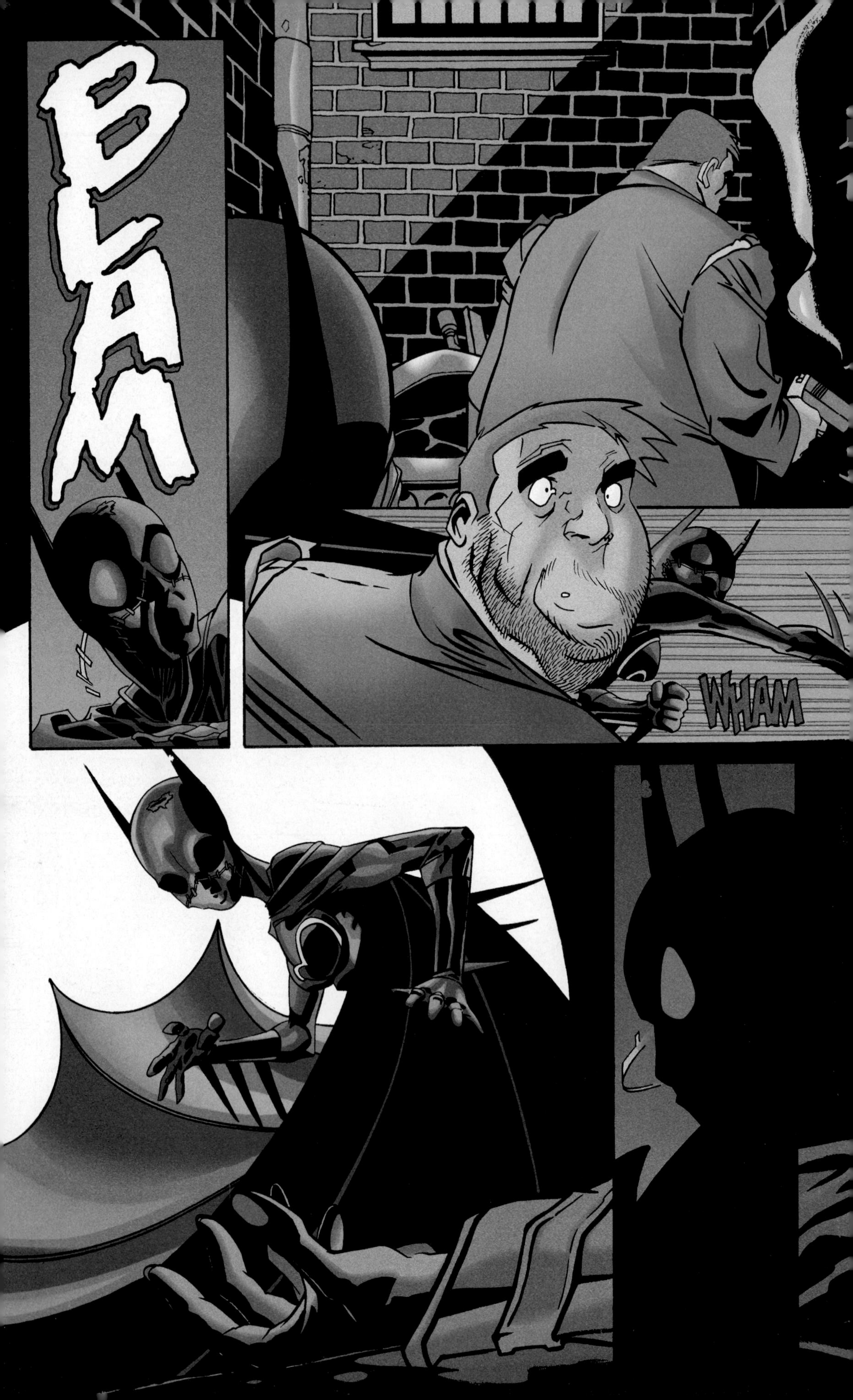
BLAM
WHAM

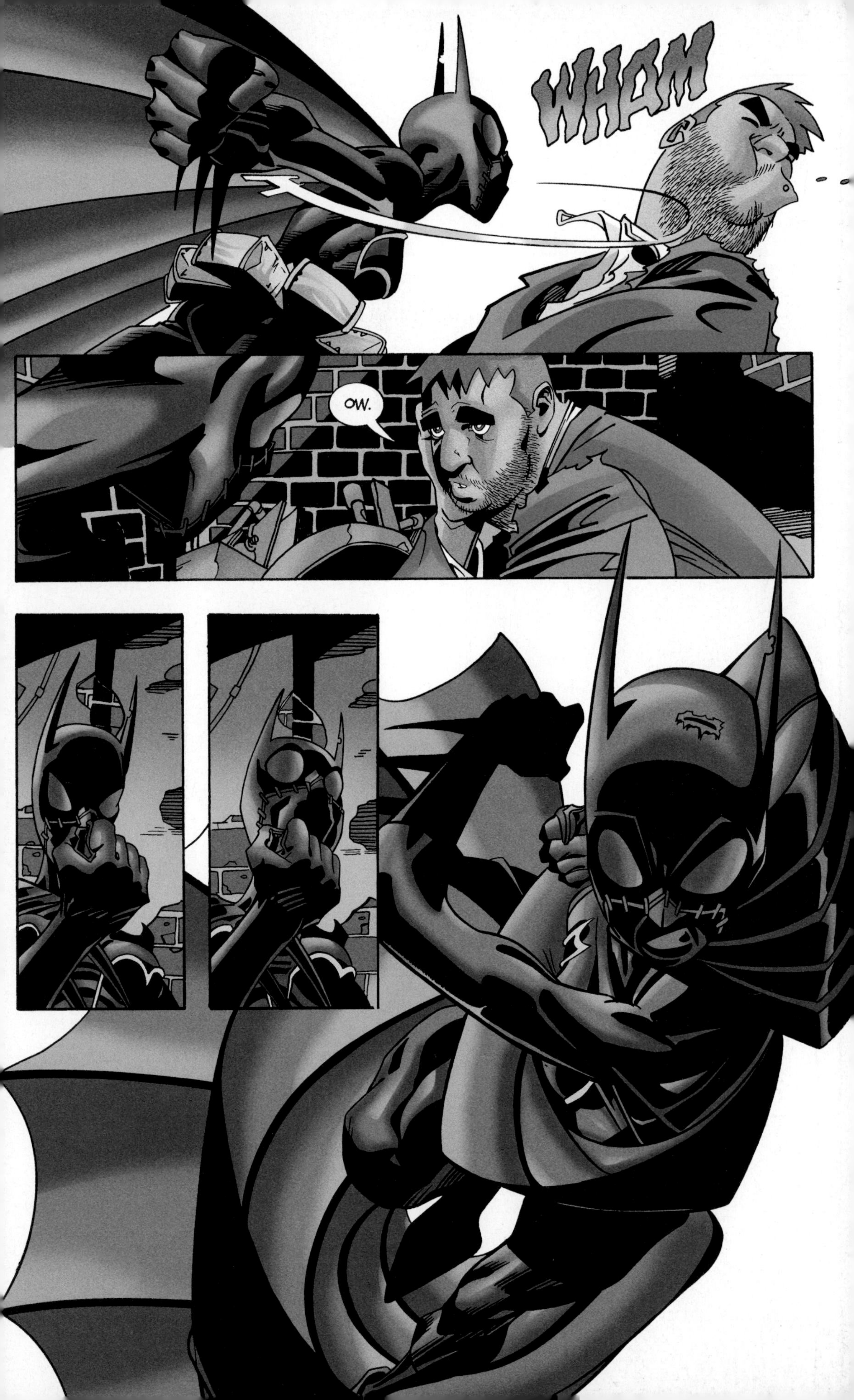
WHAM
OW.

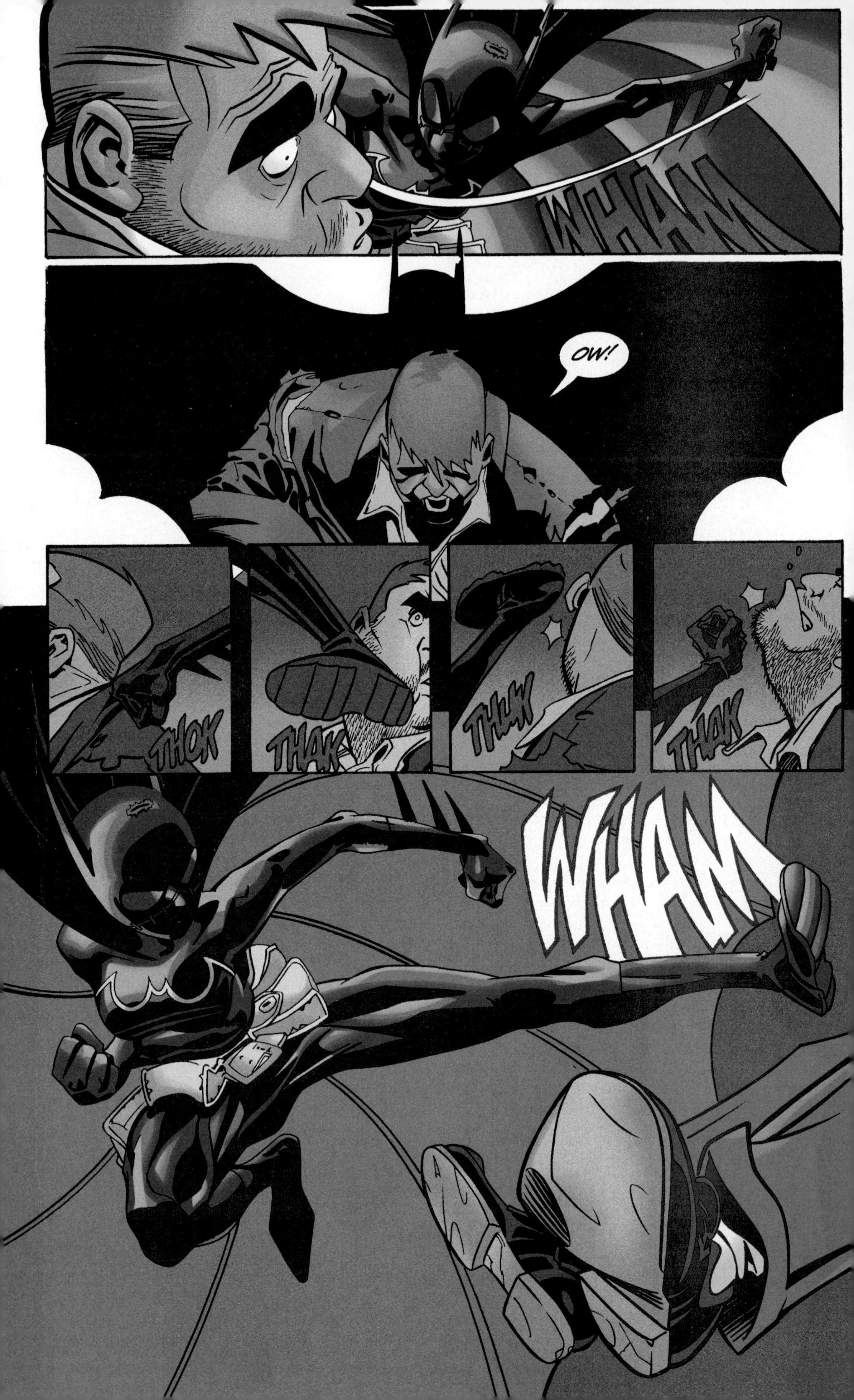
WHAM
OW!
THOK
THAK
THUK
THAK
WHAM

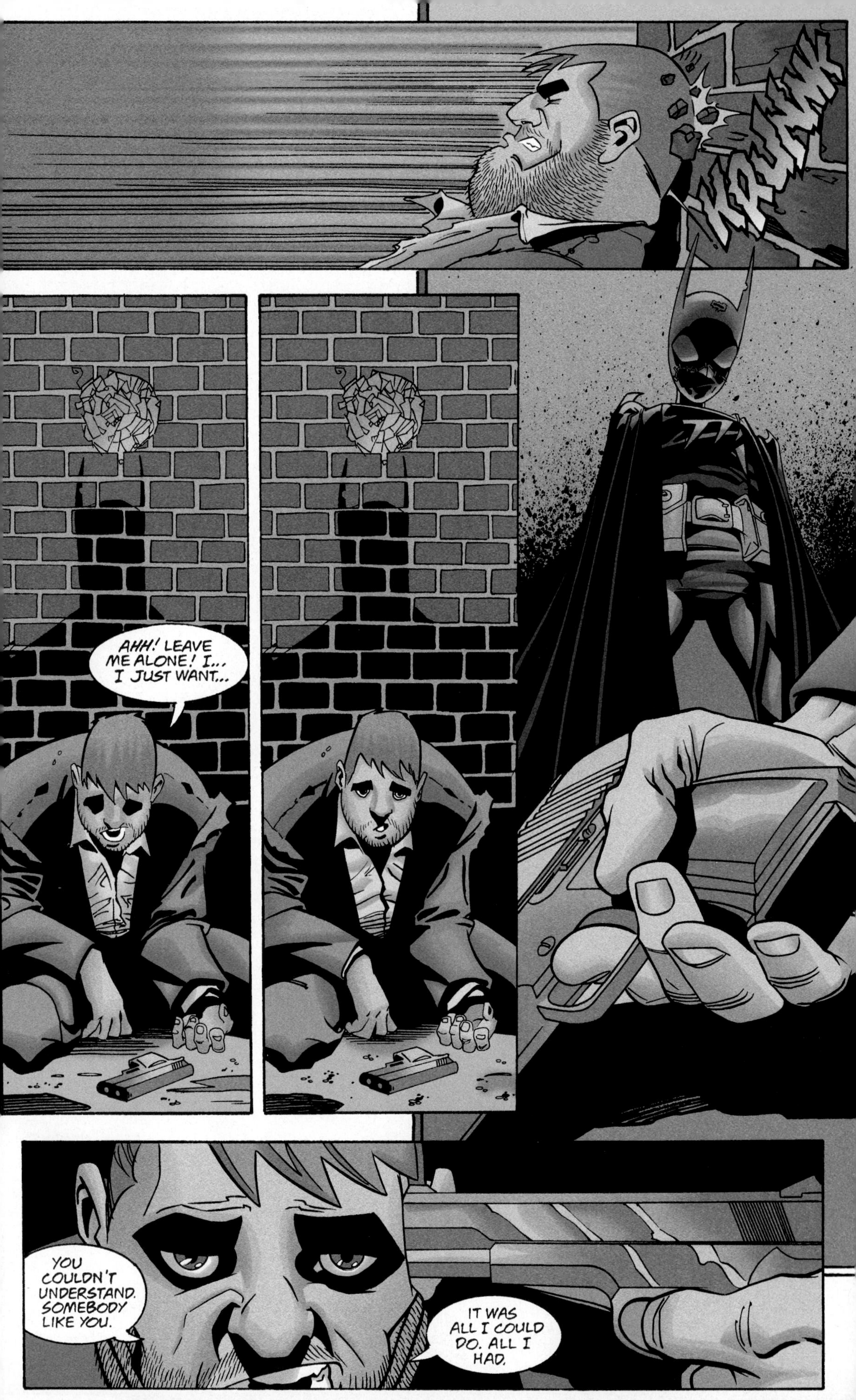
KRUNK
AHH! LEAVE ME ALONE! I... I JUST WANT...
YOU COULDN'T UNDERSTAND. SOMEBODY LIKE YOU.
IT WAS ALL I COULD DO. ALL I HAD.

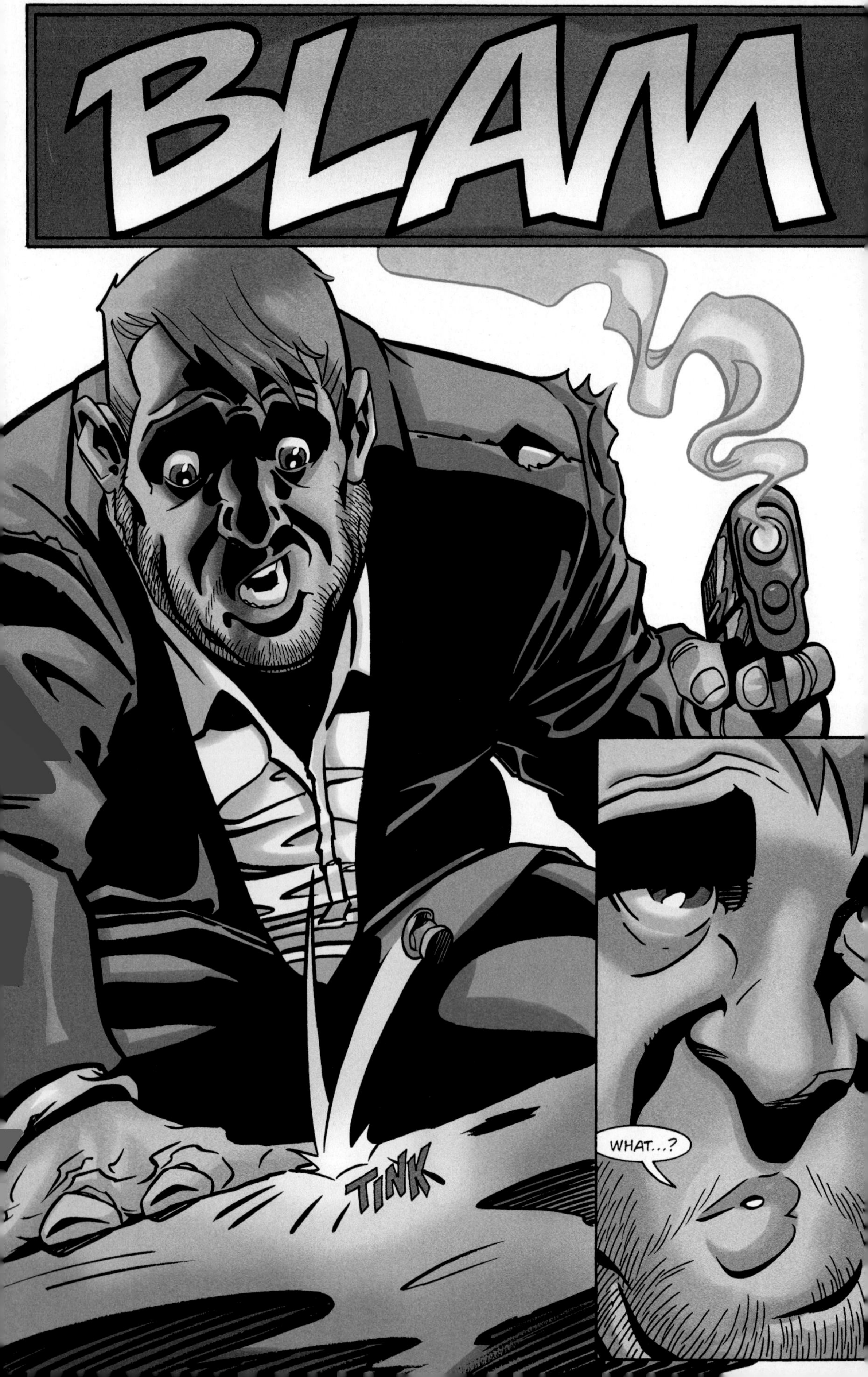
BLAM
TINK
WHAT...?

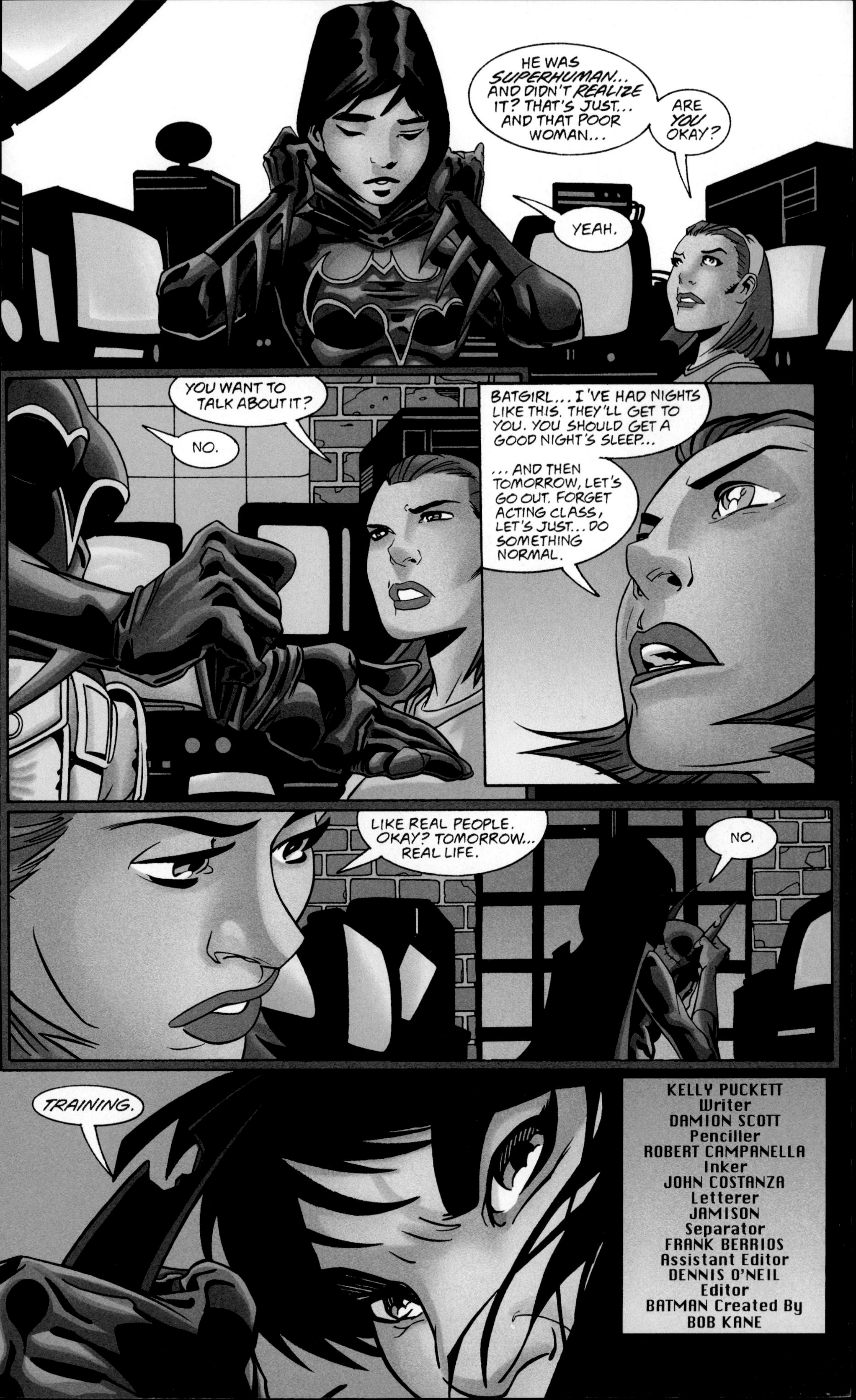
HE WAS SUPERHUMAN... AND DIDN'T REALIZE IT? THAT'S JUST... AND THAT POOR WOMAN...
ARE YOU OKAY?
YEAH.
YOU WANT TO TALK ABOUT IT?
NO.
BATGIRL... I'VE HAD NIGHTS LIKE THIS. THEY'LL GET TO YOU. YOU SHOULD GET A GOOD NIGHT'S SLEEP...
...AND THEN TOMORROW, LET'S GO OUT. FORGET ACTING CLASS, LET'S JUST... DO SOMETHING NORMAL.
LIKE REAL PEOPLE. OKAY? TOMORROW... REAL LIFE.
NO.
TRAINING.
KELLY PUCKETT Writer
DAMION SCOTT Penciller
ROBERT CAMPANELLA Inker
JOHN COSTANZA Letterer
JAMISON Separator
FRANK BERRIOS Assistant Editor
DENNIS O'NEIL Editor
BATMAN Created By BOB KANE

BATGIRL #11 cover by
Scott McDaniel & Aaron Sowd

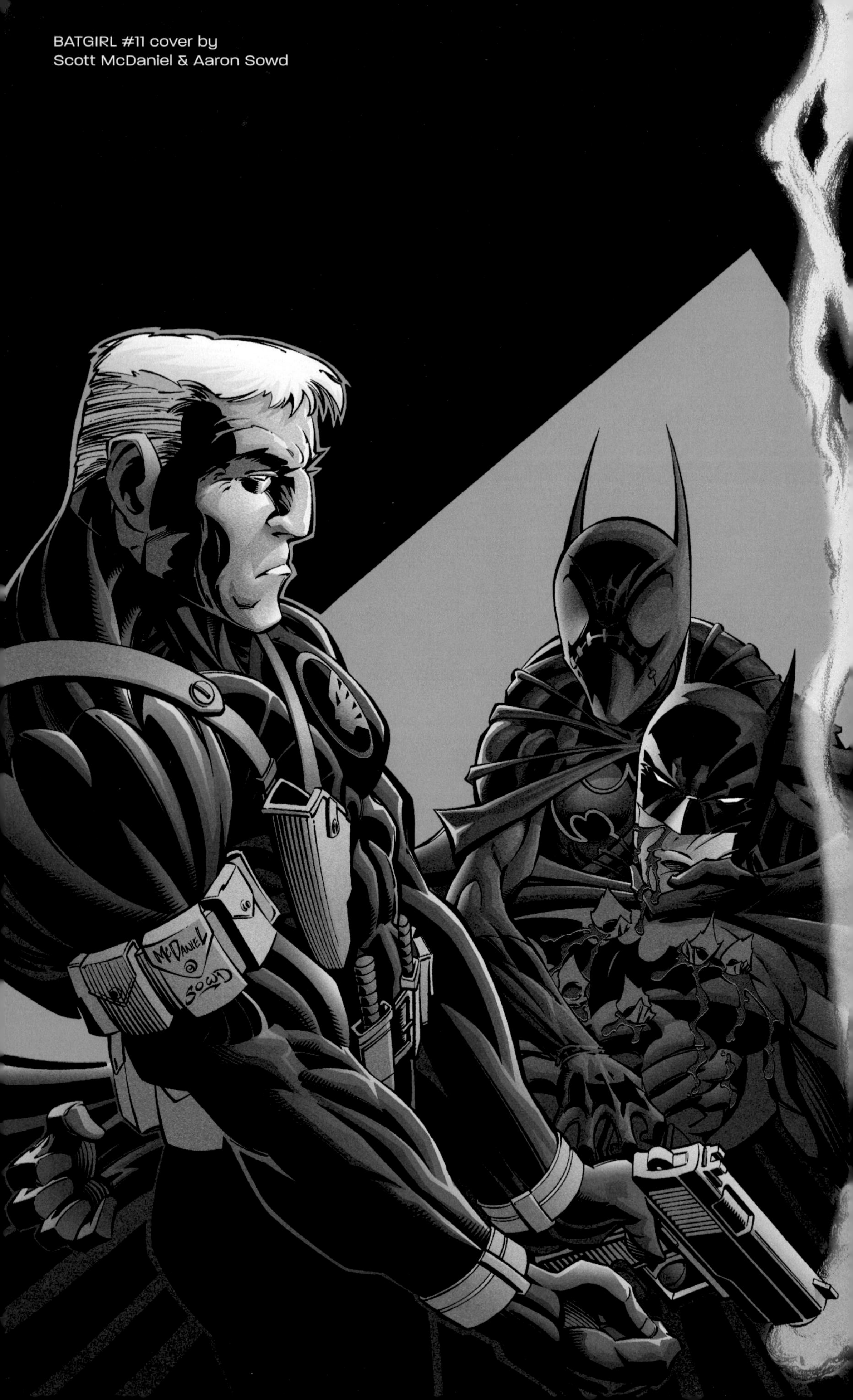
McDaniel
SOWD

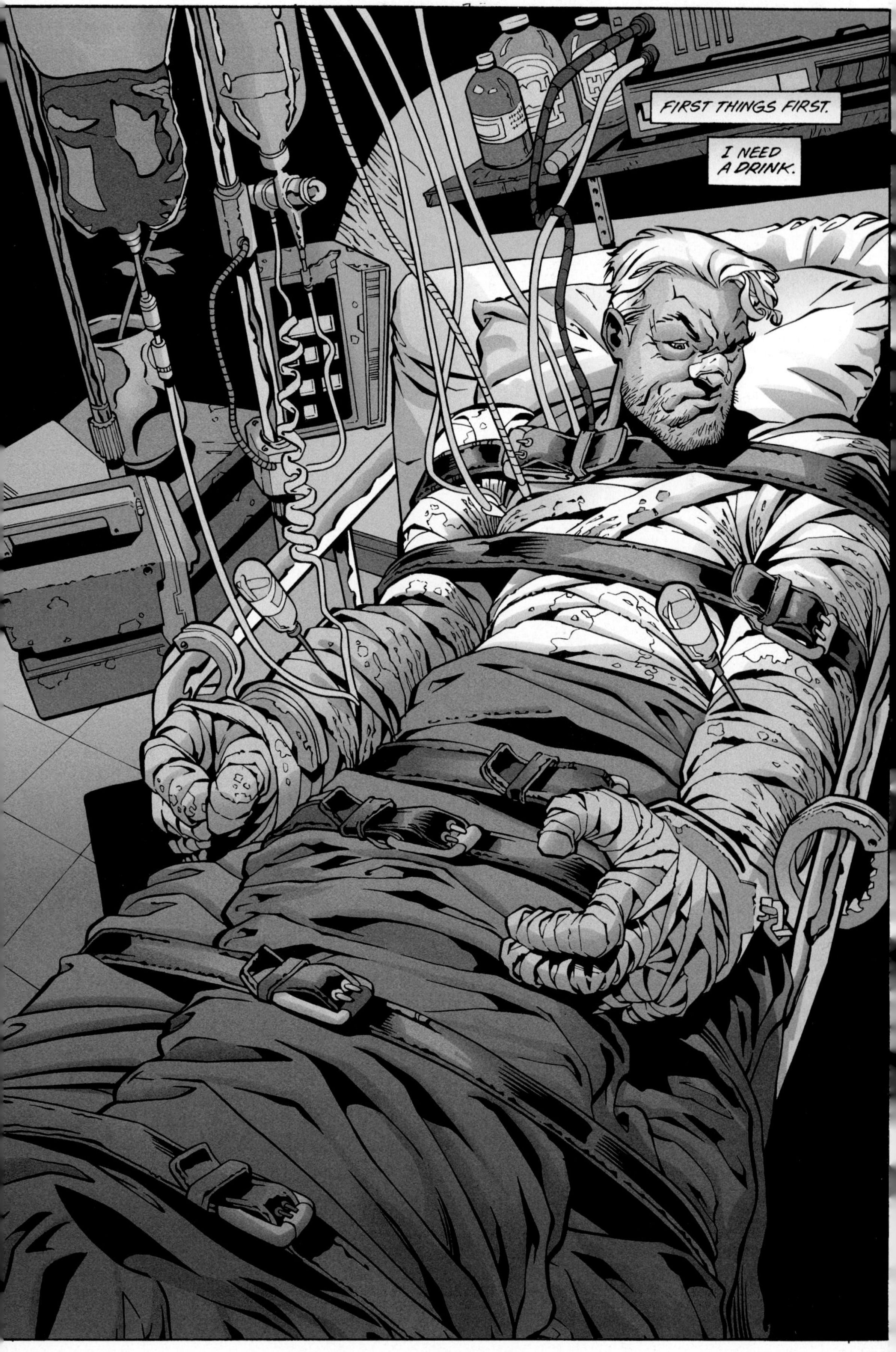
FIRST THINGS FIRST.
I NEED A DRINK.

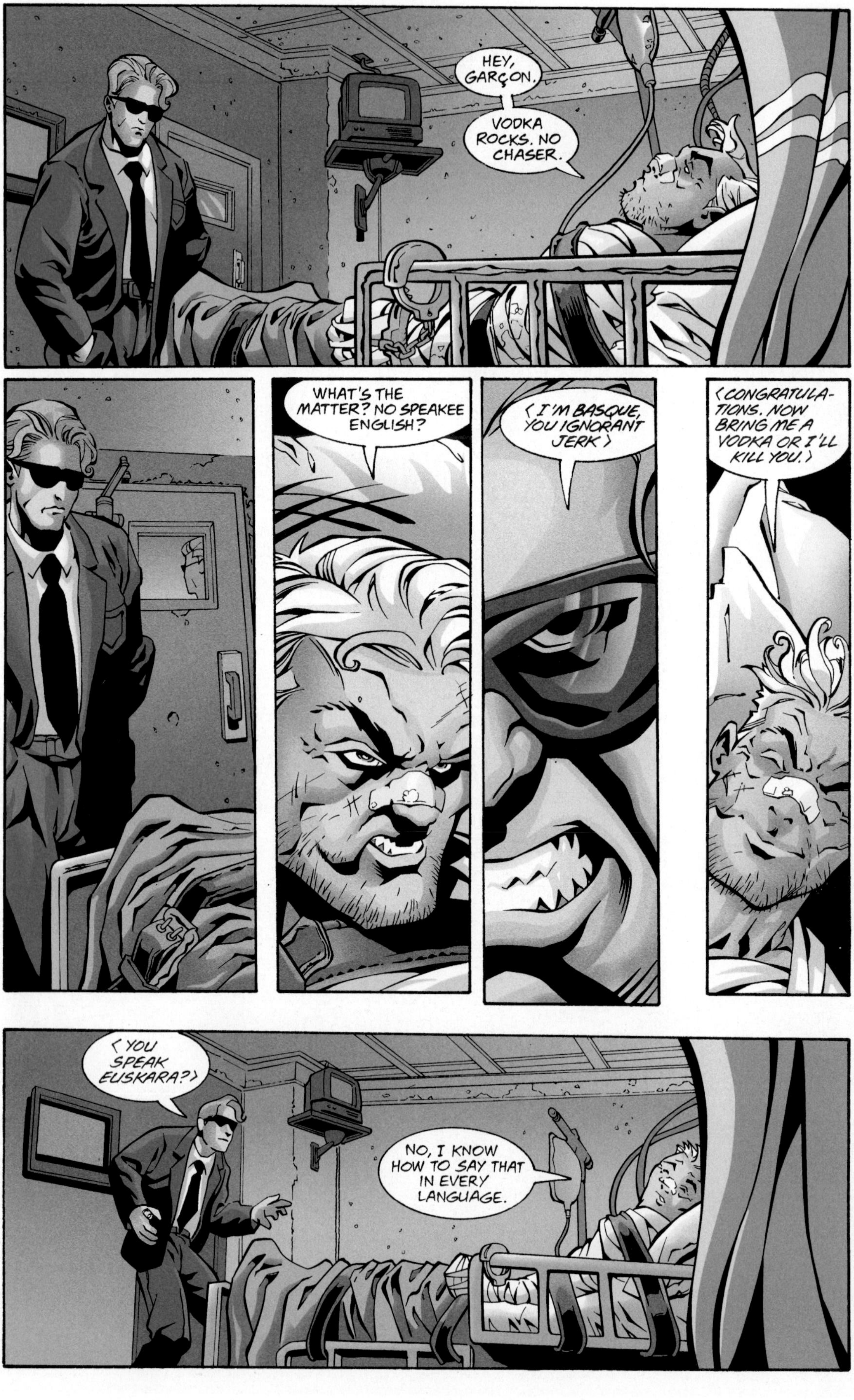
HEY, GARÇON.
VODKA ROCKS. NO CHASER.
WHAT'S THE MATTER? NO SPEAKEE ENGLISH?
< I'M BASQUE, YOU IGNORANT JERK >
< CONGRATULATIONS. NOW BRING ME A VODKA OR I'LL KILL YOU. >
< YOU SPEAK EUSKARA? >
NO, I KNOW HOW TO SAY THAT IN EVERY LANGUAGE.

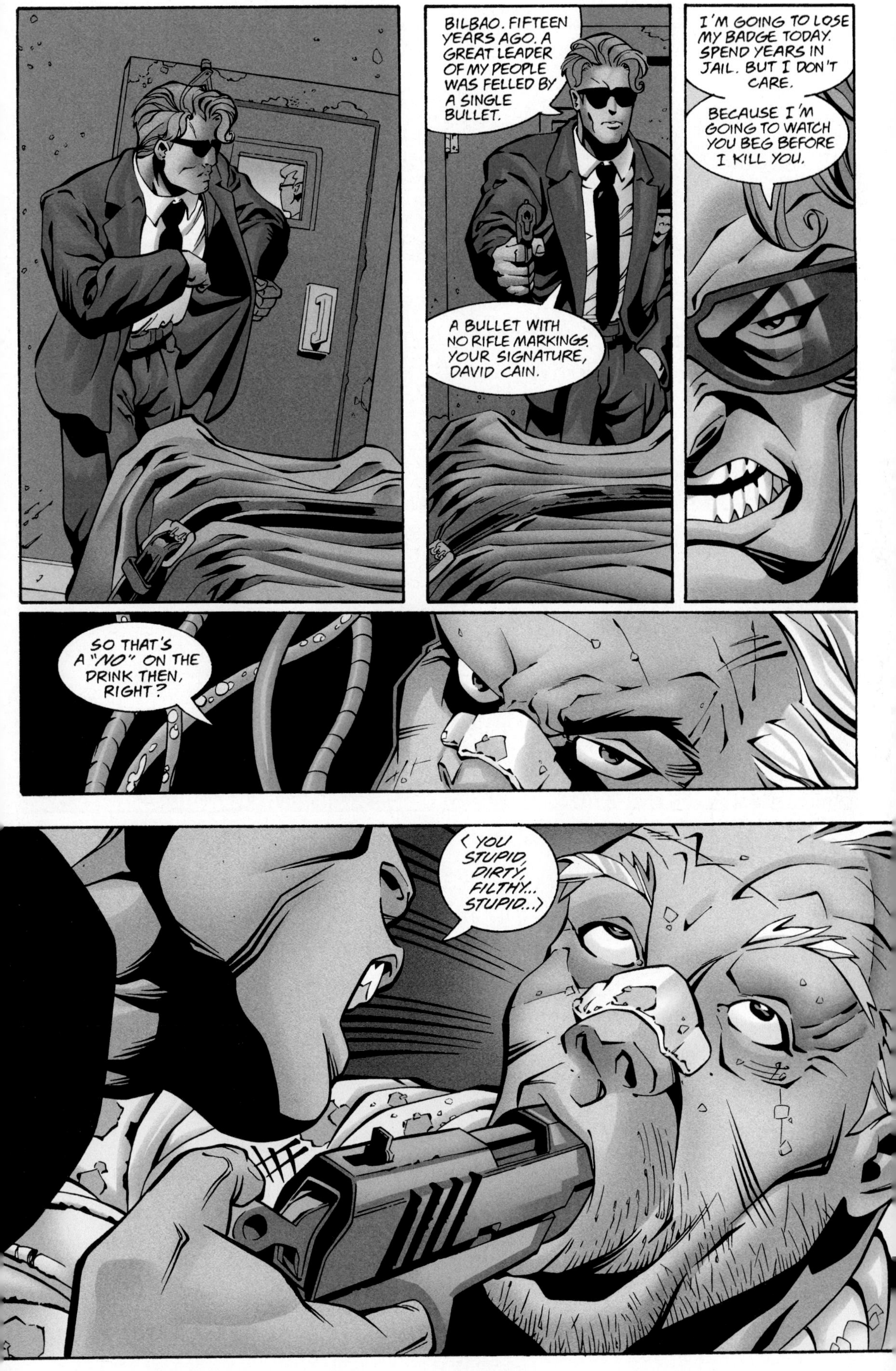
BILBAO. FIFTEEN YEARS AGO. A GREAT LEADER OF MY PEOPLE WAS FELLED BY A SINGLE BULLET.
A BULLET WITH NO RIFLE MARKINGS. YOUR SIGNATURE, DAVID CAIN.
I'M GOING TO LOSE MY BADGE TODAY. SPEND YEARS IN JAIL. BUT I DON'T CARE.
BECAUSE I'M GOING TO WATCH YOU BEG BEFORE I KILL YOU.
SO THAT'S A "NO" ON THE DRINK THEN, RIGHT?
< YOU STUPID, DIRTY, FILTHY... STUPID...>

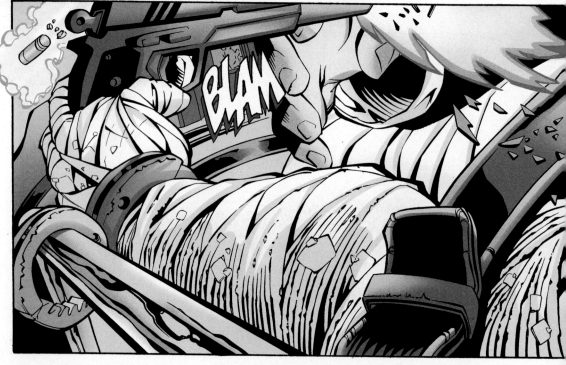

BLAM

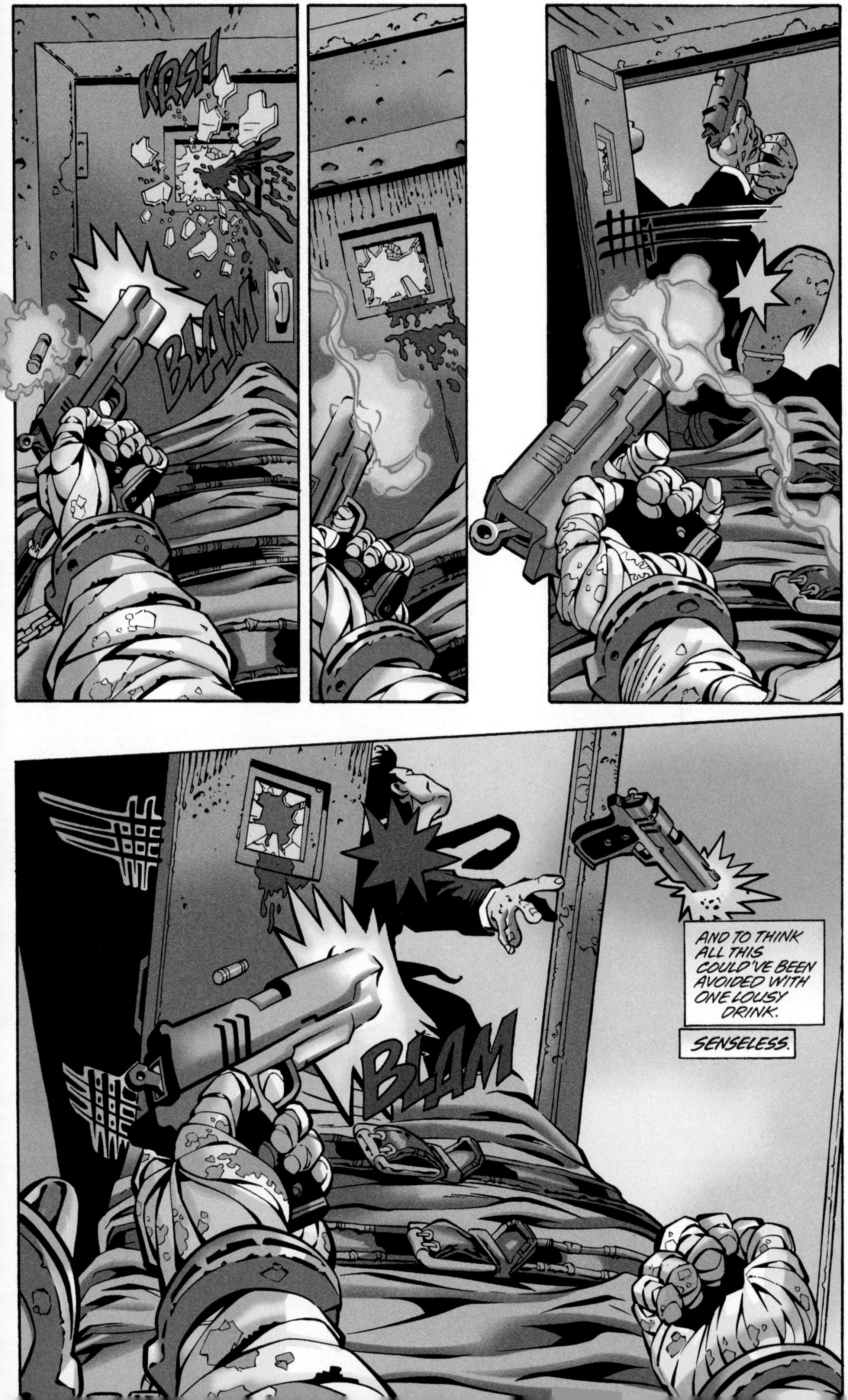
KRSH
BLAM
BLAM
AND TO THINK ALL THIS COULD'VE BEEN AVOIDED WITH ONE LOUSY DRINK.
SENSELESS.

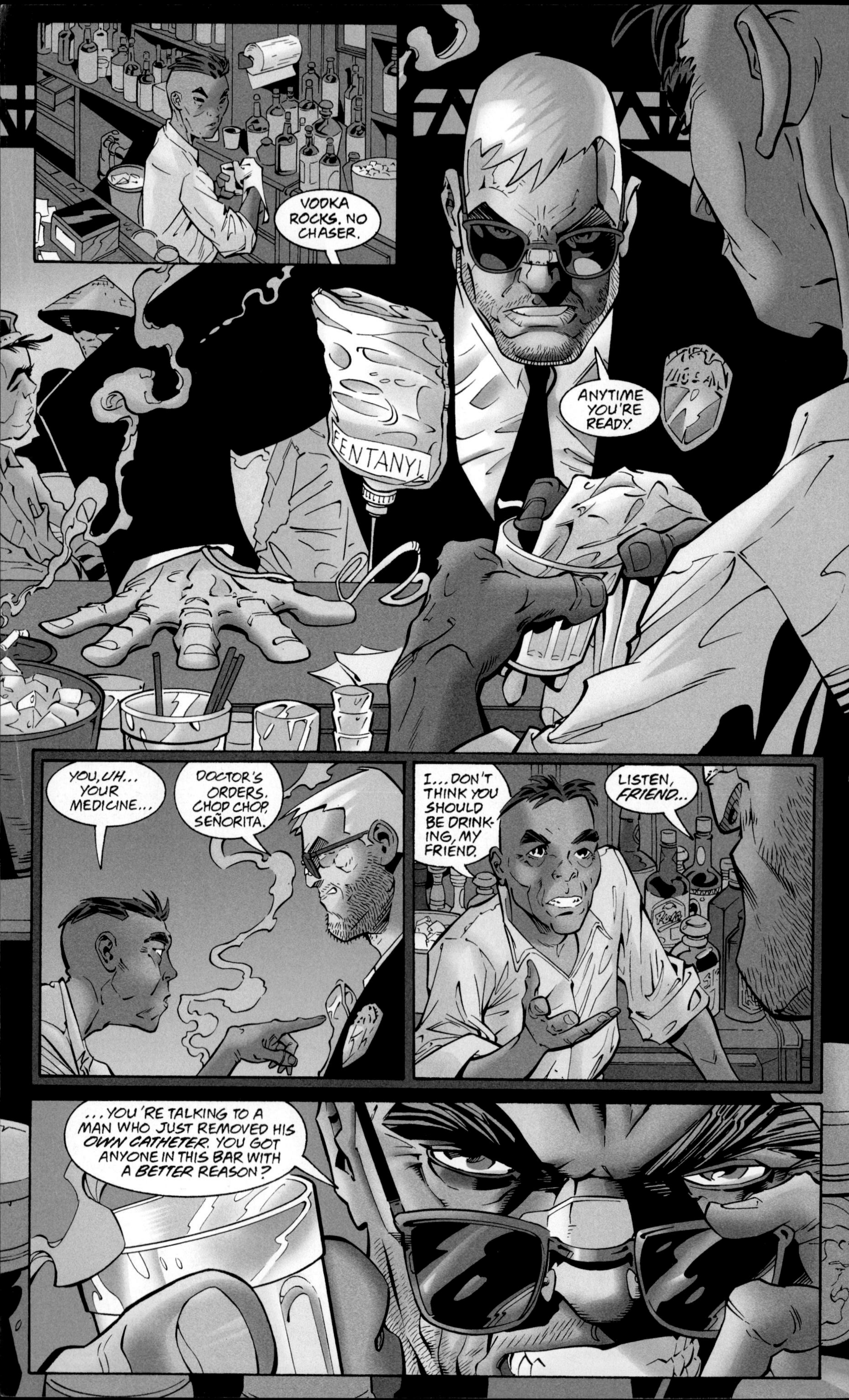
VODKA ROCKS. NO CHASER.
FENTANYL
ANYTIME YOU'RE READY.
YOU, UH... YOUR MEDICINE...
DOCTOR'S ORDERS. CHOP CHOP, SEÑORITA.
I... DON'T THINK YOU SHOULD BE DRINKING, MY FRIEND.
LISTEN, *FRIEND*...
...YOU'RE TALKING TO A MAN WHO JUST REMOVED HIS *OWN CATHETER*. YOU GOT ANYONE IN THIS BAR WITH A *BETTER REASON*?

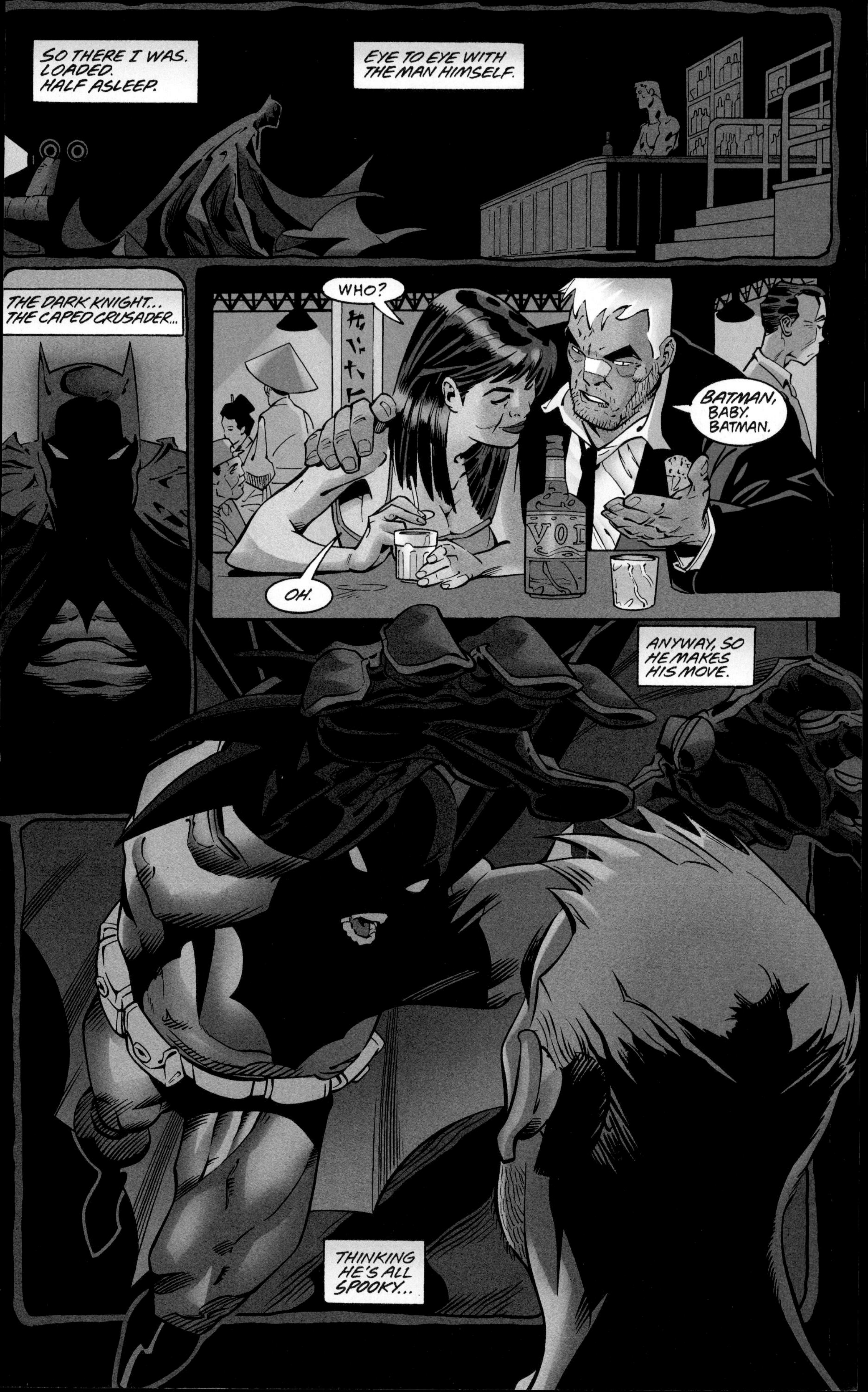
SO THERE I WAS. LOADED. HALF ASLEEP.
EYE TO EYE WITH THE MAN HIMSELF.
THE DARK KNIGHT... THE CAPED CRUSADER...
WHO?
BATMAN, BABY. BATMAN.
OH.
ANYWAY, SO HE MAKES HIS MOVE.
THINKING HE'S ALL SPOOKY...

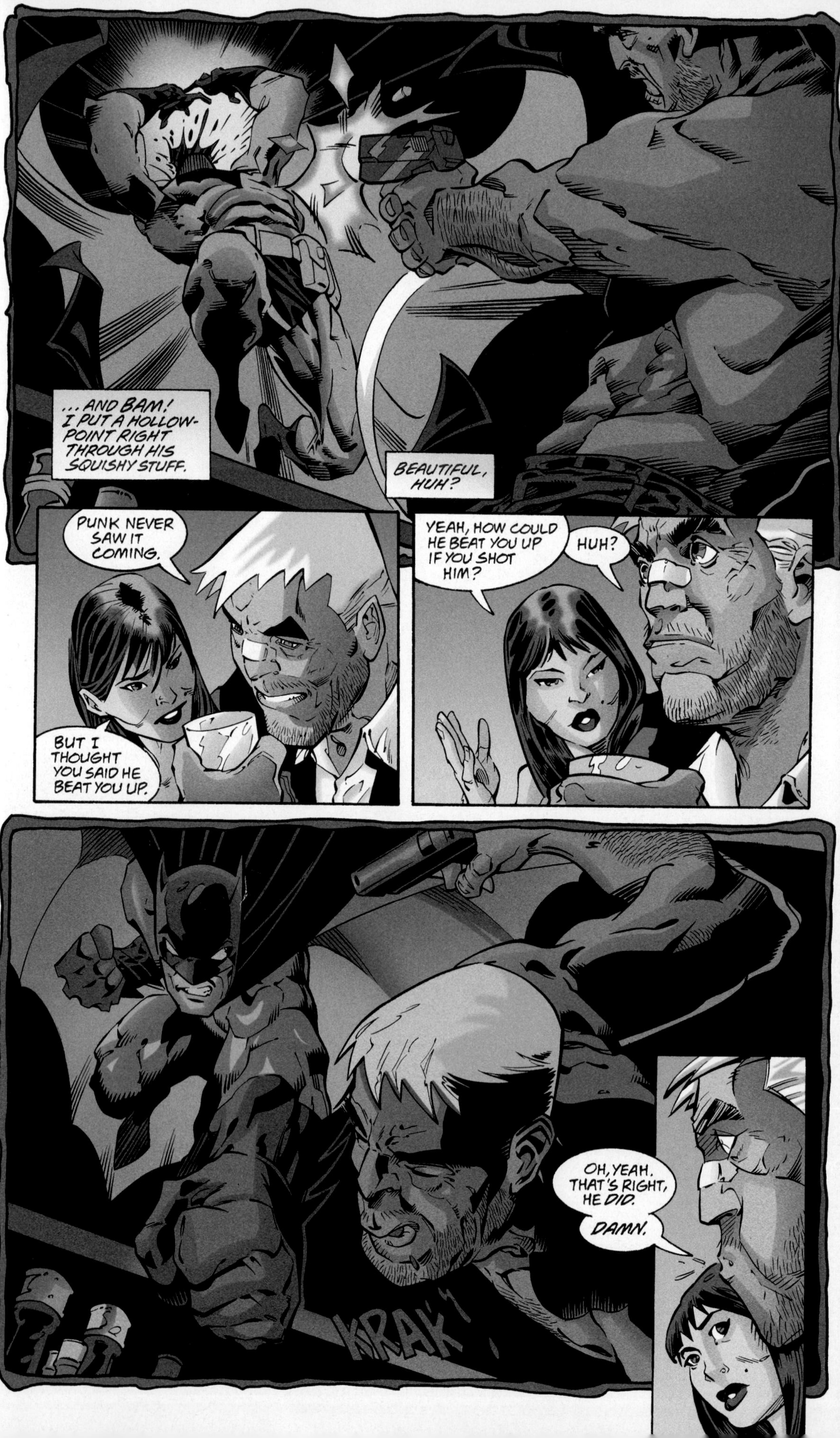
...AND BAM! I PUT A HOLLOW-POINT RIGHT THROUGH HIS SQUISHY STUFF.
BEAUTIFUL, HUH?
PUNK NEVER SAW IT COMING.
BUT I THOUGHT YOU SAID HE BEAT YOU UP.
HUH?
YEAH, HOW COULD HE BEAT YOU UP IF YOU SHOT HIM?
KRAK!
OH, YEAH. THAT'S RIGHT, HE DID.
DAMN.

"SO WHAT WERE YOU TWO FIGHTING ABOUT, ANYWAY?"

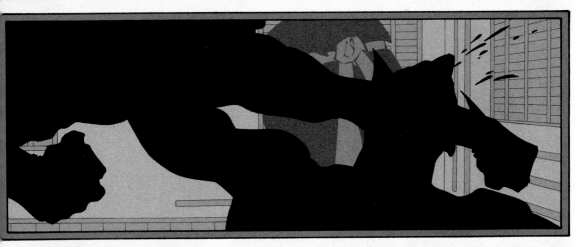

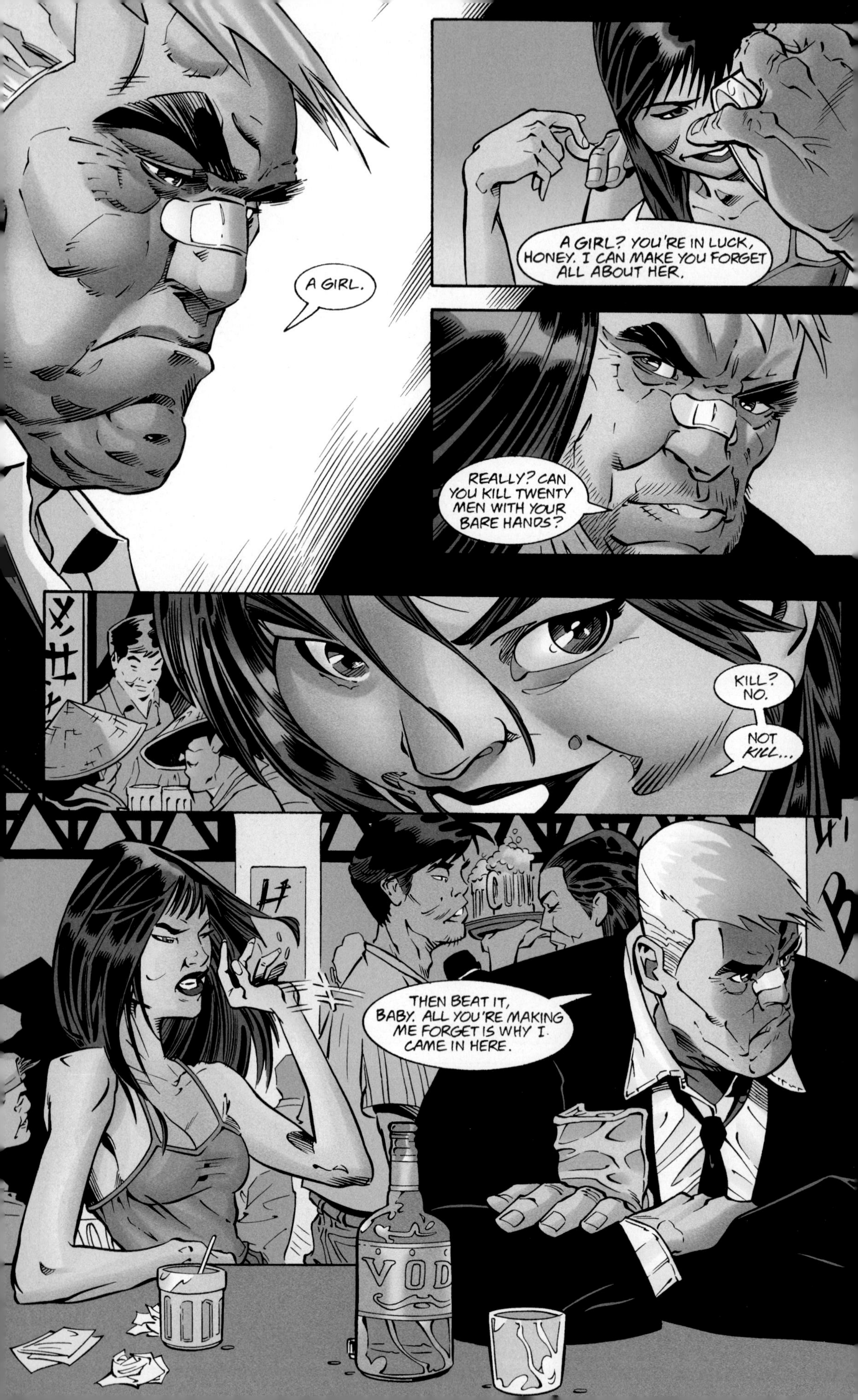
A GIRL.
A GIRL? YOU'RE IN LUCK, HONEY. I CAN MAKE YOU FORGET ALL ABOUT HER.
REALLY? CAN YOU KILL TWENTY MEN WITH YOUR BARE HANDS?
KILL? NO.
NOT KILL...
THEN BEAT IT, BABY. ALL YOU'RE MAKING ME FORGET IS WHY I CAME IN HERE.

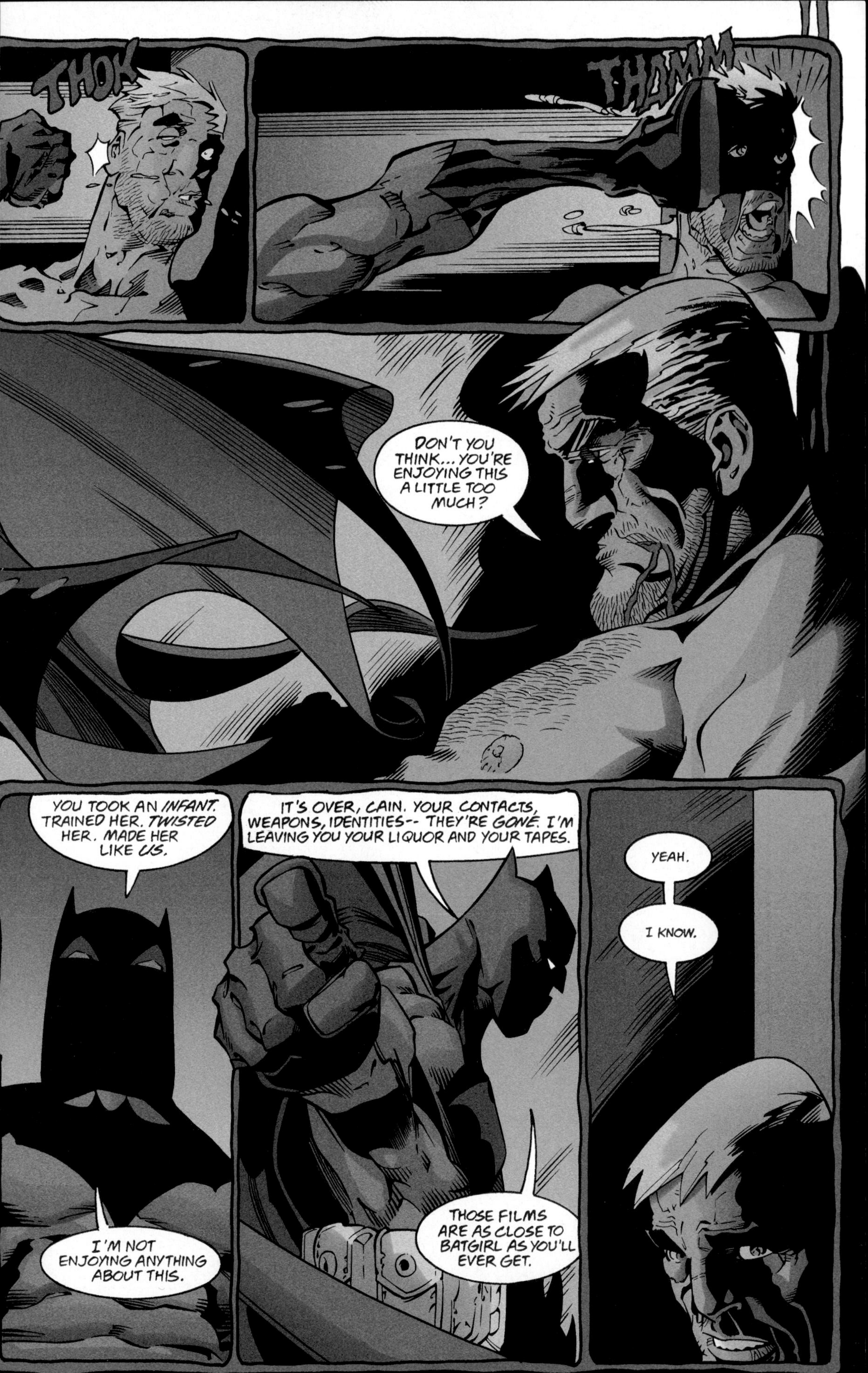
THOK
THMM
DON'T YOU THINK... YOU'RE ENJOYING THIS A LITTLE TOO MUCH?
YOU TOOK AN INFANT. TRAINED HER. TWISTED HER. MADE HER LIKE US.
I'M NOT ENJOYING ANYTHING ABOUT THIS.
IT'S OVER, CAIN. YOUR CONTACTS, WEAPONS, IDENTITIES-- THEY'RE GONE. I'M LEAVING YOU YOUR LIQUOR AND YOUR TAPES.
THOSE FILMS ARE AS CLOSE TO BATGIRL AS YOU'LL EVER GET.
YEAH.
I KNOW.

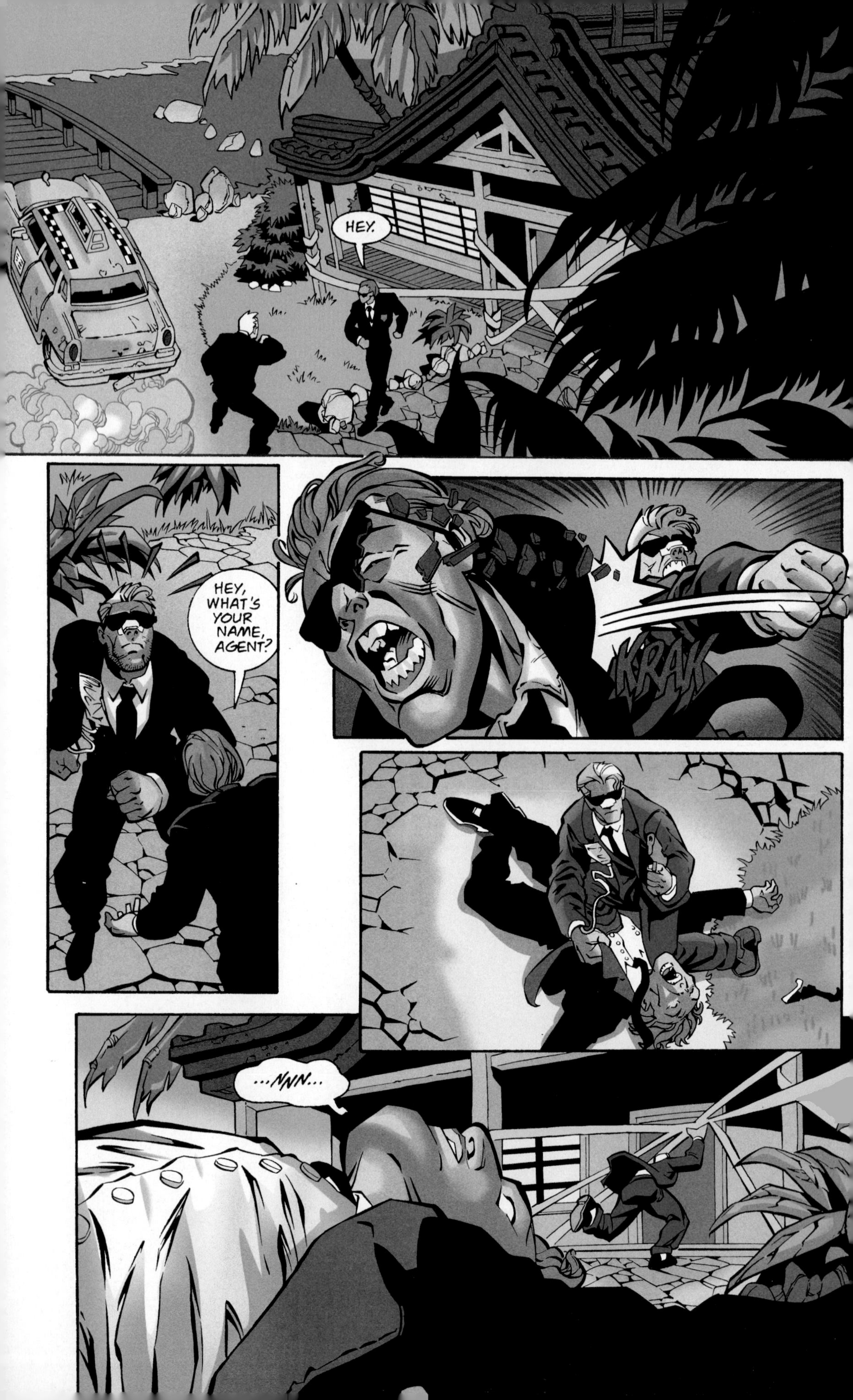
HEY.
HEY, WHAT'S YOUR NAME, AGENT?
KRAK
...NNN...

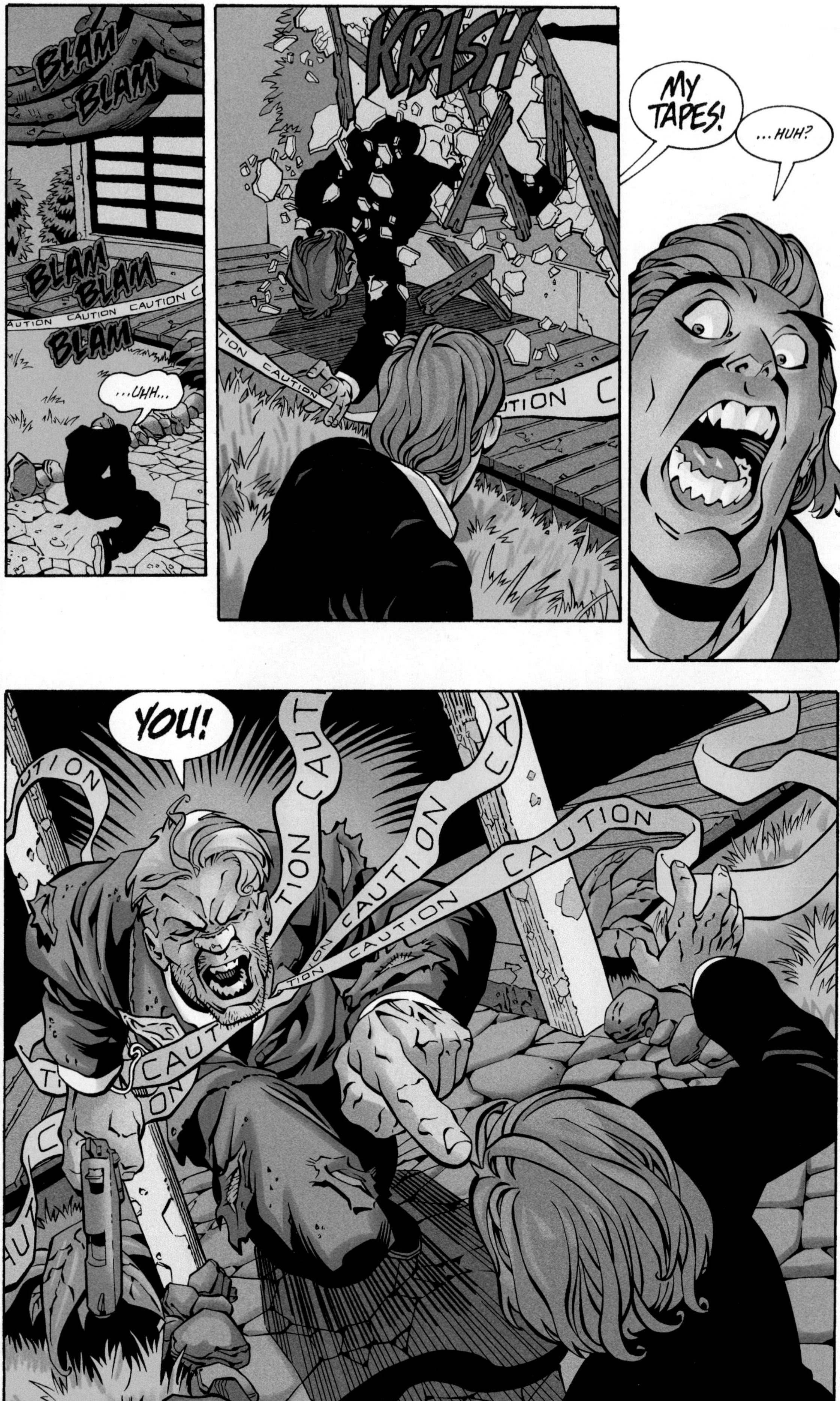
BLAM
BLAM
BLAM
BLAM
BLAM
CAUTION CAUTION CAUTION
...UHH...
KRASH
MY TAPES!
...HUH?
YOU!
CAUTION CAUTION CAUTION

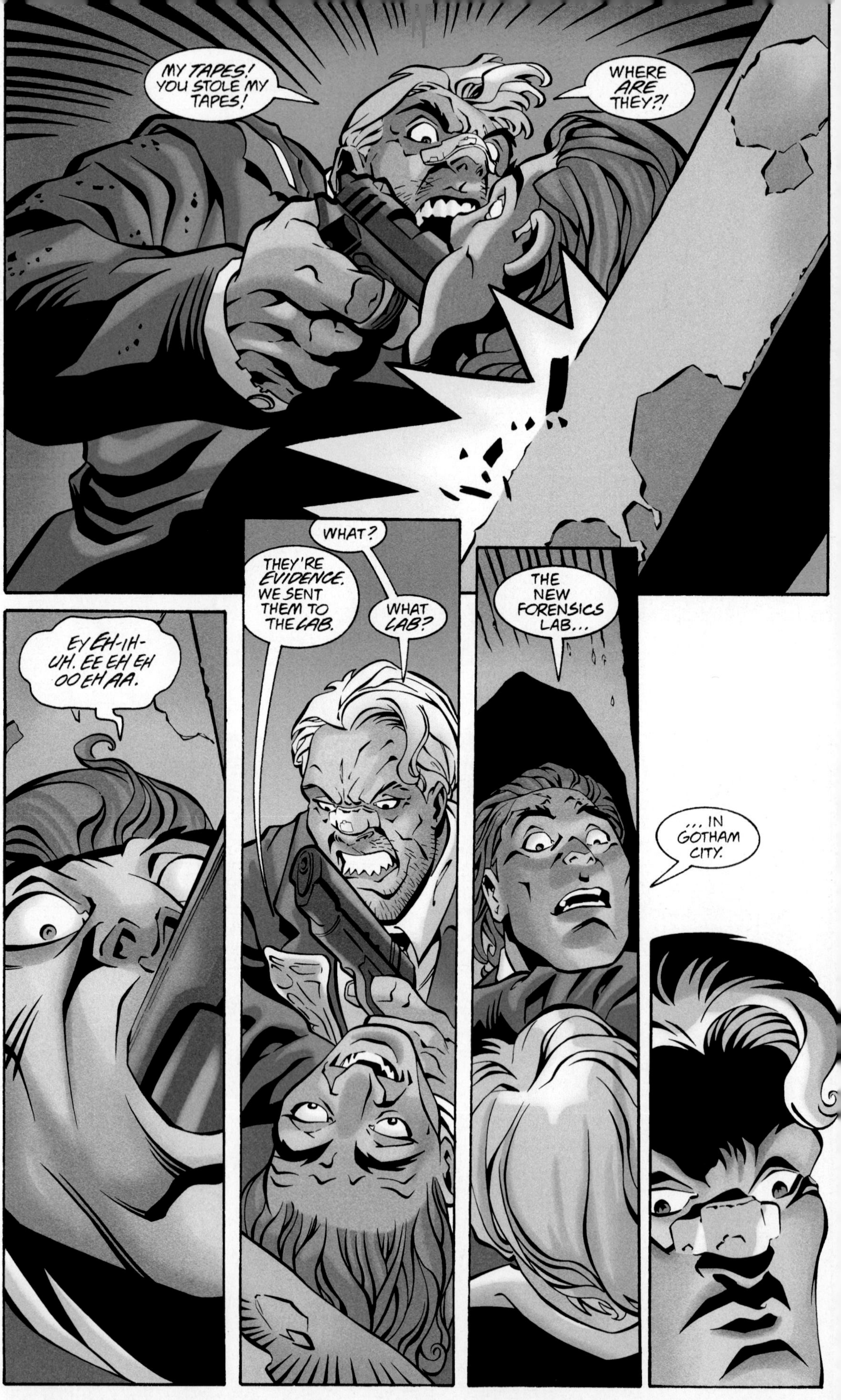
MY TAPES! YOU STOLE MY TAPES!
WHERE ARE THEY?!
EY EH-IH-UH. EE EH EH OO EH AA.
WHAT?
THEY'RE EVIDENCE. WE SENT THEM TO THE LAB.
WHAT LAB?
THE NEW FORENSICS LAB...
...IN GOTHAM CITY.

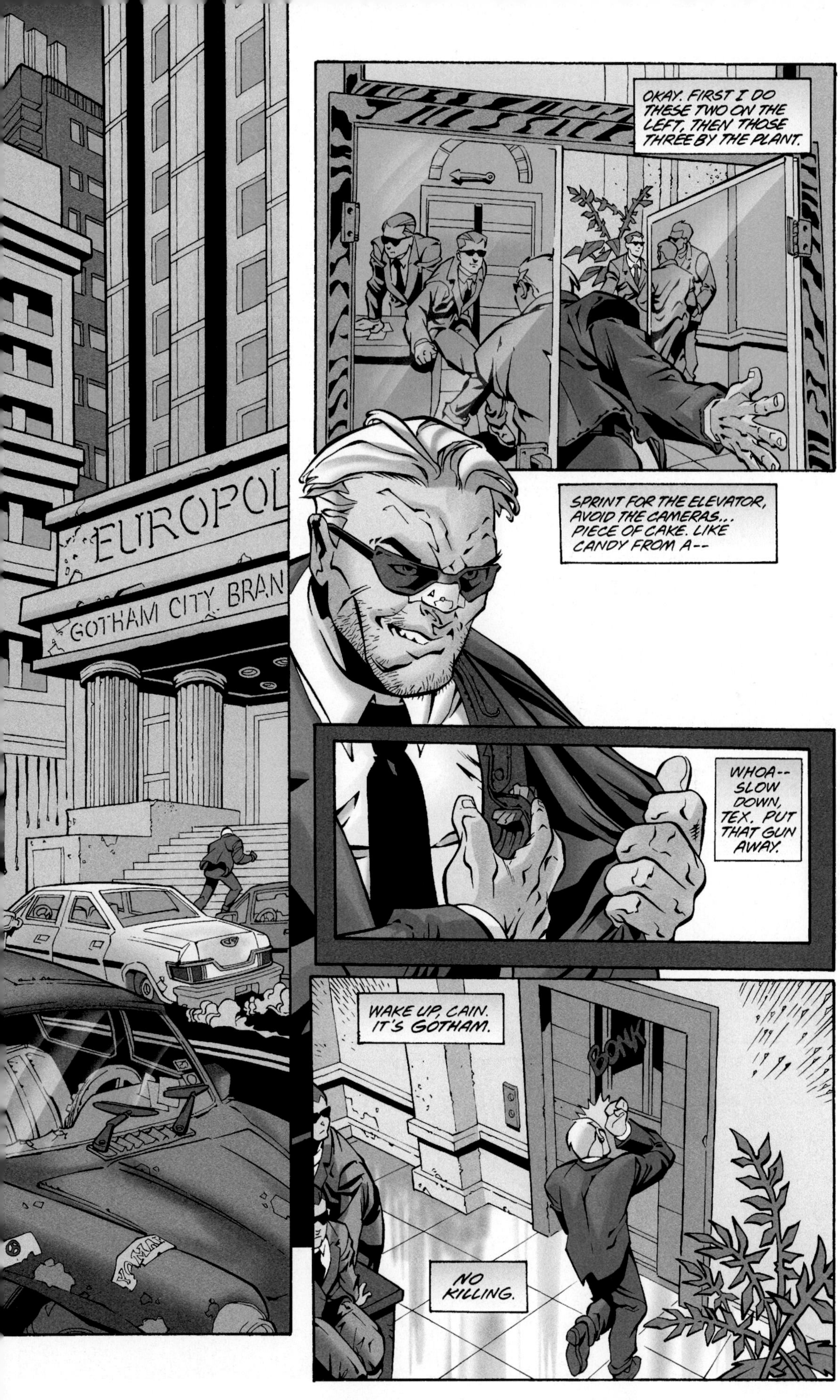
EUROPOL
GOTHAM CITY BRAN
OKAY. FIRST I DO THESE TWO ON THE LEFT, THEN THOSE THREE BY THE PLANT.
SPRINT FOR THE ELEVATOR, AVOID THE CAMERAS... PIECE OF CAKE. LIKE CANDY FROM A--
WHOA-- SLOW DOWN, TEX. PUT THAT GUN AWAY.
WAKE UP, CAIN. IT'S GOTHAM.
BONK
NO KILLING.

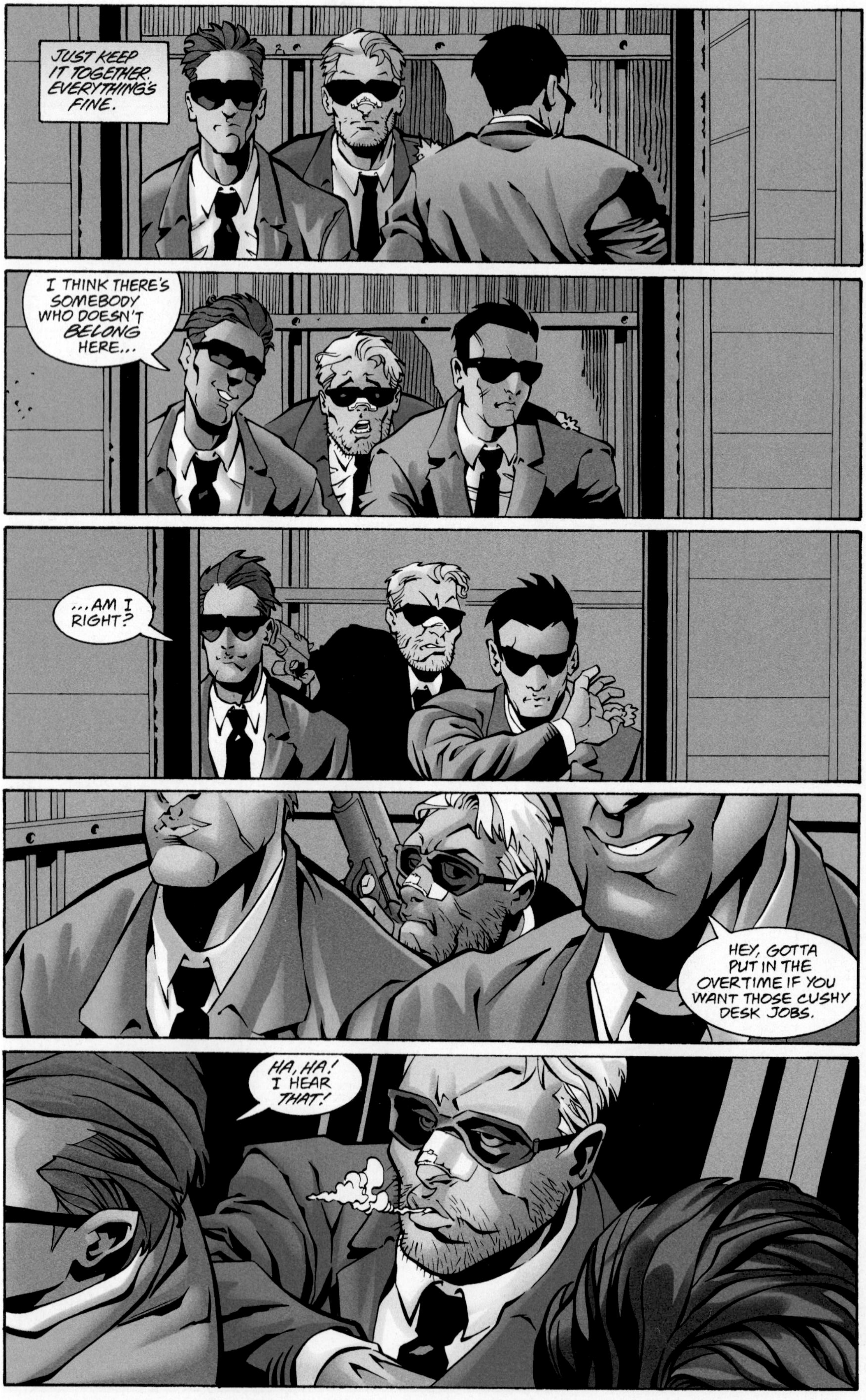
JUST KEEP IT TOGETHER. EVERYTHING'S FINE.
I THINK THERE'S SOMEBODY WHO DOESN'T BELONG HERE...
...AM I RIGHT?
HEY, GOTTA PUT IN THE OVERTIME IF YOU WANT THOSE CUSHY DESK JOBS.
HA, HA! I HEAR THAT!

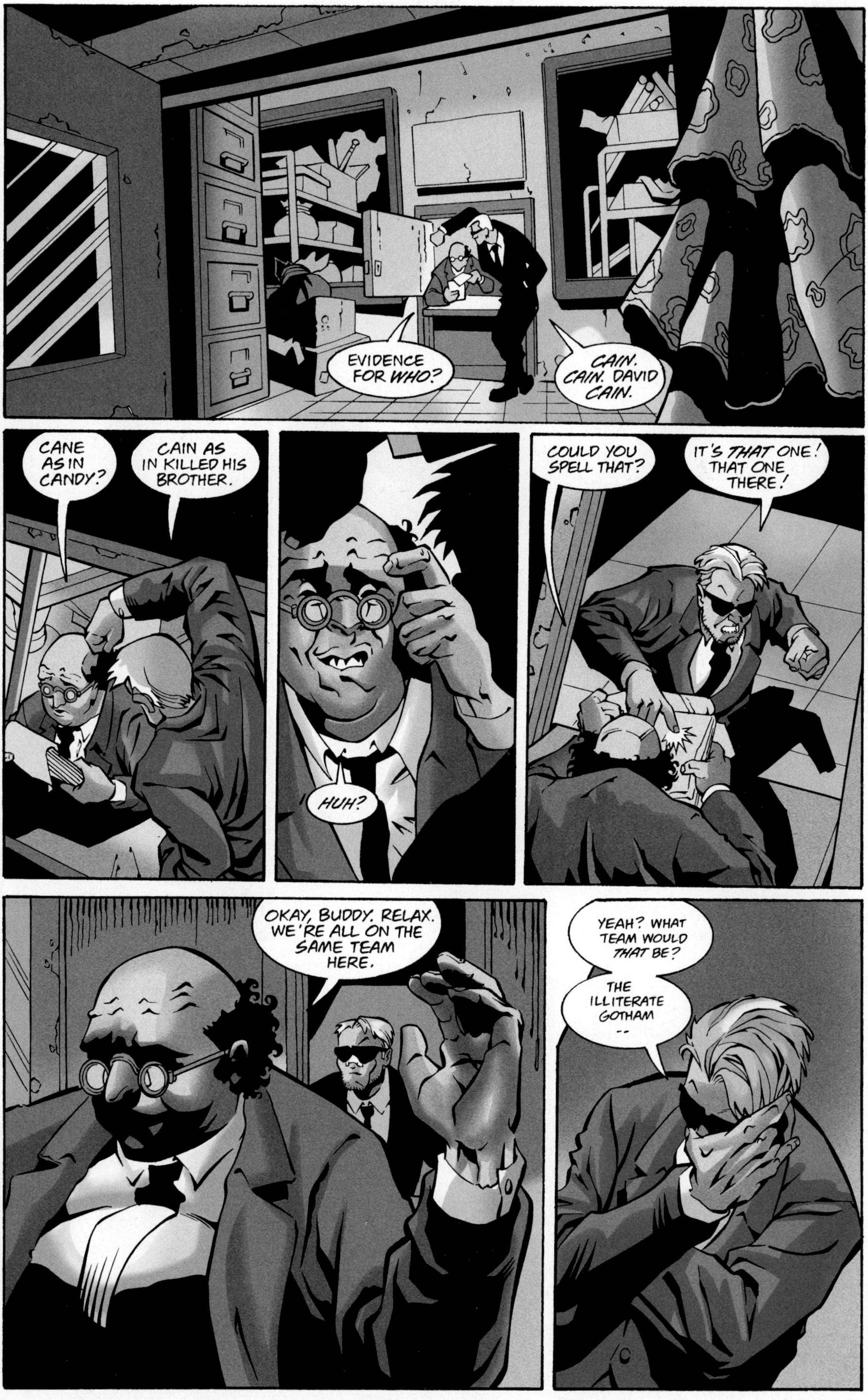
EVIDENCE FOR WHO?
CAIN. CAIN. DAVID CAIN.
CANE AS IN CANDY?
CAIN AS IN KILLED HIS BROTHER.
HUH?
COULD YOU SPELL THAT?
IT'S THAT ONE! THAT ONE THERE!
OKAY, BUDDY. RELAX. WE'RE ALL ON THE SAME TEAM HERE.
YEAH? WHAT TEAM WOULD THAT BE?
THE ILLITERATE GOTHAM --

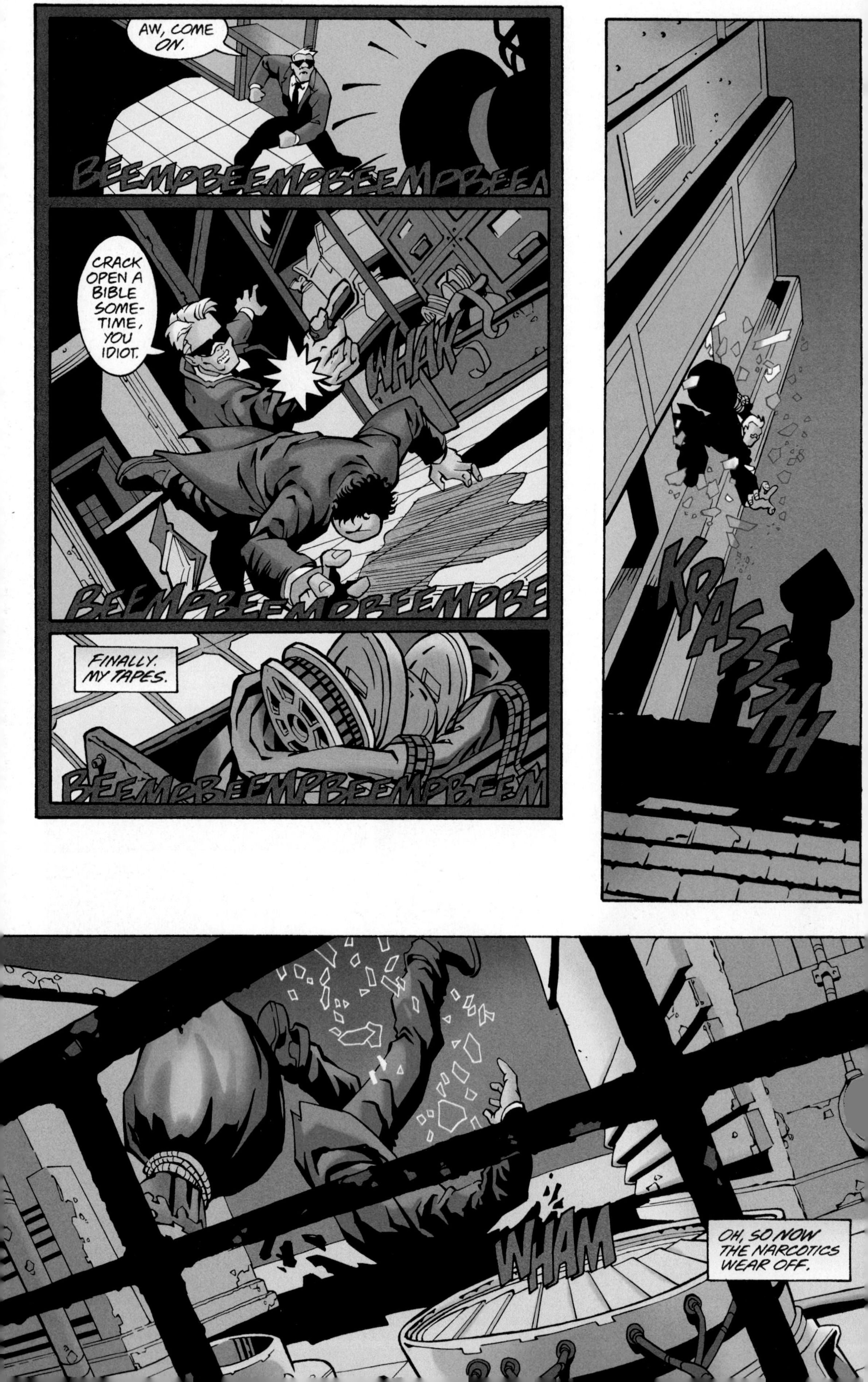
AW, COME ON.
BEEMPBEEMPBEEMPBEEA
CRACK OPEN A BIBLE SOME-TIME, YOU IDIOT.
WHAK
BEEMPBEEMPBEEMPBE
FINALLY. MY TAPES.
BEEMPBEEMPBEEMPBEEM
KRASSSHH
WHAM
OH, SO NOW THE NARCOTICS WEAR OFF.

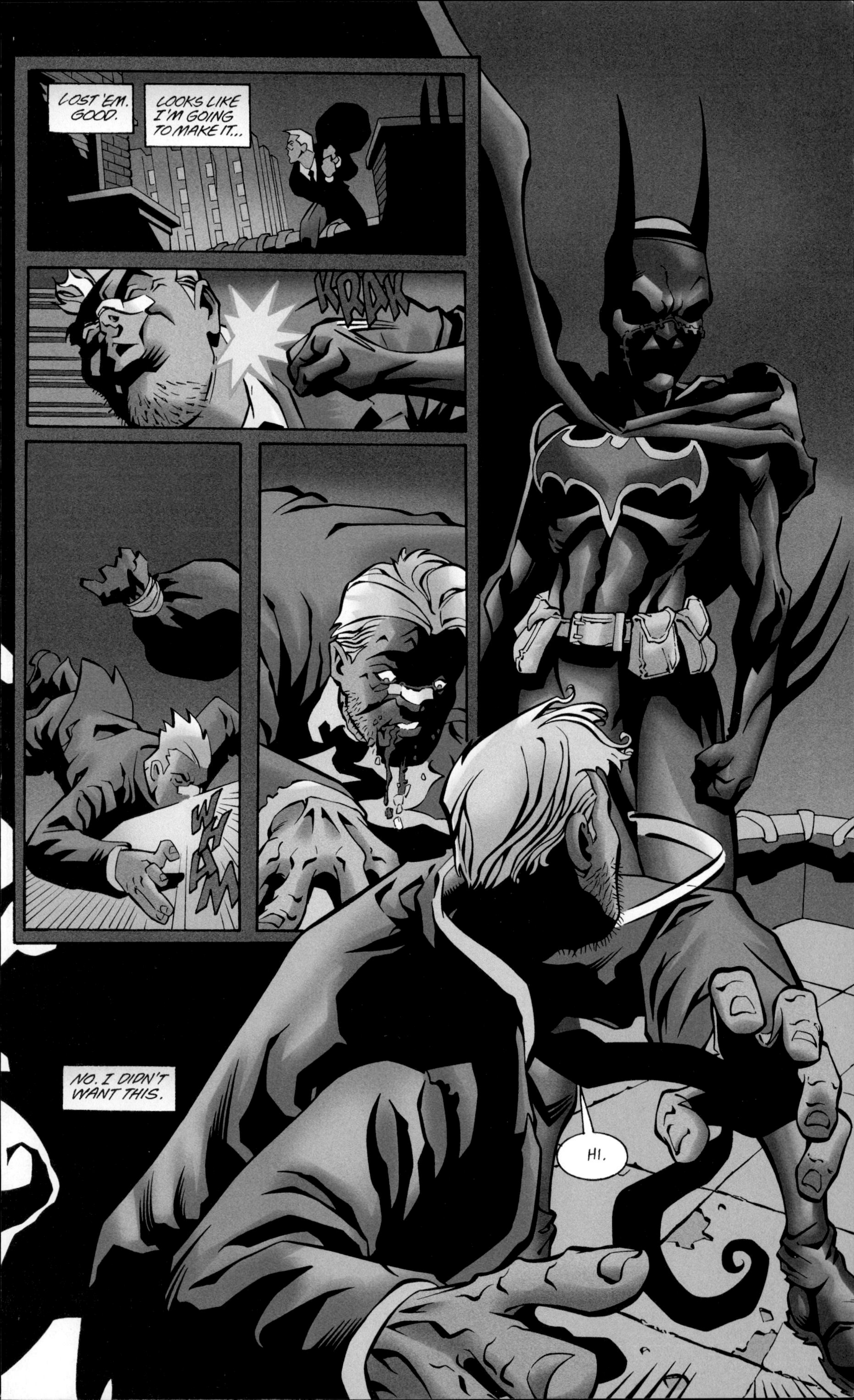
LOST 'EM. GOOD.
LOOKS LIKE I'M GOING TO MAKE IT...
KRAK
WHAM
NO. I DIDN'T WANT THIS.
HI.

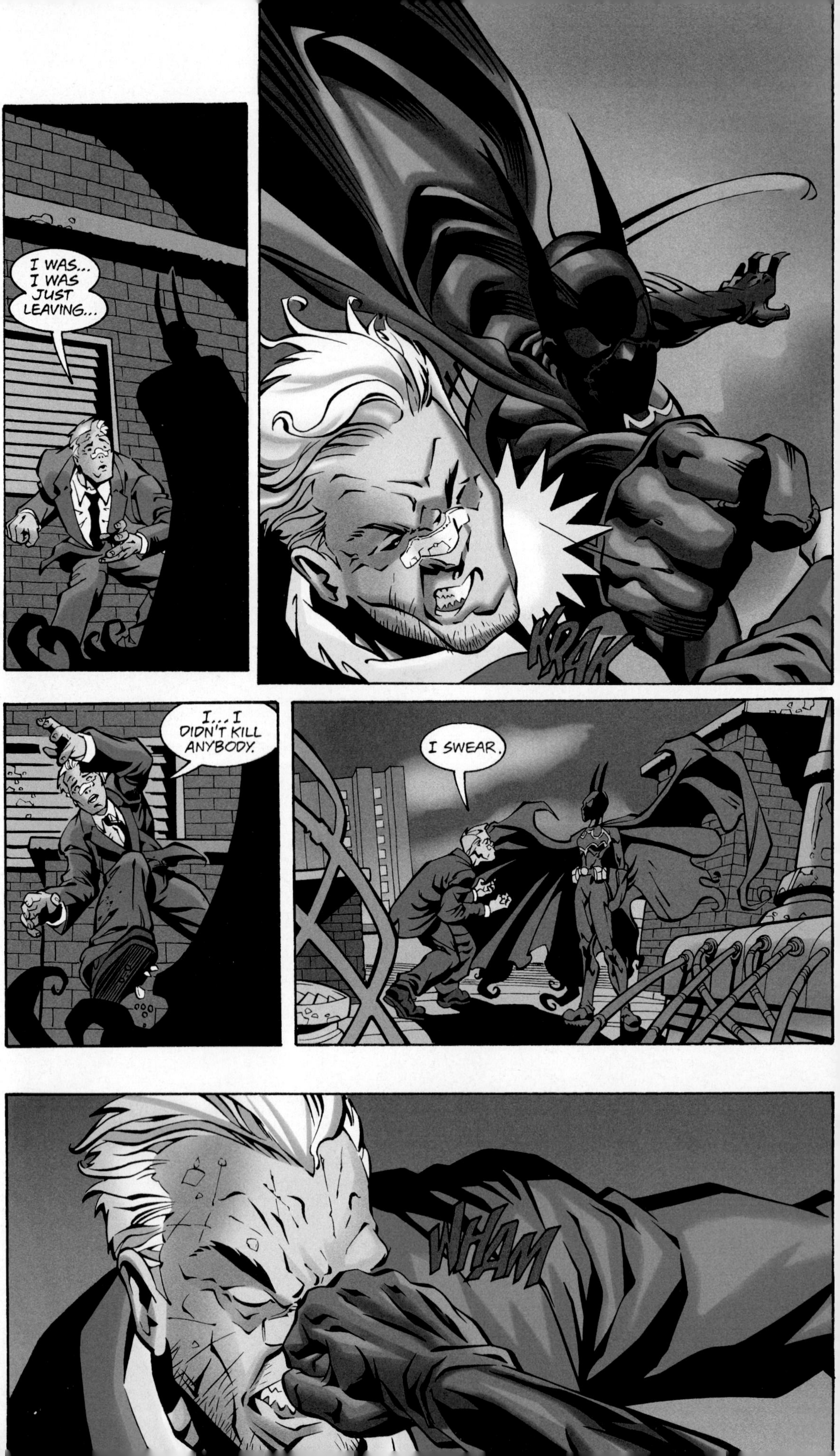
I WAS...
I WAS
JUST
LEAVING...
KRAK
I... I
DIDN'T KILL
ANYBODY.
I SWEAR.
WHAM

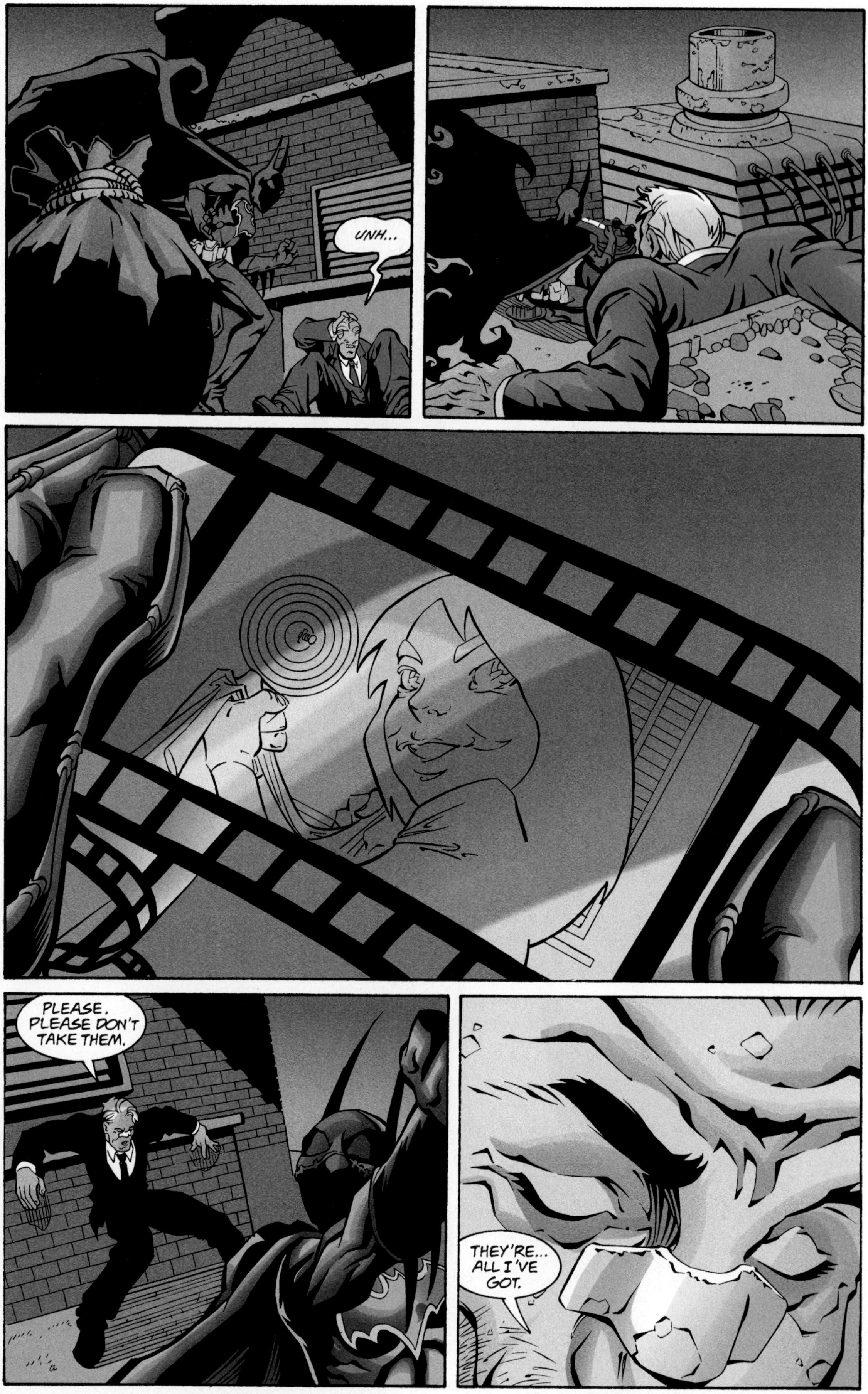
UNH...
PLEASE. PLEASE DON'T TAKE THEM.
THEY'RE... ALL I'VE GOT.

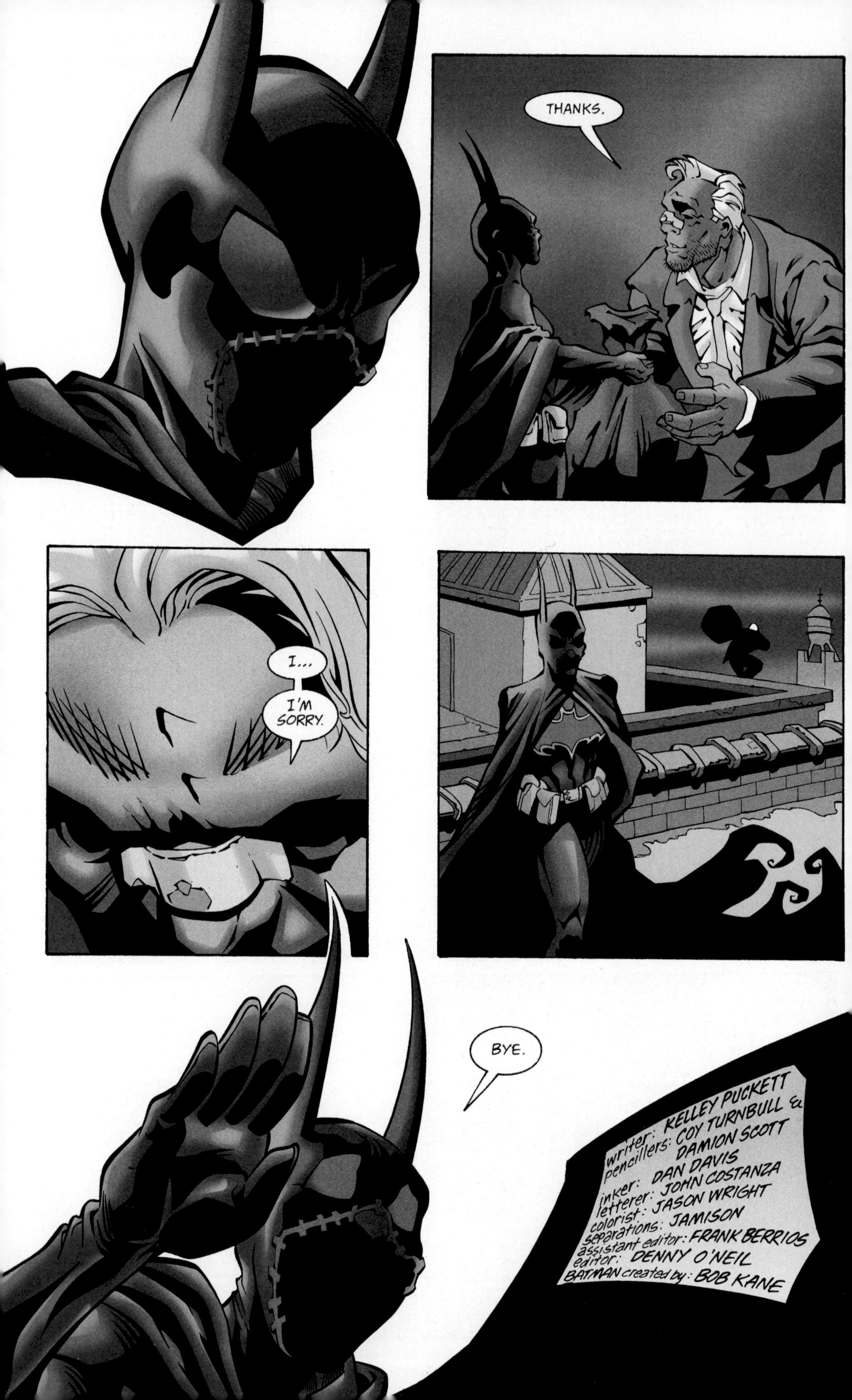
THANKS.
I...
I'M SORRY.
BYE.
writer: KELLEY PUCKETT
pencillers: COY TURNBULL & DAMION SCOTT
inker: DAN DAVIS
letterer: JOHN COSTANZA
colorist: JASON WRIGHT
separations: JAMISON
assistant editor: FRANK BERRIOS
editor: DENNY O'NEIL
BATMAN created by: BOB KANE

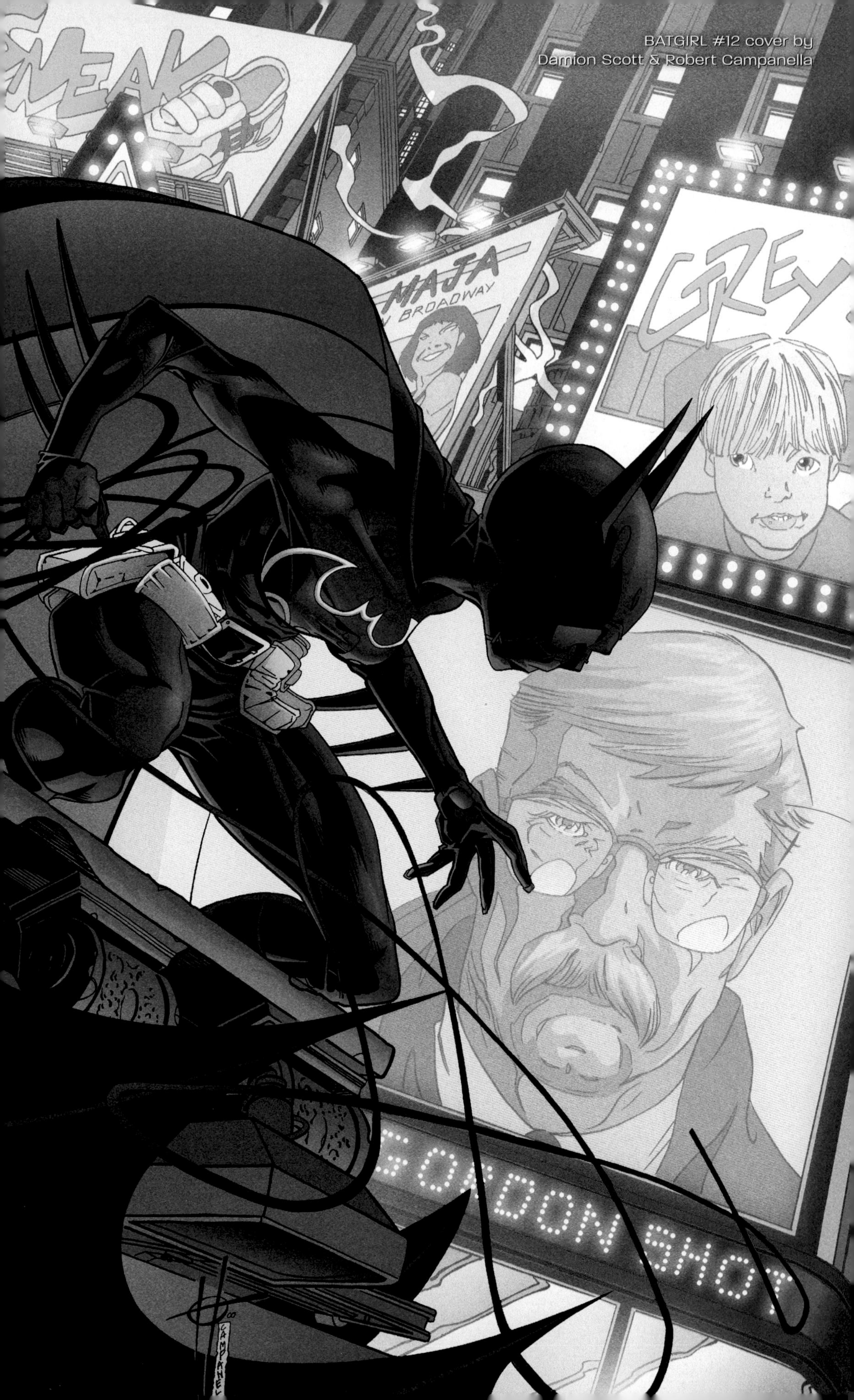
MAJA
BROADWAY
GORDON SHOT
BATGIRL #12 cover by
Damion Scott & Robert Campanella

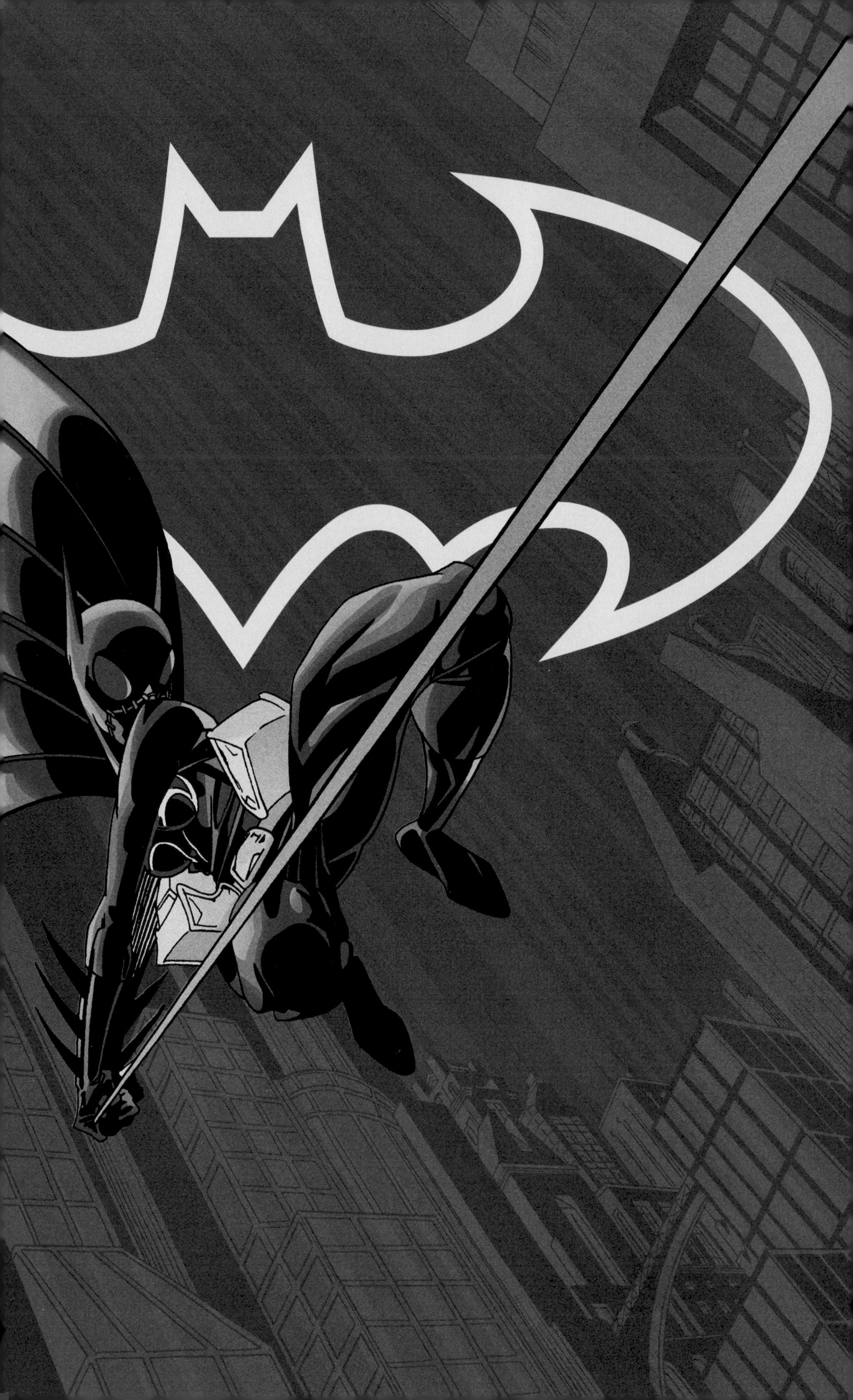

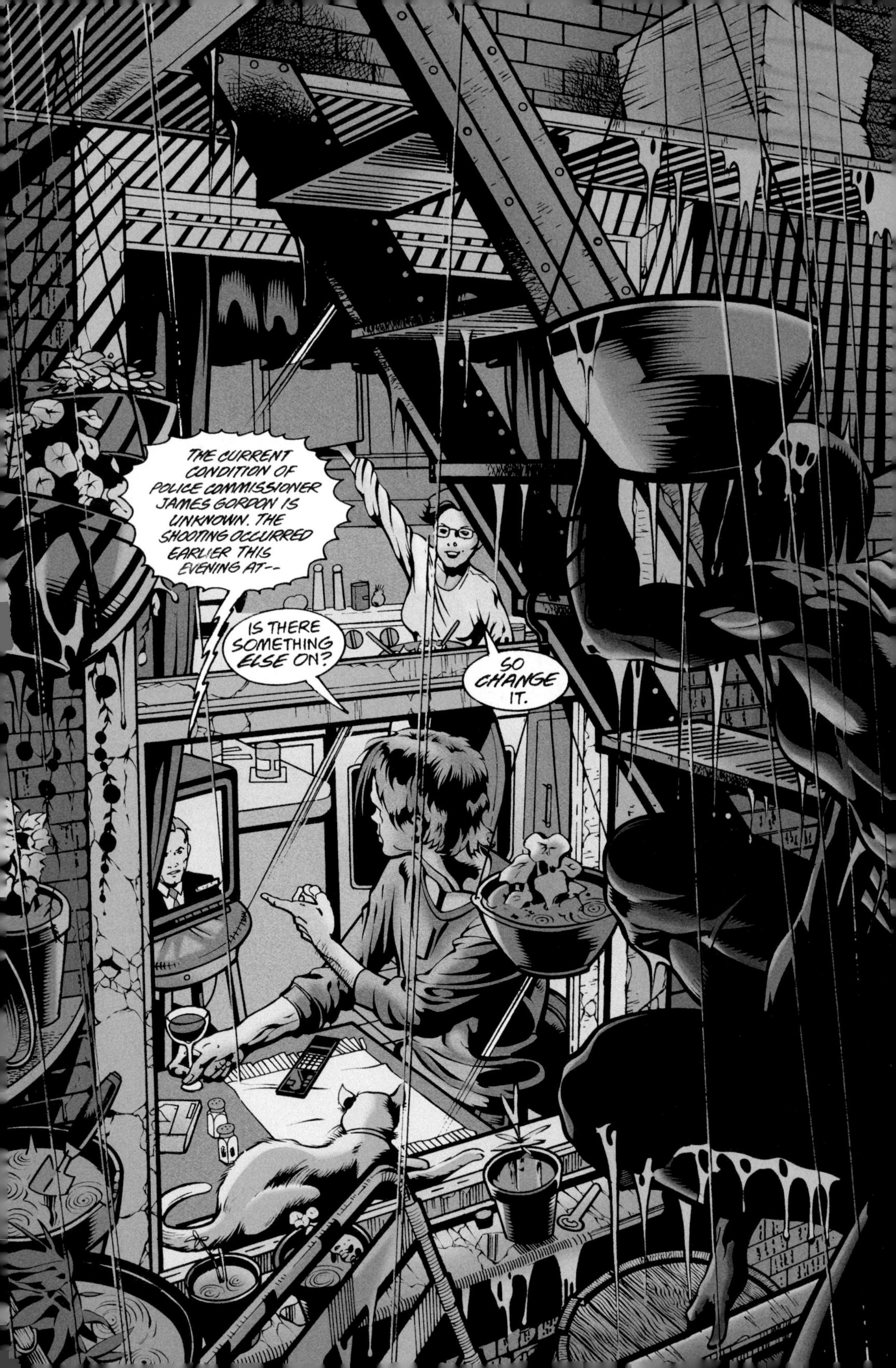
THE CURRENT CONDITION OF POLICE COMMISSIONER JAMES GORDON IS UNKNOWN. THE SHOOTING OCCURRED EARLIER THIS EVENING AT--
IS THERE SOMETHING ELSE ON?
SO CHANGE IT.

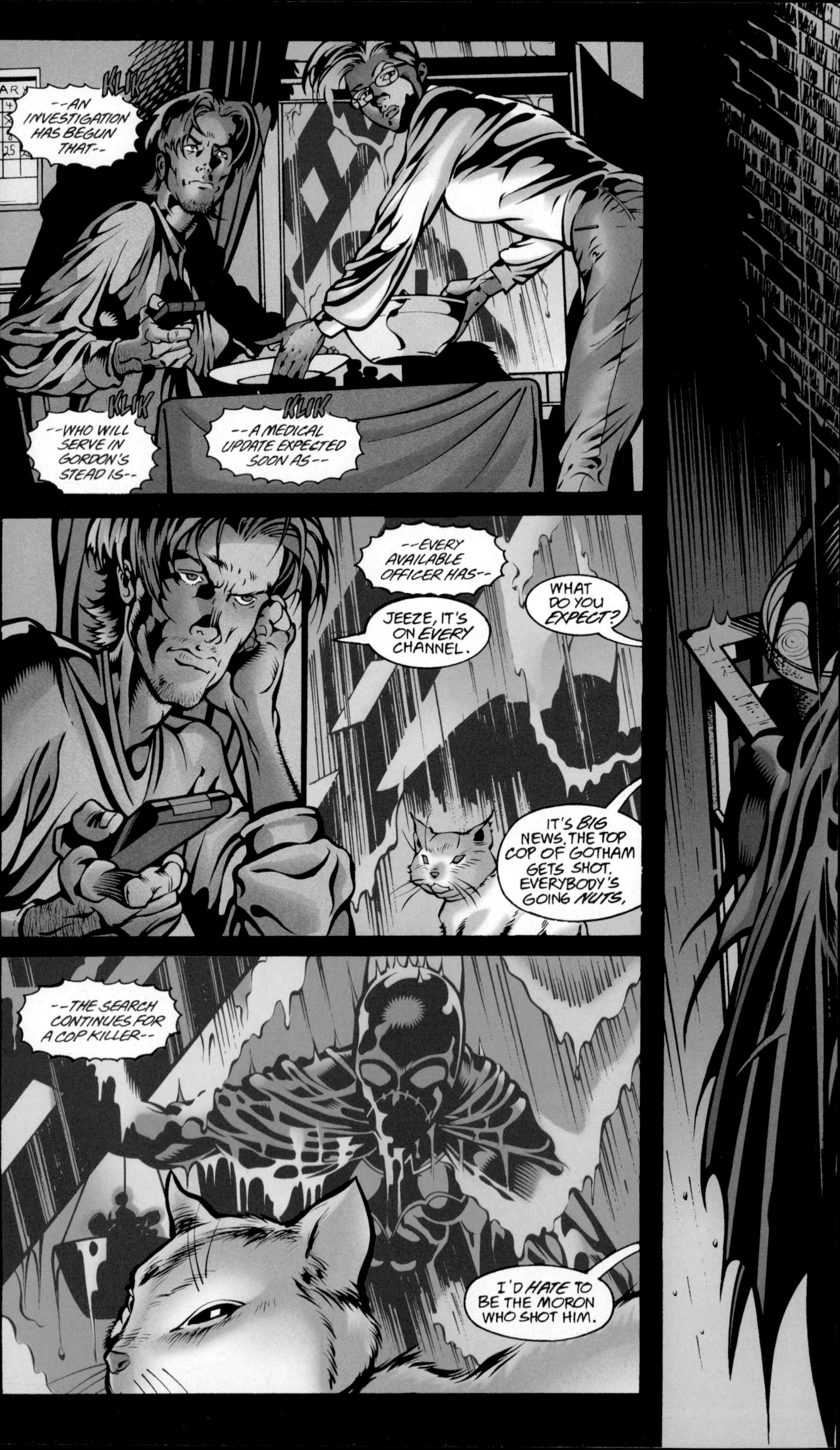
KLIK
--AN INVESTIGATION HAS BEGUN THAT--
KLIK
--WHO WILL SERVE IN GORDON'S STEAD IS--
KLIK
--A MEDICAL UPDATE EXPECTED SOON AS--
--EVERY AVAILABLE OFFICER HAS--
JEEZE, IT'S ON EVERY CHANNEL.
WHAT DO YOU EXPECT?
IT'S BIG NEWS. THE TOP COP OF GOTHAM GETS SHOT. EVERYBODY'S GOING NUTS.
--THE SEARCH CONTINUES FOR A COP KILLER--
I'D HATE TO BE THE MORON WHO SHOT HIM.

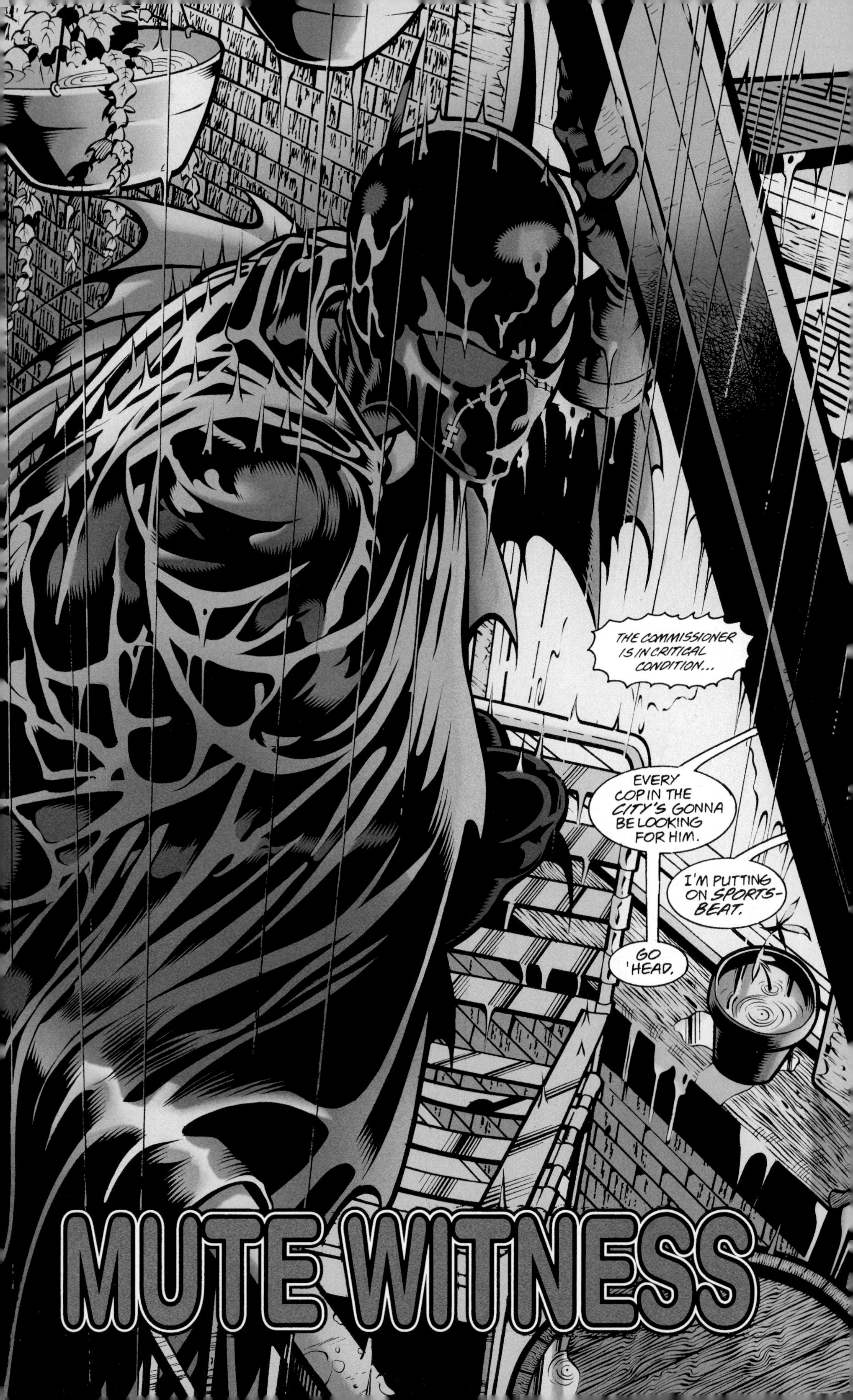
THE COMMISSIONER IS IN CRITICAL CONDITION...
EVERY COP IN THE CITY'S GONNA BE LOOKING FOR HIM.
GO 'HEAD.
I'M PUTTING ON SPORTS-BEAT.
MUTE WITNESS

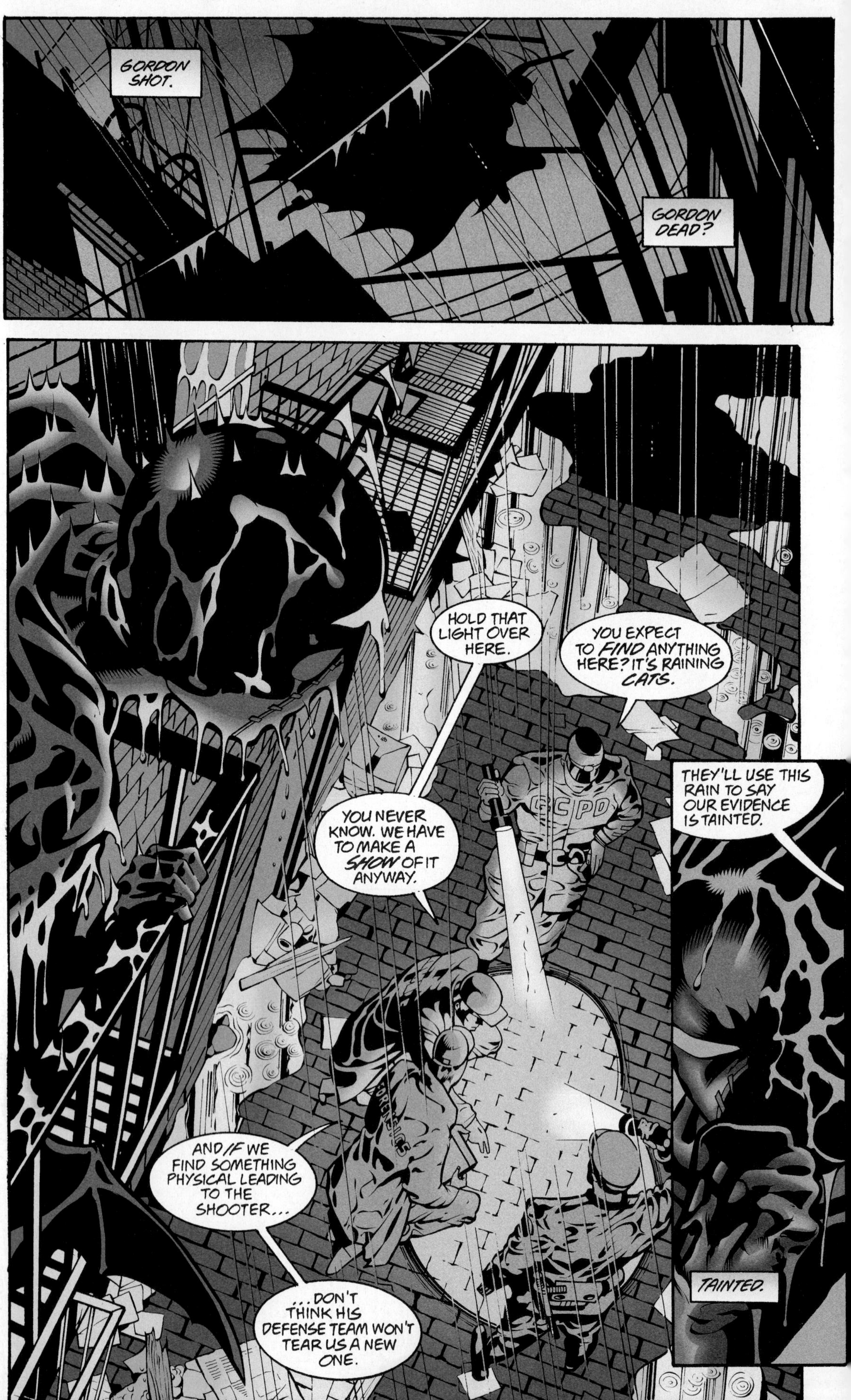
GORDON SHOT.
GORDON DEAD?
HOLD THAT LIGHT OVER HERE.
YOU EXPECT TO FIND ANYTHING HERE? IT'S RAINING CATS.
YOU NEVER KNOW. WE HAVE TO MAKE A SHOW OF IT ANYWAY.
AND IF WE FIND SOMETHING PHYSICAL LEADING TO THE SHOOTER...
...DON'T THINK HIS DEFENSE TEAM WON'T TEAR US A NEW ONE.
THEY'LL USE THIS RAIN TO SAY OUR EVIDENCE IS TAINTED.
TAINTED.

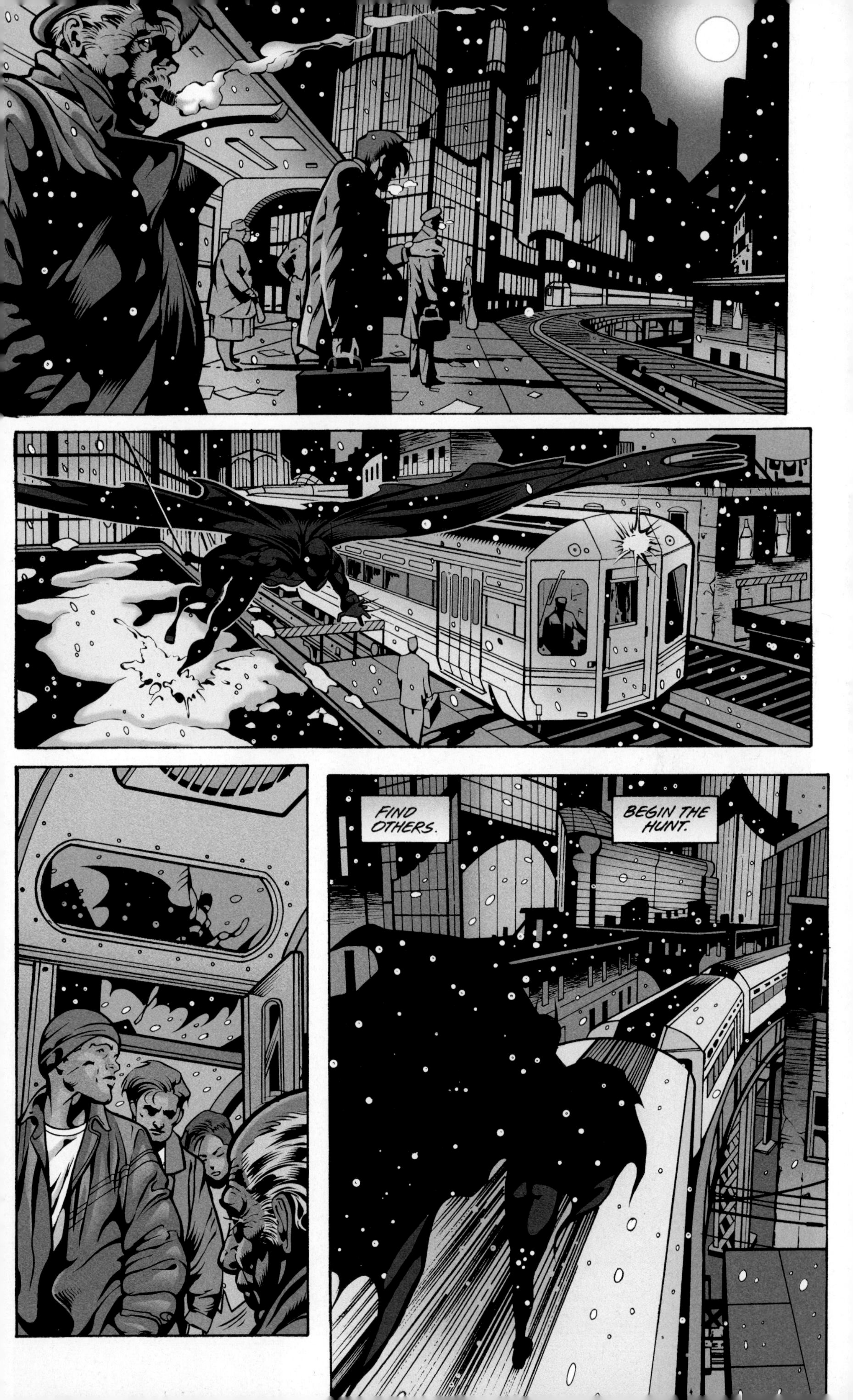
FIND OTHERS.
BEGIN THE HUNT.

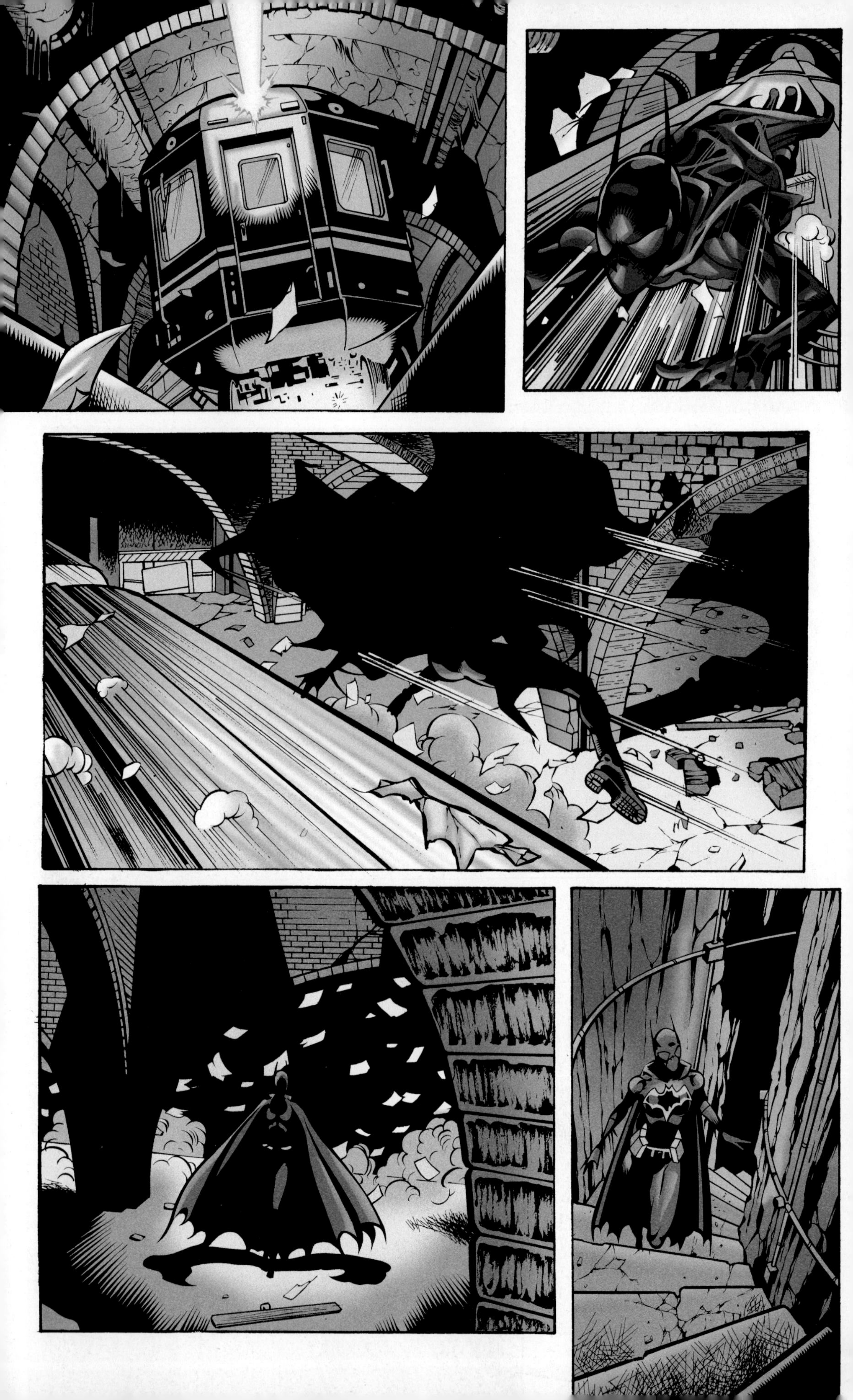

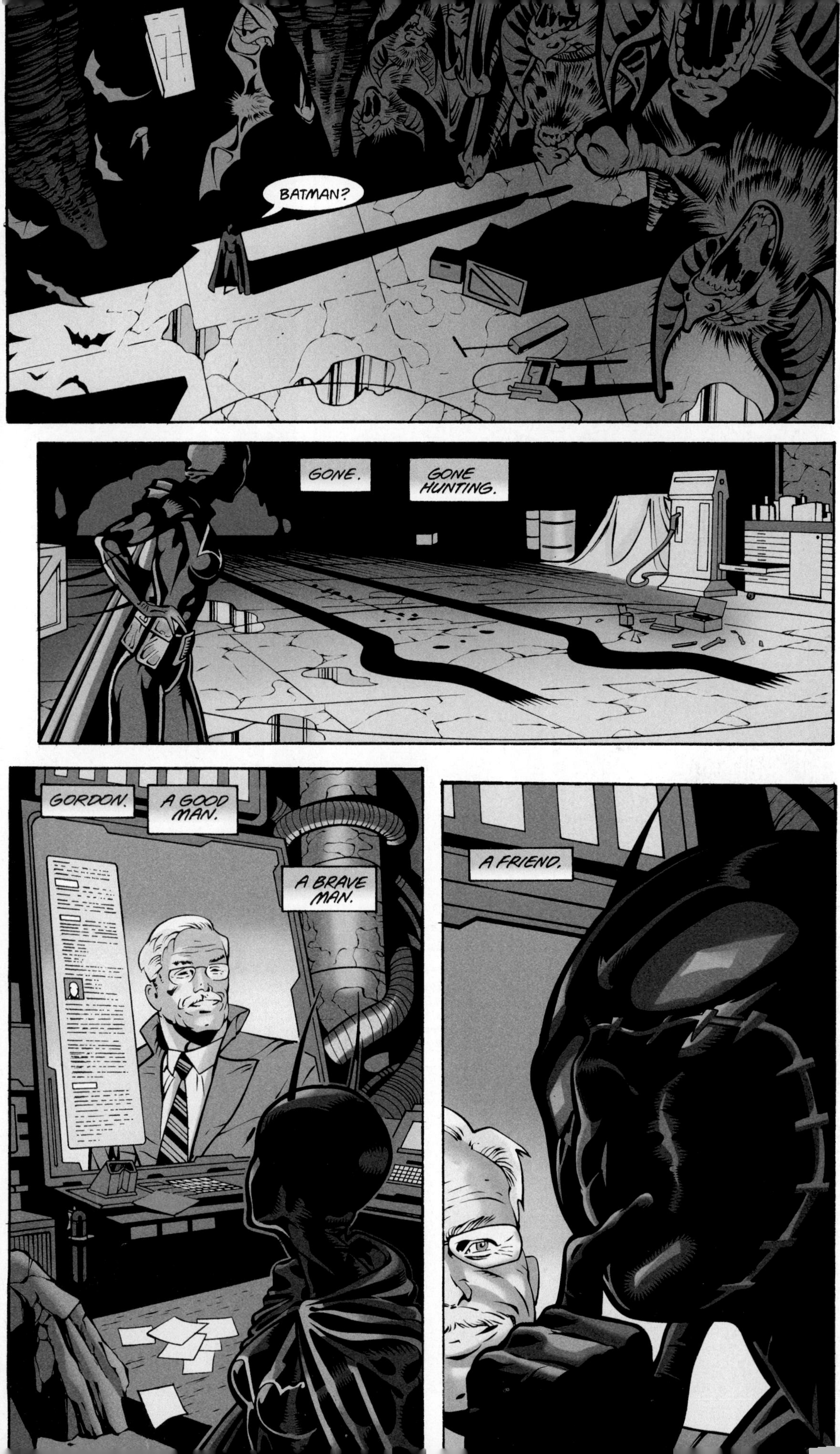
BATMAN?
GONE.
GONE HUNTING.
GORDON.
A GOOD MAN.
A BRAVE MAN.
A FRIEND.

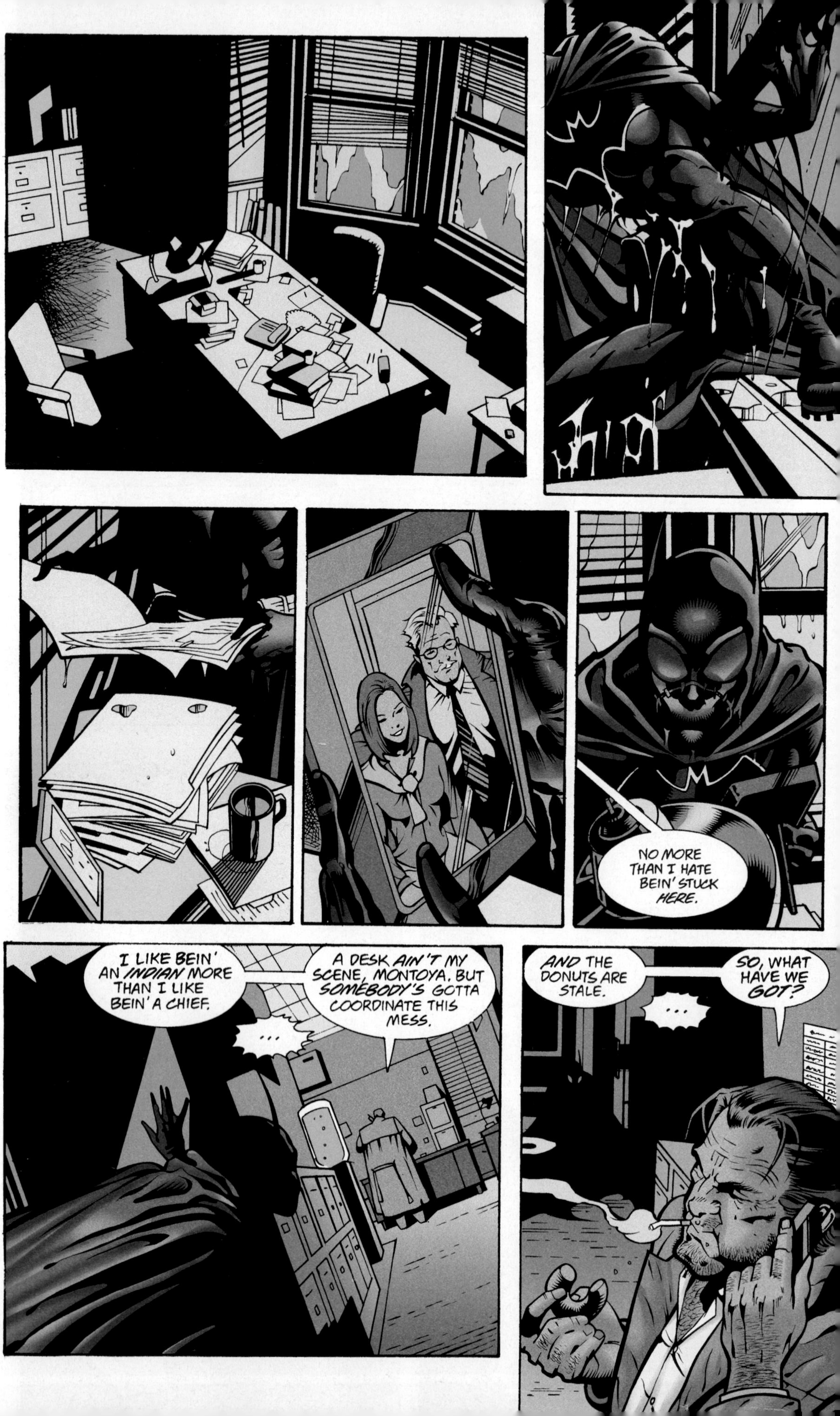
NO MORE THAN I HATE BEIN' STUCK HERE.
I LIKE BEIN' AN INDIAN MORE THAN I LIKE BEIN' A CHIEF.
...
A DESK AIN'T MY SCENE, MONTOYA, BUT SOMEBODY'S GOTTA COORDINATE THIS MESS.
AND THE DONUTS ARE STALE.
...
SO, WHAT HAVE WE GOT?

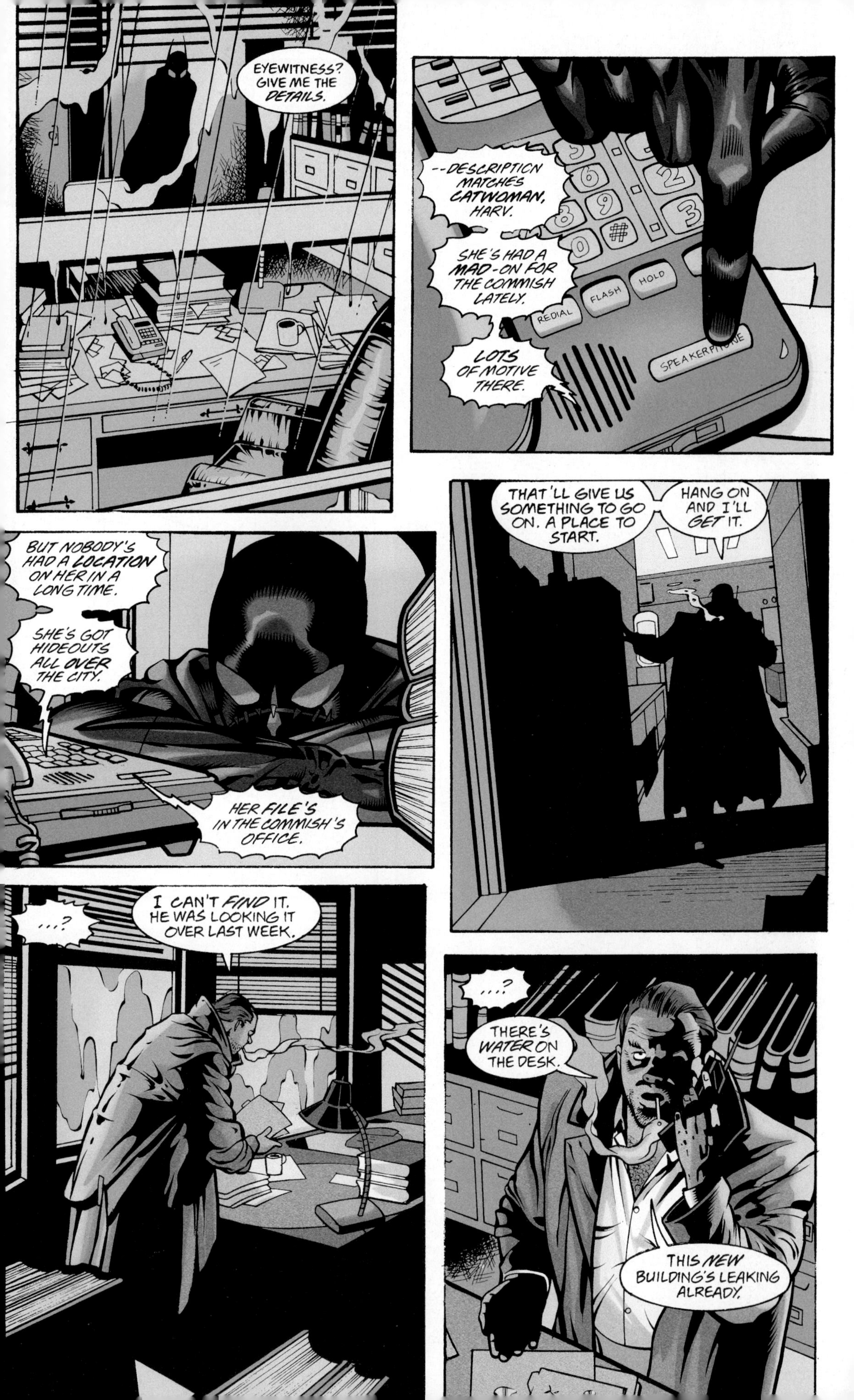
EYEWITNESS? GIVE ME THE DETAILS.
--DESCRIPTION MATCHES CATWOMAN, HARV.
SHE'S HAD A MAD-ON FOR THE COMMISH LATELY.
LOTS OF MOTIVE THERE.
REDIAL
FLASH
HOLD
SPEAKERPHONE
BUT NOBODY'S HAD A LOCATION ON HER IN A LONG TIME.
SHE'S GOT HIDEOUTS ALL OVER THE CITY.
HER FILE'S IN THE COMMISH'S OFFICE.
THAT'LL GIVE US SOMETHING TO GO ON. A PLACE TO START.
HANG ON AND I'LL GET IT.
...?
I CAN'T FIND IT. HE WAS LOOKING IT OVER LAST WEEK.
...?
THERE'S WATER ON THE DESK.
THIS NEW BUILDING'S LEAKING ALREADY.

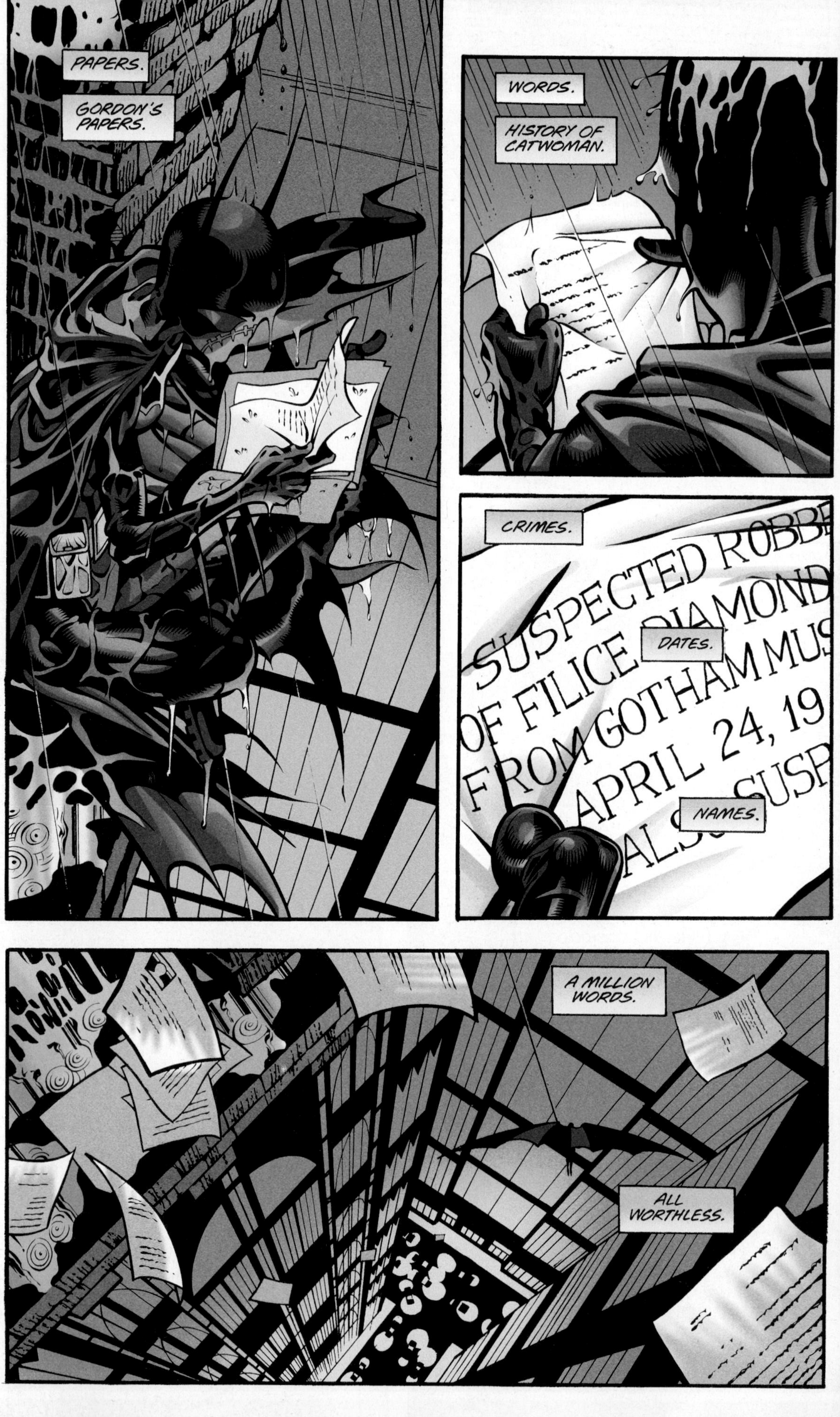
PAPERS.
GORDON'S PAPERS.
WORDS.
HISTORY OF CATWOMAN.
CRIMES.
SUSPECTED ROBB
OF FILICE DIAMOND
FROM GOTHAM MUS
APRIL 24, 19
DATES.
NAMES.
A MILLION WORDS.
ALL WORTHLESS.

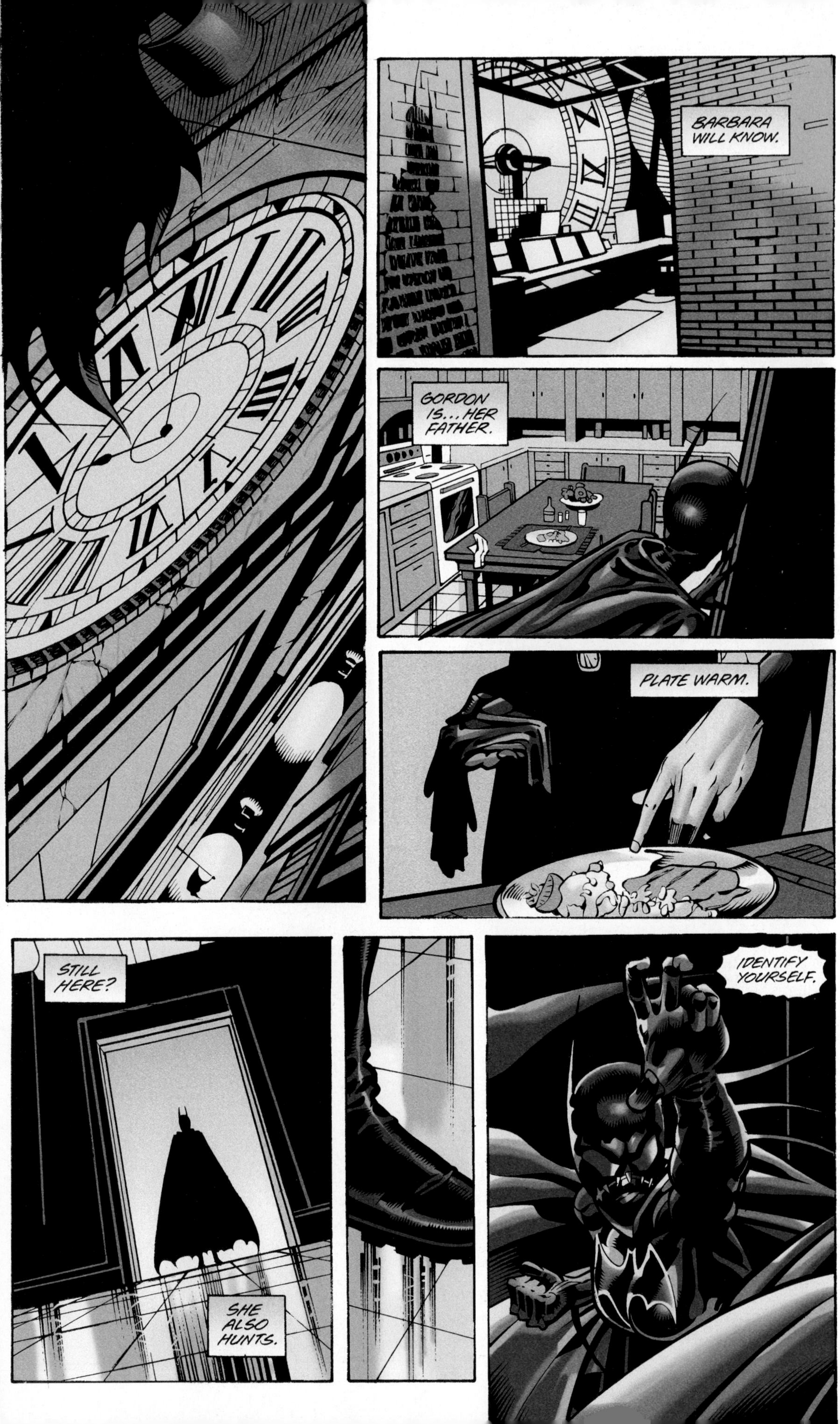
BARBARA WILL KNOW.
GORDON IS... HER FATHER.
PLATE WARM.
STILL HERE?
SHE ALSO HUNTS.
IDENTIFY YOURSELF.

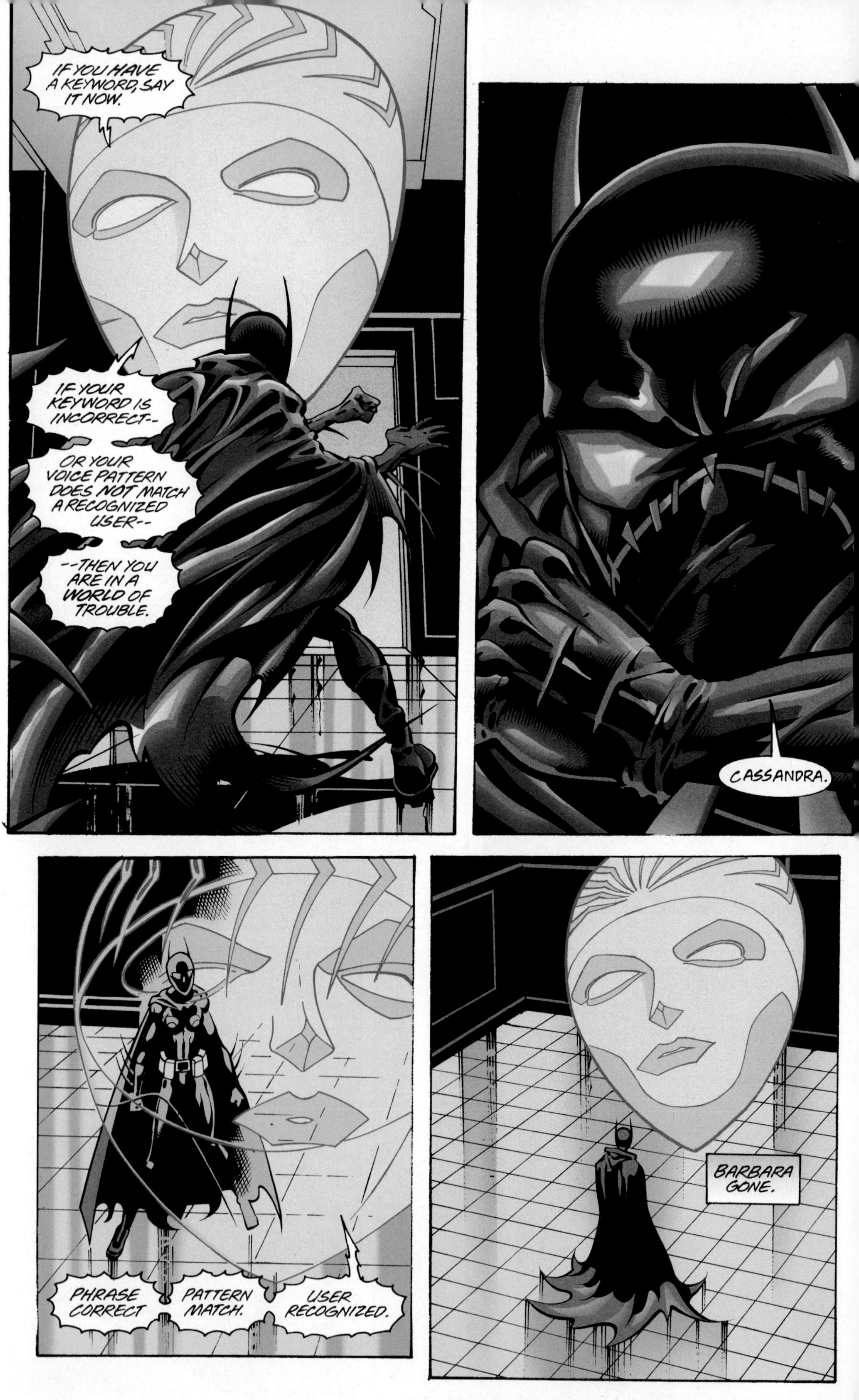
IF YOU HAVE A KEYWORD, SAY IT NOW.
IF YOUR KEYWORD IS INCORRECT--
OR YOUR VOICE PATTERN DOES NOT MATCH A RECOGNIZED USER--
--THEN YOU ARE IN A WORLD OF TROUBLE.
CASSANDRA.
PHRASE CORRECT
PATTERN MATCH.
USER RECOGNIZED.
BARBARA GONE.

WHAT FUNCTION DO YOU NEED PERFORMED?

CATWOMAN.

SEARCHING.

REFINE SEARCH?

LOCATION.

RECORD JEWEL HEIST

PRICELESS ARTIFACT STOLEN

TRAIL COLD BREWERMAN ROBBERY

POSSIBLE LOCATIONS FOR SELINA KYLE aka CATWOMAN. Residences held under assumed names

UNIT C-28, STEADFAST SELF STORAGE, TRICORNER, HARBOR HOUSE APARTMENTS, B-14, 998 HARBORDON LANE, GOTHAM HEIGHTS. PETS N' MOR BUSINESS, AVENUE

MORE WORDS.

COMPUTER, AUDIO.

WEST PARIS STREET, THAM. APT. 66-12, GOTHAMVIEW TOWER, MIDTOWN.

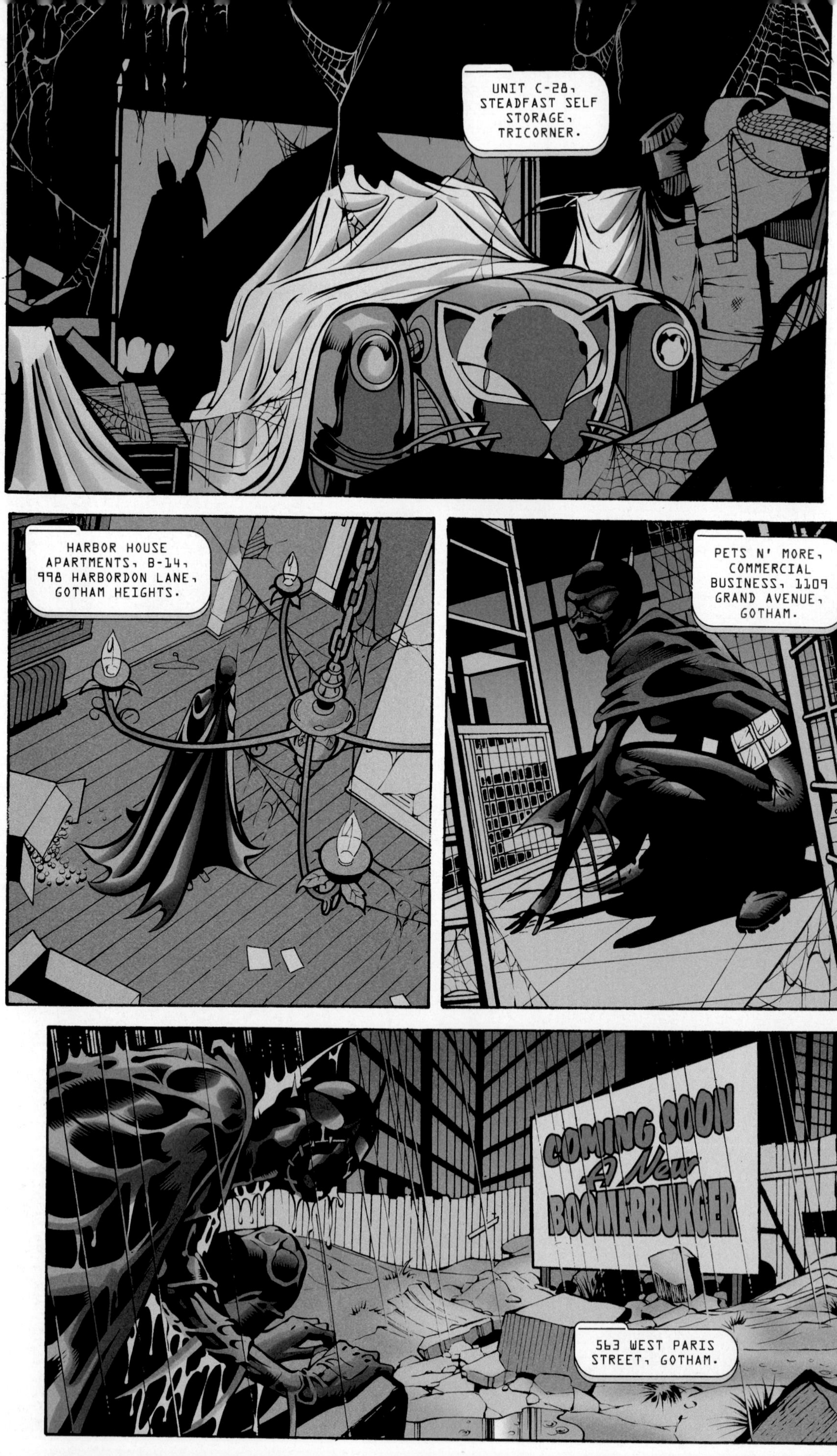
UNIT C-28, STEADFAST SELF STORAGE, TRICORNER.
HARBOR HOUSE APARTMENTS, B-14, 998 HARBORDON LANE, GOTHAM HEIGHTS.
PETS N' MORE, COMMERCIAL BUSINESS, 1109 GRAND AVENUE, GOTHAM.
COMING SOON A New BOOMERBURGER
563 WEST PARIS STREET, GOTHAM.

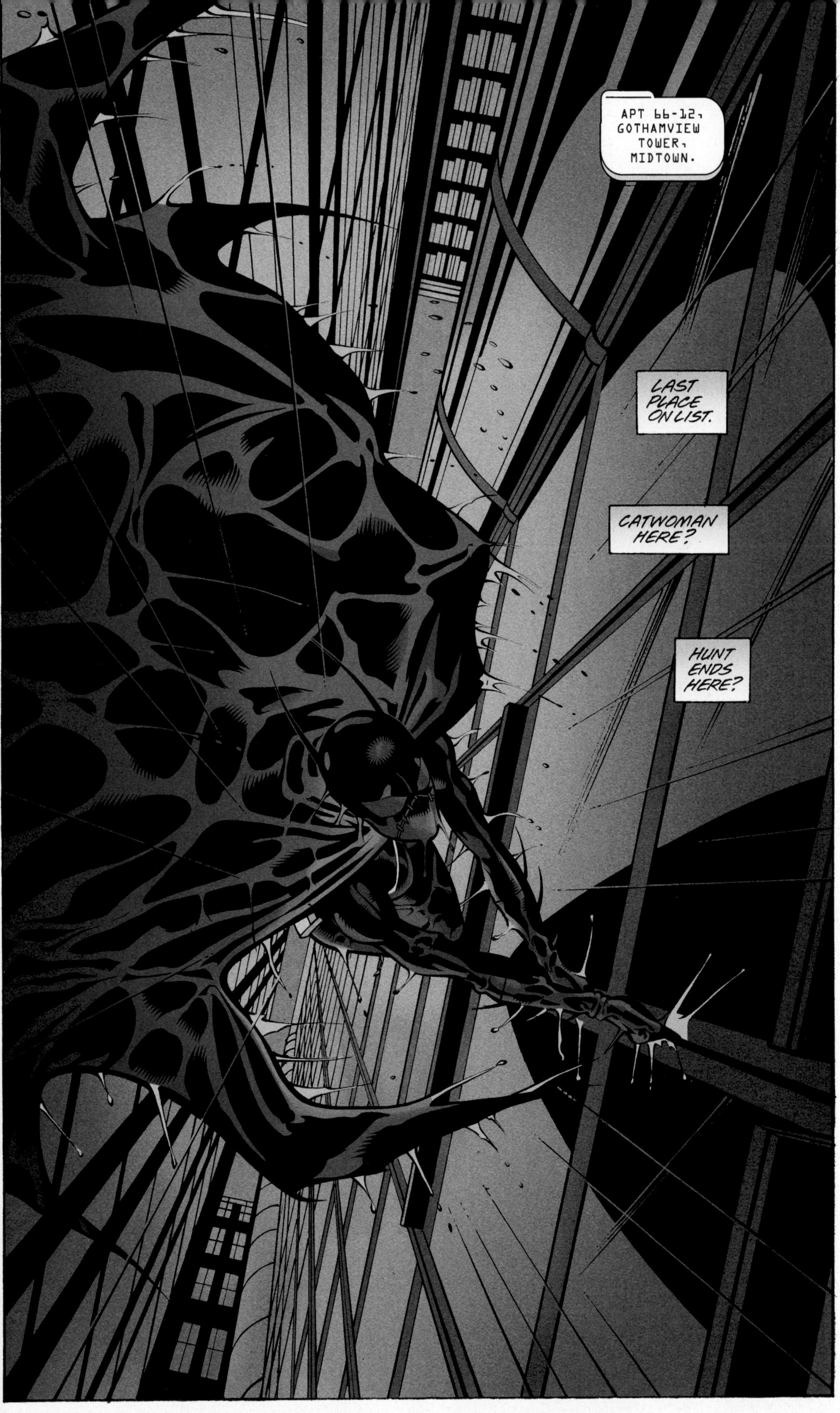
APT 66-12, GOTHAMVIEW TOWER, MIDTOWN.
LAST PLACE ON LIST.
CATWOMAN HERE?
HUNT ENDS HERE?

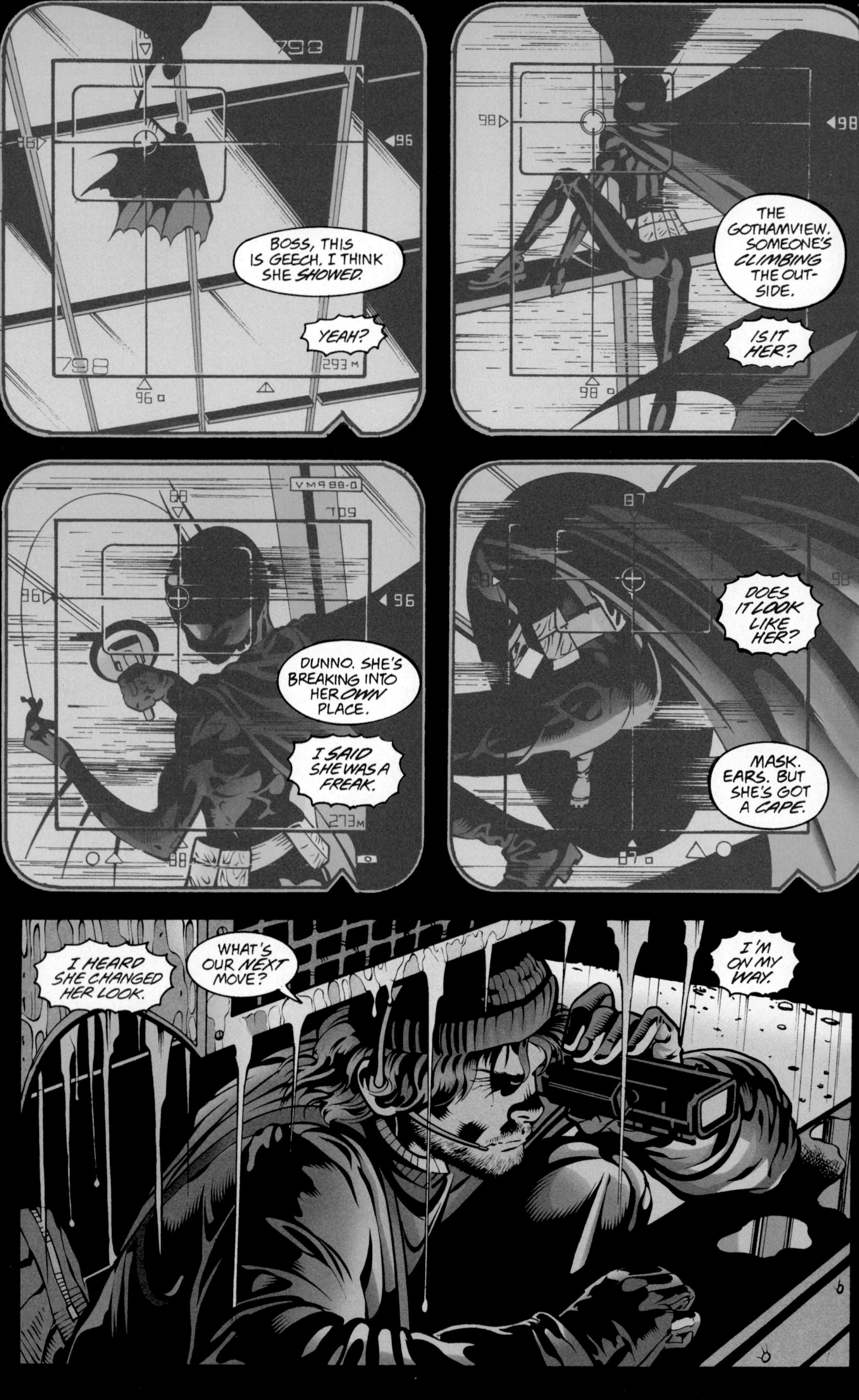
BOSS, THIS IS GEECH. I THINK SHE SHOWED.
YEAH?
THE GOTHAMVIEW. SOMEONE'S CLIMBING THE OUT-SIDE.
IS IT HER?
DUNNO. SHE'S BREAKING INTO HER OWN PLACE.
I SAID SHE WAS A FREAK.
DOES IT LOOK LIKE HER?
MASK. EARS. BUT SHE'S GOT A CAPE.
I HEARD SHE CHANGED HER LOOK.
WHAT'S OUR NEXT MOVE?
I'M ON MY WAY.

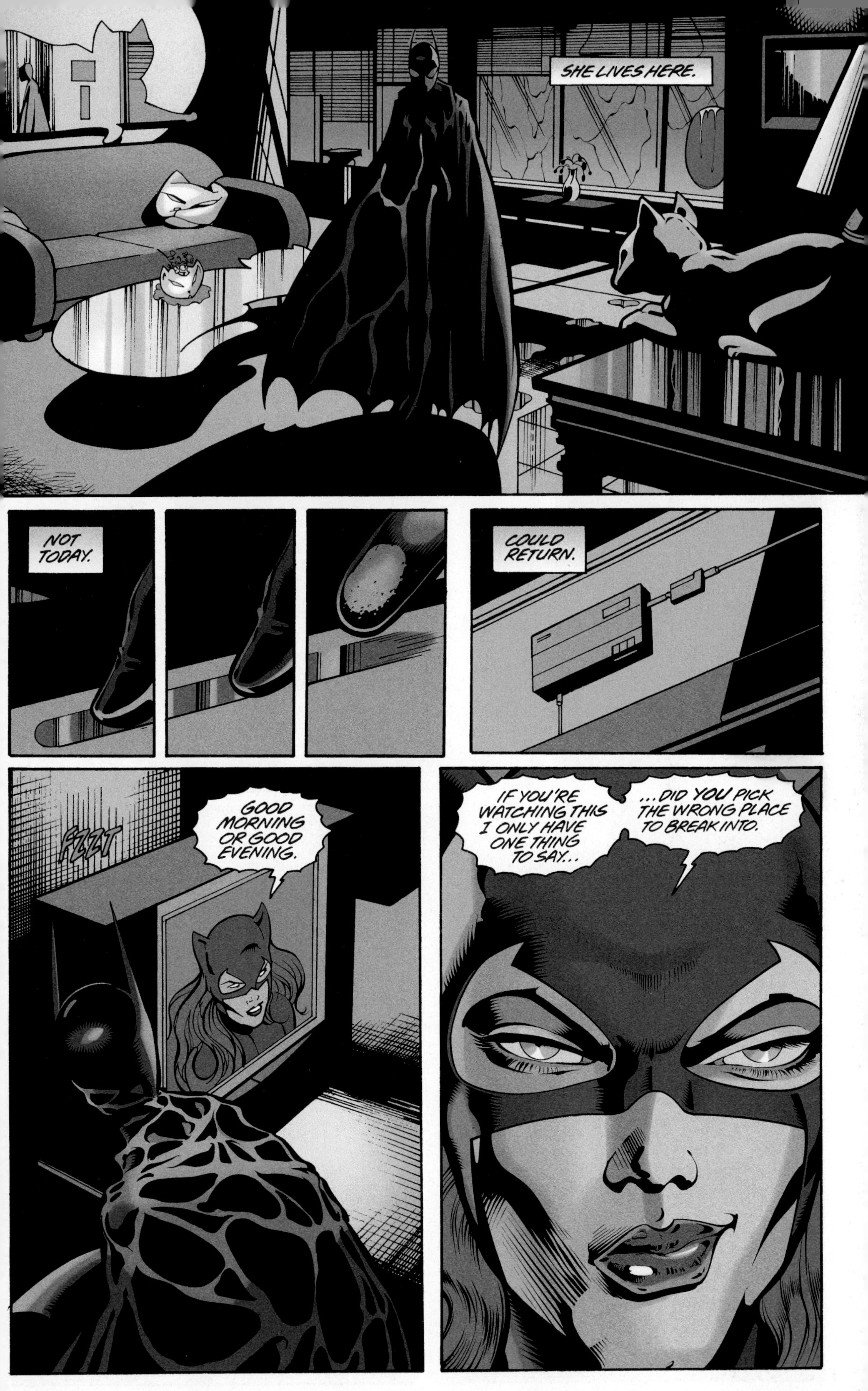
SHE LIVES HERE.
NOT TODAY.
COULD RETURN.
FZZT
GOOD MORNING OR GOOD EVENING.
IF YOU'RE WATCHING THIS I ONLY HAVE ONE THING TO SAY...
...DID YOU PICK THE WRONG PLACE TO BREAK INTO.

IT'S STUPID.

IT'S DANGEROUS.

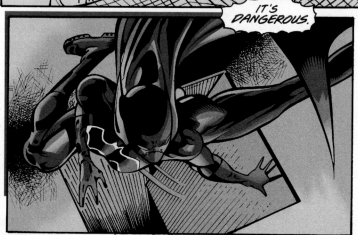

NEVER TRY TO STEAL FROM A THIEF.

AND YOU'RE NOT LEAVING HERE.

AND NOW FOR YOUR VIEWING PLEASURE-- --A SIX-HOUR MARATHON OF SCOOBY-DOO.

KRRIIISSHH!

BLAMBLAMBLAMBLAMBLAM

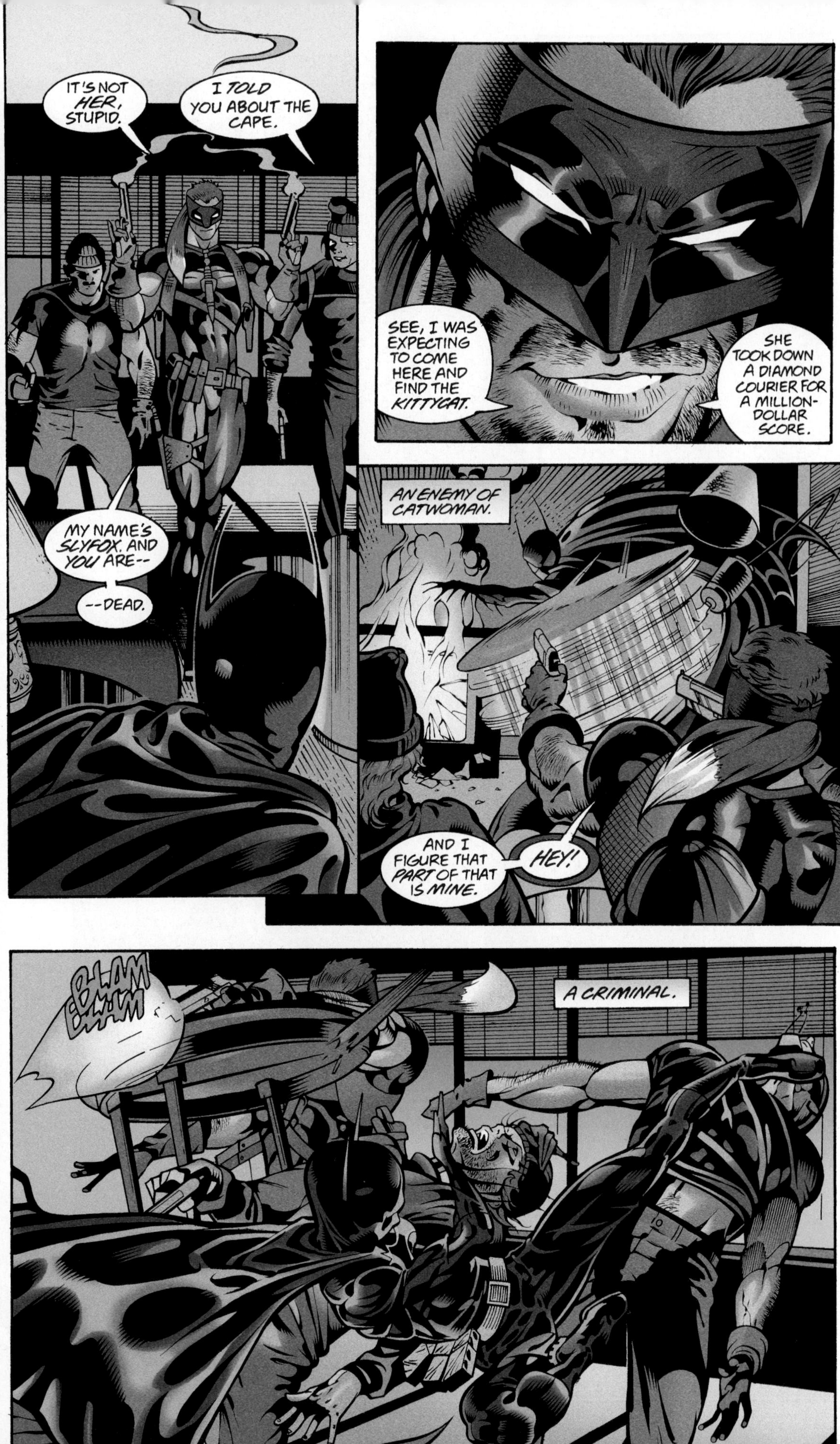
IT'S NOT HER, STUPID.
I TOLD YOU ABOUT THE CAPE.
SEE, I WAS EXPECTING TO COME HERE AND FIND THE KITTYCAT.
SHE TOOK DOWN A DIAMOND COURIER FOR A MILLION-DOLLAR SCORE.
MY NAME'S SLYFOX. AND YOU ARE--
--DEAD.
AN ENEMY OF CATWOMAN.
AND I FIGURE THAT PART OF THAT IS MINE.
HEY!
A CRIMINAL.
BLAM BLAM

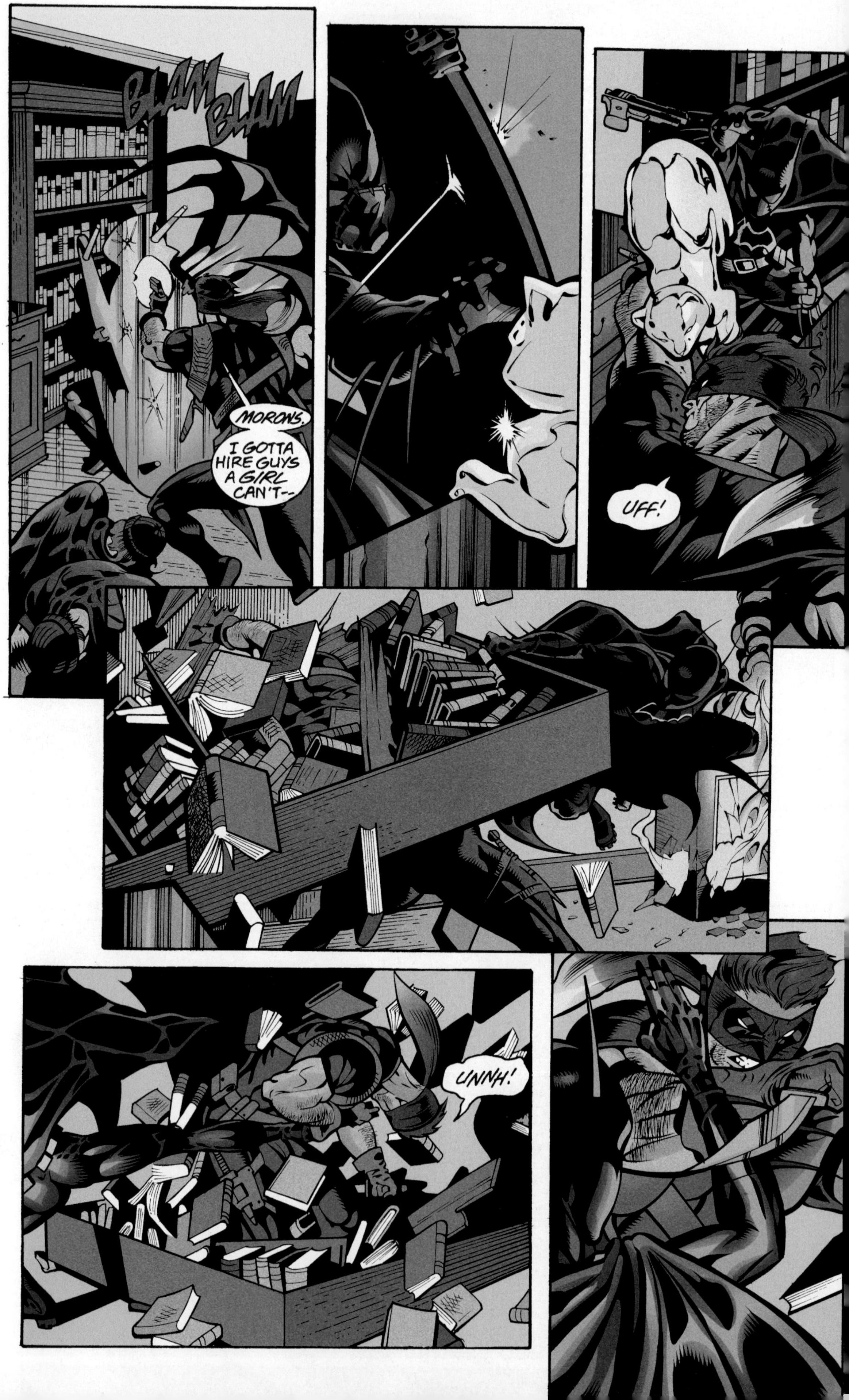
BLAM BLAM
MORONS.
I GOTTA HIRE GUYS A GIRL CAN'T--
UFF!
UNNH!

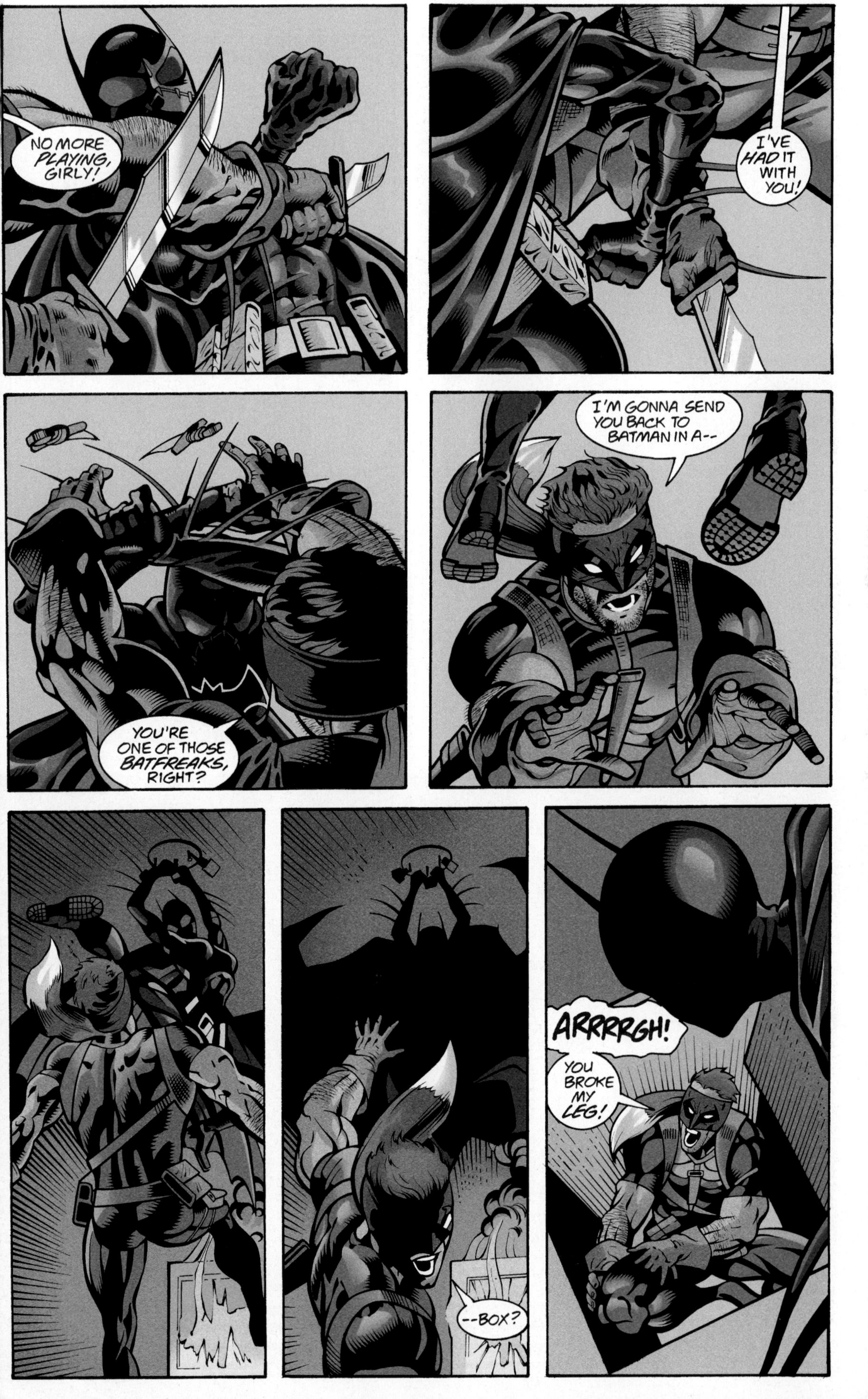
NO MORE PLAYING, GIRLY!
I'VE HAD IT WITH YOU!
YOU'RE ONE OF THOSE BATFREAKS, RIGHT?
I'M GONNA SEND YOU BACK TO BATMAN IN A--
--BOX?
ARRRRGH!
YOU BROKE MY LEG!

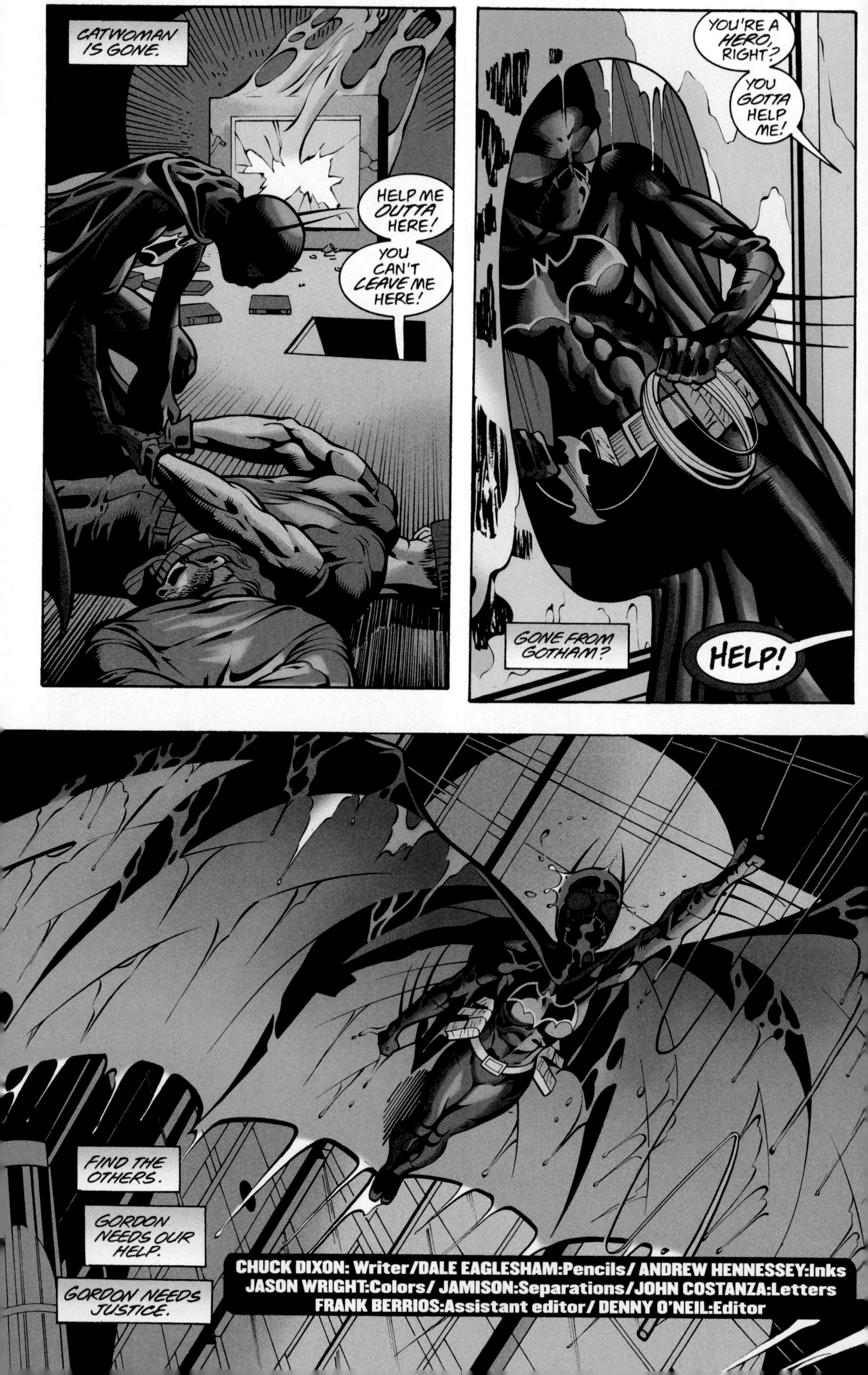
CATWOMAN IS GONE.
HELP ME OUTTA HERE!
YOU CAN'T LEAVE ME HERE!
YOU'RE A HERO, RIGHT?
YOU GOTTA HELP ME!
GONE FROM GOTHAM?
HELP!
FIND THE OTHERS.
GORDON NEEDS OUR HELP.
GORDON NEEDS JUSTICE.
CHUCK DIXON: Writer/DALE EAGLESHAM:Pencils/ ANDREW HENNESSEY:Inks
JASON WRIGHT:Colors/ JAMISON:Separations/JOHN COSTANZA:Letters
FRANK BERRIOS:Assistant editor/ DENNY O'NEIL:Editor

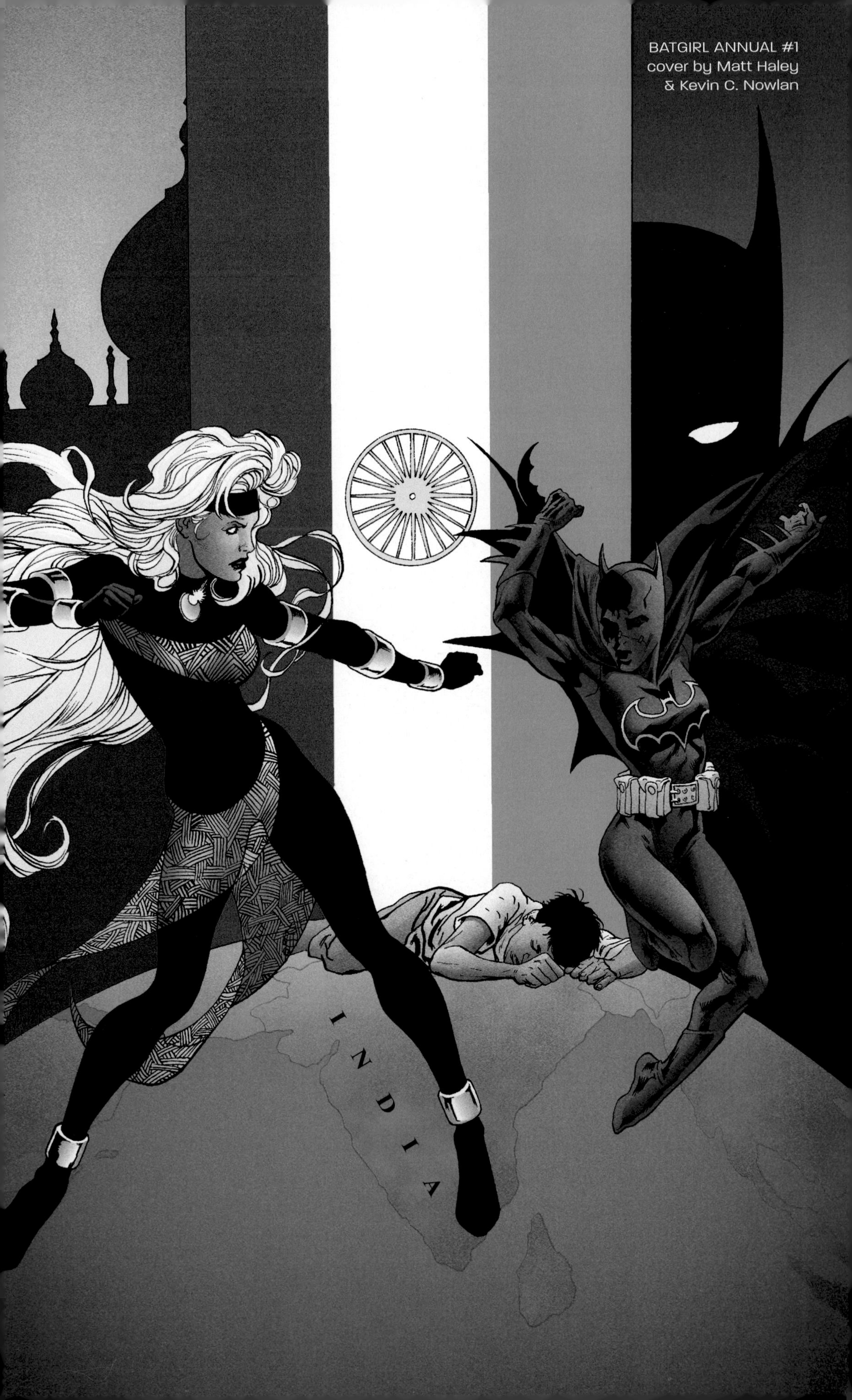
INDIA

BATGIRL ANNUAL #1
cover by Matt Haley
& Kevin C. Nowlan

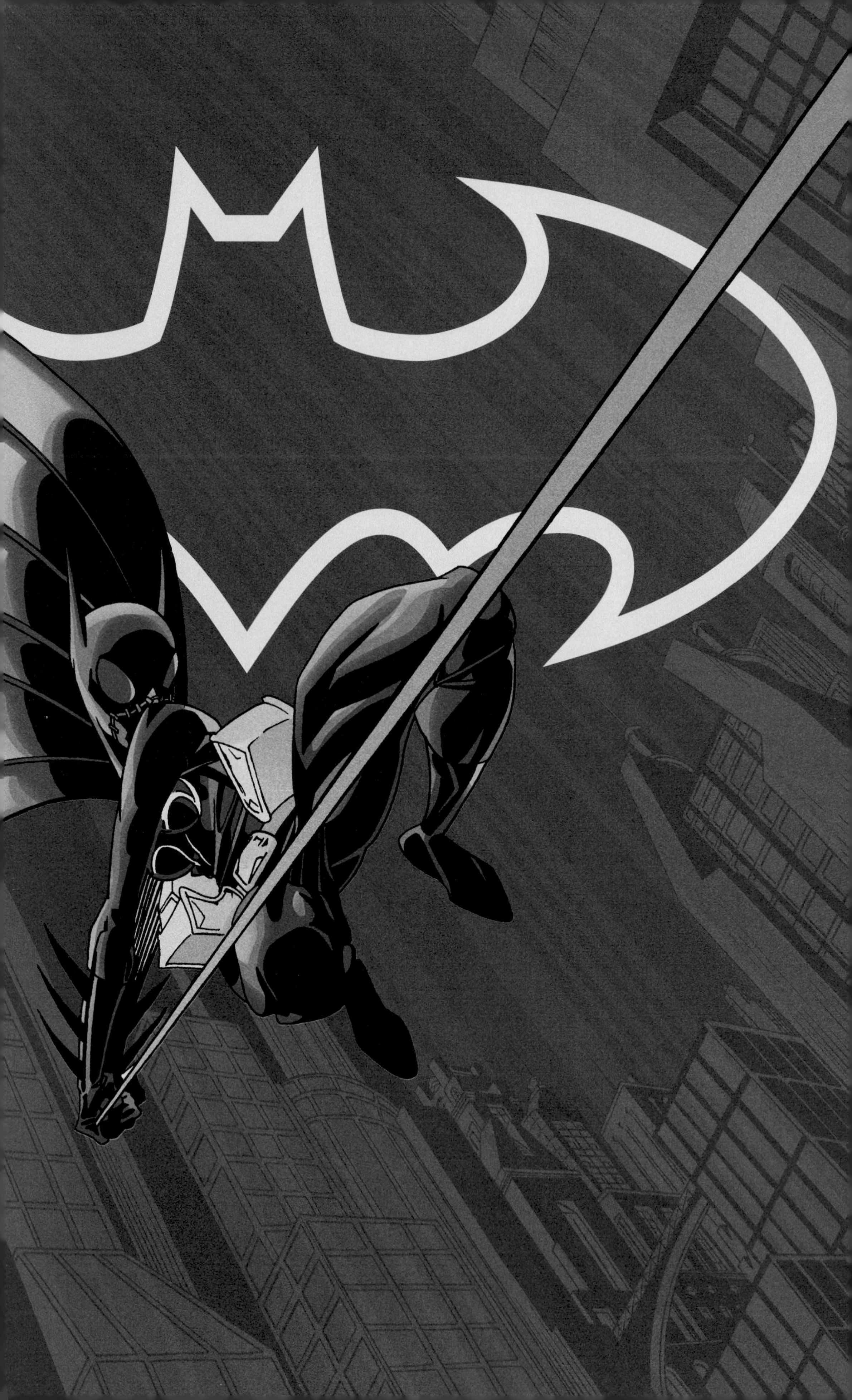

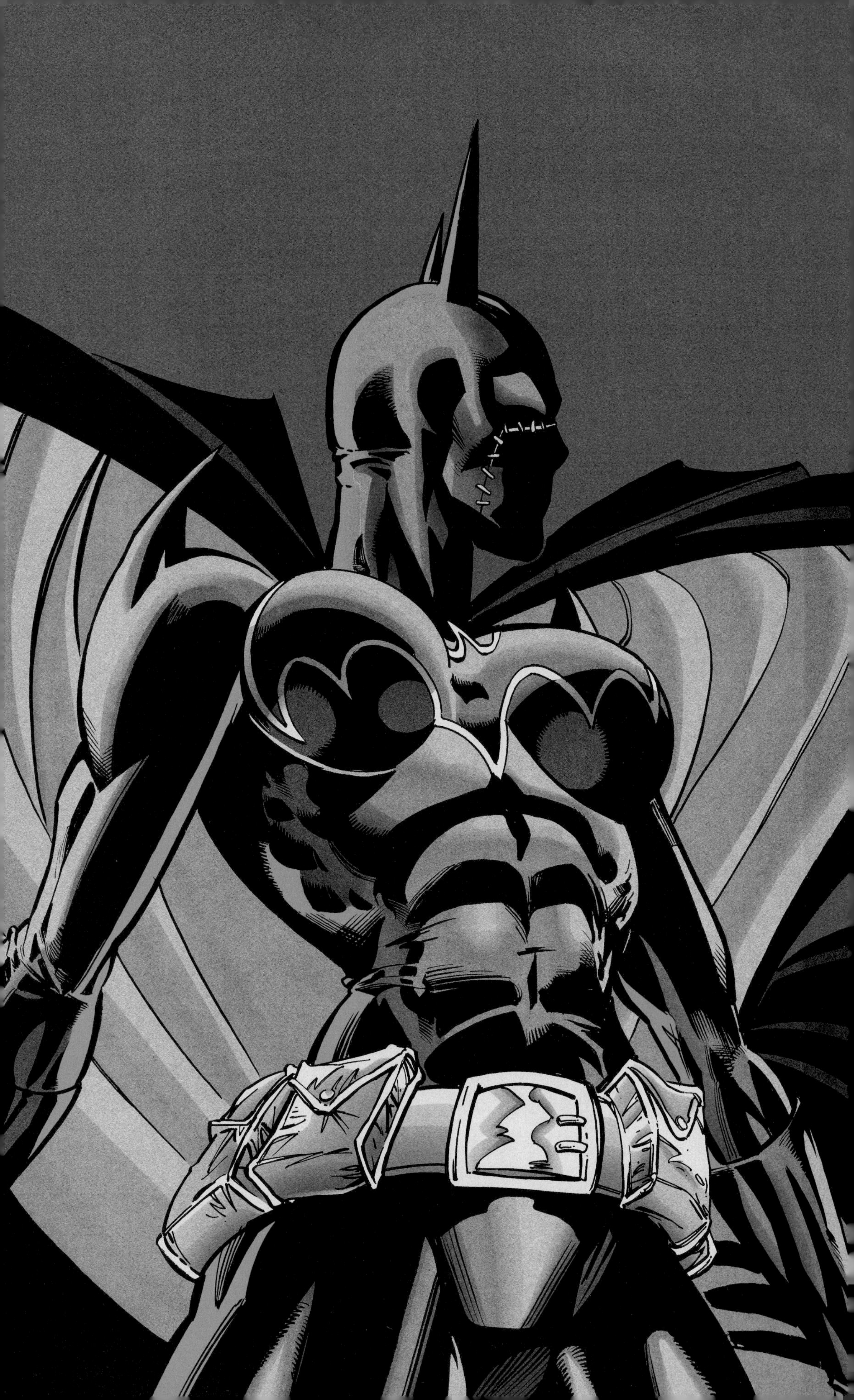

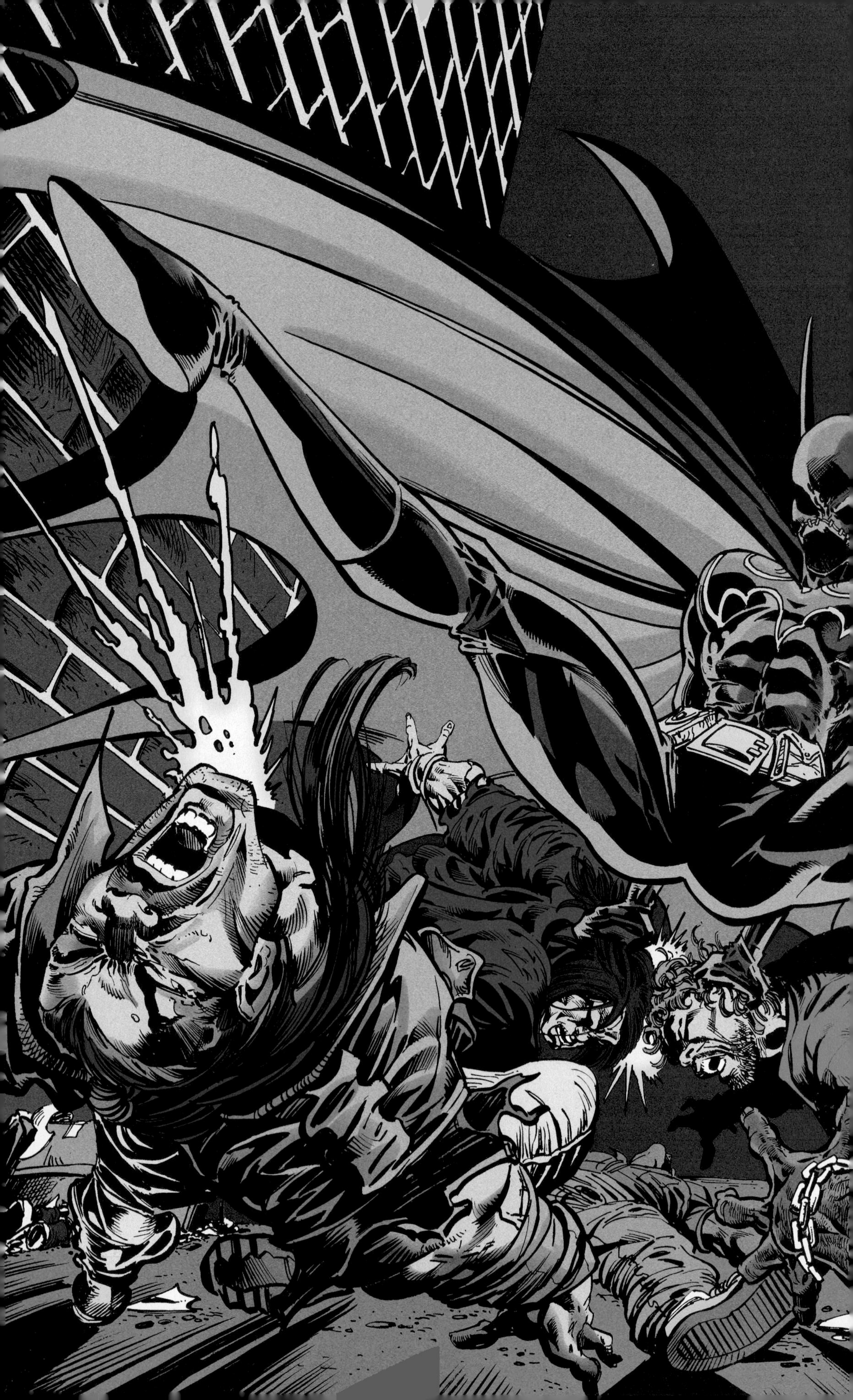

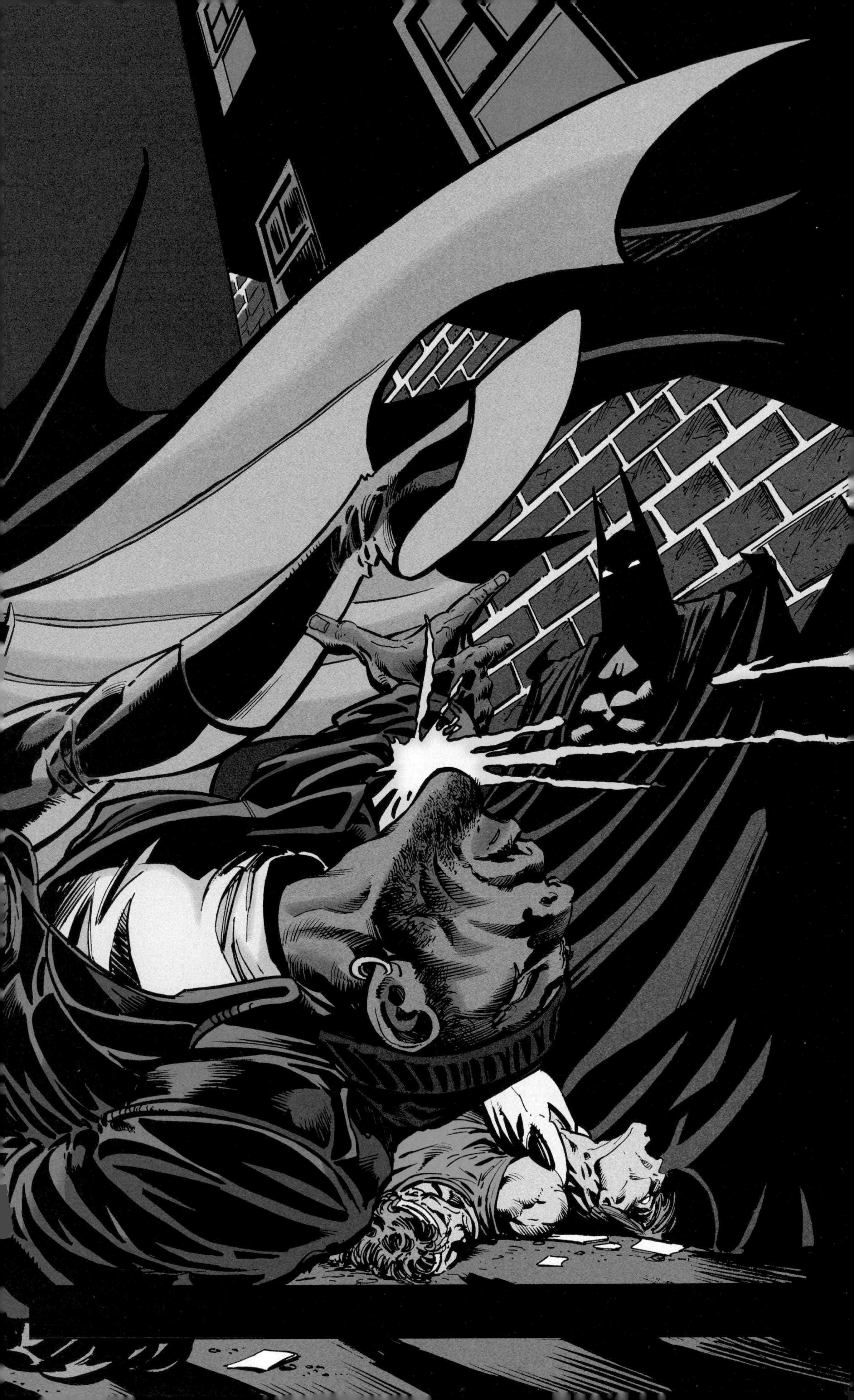

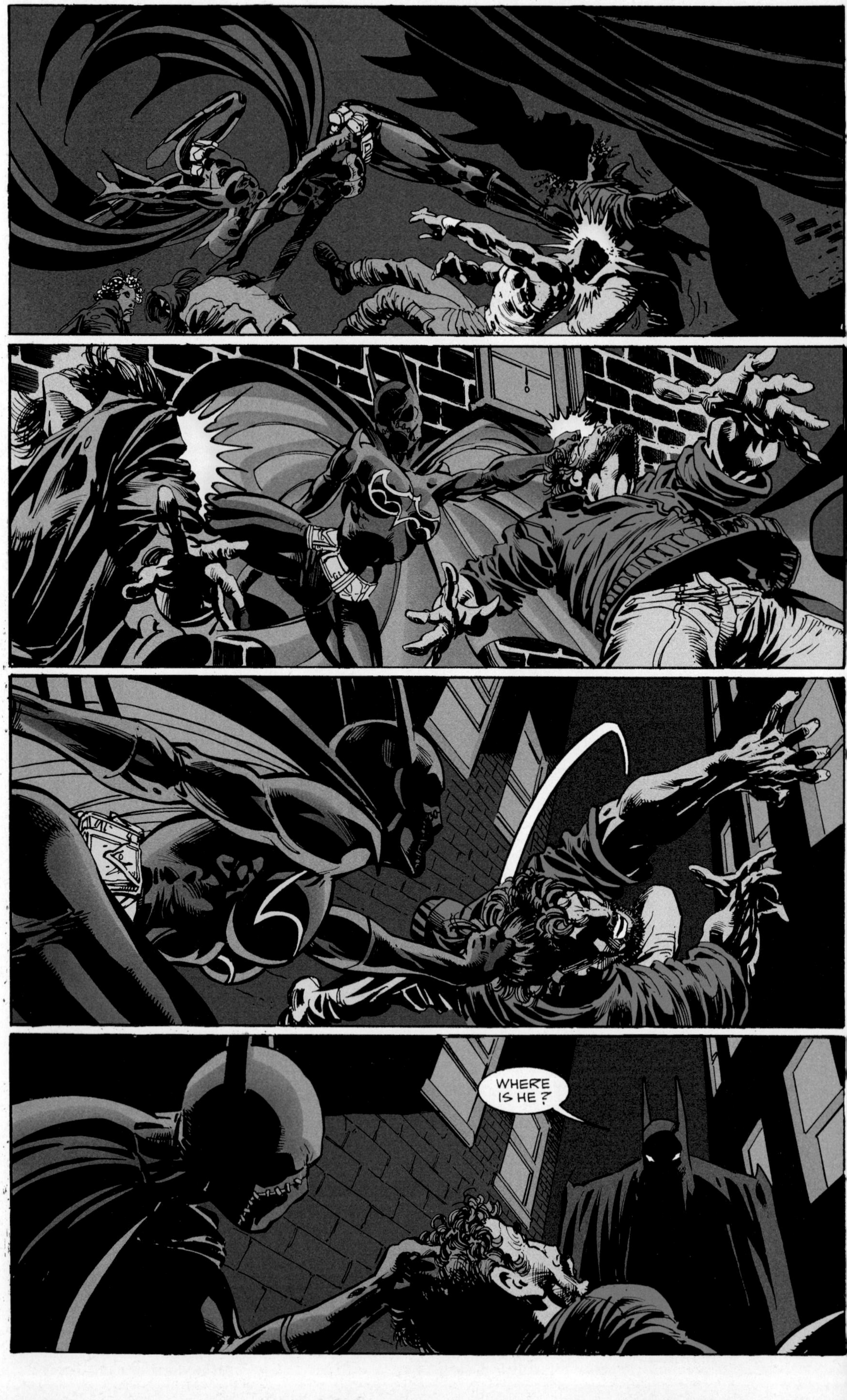
WHERE IS HE?

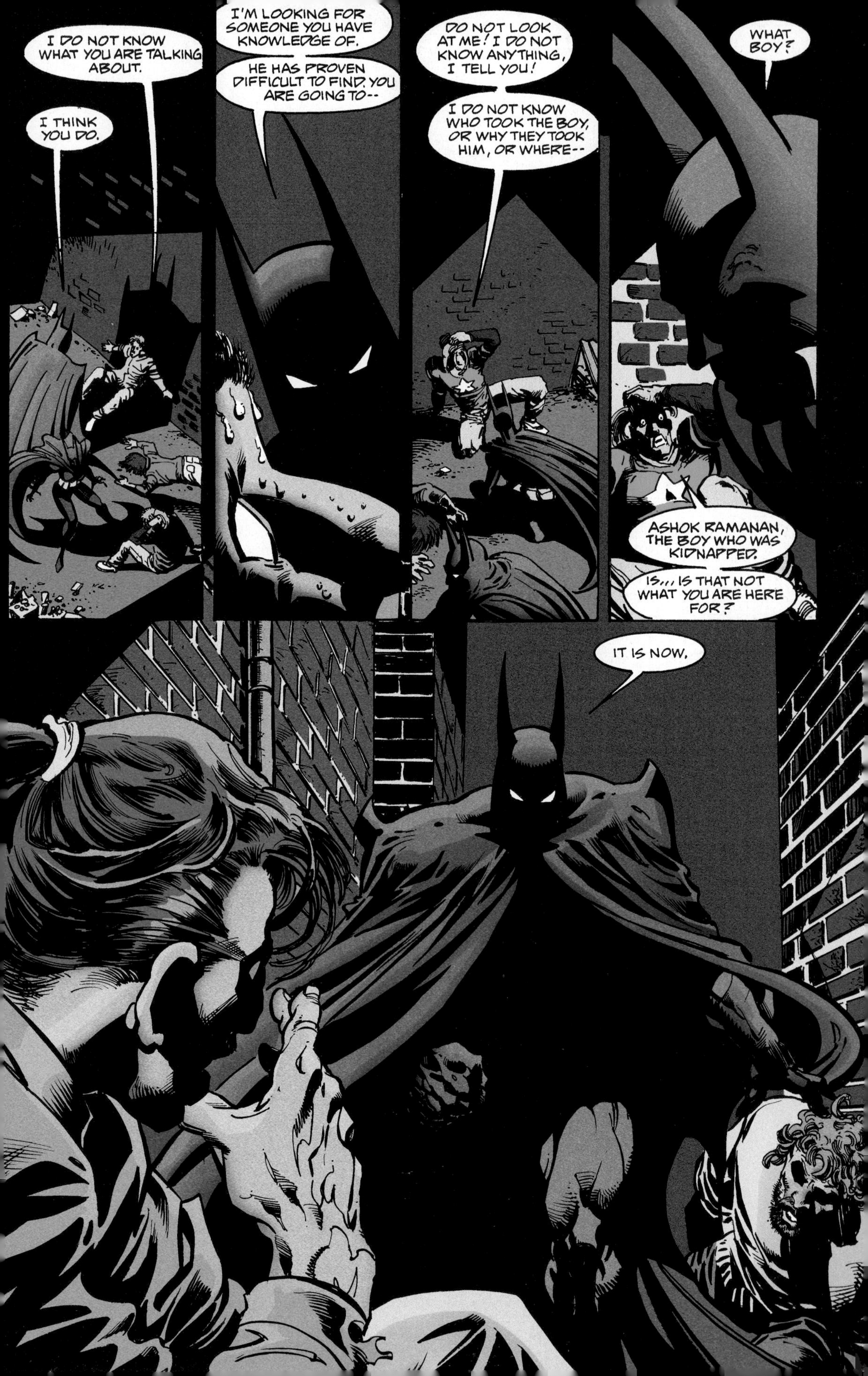
I DO NOT KNOW WHAT YOU ARE TALKING ABOUT.
I THINK YOU DO.
I'M LOOKING FOR SOMEONE YOU HAVE KNOWLEDGE OF.
HE HAS PROVEN DIFFICULT TO FIND. YOU ARE GOING TO--
DO NOT LOOK AT ME! I DO NOT KNOW ANYTHING, I TELL YOU!
I DO NOT KNOW WHO TOOK THE BOY, OR WHY THEY TOOK HIM, OR WHERE--
WHAT BOY?
ASHOK RAMANAN, THE BOY WHO WAS KIDNAPPED.
IS... IS THAT NOT WHAT YOU ARE HERE FOR?
IT IS NOW.

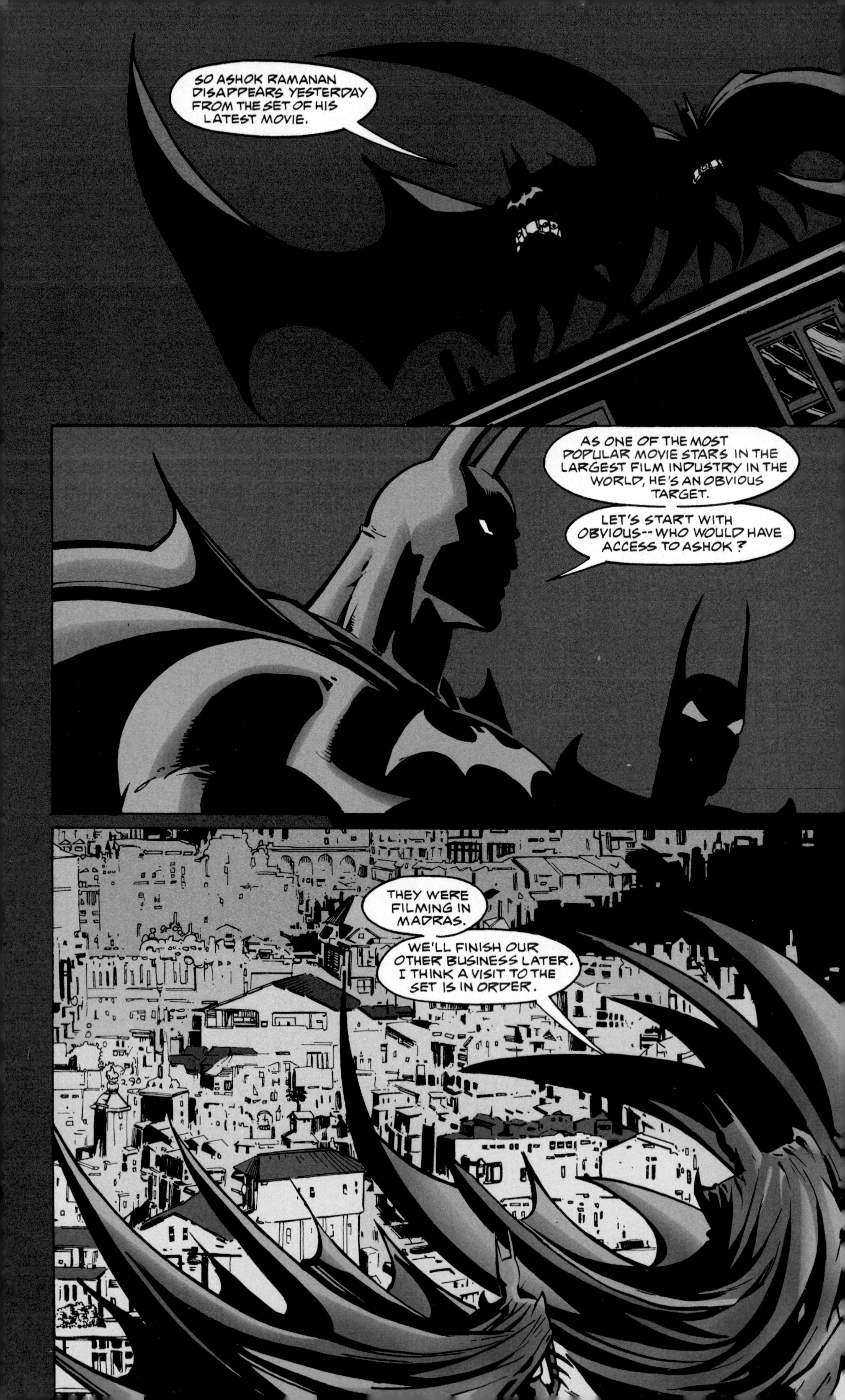
SO ASHOK RAMANAN DISAPPEARS YESTERDAY FROM THE SET OF HIS LATEST MOVIE.
AS ONE OF THE MOST POPULAR MOVIE STARS IN THE LARGEST FILM INDUSTRY IN THE WORLD, HE'S AN OBVIOUS TARGET.
LET'S START WITH OBVIOUS-- WHO WOULD HAVE ACCESS TO ASHOK?
THEY WERE FILMING IN MADRAS.
WE'LL FINISH OUR OTHER BUSINESS LATER. I THINK A VISIT TO THE SET IS IN ORDER.

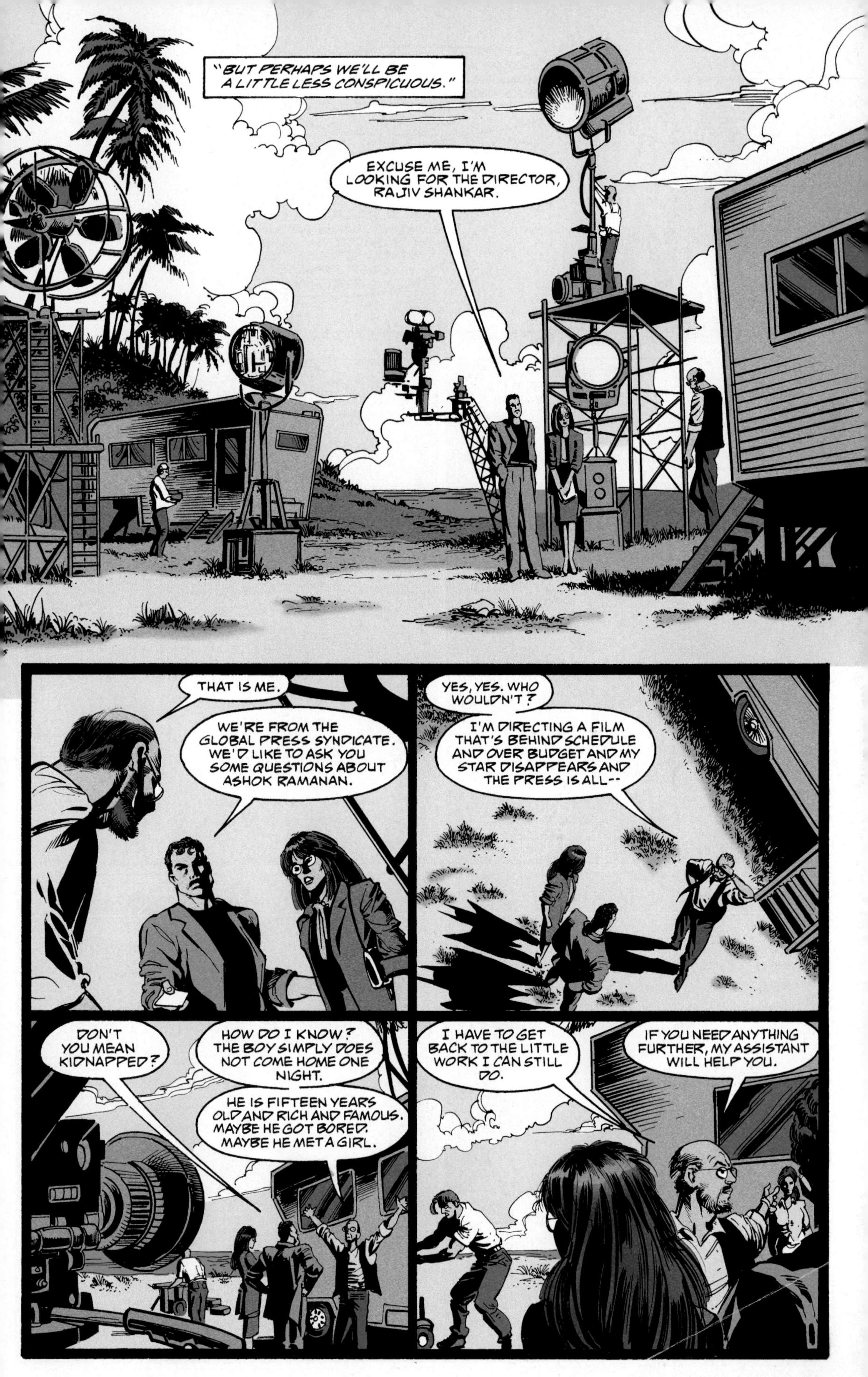
"BUT PERHAPS WE'LL BE A LITTLE LESS CONSPICUOUS."
EXCUSE ME, I'M LOOKING FOR THE DIRECTOR, RAJIV SHANKAR.
THAT IS ME.
WE'RE FROM THE GLOBAL PRESS SYNDICATE. WE'D LIKE TO ASK YOU SOME QUESTIONS ABOUT ASHOK RAMANAN.
YES, YES. WHO WOULDN'T?
I'M DIRECTING A FILM THAT'S BEHIND SCHEDULE AND OVER BUDGET AND MY STAR DISAPPEARS AND THE PRESS IS ALL--
DON'T YOU MEAN KIDNAPPED?
HOW DO I KNOW? THE BOY SIMPLY DOES NOT COME HOME ONE NIGHT.
HE IS FIFTEEN YEARS OLD AND RICH AND FAMOUS. MAYBE HE GOT BORED. MAYBE HE MET A GIRL.
I HAVE TO GET BACK TO THE LITTLE WORK I CAN STILL DO.
IF YOU NEED ANYTHING FURTHER, MY ASSISTANT WILL HELP YOU.

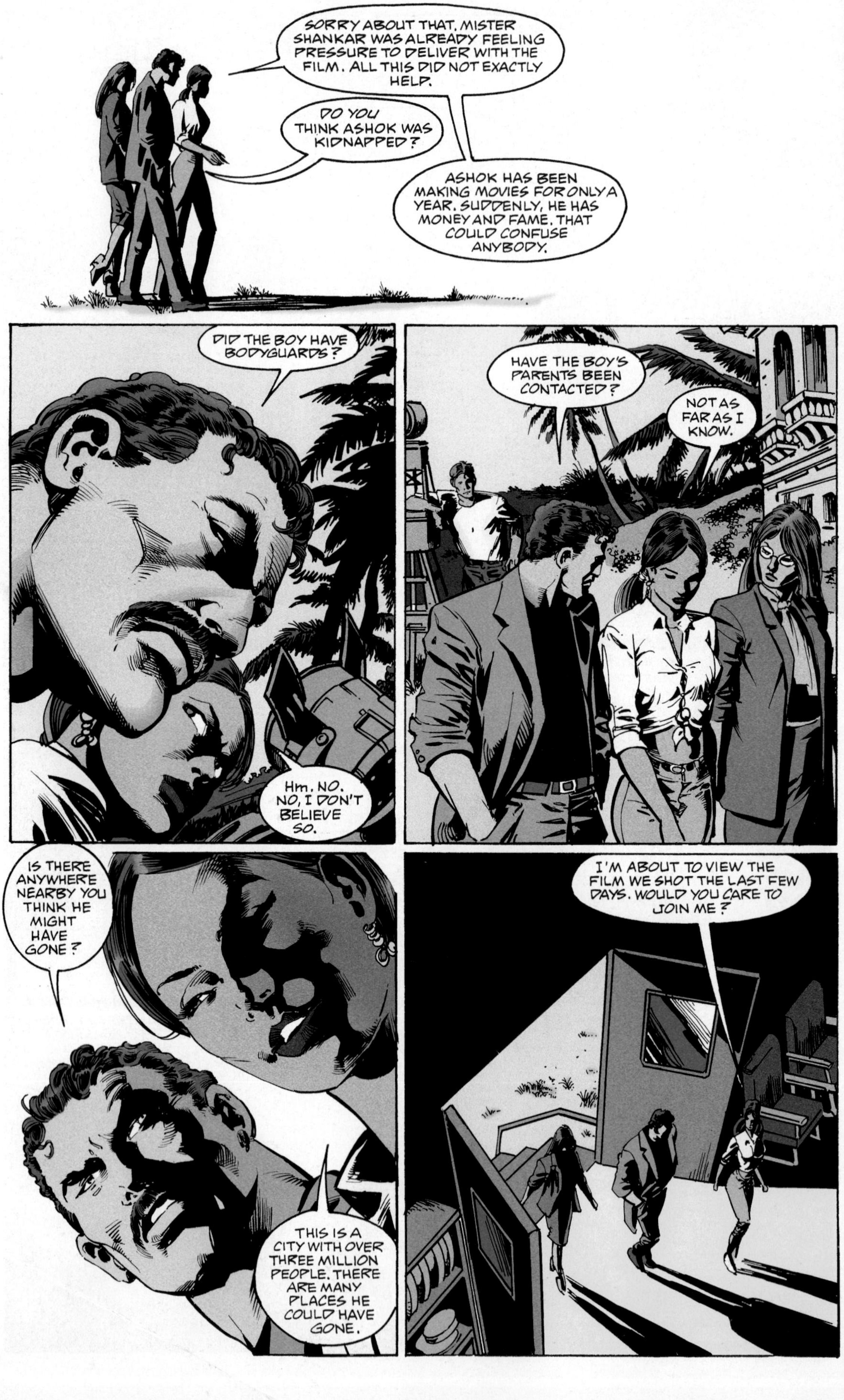
SORRY ABOUT THAT. MISTER SHANKAR WAS ALREADY FEELING PRESSURE TO DELIVER WITH THE FILM. ALL THIS DID NOT EXACTLY HELP.
DO YOU THINK ASHOK WAS KIDNAPPED?
ASHOK HAS BEEN MAKING MOVIES FOR ONLY A YEAR. SUDDENLY, HE HAS MONEY AND FAME. THAT COULD CONFUSE ANYBODY.
DID THE BOY HAVE BODYGUARDS?
Hm. NO. NO, I DON'T BELIEVE SO.
HAVE THE BOY'S PARENTS BEEN CONTACTED?
NOT AS FAR AS I KNOW.
IS THERE ANYWHERE NEARBY YOU THINK HE MIGHT HAVE GONE?
THIS IS A CITY WITH OVER THREE MILLION PEOPLE. THERE ARE MANY PLACES HE COULD HAVE GONE.
I'M ABOUT TO VIEW THE FILM WE SHOT THE LAST FEW DAYS. WOULD YOU CARE TO JOIN ME?

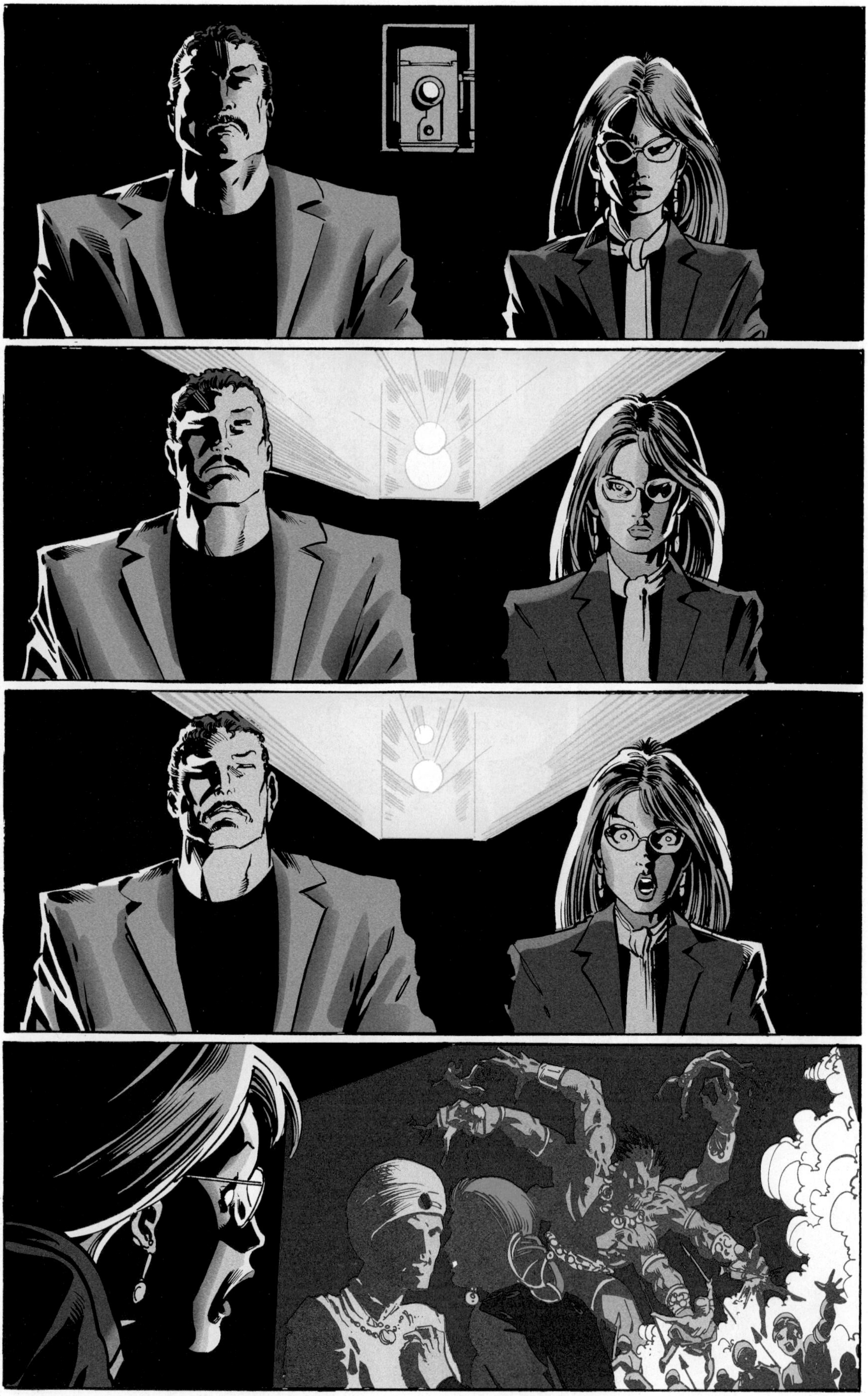

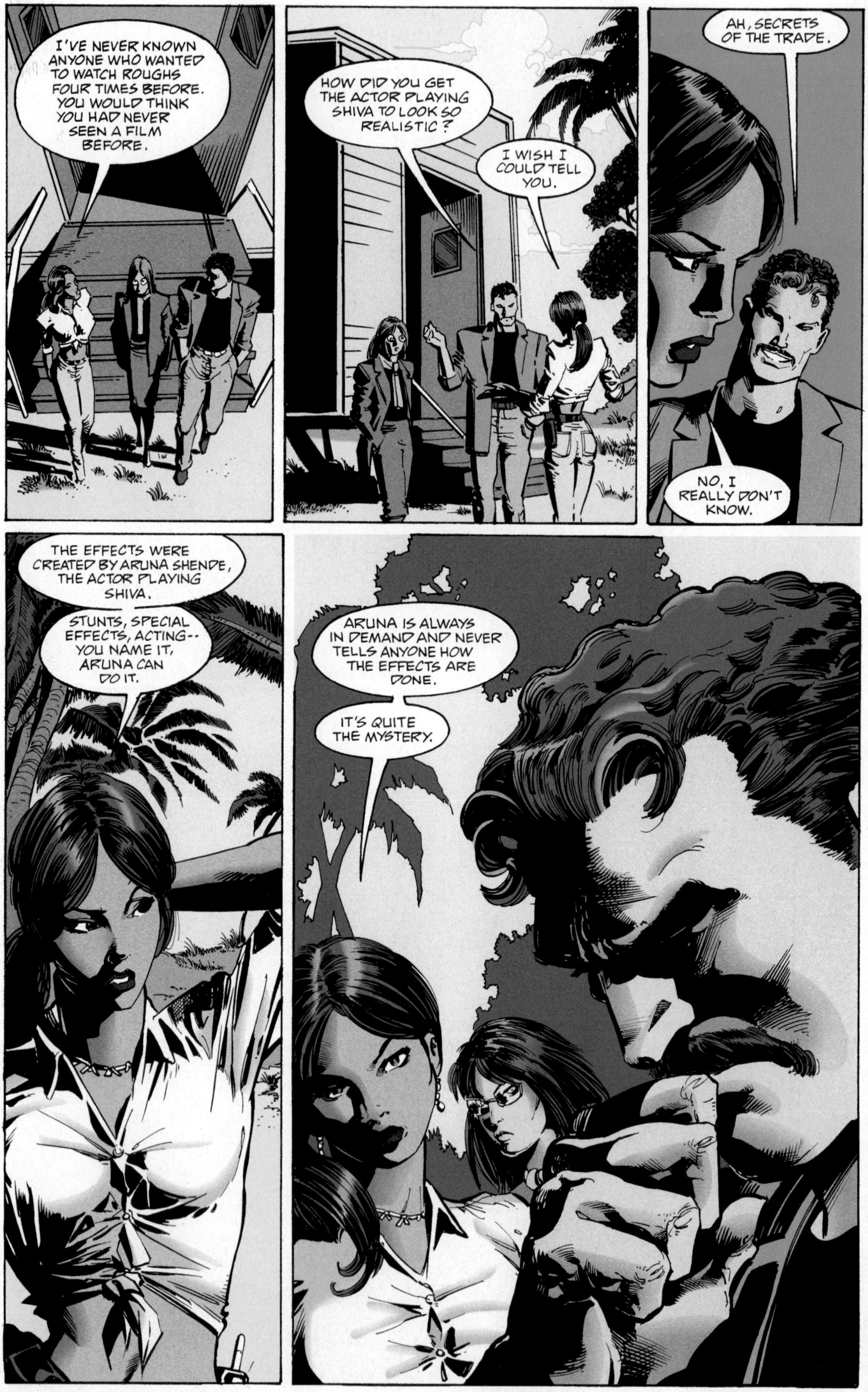
I'VE NEVER KNOWN ANYONE WHO WANTED TO WATCH ROUGHS FOUR TIMES BEFORE. YOU WOULD THINK YOU HAD NEVER SEEN A FILM BEFORE.
HOW DID YOU GET THE ACTOR PLAYING SHIVA TO LOOK SO REALISTIC?
I WISH I COULD TELL YOU.
AH, SECRETS OF THE TRADE.
NO, I REALLY DON'T KNOW.
THE EFFECTS WERE CREATED BY ARUNA SHENDE, THE ACTOR PLAYING SHIVA.
STUNTS, SPECIAL EFFECTS, ACTING-- YOU NAME IT, ARUNA CAN DO IT.
ARUNA IS ALWAYS IN DEMAND AND NEVER TELLS ANYONE HOW THE EFFECTS ARE DONE.
IT'S QUITE THE MYSTERY.

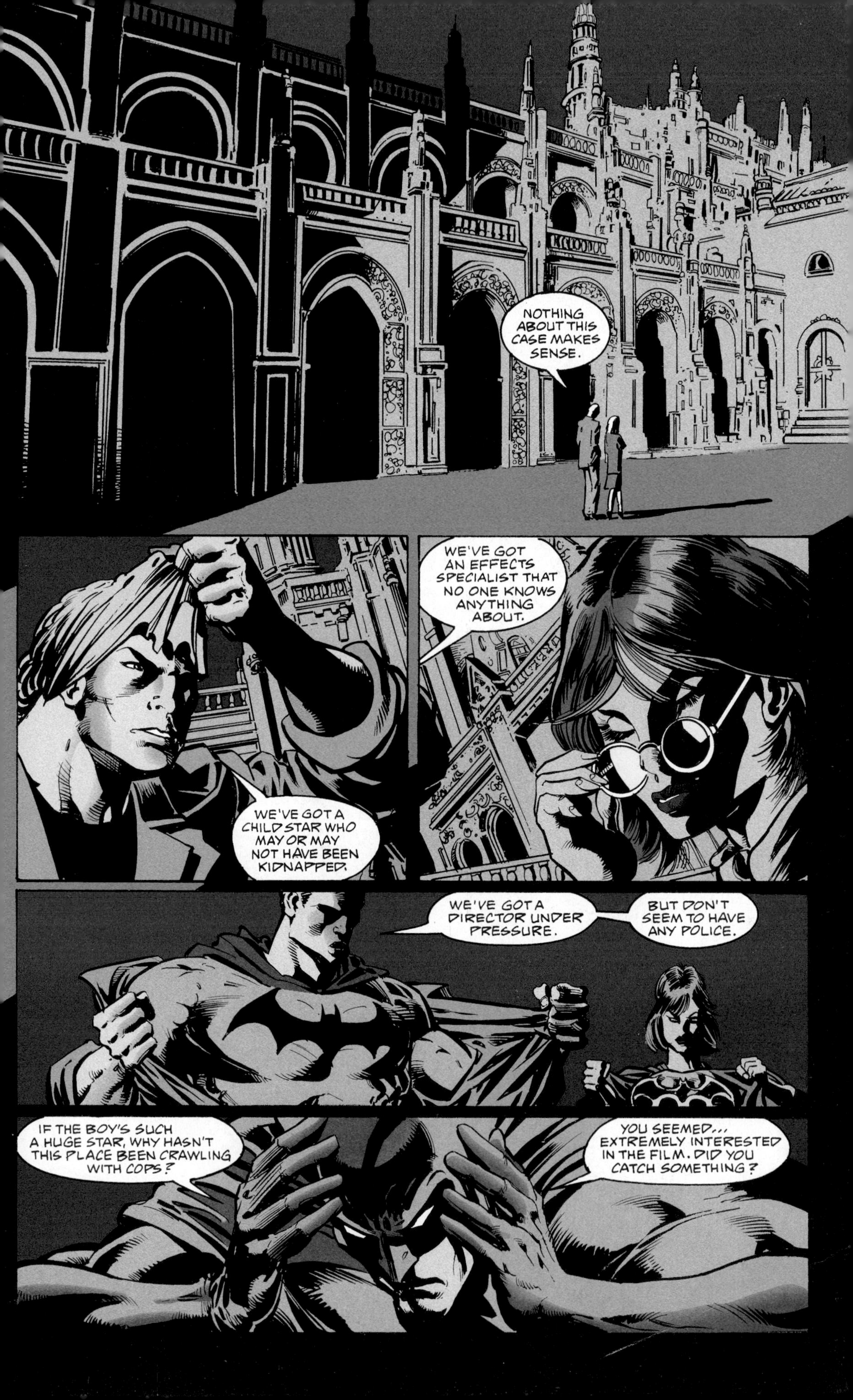
NOTHING ABOUT THIS CASE MAKES SENSE.
WE'VE GOT A CHILD STAR WHO MAY OR MAY NOT HAVE BEEN KIDNAPPED.
WE'VE GOT AN EFFECTS SPECIALIST THAT NO ONE KNOWS ANYTHING ABOUT.
WE'VE GOT A DIRECTOR UNDER PRESSURE.
BUT DON'T SEEM TO HAVE ANY POLICE.
IF THE BOY'S SUCH A HUGE STAR, WHY HASN'T THIS PLACE BEEN CRAWLING WITH COPS?
YOU SEEMED... EXTREMELY INTERESTED IN THE FILM. DID YOU CATCH SOMETHING?

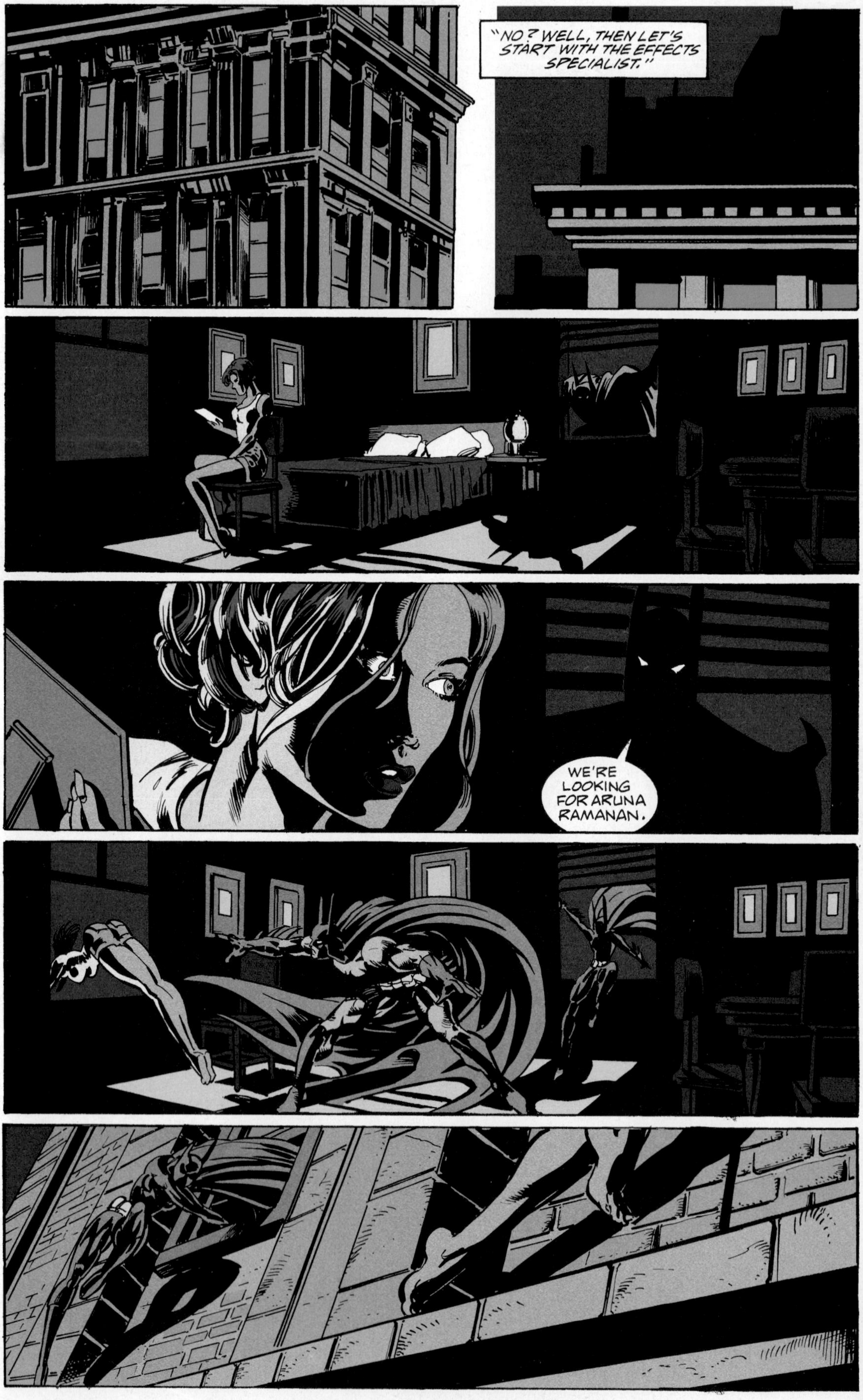
"NO? WELL, THEN LET'S START WITH THE EFFECTS SPECIALIST."
WE'RE LOOKING FOR ARUNA RAMANAN.

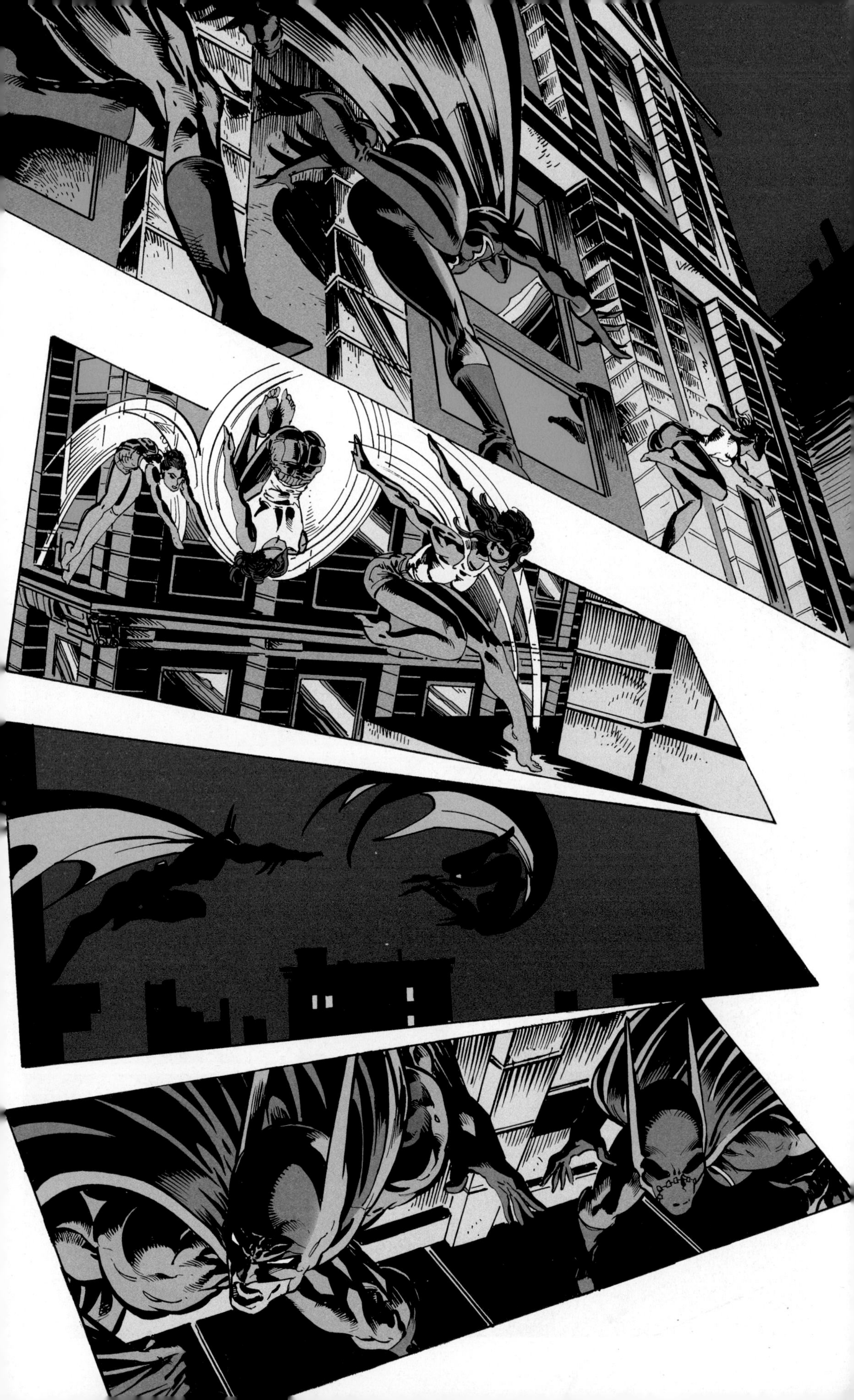

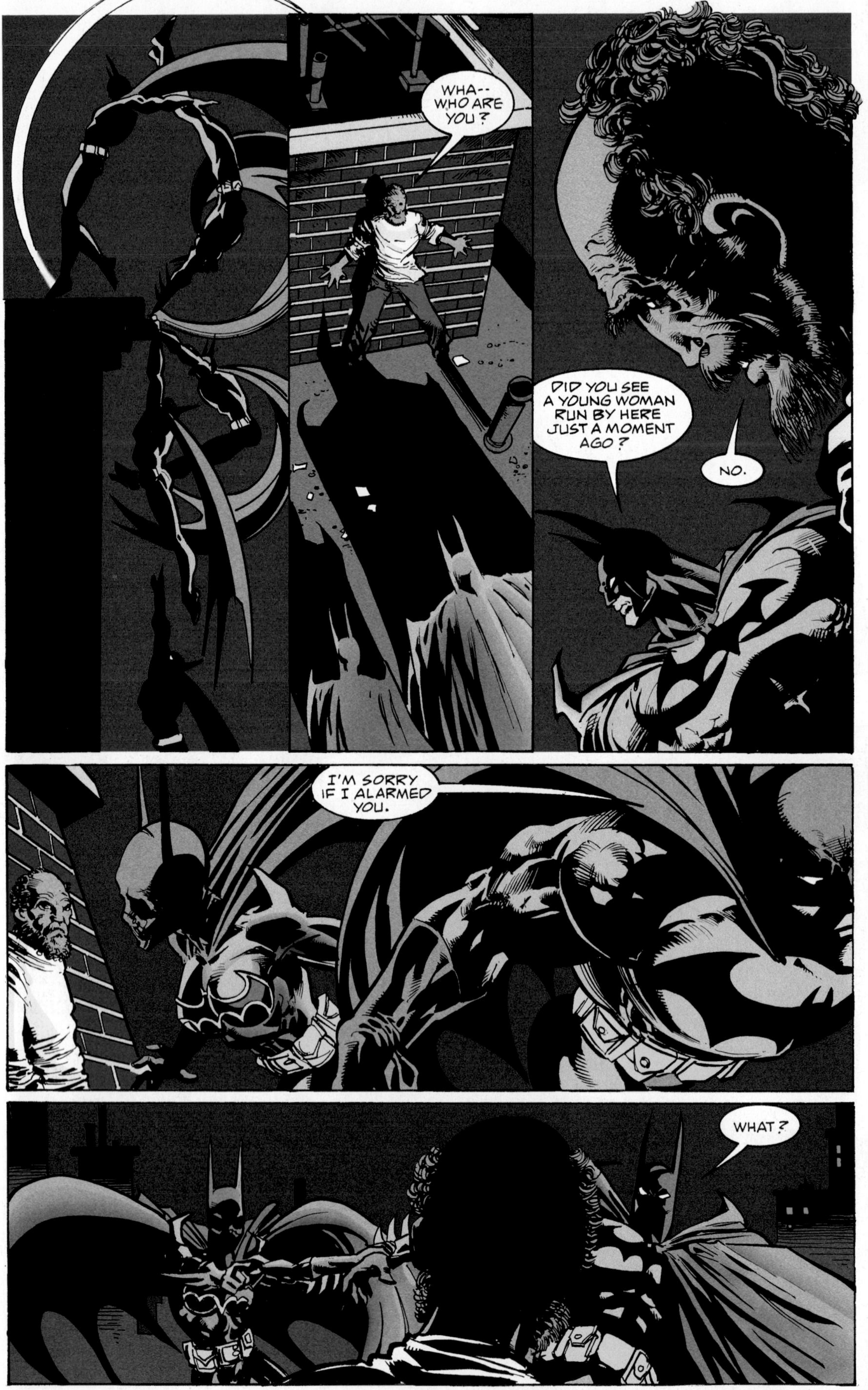
WHA--
WHO ARE YOU?
DID YOU SEE A YOUNG WOMAN RUN BY HERE JUST A MOMENT AGO?
NO.
I'M SORRY IF I ALARMED YOU.
WHAT?

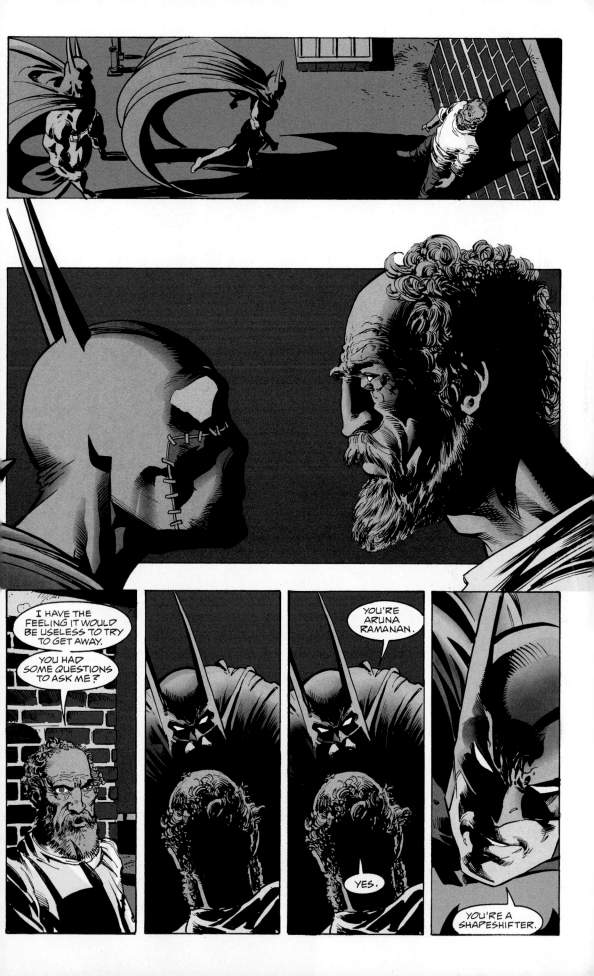

I HAVE THE FEELING IT WOULD BE USELESS TO TRY TO GET AWAY.

YOU HAD SOME QUESTIONS TO ASK ME?

YOU'RE ARUNA RAMANAN.

YES.

YOU'RE A SHAPESHIFTER.

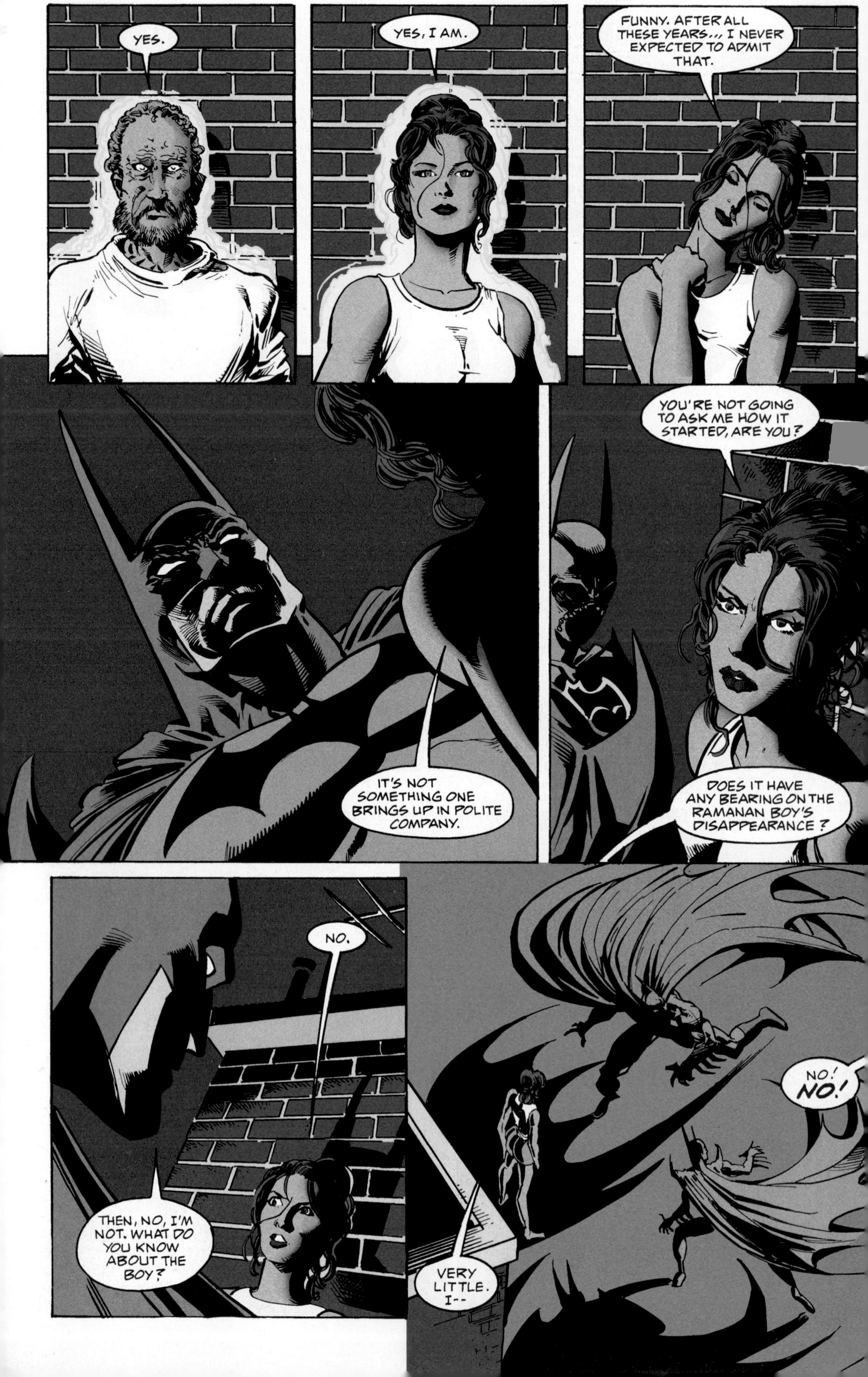
YES.
YES, I AM.
FUNNY. AFTER ALL THESE YEARS.., I NEVER EXPECTED TO ADMIT THAT.
IT'S NOT SOMETHING ONE BRINGS UP IN POLITE COMPANY.
YOU'RE NOT GOING TO ASK ME HOW IT STARTED, ARE YOU?
DOES IT HAVE ANY BEARING ON THE RAMANAN BOY'S DISAPPEARANCE?
NO.
THEN, NO, I'M NOT. WHAT DO YOU KNOW ABOUT THE BOY?
VERY LITTLE. I--
NO! NO!

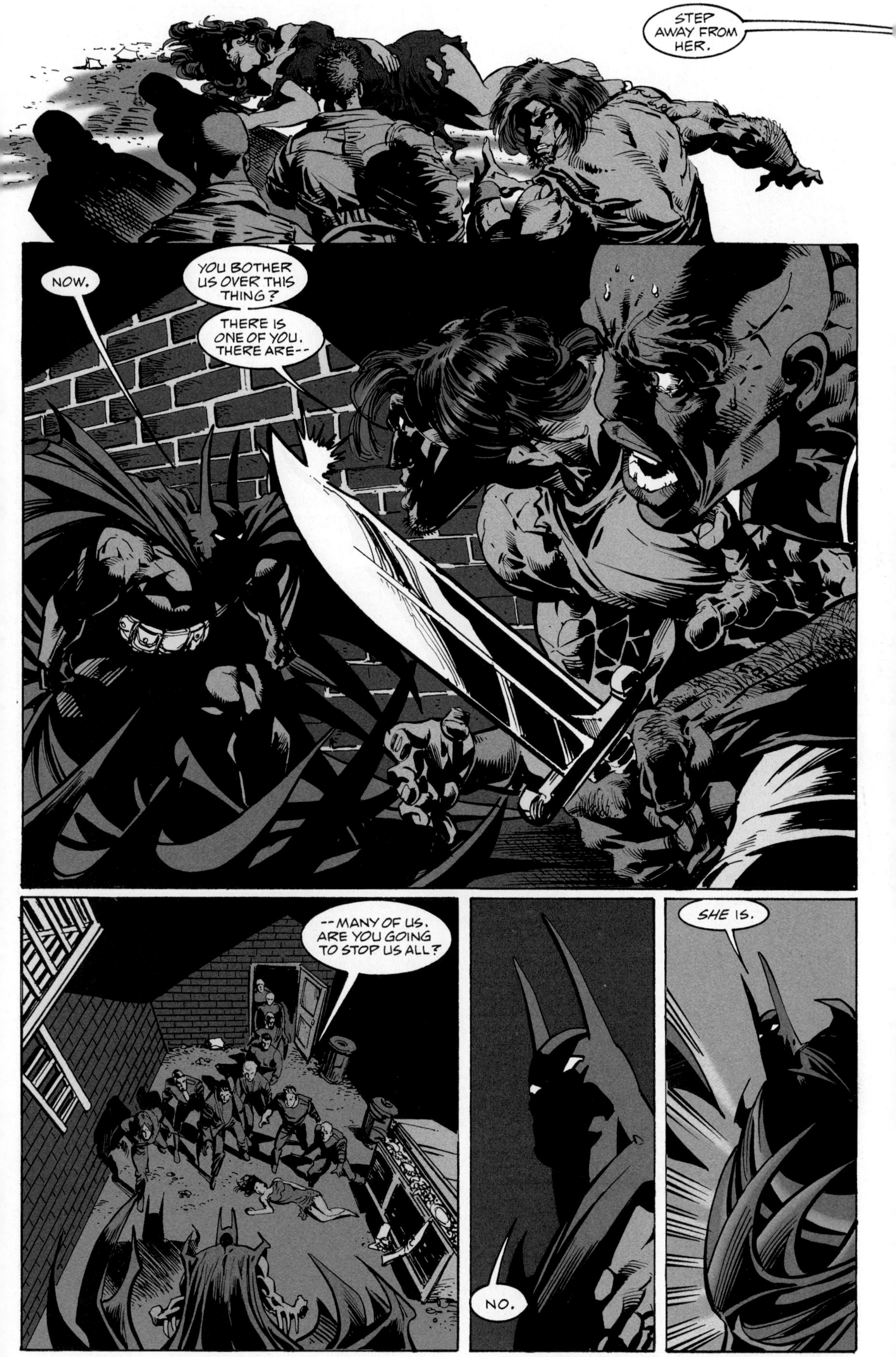
STEP AWAY FROM HER.
NOW.
YOU BOTHER US OVER THIS THING?
THERE IS ONE OF YOU. THERE ARE--
--MANY OF US. ARE YOU GOING TO STOP US ALL?
NO.
SHE IS.

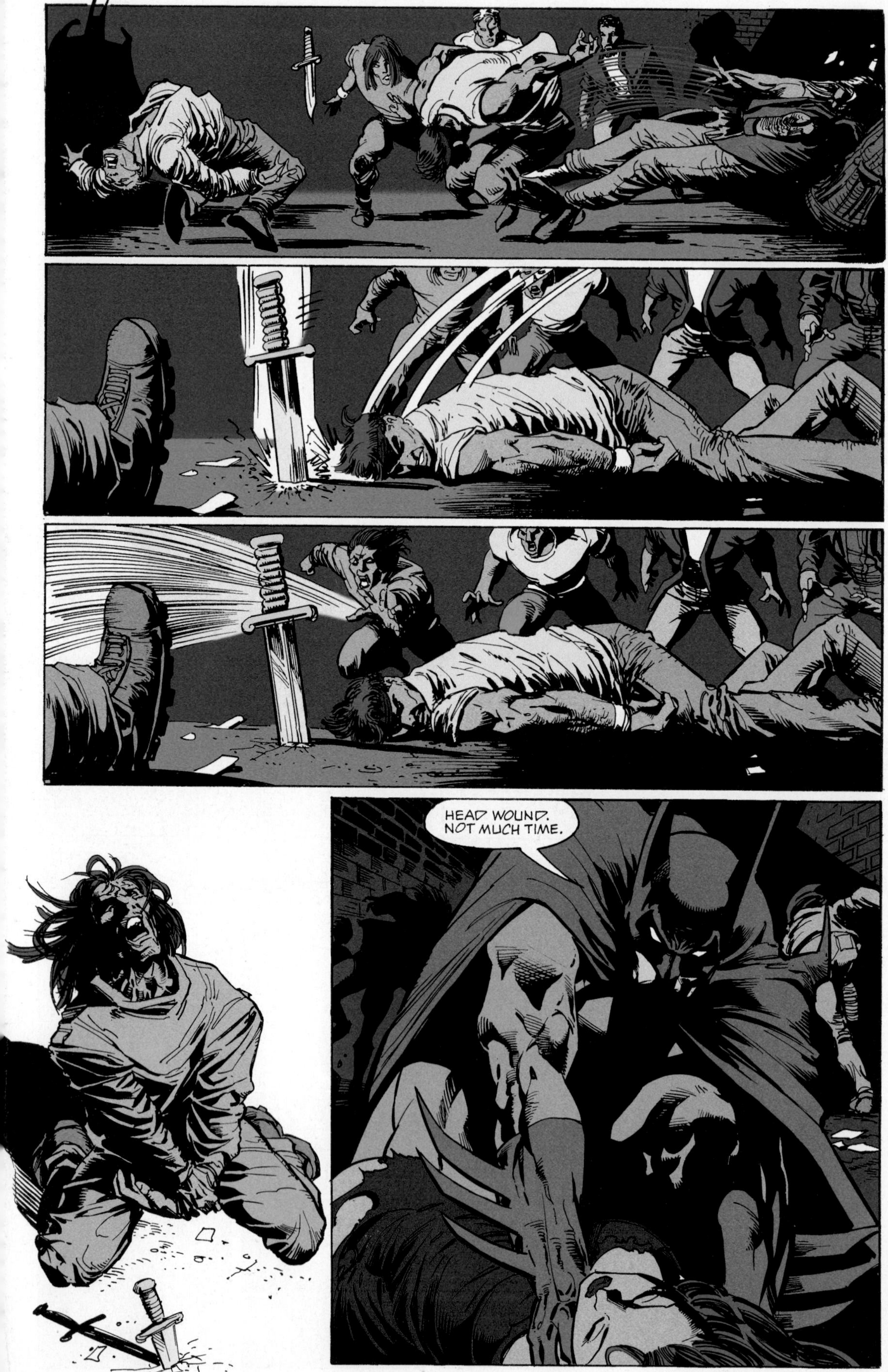
HEAD WOUND. NOT MUCH TIME.

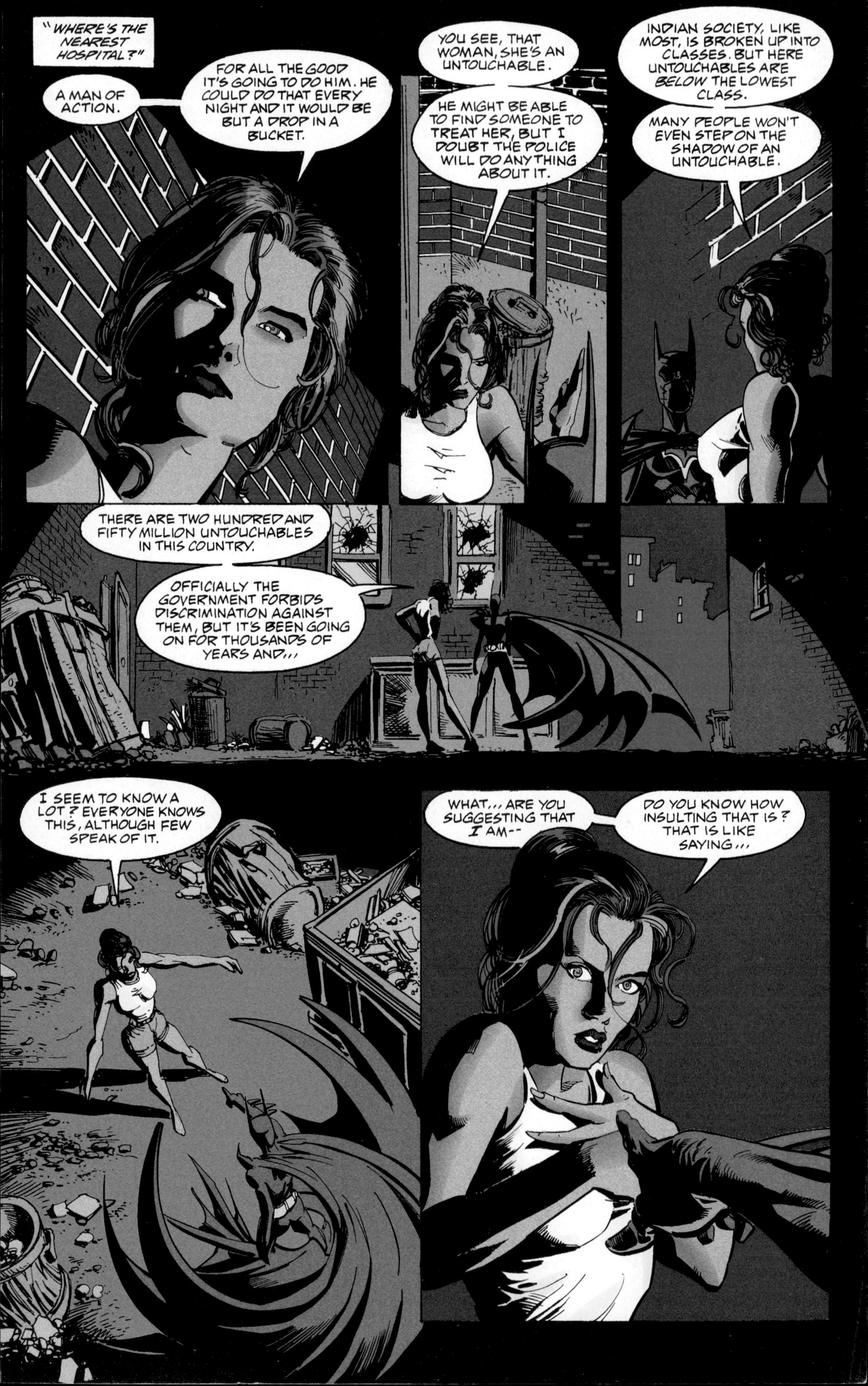
"WHERE'S THE NEAREST HOSPITAL?"
A MAN OF ACTION.
FOR ALL THE GOOD IT'S GOING TO DO HIM. HE COULD DO THAT EVERY NIGHT AND IT WOULD BE BUT A DROP IN A BUCKET.
YOU SEE, THAT WOMAN, SHE'S AN UNTOUCHABLE.
HE MIGHT BE ABLE TO FIND SOMEONE TO TREAT HER, BUT I DOUBT THE POLICE WILL DO ANYTHING ABOUT IT.
INDIAN SOCIETY, LIKE MOST, IS BROKEN UP INTO CLASSES. BUT HERE UNTOUCHABLES ARE BELOW THE LOWEST CLASS.
MANY PEOPLE WON'T EVEN STEP ON THE SHADOW OF AN UNTOUCHABLE.
THERE ARE TWO HUNDRED AND FIFTY MILLION UNTOUCHABLES IN THIS COUNTRY.
OFFICIALLY THE GOVERNMENT FORBIDS DISCRIMINATION AGAINST THEM, BUT IT'S BEEN GOING ON FOR THOUSANDS OF YEARS AND...
I SEEM TO KNOW A LOT? EVERYONE KNOWS THIS, ALTHOUGH FEW SPEAK OF IT.
WHAT... ARE YOU SUGGESTING THAT I AM--
DO YOU KNOW HOW INSULTING THAT IS? THAT IS LIKE SAYING...

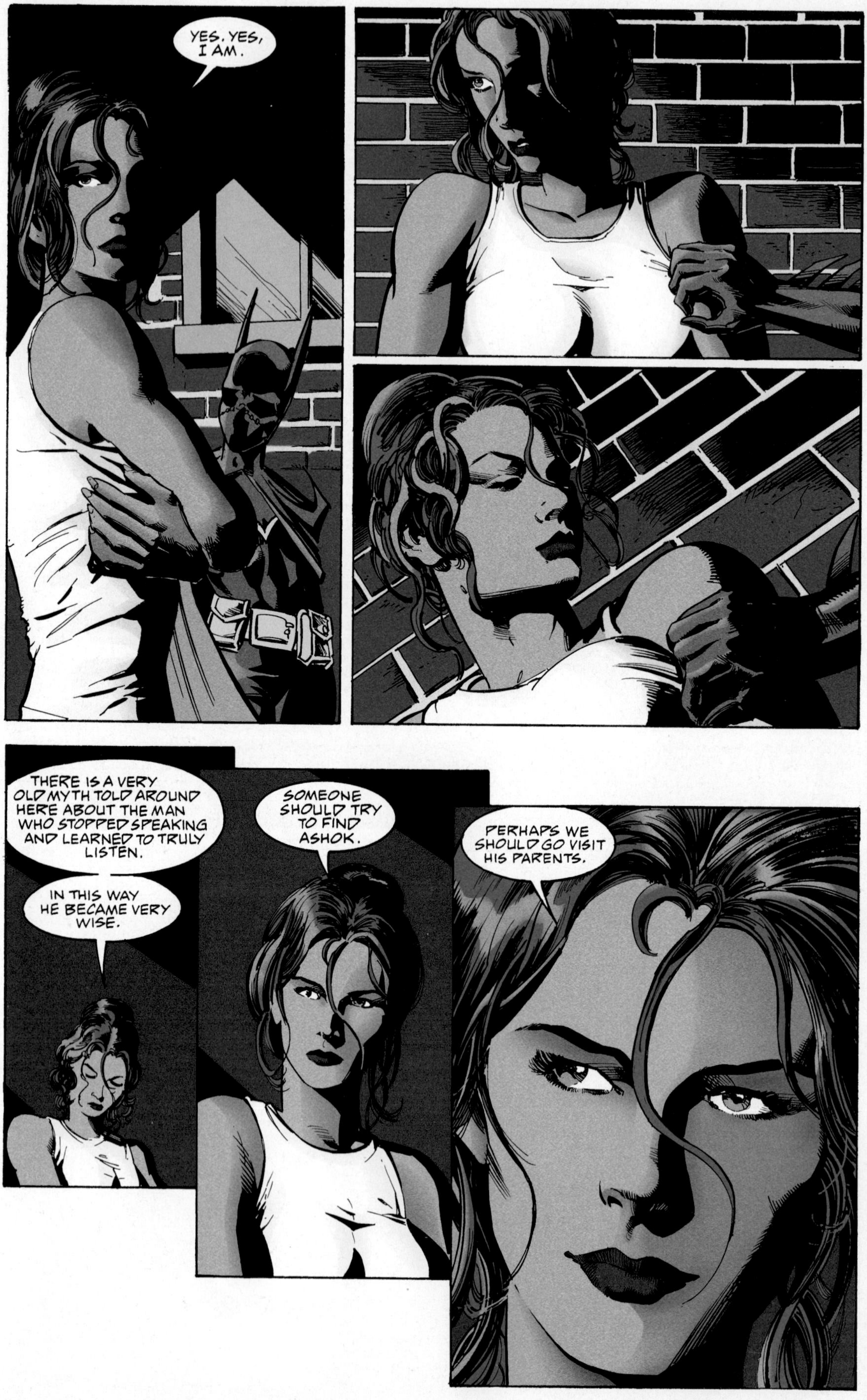
YES. YES, I AM.
THERE IS A VERY OLD MYTH TOLD AROUND HERE ABOUT THE MAN WHO STOPPED SPEAKING AND LEARNED TO TRULY LISTEN.
IN THIS WAY HE BECAME VERY WISE.
SOMEONE SHOULD TRY TO FIND ASHOK.
PERHAPS WE SHOULD GO VISIT HIS PARENTS.

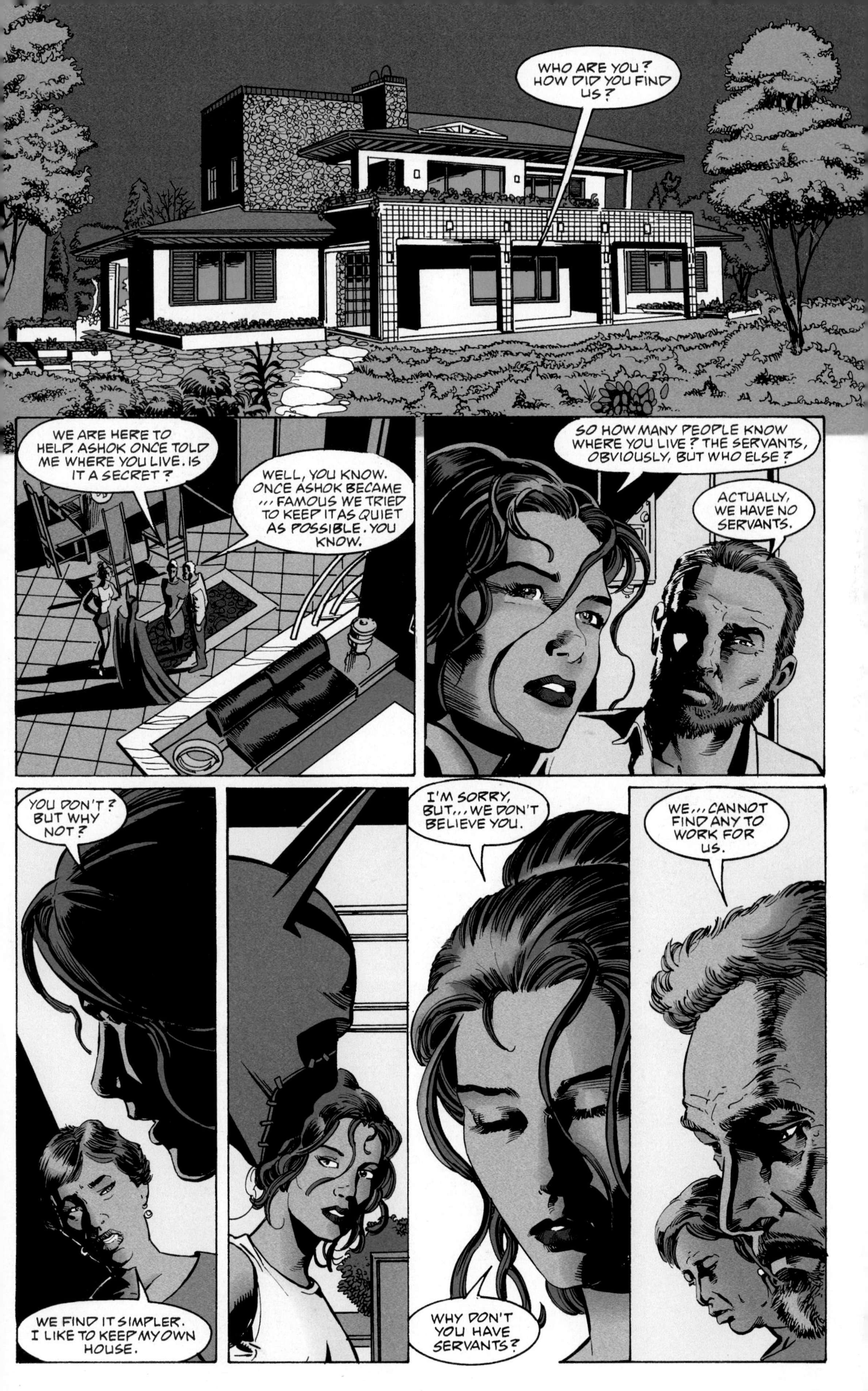
WHO ARE YOU? HOW DID YOU FIND US?
WE ARE HERE TO HELP. ASHOK ONCE TOLD ME WHERE YOU LIVE. IS IT A SECRET?
WELL, YOU KNOW. ONCE ASHOK BECAME ... FAMOUS WE TRIED TO KEEP IT AS QUIET AS POSSIBLE. YOU KNOW.
SO HOW MANY PEOPLE KNOW WHERE YOU LIVE? THE SERVANTS, OBVIOUSLY, BUT WHO ELSE?
ACTUALLY, WE HAVE NO SERVANTS.
YOU DON'T? BUT WHY NOT?
WE FIND IT SIMPLER. I LIKE TO KEEP MY OWN HOUSE.
I'M SORRY, BUT... WE DON'T BELIEVE YOU.
WHY DON'T YOU HAVE SERVANTS?
WE... CANNOT FIND ANY TO WORK FOR US.

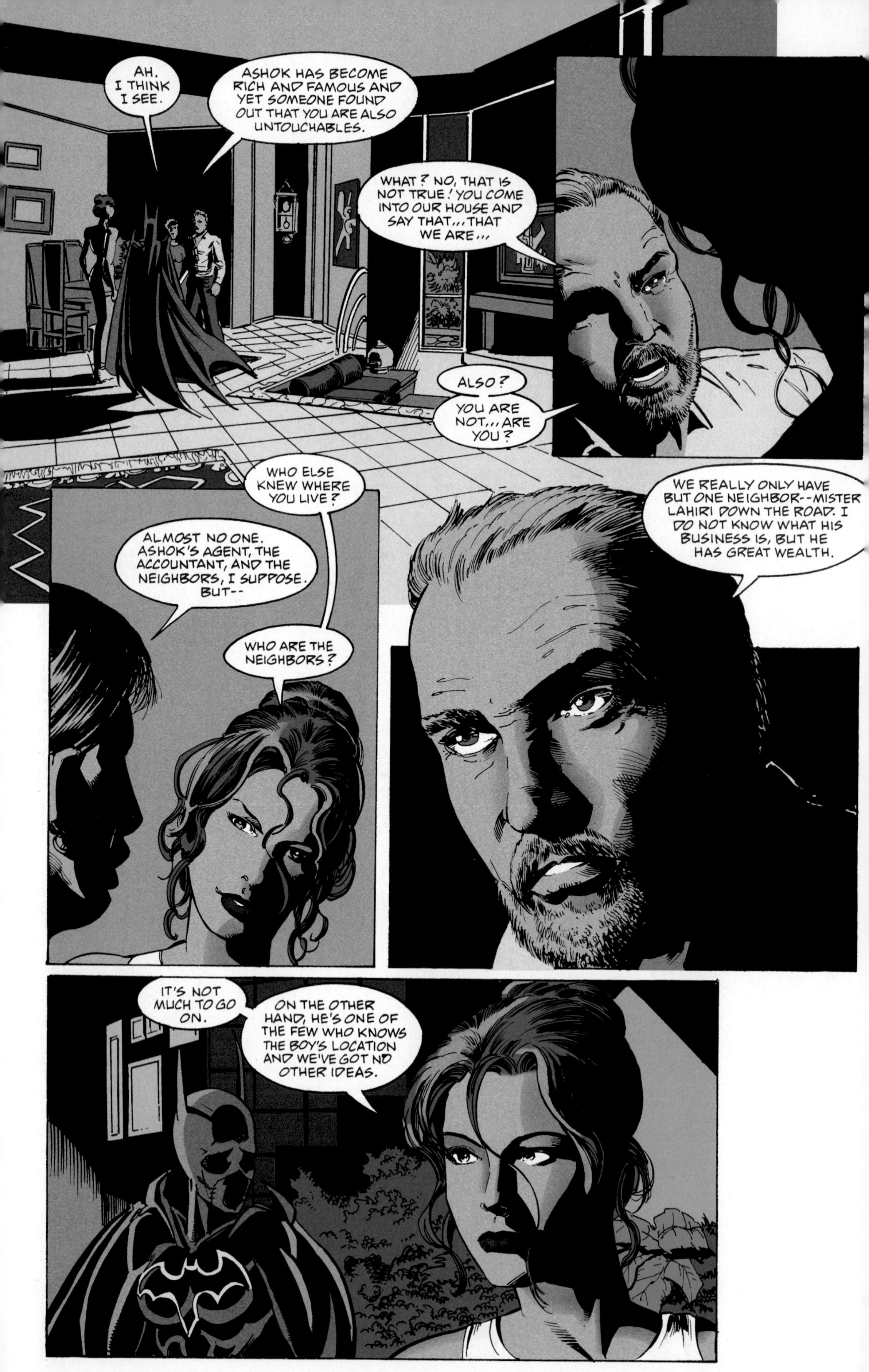
AH. I THINK I SEE.
ASHOK HAS BECOME RICH AND FAMOUS AND YET SOMEONE FOUND OUT THAT YOU ARE ALSO UNTOUCHABLES.
WHAT? NO, THAT IS NOT TRUE! YOU COME INTO OUR HOUSE AND SAY THAT... THAT WE ARE...
ALSO?
YOU ARE NOT... ARE YOU?
WHO ELSE KNEW WHERE YOU LIVE?
ALMOST NO ONE. ASHOK'S AGENT, THE ACCOUNTANT, AND THE NEIGHBORS, I SUPPOSE. BUT--
WHO ARE THE NEIGHBORS?
WE REALLY ONLY HAVE BUT ONE NEIGHBOR--MISTER LAHIRI DOWN THE ROAD. I DO NOT KNOW WHAT HIS BUSINESS IS, BUT HE HAS GREAT WEALTH.
IT'S NOT MUCH TO GO ON.
ON THE OTHER HAND, HE'S ONE OF THE FEW WHO KNOWS THE BOY'S LOCATION AND WE'VE GOT NO OTHER IDEAS.

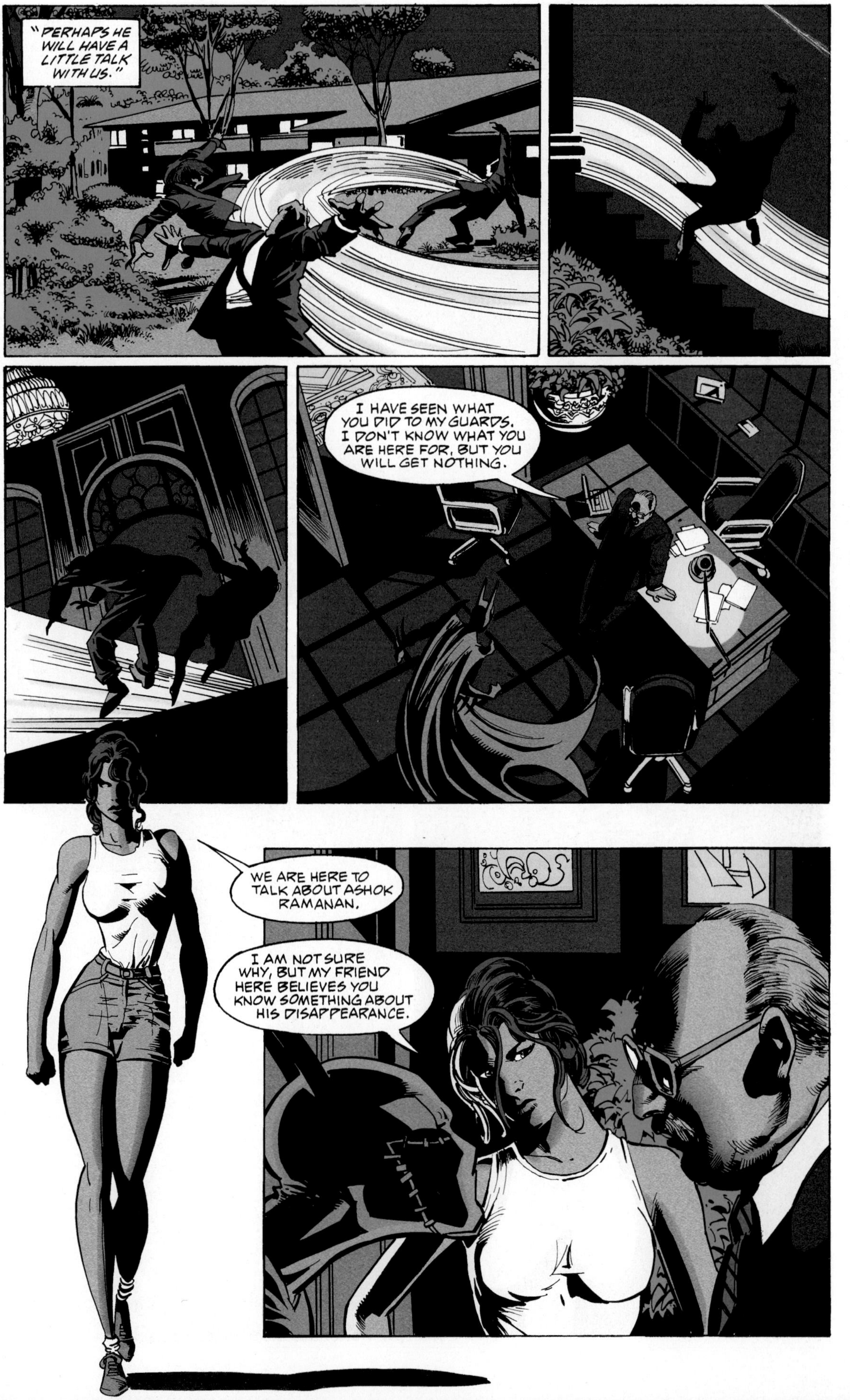
"PERHAPS HE WILL HAVE A LITTLE TALK WITH US."
I HAVE SEEN WHAT YOU DID TO MY GUARDS. I DON'T KNOW WHAT YOU ARE HERE FOR, BUT YOU WILL GET NOTHING.
WE ARE HERE TO TALK ABOUT ASHOK RAMANAN.
I AM NOT SURE WHY, BUT MY FRIEND HERE BELIEVES YOU KNOW SOMETHING ABOUT HIS DISAPPEARANCE.

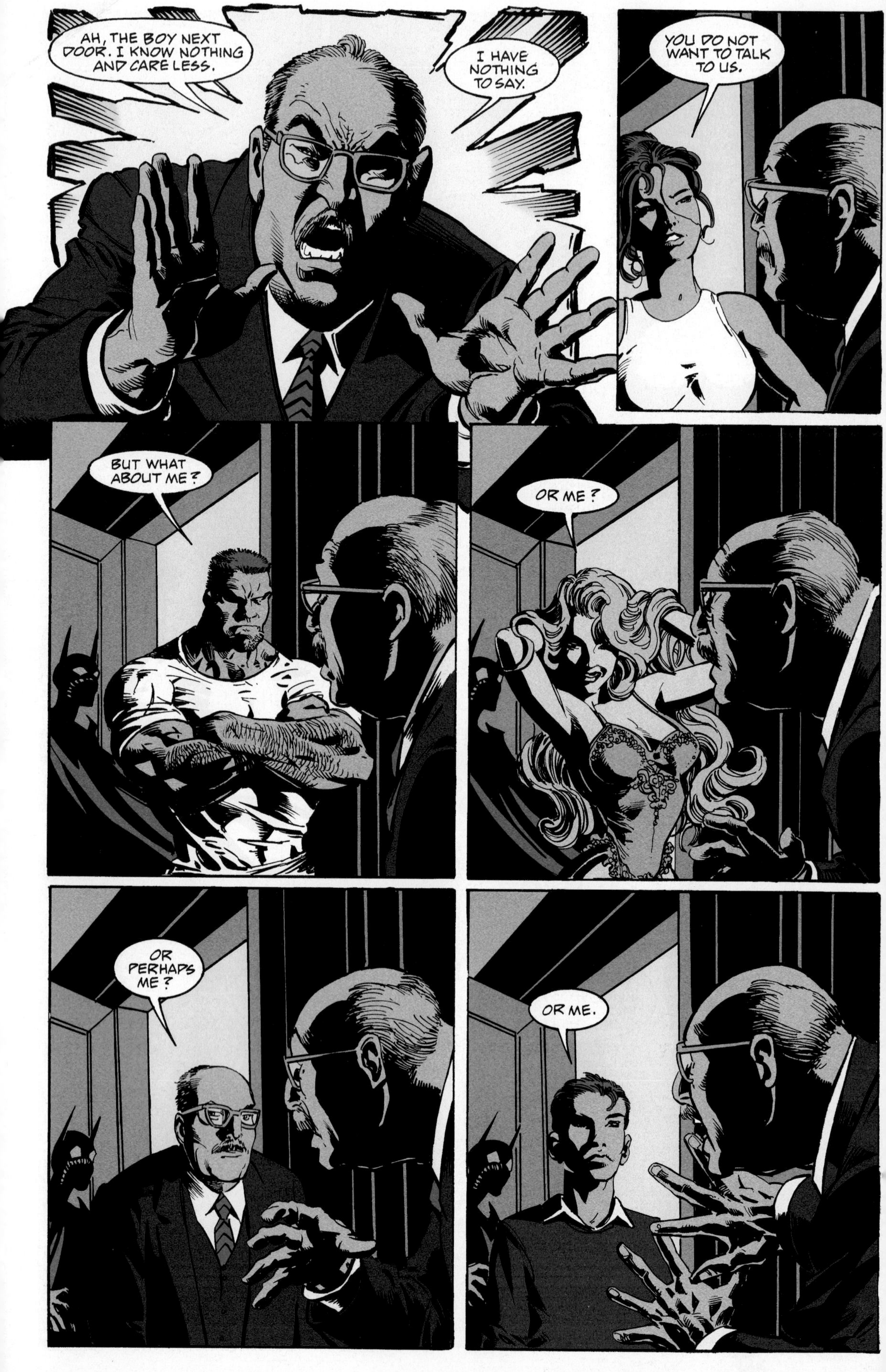
AH, THE BOY NEXT DOOR. I KNOW NOTHING AND CARE LESS.
I HAVE NOTHING TO SAY.
YOU DO NOT WANT TO TALK TO US.
BUT WHAT ABOUT ME?
OR ME?
OR PERHAPS ME?
OR ME.

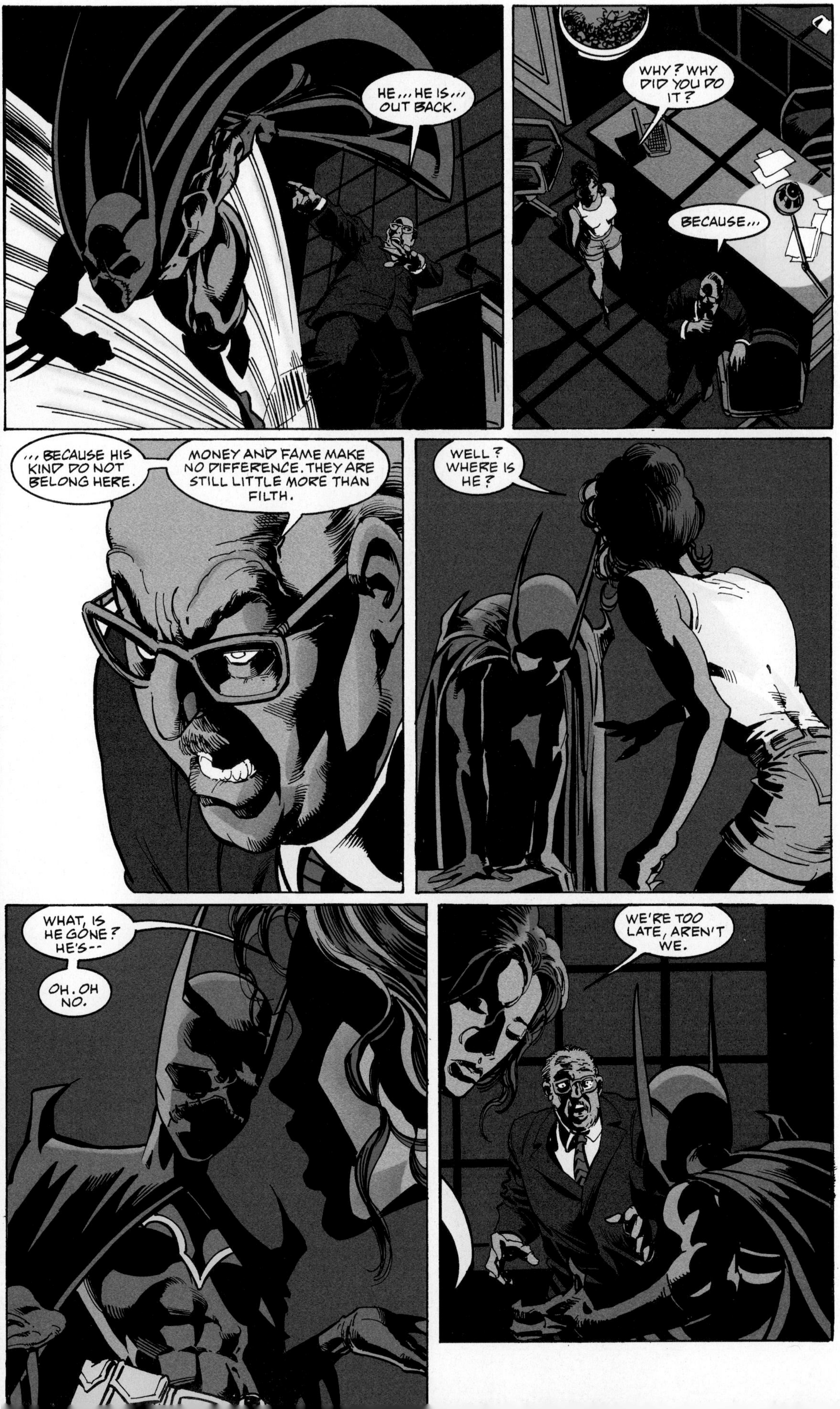
HE... HE IS... OUT BACK.
WHY? WHY DID YOU DO IT?
BECAUSE...
...BECAUSE HIS KIND DO NOT BELONG HERE.
MONEY AND FAME MAKE NO DIFFERENCE. THEY ARE STILL LITTLE MORE THAN FILTH.
WELL? WHERE IS HE?
WHAT, IS HE GONE? HE'S--
OH. OH NO.
WE'RE TOO LATE, AREN'T WE.

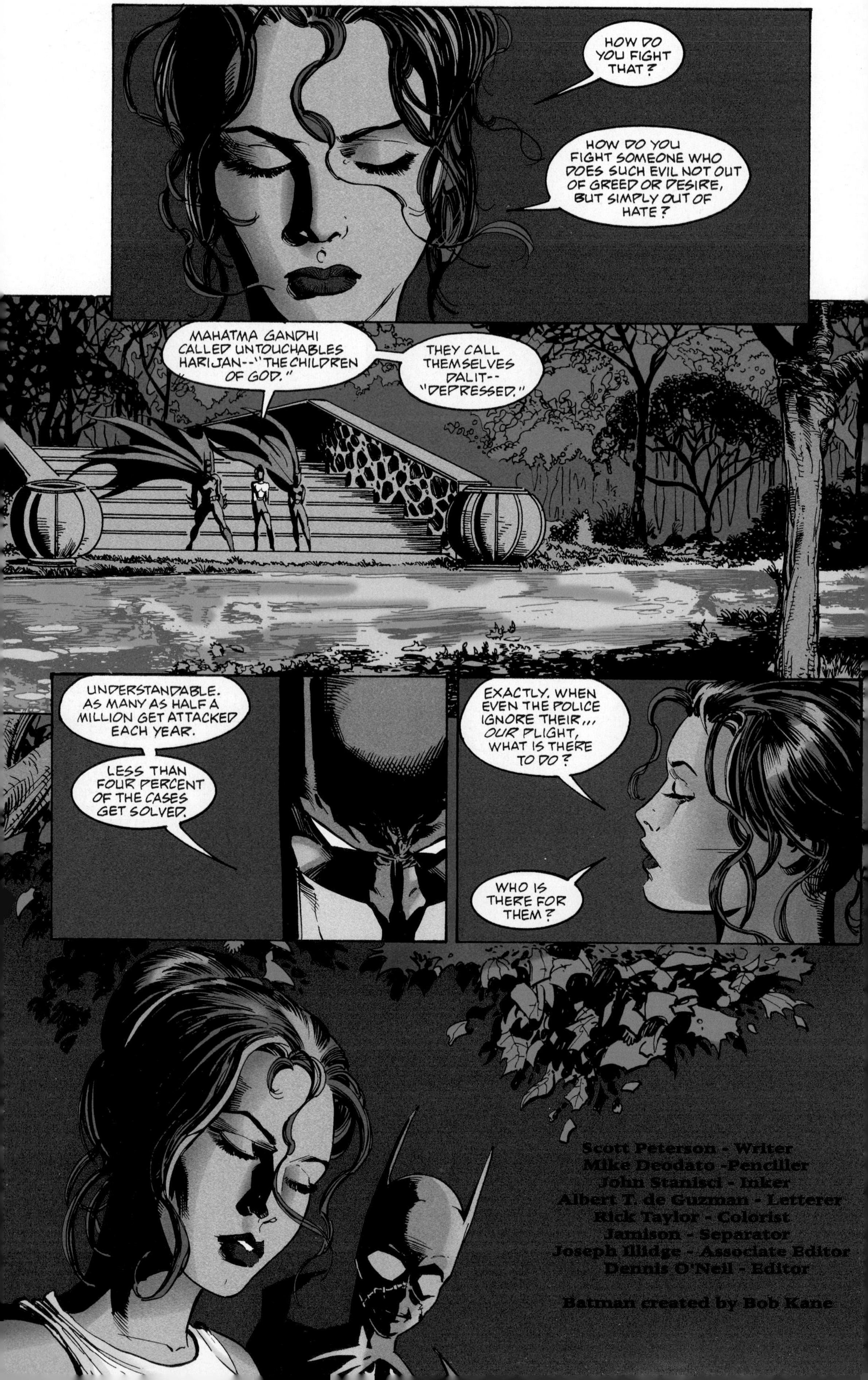
HOW DO YOU FIGHT THAT?
HOW DO YOU FIGHT SOMEONE WHO DOES SUCH EVIL NOT OUT OF GREED OR DESIRE, BUT SIMPLY OUT OF HATE?
MAHATMA GANDHI CALLED UNTOUCHABLES HARIJAN--"THE CHILDREN OF GOD."
THEY CALL THEMSELVES DALIT--"DEPRESSED."
UNDERSTANDABLE. AS MANY AS HALF A MILLION GET ATTACKED EACH YEAR.
LESS THAN FOUR PERCENT OF THE CASES GET SOLVED.
EXACTLY. WHEN EVEN THE POLICE IGNORE THEIR,,, OUR PLIGHT, WHAT IS THERE TO DO?
WHO IS THERE FOR THEM?
Scott Peterson - Writer
Mike Deodato -Penciller
John Stanisci - Inker
Albert T. de Guzman - Letterer
Rick Taylor - Colorist
Jamison - Separator
Joseph Illidge - Associate Editor
Dennis O'Neil - Editor
Batman created by Bob Kane

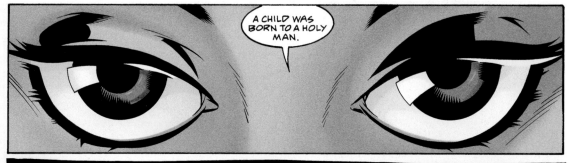

A CHILD WAS BORN TO A HOLY MAN.

"NOW, WHENEVER A BABY IS BORN, THE GOD BRAHMA COMES AND WRITES THE CHILD'S FATE ON ITS FOREHEAD."

"THIS MAN WAS SO WISE HE COULD ACTUALLY SEE BRAHMA.

"THE WISE MAN ASKED WHAT FATE THE GOD HAD WRITTEN ON HIS SON'S FOREHEAD."

"'THIS CHILD WILL GROW UP TO OWN NOTHING BUT A BUFFALO AND A BAG OF RICE.'

"'THAT'S IT?' THE WISE MAN CRIED. 'THAT IS MY SON'S FATE? SURELY IF HE--'"

"'NO,' BRAHMA SAID. 'WHAT IS SOWN IN THE PAST MUST BE REAPED IN THE PRESENT.'"

FATE CANNOT BE CHANGED.

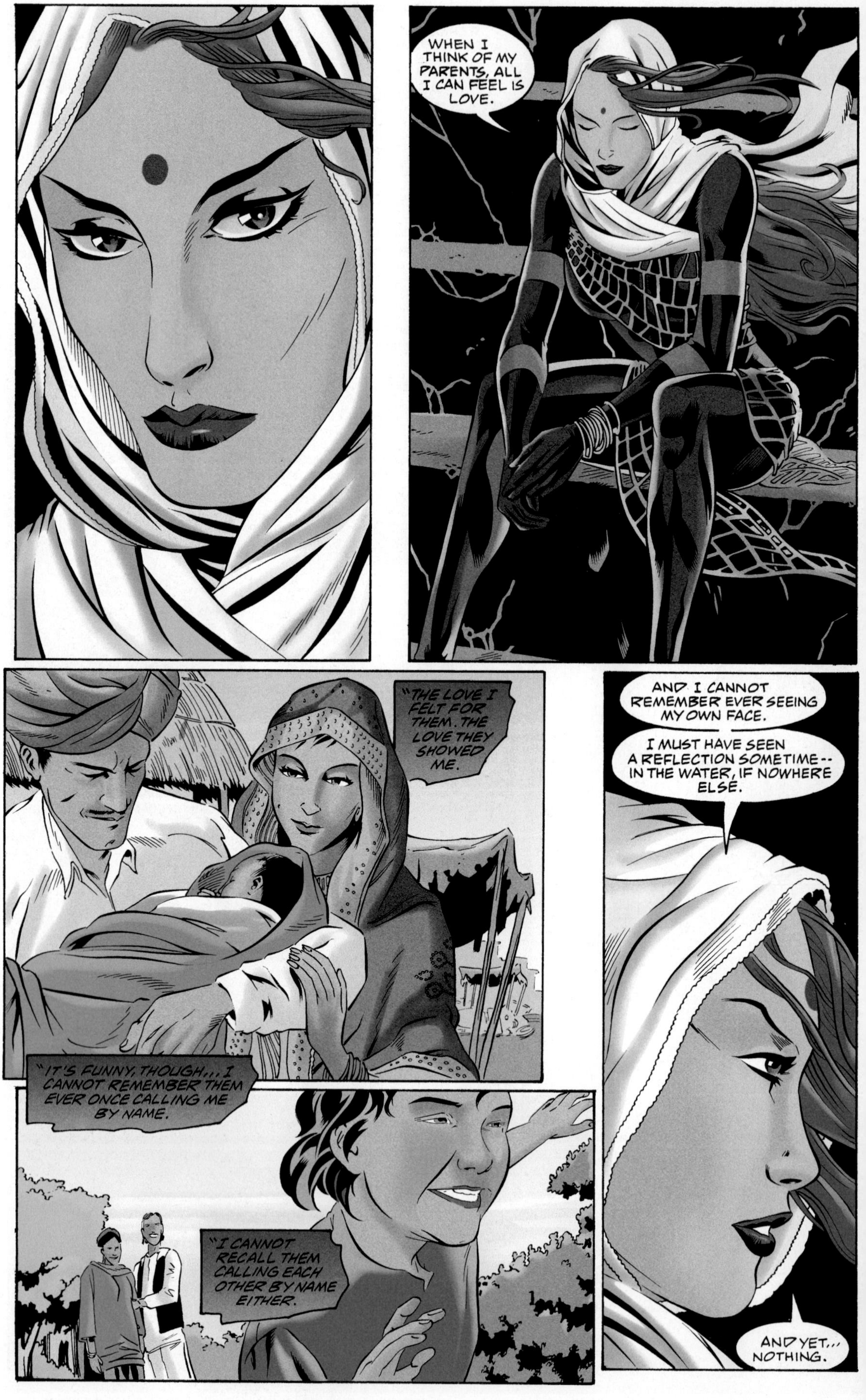

WHEN I THINK OF MY PARENTS, ALL I CAN FEEL IS LOVE.
"THE LOVE I FELT FOR THEM. THE LOVE THEY SHOWED ME.
"IT'S FUNNY, THOUGH... I CANNOT REMEMBER THEM EVER ONCE CALLING ME BY NAME.
"I CANNOT RECALL THEM CALLING EACH OTHER BY NAME EITHER.
AND I CANNOT REMEMBER EVER SEEING MY OWN FACE.
I MUST HAVE SEEN A REFLECTION SOMETIME-- IN THE WATER, IF NOWHERE ELSE.
AND YET... NOTHING.

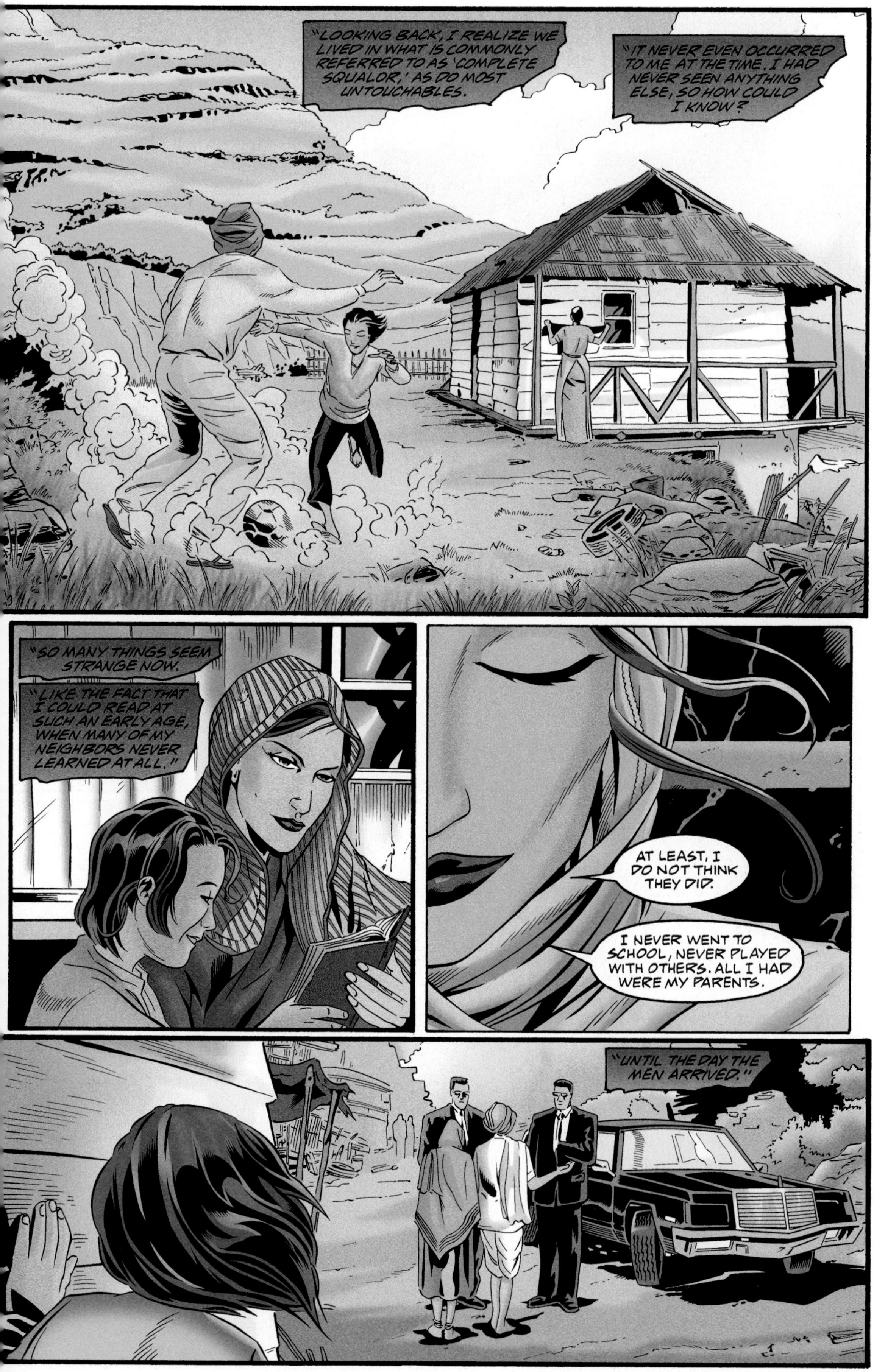
"LOOKING BACK, I REALIZE WE LIVED IN WHAT IS COMMONLY REFERRED TO AS 'COMPLETE SQUALOR,' AS DO MOST UNTOUCHABLES.
"IT NEVER EVEN OCCURRED TO ME AT THE TIME. I HAD NEVER SEEN ANYTHING ELSE, SO HOW COULD I KNOW?
"SO MANY THINGS SEEM STRANGE NOW.
"LIKE THE FACT THAT I COULD READ AT SUCH AN EARLY AGE, WHEN MANY OF MY NEIGHBORS NEVER LEARNED AT ALL."
AT LEAST, I DO NOT THINK THEY DID.
I NEVER WENT TO SCHOOL, NEVER PLAYED WITH OTHERS. ALL I HAD WERE MY PARENTS.
"UNTIL THE DAY THE MEN ARRIVED."

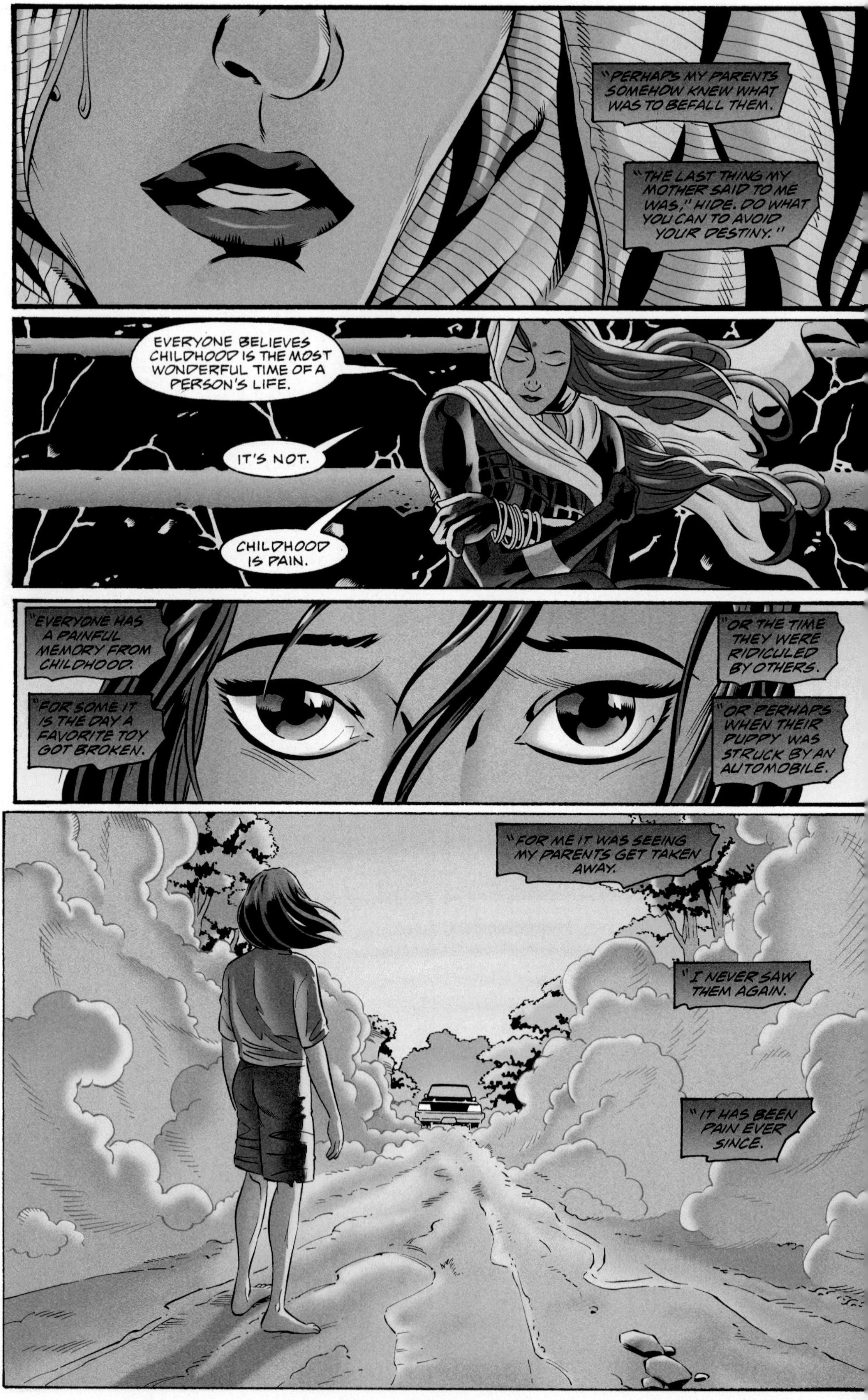
"PERHAPS MY PARENTS SOMEHOW KNEW WHAT WAS TO BEFALL THEM.
"THE LAST THING MY MOTHER SAID TO ME WAS," HIDE. DO WHAT YOU CAN TO AVOID YOUR DESTINY."
EVERYONE BELIEVES CHILDHOOD IS THE MOST WONDERFUL TIME OF A PERSON'S LIFE.
IT'S NOT.
CHILDHOOD IS PAIN.
"EVERYONE HAS A PAINFUL MEMORY FROM CHILDHOOD.
"FOR SOME IT IS THE DAY A FAVORITE TOY GOT BROKEN.
"OR THE TIME THEY WERE RIDICULED BY OTHERS.
"OR PERHAPS WHEN THEIR PUPPY WAS STRUCK BY AN AUTOMOBILE.
"FOR ME IT WAS SEEING MY PARENTS GET TAKEN AWAY.
"I NEVER SAW THEM AGAIN.
"IT HAS BEEN PAIN EVER SINCE.

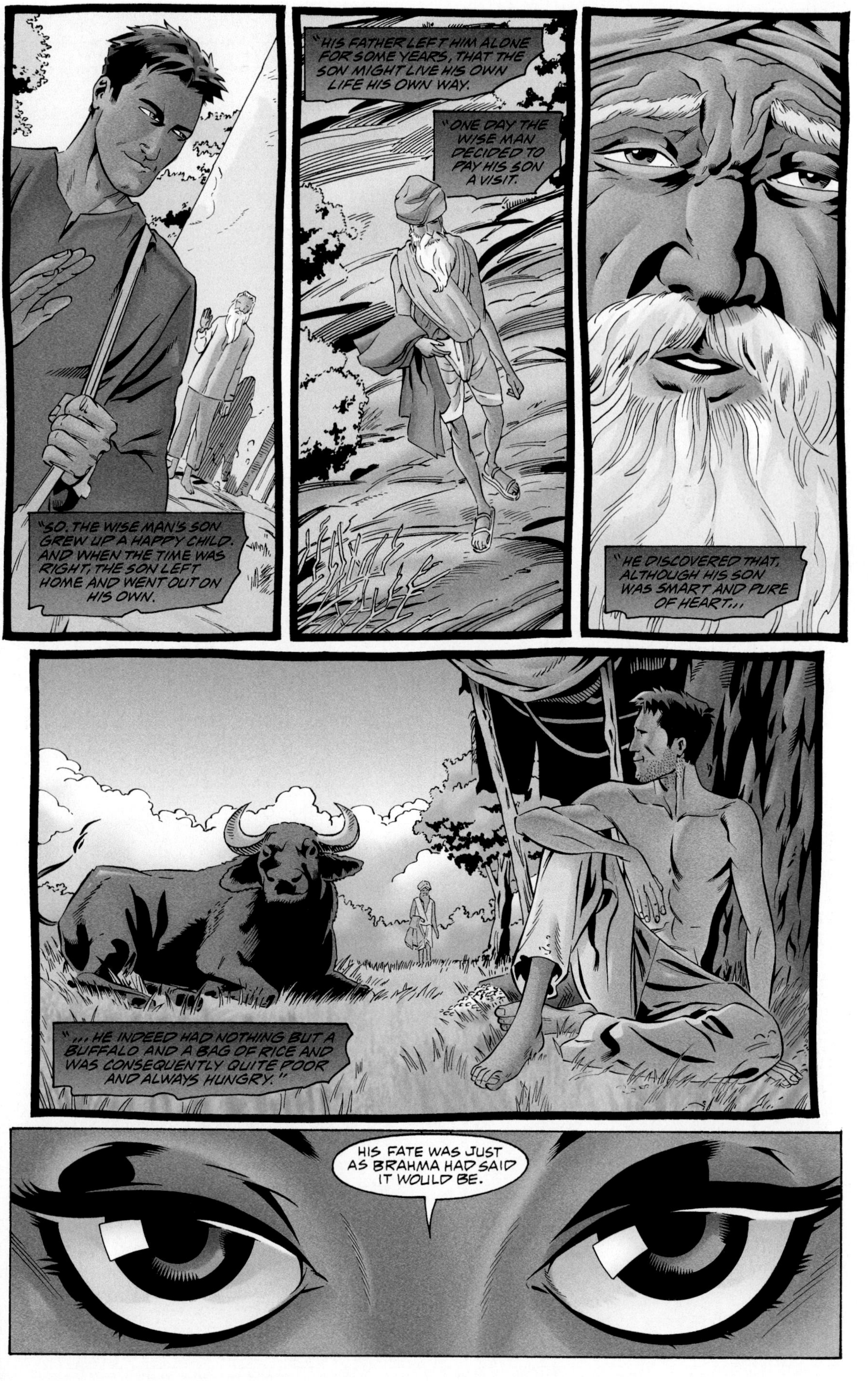
"SO. THE WISE MAN'S SON GREW UP A HAPPY CHILD. AND WHEN THE TIME WAS RIGHT, THE SON LEFT HOME AND WENT OUT ON HIS OWN.
"HIS FATHER LEFT HIM ALONE FOR SOME YEARS, THAT THE SON MIGHT LIVE HIS OWN LIFE HIS OWN WAY.
"ONE DAY THE WISE MAN DECIDED TO PAY HIS SON A VISIT.
"HE DISCOVERED THAT, ALTHOUGH HIS SON WAS SMART AND PURE OF HEART...
"...HE INDEED HAD NOTHING BUT A BUFFALO AND A BAG OF RICE AND WAS CONSEQUENTLY QUITE POOR AND ALWAYS HUNGRY."
HIS FATE WAS JUST AS BRAHMA HAD SAID IT WOULD BE.

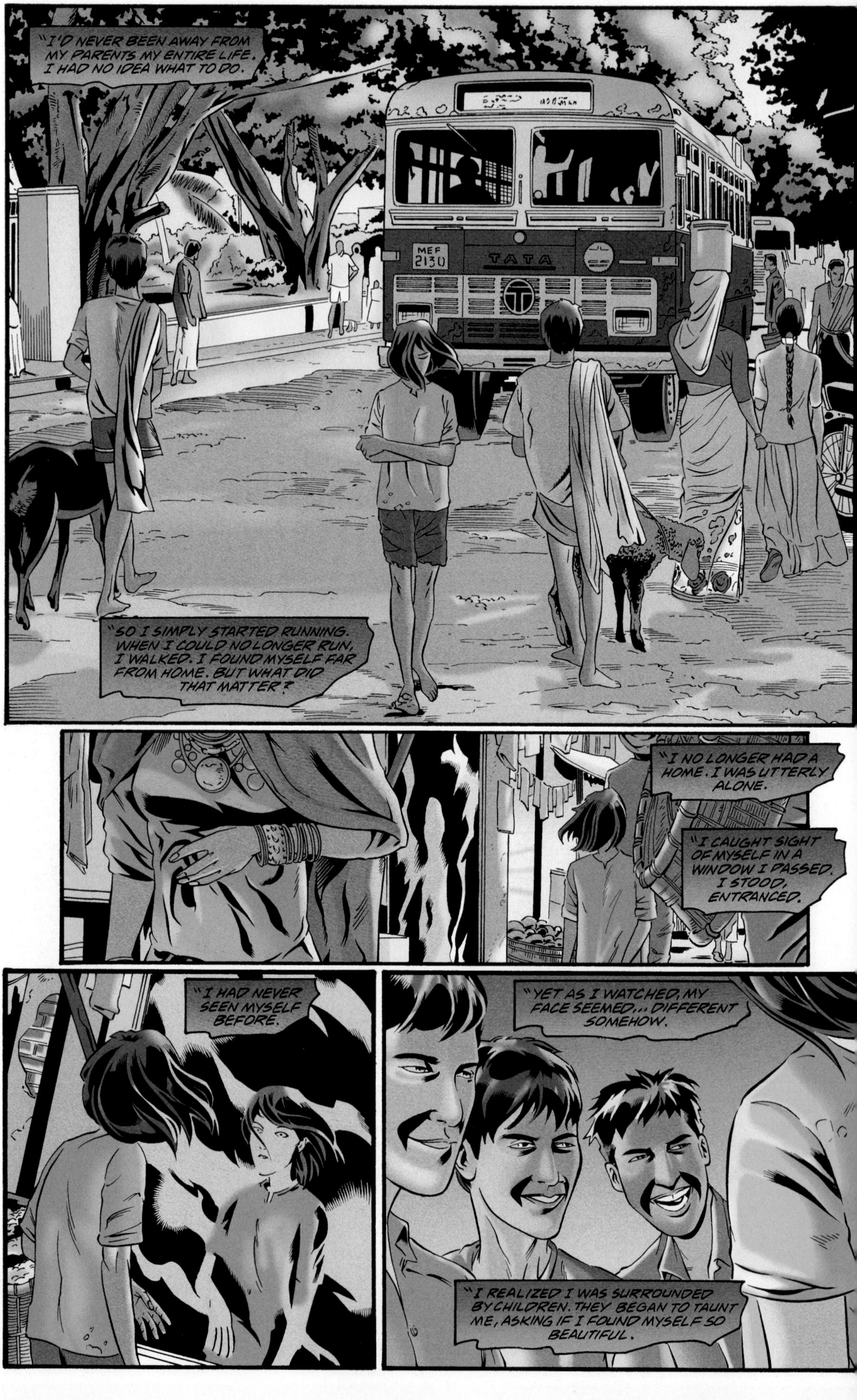
"I'D NEVER BEEN AWAY FROM MY PARENTS MY ENTIRE LIFE. I HAD NO IDEA WHAT TO DO.
MEF 2130
TATA
"SO I SIMPLY STARTED RUNNING. WHEN I COULD NO LONGER RUN, I WALKED. I FOUND MYSELF FAR FROM HOME. BUT WHAT DID THAT MATTER?
"I NO LONGER HAD A HOME. I WAS UTTERLY ALONE.
"I CAUGHT SIGHT OF MYSELF IN A WINDOW I PASSED. I STOOD, ENTRANCED.
"I HAD NEVER SEEN MYSELF BEFORE.
"YET AS I WATCHED, MY FACE SEEMED... DIFFERENT SOMEHOW.
"I REALIZED I WAS SURROUNDED BY CHILDREN. THEY BEGAN TO TAUNT ME, ASKING IF I FOUND MYSELF SO BEAUTIFUL.

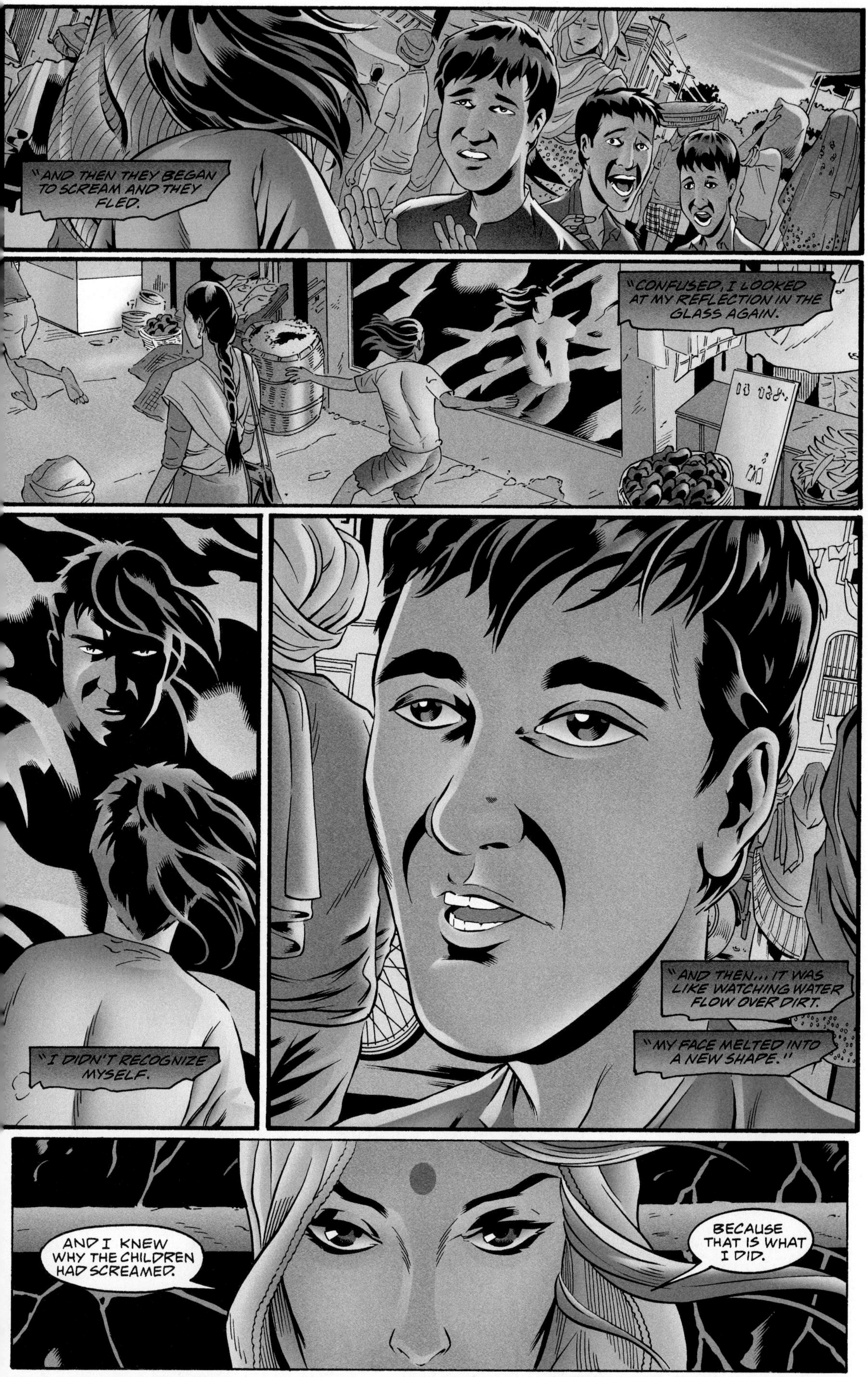
"AND THEN THEY BEGAN TO SCREAM AND THEY FLED.
"CONFUSED, I LOOKED AT MY REFLECTION IN THE GLASS AGAIN.
"I DIDN'T RECOGNIZE MYSELF.
"AND THEN... IT WAS LIKE WATCHING WATER FLOW OVER DIRT.
"MY FACE MELTED INTO A NEW SHAPE."
AND I KNEW WHY THE CHILDREN HAD SCREAMED.
BECAUSE THAT IS WHAT I DID.

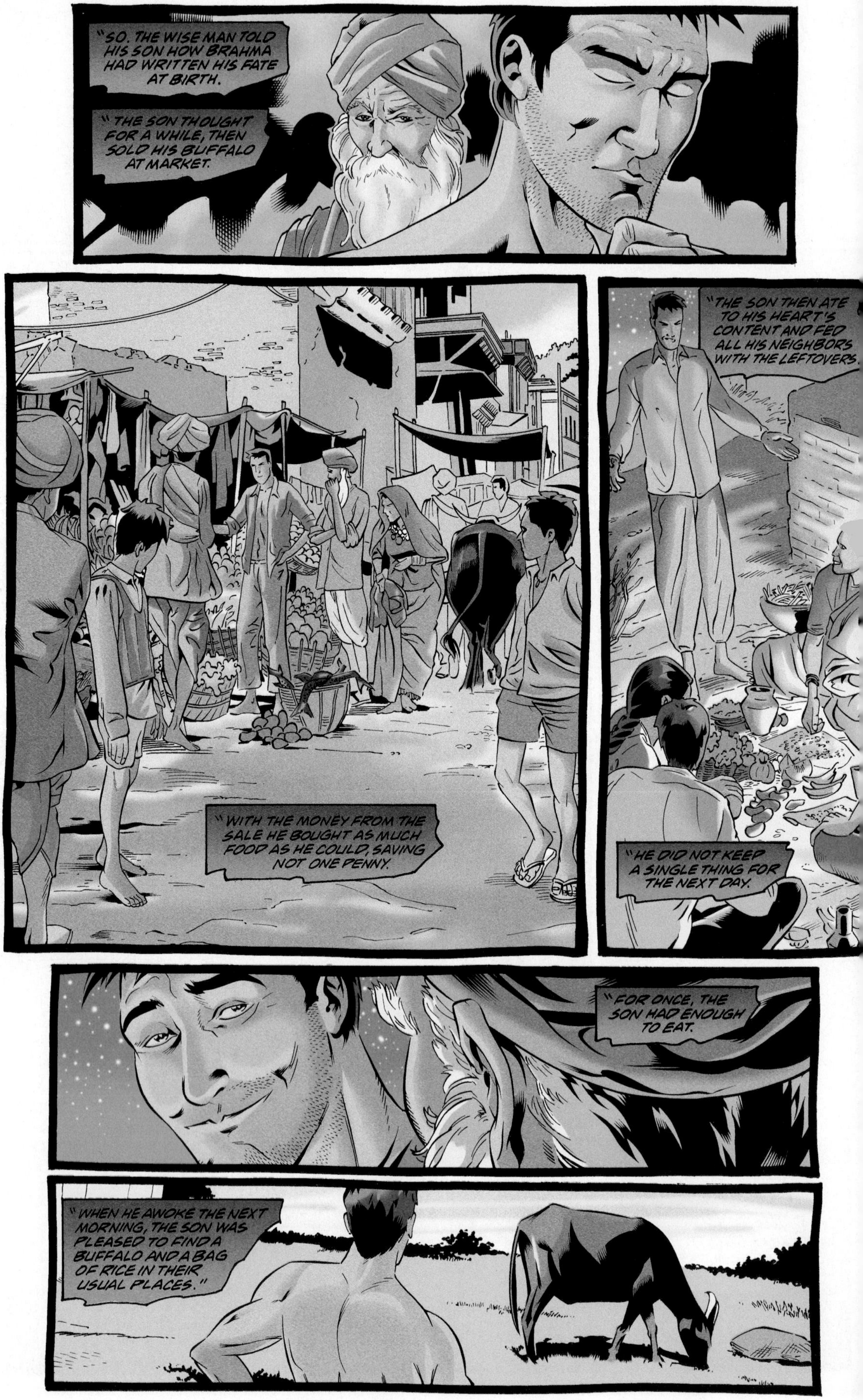
"SO. THE WISE MAN TOLD HIS SON HOW BRAHMA HAD WRITTEN HIS FATE AT BIRTH.
"THE SON THOUGHT FOR A WHILE, THEN SOLD HIS BUFFALO AT MARKET.
"WITH THE MONEY FROM THE SALE HE BOUGHT AS MUCH FOOD AS HE COULD, SAVING NOT ONE PENNY.
"THE SON THEN ATE TO HIS HEART'S CONTENT AND FED ALL HIS NEIGHBORS WITH THE LEFTOVERS.
"HE DID NOT KEEP A SINGLE THING FOR THE NEXT DAY.
"FOR ONCE, THE SON HAD ENOUGH TO EAT.
"WHEN HE AWOKE THE NEXT MORNING, THE SON WAS PLEASED TO FIND A BUFFALO AND A BAG OF RICE IN THEIR USUAL PLACES."

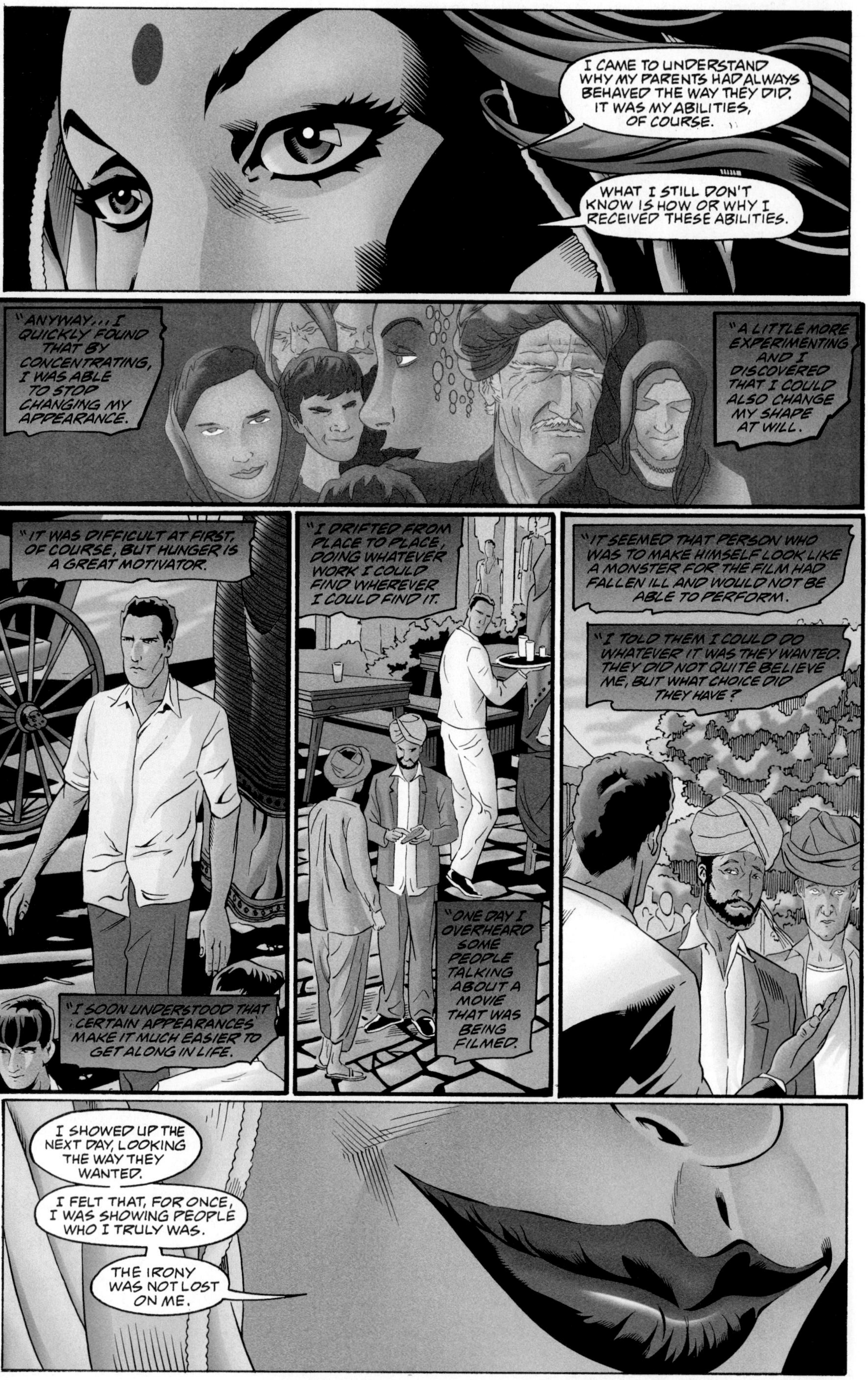

I CAME TO UNDERSTAND WHY MY PARENTS HAD ALWAYS BEHAVED THE WAY THEY DID. IT WAS MY ABILITIES, OF COURSE.
WHAT I STILL DON'T KNOW IS HOW OR WHY I RECEIVED THESE ABILITIES.
"ANYWAY... I QUICKLY FOUND THAT BY CONCENTRATING, I WAS ABLE TO STOP CHANGING MY APPEARANCE.
"A LITTLE MORE EXPERIMENTING AND I DISCOVERED THAT I COULD ALSO CHANGE MY SHAPE AT WILL.
"IT WAS DIFFICULT AT FIRST, OF COURSE, BUT HUNGER IS A GREAT MOTIVATOR.
"I SOON UNDERSTOOD THAT CERTAIN APPEARANCES MAKE IT MUCH EASIER TO GET ALONG IN LIFE.
"I DRIFTED FROM PLACE TO PLACE, DOING WHATEVER WORK I COULD FIND WHEREVER I COULD FIND IT.
"ONE DAY I OVERHEARD SOME PEOPLE TALKING ABOUT A MOVIE THAT WAS BEING FILMED.
"IT SEEMED THAT PERSON WHO WAS TO MAKE HIMSELF LOOK LIKE A MONSTER FOR THE FILM HAD FALLEN ILL AND WOULD NOT BE ABLE TO PERFORM.
"I TOLD THEM I COULD DO WHATEVER IT WAS THEY WANTED. THEY DID NOT QUITE BELIEVE ME, BUT WHAT CHOICE DID THEY HAVE?
I SHOWED UP THE NEXT DAY, LOOKING THE WAY THEY WANTED.
I FELT THAT, FOR ONCE, I WAS SHOWING PEOPLE WHO I TRULY WAS.
THE IRONY WAS NOT LOST ON ME.

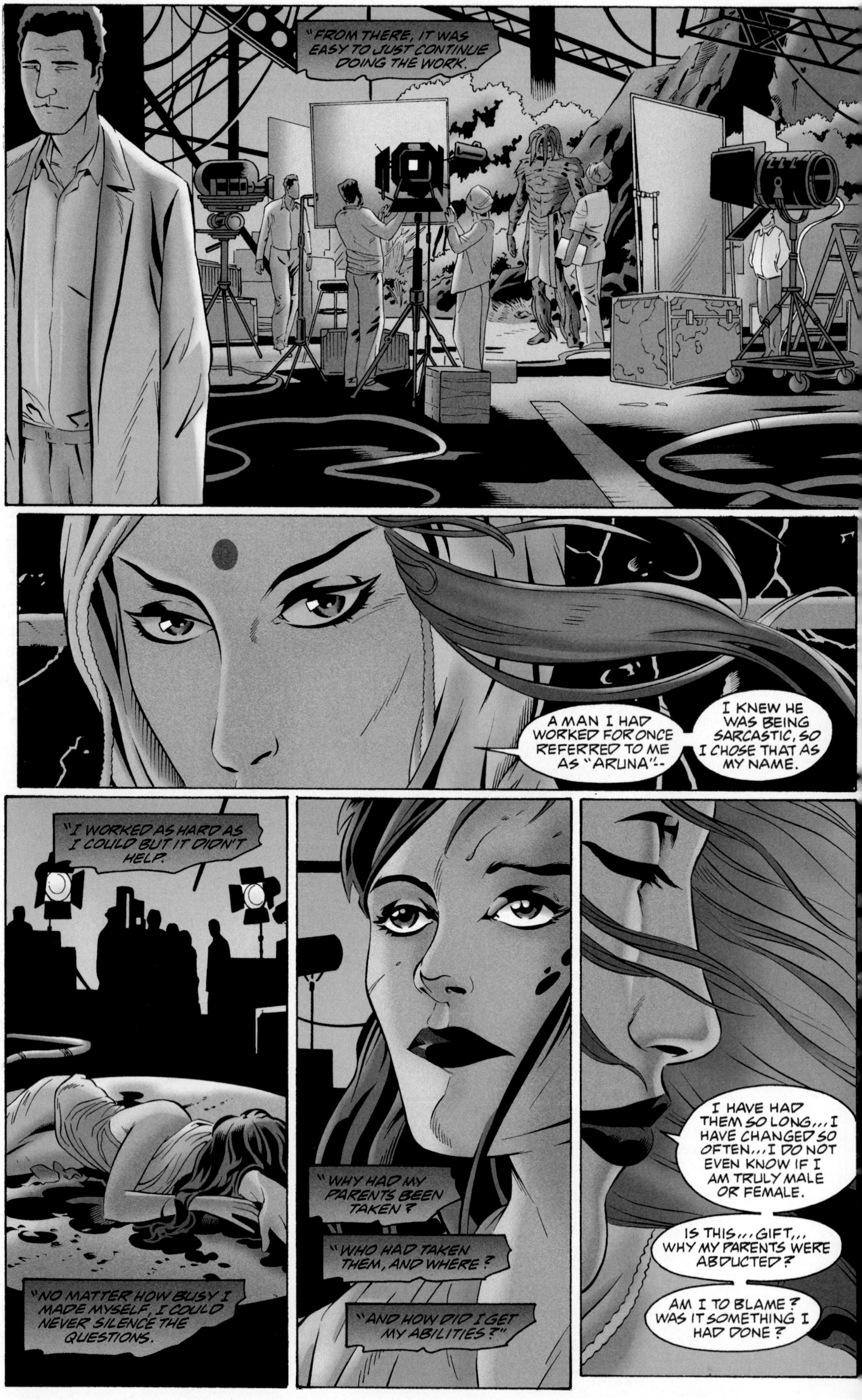
"FROM THERE, IT WAS EASY TO JUST CONTINUE DOING THE WORK.
A MAN I HAD WORKED FOR ONCE REFERRED TO ME AS "ARUNA"-
I KNEW HE WAS BEING SARCASTIC, SO I CHOSE THAT AS MY NAME.
"I WORKED AS HARD AS I COULD BUT IT DIDN'T HELP.
"NO MATTER HOW BUSY I MADE MYSELF, I COULD NEVER SILENCE THE QUESTIONS.
"WHY HAD MY PARENTS BEEN TAKEN?
"WHO HAD TAKEN THEM, AND WHERE?
"AND HOW DID I GET MY ABILITIES?"
I HAVE HAD THEM SO LONG... I HAVE CHANGED SO OFTEN... I DO NOT EVEN KNOW IF I AM TRULY MALE OR FEMALE.
IS THIS... GIFT... WHY MY PARENTS WERE ABDUCTED?
AM I TO BLAME? WAS IT SOMETHING I HAD DONE?

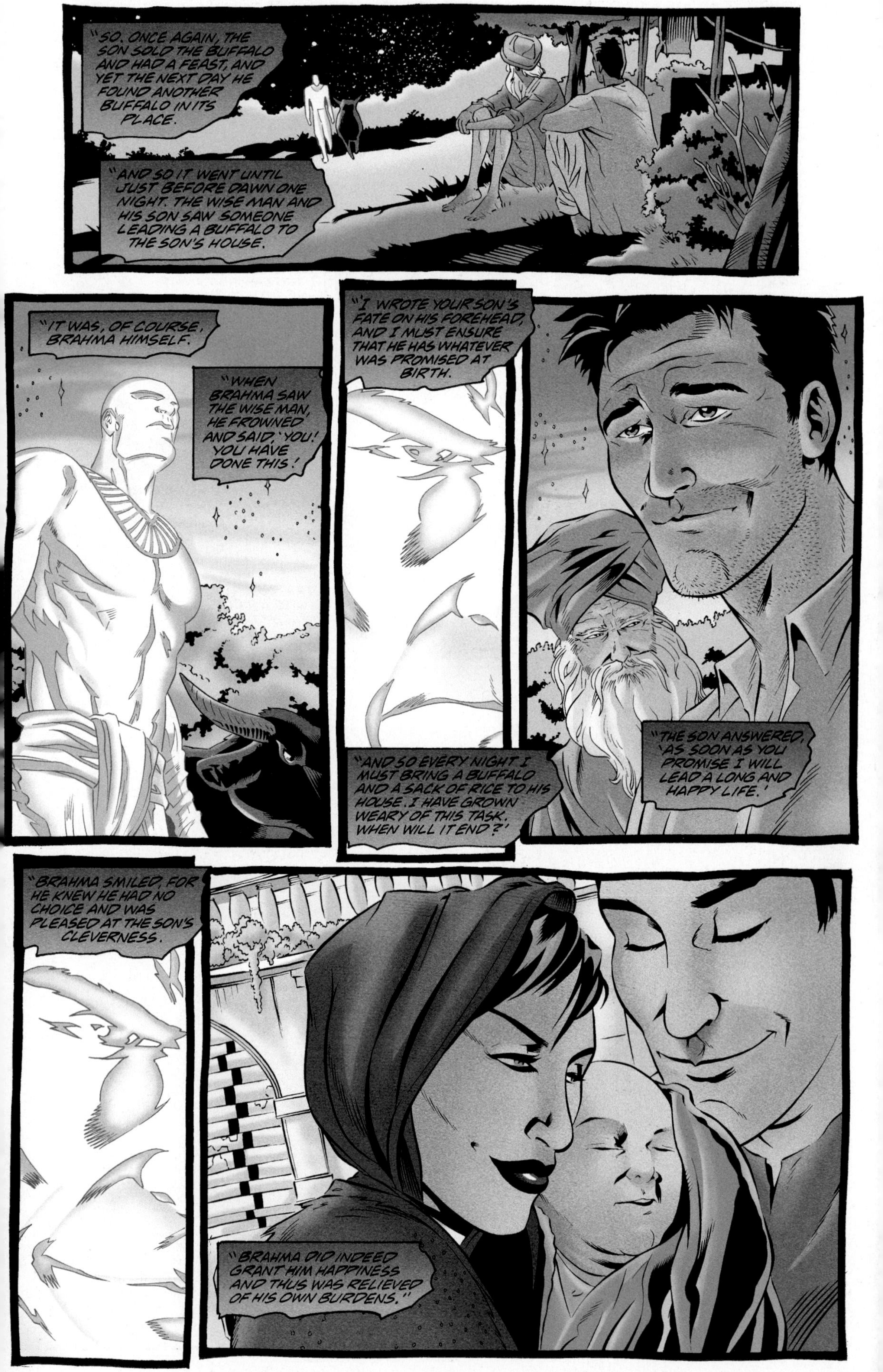
"SO, ONCE AGAIN, THE SON SOLD THE BUFFALO AND HAD A FEAST, AND YET THE NEXT DAY HE FOUND ANOTHER BUFFALO IN ITS PLACE.
"AND SO IT WENT UNTIL JUST BEFORE DAWN ONE NIGHT. THE WISE MAN AND HIS SON SAW SOMEONE LEADING A BUFFALO TO THE SON'S HOUSE.
"IT WAS, OF COURSE, BRAHMA HIMSELF.
"WHEN BRAHMA SAW THE WISE MAN, HE FROWNED AND SAID, 'YOU! YOU HAVE DONE THIS!
"I WROTE YOUR SON'S FATE ON HIS FOREHEAD, AND I MUST ENSURE THAT HE HAS WHATEVER WAS PROMISED AT BIRTH.
"AND SO EVERY NIGHT I MUST BRING A BUFFALO AND A SACK OF RICE TO HIS HOUSE. I HAVE GROWN WEARY OF THIS TASK. WHEN WILL IT END?'
"THE SON ANSWERED, 'AS SOON AS YOU PROMISE I WILL LEAD A LONG AND HAPPY LIFE.'
"BRAHMA SMILED, FOR HE KNEW HE HAD NO CHOICE AND WAS PLEASED AT THE SON'S CLEVERNESS.
"BRAHMA DID INDEED GRANT HIM HAPPINESS AND THUS WAS RELIEVED OF HIS OWN BURDENS."

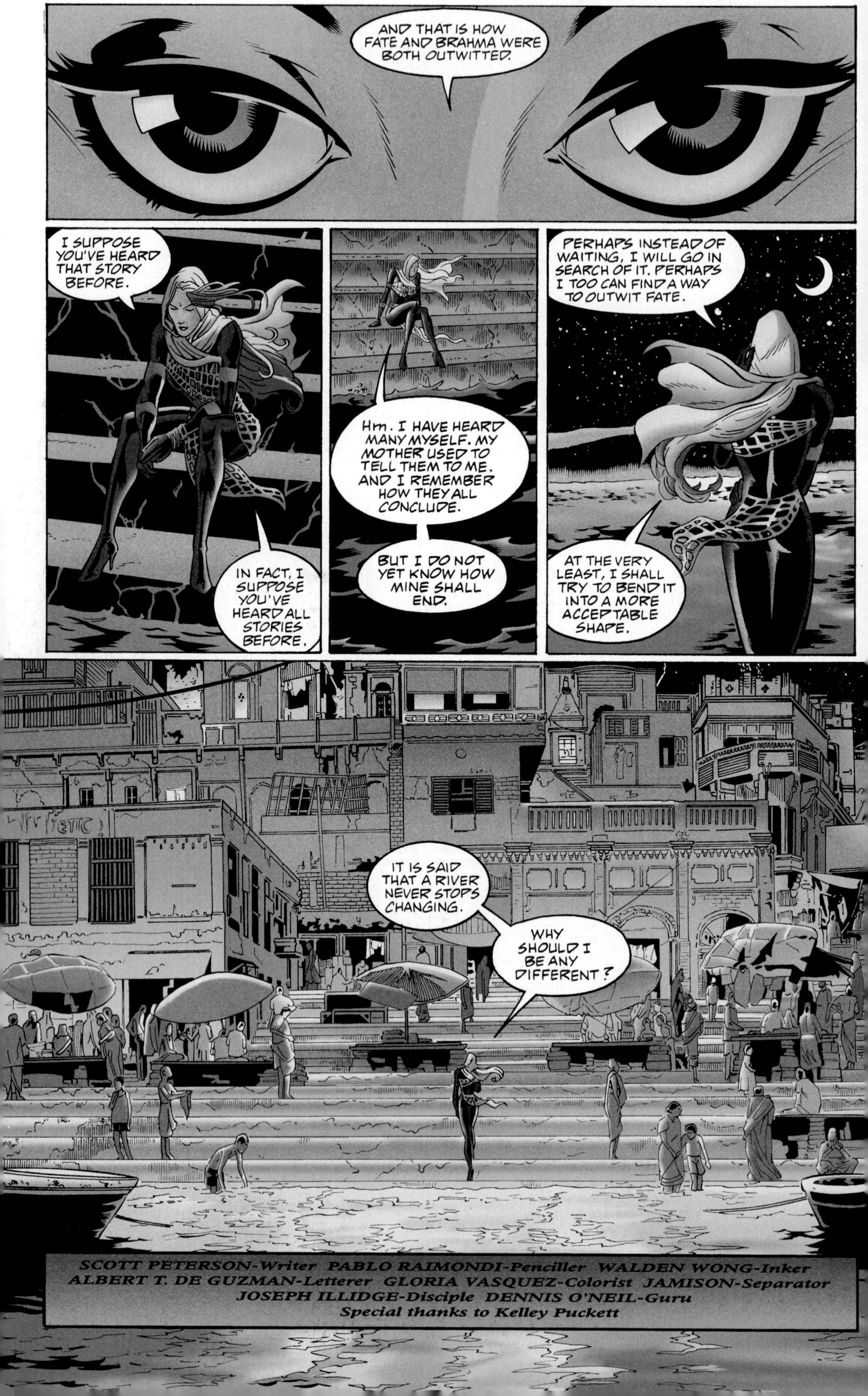
AND THAT IS HOW FATE AND BRAHMA WERE BOTH OUTWITTED.
I SUPPOSE YOU'VE HEARD THAT STORY BEFORE.
IN FACT, I SUPPOSE YOU'VE HEARD ALL STORIES BEFORE.
Hm. I HAVE HEARD MANY MYSELF. MY MOTHER USED TO TELL THEM TO ME. AND I REMEMBER HOW THEY ALL CONCLUDE.
BUT I DO NOT YET KNOW HOW MINE SHALL END.
PERHAPS INSTEAD OF WAITING, I WILL GO IN SEARCH OF IT. PERHAPS I TOO CAN FIND A WAY TO OUTWIT FATE.
AT THE VERY LEAST, I SHALL TRY TO BEND IT INTO A MORE ACCEPTABLE SHAPE.
IT IS SAID THAT A RIVER NEVER STOPS CHANGING.
WHY SHOULD I BE ANY DIFFERENT?
SCOTT PETERSON-Writer PABLO RAIMONDI-Penciller WALDEN WONG-Inker
ALBERT T. DE GUZMAN-Letterer GLORIA VASQUEZ-Colorist JAMISON-Separator
JOSEPH ILLIDGE-Disciple DENNIS O'NEIL-Guru
Special thanks to Kelley Puckett

"Simone and artist Ardian Syaf not only do justice to Babs' legacy, but build in a new complexity that is the starting point for a future full of new storytelling possibilities. A hell of a ride."—IGN

START AT THE BEGINNING!

BATGIRL
VOLUME 1: THE DARKEST REFLECTION

**BATGIRL VOL. 2:
KNIGHTFALL
DESCENDS**

**BATGIRL VOL. 3:
DEATH OF THE FAMILY**

**BATWOMAN VOL. 1:
HYDROLOGY**

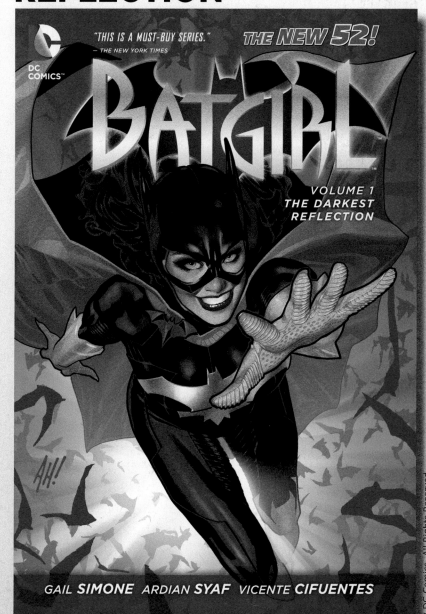

GAIL **SIMONE** ARDIAN **SYAF** VICENTE **CIFUENTES**

START AT THE BEGINNING!

WONDER WOMAN VOLUME 1: BLOOD

WONDER WOMAN
VOL. 2: GUTS

by BRIAN
AZZARELLO and
CLIFF CHIANG

WONDER WOMAN
VOL. 3: IRON

by BRIAN
AZZARELLO and
CLIFF CHIANG

SUPERGIRL VOL. 1:
LAST DAUGHTER OF
KRYPTON

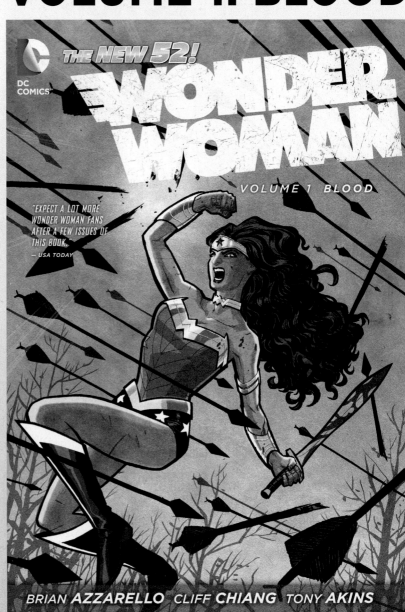

THE NEW 52!
DC COMICS™
WONDER WOMAN
VOLUME 1 BLOOD

"EXPECT A LOT MORE WONDER WOMAN FANS AFTER A FEW ISSUES OF THIS BOOK."
— USA TODAY

BRIAN **AZZARELLO** CLIFF **CHIANG** TONY **AKINS**

"Chaotic and unabashedly fun."—IGN

*"I'm enjoying HARLEY QUINN a great deal;
it's silly, it's funny, it's irreverent."*
—COMIC BOOK RESOURCES

HARLEY QUINN
VOLUME 1: HOT IN THE CITY

**SUICIDE SQUAD VOL. 1:
KICKED IN THE TEETH**

**with ADAM GLASS and
FEDERICO DALLOCCHIO**

**HARLEY QUINN:
PRELUDES AND
KNOCK-KNOCK JOKES**

**with KARL KESEL and
TERRY DODSON**

**BATMAN: MAD LOVE
AND OTHER STORIES**

**with PAUL DINI
and BRUCE TIMM**